OLD TESTAMENT THEOLOGY

THE OLD TESTAMENT LIBRARY

Editorial Advisory Board

Gerhard von Rad

OLD TESTAMENT THEOLOGY

Volume II

The Theology of Israel's Prophetic Traditions

Translated by
D. M. G. Stalker

Introduced by
Walter Brueggemann

Westminster John Knox Press
LOUISVILLE
LONDON · LEIDEN

A translation of *Theologie des Alten Testaments,* Bd. II, *Die Theologie der prophetischen Überlieferungen Israels,* published by Chr. Kaiser Verlag, Munich, in 1960.

Theology of the Old Testament, Vol. II, by Gerhard von Rad. © Oliver and Boyd Ltd 1965. Published by arrangement with HarperSanFrancisco, a division of HarperCollins Publishers, Inc. All rights reserved.

Published by Westminster John Knox Press
Louisville, Kentucky

This book is printed on acid-free paper that meets the American National Standards Institute Z39.48 standard. ∞

PRINTED IN THE UNITED STATES OF AMERICA

01 02 03 04 05 06 07 08 09 10 — 10 9 8 7 6 5 4 3 2 1

Library of Congress Cataloging-in-Publication Data

A catalog record for this book is available from the Library of Congress.
ISBN 0-664-22407-5 (vol. I)
ISBN 0-664-22408-3 (vol. II)

CONTENTS

Part Two

CLASSICAL PROPHECY

Part Three

THE OLD TESTAMENT AND THE NEW

OLD TESTAMENT LIBRARY CLASSICS

PREFACE

A library is incomplete without classics. If the only literature that a library holds is that which is currently published, then the appreciation of contemporary works will lack perspective and the understanding of the subject matter will be impoverished. Wisdom comes as much from reading across time as it does from reading within one time. In any field, the present builds upon and includes the past, even as it moves on into the future. That situation holds especially for the study of the Old Testament, which is itself both classic literature and a remarkable library.

In the history of published resources in the field of Old Testament studies, many books have appeared whose life in print was deservedly short. Occasionally, however, volumes have been published that have exerted significant influence upon the ways in which the Old Testament was read and understood. Some are works that include and conclude previous lines of thought, offering a seminal synthesis. Others, by dint of a bold thesis, opened thinking about the Old Testament in new and important ways. When one looks back over the past century and a half, during which study of the Old Testament came of age as an intellectual discipline, the classics are those volumes that provide the major landmarks on the terrain.

A classic work, by its very nature, does not become obsolete. It is never out of date. A classic has abiding worth in and for the present as well as implications for future work.

The editors of the Old Testament Library have identified volumes that not only have had signal importance in the past but continue to be valuable resources for the present. Each new edition of these classics will be introduced by an essay that defines its importance in the history of Old Testament study and discusses its value for contemporary readers. The inclusion of such classics will make the Old Testament Library a deeper and broader resource for the study of the Old Testament.

JLM
CAN
DLP

PREFACE TO THE 1965 EDITION

This volume, which brings the Old Testament Theology which I began a few years ago to its conclusion, will, I hope, answer numerous questions concerning the theological *modus progrediendi* which necessarily still remained open for the reader of VOL. I.

The sketch offered here is to be understood in the light of a definite perplexity which has arisen within the history of Old Testament theology up to date. No one who attempts to assess what has already been achieved and what still remains to be accomplished can fail to see that, by and large, the conceptions of a theology of the Old Testament oscillate between two very different possibilities. These are to approach Old Testament Theology either *via* Israel's religious ideas or *via* saving history. Vatke, the publication of whose *Religion des Alten Testamentes* in 1835 marked the first full-scale appearance of this branch of Biblical scholarship, wished to handle Israel's spiritual and religious development as a unit, that is to say, as a coherent evolution; and what he wanted to do was to bring out the way in which this material, unique though it is, nevertheless exhibits the universal elements in the religions of mankind. This interest in the common truths of religion continued to play a part long after Vatke, and can still be found to-day. Even where investigation and comparison of the history of religions led to a keener appreciation of the unique elements in the religion of Israel and to a diminution of the influence of philosophic thought, the chief interest of theology was still largely in Israel's spiritual and religious achievement. This is particularly clearly seen in the *Theologies* of Schultz, Dillmann, Sellin, and Procksch, with their division of Old Testament theology into two sections, the one dealing with its history and the other with its religious ideas. These *Theologies* most certainly claim that Israel was granted a special revelation; for them, however, the divine condescension— Vatke himself spoke of a divine *synkatabasis*—took place wholly in the spiritual sphere, and also, it was this internal religious movement of ancient Israel towards Christianity that was then regarded as the properly eschatological element in the Old Testament. In contrast, Eichrodt's *Theology,* with its key-note "the breaking in of the kingdom of God," constituted a decisive turning-point. (Vischer's warning cries, which were on the whole effective, ought also to be remembered.) The only really important question is whether Eichrodt's treatment of the material does justice to the close relationship with history which is characteristic of Old Testament utterances.

This dominant view which concentrated on the spiritual and inward life of Israel was opposed by a small number of scholars (J. T. Beck, G. Menken, J. C. K. von Hofmann, F. Delitzsch, and others). For them the starting-point is the primacy of the historical saving acts. Very definite facts are "what we are presented with as the source of the religious ideas. . . . The growing-point in the objective demonstration of religion is not provided by man's consciousness. It was not consciousness that created what is set forth as fact, but rather the reverse, the facts created the consciousness of them."[1] However, definite contemporary philosophic ideas which, as we can see to-day, are not drawn at all from the Old Testament itself, contributed even to this way of regarding the subject, especially so in the case of Hofmann. In particular, what arouses the greatest misgivings from the theological point of view is these men's interest in an "objective saving history," for that latter does not derive from the Old Testament itself. We certainly find there the greatest possible interest in various historical data, as well as in the historical developments which follow after them. The crucial thing however is the way in which the saving data are constantly applied to, and made relevant for, contemporary situations. There is absolutely nothing of that objectification to which this "saving history" school attached so such weight. In view of all this, it must be apparent that even to-day the old question concerning a theology of the Old Testament is still an open one, and that much still remains to be done and elucidated before such a theology can be written as it ought to be.

Here the present writer must once again emphasise that he does not consider what he offers to be a complete and comprehensive theology of the Old Testament. For example, much more could have been said about the way in which the various concepts were developed. On this point, however, there is so much excellent material in recent special studies, in *Theologisches Wörterbuch zum Neuen Testament,* edd. G. Kittel and G. Friedrich, and also in the *Theologies* of Eichrodt and Köhler, that I could afford to be brief here. On the other hand, my own method of developing the theology of the Old Testament might be the very thing to help to create recognition of the limits inherent in these examinations of concepts which are still so popular. I do not, of course, for a moment mean that such examinations are unnecessary. They are important both to orient exegesis and as correctives. But whether their results—knowledge of the concepts of "faith," "righteousness," "the covenant," "the sacrifices," "zeal," "the glory of God," etc.—play a part as constitutive elements in a theology of the Old Testament is another question. Investigation of such concepts might laboriously produce an overall idea within which the greatest possible number of separate occurrences of them could be included. Yet, this investigation can only arrive at such a complex of ideas by way of generalisation and abstraction. If, however,

[1]J. C. F. Steudel, *Vorlesungen über die Theologie des Alten Testaments,* Berlin 1840, pp. 18f.

what we wished broadly to demonstrate here is correct, that is, that a statement made in the Old Testament is initially to be understood as standing in the space between a quite particular past in the divine action and a quite particular future, and that this is the only place from which one can determine what faith, unfaith, righteousness, or the covenant are in this realm of tension between promise and fulfilment—then one will have no illusions about the limits of such necessarily generalised and abstract investigations of concepts.

If I may ask one thing of the reader, it is that he should not take the last four sections of this volume in isolation. They stand or fall according as what preceded them is valid, in particular what is said about the history of tradition and its continuous re-interpretation. There is to-day no overall interpretation of the Old Testament which does not constantly have to justify itself at the bar of a detailed interpretation which exactly corresponds to it. Otherwise it is idle chatter. Yet, the theological interpretation of Old Testament texts does not start only at the point where the exegete trained (more or less) in literary criticism and history has done his work, which would mean that we have two processes at work, one concerned with literary criticism and, after it, another occupied with "theology." The theological interpretation which seeks to understand a statement about God made in the text is at work from the very beginning of the process of understanding. Less than ever to-day can anything be effected by means of Biblical and theological formulae or slogans. What characterises the nature of the problem before us now is the great closeness of exegesis and "introduction" on the one hand and the theology of the Old Testament on the other. Theology's interest in exegesis and the methods of understanding used there is a keen one, because it is here that the decisions which are important for itself are taken. It cannot unfold itself without constantly referring to detailed exegesis and its results, and it only becomes trustworthy as it constantly allows the reader to see exegesis, which is its proper basis. For there is still very little agreement on the matter of what exegesis should understand as the proper *statement* made by a text and how it should extract this, freed as far as can be from modern prejudice and inapposite blue-prints. However, quite apart from this interest in exegesis, of which particular account has to be taken to-day in any theology of the Old Testament, in such a conception of the Old Testament which is so based on the history of tradition and on eschatology as the one offered here, the essential problems of a theology of the Old Testament quite automatically moved to the end, that is to say, to the point in the saving history where the question of the relationship between the accumulated promise of the Old Testament and the Christ-event in the New is most acute. The difference— again of necessity simplified—is of course clear. If I view the Old Testament "genetically," *i.e.,* as a comprehensive process of religious and spiritual evolution, I can view it as, to some extent, a self-contained entity. But if what I principally see in it is the ceaseless saving movement of promise and fulfilment, then it becomes apparent how the expectations it contains fan out ever wider, then it is no self-contained entity, then it is absolutely open, and the question of its relationship to the New Testament becomes the question *par excellence.*

I had the honour of delivering the section beginning at p. 99, and parts of the sections beginning at pp. 319, 336, and 357, to the theological faculty of the Royal University of Utrecht as Obbink Lectures on 29 February and 1 March 1960.

I have once again to thank Herr Pfarrer Eduard Haller (Neuendettelsau), and on this occasion also Dr Diethelm Michel (Heidelberg), for preparing the manuscript for the press and for careful assistance in proof-correction. The index, which includes both volumes, was prepared for VOL. I by one of my students, Herr S. Kappus (Reutlingen), and for VOL. II by Dr R. Knierim (Heidelberg). I am very grateful for their help, which makes the two volumes easier to use. I should not like to end without mentioning that I remember with great gratitude several conversations with Otto Weber, because they helped me with the elucidation of certain questions which were to be taken up in the final sections of this volume.

Heidelberg, 1 June 1960   GERHARD VON RAD

PREFACE TO THE ENGLISH TRANSLATION

I have some hesitation in allowing these volumes to appear in a foreign dress. Theological writings are like others—their roots are often more exclusively bound up than we are aware with the country and language in which they were written, for a specific country and language always imply as well a specific mode of thought. These volumes have their origin in a theological situation, a phase in theological discussion—I should prefer to call it a certain impasse—which has been felt with particular force in Germany. Perhaps, then, if they had been intended to meet the needs of scholars in other countries, they should not have been written in the way they are.

I wish particularly to thank Mr Stalker, the translator, for the time he has given to this work and the excellence of his rendering. He has done everything he could to bridge the difficult gulf between the two languages. If obscurities still remain, the reader should lay them at the author's and not at the translator's door.

The fourth edition of VOL. II, which is expected to be published in Germany before the end of this year, will contain some alterations to which the lively discussion, both appreciative and critical, which greeted the book's first appearance, gave rise. Unfortunately it has not been possible to include all of them in this translation.

Heidelberg, February 1965   GERHARD VON RAD

TRANSLATOR'S NOTE

I wish again to thank many friends in the University of Edinburgh and elsewhere who have helped me, in particular Miss E. B. F. Kinniburgh, B.D., who has greatly improved the English style, Miss Sheena M. Osler, M.A., who has verified the Scripture references and made the English Index of them, and Frl. Reinhild Schmidt, Lübeck.

D. M. G. STALKER

PART ONE

General Considerations in Prophecy

Remember not the former things nor consider the things of old.
For behold, I purpose to do a new thing.

Isaiah XLIII. 18f.

CHAPTER A

INTRODUCTION

THE fact that the present *Old Testament Theology* is divided into two volumes suggests that there is a definite break between the message of the prophets and the ideas held by earlier Jahwism, but proof of this cannot be given at once or in a single sentence: it can only appear with the development of the whole subject which follows.[1]

The road towards the recognition of the break had, of course, been in preparation for some considerable time. Critical investigation of prophecy is still in its early stages: only in the nineteenth century was prophecy seen to be *sui generis* in religion—we may even say it was not discovered till then. The result was something rare in the history of Biblical interpretation—a whole vast realm of the Bible was for the first time understood, and this at once began to make an impact beyond the limits of professional scholarship, and to deliver a message to the era which had so discovered it. The names which will always be associated with this discovery are those of Ewald, Wellhausen, and Duhm.

It was of very great importance for this new understanding of prophecy that its message was now studied independently from the "law" which, up to now, had been thought to antedate it.[2] The moment that source criticism found a deposit of the prophetic teaching

---

[1] Cp. VOL. I, p. 128.

[2] In Protestant circles the idea that the prophets were exponents of the Mosaic law persisted from the time of Luther down to the middle of the nineteenth century. "Prophetia enim nihil aliud quam expositio et (ut sic dixerim) praxis et applicatio legis fuit" (Luther's *Works*, Weimar 1923–48, VOL. VIII, pp. 105, 106ff.). Prophecy is "deeply rooted in the law, is its child, and is simply its further unfolding applied to the people's present and future" (H. A. C. Hävernick, *Vorlesungen über die Theologie des Alten Testamentes*, Erlangen 1848, p. 16). Compare Wellhausen's account of his efforts to understand prophecy as preceded by the law: he studied the Pentateuch through and through, he says, but it was in vain that he looked for the light which was to be shed from this source on the prophetical books. "On the contrary, my enjoyment of the latter was marred by the Law; it did not bring them any nearer me, but intruded itself uneasily, like a ghost that makes a noise indeed, but is not visible and really effects nothing." *Prolegomena to the History of Israel*, henceforth cited as *Prolegomena*, trans. J. S. Black and Allan Menzies, Edinburgh 1885, p. 3.

in Deuteronomy and the Priestly Document, thus doing away with the need to understand the prophets in the light of the Pentateuchal tradition, a new approach to the prophets was open. This change of ground in dating was revolutionary. It meant that at one fell swoop the prophets were brought out of their position in the shadows where their distinctive characteristics could never possibly be realised.

But the pendulum swung too far. For the prophets were never as original, or as individualistic, or in such direct communion with God and no one else, as they were then believed to be. As we now see, they were in greater or lesser degree conditioned by old traditions which they re-interpreted and applied to their own times. Indeed, at the end of the volume we shall even be faced with the task of restoring them their share of the law.[3]

The corrections which the passage of time has forced on the picture painted by "classical prophetic criticism" are of profound importance. What was then regarded as constituting the very essence of prophecy was the prophets' intellectual and spiritual independence and religious immediacy, but, as we to-day are well aware, this arose solely from the critics' use of modern ideas of the freedom and spirituality enjoyed by religious genius. Research has meanwhile clearly shown that the prophets were much more directly involved in concepts common to the ancient east, in cult and in myth, and even in what were termed primitive "magical" ideas, than was at that time supposed. And this attachment to inherited traditions and ideas generally current at that time did not simply affect the circumference of their message: it went right to its heart. Consequently, the classical definition of the specific essence of prophecy, based as it then was, in particular, on the new ideas conceived by the prophets out of their own intimate communion with the deity, has been largely discredited. We have also abandoned the whole idea of a "religion of the prophets" as a religion of the spirit diametrically opposed to the "cultic religion of the priests." In this connexion, Biblical criticism is even to-day still busy demolishing an idea of prophecy which may be said to have reached its full growth in Duhm's *Israels Propheten* (1916). However, the more criticism has moved away from the psychological, personal, and idealistic considerations involved in the classical picture of the prophets, the less certain has it become of what constitutes the original element in their message. The recognition of the deep debt which their teaching owes to

[3] See below, pp. 395ff.

tradition has in itself almost thrown criticism back upon the old question from which it started out. Criticism has now, in the light of its new focus, to try to re-define what is specifically "prophetic." If the prophets' teaching can no longer be derived simply from their religious experience, the question of its origin has to be put in a different way—in what theological *milieu* was their unique independence and religious authority active?

The answer to these basic questions demands that we describe the teaching of the various prophets in chronological sequence. A brief pre-history of the "prophetic movement" may also help us to arrive at an exact understanding of the nature of prophecy.[4]

[4] General works: G. Hölscher, *Die Profeten*, henceforth cited as *Profeten*, Leipzig 1914; B. Duhm, *Israels Propheten*, Tübingen 1916; T. H. Robinson, *Prophecy and the Prophets in Ancient Israel*, henceforth cited as *Prophecy*, London 1923; A. Jepsen, *Nabi*, henceforth cited as *Nabi*, Munich 1934; M. Buber, *The Prophetic Faith*, trans. C. Witton-Davies, New York 1949; C. Kuhl, *The Prophets of Israel*, trans. Rudolf J. Ehrlich and J. P. Smith, Edinburgh and London, 1960; A. Neher, *L'Essence du prophétisme*, Paris 1955. Cp. also R. Rendtorff, in *Theologisches Wörterbuch zum Neuen Testament*, henceforth cited as *Th.W.B.N.T.*, edd. G. Kittel and G. Friedrich, Stuttgart 1933ff., VOL. VI, pp. 796ff.; G. Fohrer, "Neuere Literatur zur alttestamentlichen Prophetie," in *Theologische Rundschau*, henceforth cited as *Th.R.*, XIX (1951), pp. 277ff., XX (1952), pp. 193ff., 295ff.

PROPHECY BEFORE THE CLASSICAL PERIOD

I. ORIGINS

IT was in the ninth century, with Elijah and Elisha, that prophecy, the subject of this volume, first began to make its voice heard. This was therefore at a fairly advanced stage in ancient Israel's faith and worship. Indeed, prophecy, with its specific functions, made a late appearance compared with the age-old institutions of the priesthood or of sacral law, though its origins can be traced to considerably earlier times. In particular is this true of eighth-century prophecy, that is, the messages of Amos, Hosea, or Isaiah, with whom the movement reached its first high-point. Yet the term "prophetic movement" may be misleading, though, of course, we can hardly do without it altogether. For prophecy gains a much more complex appearance the more deeply criticism enquires into it. The straight line of development which once was drawn from the ecstatic bands met with in I Sam. x. 5ff. down through Samuel and Elijah to Isaiah and Jeremiah has for long now been recognised as an inadmissible oversimplification. The origins of prophecy are themselves a difficult problem: there is not enough source material, and what there is is not sufficiently homogeneous, to allow us to draw up anything like a history of the movement, or even a rough sketch of its first beginnings. Indeed, our use of the general term "prophets" gives the impression of a uniformity which did not in fact exist. In the sources Nathan is everywhere designated as prophet (נביא), but on the other hand Gad sometimes functions as "David's seer" (חזה, II Sam. XXIV. 11), and sometimes as prophet (נביא, I Sam. XXII. 5; II Sam. XXIV. 11). Amaziah addresses Amos as "seer" (חזה), whereupon the latter retorts that he is no "prophet" (נביא, Am. VII. 12, 14). In I Sam. IX. 9 prophet and seer (ראה) are designated as synonymous terms, though it is said that the use of the terms had changed with the passage of time. Elijah is very frequently given the title of "man of God" (איש האלהים),[1] but the disciples who gather round him are called "sons of the prophets" (בני הנביאים, II Kings II. 3, 5, 7, 15, IV. 1, 38, etc.). I Kings XIII tells of the "man of God" from

[1] II Kings IV. 7, 9, 16, 21f., 25, 27, 40, 42, V. 8, 14f., 20 etc.

Judah, but designates his colleague in Bethel as *nabi'*—though it goes on to cancel out the distinction by making the man from Judah say, "I too am *nabi'* as you are" (1 Kings XIII. 18). This remarkable fluctuation in the terms employed warns us against regarding any specific text as an altogether direct reflexion of what the actual usage was. The narrators' own preconceptions always play a part; and, more particularly, the terms used in the various text-groups are those current in the places where the texts originated.[2] Again, why should we ever expect that the same thing would always be called by the same name at all times and in different places? And was it in fact the same thing at all times? We can be perfectly sure that, if the sources use a number of different terms for prophet, this indicates in the last analysis that there were different kinds of prophets and different kinds of prophecy. We must not therefore look for any consistency or system in the way in which the terms are used in the Old Testament as it now exists.

By far the commonest term used in *nabi'*. This however makes things harder rather than easier, for there is no doubt that the increasing use made of it, particularly by later authors writing about the past, is the result of a process which ironed differences out and reduced the various terms to a common denomination. One of our special tasks here will be to show how a number of different concepts of the prophets' office and teaching current from the eighth to the sixth centuries came to be embraced by the one term *nabi'*. To translate this by the Greek word "prophet" does not bring us one inch further forward in our understanding of the matter.[3]

We may take it for granted that men possessed by the spirit only

---

[2] A good example of this difference in concepts and of the obscurities to which it gives rise is furnished by the tradition about Samuel in 1 Sam. Although the writers only use the designation נביא in the accounts of his youth, there is no doubt that they regard him throughout as one endowed with mantic powers and as a prophet. The man who composed the accounts of Samuel's youth and of his call (1 Sam. I–III) only describes him as נביא in one solitary instance (1 Sam. III. 20). The other writer who composed 1 Sam. XIX. 18ff. regards him as the leader of a group of ecstatics, while the author of 1 Sam. IX designates him as seer and man of God (6, 8, 11). The Deuteronomist pictures him as the last of the judges (1 Sam. VII. 15). It is very likely however that the historical Samuel was no single one of all these, but a preacher of the law. See VOL. I, pp. 33, 60; H. Wildberger, "Samuel und die Entstehung des israelitischen Königtums," in *Theologische Zeitschrift*, henceforth cited as *Th. Z.*, Heft 6 (1957), pp. 464f.

[3] Details and references in Rendtorff in *Th. W.B.N.T.*, VOL. VI, pp. 796ff., and *Nabi*, pp. 5ff.

appeared in Israel after the conquest of Canaan. In eleventh-century Syria and Palestine there are signs of the rise of an ecstatic and mantic movement whose origins are apparently outside that area, and perhaps lie in the mantic of Thrace and Asia Minor.[4] Canaanite religion must, then, have been the medium by which the movement came to Israel. The earliest Old Testament evidence for its appearance are the accounts of the Dervish-like enthusiasts who from time to time emerged up and down the land, probably to be eyed askance by the settled Israelite farmers (I Sam. x. 5ff.). Their ecstatic excitement was infectious: it could even suddenly communicate itself to someone who merely approached a band of them while they were in their frenzy (I Sam. xIx. 18ff.). The use of the term "slavering," "dribbling," in the sense of prophesying (הטיף, Am. vII. 16; Mic. II. 6. 11), or what was even possible as well, designating a prophet as משגע, a "mad fellow," (II Kings. IX. 11), speak for themselves. In the earliest times this ecstatic excitement may normally have found expression in articulate speech, but it may also have been an end in itself, proof of divine possession—we do not know. The very graphic description of the frenzy of the priests of Baal, which went on growing greater for hours on end, takes notice of cries of appeal to their god which they uttered as they mutilated themselves and, in their enthusiasm, lost all sense of pain (I Kings xvIII. 26ff).

The story in Num. xI. 10ff., an Elohist text, throws light on the theological judgment passed upon these ecstatic conditions. In words of utter dejection and even despair, Moses complains of the burden of his office. Jahweh thereupon commands seventy of the elders to come to the holy tent, takes some of the spirit of Moses, and portions it amongst them. This has a most astounding effect—they at once fall into a state of continuous prophetic ecstasy (ויתנבאו). Why, two of them, who for some reason did not come out to the tent, were transported in this way while remaining inside the camp! Joshua, alarmed at this

---

[4] *Profeten*, pp. 132ff. Cp. the classical description of ecstatic conditions amongst the mantics of Thrace and Asia Minor in E. Rohde, *Psyche*, 4th edn., Tübingen 1907, VOL. II, pp. 8–22. *Prophecy*, pp. 33ff. For the early history of prophecy see J. Lindblom, "Zur Frage des kanaanäischen Ursprungs des altisraelitischen Prophetismus," in *Von Ugarit nach Qumran: Beiträge zur alttestamentlichen und altorientalischen Forschung Otto Eissfeldt zum 1. September, 1957, dargebracht von Freunden und Schülern*, edd. W. F. Albright, W. Baumgartner, J. Lindblom and H. H. Rowley, *Beihefte zur Zeitschrift für die alttestamentliche Wissenschaft*, henceforth cited as B.Z.A.W., 77 (1958), pp. 89ff.

state of affairs, begs Moses to forbid them, but the latter sees it with very different eyes. "Would that all Jahweh's people were prophets, that Jahweh would put his spirit upon them!" This is not, of course, evidence that prophetic frenzy was known in Israel as early as the "wilderness period." The story is rightly regarded as being, in the Pentateuchal tradition, a comparatively late one[5] : yet it is also early in the sense in which it supplies evidence of an encounter with the prophetic movement and some discussion of it. It still preserves echoes of the amazement to which this strange event gave rise, and of the effort to come to some intellectual understanding of such an unprecedented phenomenon. Does it not make for disorder? Or is it perhaps after all compatible with Jahwism? To an astonishing degree the verdict is favourable—the spirit of these frenzied individuals is taken from Moses's spirit. The end which the story tries to serve is therefore that of the legitimation of this new religious phenomenon which may have caused the orthodox a good deal of perplexity. The story may actually be taken as evidence of an acceptance of the ecstatic movement into the institutions of Jahwism, or at least as an etiology of the prophetic movement which gave it legitimation. In Moses's answer where the difficult question has so positive a solution given it, Jahwism begins to interpret itself in a completely new way. It now measures itself against a previously unknown standard—it assesses itself according to the measure in which it possesses the prophetic spirit, of which, the story implies, there can never be too much.

This story is immediately followed by another which again deals with a particular manifestation of early prophecy, this time in the form of a gnomic saying. "If there is a prophet among you, I make myself known to him in visions, and speak to him in dreams. Not so with my servant Moses . . ." (Num. XII. 6ff.). Here too, a connexion is made between the $n^e bi'im$ and Moses, but at the same time of course, the emphasis is now on the differences between them and Moses—in the first story it had lain on the similarities, and had tried to show the closest possible relationship between them. The rather curious words just quoted probably refer, however, to a different kind of *nabi'*, for the prophets envisaged here are not simply vessels for the divine spirit, but subjects whom the deity addresses in an articulate way, and the two

[5] H. Gressmann, *Mose und seine Zeit*, henceforth cited as *Mose*, Göttingen 1913, p. 179; M. Noth, *Überlieferungsgeschichte des Pentateuch*, henceforth cited as *Pentateuch*, Stuttgart 1948, pp. 141ff.

can hardly be identical. Moreover, this prophet, as the oracle speaks of him, comes with a message to deliver. Admittedly—and this is emphasised—his illumination is somewhat indirect. It comes in dreams and enigmatic utterances, and so there is a certain gap between inspirer and inspired. Moses's relationship to God is much more direct, since his knowledge originates in face-to-face converse with God, and immediate vision. Unfortunately, much in the passage is obscure. What is meant by beholding the "form of Jahweh"? Above all, who is the "Moses" who is so insistently given precedence over the $n^e bi'im$?[6]

At one period in the critical investigation of prophecy, prophets and ecstatics were thought to be identical in origin and equally old in time. To-day however the idea that the prophets shared this single ancestry, and that the vast tree of prophecy grew from this single root, is regarded as very doubtful. Once we have freed ourselves from this highly artificial view of the development of prophecy, it soon becomes clear that several very diverse elements were characteristic of the $n^e bi'im$ even at their earliest appearances in the Old Testament. There seems no reason to doubt the existence of bands of ecstatics as late as the time of David. But if this was so, such "prophets" were then the contemporaries of Nathan; what, apart from the title $nabi'$, did they have in common with him?[7] The differences between the two are so great that it has even been suggested that Nathan ought not to be called a prophet at all, but should simply be regarded as the tutor of Solomon.[8] Texts from the archives of Mari, a city state on the middle Euphrates in the time of Hammurabi (c. 1700 B.C.), have, however, thrown new light on this very matter of Nathan's function as a prophet, for we read there of a mantic prophet ($muhhum$) of the god Dagan who passes on to high officials of state communications which he has received in dreams from the god. These texts have, however, a peculiar feature. They are not oracles of the ordinary sort. They are vexatious interventions, remonstrances, and commands of the deity which this man of god, who obviously had close connexions with the court, passes on.[9] A second Mari text is even closer to the state of affairs in early Israel, for

[6] See VOL. I, p. 291.

[7] II Sam. VII. Iff., 12; I Kings I. 8, 23. Gad also filled the role of court prophet as well as Nathan. See I Sam. XXII. 5; II Sam. XXIV. 11–13.   [8] *Profeten*, p. 124.

[9] Cp. W. von Soden, "Die Verkündigung des Gotteswillens durch prophetisches Wort in den altbabylonischen Briefen aus Mari," in *Welt des Orients*, 3 (1950), pp. 397ff. M. Noth, "History and the Word of God in The Old Testament," in *Bul-*

in it, using a prophet as his mouthpiece, the god—in this case the Syrian weather-god Hadad—not only claims to have put the king on his throne, but as well informs the latter that he can also revoke the appointment at will. "What I gave, I shall take away."[10] Nathan too received his revelations by night (II Sam. VII), spoke in the name of his God a word which founded a dynasty, and appeared unbidden at court to remonstrate in that same name (II Sam. XII). The text also reminds us of the seer Gad, who had to inform David of the divine displeasure at the census which the king had taken (II Sam. XXIV. 11ff.).

Even if these parallels outside Israel allow us to postulate the historicity of Nathan as both a mantic prophet and a politician at the court of David, yet the internal source, the Old Testament itself, does not give a sufficiently clear picture of his office to allow us to differentiate between it and other manifestations of contemporary *nabi'*-prophecy. The one thing we can still see is that Nathan was no ecstatic, and that he had no connexions with the impassioned, enraptured prophets who were active in the land at the same time.

The case of Ahijah of Shiloh provides a parallel. I Kings XIV. 1ff. (cp. I Sam. IX. 7f.) shows that he was consulted by people even over domestic misfortunes, and was paid a fee for his advice. Yet he too intervened in politics, and designated Jeroboam king of Israel (I Kings XI. 29ff.). There are, in fact, great affinities between the prophets of Mari and those who later work in Israel, and these should not be set aside simply because there are also considerable differences between them.[11] Even in the great Isaiah himself we are still aware of vivid reminiscences of those prophets who, in the name of their God, dealt with kings in matters of war, or of the succession, or of foreign policy.

Even if we were to examine the relevant texts in much more detail than is done here, it would still be impossible to arrive at a picture of the earliest "prophets" which would allow them to be seen as a

Studien zum Alten Testament, henceforth cited as *Ges. St.*, Munich 1st edn., 1957, [2nd edn. 1960], pp. 230ff.

[10] A. Lods, "Une tablette inédite de Mari, intéressante pour l'histoire ancienne du prophétisme sémitique," in *Studies in Old Testament Prophecy*, ed. H. H. Rowley, Edinburgh 1950, pp. 103ff.

[11] S. Herrmann has drawn particular attention to Elijah's relationship to Obadiah, the "governor of the house," since, exactly as in Mari, the prophet's dealings with the king are *via* a highly placed official of state (I Kings XVIII. 1ff.). (*Die Ursprünge der prophetischen Heilserwartung im Alten Testament*, Theological Dissertation, Leipzig 1957, pp. 58ff.)

reasonably clearly contoured historical phenomenon. The sources give no answer to the questions which we so urgently ask. There is actually a good deal of evidence that a mantic and ecstatic movement appeared in Syria in the eleventh century, and that, in spite of the fact that it was probably not Semitic in origin, it was accepted by Israel. But there is no reason to suppose that for Jahwism this was the spark which kindled Israel's own specific prophetic movement. Beyond doubt, when the title of prophet is given to Abraham (Gen. xx. 7), or to Moses (Deut. XVIII. 15, XXXIV. 10, etc.), or to Aaron (Ex. VII. 1), or to Miriam (Ex. xv. 20), this is to be taken as representing the way in which a much later age looked upon these people. It is an anachronism. At the same time it is difficult to prove the truth of what is said in 1 Sam. IX. 9—a text which in itself is far from clear—that the *nabi'* superseded the seer.[12] We have already seen that the main obstacle to a clearer understanding of the position during the early period is a semantic one—for within a very short period every kind of prophet was included in the general term *nabi'*. But was *nabi'* originally used simply for the ecstatic who now and then was "turned into another man" (1 Sam. x. 6) and whose words were then prompted by his frenzy? We cannot say for certain to which of the manifestations of prophecy the term was originally attached, and to which of them it was later transferred. The pictures given of Nathan, Gad, or Ahijah do, however, make it possible to maintain that these men were already dealing in embryo with some of the great themes which were to be taken up by the prophets who followed them—Jahweh's designs with the monarchy, the promise that the monarchy would continue in being, the announcement of chastisements which would overtake the anointed kings, and even the repudiation of a royal house (1 Kings XIV. 7ff.).

Here we may recall the oracle on Judah in the Blessing of Jacob (Gen. XLIX. 8–12), a passage which has always been extremely difficult to interpret. The generally accepted view is that the verses comprise a prophetic oracle referring to the kingship of David, but if this is so, is it not odd that this kingship is represented as belonging specifically to Judah? When he became king of Israel David certainly ruled over more than a single tribe, and it has therefore been suggested that the oracle should be connected with his period of rule at Hebron.[13] All the

---

[12] For the debate on 1 Sam. IX. 9, see H. H. Rowley, *The Servant of the Lord*, London 1952, pp. 99ff.

[13] J. Lindblom, in Supplement to *Vetus Testamentum*, henceforth cited as *V.T.*

difficulties lie in vs. 10b. It is said there that the sceptre and the ruler's staff shall "not depart" from Judah. The question is: what is the meaning of "until" in the phrase "until Shiloh comes"? Does it allude to one who appears *after* this "departure"—that is to say, to one who only "comes" after the rule of the sceptre of Judah has ceased? If so, we have here a genuine prophecy which foretells the coming of a ruler distinct from those who have preceded him. But it is also possible to take "until" not as exclusive but as inclusive: in this case the meaning is that the prophecy attains its goal and climax in David—even when he comes to the throne the rule of the sceptre of Judah does not cease. The answer all depends on the meaning given to the word שִׁילֹה in vs. 10. If we allow recourse to the generally accepted, though of course rather colourless, emendation מֹשְׁלֹו, the verse runs: "until his ruler comes, and to him belongs the obedience of the peoples." Taking "until" in the inclusive sense, this could be interpreted as a *vaticinium ex eventu* with reference to David and the empire he established, and the description of the really paradise-like fertility of the land of Judah—the man who can without a thought bind his mount to a vine and wash his garments in wine is living in paradise—could derive from the style of diction current at court.[14] Recently however, thanks to Lindblom, there has been a reaction in favour of letting the text as we have it stand. In this case the implication is that it was expected that David would come to Shiloh, the centre of the Amphictyony. (He did not, of course, do so, for, as Eissfeldt points out, he gave his kingdom a new centre, Jerusalem, and had the Ark brought there from Shiloh.[15]) This interpretation does not answer the question whether, as Eissfeldt himself believes, the oracle dates from before the destruction of Shiloh (1050). It could, indeed, also be interpreted as an example of wishful thinking: that Shiloh was to be restored to its former position of honour.

The oracle on Judah in Gen. XLIX may therefore be taken as completely prophetic in the narrower sense of that term, or as simply celebrating the rise of David—we cannot be sure. There is, however,

VOL. I (1953), p. 78. There is, of course, this defect in Lindblom's argument. To fix the date of the oracle on Judah he adduces oracles concerning other tribes as well. But the form and content of Gen. XLIX give no guarantee that the individual oracles are to be related to the same historical era.

[14] See VOL. I, pp. 320f.

[15] Eissfeldt, "Silo und Jerusalem," in Supplement to *V.T.*, VOL. IV (1957), pp. 138ff.

no doubt about the oracle of Balaam in Num. xxiv. 15–19: the form in which it is given is clearly that of the prophetic oracle. It, too, is generally assumed to refer to David,[16] and provides a fleeting glimpse of the style used in delivering royal oracles in honour of the new dynasty. Once again much of the detail is obscure. The description of the monarch as a star or a comet only occurs again in Is. xiv. 12f.

If, as is generally assumed, the two oracles are *vaticinia ex eventu*, which means that they sing the praises of something which already exists in order to give it their blessing, they may be described as "Messianic" in so far as they make reference to the anointed one,[17] but quite obviously they have to be distinguished from the later prophets' Messianic predictions which start from the assumption that that which at present exists is superseded, and that men have now to adjust themselves to something new.

2. ELIJAH

The pictures drawn in the Old Testament of Nathan or Ahijah of Shiloh may seem curiously lifeless: but in the stories about Elijah we are suddenly confronted with a clearly drawn historical figure.[18] Admittedly, the traditions about him are far from homogeneous. The large block I Kings xvii. 1 – xix. 18 is itself made up of six separate stories which have obviously been edited and harmonised sometime after their original drafting; and the stories of Naboth's vineyard in I Kings xxi and of Ahaziah's sickness in II Kings i belong to a rather different category. Though there is still some schematisation and use of standard types, this is for the particular purpose of bringing out sharp contrasts where that is necessary, and the details of the story bear the stamp of history and individuality. This applies especially to Elijah himself: he is unapproachable, unpredictable, feared, and even hated, but always someone to be reckoned with. The impression given, however differently, in all these stories is of a man of enormous powers. Such a figure cannot simply have been invented, and can only be explained by saying

---

[16] At least this is what the reference to the subjection of Moab and Edom suggests. On the other hand it is remarkable that so old a piece of writing—it is perhaps even contemporary with the events it describes—should speak of David, who was a Judean, as a star from "Jacob," that is to say, from Israel.

[17] See VOL. I, p. 316, n. 13.

[18] G. Fohrer, *Elia*, Zürich 1957; R. S. Wallace, *Elijah and Elisha*, Edinburgh 1957; J. Steinmann, in *Elie le prophète*, Bruges 1956, pp. 93ff.

that the stories reflect a historical figure of well-nigh superhuman stature. True, they tell us nothing about his personal circumstances, the religious and social *milieu* to which he belonged, or his origins. They speak of him as if he were known universally: but at the same time they do not assume that the people who read them, or who heard them told, had anything like our modern interest in the prophet's "personality." We are told that he came from Gilead, and this should remind us that in this territory east of Jordan, which had never been the seat of an earlier Canaanite civilisation but was land colonised by Israel herself, Jahwism would have preserved its intransigence towards other cults much more than was the case to the west of the river, where it had grown more and more ready to open its doors to the cult of Baal. Since Elijah grew up in what was still the Jahwism of the patriarchs, we can well understand his horror at the syncretism with which he was brought into contact later.

As we have already seen, this was a syncretism which had its roots deep in the past. It really began as early as the entry into Canaan, but entered upon a new phase when David incorporated into the empire of Israel large tracts of Canaanite territory which were then "evangelised," though not in any systematic way.[19] Yet, even if Jahwism extended into these areas—as, in time, it certainly did—the effect of the co-incidental increase in the population of Israel was to swell the Canaanite element to dangerous proportions. This was not noticed at the time; for the crumbling away of the old ideas held about Jahweh, about the distinctive way in which he was worshipped, and about his will as expressed in law, was a gradual process, and only a very few were aware of it. Looked at from the outside, almost everything connected with the cult was still what is had always been. The altars sent up their smoke, the customary prayers were offered, and the religious language and concepts which spoke to men's minds of Jahweh's self-revelation and of his acts may scarcely have changed. But were people still worshipping *Jahweh*? Was it not rather Baal, with his control over the blessings of the world of nature, who was now in their minds? For Baal was nonetheless Baal, even when invoked by the name Jahweh. Or was the object of worship some indeterminate third party who belonged somewhere between the two?

This was what had happened to Jahwism in the hundred and fifty years since the end of David's reign. Then, as a result of the policies

[19] See VOL. I, pp. 61f.

and Ahab, the whole situation suddenly took a turn for the worse. What had always been a danger now became an acute one. The cause was the action of Omri in giving his kingdom a new central point by founding Samaria. Very likely Samaria had so far been a relatively independent city-state with a political constitution and cultic usages of its own.[20] At all events, it possessed a temple of Baal (I Kings xvi. 29, 32; II Kings x. 18ff.), and it certainly had none dedicated to Jahweh. To give his kingdom additional strength, Omri had already entered into alliances with his neighbours on the north-east and north-west, and the political and economic ties with Tyre grew still closer when Jezebel was married to Omri's son Ahab, for she was of the royal house of Tyre. In antiquity, however, such relationships were never solely secular matters, because political recognition always also involved the partners in the alliance in certain cultic concessions, and the Elijah stories make it perfectly clear not only that Jezebel herself continued to practise the Phoenician form of worship in which she had been brought up, but also that, even in Israel, she was able to support "prophets," the officials of this cult (I Kings xviii. 19). In the country districts, people still worshipped Jahweh—or rather, the deity whom they still thought of as Jahweh—but at court and in the upper classes in the city worship was given to Baal. As a result, any genuine worship of Jahweh which still persisted in the land was thrown completely on to the defensive.

Just at this time, when the peril confronting Jahwism was serious indeed, there came Elijah. The great religious assembly on Mount Carmel, to which the faithful came hastening from far and wide, and of which a detailed account is given in I Kings xviii. 17–40, suggests that Elijah had been able to force the authorities to take action on the question of who was to be God in Israel.[21] It looks as if, even at this late date, this was something which resembled a muster of the Amphictyony at which Elijah was determined to settle once for all the issue between

---

[20] A. Alt, "Der Stadtstaat Samaria," in *Kleine Schriften zur Geschichte Israels*, henceforth cited as *K.S.*, Munich 1953–9, VOL. III, pp. 270ff.

[21] Alt, "Das Gottesurteil auf dem Karmel," in *K.S.*, VOL. II, p. 135, and also VOL. III, p. 276f.; Otto Eissfeldt, "Der Gott Karmel," in *Sitzungsberichte der Deutschen Akademie der Wissenschaften zu Berlin, Klasse für Sprachen, Literatur und Kunst*, I (1953), pp. 31ff.; K. Galling, "Der Gott Karmel und die Ächtung der fremden Götter," in *Geschichte und Altes Testament* (Beiträge zur historischen Theologie), XVI, Tübingen 1953, pp. 105ff.

the two religions. It must nevertheless have come as a great surprise to his fellows that Elijah viewed the matter as a case of "either-or." At the time, no one else saw as he did that there was no possibility of accommodation between the worship of Baal and Israel's ancient Jahwistic traditions. We should not imagine, then, that the stark choice involved in the question "either Jahweh or Baal" was familiar to the audience or a current ultimatum.[22] The story says that the people heard it in silence, and this argues lack of understanding of the question rather than any feeling of guilt (vs. 21). Elijah had to make a Herculean effort before he succeeded in forcing them to make a decision for which no one saw any need.

If we want to know exactly what happened on Mount Carmel, we must follow the lead given by Alt and start from what appears at first sight to be no more than an incident mentioned in passing, the destruction of the altar dedicated to Jahweh (vs. 30). Since Carmel lay outside the area settled by the Amphictyony, the altar can only have been erected after the time of David. There, therefore, the worship of Jahweh must have represented an invasion: Carmel must have been an advance post in Canaanite territory, for from time immemorial the mountain had been the domain of the cult of the Baal of Carmel. How and when the advance was made is not known. Jahwism may at first simply have ousted the worship of Baal, but later the old indigenous cult revived; and of course Israel was often to experience what now resulted—once the two altars were established side by side, Jahweh's was inevitably deserted in favour of Baal's. This was the situation with which Elijah found himself faced on Carmel. As has just been said, the absolutely new factor was that for him the co-existence, or rather the coalescence, of the two forms of worship, in which the rest of the people were perfectly at home, was intolerable. Thus the whole story turns on the answer given to the prophet's question. Yet, who was it who answered? Certainly not the people. (Here the story goes its own road compared with the otherwise very similar story in Josh. xxiv. 14ff.) Nor was it Elijah. It was Jahweh himself who gave the answer. Obviously what the narrator of the story wanted to make clear was that this was the only possible way by which Israel could have been saved, and that she could never of herself have been delivered from her neglect of her faith and worship, unless Jahweh himself had once again borne great

[22] The rather obscure words "limping with two different opinions" may have an allusion to a cultic dance, to bending the knees (so Galling, *op. cit.*, p. 107).

and glorious witness to himself. Such a declaration was, of course, a far more wonderful and more decisive answer to the question of who was God in Israel than any human reply, however solemn, would have been. The story does all it can to give a wider importance to what was, after all, a local incident, and to make it a touchstone of action for the whole nation.

To digress for a moment: from the first beginning, the whole story is based on the irreconcilable antithesis which existed between the two forms of worship. This is, in a sense, unfortunate, for it means that we take as the starting-point what was in fact the outcome of the incident. We are only given Elijah's view of the situation. On the other hand, this does mean that the complete irreconcilability of the two religions is clearly brought out, though in conventional terms. Baalism leads to extremes, and the loss of personal identity, as is shown by the hopeless attempts of the priests of Baal to do something that will attract their god's attention. Compared with this frenzy, Elijah's composure gives an impression of downright inertia. Israel's God was ready to give proof of himself, and Israel knew it! She knew that he sought her out, and that she did not need to seek him or beg his attention. But if this aspect of the story contains a certain amount of "teaching," there is also a different, more old-fashioned aspect illustrated by the full belief in miracles and, more particularly, by the way in which everything is made to depend on Elijah, a figure of absolutely primeval force, with stupendous confidence in his own prophetic powers ("as Jahweh the God of Israel lives, in whose service I am, there shall be neither dew nor rain these years, except by my word"—I Kings XVII. I).

The next aspect of the story to be considered is that the slaughter of the priests of Baal was in no sense an act of vengeance or fanaticism to which Elijah let himself be driven by the force of passion. It has very properly been pointed out that he was only giving effect to an ancient, though now largely forgotten, amphictyonic law which imposed the death penalty on any form of apostasy from Jahweh: "whoever sacrifices to other gods shall be put to death" (Ex. XXII. 19 (20)).[23] Deuteronomy, two hundred years after Elijah, still retains the provision (Deut. XIII. 7–12 [6–11]). It even envisages the possibility of whole cities together renouncing the worship of Jahweh, and for this prescribes the extremest penalty, the "ban," the total destruction of every living thing (Deut. XIII. 13ff. [12ff.]).[24]

[23] See VOL. I, p. 204, n. 30.   [24] Galling, *op. cit.*, pp. 122ff.

As it stands, the account of the theophany at Horeb (1 Kings xix), which follows the scene on Carmel, purports to be its immediate sequel, for with great artistry the story sets in the foreground the one actor in the drama who had neither been convinced nor overpowered by Jahweh's self-revelation on Carmel and who had now resolved to take extreme measures, namely Queen Jezebel. Quite obviously this story originally stood on its own, and in some respects it in fact runs parallel to the other. It too takes as its starting point the desperate plight into which Jahwism had come (vs. 10), it too gives an account of a manifestation of Jahweh, and finally it too ends with a pronouncement of penalty, which in this case however is only proclaimed and not carried out.[25] The extermination of Jahwism which he sees staring him in the face is of course the real reason for Elijah's despair. The picture of a prophet so enervated and resigned as to be at the point of contemplating suicide was an extremely bold and thrilling subject for a story teller of the time to attempt. This is truly weakness at its weakest, in fact the very epitome of weakness. For who can plumb such depths of weakness as a prophet who knows that his one and only help lies in what God can say and do? The description of the theophany itself has certainly been worked over in places, but even as it stands, its realism vouches for its great age.[26] Its interpretation is fairly generally agreed upon, but with a subject of this kind, the important questions are those put by hermeneutics: what possible interpretations are there which agree with the story itself, and where does it impose limits on our eagerness to discover its various meanings? No one can accept the widely held idea that the "still, soft whisper" expresses a more elevated, more ethical and spiritual, concept of God, and is therefore a rebuke to Elijah and his zeal. For one thing, it is out of keeping with the task itself which is laid upon the prophet, which reveals absolutely no trace of any such gentle spirituality. With an Old Testament theophany everything depends upon the pronouncement: the phenomena which accompany it are always merely accessories. This is particularly true in cases where the narrator does not give any interpretation of them, and it is very doubtful if descriptions of the phenomena accompanying a theophany are really meant to be explained in such a symbolic way.

To say this is not, of course, to deny that the contrast between storm,

[25] H. Gunkel, *Elias, Jahwe und Baal*, Halle 1906, pp. 20f.

[26] It is perfectly obvious that vss. 9–14 are not a unity. But the whole thing falls into place if vss. 9b–11a are taken as a maladroit anticipation and struck out.

earthquake, and fire and the "voice of a thin silence" is extremely strange and effective: but it is part of the nature of such stories that, while trying to understand this contrast, we should keep strictly to the facts stated, and not read any dubious symbolical meaning into them.[27] One obvious interpretation of this strange series of natural phenomena is that the powers of nature lying in the foreground of the story should make the reader aware of another world lying behind them, which is not, of course, conceived in terms of metaphysics, and is also not their extension or intensification, but rather their reverse side. The narrator cannot, of course, indulge in the abstractions of philosophy; even when he wants to suggest some quite immaterial and out of the way phenomenon, he has to keep within the realm of sense-perception. He therefore describes the manifestation of Jahweh in terms of "air, breath," which though still lying within the natural realm, represent the extreme limit of apprehension by the senses.[28] As to the effects, however, of this appearance of Jahweh, the atmosphere became no easier when the gentle sigh of the wind was heard after storm, earthquake, and fire had come and gone: indeed, the result of the manifestation, at least on Elijah, was actually to increase the tension (vs. 13).

The wording of I Kings XIX suggests that the theophany there recorded should be compared with the one given in Ex. XIXf., but as I see it, we should be very careful here. The very mention of a mountain of God implied, we must realise, the idea of a theophany and all the paraphernalia which regularly belonged to it and which everyone who heard the story expected as a matter of course. Thus, I Kings XIX does not necessarily derive from Ex. XIX. If, however—and this is by no means certain—the narrator did intend to remind people of the events which had taken place long ago at Sinai, and to have what he told regarded as parallel to them and as their sequel, the tradition and picture of Sinai which he took up is unknown. It may have had features other than those which appear in Ex. XIXf.

The reason why Elijah undertook the long journey to Horeb is not made particularly clear. Is it to be regarded as a pilgrimage?[29] He obviously wanted to pour out his troubles to Jahweh at the place where Jahweh had already shown himself so plainly, and where Moses, too,

[27] See VOL. I, p. 181, n. 13.

[28] Ps. CVII. 29 also suggests that the word דממה has to do with atmospheric conditions, a gentle movement of the wind. So also LXX, which renders by φωνὴ αὔρας λεπτῆς.   [29] See VOL. I, pp. 9f.

had worked. Elijah's most grievous plaint was his conviction that the cause of Jahwism was utterly lost in Israel. The answer he received was in the highest degree surprising—and this leads us back to the statement that the prime consideration in interpreting a theophany is the actual pronouncement. Jahweh has not finished with Israel: there is still much he plans to do with her. First, she must suffer dreadful havoc at the hands of Hazael of Syria and Jehu, and Elijah himself is to appoint these two avengers to their task. The one is to chastise the nation from without, the other from within.[30] But this does not mean the end for Israel, for Jahweh intends to "leave seven thousand, all the knees that have not bowed to Baal, and every mouth that has not kissed him" (1 Kings xix. 18). These words are at once the climax of the story and the key to its meaning, for they are, of course, the answer to Elijah's complaints that he was the only remaining loyal worshipper of Jahweh. There are certainly to be terrible chastisements: nevertheless an Israel will survive to stand before Jahweh. Of course—and here a new note is struck in Israel's story—it will only consist of a remnant. But it is to be noted that this is spoken of as if it already existed: there is no antecedent condition (a remnant will remain if some are found who have not bowed the knee to Baal). God appoints the remnant, and he already knows people of whom Elijah knew nothing. The remnant doubtless consists of those who had remained faithful: but their preservation had been decided even before the start of the coming troubles.

Jahweh's revelation of his designs for Israel also means the end of Elijah's prophetic office. He has still to implement the three commissions which had been laid upon him, but thereafter Jahweh has no further need of him. He is, however, permitted to know that even so Jahweh is to continue to bless Israel, for from the remnant a new Israel will arise.[31]

Some discussion of the remnant may be given here. As Müller's study, which is still authoritative, proved, the origins of the remnant concept are not to be looked for in the religious or cultic sphere, but in civil life.[32] At the time when the concept came into being, warfare

[30] Hazael, 11 Kings VIII. 7ff.; Jehu, 11 Kings IX. 1ff.

[31] Could the collection of stories about Elijah have ended without giving some account of the carrying out of the orders? It is an old question, and, because of 11 Kings VIII. 7ff. and IX. 1ff., we have in fact to reckon with the possibility that part of the original text has been lost. A redactor took the view that Hazael and Jehu were not anointed by Elijah, but by Elisha.

[32] For what follows cp. W. Müller, *Die Vorstellung vom Rest im Alten Testament*, Theologische Dissertation Leipzig 1939.

aimed in principle at total annihilation. Very often, however, the enemy was not utterly wiped out, and in such cases a remnant remained. Early eastern monarchs, in particular kings of Assyria, frequently boast that a campaign was so successful that the vanquished were left without a remnant. In other cases they admit that a remnant did survive, though stressing that it was no more than a remnant. Israel too used the term in this civil sense, for example, a "remnant of Edom" (Am. ix. 12), the "remnant of the Rephaim" (Josh. xiii. 12), the "remnant of the kingdom of Sihon" (Josh. xiii. 27), the "remnant of the Amorites" (ii Samuel xxi. 2), the "remnant of Ashdod" (Jer. xxv. 20), etc. In general the fate of a remnant was wretched. If it managed to escape dispersal, or eviction, or death from starvation, it was still condemned to complete political insignificance. Sometimes of course, a remnant became the nucleus of a people's rebirth. A remnant which remains can therefore be a stricken nation's badge of hope, and because of this, was always carefully watched by other nations. During the Monarchy, Israel learned at the hands of the Philistines, "the remnant of the coast-land of Caphtor," what an uncomfortable neighbour even a stricken and decimated people could be (Jer. xlvii. 4; Ezek. xxv. 15f.).

In no sense, therefore, is the remnant concept peculiar to the preaching of the prophets, as Gressmann believed it to be.[33] Müller is also right in saying that Elijah was not the first to transfer it to the language and ideology of religion, for the concept is obviously used by J in his attempt to explain Jahweh's paradoxical designs in history[34]—Noah and his sons are simply a remnant preserved: Lot and his family are the same, a remnant escaped from Sodom: Jacob divided his possessions in such a way that, if the worst came to the worst, the company which was left might be a "remnant which escaped" (Gen. xxxii. 9 [8]): and in a solemn hour Joseph declared to his brethren that the reason why Jahweh had led him in the strange way he had was "in order to preserve a remnant on earth, and to keep you alive as a great remnant which escaped" (Gen. xlv. 7). The only new thing in Elijah's use of the concept is that he refers it to preservation from calamities which are still to come and which Jahweh himself is to bring about.

The picture of Elijah is rounded off by the story of Naboth (i Kings xxi) and the account of Ahaziah's search for a cure (ii Kings i). In the first of these the point at issue is the unconditional validity of God's

---

[33] H. Gressmann, *Der Ursprung der israelitisch-jüdischen Eschatologie*, Göttingen 1905, pp. 229ff.   [34] Müller, *op. cit.*, pp. 40ff.

law, before which all men are equal, and to which even a king is subject. The incident illustrates the contrast between two different concepts of law. The very much more arbitrary interpretation of the rights and privileges of a monarch which was characteristic of the Canaanite city states is contrasted with the concept which existed in Israel. The latter was, in a sense, democratic, and it certainly made much more stringent demands: without respect of persons, a man's rights and property, and in particular his life, were regarded as under divine protection.[35] The second story shows conflict breaking out in just the same way though in a different field, the sphere of sacral medicine. King Ahaziah had fallen out of the window. He knew that if he wanted to get better, he must have recourse to a divine being, but the one to whom he went was Beelzebub of Ekron who was, it seems, renowned far and wide as the possessor of the power of miraculous healing. Elijah at once reacts, and in his own person displays that absolute intolerance of any other god which characterised Jahwism. As with law so with healing—it belongs to Jahweh alone: and Ahaziah's recourse in his extremity to a foreign god and not to Jahweh was tantamount to disbelief in him and apostasy from him, and a sin against the first commandment.[36]

Looked at from our point of view, the pictures of Elijah do not properly speaking represent him as a subject, a "figure" in the modern literary sense of the term, in any way worthy of consideration for his own sake, or meriting any special interest. The stories regard him rather as a part of a mighty event, namely the amazing witness borne by Jahweh to himself after a time of syncretism and apostasy. In this,

[35] The discovery of the royal archives of Ugarit and Alalakh in northern Syria have shed new light on the economic conditions and the conditions of land tenure which clearly had long been in existence in these places. See J. Nougayrol in *Mission de Ras Shamra VI: Le Palais Royal d'Ugarit*, ed. C. F. A. Schaeffer, Paris 1955, pp. 31, 283ff.; D. J. Wiseman, *The Alalakh Tablets* (British Institute of Archaeology at Ankara. Occasional Publications, II. London 1953). In practice the whole economic life was under the control of the king, and he consistently strove for his own part to extend his own private estates. One of the things which the Alalakh texts reveal is the frequency of excambion. This sheds a new light on I Kings XXI. The prophets opposed it, and advocated the economy which had obtained in early Israel, and which was incompatible with the idea of law current in Canaan. The kings of Israel and Judah increasingly adopted the latter. See Alt, "Der Anteil des Königtums an der sozialen Entwicklung in den Reichen Israel und Juda," in *K.S.*, VOL. III, pp. 348ff.

[36] See VOL. I, p. 274f. Also J. Hempel, "Ich bin der Herr, dein Arzt," in *Theologische Literaturzeitung*, henceforth cited as *Th. Lz.*, 82 (1957), col. 809ff.

of course, Elijah played an important part, but not in such a way as would allow him to be taken as the chief subject of the story. In the writer's view, he was what he was not because of any remarkable powers or qualities which made him eminent, but because he was used by Jahweh at a momentous hour as a figure in the interplay of political and religious forces. Elijah sometimes describes himself as one who "attends upon Jahweh as servant" (I Kings XVII. 1, XVIII. 15, XIX. 11: R.S.V., "before whom I stand"), but at the same time it is not altogether easy to determine what kind of service this was, the reason being that the stories no sooner bring him on the scene than they make him disappear into the background by wresting the action out of his hands as Jahweh takes it directly into his own. Again, the world in which Elijah lived was chock-full of miracles, yet he himself never works a single one, in striking contrast to Elisha, who was quite ingenuously extolled as a worker of miracles. But was not Elijah unique in his zeal for Jahweh? He certainly was, but this zeal cannot possibly be put forward as the quality for which the stories sing his praises. Is it not significant that the one occasion on which he speaks of his zeal is not after the drama on Carmel, but at the very moment when he sees himself at the end of everything, and realises that, for all his zeal, he has failed (I Kings XIX. 10)? The fact is that the subject of the Elijah stories is basically not the prophet himself, but Jahweh. He it was who brought everything to pass, and he, and he alone, gave the answer to the momentous question: who was to be God in Israel. Elijah always comes into the action only momentarily, and he does so only to vanish and then, mysteriously and for no apparent reason, to reappear elsewhere. He seems to have lived a different life from Elisha, shunning society and living entirely alone, with no fixed abode but roaming from place to place. However, these apparent differences in their modes of life may be explained by differences in the literary methods used by the writers of each of the stories.

Since the Elijah stories centre in the acts of Jahweh and not those of the prophet, this gives them, despite their great variety of content, a certain uniformity which the Elisha stories completely lack. The central theme of them all is the irreconcilable antagonism between Jahweh and Baal which quite suddenly flared up again after the two had apparently come to terms, and tore open a deep gulf in the midst of Israel. Was the bestowal of the rain no longer to be Baal's province, or the healing of sickness Beelzebub's? For Elijah, of course, the question did not even arise: the whole thing was perfectly simple; and so he entered the lists on behalf of Jahweh who alone possessed these powers and in opposition to Baal who utterly lacked them. His insistence that power is the central issue in the contest may raise some doubt as to whether it is proper to speak of his as a monotheist. The keen edge to his polemic makes it perfectly possible that he would have allowed that Baal did exercise divine power, though of a relative and naturally much inferior sort. But the question is really irrelevant, for in any case Baal's writ did not apply to Israel.[37] The proposition that Israel belonged to Jahweh and to him alone, a belief deriving from the people's earliest days, no doubt found in Elijah a champion such as it had never had before, but at the same time he also was to say something about this relationship between Jahweh and Israel which went far and away beyond the nation's whole experience with Jahweh up to this time— Jahweh is resolved not to tolerate the apostasy of his people, but is about to rise up against them. Three men, Hazael of Syria, Jehu, who was to seize the throne in Israel, and the prophet Elisha have been commissioned to execute his judgments and crush Israel in pieces. They are not entirely to eradicate her from the pages of history, but only a remnant will be left for Jahweh to act upon in the future. Seven thousand is, of course, to be taken as a round number: compared with Israel as a whole it was an infinitesimal minority. Even before Elijah's day the faithful believed that in certain circumstances Jahweh might chastise his people as well as help them, but we must stress again that the idea that he might resolve to destroy them, leaving only a remnant, was absolutely new. Yet this was merely a foretaste of what the prophets who followed Elijah were to have to declare![38]

3. ELISHA

The collection of stories about Elisha may originally have been a literary unit, but because of the manner in which the Deuteronomistic histories were edited, it is even more disjointed than the Elijah collection.[39] It opens with the translation of Elijah and the passing of his

[37] On the recurrent question of the prophets and monotheism see Buber, *Prophetic Faith*, p. 110. "It may be uncertain whether he (the prophet Amos) reached some 'ism' or other; all the pretension of such distinctions comes to nothing when it tries to assert itself in face of what is to be found here; a man, given up to the oneness of his God."

[38] One of Elijah's contemporaries was Micaiah ben Imlah. I Kings XXII. 9ff. gives a detailed account of his prophecy of doom and of the conflicts to which it gave rise.

[39] The Elisha stories are to be found in II Kings II. I – XIII. 21.

charisma over to Elisha. (Because of this, II Kings II should be read in the context of Elisha and not of Elijah.)⁴⁰ And it closes with the miracle wrought by the prophet's dead body in its grave (I Kings XIII. 20f.). The majority of stories show Elisha in the company of people who are described as "disciples of the prophets" (בְּנֵי הַנְּבִיאִים) and who are, from the sociological point of view, a highly interesting separate group within the framework of Israelite society. We encounter them at several different places in the southern part of the Kingdom of Israel, and it may well be that their settlements there were closely associated with local sanctuaries.⁴¹ They seem actually to have formed themselves into separate congregations which lived according to rule. At all events, we sometimes read of assemblies held for teaching purposes (II Kings IV. 38, VI. I). Elisha is clearly their master and is called "father" by way of honour (II Kings VI. I, 5, 12, 21, cp. II. 12). The stories give us such a clear picture of this strange group's whole *milieu* that we can be sure that its members were drawn from a very low economic and social stratum in the population and indeed, that they were most likely without any status whatsoever. Their standards of eating and housing are miserable in the extreme. A case of debt is mentioned on one occasion (II Kings IV. 1–7). It may very well be that the function of sanctuaries as places of asylum had some meaning for these associations. At any rate, we must seriously consider whether the people who joined them made the choice entirely of their own free will. Insolvency was possibly the reason why they turned their backs on middle-class and peasant life. Or did their withdrawal conceivably owe more to religious than to economic factors? Perhaps the people in question still clung to the patriarchal mode of life sanctioned by Jahwism, in which they had a title to land, and had been unable to maintain themselves within the framework of the more feudal economy of the Canaanites. We are probably right in thinking that these bands of prophets were almost the last representatives of pure, uncontaminated Jahwism and its divine law,

---

⁴⁰ The meaning of Elisha's request in II Kings II. 9 is not altogether clear. What he most probably wants is the first-born's share of the *charisma*, which is according to Deut. XXI. 17 a double portion in the inheritance. The idea that he requests the double of the *charisma* of Elijah is certainly wrong. On the question of a prophetic succession, see H. J. Kraus, *Die prophetische Verkündigung des Rechts in Israel, Theologische Studien, Heft 51*, Zürich Zollikon 1957, p. 25.

⁴¹ I Sam. XIX. 8ff. presupposes the existence of such an association of prophets at Ramah. According to I Kings XX. 38, 41 the members of such associations were apparently recognisable by their tattoo marks (cp. Zech. XIII. 6).

and they were therefore of extreme importance for its survival, and especially for the particular character which it was to have from this time on. In the long run, these men were the parents of that stupendous radicalisation of Jahwism and its law which we find in the later prophets. They laid the foundations of that mysterious social and economic detachment and that disregard for the considerations of state policies which were the unquestioned preconditions for the rise of the later prophetic movement. These outcasts accumulated the vast capital on which the latter lived, for it was they who set the stamp on the idea of what it meant to be a *nabi'* and what it meant to speak to Israel in the name of Jahweh. Amos and Isaiah after them had only to adopt these ideas as their own.[42]

What was Elisha's office? To what tasks was he called as a prophet? The sources are in no doubt about the answer: he was a worker of miracles. He made iron float, made a spring of water wholesome, struck an enemy army with blindness, healed a leper, even brought a dead man back to life, and so on.[43] Nowhere in the Old Testament are so many miracles crowded into so small a space, and nowhere is such open pleasure taken in the miraculous, or such sheer delight shown at the repeated and astonishing proofs of the prophet's *charisma*. This means, of course, that Elisha's own person occupies the centre of the stage much more than was the case with Elijah. But "person" in this context does not carry the same full meaning as in our modern speech. Elisha's possession of a *charisma* which gives him the power to perform miracles is the real subject of the stories.[44]

[42] The Dead Sea Scrolls, which have not only given us information about a monastic-like settlement of Essenes, but also, in the Manual of Discipline, a precise account of the strict rules which regulated its common life, set the accounts of the associations of prophets in the time of Elisha in a new light, for we are now enabled to see them in a wider sociological context. This does not mean that we can simply call these associations the forerunners of the Essenes, but what we do see more clearly is that such groups of religious radicals occasionally existed in Israel, and that it was natural for such schismatics as the Essenes were to revive this old form of community, in order to preserve their own particular religious points of view. Cp. L. Rost, "Gruppenbildungen im Alten Testament," in *Th. Lz.*, 85 (1955), cols. 1ff.

[43] Comparison of 1 Kings XVII. 17–23 and 11 Kings IV. 29–37 shows that the version which ascribes the miracle to Elisha lays much greater stress upon the fact that it is a miracle and enters in much greater detail in its description of the technicalities of all that was done.

[44] In addition to miracles proper, the stories also credit the prophet with different kinds of parapsychic capabilities, such as clairvoyance and seeing from afar (11 Kings VI. 12, 32f., V. 26, VIII. 10ff.). G. Widengren, *Literary and Psychological Aspects of the*

Yet although the miracle stories account for a large part of what we know about Elisha, they certainly only give a very one-sided picture of his work. Indeed, what they portray was possibly not his real work at all, but only that aspect of it which was remembered by popular tradition. One story about him perhaps implies that on the Sabbath or at the new moon, people used to come from far and wide to the man of God to consult him (II Kings IV. 23). More than one passage gives clear evidence of another aspect of his work—politics; and this was very probably the real focal point of his whole life. Though these bands of prophets turned their backs on the ordered structure of society, this did not mean that they ceased to take any interest in Israel's public affairs and devoted themselves entirely to private contemplation. The opposite would rather be the case. In the east, groups like these have always shown a particularly keen concern for the problems of the community at large, and from time to time their initiative has had far-reaching consequences. The story which tells of Hazael's seizure of the throne credits Elisha with having influence in as distant a city as Damascus (II Kings VIII. 7-15). Naturally there is no proof of this: but even if the basis for this tradition is merely legendary, we can still gather from it something of the scope and the extreme daring of the conspiracies upon which these prophets embarked. The kind of political strings which Elijah manipulated can be seen still more clearly in the account of the anointing of Jehu and the fall of the then reigning dynasty, since for this event there is really sound historical evidence. Elisha was directly behind this act of horror. It was he who designated as king this eager partisan of uncontaminated Jahwism, and it is hard to imagine that he could have been blind to the fact that in the struggle against Baal and his worshippers, Jehu was to wade through a sea of blood (II Kings IX-X). The monarchy in the Northern Kingdom was based upon a *charisma*, and when prophets like Elisha appointed kings or hatched revolutions, they saw themselves as direct instruments of the God who guided history.[45] As they appear in the Old Testament, Elisha and Elijah, and many other key-figures of Jahwism also, were not simply devoted to what we think of as the world of religion and the spirit—faith, instruction, and worship—not even in their role as reformers: they were the servants of Israel, and the life of Israel did not

Hebrew Prophets, henceforth cited as *Aspects*, Uppsala Universitets Årsskrift 10, Uppsala and Leipzig 1948, p. 97.

[45] Alt, *K.S.*, VOL. II, pp. 121f.

have only a religious aspect. She had a political life as well. She was an historical entity, living not only in the realm of the spirit but also in the world of politics: the dangers to which she was exposed were equally great in both of these, and in each she required guidance and protection. Now Elisha regarded himself, and was regarded by others, precisely as the chosen instrument for Israel's defence and preservation—and by "Israel" is meant the true Israel, the Israel to which alone God granted the right to exist. This comes out clearly in its words applied to him and usually rendered as "my father, the chariots of Israel and her horsemen."[46] The legend shows that the man of God did in fact on occasion engage in enterprises of war whose sacral character is still discernible, and in which he intervened to give counsel, and use his supernatural knowledge to save his people (II Kings VI. 8–23). At the same time, however, this description of the prophet as Israel's true defence is a very forthright slogan, almost in fact a religious programme, whose influence far transcended the hour in which it was born. It preserves a memory of the days of the holy wars when Israel was confronted with the chariots of the Canaanites, and, herself not possessing these, was thrown back upon Jahweh alone. This was the time of origin of the stories which increasingly elaborated the theme that Israel's help lay not in chariots and horses, but solely in Jahweh.[47] Then, in an age which had long forgotten such holy wars, the emergence of men like Elisha put the stamp of truth on the experience of the past. Jahweh was still with Israel. True, great changes were in store. Dire disasters were to come upon her, to chastise and sift her, to make her once more a people in whom Jahweh took pleasure. A century later Amos, Hosea, Isaiah, and Micah developed this idea in such a way as to make Elijah's and Elisha's view of the future seem naïve and almost embryonic.[48]

[46] On II Kings XIII. 14, II. 12 see von Rad, *Der heilige Krieg im alten Israel*, 2nd edn. henceforth cited as *Heilige Krieg*, Zürich 1958, p. 55f. Also K. Galling, "Der Ehrenname Elisas und die Entrückung Elias," in *Zeitschrift für Theologie und Kirche*, henceforth cited as *Z. Th. K.*, Heft 2 1956, pp. 129ff. As Galling made clear, at this time there can be no talk of horsemen; the phrase is more accurately rendered, "chariots of Israel and their teams."

[47] See *Heilige Krieg*, pp. 14ff., 33ff.

[48] The *logia*, *i.e.*, the elements of proclamation proper contained in these narratives about prophets, have been examined by W. Reiser; he designates the prophetic words spoken in each case when a miracle was performed—for example, the prophecy concerning the meal in the jar (I Kings XVII. 14), or the announcement of cheap prices to-morrow (II Kings VII. 1)—as eschatological oracles, and forerunners of predictions

Two of the Elisha stories seem to stand out prominently from the rest, Elisha's meeting with Hazael (II Kings VIII. 7–15), and with Naaman (II Kings v). In the first, where the prophet meets the future usurper of the throne, high political tension and human woe are so concentrated that the result is a most sublime and moving scene. This is especially so where Hazael and the prophet are made to speak together in words of extreme restraint and delicacy. The second story gives a sympathetic portrayal of one aspect of the prophet's work, the pastoral guidance of an individual—the only occasion on which this particular aspect is shown.

In II Kings v the story's very opening gives a clearly drawn portrait of Naaman the Syrian: he is not only one of the chief officials of state, but he is also an upright man; and because of him Jahweh lent his aid to the Syrians. Thus, throughout the world Jahweh's eyes are upon the righteous, and he blesses all that they do. At the same time, however, Naaman is a leper.

First of all, the story contrasts the hiddenness of God's ways and the insignificance of the means which he employs—it is a little slave-girl from Israel who makes the first move that leads to the healing of Naaman—with the behaviour of the human beings concerned. The Syrian king makes the matter an affair of state and sends the king of Israel a diplomatic note requesting him to cure Naaman. The Syrians were, of course, unaware that in Israel Jahweh's bestowal of gracious gifts took no consideration of social status and position. Nor does the King of Israel himself know what to make of this strange request. "Does he take me for a god? No, all he seeks is a quarrel." There is almost an element of the grotesque in the description of the events which led up to this first fiasco, and even after these preliminary troubles were cleared up, the solution was far from being a speedy one. On the contrary, when Naaman, accompanied by a large suite of attendants, drives up to Elisha's door, there is a further clash of opposite points of view. Elisha made no attempt to appear in person, and to Naaman, who was expecting some solemn mumbo-jumbo, the message the prophet sent by his servant must have seemed very cavalier treatment indeed. But it was precisely this desire for a miracle which he meant to disappoint and smash: it was not to be a case of one mythology

such as Am. IX. 13. (W. Reiser, "Eschatologische Gottessprüche in den Elisalegenden" in Th. Z. (1953), pp. 321ff.). How far it is already correct to speak of eschatology here depends of course on how this term is to be defined. See below, pp. 115f.

out-bidding another. So the prophet completely dissociated himself physically from the healing, and by his command to wash in Jordan called instead for obedience. Oddly enough, though the healing did take place, it is not the focal point of the story. There is, in fact, a double climax: Naaman's first unhappy clash with Elisha, and their friendly conversation following the healing. The healing hangs suspended between these two high points.

After washing in the Jordan, Naaman came back to Elisha, and when he was unsuccessful in pressing his gifts upon the prophet, he made two requests of this apparently inexorable man. The first was that he might take two mules' burdens of earth back with him to Damascus, to make it possible for him to pray to Jahweh there. The request has more than once led commentators to express a poor opinion of Naaman's faith. But they are wrong, and their mistake is due to their tacit philosophic assumption that, like ourselves, Israel made a clear division of the world into material and spiritual spheres. Admittedly, even an Israelite reading the story must have felt that there was something odd in the request for a load of earth, but he would not have been taken aback in the slightest at Naaman's inability to rise to the level of the spiritual. He would have been touched by the way in which a man who had encountered the God of Israel here expresses his eager desire to be able to continue to worship him on heathen soil. Indeed, since he believed that the land which Jahweh granted was the saving gift *par excellence*, he would have felt that, in the difficult situation in which Naaman was placed, the latter was perfectly in order in seeking to give his faith what might be called a point of sacramental attachment, even if he took an unusual way of doing this. (This same load of earth has its contribution to make to the theological discussions between the spirit of Greece and the faith of the Bible, a necessary and recurrent subject of discussion for modern thought.)

Naaman's second request now that he is a worshipper of Jahweh also raises difficulties, because of the importance for Israel of the First Commandment. For he asked Elisha's permission to bow down at the King of Syria's side in the temple of Rimmon when his official position made this necessary. Naaman is already well aware that, once he is back home, it will be impossible to dissociate himself completely from pagan practices. This being so, will Jahweh's law slay him? To appreciate how acute the dilemma was, one has to realise that the request came from the lips of one who had no idea of the modern retreat of religion into the confines of the individual heart and spirit, for which the external accompaniments of worship are no longer essential.

Elisha's reply, eagerly awaited by Naaman, is brief and restrained in the extreme, but it is inspired by a profound pastoral insight. "Go in peace." To say that the prophet dodged the issue, or that he in fact sanctioned laxness, is to mistake its meaning. On the contrary, the main thing in it is that no law of any kind was imposed upon Naaman. How easy it would have been to furnish him with a shield of commandments! Instead, Elisha sent him back to his pagan environment, and put him and his faith under the guidance of Jahweh, in whose service he had pledged himself to continue. The prophet's initial reception of the Syrian had been harsh, but his dismissal of him is marked by generosity. The story deserves attention for the way in which it touches upon questions which transcend the healing of Naaman and in fact do really go beyond what is narrated.

While the pagan stranger comes out of the story very well, it ends with a sorry tale of how one of Elisha's closest associates was found wanting (vss. 20-7). Here too, as he leaves the scene, Naaman again appears in the best of lights when compared with the mendacious and greedy Gehazi.

CHAPTER C

THE ORAL TRADITION OF PROPHECY

ABOUT a century after Elijah, Amos, Hosea, Isaiah, and Micah appeared on the scene. If the source material for them is compared with that available for their predecessors, we find that in the eighth century a new factor has emerged. The narrative form of report, which is the only kind of source we have for Elijah and Elisha, markedly diminishes, and its place is taken by collections of disconnected *logia*. This difference in the way in which the account of the prophets' activity has been handed on forces us to give some consideration to the literary "form" in which the memory of their work and preaching has ultimately come down to us, for upon this largely depends the theological evaluation of later ages.

Like the historical tradition, the prophetic corpus lies before us in what are, to some extent, very shapeless collections of traditional material, arranged with almost no regard for content or chronological order, and apparently quite unaware of the laws with which we are familiar in the development of European literature.[1] Ezekiel is the first to give us the benefit of an arrangement according to a chronology based on the time at which the oracles were delivered. Nevertheless, within this vast body of material a differentiation, at once simple and at the same time of great theological importance, is immediately forced upon the reader's notice. This is the distinction between passages in poetry and passages in prose. While there are exceptions, the prophets' own way of speaking is, as a rule, in poetry: that is to say, it is speech characterised by rhythm and parallelism. In contrast, passages in which they are not themselves speakers but are the subjects of report, are in prose. There are thus two ways in which the prophets made their

---

[1] On the confusing impression which the literary legacy of the prophets makes on the uninitiated, Luther says: "They (the prophets) have a queer way of talking, like people who, instead of proceeding in an orderly manner, ramble off from one thing to the next, so that you cannot make head or tail of them or see what they are getting at." (I am indebted to Professor Eudo C. Mason for this rendering. Trs.) *Works.* Weimar Edn., VOL. XIX, p. 350.

contribution to the literature of the Old Testament, or at any rate to the traditions contained in it; on the one hand there are narratives or collections of narratives which tell of what they did, and on the other oracles or collections of oracles which they themselves delivered. Accordingly there are two reasons why they attracted the attention both of their own contemporaries and of those who came after them. One was the content of their preaching; the other was the circumstances of their appearance, the conflicts in which they were involved, the miracles they performed, and their particular encounters with particular people. In cases where both what a prophet himself said and what was reported about him are preserved, it is obviously not always possible to harmonise the accounts, for the point of view of a narrator who sees the prophet involved in the tensions and dramas of public life may be different from that of a group of disciples whose sole interest was to record in correct form oracles whose historical context had been forgotten. This explains, for example, the marked dissimilarity between the picture of Isaiah given in the stories told about him and that conveyed by his own oracles. The former is much closer to the popular estimate of him, and scarcely gives any indication of the enormous intellectual sweep of his preaching as reflected in the oracles. It must also be self evident that of these two forms in prophetic literature, that of the report is the earlier. Time, some degree of familiarity with the phenomenon of prophecy itself, and some education into a more spiritual outlook were all needed before it became possible to collect only the prophets' bare words, and to view them in detachment from their historical context, and evaluate them on their own intrinsic merits.

1. The first stage was undoubtedly that stories were told about the prophets,[2] and in this respect the stories about Elisha give the impression of coming from a distant past. On the other hand, the very considerations just noticed should warn us against allowing these popular miracle stories to lead us into forming too naïve a picture of this prophet as he really was. He gave formal lectures to disciples (II Kings IV. 38, VI. 1). If we had a collection of his lectures or his *logia*, our picture of him might well be different. The same would be true of Elijah. By the time

---

[2] The stories too can be separated into accounts of prophetic acts (*e.g.*, I Kings XVII 1–7, 8–16, 17–24) and accounts of prophetic words (*e.g.*, I Kings XXI. 17–20; II Kings I. 3f.). O. Plöger, *Die Prophetengeschichten der Samuel- und Königsbücher*, Dissertatiou, Greifswald 1937, pp. 38ff.

of Amos, however, people had learned to take a prophet's words by themselves and to write them down. This meant that the centre of gravity in the prophetic tradition now moved from the story told about the prophet to the collection and transmission of his *logia*. This development did not, however, lead to the disappearance of the custom of telling stories about the prophets, or indeed, to any decline in such a practice. This literary category still remained influential, for, in spite of what so many theologies of the Old Testament apparently believe, when she came to a more spiritual understanding of prophecy, Israel never went so far, in the interest of reducing the prophetic message to its ideal truths, as to sever it from its original roots in concrete events. On the contrary, she never ceased to see each of the prophets in his own historical situation, either as one who initiated historical movements or as one who was crushed to powder in the conflicts of history. The largest number of stories about a prophet is to be found in the book of Jeremiah, which is comparatively late.[3] When we come to it, we shall have to consider the importance of these as a supplement to Jeremiah's own oracles.

In reading the prophets to-day we must, of course, realise that what chiefly interests us, biographical detail, imports into these stories a viewpoint which is foreign to them themselves. Even the idea of "prophetic personalities" which so readily comes to our minds is very far from being what the sources themselves offer us. In all probability, the writers were much less concerned than we imagine to portray a prophet as a "personality," that is to say, as a unique human being who possessed special qualities of mind and spirit. The same is true of interest in biographical detail. We can even feel that the sources are opposed to any attempt to write "lives" of the prophets. Had the writer of Amos VII. 10ff. had any intention of giving information about Amos's own life, he would never have ended his account as he does, and have failed to inform the reader whether or not the prophet complied with the deportation order. If the story is to be read as a fragment taken from a biography, the only possible verdict on such an ending is "unsatisfactory." Amos is here only described from the point of view of his being a prophet, that is to say, as the holder of an office, and because of this the writer had no interest beyond describing the clash between the

---

[3] In connexion with the so-called Temple address in the year 609, the tradition contains the prophet's words (Jer. VII. 1–15) and independently a story which describes the incident (Jer. XXVI).

bearer of a *charisma* and the high priest, and recording the oracle of doom to which this gave rise.

The stories about Elijah, Elisha, and Isaiah also provide examples both of a similar lack of interest in biographical detail and of a concentration upon how a prophet acted in virtue of his calling. A change comes about with Jeremiah. Jeremiah the man and his *via dolorosa* are now really described for their own sake. This, however, is closely connected with the fact that with Jeremiah prophecy entered upon a critical phase of its existence, and that a new concept of a prophet was beginning to appear. Probably the first to realise that suffering was to be regarded as an integral part of a prophet's service was Baruch. There was more to being a prophet than mere speaking. Baruch saw a completely new aspect of the office. Not only the prophet's lips but also his whole being were absorbed in the service of prophecy. Consequently, when the prophet's life entered the vale of deep suffering and abandonment by God, this became a unique kind of witness-bearing. Yet even this does not mean that in narrative portions of Jeremiah the account of the prophet's life is given for its own sake. It is given because in his case his life had been absorbed into his vocation as a prophet, and made an integral part of the vocation itself. But, as I have already stressed, this insight was only reached after some time and must therefore be dealt with at a later stage.[4]

2. Prophecy ultimately employed the "messenger formula" as the most direct means of expressing its function.[5] But since from its very first appearance in Israel there were more kinds of prophecy than one, it is practically impossible to point to any single basic "form" of prophetic speech and to identify it, from the point of view of form criticism, as prophecy's original starting-point.[6] Yet, even though the

[4] See below, pp. 206ff.

[5] L. Köhler, *Kleine Lichter* henceforth cited as *Kleine Lichter*, Zürich 1945, pp. 11ff.; . Lindblom, *Die literarische Gattung der prophetischen Literatur*, Uppsala 1924; J. Hempel, *Die althebräische Literatur und ihr hellenistisch-jüdisches Nachleben*, Potsdam 1930–4, pp. 56ff.; H. W. Wolff, *Das Zitat im Prophetenspruch* henceforth cited as *Das Zitat*, Munich 1937.

[6] An old form, perhaps one of the oldest, is preserved in the cries uttered by the prophets in the context of sacral war enterprises, as has been pointed out by R. Bach (R. Bach, *Die Aufforderung zur Flucht und zum Kampf im alttestamentlichen Prophetenspruch*, Doctoral Dissertation, Bonn 1956). What is under discussion here is, for one thing, the stereotyped command to get ready for battle (cp. 1 Kings xx. 13f.; Hos. v. 8; Is. XIII. 2; Jer. XLVI. 3f., XLIX. 8, 14, 30f., L. 14f., 21, 29, LI. 11, 27); for another, the

"messenger formula" cannot be taken as this, it should be considered first, since it persists as a constant factor in all O.T. prophecy from Elisha to Malachi, and is, too, the most consistently used of all the many different prophetic literary categories.

As everyone knows, it was a common custom in the ancient world for a messenger with some announcement to make to discharge his errand when he came into the recipient's presence, by speaking in the first person, the form in which the message had been given to himself, that is to say, he completely submerged his own *ego* and spoke as if he were his master himself speaking to the other. Examples of this entirely secular use of the "messenger formula" introduced by the words "thus says so and so" are still to be found within the Old Testament itself.[7] This is the form which the prophets used more frequently than any other to deliver their messages, and the fact is important for the understanding of their own conception of their role. They saw themselves as ambassadors, as the messengers of Jahweh.

As a rule, however, the prophets prefaced this messenger formula with another form of words whose purpose was to draw the recipient's attention to the message and which, indeed, gave the first precise designation of those for whom it was intended. In the case of a divine threat, what was prefixed was a diatribe, in the case of a promise, an exhortation. These two, the messenger formula and the prefaced clause, must both be present before we have the literary category "prophetic oracle." To understand the category, we must remember that down to the time of Jeremiah, with whom there is a change, the prophets always made a clear distinction between the messenger formula and the diatribe or exhortation which introduced it. The former alone was the direct word of God: the other was a human word whose purpose was to lead up to and prepare the way for God's word and give it its reference. The divine word was, of course, primary in point of time: this was what came to the prophet in a moment of inspiration, to be passed on to those whom it concerned. This the prophet did by prefixing to it a diatribe which identified the people addressed. What makes the inner connexion between diatribe and threat is the character-

commands to flee directed to people against whom there was no hostile intent, but who lived in the zone chosen for military operations (cp. 1 Sam. xv. 6f.; Jer. iv. 6f., vi. 1, xlix. 8, 30, l. 8, li. 6).

[7] *E.g.*, Gen. xxxii. 4ff. [3ff.], xlv. 9; Num. xxii. 16; 1 Kings ii. 30; Is. xxxvii. 3.

istic "therefore" (לכן), justifying the latter and leading on to the words "Thus hath Jahweh spoken."[8]

But the messenger formula, frequent though it is, is still only one among many forms used by the prophets in their preaching.[9] In fact, they showed no hesitation in availing themselves of all manner of forms in which to clothe their message. None, secular and sacred alike, was safe from appropriation as a vessel for the discharge of his task by one prophet or another. What these men wanted to do, of course, was to attract attention: indeed sometimes, as when, for example, they laid violent hands on some time-hallowed sacral form of expression, their express intention was to shock their audience. Thus their utterances can be couched as a priestly direction concerning sacrifice (Is. I. 16f.; Am. v. 21ff.), as a cultic hymn, or as a pronouncement in a court of law.[10] Deutero-Isaiah took the priestly oracle of weal and reshaped it into something more sweeping and made it *the* "form" of his preaching. His well-known phrases, "Fear not, I have chosen you, redeemed you, I call you by name, you are mine" (Is. XLI. 10ff., XLIII. 1f., XLIV. 1f., etc.) are modelled on the liturgical language used by the priest in the cult in response to an individual prayer of lamentation.[11] In other cases the message was clothed in the form used by the teachers of wisdom (Is. XXVIII. 23ff.; Am. III. 3ff.), or of a popular song (Is. v. 1ff.). The best example of the changes which these literary categories underwent at the hands of the prophets, who sometimes even expanded them into really grotesque shapes, is the dirge: the later prophets actually turned it upside down and parodied it.[12] Exegesis has therefore to be particularly careful here, because a great deal depends on correct determination of "form," and in particular on the correct delimitation of the begin-

[8] Cp. for example Am. III. 11, IV. 12, v. 11, 16, VI. 7, VII. 17; Hos. II. 8 [9]; Is. v. 13, x. 16; Mic. II. 3, III. 12; Jer. II. 9, v. 6, 14, etc. Since in point of time the receipt of the word preceded the prophet's address, כה אמר should be translated by a past tense.

[9] According to Köhler, *Kleine Lichter*, p. 13, it is found 14 times in Amos, 44 times in Isaiah, 157 times in Jeremiah and 125 times in Ezekiel.

[10] Is. I. 2f., 18–20, III. 13–15; Hos. IV. 1–4a; Mic. I. 2–7, VI. 1–8; Jer. II. 4–9; Is. XLI. 1–5, 21–9, XLIII. 8–13, 22–8, XLIV. 6–8, XLVIII. 1–11, L. 1–2a. The cases where Jahweh speaks as the person accused, Mic. VI. 3–5; Jer. II. 4–13, 29f.; Is. L. 1–2a, are particularly noteworthy.

[11] J. Begrich, "Das priesterliche Heilsorakel," in *Z.A.W.*, LII (1934), pp. 81ff.

[12] Am. v. 1; Is. XXIII. 1ff.; Ezek. XIX. 1ff., 10ff.; parodies of dirges, Ezek. XXVII. 2ff, XXVIII. 11ff., XXXII. 17ff.; Is. XIV. 4ff. Cp. H. Jahnow, *Das hebräische Leichenlied im Rahmen der Völkerdichtung*, Giessen 1923.

ning and end of the unit under discussion. To add a verse from the unit which follows, or to omit one which properly belongs to the close of an oracle, can alter the whole meaning.[13]

The form in which a particular message is cast is also important in a still stricter sense of the word "form," for a "form" is never just something external, concerned with literary style alone; in the last resort, form cannot be separated from content. What determined the choice of the form was primarily the subject-matter of the message. But the content of the prophetic preaching could not possibly be housed in any traditional form—not even a specifically prophetic one—for it completely transcended the whole of Israel's previous knowledge of Jahweh. The very nature of the subject-matter itself demanded nothing short of a bold method of expression—it was always, so to speak, an *ad hoc* improvisation—simply because the prophets' message thrust out at every side beyond each and all of Israel's sacral institutions, the cult, law, and the monarchy. In the same way, the very nature of prophecy also demanded the right to make use of what were entirely secular forms with exactly the same freedom as with religious ones, as if there were no difference at all between them, for ultimately prophecy moved in a direction which transcended the old distinctions: when it prophesied judgment, it also announced the end of the established sacral order, and when it foretold salvation, it spoke increasingly of a state of affairs in which all life would be ordered, determined, and sustained by Jahweh, and this would, of course, result in the removal of the old distinction between sacral and secular.

3. The separate units consisting of oracles or songs were very soon gathered together into little complexes.[14] Whether such "divans," as Hempel calls them, were arranged by the prophet himself or by his disciples, is for the most part unknown. Although our information about such possible disciples is limited, present-day criticism is certainly right in crediting them with an important part in the collection and

[13] In this respect the Old Testament division into pericopes requires drastic correction.

[14] H. Birkeland, *Zum hebräischen Traditionswesen* (*Die Komposition der prophetischen Bücher des Alten Testaments*) *Avhandlinger utgitt av Det Norske Videnskaps-Akademi in Oslo*, henceforth cited as *Traditionswesen*, II, Oslo (1938); S. Mowinckel, "Prophecy and Tradition. The Prophetic Books in the Light of the Study of the Growth and History of the Tradition," henceforth cited as "Prophecy and Tradition," *A.N.V.A.O.* II (1946), No. 3; J. Hempel, *Worte der Profeten*, Berlin 1949, pp. 53ff.

series of oracles each beginning with the words "Woe to," which we may be sure were no more delivered consecutively than were those in Matthew XXIII. 13ff.—the connexion is editorial. The same is true of Jeremiah's oracles against the false prophets (Jer. XXIII. 9ff.), or the royal house (Jer. XXI. 11 - XXIII. 8). In the complex made up of Isaiah VI. 1–IX. 6 [7], the editor grouped on chronological grounds, for, apart from the prophet's call which stands at the beginning, the oracles and the incidents dealt with date from the time of the Syro-Ephraimitic war. Ezekiel IV–V is a collection of the prophet's so-called symbolic actions.[15] In many cases, however, there is no recognisable principle of arrangement. This is particularly true of the formation of more elaborate complexes, that is to say, where it is a case of the collection of collections. Almost all the help we have towards insight into how this redactional process progressed are a few headings within the prophetic books.[16]

For all the immense range of the prophetic tradition, there are really only three passages, two in Isaiah (VIII. 16–18, XXX. 8–17) and one in Jeremiah (XXXVI), which describe in somewhat greater detail how the prophet's message was put into written form and handed on. Yet, so many are the conclusions which they allow concerning the nature of the prophets' teaching in general, and of the prophets' own conception of that teaching, that they must be considered here, however briefly.

"I will bind up the testimony, seal the teaching among my disciples, and will wait for Jahweh, who is hiding his face from the house of Jacob, and I will hope in him. Behold, I and the children whom Jahweh

[15] Sometimes the "principle" of catchword arrangement may also have been in operation. In Deutero-Isaiah, where Mowinckel believed it could be demonstrated, the basis of theological concepts is of course much narrower than it is with, for example, Isaiah, Jeremiah, or Ezekiel, and in proportion it is naturally much easier to recognise a connexion between the units (Z.A.W. XLIX (1931), pp. 87ff.). Nevertheless, In Is. I. 9 and 10 the sequence may have been determined by the catchword "Sodom," and in Is. VIII. 8 and 9f. by the catchword "Immanuel." Similar observations have been made in the exegesis of Hosea (H. W. Wolff, Dodecapropheten, Biblischer Kommentar, ed. M. Noth, Neukirchen 1956ff., henceforth cited as Bib. Komm., p. 90). These instances are however too isolated to serve to clarify the process of redaction in general.

[16] There can have been cases where what the prophet left behind was handed on initially by way of oral tradition. In others the reduction to writing had already begun in the prophet's lifetime ("Prophecy and Tradition," pp. 62ff.). As early as the second millennium, Palestine was one of the places where writing had an important function in intellectual life and the exchange of ideas. G. Widengren, Aspects, x.

hās given me are signs and portents from Jahweh of hosts, who dwells on Mount Zion" (Is. VIII. 16–18).

Isaiah VI. 1–IX. 6 [7] deals with the stirring events of the Syro-Ephraimitic war, and records the threats, warnings, and promises which Isaiah delivered at that time. To our surprise, however, right in the middle of these, the prophet suddenly speaks of himself, and directs the reader's thoughts to his own person and to a group of people gathered round him. But the particular situation revealed in the passage at once makes the whole thing clear. The prophet is to "seal" and "bind up" his "teaching" in just the same way as we "record something in the minutes," and then have the document officially put into safe keeping. The words can therefore only mean that at the time when Isaiah wrote them down, he thought of himself as discharged from office. The glimpse here given of his thoughts and expectations on his withdrawal from his first public activity makes the passage unique indeed. He has delivered the message that was given him. The rest lies in the hands of Jahweh who—as Isaiah is perfectly sure—will follow what his ambassador has revealed by word with his own revelation in action. The message tore open a deep gulf in the nation. It made it obdurate (Is. VI. 9f.), and made Jahweh himself a snare to his people (Is. VIII. 14); and yet, by a tremendous paradox, it is on this very God who has hidden his face from the house of Israel that Isaiah sets his hope.[17] What confidence in face of the absence of faith! But the surprise is rather that the message actually brought faith forth, even if only within a very narrow circle. Thus, even when Isaiah withdraws into the anonymity of civil life, he still remains of importance as a sign—the narrow circle of the faithful is the surety that Jahweh is still at work and that he has not abandoned his purpose in history. Significantly enough, these purposes Isaiah regarded as, in the last analysis, good: otherwise, how could he have "placed his hope" in the coming revelation of Jahweh in person? In this connexion, although the prophet's words about "binding" and "sealing" his message are only figurative and allusive, Isaiah presumably did in actual fact go on to make a written record of all he had said up to the time when he was relieved of office, and—also presumably—this record forms the first point of crystallisation of the book of Isaiah.[18]

[17] On the hardening of Israel's heart, see below, pp. 151ff.

[18] The theory that in the last analysis the tradition of Isaiah goes back to two sketches written by the prophet himself, one in his early period (Is. VIII. 16) and one in the later one (Is. XXX. 8), have already been formulated by Duhm.

"Now go and write it before them on a tablet and inscribe it in a book, that it may be for a time to come as a witness for ever, for they are a rebellious people, lying sons who will not hear the instruction of Jahweh. . . . Therefore thus says the Holy One of Israel, 'Because you have despised this word, and trust in oppression and perverseness, and rely on them; therefore this iniquity shall be to you like a break in a high wall, bulging out and about to collapse, whose crash comes suddenly, in an instant.'. . . For thus said the Lord Jahweh, the Holy One of Israel, 'In returning and rest you shall be saved; in quietness and trust is your strength.' But you would not . . ." (Is. xxx. 8–15).

This passage, which comes from the latter period of Isaiah's life, makes the transition of prophecy from oral proclamation to its reduction to writing, that is to say, to the second, the literary, form of its existence, still more clear. Here the prophet is no ambassador. He is not to go out, but is to "go into" his house, and he is not to speak, but to write "for a time to come." The situation is clearly the same as that in Is. VIII. 16ff. The message has been delivered. Once again a phase of the prophet's work has come to an end, and once again it has resulted in failure. Isaiah had not succeeded in kindling faith; his hearers were far too preoccupied with political projects to listen. Indeed, things were even worse. They "would not" do so, and deliberately decided against Jahweh and his pleading. And this time there are no comfortable words about a small group of disciples. The atmosphere is much more laden with rejection than it was on the other occasion. A far deeper darkness enfolds the prophet. In one respect the passage goes much further than Is. VIII, for it shows the decision against Jahweh and his pleading as one which has already been taken.[19] This is important for the message of Isaiah, for this is one of the very few places where the prophet himself recapitulates the essential content of that message in one or two words and summarises the ideas. His wish had been to move people to turn to Jahweh, and to seek security in his protection, and to find confidence and "calm" (taking the sense given to נחת by Procksch). As it was, since they had rejected it all, it will be their lot to lose all stability, as Isaiah so magnificently depicts it in the picture of a wall suddenly bulging out and collapsing.

Why does the prophet write down his message as a "testament," as it is generally called? How far is it intended for "a time to come"? What he thought of initially was certainly the fulfilment of his threat.

[19] See note 17 above.

Those who came after him would be able to see in retrospect that his prophetic word had been no empty one. It may also well be that, as he made the record, his thoughts ranged considerably wider than the immediate fulfilment. His own generation was written off—"suddenly, in an instant," ruin would overtake it. Yet, even if the fate he foretold for it actually came to pass, this was after all only one part of his prophetic message. The promise of blessing it contained, its invitation to seek security in the protection of Jahweh, also remained valid. Though one generation turns a deaf ear to it, it does not fail. Jahweh does not abandon his purposes: the only difference is that these now reach forward to a more distant future in the nation's history, and for this reason the message required to be written down.

What gives the passage its great interest is that it shows how in certain circumstances the prophet broke the connexion between his words and their original hearers and, without the slightest alteration, carried the message over to apply to hearers and readers of a more distant future. At the time when Isaiah wrote down his preaching, possibly after 701, history had certainly overtaken many of his prophecies. Looked at from the point of view of their obvious and immediate fulfilment, they had apparently failed. This was not, however, a reason for regarding them as things of the past, for they retained their significance for more than merely the time to which they were addressed initially. Nor was it any more a reason for altering their content or recasting them to suit their new recipients. The same thing had happened with Hosea. When it was originally delivered, his whole message was directed to the then northern kingdom. But sometime later very slight editing—the insertion of the name "Judah" at several places—gave it a new address, to the southern kingdom.[20] It was never presumed that the prophet's oracles were addressed to one set of people and one only, and were thereafter to be wrapped up in their rolls and deposited among the records. There must have been people who never forgot that a prophet's teaching always remained relevant for a coming day and generation, and who themselves played their part in making it appear relevant—in many cases their work can be clearly seen in the various secondary additions which they made. A clearer instance than most showing what took place during the process of transmission is the relationship of Trito-Isaiah to Deutero-Isaiah. The former's dependence upon the latter is so striking that it has been correctly assumed that their

[20] See VOL. I, p. 71.

relationship was one of master and pupil. But the situation in which the younger man voiced the elder's words was very different from that in which they had first been coined; and consequently, the master's sayings were radically modified.[21] In the first phase of his activity Jeremiah too is a disciple—that of Hosea.[22] Again, scholars long ago marked off a large section of prose passages in his book whose diction and theological ideas approximate very closely to the tradition associated with Deuteronomy and the Deuteronomists. Obviously, we have here a characteristic reshaping by a second hand of material belonging to Jeremiah, though we do not, of course, know who was responsible for it or why he acted as he did.[23]

Baruch's long, detailed account of how Jeremiah's preaching was set down in writing, and of the several readings of the roll, parallels the two passages from Isaiah discussed above to the extent that it describes the transition from oral preaching to written word. But it goes much further in that it tells of the strange fate which overtook the book. Like Isaiah, Jeremiah derived the order to make a written record from Jahweh's express command: what however is significant is the purpose of this undertaking as revealed in the account (Jer. xxxvi). It was a final attempt to move Israel to repentance, and so to make it possible for Jahweh to forgive her. But this is only the introduction to the account of the book's fate once it had been produced. Baruch shows great artistry as he leads up to the climax. He tells how the roll was read three times. The first occasion is fairly lightly touched on. This was a public reading during a fast before Jahweh in 605. The second reading, held in the secretary of state's office in the presence of the chief state officials, is given a fuller description. The audience then was alarmed at what they

---

[21] K. Elliger, "Deuterojesaja in seinem Verhältnis zu Tritojesaja," henceforth cited as "Deuterojesaja," *Beiträge zur Wissenschaft von Alten und Neuen Testament*, henceforth cited as *B.W.A.N.T.*, IV, 11, Stuttgart 1933; W. Zimmerli, "Zur Sprache Tritojesajas" in *Schweizer Theologische Umschau, Festschrift für L. Köhler*, Zürich 1950, pp. 62ff.

[22] K. Gross, *Die literarische Verwandtschaft Jeremias mit Hosea*, Dissertation, Berlin 1930. On the other hand, because of its entirely different roots in the tradition, it is difficult to connect the prophecy of Deutero-Isaiah with the disciples of First Isaiah.

[23] On this strand of tradition designated by Mowinckel as "Source C," cp., as well as the introductions and commentaries, S. Herrmann, *Der Gestaltwandel der prophetischen Heilserwartung im Alten Testament*, Doctoral Thesis, Leipzig 1959, pp. 5ff. Is this "source C" to be equated with "Baruch's roll" (Jer. xxxvi. 32)? T. H. Robinson, "Baruch's Roll" in *Z.A.W.*, XLII (1924), pp. 209ff.; O Eissfeldt, *Einleitung in das Alte Testament*, 2nd edn., Tübingen 1956, pp. 424ff.

heard, they cross-examined Baruch, and the roll itself was put into "official safe-custody." While there was marked goodwill towards Baruch personally, the matter itself had to be reported to the king. What a consummate artist Baruch is as he thus prepares the way for the climax of his story! What is the king's attitude going to be? For his decision will determine whether the whole people—not just he him-self—are to stand or fall. Now the story gives a detailed account. The king is in the winter-house, sitting beside the brazier, with his ministers around him. Yet in the end it is not he who is the centre of interest, but the roll itself, which he cuts up and throws piece by piece into the fire. Thereupon Jeremiah dictates his preaching to Baruch anew, and makes the second roll more comprehensive still than the first.

The story is unique in the Old Testament, since its subject is neither a person, nor an act of Jahweh's providence or appointment, but a book. But the book's fortunes epitomise the fortunes of the message it con-tained. Once more the *motif* is that of the great failure, which Jeremiah plays with his own particular variations. We might therefore almost speak of a "passion" undergone by the book as well as by its author. At one point, however, the parallel with Jeremiah's own *via dolorosa* breaks down. The scroll is torn and burnt, but it is renewed. Jahweh's word does not allow itself to be brought to naught.

These three passages show, of course, only the first step in the forma-tion of tradition, that from oral proclamation to written record, a step sometimes taken by the prophets themselves. This was, however, a long way from the final stage in the process of making a permanent record of a prophet's message; instead, it ought to be called only its beginning. As we have already seen, a prophet's preaching was not restricted to its original audience. As Israel journeyed through time, the message accom-panied her, even if the historical circumstances to which it had originally been spoken had changed in the interval. The basic conviction under-lying the process of tradition was that, once a prophet's word had been uttered, it could never in any circumstances become void. The time when, and the way by which, it reached fulfilment were Jahweh's concern; man's part was to see that the word was handed on. And we must notice particularly that even the prophecies which had plainly found their historical goal, and had thus clearly been fulfilled, were retained as prophecies which concerned Israel and could always have fresh meaning extracted from them.

A particularly revealing instance of this centuries long incessant process of continual reinterpretation of tradition is furnished by so-called Nathan prophecy (II Sam. VII). Verses 11 and 16 show what is perhaps the oldest strand, a prophecy aimed directly at David himself. Compared with it, the ideas expressed in vss. 12a, 14–16 are later—the advance in point of time comes out in the interest shown in "the son after you, who shall come forth from your body," when David "will have lain down with his fathers": the point is now Jahweh's relationship to David's descendants.[24] Then, considerably later, the Deuteronomistic theology of history connected this whole prophecy with Solomon's building of the temple (vs. 13), while later still Deutero-Isaiah severed the tie with the house of David and applied the saying to Israel as a whole (Is. LV. 3f.). Even after this, the old reference of the promise to the seed of David himself is not wide enough for the Chronicler: he speaks of "the seed which shall come forth from thy sons," and thus adds a further stage in the prophecy's scope (I Chron. XVII. 11). In this way an oracle first spoken in the long distant past continued to have a present message considerably later than the exile.

The way in which tradition mounts and grows can be closely followed in the prophetic writings. Exegesis must be less ready than at present to look on this infusion of new blood into the prophetic tradition as "spurious" or an unhappy distortion of the original. The process is in reality a sign of the living force with which the old message was handed on and adapted to new situations. Adaptation was in some cases effected by adding threats against foreign nations which had meantime come within the orbit of Israel's history. Thus, for example, the very old prophecy of Balaam was finally even made to refer to the Greeks (Num. XXIV. 24).[25] In Isaiah XXIII a few later additions made an earlier oracle against Sidon refer to Tyre. To the Messianic prophecy of Is. XI. 1ff. was added in a later day vs. 10, and it was applied to the Gentile world, and was taken up by Paul in this reinterpreted form (Rom. XV. 12). In just the same way the Messianic prophecy in Amos (IX. 11f.) passed over into the New Testament in its less restricted LXX version (Acts XV. 16f., reading אָדָם instead of אֱדוֹם).

When, however, in the course of adaptation of this kind an old

[24] The analysis given by L. Rost, *Die Überlieferung von der Thronnachfolge Davids*, B.W.A.N.T., III. 6, 1926, pp. 47ff. From a rather different point of view M. Noth, "David und Israel in 2 Sam. 7," in *Ges. St.*, 2nd edn., pp. 334ff.

[25] L. M. v. Pákozdy, "Theologische Redaktionsarbeit in der Bileampericope," Bei. Z.A.W., 77 (1958), pp. 161ff.

oracle is converted into its opposite—when for instance an oracle of judgment is made into one of salvation—doubts begin to arise, at least for the modern reader. Isaiah proclaimed "woe" to the Egyptians, "the nation tall and smooth, feared near and far," and threatened them with destruction (Is. xvIII. 1–6). But as it now stands, the oracle goes on to prophesy that "at that time" gifts will be brought to Jahweh from "the people tall and smooth, feared near and far" (vs. 7). Yet even such a conversion of an older message of judgment into one of salvation is not the plagiarism, on principle illegitimate, of a later writer who is himself devoid of inspiration. There is in the Isaiah text a genuine sense of continuity, and a genuine belief that authority has been given to reinterpret an earlier oracle, even if in opposite terms, because of the very different historical situation.[26] The very fact that oracles are so often inverted in this way might suggest that we should regard it as a perfectly normal and theologically legitimate procedure.[27] For example, in the composite passage Isaiah xxII. 15–25 three stages of growth stand out in clear relief. In the first section, vss. 15–18, the wrath of Jahweh and of the prophet himself were poured out on Shebna, one of the chief officials of Judah. He shall not some day be laid to rest in his newly hewn tomb. Jahweh will toss his mummified corpse into a foreign land as if it were a ball. This is the end of the oracle spoken by Isaiah himself, but it continues: "I will thrust you from your office and cast you down from your station. This will come to pass on the day when I call Eliakim the son of Hilkiah my servant. I will clothe him with your robe, and bind your girdle on him, and commit your authority to his hand, that he may be a father to the inhabitants of Jerusalem and to the house of Judah. And I will place on his shoulder

[26] On the traditions of interpretation of Is. LIII, see H. Hegermann, *Jesaja 53 in Hexapla, Targum and Peschitta*, Gütersloh 1954.

[27] "This secondary tradition cannot be understood under the categories of genuine and false. Its point of reference is rather the immediate vitality of the prophet's word amongst his disciples. At a somewhat later date these seek to understand the word in the light of the whole word of God heard in Ezekiel!" W. Zimmerli, "Ezechiel," *Bib. Komm.*, p. 111. On the subsequent history of prophetic texts see H. W. Hertzberg, "Die Nachgeschichte alttestamentlicher Texte innerhalb des Alten Testaments," Bei. Z.A.W. LXVI (1936), pp. 110ff.; J. Hempel, *Die Mehrdeutigkeit der Geschichte als Problem der prophetischen Theologie, Nachrichten der Akad. d. Wiss. in Göttingen (Phil. hist. Klasse)*, Göttingen 1936, pp. 24ff.; Douglas Jones, "The Tradition of the Oracles of Isaiah of Jerusalem" in *Z.A.W.*, LXVII (1955), pp. 226ff.; "Prophecy and Tradition"; Birkeland, *Traditionswesen*.

the key of the house of David; when he opens, none shall shut, and when he shuts, none shall open. I will fasten him like a peg in a sure place, and he will become a throne of honour to his father's house" (Is. XXII. 19–23). The very change in the style—there is a sudden transition to the first person singular—betrays that a fresh start had been made. In addition, vs. 19a makes a poor transition: Shebna has already been rejected, and talk about his dismissal is out of place. The centre of interest is now Shebna's successor Eliakim and his installation in office (the few verses are a veritable gold-mine for information about the ceremonial language in use at the court). But there was something else to be said about Eliakim, and it was something which was quite unknown at the time of his appointment. This brings us to the third phase in the development of the Shebna texts. "And the whole weight of his father's house will hang upon him, the offspring and the issue, every small vessel, every cup and flagon. In that day, says Jahweh of hosts, the peg fastened in a sure place will give way, it will break off and fall down, and the burden that is upon it will be destroyed, for Jahweh has said so" (Is. XXII. 24–5).

This expansion hinges on the "peg" of vs. 23, but understands the metaphor in a completely different way. Eliakim is certainly to be a peg, for all his kinsmen are to hang upon him. Therefore what happens to a peg on which too many pots and pieces of kitchen-ware are hung will also happen to him. He will give way, and the whole collection will be smashed to pieces on the floor. A delightful satire on the nepotism of highly placed officials!

This way of dealing with traditions brings us up against a hermeneutic problem which can only be noticed briefly here. If a prophet's words thus accompanied Israel on her journey through history, and if they retained their character as addresses to her even long after the time of their original delivery, later ages must have felt themselves at liberty to reinterpret them freely, for the only way in which the word reaches those to whom it was later addressed was by "adaption" of its content.[28] Present-day exegesis is concerned above all else to discover the content of each specific oracle as it was understood by the prophet himself. But, while not abandoning this effort, ought it not perhaps to be more aware that this is only one possible way among many of

[28] On this process of "adaptation" see I. L. Seeligmann, "Voraussetzungen der Midraschexegese," henceforth cited as "Midraschexegese," in Suppl. to *V.T.*, 1 (1953), pp. 150ff., particularly pp. 167f.

understanding an oracle? By being referred to subsequent generations and the situations confronting them, fresh possible ways of taking the prophet's oracles were opened up, and this process continued right down to the time when, in the New Testament, the prophets' preaching was for the last time reinterpreted in the light of present events. Ought we not also to remember that when a prophecy came into the hands of those who transmitted the traditions, this itself meant that the time when the prophecy could be taken in the strict sense which it had when it was originally delivered was already a thing of the past?

CHAPTER D

THE PROPHETS' CALL AND RECEPTION
OF REVELATION

THE prophets themselves believed that their calling, to which we shall now turn, confronted them with a range of tasks and duties. We may, indeed, quite properly speak of the prophetic "office" consisting on the one hand of binding commitments and on the other of liberties and powers. Of course, since this is a very general term, it will have to be more precisely defined as we proceed, for we cannot presume that each and every prophet held an identical view of it. There were very many shades of difference indeed, of which only a few can be noticed in what follows. Not only did the prophets' own conception of their office clearly change, it was also possible for a prophet even to come into conflict with his office: a further cause of conflict might be where the prophet's definition of his office differed from the ideas of others. For example, in the case of Isaiah, the idea of his office which he himself held was not at all the same as the one which forms the background of the stories told about him in chs. xxxvi-xxxix. The latter version is determined by the narrator's own idea of it. In principle, behind every prophetic tradition and behind even the most insignificant mention, lies a well-defined idea of what constitutes a prophet and his office. If scholarship had a still keener awareness than it has of these questions, its eyes would be much more open to the enormous variety in the idea of what a prophet was.[1]

1. As the result of a new understanding of the cult, the question has recently been asked whether even the prophets were not much more closely connected with this institution than was once thought possible

---

[1] A classic simplicity is to be seen in what is said about the prophet s relationship to God as this is reflected in Aaron's relationship to Moses in Ex. iv. 16 (?J) and vii. 1: Moses is Elohim for Aaron, Aaron is a mouth for Moses. God does not himself speak, but the prophet is a mouth for him. The fact that it was possible to go back in such a way to this determination of the relationship as if it were a definition of it, in order to clarify the peculiar quality of a relationship of an entirely different kind, shows how settled and generally accepted this "definition" must have already become by the time. At the same time there was also room for quite different views of it.

and, on the basis of what is in some degree a very original interpretation of evidence both inside and outside the Old Testament, the view has been put forward that the majority of the prophets mentioned in the Old Testament were official spokesmen of the cult, and were therefore members of the cultic personnel of the sanctuaries.[2]

It has never been doubted that the prophets liked to pay visits to sanctuaries, both because great numbers of pilgrims resorted to them and also because the catchwords and the points to which they could link their oracles were given them in the religious excitement of the crowds, who would only be met with in such numbers at these shrines. This in itself, however, is no reason for talking about "cult-prophets." It may also be taken for granted that an ever-growing number of bands of $n^e bi'im$ were present at the sanctuaries during festivals. These sometimes made such a nuisance of themselves to the priests that special means of supervising them had actually to be set up (Jer. xxix. 24ff.). But the real question is this—were the prophets members of the cultic personnel in the narrow sense of the term, that is, as its authorised spokesmen? In the case of pre-classical prophecy, it is extremely difficult to give any clear answer, for the simple reason that the material which has come down to us is so scanty. Moreover, we tend to look on these early $n^e bi'im$, and also on their successors, as a much more uniform body than they in fact were. Elisha's station in life was obviously quite different from Elijah's: and both these prophets are clearly very different again from such a man as Nathan. The ecstatics mentioned in I Sam. x. 10f. came from a shrine, but it is difficult to believe that they themselves held a cultic office there. The same is true of the group which gathered round Elisha, and in an even greater degree of Elijah also. No doubt Elijah offered sacrifice on one occasion (I Kings xviii. 30ff.), but this proves nothing, for at that time any Israelite could do the same.

The picture changes, however, when we also recognise the fairly firmly rooted idea that at least one main function of the $nabi'$ was intercession.[3] Since so far as we can see this was requested on occasions of

---

[2] The foundation was laid by Mowinckel, *Psalmenstudien*, VOL. III (*Kultprophetie und prophetische Psalmen*), Oslo 1923; see also A. R. Johnson, *The Cultic Prophet in Ancient Israel*, Cardiff 1944; A. Haldar, *Associations of Cult Prophets among the Ancient Semites*, Uppsala 1945; cp. however H. H. Rowley, "Ritual and the Hebrew Prophets" in *Journal of Semitic Studies*, I (1956), pp. 338ff.

[3] I Sam. xII. 19, 23, xv. 11. In a different way however with Isaiah and Jeremiah: II Kings xIX. 1ff.; Jer. vII. 16, xLII. 2.

OTT E

public emergency and therefore concerned "Israel," the prophet must at that time have been regarded as in fact a duly authorised spokesman of the whole body of the people. It is also perfectly possible that such intercession by a *nabi'* was sometimes made in the solemn context of an official act of worship. It may be, too, that on such occasions he delivered oracles against foreign nations and called down curses against particular enemies. There is also reason to believe that prophets of a certain kind had an important role assigned them in warfare—it was they who gave the command to attack (i Kings xx. 13f., 22, 28, xxii. 6, 12, 15; ii Kings iii. 16f., vi. 9). Further, the official ultimatum issued to the neighbours of a people against whom Israel was waging war and to the aliens resident in its midst, warning them to flee from the threatened region (i Sam. xv. 6), was a matter for the prophets.[4] Here, too, the prophets are seen as authorised spokesmen of the whole body of the people, and this in the context of an event which was at that time still regarded as sacral and cultic.

These and other facts show that in the ninth century the *nabi*'s were still in various ways incorporated within the official cult. At the same time, however, it is impossible to imagine that their function was as much subject to rules and regulations as that of the priests. For another thing, their office was not hereditary but charismatic, and therefore *a priori* on a different footing. Again, is it entirely without significance that Deuteronomy gives regulations for the revenues of the priests and levites, but that nothing of the kind occurs in connexion with those of the prophets?[5] Further, the fact that women are quite naturally spoken of as prophets (Ex. xv. 20; ii Kings xxii. 14; Neh. vi. 14), whereas the idea of women priests was quite inconceivable, rather militates against the thesis of cultic prophets. Nevertheless, it is clear that there were still large numbers of such temple-*nabi*'s as late as the time of Jeremiah, and, most probably, they came forward as the spokesmen both of Jahweh and the people. However, the prophets who have been called the "writing prophets," Amos, Isaiah, Micah, Jeremiah, and the rest of them, were not of their number, as their bitter attacks on these cult prophets makes abundantly clear. They were instead members of a radical wing which increasingly declared its independence from the operation of the official cult.[6] Proof of this must, of course, be drawn

---

[4] See above, p. 36, n. 6.

[5] O. Plöger, "Priester und Prophet," in *Z.A.W.*, LXIII (1951), pp. 179, 186.

[6] "Because we think that the freedom of the prophetic office should be funda-

primarily from the content of their preaching and their general outlook, but it can also be demonstrated in the very forms which they used. These are characterised by the extreme boldness of their newly-minted rhetorical devices and of the comparisons they employed, which they chose solely to scandalise and startle the people who heard them, by the way in which so often they couched their messages in perfectly secular literary forms—selected *ad hoc* and subsequently abandoned— and in particular by the incredible variety of forms they used in their preaching, ranging over the whole field of expression then available. Such improvisation was quite unknown in the cultic sphere where all utterance, be it of God or of man, was regulated by convention and standardisation. Moreover, there was no place in the cult for the idea that Jahweh would enter into judgment with his own people.[7] These quick transitions which the great prophets make from form to form are, however, merely the symptom of a radical process which was at work in the very heart of their preaching. This was a totally new understanding of God, of Israel, and of the world, which the prophets each in turn cumulatively developed to a degree which went far beyond anything that there had ever been in the past. More will be said of this later.[8] Our main reason, however, for thinking that the prophets were much more independent than those who held a fixed office in the organised life of a sanctuary comes from the accounts of their calls, and to these we must now turn.

2. The Old Testament often tells of how a prophet was called to his office. The accounts all come from a comparatively short period

mentally maintained we do not deny that in certain periods many prophets were connected with the temple ... but we do deny that the prophets as such were official assistants at the cult. Not only from the character of Elijah, the remark of Amos (VII. 14) the figure of Huldah, the wife of a palace official (II Kings XXII. 14) is it evident that there was no unbreakable connection between prophecy and the priestly office, but from the general tone of the prophecies of Micah, the activity of Haggai (II. 12f.) and particularly from the well-known story of Eldad and Medad in Num. XI, the expectation of Joel II. 28ff., etc." C. Vriezen, *An Outline of Old Testament Theology*, trs. S. Neuijen, Oxford 1958, henceforth cited as *Theology*, pp. 261f.

[7] So—and rightly—F. Hesse, "Wurzelt die prophetische Gerichtsrede im israelitischen Kult?" in *Z.A.W.*, LXV (1953), pp. 45ff. Also, the cases in which prophets were enquired of by an official deputation or requested to make intercession (II Kings XIX. 1ff.; Jer. XXXVII. 3), do not show that their answers were given within the framework of the cult. Jeremiah once had to wait ten days for God's answer, and only then could he summon the deputation to give it them (Jer. XLII. 1ff.).

[8] See below, pp. 112ff., 297ff.

of time in Israel's history, the period of the Monarchy. This shows both how far outside the normal range of Israel's religious experience such calls lay and that they were not characteristic of the representatives of Jahwism from the very beginning.[9] Moreover, in the ancient east people did not write things down simply for the sake of writing them down—the written record was always used as a means to a very definite end—so that the very fact that a call was recorded in writing shows that it was regarded at the time it occurred as something unusual.

The prophetic call in fact gave rise to a new literary category, the account of a call. In Israel the connexion between a person's experiences in his religious and cultic life and the way in which he expressed himself by means of the spoken or the written word was such a direct and living one that any innovation of importance at once made itself apparent in the realm of form: an old form was modified, or a new one was brought into being. Here I mean the innovation by which the accounts of prophetic calls were given in the first person singular. Of course, men of Israel had said "I" in the presence of God even before the prophets appeared on the scene—for example in laments and thanksgivings. But this was quite a different use of "I." The old cultic forms made first personal singular statements about the relationships between God and man which almost anyone could have taken on his lips—indeed he should have done so. It was broadly a collective and inclusive first person. But the "I" the prophets speak of is expressly exclusive. The men who speak to us in these accounts were men who had been expressly called upon to abandon the fixed orders of religion which the majority of the people still considered valid—a tremendous step for a man of the ancient east to take—and because of it the prophets, in their new and completely unprecedented situation, were faced with

---

[9] F. Giesebrecht, *Die Berufsbegabung der alttestamentlichen Propheten*, Göttingen 1897; H. Gunkel, "Die geheimen Erfahrungen der Propheten" in *Die Schriften des Alten Testaments II*, 2, 2nd edn., Göttingen 1923, pp. xviiff.; J. Hänel, "Das Erkennen Gottes bei den Schriftpropheten," *B.W.A.N.T.*, Neue Folge, 4), Stuttgart 1923; F. Häussermann, "Wortempfang und Symbol in der alttestamentlichen Prophetie. Eine Untersuchung zur Psychologie des prophetischen Erlebnisses," Bei. *Z.A.W.*, LVIII (1932); A. Heschel, *The Prophets*, London 1962; S. Mowinckel, *Die Erkenntnis Gottes bei den alttestamentlichen Propheten*, henceforth cited as *Erkenntnis Gottes* (Supplement to *Norsk Teologisk Tidsskrift*), Oslo 1942; J. P. Seierstad, *Die Offenbarungserlebnisse der Propheten Amos, Jesaja und Jeremia, Skrifter utgitt av Det Norske Videnskaps-Akademi i Oslo*, II (1946), 2, Oslo 1946; Widengren, *Aspects*.

the need to justify themselves both in their own and in other people's eyes. The event of which the prophet tells burdened him with a commission, with knowledge and responsibility which placed him in complete isolation before God. It forced him to justify his exceptional status in the eyes of the majority. This makes clear that the writing down of a call was something secondary to the call itself, and that it served a different end than did the latter. The call commissioned the prophet: the act of writing down an account of it was aimed at those sections of the public in whose eyes he had to justify himself. No doubt these accounts are of great importance because of the insight they give us into the experience which made a man a prophet, and they do this far more directly than does any hymn used in the cult. At the same time, however, exegesis has always to remember that these narratives are probably not simply transcripts of what was experienced at the time. They are as well accounts designed to serve certain definite ends and they no doubt to a certain extent stylise the call. There must have been many features in a call which would be of enormous interest to us, but the prophets do not mention them because in their view they were of no particular interest.[10]

Did then the writing prophets hold a regular cultic office? As I see it, the accounts of their call answer this question with a decided "No." If a prophet had held a definite position in the cult, would he have laid so much stress upon his call? The importance which the prophets attached to their call makes it quite clear that they felt very much cut off from the religious capital on which the majority of the people lived, and dependent instead on their own resources.

The source material here is well known. First of all there are the accounts in the first person singular in Amos VII–IX, Isaiah VI, Jeremiah I, Ezekiel I–III, Isaiah XL. 3–8, and Zechariah I. 7 – VI. 8, but to these should be added such a story as the call of Elisha (1 Kings XIX. 19ff.) or that of the youth Samuel at a time when the word of Jahweh "had become rare in the land" (1 Sam. III. 1ff.), for, whatever office the historic Samuel actually held, what the narrator wished to relate was the way in which a young man was raised up as a prophet (vs. 20). The

---

[10] This is equally true of the question whether the reception of a revelation was preceded and prepared for by meditation, as it is also of the question of the particular psychical condition (ecstasy) in which the prophet received it. And above all we should welcome more precise knowledge of the form in which the content of each revelation appeared to the prophet, and of the way by which he ascertained its reality.

same is true of the call of Moses in Ex. III–IV, particularly in E's version of it; for the account of the commissioning, the divine promise, "I will be with your mouth" (Ex. IV. 12), and Moses's reluctance are all obviously told so as to make them agree with the ideas about prophetic call current in the narrator's own time. It is amazing to see such a wealth of psychological and theological nuance in ideas which may well belong to the ninth century, and it is equally amazing that the question of legitimation was even then given such importance ("But if they do not believe me," Ex. IV. 1), though, of course, it is only with Jeremiah, of the writing prophets, that the question becomes acute. There is a frank admission, also astounding at this early date, that it was possible for one who was called to office to refuse that call (Ex. IV. 10ff.). Finally, we have also to consider 1 Kings XXII. 19–22. Micaiah ben Imlah's idea of the way in which the call to be a prophet came about— that is, as the result of deliberation in the privy council of heaven—can hardly have been unique. It must have conformed to what were fairly widely held views. These ninth-century references in themselves warn us not to underrate early prophecy, or to assume that Amos or Isaiah imported something completely new into Israel when they made their appearance.

The event which led to a man's call to be a *nabi'* is described in a considerable number of different ways, and it is also plain that there was no conventional fashion in which it came about. Moreover, each individual prophet was conditioned by his own particular gifts of mind and spirit, and this led to different reactions to the event. Yet, in spite of this, it is possible to pick out certain common features in those cases in which the prophets themselves tell us anything about their call.

The call of Elisha is admittedly somewhat different from the rest, because here it is one human being—Elijah—who presses another— Elisha—into the service of Jahweh (1 Kings XIX. 19ff.). Elisha is called to "follow" a human being (הלך אחרי), that is, he was to be Elijah's disciple. And the story of the way by which Elijah's *charisma* was transferred to Elisha is also unique (II Kings II. 15), for strangely enough the prophets from Amos onwards do not think of themselves as bearers of the spirit, but as preachers of the word of Jahweh. For reasons at which we can only guess, the concept of the spirit, which was obviously still constitutive in making Elisha a prophet, lapses almost completely, and, as we might think, rather abruptly, into the background. For the ninth-century prophets, however, the presence of "the spirit of Jahweh" was absolutely constitutive. Elisha had to request Elijah for possession of it (II Kings II. 9); and only after it rested upon him is he reckoned a prophet. It is emphasised, however, that his possession of the spirit was attested by his associates, and this legitimated him in their eyes (vs. 15). Delusion can only come about when the "spirit" leads the prophets astray. This raises the question whether the spirit "went" from one prophet to the other (I Kings XXII. 21f., 24). Again, the spirit could suddenly take a prophet from where he was and carry him off elsewhere (I Kings XVIII. 12; II Kings II. 16). The almost instantaneous disappearance of this well-defined concept is not only striking: it is also important theologically, for when this objective reality, the spirit, whose presence had to be attested by a prophet's associates, ceased to operate, then the prophet of the word had to rely much more on himself and on the fact that he had received a call.[11]

As far as we can see, the prophets of the eighth and seventh centuries received their call through God's direct and very personal address to them, and this created a totally new situation for the man concerned. The work on which he was sent was not just limited to a fixed period. The office to which he was commissioned, though perhaps not in every instance regarded as lifelong, at all events removed these men from all their previous mode of life for at least a considerable time. Being a prophet was a condition which made deep inroads into a man's outward as well as his inner life—we shall later have to remember the consequences involved in the fact that from the very beginning not only the prophets' lips but also their whole lives were conscripted for special service. The complete absence of any transitional stage between the two conditions is a special characteristic of the situation. Being a prophet is never represented as a tremendous intensification or transcendence of all previous religious experience. Neither previous faith nor any other personal endowment had the slightest part to play in preparing a man who was called to stand before Jahweh for his vocation. He might by

[11] Mowinckel in particular drew attention to the absence of this concept of the spirit in classical prophecy, *Erkenntnis Gottes*, pp. 16f. Cp. also (by the same author) "The Spirit and the Word in the Pre-exilic Reforming Prophets," in *Journal of Biblical Literature*, henceforth cited as *J.B.L.*, LIII (1934), pp. 199ff. Mowinckel explains this difference as due to the "reforming prophets" being on the defensive against the popular prophets, whose appeal was to the spirit. This is at all events a possible explanation. Unfortunately the words of the prophets themselves do not admit the deduction of this polemic as clearly as one would wish for. Perhaps the concept of the spirit was a characteristic of North Israelite prophecy (cp. Hos. IX. 7).

nature be a lover of peace, yet it might be laid upon him to threaten and reprove, even if, as with Jeremiah, it broke his heart to do so. Or, if nature made him prone to severity, he might be forced, like Ezekiel, to walk the way of comforting men and saving them. So deep is the gulf which separates the prophets from their past that none of their previous social relationships are carried over into the new way of life. "I was a herdsman, and a dresser of sycamore trees; but Jahweh took me from following the flock and said to me, 'Go, prophesy against my people Israel' " (Am. VII. 14f.). This was more than simply a new profession: it was a totally new way of life, even at the sociological level, to the extent that a call meant relinquishing normal social life and all the social and economic securities which this offered, and changing over instead to a condition where a man had nothing to depend upon, or, as we may put it, to a condition of dependence upon Jahweh and upon that security alone. "I do not sit blithely in the company of the merrymakers. Because thy hand is upon me, I sit alone; for thou hast filled me with indignation" (Jer. xv. 17).

Flesh and blood can only be forced into such a service. At all events, the prophets themselves felt that they had been compelled by a stronger will than theirs. Admittedly, the early prophets only rarely mention these matters affecting their call. The first to break the silence is Jeremiah.

Thou didst deceive me, and I let myself be deceived;

Thou wast too strong for me, and didst prevail over me (Jer. xx. 7)
What is here said in open rebellion, the avowal that he was compelled, with no possibility of refusal, was also expressed by Amos.

The lion has roared—who is not afraid?

The Lord Jahweh has spoken—who does not prophesy? (Am. III. 8)
This verse has been rightly called a "word of discussion." That is to say, it is the answer to a query whether Amos could bring proof of his right to speak in the name of Jahweh. The prophet refuses to allow his prophecy to be called in question in this way. What he says is in no sense the product of reflexion or personal resolve. It is something which bears witness to itself, and so is not unlike some unconscious reflex action which even the person concerned cannot himself explain.

3. The call to be a prophet in which, as we have said, an individual was personally addressed by God, was as a rule associated with another factor which made the future ambassador of God acquainted with the will and purpose of Jahweh in an extremely vivid way. This was a

vision. Of course, in the fairly large number of visions which occur in the Old Testament there is no instance where a vision is not immediately followed by an audition and where it does not culminate in God's addressing the prophet. Nonetheless, the fact that Jahweh claimed not only the prophet's lips but also his eyes for the service of his new task is of prime importance. The purpose of the vision was not to impart knowledge of higher worlds. It was intended to open the prophet's eyes to coming events which were not only of a spiritual sort, but were also to be concrete realities in the objective world. Contrary to popular misconception, the prophets were not concerned with the being of God, but with future events which were about to occur in space and time—indeed, in Israel's own immediate surroundings. Yet even to the theologian this massive concentration upon historical events, as also the complete absence of any sort of "speculative" inclinations even in those visions where Jahweh is seen in person, must be a source of constant wonder. For example, Amos says that he saw Jahweh holding a plumb-line to a wall. But when Jahweh asked him what he saw, his answer was "a plumb-line" (Am. VII. 7f.)! Again, in his fifth vision, where he sees Jahweh standing upon the altar, he shows an astonishing lack of interest in what Jahweh looked like (Am. IX. 1). The same is also true of Isaiah's great throne vision (Is. VI). The first prophet to attempt anything like a detailed picture of the "glory of Jahweh" as it broke upon him from the realm of the transcendent at his call is Ezekiel. And yet how circumspect he too is as he describes what he perceived above the throne and "what was like as it were a human form" (Ezek. I. 26ff.).

The reception of revelation itself, that is to say, the more immediate circumstances in which this event in the prophet's inner self-consciousness took place, are only occasionally mentioned in the sources, and so much that we should like to know is left unanswered. On one point, however, there is universal agreement, that visions and auditions came to the prophets from outside themselves, and that they came suddenly and completely without premeditation. Only once is there mention of any technical preparation for the reception of a revelation—through a minstrel (II Kings III. 15). This however was exceptional. Inspiration might come to a prophet as he sat at table (I Kings XIII. 20). On the other hand, he might have to wait as long as ten days for an answer from Jahweh (Jer. XLII. 7). There is no doubt that, at the moment when the prophets received a revelation, they believed that they heard themselves addressed in words. There was *alloquium vocis articulatae*. Perhaps as a rule they first heard their name called (I Sam. III. 4ff.). The sources also allow us to make the further inference that, very frequently at least, such reception of revelation was something which caused the prophet a severe bodily shock. It is true that the earlier prophets have very little to say about this aspect of their office. But when it is told of a prophet that the hand of Jahweh came upon him or fell upon him (I Kings XVIII. 46; Ezek. VIII. 1), or when a prophet himself even says that the hand of Jahweh seized him (בחזקת יד Is. VIII. 11), there is every reason for believing that behind these brief notices lie experiences which not only shook his soul but caused bodily disturbances as well. Ezekiel relates how he sat on the ground awe-struck and unable to speak a word for seven days after his call (Ezek. III. 15). Daniel too says that all the blood drained from his face, that he fell to the ground (Dan. x. 8f.), and that after one such experience he lay sick for some days (Dan. VIII. 27). By the time of Apocalyptic such language may have become to some extent stereotyped and conventional, but in earlier days a prophet's bodily sufferings were something very real and painful.

As whirlwinds sweeping in from the Negeb
   it comes from the desert, from a terrible land.
A stern vision is told to me:
"The plunderer plunders, the destroyer destroys.
   To the attack, O Elam, lay siege, O Media."
Therefore my loins are filled with cramp,
   pangs have seized me, like the pangs of a woman in travail.
I am troubled, so that I cannot hear, dismayed, so that I cannot see,
   my mind reels, horror has laid hold upon me.
The twilight for which I look, it has turned for me into horror.
"They prepare the table . . .
   they eat and drink.
Up, ye princes, oil the shield!"
For thus the Lord said to me:
"Go, set the watchman,
   Let him announce what he sees. . . ."
And behold, here come chariots,
   men and teams of horses.
And he answered and said: Fallen, fallen is Babylon,
   all the images of her gods have been shattered to the ground.

O my threshed one,
  O my son of the threshing floor,
What have I heard from Jahweh of hosts,
  the God of Israel, that I announce to you.

(Is. XXI. 1–10)

This passage, which comes from the second half of the sixth century and is therefore not from Isaiah himself, lets us see as no other does something of the prophet's very deeply agitated and tormented state as he received a "stern vision." He is greatly disturbed. Pictures thrust themselves upon his inner eye. Their outlines are scarcely fixed before they break up again. With them mingle cries complaining of the unbearable anguish and bodily pains which have overtaken him as he sees the vision (cp. Hab. III. 16). In the end all is resolved in the "cry of deliverance" (Procksch) telling of the fall of the impious world-power. The prophet is now exhausted, and the last thing he summons up is a feeling of sympathy with his own threshed people, the "son of the threshing-floor."

How such and similar processes in the prophet's self-consciousness are to be more precisely defined psychologically is a question to which the investigations of present-day psychology are still unable to give a satisfactory answer. The idea that the prophets were "ecstatics," an idea widely accepted as a result of Hölscher's great work, is now out of favour, for the concept of ecstasy has proved to be too general and imprecise. In particular, the way in which it was used suggested that while the prophet was in this state his self-consciousness disappeared, and that, ceasing to have a will of his own, he became the scene in which processes external to his own personality were played out. This, of course, put the whole thing the wrong way round; for when, in a way hitherto unknown in Israel and in the entire ancient east, the individual with his responsibility and power to make decisions came in prophecy to occupy the centre of the stage—one might almost say when the individual was discovered—it was only to be expected that it would be precisely in the event of the prophet's reception of revelation that this new factor would be apparent. And as far as we can tell with any certainty from the sources, this is absolutely the case. The literary form in which the prophets describe their visions, the first person singular, is itself evidence. Even so, this in no way excludes the possibility of a "condition of abnormal excitation during which the normal wakeful consciousness of the man upon whom it comes is put out of action and his relationships to ordinary life diminished to the point at which they no longer exist."[12] In such a condition, that of direct encounter with God and with his purposes in history, might not the normal consciousness have been raised to an intensity never experienced in the ordinary way? If so, the term "ecstasy" is much too rigid. Lindblom tried to find a way out of the difficulty by drawing a sharp distinction between the "ecstasy of concentration" and the "ecstasy of absorption."[13] It is quite true that none of the prophets ever in fact had any kind of experience of becoming one with the Godhead. Nevertheless, there are grave objections to Lindblom's comparison of the prophets' experience with certain forms of medieval mysticism; for even in their most sublime experiences the mystics always remained within the limits of the accepted dogmas of their own day, whereas the prophets, precisely in their inaugural visions, were led out to new vistas of belief. With Amos, Isaiah, and Jeremiah the material which we could use directly in this connexion is both too scanty and too obscure, but if we take the well-attested occurrences in the pre-classical *nabi*'s on the one hand and, on the other, the more numerous references in Ezekiel, impartial examination will lead to the conclusion that nearly all the prophets experienced such temporary states of consciousness in which the senses were intensified. The fact that these occur so very much more frequently in Ezekiel than in the others is no reason for regarding him as exceptional in this respect.

If, then, we have to reckon with such abnormal states of consciousness in the prophets, it is mistaken to suppose, as is sometimes done, that these have no particular importance for the theologian. Here as everywhere else, to detach matters which belong to the central substance of Jahwism from their contingent links with history or with a person, and to regard them as no more than abstract truths, is to distort them. If Jahweh chose such a singular realm as the prophet's spirit, if he chose none of the already existing institutions for his new word to

[12] This definition is taken from F. Maass' article, "Zur psychologischen Sonderung der Ekstase," in *Wissenschaftliche Zeitschrift der K. Marx Universität Leipzig, 1953/54, Gesellschafts- und sprachwissenschaftliche Reihe, Heft 2/3*.

[13] J. Lindblom, "Einige Grundfragen der alttestamentlichen Wissenschaft," in *Festschrift für Bertholet*, edd. W. Baumgartner, O. Eissfeldt, K. Elliger und L. Rost, Tübingen 1950, pp. 323ff.; see also "Die Religion der Propheten und die Mystik," in *Z.A.W.*, LVII (1939), pp. 65ff.

Israel, and if in this psychic realm which had been so singularly kept open he brought such a singular thing to pass, this must stand in relationship to other matters which theology cannot ignore. It actually means nothing less than that in the states where the prophet saw visions and heard himself addressed, he became in a strange way detached from himself and his own personal likes and dislikes, and was drawn into the emotions of the deity himself. It was not only the knowledge of God's designs in history that was communicated to him, but also the feelings in God's heart, wrath, love, sorrow, revulsion, and even doubt as to what to do or how to do it (Hos. VI. 4, XI. 8; Is. VI. 8). Something of Jahweh's own emotion passed over into the prophet's *psyche* and filled it to bursting-point.[14] Once it is seen that the primary reference of the condition is a theological one, it becomes very doubtful whether any special psychic preparation on the prophet's part was required, or even whether it was at all possible. The highest degree of being absorbed into the emotions of the Godhead in this way was reached by Jeremiah and Ezekiel, but there is evidence that the majority of the prophets experienced it to some degree.

A revelation received in such an unusual way can never have been an end in itself. Least of all was it given to the prophet to let him know that God was near to him. Its purpose was to equip him for his office. On the other hand, when a prophet did receive such a revelation, it was in every case something purely personal. It lifted him right out of the common ruck. He was allowed to know God's designs and to share in God's emotions; but he never thought of holding his status before God up to other people as normative for them. It is significant that no prophet ever instructed or exhorted those to whom he spoke to reach out to a direct experience of God such as he himself had had. Joel was the first to look forward to the day when everyone in Israel would be like those rare beings who are endowed with the spirit (Joel III. 1ff. [II. 28ff.]). In an earlier passage, the only one of its kind, the same wish is put into the mouth of Moses (Num. XI. 29, E).

4. From the point of view of the history of tradition, among the receptions of visions more elaborately described in the Old Testament, those of Micaiah ben Imlah (1 Kings XXII. 19ff.), Isaiah (Is. VI), and Ezekiel (Ezek. I–III) fall into the same class, for they follow what was

---

[14] The great significance of the idea of the emotions, the prophetic "sympathy," was pointed out by A. Heschel in his important *Die Prophetie*, Krakow 1936 (see above, n. 9).

obviously a given basic concept, that of solemn commissioning by Jahweh as he sat enthroned in the midst of his heavenly entourage.[15] Each of the three, however, adapts the "schema" in its own particular way. In 1 Kings XXII. 19ff. the occasion is a regular session of the assembly of the notable personages in heaven ("one said one thing, and another said another," vs. 20), until "the spirit" comes forward and makes the proposal to delude Ahab's prophets by means of a lying spirit, to which Jahweh agrees. The spirit was then forthwith sent out. Isaiah too says that he saw Jahweh in the heavenly temple, seated upon his throne. The seen element, of course, plays only a small part in the narrative. When the prophet describes what he beheld, all that he mentions is the hem of the garment which reached to Jahweh's feet. Quite obviously, he had not dared to lift up his eyes. Moreover, smoke quickly clouded the scene from him. But this enhanced what he heard. He heard the seraphim's *Trisagion*, the thunder of which made the palace shake. At this direct encounter with supreme holiness and in this atmosphere of sheer adoration, Isaiah became conscious of his own sinfulness and was appalled—indeed, the sin of his whole nation seemed to be made manifest in his own person. At his confession of sin Jahweh made a sign—Isaiah did not, of course, see this—and a rite of atonement, which now made it possible for him to raise his voice in this holy place, was performed upon his lips. On hearing Jahweh ask whom he could send (the term "send" is used very absolutely), Isaiah with a minimum of words and without more ado put himself at his Lord's disposal, and was forthwith given his commission, which was to make his nation stubborn and harden their hearts by the very message he was to proclaim "until cities are laid waste and the fields in the open country are like waste land"; a holy seed was, however, to remain. Even in the prophetic literature, where the extraordinary is not the exception but the rule, there is very, very little to compare with the grandeur of the verses in which Isaiah describes his call. Does this lie in the overwhelming splendour of its outward accompaniments, or in the mighty power of the spiritual experience? Yet even to put such a question is to tear apart the classic balance between external and internal. The description of the external embraces all the inward experience, and *vice versa*.

[15] W. Zimmerli, *Ezechiel*, Bib. Komm., pp. 18ff. Attention was drawn to the connexion between Is. VI and 1 Kings XXII. 19ff. by M. Kaplan, "Isaiah 6. 1-11," in *J.B.L.*, 45 (1926), pp. 51 2ff. Cp. also I. Engnell, *The Call of Isaiah. An Exegetical and Comparative Study (U.U.A.*, 1949: 4), pp. 28ff.

Ezekiel too sees Jahweh sitting on his throne. With him, however, the description of the vision is much more involved, since in his case the throne vision is united with what was originally an entirely different and independent idea, that of the descent of the "glory of God," to form a single complex unit.[16] Here, therefore, the heavens open, and Jahweh's throne, borne by four heavenly beings, comes down to earth on storm-clouds. The manner of the prophet's call to office is similar to that of Isaiah except that in this case there is a still stronger impression that he received his commission in the form of what could almost be called a state-paper. For the king on the throne hands the waiting ambassador a scroll containing his instructions. There is also another similarity between the calls of Ezekiel and Isaiah. The prophet is repeatedly reminded of the difficulty and even hopelessness of his position by the words with which Jahweh accompanies the delivery of the note: the people to whom he is sent are of a hard forehead and a stubborn heart. This whole commissioning is hedged about with words which prepare Ezekiel for the failure of what he undertakes, though the latter lays much greater stress than does Isaiah on his hearers' freedom to refuse to listen to him (Ezek. III. 7, 11).

The three visions just considered thus end by indicating a completely negative result—in no sense will the prophet's work lead to deliverance; it will only hasten on the inevitable disaster. The ideas which the three men each held about the nature of their calling must have been very much alike: there must have been some kind of common call-experience which put a stamp upon their work from the very outset. Their devastatingly negative outlook on the future of their work, and the way in which, without any illusions, they faced up to its complete failure, are again a factor which compels us to look for these prophets outside the cult. For cult always implies at least a minimum of effect; it is action which has beneficial results in one way or another.

The call of Jeremiah begins with a dialogue in which Jahweh gently but firmly breaks down the other's shrinking resistance to his commission. Then follow the two visions of the rod of almond and the seething cauldron, which indeed fall very short of the forcefulness of the other three which have just been discussed. In other respects Jeremiah was a master of expression. Here, however, his creative power is clearly less than usual. Even in the dialogue which precedes the visions Jeremiah surprises us. He says that Jahweh touched his mouth. There is no in-

[16] On the *mo'ed* concept, see VOL. I, pp. 235ff.

dication, however, that he saw Jahweh as well as heard him. It was not in Jeremiah's power to give a visual picture of the presence of Jahweh.

In the visions themselves he beheld two static objects—there is no motion—which in themselves are quite unremarkable. It is only the words of Jahweh which follow the visions and interpret them that indicate the objects' symbolic character—Jahweh is watching over his word, it is never out of his sight: and evil is to break upon Jerusalem and Judah from the north. Here too something of the magnificent realism which elsewhere characterises the descriptions of the dealings between Jahweh and Jeremiah is missing. In Jeremiah's visions nothing at all is done. The rod of almond and the seething cauldron are both simply things: what the prophet sees is little more than an illustrative and symbolic picture which serves to corroborate the message given to him. The substance of Jeremiah's visions is no longer some irrevocable act which Jahweh is about to do. Compared with the visions in I Kings XXII, Is. VI, and Ezek. I-III, those of Jeremiah display a distinct lack of action. Their content is rather the symbolic illustration of more general insights which are to dominate his preaching from now on.[17]

Deutero-Isaiah received his call by means of two auditions. He had no vision, nor was he directly called by Jahweh. Instead, his ear caught something of the movement that had made itself felt in the heavenly places. He heard the summons given to the angelic beings to build the wondrous way over valley and mountain to prepare for that coming of Jahweh in which he would manifest himself to the world (Is. XL. 3–5). This first audition therefore only allowed the prophet to learn something of the preparations which were already being made in heaven for Jahweh's imminent advent—and this before there was even the slightest indication of it upon earth. In the second, however, he was directly addressed—obviously by an angel—and given the theme of his preaching: amid the transience of "all flesh," a transience which was caused by Jahweh's own fiery breath, Jahweh's word

[17] In the last analysis, this diminution in the power to delineate what was beheld in vision rests on a loss in the event itself. The more immediate circumstances in which Jeremiah hands the nations a cup of the wine of wrath in the vision in ch. xxv. 15ff. remain completely obscure. In the case of the older prophets, everything is clear and logical, even in their visions. In the case of the pots (Jer. XVIII) Jeremiah had admittedly no experience of vision; but this passage too is very characteristic of the lessening in the event itself just mentioned, for what Jeremiah sees with his eyes becomes a symbol, yet not a symbol of concretely impending event, but of something potentially feasible for Jahweh, that is to say, something in the realm of the mind.

alone is permanent, and is the guarantee of permanency (Is. XL. 6–8).[18]

Little can be said about the frequency with which the various prophets received such extraordinary revelations. The number of visions and auditions reported in grand literary style is certainly nothing to go on. As we saw, such subsequent elaborations had a definite purpose to serve with visions received at a call. In other cases there was no interest in giving an express and studied description of what the prophet had seen; then he simply confined himself to communicating its contents. There are plenty of oracles of this kind which quite clearly derive from genuine visionary or auditory experiences. This can certainly be presumed in the case of the description of the onslaught of the nations against Zion and their miraculous repulse in Is. XVII. 12ff. The same is true of the theophany in Is. XXX. 27f. or in Is. LXIII. 1ff., as it is also of descriptions of anguish such as Nah. II. 2ff. [1ff.], where the visual element is particularly conspicuous. It also holds good of Jeremiah's anticipations of the wars to come (Jer. IV–VI): they are so shot through with the prophet's sensory perceptions as to leave no doubt of their visionary and auditory character.[19]

It is impossible exactly to separate out visionary experiences which were genuinely ecstatic from other forms of the reception of revelation. Jahweh had assuredly more ways than one of communicating with the prophets, but it is hopeless to try to gain clear ideas about the psychical side of the processes. Isaiah says that Jahweh revealed himself "in his ears" (Is. V. 9, XXII. 14); so too Ezekiel (Ezek. IX. 1, 5), and elsewhere.[20] Thus, there were also revelations which took the form of an auditory experience and nothing more. Jeremiah makes a clear distinction between oral revelation and revelation by means of a dream, and sets little store by the latter (Jer. XXIII. 28). The experience of receiving a word also occasionally attained a high degree of vehemence; otherwise, how could Ezekiel have likened the sound of the wings of the cherubim which could be heard from afar with the resounding of the voice of Jahweh, "when he speaks" (Ezek. X. 5)? On the other hand we have good reason to believe that the prophets were also given inspiration in which no kind of change came over their ordinary consciousness, that is to say, in which the revelation was a mental process. This is probably so in the great majority of those cases in which the prophet speaks only

---

[18] On Zechariah's visions in the night, see below, pp. 286ff.

[19] Jer. IV. 23–6 is particularly characteristic in this respect; see below, p. 196.

[20] Jahweh "uncovers" or "wakens" the ear, 1 Sam. IX. 15; Is. L. 4.

of the word of Jahweh which had come to him. Nevertheless, even here the element of "event" which the revelation had for the prophet ought not to be overlooked. It is not simply a matter of mental perception, but of the "coming" of the word of Jahweh (ויהי דבר יהוה אלי), and consequently even with this quite unsensational form of revelation the prophets never lost the feeling that there was something strange in the experience.[21]

Oddly enough, Job's friend Eliphaz also gives an account of an experience in which he received a revelation similar to that of the prophets.

> A word stole to me,
>   my ear perceived a whisper of it,
> in disquieting thoughts, amid visions of the night,
>   when deep sleep falls on men.
> Dread seized me and trembling,
>   it made all my limbs shake;
> a spirit glided over my face,
>   the hair of my flesh stood up.
> It stood still—; but I could not discern its appearance;
>   a form was before me, I heard a still low voice:
> "Can a mortal man be in the right before God,
>   or a man be pure before his Maker?"   (Job IV. 12–17)

This is easily our most comprehensive and detailed description of the outward circumstances which accompanied a revelation. It certainly cannot be dismissed by saying that Eliphaz was not of course a prophet. The clearest proof of how little a prophet he was is the "oracle" in vs. 17, which is in fact not an oracle at all, but runs counter to the whole prophetic tradition and takes the form of a rhetorical question; this means that it is a saying of the kind found in the wisdom literature. None the less, it may be assumed that when Eliphaz describes the psychical accompaniments of a revelation, he takes as his basis genuine prophetic tradition. The time for receiving a revelation of the kind is the night. It is heralded by disquiet and feelings of fear. Then little by little the sensory organs are stimulated, first touch, then sight, and finally hearing.

The frequency with which such revelations were received is a

[21] Mowinckel paraphrases the formula ויהי דבר יהוה as "the word of Jahweh became active reality with so and so." *Erkenntnis Gottes*, p. 19.

question about which little can be said so far as each individual case is concerned, but a general survey of prophecy from the eighth to the sixth century does lead to one important result. Basically Amos had one task and one alone to do: "Go and prophesy against my people Israel" (Am. VII. 15). No doubt this embraced a considerable number of word-revelations which may have come hard on each other's heels during the time in which he was active. Yet his activity may well have been limited in duration: it was conceivably only a matter of months; then—perhaps because he was expelled by Amaziah—he went back home and his *charisma* thereafter ceased. With Isaiah it was different. His prophecy surges up in a number of separate waves, which were in each case determined by specific political situations. Yet, what we know of his activity makes perfectly clear that even he regarded the various occasions on which he came forward as of limited duration, and that, as each ended, he could consider himself released from office.[22] With Jeremiah, however, the calling meant a lifelong office. Later on we shall have to consider in more detail the great change which came over the whole idea of the nature of prophetic service at this point— how the prophet's whole life became bound up with Jahweh's dealings with his people, and how this exhausted him. Here—at least in principle —there were no distinct phases in the exercise of his office, no several stages ending when a specified task had been duly performed. Jeremiah was a prophet because Jahweh had conscripted his whole life.[23]

As far as the reception of revelation is concerned, Jeremiah makes it clear that he sometimes had to wait a considerable time for an answer (Jer. XXVIII. 12, XLII. 7). When in contrast with this the Servant in Deutero-Isaiah—and his office was above all else *munus propheticum*— says that Jahweh "morning by morning awakens his ear" (Is. L. 4), this undoubtedly marks a decisive advance upon what Jeremiah could say about himself. Indeed, it signifies the climax of prophecy in the Old Testament. For what the Servant is trying to say is that his reception of revelation was continuous, and his converse with Jahweh unbroken.

[22] See above, p. 41.

[23] See below, pp. 204f., 274f. This change is also connected with the fact that in Jeremiah a formal separation between the words of Jahweh proper and the diatribes or other utterances of the prophet himself is much less clearly perceptible. With Jeremiah not only do the oracles in the narrower sense of this term receive the status of divine revelation; with him there is the tendency to give out his own words and compositions as well as a word of Jahweh.

CHAPTER E

THE PROPHET'S FREEDOM

TO speak of the prophets' call, their visions, and the other ways in which they received revelations leads on to the discussion of that mysterious compulsion which came over them often quite unexpectedly, depriving them temporarily of the free exercise of their faculties, and which they were quite unable to resist. In Jeremiah in particular there are utterances in which the prophet very realistically—indeed almost literally—sees himself as a vessel into which wrath has been poured, wrath which he cannot suppress even if he so desires.

> But I am full of the wrath of Jahweh,
>   I am powerless to hold it in.
> I pour it out upon the children in the street,
>   upon the gathering of young men. . . .
>   (Jer. VI. 11; cp. XV. 17, XX. 9)

Yet the discovery of these abnormal psychical conditions and the novelty of this aspect of the prophets' life have sometimes led to a thorough misconception of what these men were and what they did. The compulsive element in their preaching which gave them a complete lack of feeling and, indeed, made them almost lose consciousness as they functioned as God's instrument is taken to be that which gives them their peculiar character. This view, with its insistence on the element of subjugation and on the aspects which lie quite outside the normal activities and experiences of mind and spirit was itself, of course, a reaction against the naïve picture of the prophets as national teachers and the great pioneers of an ethical and spiritual concept of religion. Nevertheless it is misleading. To counter it, we must discuss the freedom which the prophets enjoyed—itself of supreme theological interest. This is never concretely defined, and the prophets never take it as the subject of preaching. Yet they made the fullest possible use of it in practice, as is clearly shown in connexion with their call.

While it is true that the accounts given by Isaiah and Jeremiah are the only direct evidence of the large measure of free choice allowed to the prophet in the whole matter of his call, there is no reason to suppose that these two cases were different from the rest.[1]

It is generally believed—and rightly so—that in this respect the experience of Isaiah surpasses anything that was possible for other prophets. Isaiah was allowed to see and hear what took place in the heavenly council assembled around the throne of Jahweh. He was not, however, addressed in person, as was generally the case at a prophet's call. He only heard the question put by Jahweh to the assembly as to who might be sent. Whereupon he offered himself: "Here am I! Send me!" (Is. VI. 8). It was a general question, but it struck home to Isaiah like a lightning flash, and even before the assembly could begin discussion of it (cp. I Kings XXII. 20), he at once called out and put himself at Jahweh's disposal as messenger. If this is not freedom, what is? Yet this decision was not taken once and for all. The prophet had rather to take and re-take it in face of difficulties that kept arising, for freedom also implies the possibility of refusal. Isaiah himself may at times have been in danger of refusing, for he once declares that "the might of God's hand disciplined me not to walk in the way of this people" (Is. VIII. 11).

For Jeremiah, however, this borderline between obedience and disobedience was fraught, all his life long, with even greater peril. But the situation in which he was placed was so very different from that of Isaiah that any real comparison between the two is impossible. In contrast with the latter, Jahweh's address and call to Jeremiah was a direct one. At first Jeremiah shrank back in terror. In the end, however, he did go as he was commanded. Yet this did not mean that he surrendered his freedom to God—and the best proof of this lies in the so-called "Confessions" where, in spite of all his suffering, he continues in closest contact with Jahweh, questioning him, professing his faith in him, and complaining to him. The force used on Jeremiah was inconceivably harsher than that laid upon any other prophet. But this should not blind us to the other side of the question. We ought also

---

[1] Recall (see above p. 56) the story of the call of Moses (Ex. IV). It is clearly formed on the model of a prophet's call as this was conceived at the time (the time of J and E), and gives a surprisingly large place to Moses' objections, and even opposition. Elisha was called to succeed Elijah by Elijah himself, that is to say, by a human being (I Kings XIX. 19ff.); this seems to presuppose a standing rule traditional in the prophetic guilds, and is therefore to be taken separately. (See E. Würthwein, "Amos-Studien," in *Z.A.W.*, LXII (1950) p. 25.)

to appreciate the freedom which Jeremiah kept and used in his dealings with God. He used it to render a unique obedience ,and yet it occasionally led him almost to the verge of blasphemy (Jer. xx. 7, 14).

An examination of the prophetic preaching itself reveals that the case is much more complex than the widely accepted view that in most cases it was delivered under irresistible compulsion. While it is true that all the evidence suggests that at the moment when a revelation was given to a prophet he was in a state of extreme passivity, he certainly did not continue in this state. We have already discussed the extraordinary number of literary forms on which the prophets clothed their addresses as the situation demanded. Remember, however, that each instance implies a choice, and a very responsible choice at that, on the part of the prophet. For these forms into which their message had to be cast were more than just outward things. The message itself was affected by the form in which it was given—whether as a dirge, or a priestly cultic decision, or a song of the vineyard. The prophet would be very careful to find the appropriate form for each specific message. There are cases which suggest that a prophet might act in a very free and arbitrary way as he selected a form for a commission which had been given him. Ezek. xxiv. 15-27 is a good example of this. Jahweh had informed the prophet that he was about to take his wife, "the delight of his eyes," away from him, but he, the prophet, was not to weep for her nor take mourning for the dead. Later on, however, when he was asked by the people why he acted thus, he gave the message which was really intended: the sanctuary in Jerusalem, "the desire of your eyes," is to be profaned, and sons and daughters are to perish without mourning being made for them. There is therefore a certain gulf between the divine command (vs. 15–19) and the means by which the prophet carried it out (vs. 20–7). The prophet used great freedom in interpreting the command. He made the words "the delight of your eyes" refer to the temple, and the command to make no mourning refer to a disaster in war.[2]

The case is rather different with the form called the messenger formula which is particularly frequent in classical prophecy, for here the form itself required that the divine commission be reproduced exactly and without re-shaping. The prophets, however, never passed on God's words just as they were. They prefaced them—they were generally a threat—with a diatribe, which formed an introduction: in

[2] Hänel, *Das Erkennen Gottes*, p. 28.

fact, it is the diatribe which connects the divine words with those to whom they applied. Only in exceptional cases were the divine words referred from the beginning to a definite person (as, for example, the king) or to a definite group. Usually their content was of a more general nature; they announced, for instance, the decimation of an army (Am. v. 3), the deportation of the upper classes (Am. iv. 2f.), or that the land was to be made desolate (Is. v. 8ff.). Addressing this message *ad hominem* was, then, a matter for the prophet himself. This left a wide field open for the exercise of his own judgment and pastoral vigilance. Indeed, his was the most important role of all; for what is a divine oracle without a recipient? The prophet therefore addresses the threat of deportation to a luxury-loving upper class (Am. iv. 1ff., vi. 1ff.), of devastation of the land to speculators in real estate, and so on. It is hardly possible to overrate the importance of the prophet's share, for without it the word the prophet receives does not reach its goal and therefore cannot be fulfilled. What makes it such a tremendous responsibility is the fact that the prophet is thus the one who puts the will of Jahweh into effect: Jahweh thereafter commits himself to stand by the decision of his ambassador.

What guided the prophets in their application of the divine message to the various groups of people? We have a certain amount of information. The prophets for their part did not simply speak on behalf of the social interests of a particular class—not even of their own class—nor did they speak as people who had suffered unjustly. They regarded themselves as bound to a definite fixed order which their announcement of punishment was designed to restore. This raises the question of the theological relationship between the diatribe and the threat.[3] That such a relationship does exist is shown by the לכן ("therefore"), at once frequent and characteristic, which customarily makes the logical connexion between the two component parts, the diatribe and the divine words, and which helps to give the reason for the threat which follows. The prophets here show that, to a limited degree, they did have an interest in teaching. He against whom the threat is directed has to be made aware of and understand what is in store for him and why this is so. Occasionally, even, the hope is added that he will be moved to repentance and so find safety. What he must understand is that the punishment which is about to overtake him is exactly commensurate

[3] H. W. Wolff, "Die Begründung der prophetischen Heils- und Unheilsspruche," in *Z.A.W.*, LII (1934), pp. 1ff.

with his offence, and that there is a nemesis in history whose author is Jahweh. In Old Testament terms, that is to say, Jahweh causes the evil that men set in motion to recoil on their own heads—offence and punishment strictly correspond. For example, Elijah prophesied some time before the event that the dogs would lick up Ahab's blood in the place where they licked up the blood of Naboth (I Kings XXI. 19); "therefore" the drinkers of wine will perish with thirst (Is. v. 13); "therefore" those who wished to flee away on horses shall have to flee (Is. XXX. 16); "therefore" the possessors of large estates will see the land made desolate (Is. v. 9; Mic. III. 12) or be deprived of their land (Mic. II. 4f.) and the false prophets will sit in darkness without light (Mic. III. 6f.) etc. No theological profundity is demonstrated in this logic of events: the logic is painfully obvious. In this department of prophetic utterance no esoteric experiences or other supernatural forms of insight are brought into play. In principle, what a prophet applies here is a perfectly basic piece of knowledge which is vouchsafed not only to himself but also, in principle, to everyone who has any experience of the world and of life, namely knowledge of the fundamental God-given fixed orders to which human life is subject.[4] This is the place where prophecy makes close and vital contact with the Wisdom literature.

Sometimes the logical connexion between the diatribe and the divine words is less strict, especially where, as in the poem on Assyria in Is. x. 5-19, the diatribe is elaborated to such an extent as to take ascendancy over the threat and become a relatively independent subject in itself. Its *motif*, however, the *hybris* that comes to a fall, is again one found in the Wisdom literature.

"I have made you an assayer among my people, that you may know and assay their ways" (Jer. VI. 27).

This office of assayer, which Jeremiah believed had been entrusted to him, and which all the prophets from Amos to Malachi each in his own way regarded as theirs also, demanded sustained vigilance in passing judgment upon men and circumstances. Here abnormal states of psychical excitement and the rule of thumb application of legal norms were equally valueless. This called, rather, for men of extreme intellectual versatility, whose judgment was incorruptible, who possessed a profound knowledge of human nature, and who, above all, were very familiar with the religious traditions, both those of the saving history and those found in the hymns used in worship (Deutero-Isaiah).

---

[4] These fixed orders were discussed in VOL. I, pp. 421f.

The frequent quotations which the prophets wove into their utterances and used to characterise their audience and its way of thinking and to hammer home its collective guilt, were one of the fruits of their acute observation of mankind.[5] How attentively they must have looked around them and observed people before they could have made these succinct characterisations! We must not, of course, imagine that the prophets were concerned to give an objective and faithful reproduction of what they saw. In many instances they generalised, or even caricatured, the behaviour or the utterances of those whom they attacked, in order to demonstrate the end of the evil road which they saw their audience treading.[6]

Finally, we have to consider the literary category of discussions, which have already been mentioned. If these were analysed, they would open up quite a number of other standpoints from which to view this aspect of the prophet's task in which everything depended on the cogency of the theological proofs he adduced; for here the prophet was initially on the defensive. In the tense moments when an argument flared up out of the blue, the factors which determined whether or not a prophet would succeed in passing over to the offensive were not only his superior intellectual and theological equipment, but also his quickness in repartee. Of course, the prophet was not always successful. In one such argument of Jeremiah's, to which a large audience doubtless listened with keen interest, the prophet came off second best. He could do nothing to counter Hananiah's oracle of weal played by the latter as his trump card, and had simply to quit the field (Jer. XXVIII. 1–11).

All that has been said above, and a great deal more that has been left undiscussed, may help to give some idea of how a prophet though under orders yet at the same time enjoyed a unique freedom, that is to say, a freedom which left it open to himself to take decisions of the utmost moment.

While it is important that this aspect of the prophets' words and actions should be more clearly recognised—it is often underestimated—the question nevertheless arises whether the previous discussion does in fact indicate anything more than the outward manifestations of a

[5] Wolff, Das Zitat.

[6] Examples of such harsh representations of opponents' words and actions are to be found in Is. V. 20, XXVIII. 15; Jer. II. 20, 25, 27; Am. II. 12; Zeph. I. 12; see Wolff, Das Zitat, pp. 60ff.

freedom whose roots are considerably deeper, and which is itself only a pointer to some ultimate and fundamental experience of the prophet when he encountered Jahweh and was commissioned by him. It is, of course, difficult to put this in proper theological terms, and perhaps we can do no more than grope our way, because, as everyone knows, the prophets themselves never reflected on these matters or spoke of them. We have already discussed the way in which the claim which the prophet's office made upon him became more and more all-absorbing, until, as for example with Jeremiah, it took his whole being into itself to the extent of abolishing any distinction between the vocation assigned to the prophets and their, as we might say, extra-official and private lives, a distinction which still has to be reckoned with in the case of a prophet like Amos. Yet, wherever a man's prophetic office and his private life became conjoined—and this was at least partially the case even with some of the earlier prophets—the very violence of this meeting inevitably set its stamp upon them and made them what they were. This means that the prophets were a very special type of men displaying characteristic traces of the exceptional.

Yet it is possible to say, with all due caution, that a definite pattern here and there emerges. The picture we see is of a man appointed to hear the word of God. As the result of this divine call he surrenders much of his freedom—occasionally he is completely overwhelmed by an external compulsion: but paradoxically, just because he has received this call he is able to enjoy an entirely new kind of freedom. Drawn into ever more and more close converse with God, he is privy to the divine purposes and is thereby given the authority to enter into a unique kind of converse with men. The man reflected here is not, of course, an integrated personality. He is divided and sorely troubled as God hides himself from him more and more. Yet, as the martyrdom of Jeremiah testifies, he is in some mysterious way free to choose suffering and so to stand up to God's test. We have already seen further how their office intensified all the prophets' mental capacities to the highest possible degree, so that even their treatment of poetic forms becomes perfectly daring. To put it in the language of the present day—and it is not inappropriate—we may say this: we are shown men who have become persons because God has addressed them and they have had to make a decision in his presence. This was something new in Israel. And these men were subject to the word of Jahweh in a far more intense form than ever before in Israel. We must guard against looking at this whole subject in contemporary terms: the people of the ancient world used the pronoun "I" in a sense quite different from ours. The "I" of which the prophets became conscious because Jahweh spoke to them differed both from the "I" used by the oriental rulers of the period and, to an even greater degree, from the "I" used by present-day Western man, the meaning of which has been so influenced by idealist philosophy and the romantic movement.

A remarkable facet of this attainment of personality which the prophets achieved was that their messages were issued under their own names. It is very surprising that ancient writings whose author was already dead should have been issued under his name; indeed, in view of the accepted usage of the ancient east, including Israel, it is something quite exceptional. In the editing of legal and cultic traditions we expect current practice to be followed. Again, the intellectual achievement—often considerable—of the men we rather feebly term "redactors" is anonymous in principle. And in the case of works like the Succession Document or J, where the intellectual stamp is so distinctive that we feel these writings bear the marks of individual genius, the anonymity is still more surprising.[7] Yet this is the rule throughout in the Old Testament. When, therefore, the rule is broken in the prophetic writings, the only possible explanation is that in the case of the prophets a message was uniquely bound up with the name of a single person, and he alone could be regarded as responsible for it. The same cannot, however, be said of the Jahwist or of the author of the Succession Document, because in spite of all the individual genius at work there also, and in spite of these men's great power to make their story speak to their contemporaries, they did not go in principle beyond the religious heritage which Israel already possessed. But the prophets, particularly the pre-exilic prophets, were able to do this. Here, with an exclusiveness that had never before been known in Israel, God turned to an individual and made him the instrument of a revelation that was given once and once only. One man could not take the place of another, nor was the word entrusted to him to be heard on any other lips. He was the only one who knew it, and was responsible for the conscientious delivery of the message. The logical end of the process which here began was martyrdom for the prophet, if Jahweh so willed it.

Now that we have tried to understand the prophetic office in its

[7] See VOL. I, pp. 54, 312ff. The publication of a high official's statement of his activities (Nehemiah) is of course a different case.

unique freedom, logic demands that we next consider the possibility of
a prophet's refusal or disobedience, a possibility which must in fact
have been a danger at every step he took and every decision he made.
Is all the prophecy which survives to-day the prophecy of obedience?
If not, on what side were the prophets particularly vulnerable? When
on one occasion Jeremiah complained about the sufferings and hostility
which were wearing him away, and lamented that God sent him no
help, Jahweh answered him thus:

> If you return, you may serve me again.
> If pure thoughts you utter, and not base,
> then you may again be my mouth.
>
> (Jer. xv. 19)

The complaint which prompted this answer was, then, "base"
(זולל). The particular reference is to an outbreak of despair, when
the prophet even went the length of reproaching Jahweh with leaving
him in the lurch. This leads us to a further question: did such a refusal
affect only the prophet's personal relationship with God? Did it have
no effect at all on what he said in public? Here the modern reader of
the Bible will perhaps think of certain passages in the post-exilic
prophets where enemies of Jerusalem are forewarned that their flesh
will rot fearfully away (Zech. xiv. 12), but where Israel is shown the
prospect of her enemies serving her as servants and handmaidens (Is.
xlix. 22), and even of herself treading down the wicked (Mal. iii. 21
[iv. 3]), and of wading in the blood of her enemies and becoming drunk
with it (Zech. ix. 15). Can these be called cases where a prophet's
darkness was so deep as to allow human instincts and passions to gain
the upper hand over the message from God, so that they perhaps testify
to human hatred rather than to God's will for the future? Such a judgment, however, presupposes a knowledge which we do not have of the
circumstances in which such messages were delivered, to say nothing
of the inherent element of risk involved in making use of such psychological interpretations, based as they must be on conjecture about the
prophet's spiritual state. What we must take as our starting point is the
objective content of such prophecies, and we must try to understand
them in the light of the whole teaching of the prophet concerned, and
if need be compare this with that of the other prophets. As far as the
last of these is concerned, the fact that Amos, Hosea, and Isaiah do not
strike this note may give us pause. But is there only one explanation of

the difference? In dealing with such passages exegesis has above all else to be clear about the criteria it proposes to apply. It ought to be perfectly obvious that, since these passages to some extent already verge on the bizarre conventions found in the literature of Apocalyptic, our modern Christian humanitarian ideal completely fails as a standard of judgment. But if such critical questions are left open—though there is no reason why they should be—it is, theologically, a bad sign that, as usually happens, they are asked only of aspects of the prophetic message which seems to us immoral or inhumane. The "base thing" which Jahweh rebuked in Jeremiah was certainly not his implacable feelings towards his persecutors: it was his disobedience to God and his angry rebellion against his office. Did the prophets, and in particular those whom we usually and perhaps too carelessly think of as later and feebler members of the succession, have, each in his own day, a true estimate of their office, or did they fall short of the task to which they were called? And yet, what knowledge have we of their task? Nevertheless, now that examination of tradition has revealed the extremely close link between the prophets' preaching and the perfectly well-defined traditions upon which they depended, we can make a cautious judgment about the way in which a prophet adapted his material, what he chose to include and what he relegated to the background. We know, for example, that they felt themselves free to modify the traditions they employed to suit their own day and age, and they did this more by pointing up detail than by making changes in their actual content.

CHAPTER F

THE PROPHETS' CONCEPTION OF THE
WORD OF GOD

W E must turn to a subject which is equally central for all the
prophets, namely, the "word of Jahweh." Yet, although the
word of Jahweh is both a necessary precondition of prophetic
preaching, and also forms its subject matter—though, indeed, it is the
fundamental basis of the prophet's existence—they only occasionally
made it the subject of theological reflexion. Their relationship to it was
so personal and direct, that is to say, the word was so exclusively bound
up with the specific time at which it came to them and with the
specific message which it gave them, that for the most part they found
it simply impossible to think of the word of Jahweh in objective terms
and as something having very specific properties of its own. It is only
exceptionally that they furnish us with direct information about its
nature; in general, it is only indirectly that we can reconstruct the
prophets' concept of the word of Jahweh—that is, by drawing conclusions from their preaching. A critical account of the prophetic concept is needed all the more urgently to-day in that we simply cannot
assume that our conception of "the word of God" or of the function
of words in general is identical with that held by the prophets.

In modern languages, or at least in modern European languages, the
almost exclusive function of the word as an aggregate of sounds is to
convey meaning. It is a phonetic entity which enables men to communicate with one another, and is therefore a vehicle used for purposes
of intellectual self-expression. This noetic function of the word, the
conception of it as bearing and conveying an intellectual idea, is, however, far from covering the meaning which language had for ancient
peoples. Indeed, our conception of the word, as that which conveys an
intellectual meaning, seems to be the complete opposite of the conception which we must suppose existed in the cultural state represented
by the myth. There, a word is much more than something which
indicates and designates a certain object; it is quite the reverse of a
label attached to an object at a later stage. At the early mythical level
of thought, man's apperception of the world about him is of it as a

unified entity. He makes no distinction between spiritual and material
—the two are intertwined in the closest possible way; and in consequence he is also unable properly to differentiate between word and
object, idea and actuality. Such thought is thus characterised by an
inherent absence of differentiation between the ideal and the real, or
between word and object; these coalesce as if both stood on one plane
of being.[1] In a way which defies precise rational clarification, every
word contains something of the object itself. Thus, in a very realistic
sense, what happens in language is that the world is given material
expression. Objects are only given form and differentiation in the word
that names them. This idea of the word's power of mastery was very
familiar in the ancient world. Even in J's story of the Garden of Eden,
the word of the man is noticeably given precedence over the world of
objects. It was only when man gave the animals their names that they
existed for him and were available for his use (Gen. II. 19f.).[2] Myth is
more than merely early man's way of expressing his comprehension of
the world; it is also what brings the world into being—the myth has
to be recited, because this is the only means of countering the perils
which everywhere beset the fixed orders of creation, and of guaranteeing their continued existence. From this it is only a step to what we
term "magic," though for early man, use of magic was one of the
basic ways in which he gained control over the world. A curse was
effective upon an enemy in virtue of the power inherent in its form;
and at a hunt, magical rites, or even a drawing of the hunted animal,
could be used to bring it into the power of the man who had bewitched
it, whether by word, rite, or representation. These and countless other
examples to be found in comparative religion rest on a conception of
language which we can call dynamistic, since here a word (or a symbol
or symbolic action) is thought to possess a power which extends beyond the realm of the mind and may be effective in the spatial and
material world also.[3]

[1] E. Cassirer, *Philosophie der symbolischen Formen*, 2nd edn., Freiburg im Bresgau
1956, VOL. I, pp. 56, 21; 2nd edn., Freiburg im Bresgau 1953, VOL. II, pp. 47ff.

[2] "Just because the creation of the word is itself a kind of conjuration, in which
being itself comes to light, man at all times has the obscure feeling of touching on
existence with [it]." W. F. Otto, *Die Musen und der göttliche Ursprung des Singens und
Sagens*, Darmstadt 1956, p. 80.

[3] Similarly, O. Procksch, *Th. W.B.N.T.*, IV, p. 90. He distinguishes a dianoetic
moment, which contains a νοῦς, and a dynamic element, in the word; the דבר is
filled with power. "We must keep in mind that the term *dabar* in Hebrew is much

But early civilisations did not for long remain in the stage in which the world was conceived in terms of magic and dynamism: indeed, if we follow the *schema* usually adopted for the great phases in the history of culture, this stage was soon almost entirely left behind. The *schema* does not fully exhaust itself on the issue of language and of the many functions which devolve on it within the various cultures and religions. If we try to explain this in terms of evolution, by saying that on occasion the dynamistic possibilities of language remained alive for a much longer time, and, even in advanced cultures, could automatically come to the surface again, this would hardly be a true description of what actually happened; we should then be measuring the development of language against a preconceived picture of the history of human culture, and giving the impression that, wherever language is "still" thought of as possessing power, this always indicates that initial stages or relatively unedited remainders are being carried over from a cultural level already in principle left behind, and are forcing their way into another level to which they are quite foreign. This, of course, does happen: but one could equally well ask whether language has not become impoverished because it has lost functions which at an earlier cultural level had once belonged to it. It would be an unhappy state of affairs if we had to try to make excuses for the language of the prophets because "traces of a magical use" of the word are still to be found in it. We may notice in passing that this is in no way something peculiar to Israel. It is well known that in many old and sometimes highly developed cultures language was not restricted simply to the description of objects; in out of the ordinary situations, due to a mysterious power of creation, language could produce either something new, or an intensified form of something already in existence: that is to say, language itself became creative; and this is a possibility which language has never lost, even to this day.

There are a number of different departments in the cultures of the ancient east where we meet the word of power, the chief of them being, of course, the more restricted realm of the cult, and the rituals connected with exorcism and with blessing and cursing: it is also to be found in specific theological traditions. The idea of a god's word of power played an important part in Old Babylonia and Old Egypt—these cultures go even to the length of conceiving it as a physical and cosmic

more dynamic and concrete than its Western equivalent *word*. *Dabar* is something concrete, living." Th. C. Vriezen, *Theology*, p. 94.

force.[4] Even in everyday life, however, certain words were thought of as having power inherent in them, as for example people's names. A man's name was not looked on as something additional to his personality, something which could be changed at will; on the contrary, it contained an essential part of his nature and was at times actually looked on as his double; he was therefore particularly exposed to the baleful influence of magic by its use. An ill-starred name could threaten its bearer's life. Jacob valiantly rescued one of his children from the dark fate which was beginning to descend upon him because of the ill-starred name Ben Oni ("son of sorrow"), by giving him instead a name of happy omen (Gen. xxxv. 18).

While we are taking random examples like this, we may also consider a linguistic usage, the background to which is often misinterpreted —that of etiologies which depend on etymology and the play on words. In Israel, as elsewhere, such etiologies were not treated as a literary or rhetorical pastime, but were taken very seriously as a means of reaching certain important pieces of knowledge.[5] Present-day taste dislikes the absence of a recognisable connexion, either in logic or in meaning, between the words thus co-ordinated—indeed, to our way of thinking, the choice may seem perfectly arbitrary. Are we, however, only to keep to the immediately understood meaning which attaches to a word? In such "plays on words" the word has a different and much more primitive way of acting: on solemn occasions it can release meanings and establish mental affinities which lie at the deeper level of

[4] Abundant similar material drawn from comparative religion is to be found in J. Hempel, "Die israelitischen Anschauungen von Segen und Fluch im Lichte altorientalischer Parallelen" in *Zeitschrift der morgenländischen Gesellschaft* (1925), pp. 20ff. S. Mowinckel, *Segen und Fluch in Israels Kult und Psalmendichtung V*, Oslo 1924. On the conceptions of the power of the divine word, see L. Dürr, "Die Wertung des göttlichen Wortes im Alten Testament und im antiken Orient," henceforth cited as "Die Wertung des göttlichen Wortes," in *Mitteilungen der vorderasiat.-aegypt. Gesellschaft* XLII. 1 (1938). O. Grether, "Name und Wort Gottes im AT," henceforth cited as "Name und Wort," Bei. *Z.A.W.*, LXIV (1934), pp. 59ff.

[5] M. Warburg, *Zwei Fragen zum Kratylos* (2. *Voraussetzungen zum Verständnis der griechischen Etymologie*), *Neue philologische Untersuchungen V*, Berlin 1929, pp. 65ff. There is a relatively large number of such "etymologies" in the Old Testament. In the historical books alone J. Fichtner counts about 60 ("Die etymologische Ätiologie in den Namengebung der geschichtlichen Bücher des Alten Testaments", in *V.T.*, VI [1956], pp. 272ff.). It is not of course to be maintained that the view here taken is equally applicable to every reference; probably it only applies to one section, for Israel certainly also knew of the more rhetorical use of plays upon etymology.

its magical matrix and which apparently have little or nothing to do with its obvious and everyday meaning.[6] What happens in such etymologies is rather peculiar. On the one hand, the word in question loses a certain amount of its meaning, and apparently acts as a series of sounds rather than as a way of conveying meaning; but this series of sounds, which is the word reduced to its original value, is at the same time given a greatly intensified meaning, in that it is now, in respect of its form, surrounded by new associations and new meanings. The play upon "qayis—qes" in Amos's vision has meaning for us too; but only because we also can with fair ease make the mental jump from "harvest" to the idea of "end" (Am. VIII. 2). It is probable, however, that our connexion between these two words is, from the point of view of the phenomenology of linguistics, far too modern—that is to say, far too spiritual. Again, in what is said in Jeremiah about the almond tree ("watching rod" שָׁקֵד) and about Jahweh "watching over" (שָׁקֵד Jer. I. 11f.) his word, it is only the conceptual connexion that meets our eye. It is different with the improvised word-plays in Mic. I. 10–15 and Is. x. 29–31, for here the names of the places suggest associations, and give hints at the fate in store for them, which are still only linked to them by the "outward" sound of the words. This kind of thing is done all the more easily in Hebrew in that the Hebrew speaker, even when he is using language noetically, is in general far less concerned with linguistic precision and the avoidance of ambiguity than we often assume. If in prophetic diction a phrase or a word could have several possible references, so much the better, for the saying was thereby enriched.[7]

To digress for a moment: what has here been said about the Hebrew language regarded as a phenomenon composed of sounds which almost

---

[6] B. Meissner, *Babylonien und Assyrien*, henceforth cited as *Babylonien*, BD. II, Heidelberg 1925, p. 353, still speaks of the "unfortunate love of all Semites for etymology." As against this, see Seeligmann, *Midraschexegese*, p. 157.

[7] In this connexion mention should also be made of the names of ominous import in Hos. I. 4ff. and the renaming in Hos. II. 25 [23]. Finally, paronomasia should also be mentioned here; for with its juxtaposition of words with a similar sound, this figure is also primarily based on words' sound. Linguistic assonance is not however an outward thing; a peculiar power issues from the linguistic body of the expression. The precision of the paronomastic expression is diminished in favour of its greater breadth of meaning. G. Boström, *Paronomasie i den äldre Hebreiske Maschalliteraturen*, Lund 1928; I. Gabor, "Der Urrhythmus im Alten Testament," in Bei. *Z.A.W.*, LII (1929).

possesses a creative power of its own to conjure things up also holds true, in a different way, in Greek. Here, in addition to conveying meaning, its melodiousness and rhythm affect men even in their physical nature.[8] In Greek too the gap between the word and the objective thing it denotes can be so narrowed as to give even the modern reader the impression that the objects in all their material solidity have been taken up into the word.

"The characteristic of classical Greek is that the word operates as a rhythmic and musical force and at the same time as language, as a phonetic formation, as that which conveys ideas and emotions. The word serves not only a phonetic purpose: it is at the same time something more, it is a rational art-material which is shaped for its own sake. Undoubtedly it is language like our own, inasmuch as it serves to establish semantic connexions. It has also, however, a quality which we to-day can hardly understand, that of appealing directly to the senses as music does. It is rhythm which, independently of the word's linguistically conditioned sound properties, grants it a strength which is actually based in another sphere." "What impression may the Greeks have had of their own language? They must have had the feeling that it was mightier than they."[9] A Greek word "is like a solid body that the hands can grasp. The words of a verse in Greek stone one as it were."[10] This can also be said with equal truth of many of the utterances of the Old Testament prophets.

To return: Israel too was thus aware that her language possessed possibilities other than those demanded by everyday personal conversation.[11] She was aware of a use of language in which the primary requisite was in no sense a partner in conversation, but *just* that the words should *just* be spoken, that they should simply be brought on the scene as an objective reality endowed with mysterious power. This was, of course, only one possibility among others, but Israel never abandoned it, not even at the time when she learned the use of very

[8] Th. Georgiades, *Musik und Rhythmus bei den Griechen*, henceforth cited as *Musik und Rhythmus*, Hamburg 1958, pp. 42ff.

[9] *Musik und Rhythmus*, p. 43.   [10] *Musik und Rhythmus*, p. 45.

[11] G. Gerleman, *Wort und Realität (Donum natalicum H. S. Nyberg oblatum)*, Uppsala 1954, pp. 155ff. "Words operate more powerfully than do the information and the content; on the one hand they are spirit, but on the other they have the substantial and ambiguous character of natural things." G. Benn, *Probleme der Lyrik*, 1951, p. 24. For what follows, cp. also Grether, *Name und Wort*, pp. 103ff., 126ff., 135ff.

polished and rhetorical utterance, as for example in political and diplomatic conversations or in the exchange of ideas with wise men of other nationalities. As is only to be expected, she also employed this new skill in the realm in which her intellectual activity was at its strongest, the realm of religion and theology. Both in her most ordinary and in her sublimest statements, in magic, and in the deepest insights of theology or prophecy alike, Israel took as her starting point her conviction that the word possessed creative power.

Israel's theologians and prophets were, of course, certain that, for all the mysterious possibilities inherent in every word of man, the word of Jahweh towered incomparably high above them. Moses, as we see him in Deuteronomy, is most insistent in warning his people that they should not think of Jahweh's word as "empty" (ריק, Deut. XXXII. 47), and this obviously embraces the belief that the word of man is to be regarded as, in greater or lesser degree, "empty" in comparison with the word of God. Deutero-Isaiah also says that the word of God is not "empty," but effective (Is. LV. 11). We have already noticed the part which the concept of the creative word of Jahweh played in the priestly cosmological traditions, particularly in the Priestly Document's account of creation.[12] To this there is a corresponding concept in a cultic hymn.

> By his word the heavens were made,
> and all their host by the breath of his mouth.
> For he spoke, and it came to pass;
> he commanded, and it stood forth.
>
> (Ps. XXXIII. 6, 9)

Another of the Psalms says that "Jahweh calls the stars by name" (Ps. CXLVII. 4), and this idea is taken up by Deutero-Isaiah who, as is well known, made the creation of the world by Jahweh, and creation by the word, the *leit motif* of his preaching (Is. XL. 26, XLVIII. 13, L. 2). The mention of this creative word of Jahweh in Ps. CXLVII. 15–18, a Wisdom poem whose aim is instruction, is of particular interest, since here the word of Jahweh and its "going forth" are connected with the snow, the frost, the ice, and the wind, which also come from heaven.[13]

[12] See VOL. I, pp. 142f.

[13] Here the poet is clearly determined by the scientific onomastica (see VOL. I, p. 425). The inclusion of the אמרה which God sends on earth of course corresponds to a particular application to which effect was to be given precisely in this context; the mention of the divine word within this enumeration almost feels like an interpolation.

It has long been known that in this respect Israel shares in many ways in ideas found at various points in the religions of the ancient east.[14] But this must not blind us to the fact that her ideas of the power of God's word were entirely her own, and that in this very respect she evolved a magnificent and quite unique theological achievement. We need hardly say that to make generalisations based on the theory of evolution, and to say that here is an example of a primitive or magical view of language, only hinders the proper understanding of such an exceptional phenomenon, since this reduces it to a common denominator of cultural development which does not apply here. There were archaic survivals in all religions, and Israel was certainly not exempt from them. The striking fact remains, however, that the way by which she came to make her most important statements about the properties of the divine word was not that of remaining uncritically bound to these primitive elements, but that of exercising her most concentrated reflexion; and that what is said, for example in the prophets, about the "magical" power of the divine word occurs in the context of and in closest association with a very advanced and even positively revolutionary view of the spiritual world. The reason for this, to put it briefly, is not to be looked for among the general phenomena of religion, but in the unique character of the subject itself expressed here.

The prophets' statements about the word of Jahweh are relatively independent of those made by the priestly theology. With the former we encounter what is obviously a self-contained set of ideas and traditions. The term, "the word of Jahweh" (דבר יהוה), occurs 241 times in the Old Testament writings; of these no less than 221 (93 per cent) relate to a prophetic oracle. There can, therefore, be no doubt but that this collocation was used as a technical term for an oral prophetic revelation. The phrase, "the word of Jahweh came to so and so" (ויהי דבר יהוה אל, or something similar, 123 times), is particularly characteristic, because it represents the apperception of the divine word as event, a contingent happening in history, which a man is looking for or which takes him by surprise, and which therefore in either case sets the person concerned in a new historical situation.[15] It is very significant that the phrase always appears with the definite article,

---

[14] See Dürr, "Die Wertung des göttlichen Wortes," pp. 2ff.

[15] Mowinckel paraphrased the words as follows: "the word of Jahweh became active reality with so and so," *Erkenntnis Gottes*, p. 19; W. Zimmerli speaks of the "word event," *Ezechiel*, p. 89 etc.; Grether, *Name und Wort*, p. 76; Vriezen, *Theology*,

"*the* word of Jahweh," and never in the indefinite form, "*a* word of Jahweh," as a superficial glance at the extremely large number of such "word-events" might have led one to expect.[16] The latter would however have shown a radical misunderstanding of the process, for however brief and concise the word might be, it was intended as *the* word of Jahweh for the man who received it and for his situation. The word that came on each occasion is not to be set alongside the rest of the words of Jahweh, so that it is only in the synthesis that it yields something like the message the prophet has to announce; on the contrary, for the person concerned it is the complete word of God, and has no need of tacit supplementation by the other words which the prophet had already spoken on other occasions. At different times and to different people the prophet takes different ways of saying the same thing. Paradoxical as it may seem, in principle the prophet says the same thing to everyone; he plays variations upon it only to meet differences in the conditions of his audience. This is the main reason why it is so difficult to set out a prophet's teaching. We are bound to make the attempt, but at the same time there is no possibility of achieving the result by taking, as it were, the average of his ideas from the sum total of his prophetic *logia*.[17]

But we shall be disappointed if we imagine that, in all the really abundant and varied material available, the prophets give a complete account of the phenomenology of the word of Jahweh. Indeed, we may even come to think that the prophets are the last people to provide an answer to this question, because their attitude to the word they receive is so far from neutral—the word presses in upon them, they

p. 95. The "word" belongs to the prophet in the same way as does *torah* to the priest and counsel to the wise (Jer. xviii. 18).

[16] Attention was first drawn to this remarkable fact by L. Köhler, *Old Testament Theology*, trs. A. S. Todd, 1957, p. 106.

[17] We find exactly the same state of affairs, which is of course very important for exposition, in the synoptic gospels. "The Gospels tell the story of Jesus in 'pericopae'. These story scenes give his history not only when pieced together, but each one in itself contains the person and history of Jesus in their entirety. None requires explanation in terms of previous happenings. None is directed at later events for the unfolding of what has gone before. We are always being held in the beam of this scene and this scene only. . . . This way of telling his story has its exact counterpart in the transmission of his words. Here again each word stands by itself, exhaustive in itself, not dependent on context for its meaning or requiring a commentary on it from some other word." G. Bornkamm, *Jesus of Nazareth*, trs. J. M. Robinson, London 1960, p. 25. Cp. also below, pp. 129f.

make it their own, and allow it to absorb all their emotions. In his word Jahweh meets his prophet in the most personal way possible; how could a man then talk of it as if it were a neutral thing? Thus it would be better to apply for information not to the prophets but to their audience, who were less directly involved in the word of God: but, to do this we would have still to be able to discover what impression the prophetic word made upon them!

It may be noticed in passing that this difficulty lends added importance to the verdict passed by Amaziah the high priest on the message of Amos. It is well known that he reported Amos's appearance at Bethel to the king, and, like a true official, added a note giving his own comment on the matter: "the land is not able to bear all his words" (Am. VII. 10). The verb (כול) is ordinarily used of the cubic capacity of vessels; the words therefore imply that the land—note that he speaks of the land and not of Israel—had a certain limited capacity. This was certainly no dull-witted official report: the man who wrote it was a keen-eyed observer with real insight into the force of Amos's words. Paradoxically enough, therefore, we have to allow that Amaziah had a certain understanding of the prophet's message—he saw it as a real danger to the Israel of the day and to its religious and economic life to that date.

To resume: as has been said, with the earlier prophets in particular, reflexion on the nature and properties of the word which they spoke is not *a priori* to be expected. Their feelings are intensified, and they deliver it almost as if it were a ritual, and are perfectly sure of the effects which it accomplishes. One of the oldest utterances of the prophets are the words attributed to Elijah, that there should be neither dew nor rain in Israel "except by my word" (I Kings XVII. 1). To whom, however, is this word which is to break the drought to be spoken? When the proper time comes, does he mean to speak it to Jahweh, or to the heavens and the clouds? This last is not beyond the realm of possibility. What is, however, more likely is that he expected Jahweh to give it to him to command the rain. The reader who has studied comparative religion may here feel reminded of the self-understanding of the "bearer of power" among primitive peoples and of the magical force latent in his word. Yet, to discover, as we think, such phenomena still "lingering on" in Elijah does not take us very much further forward. On the evidence available, it could equally be argued that we see in Elijah the beginning of a concept of the prophetic word which can be traced down from his own time almost to the moment when prophecy finally disappeared. We may even go further: it is easy to show how the old concept became of more and more theological importance, to reach its fullest development in Jeremiah and Deutero-Isaiah.

The verse which stands at the head of Amos's oracles (in a position which suggests that it is intended to serve as a statement of policy for the whole collection) states that Jahweh "roars" (Am. I. 2). This is a term which goes far beyond the limits of the normal language of worship or of any other department of religion. Oddly enough, it says nothing about the subject-matter of the roaring: there is no definite verbal utterance on the part of Jahweh, just as there is no mention of any human hearers to whom the oracle refers. The only thing spoken of is a sound, and all that is said of it is that it echoes. Nevertheless, the effect of this sound is tremendous, for when it goes forth from Zion it makes the pastures of the shepherds desolate and withers even the summit of distant Carmel.[18] Amos's near contemporary, Isaiah, also on occasion uses strange language about the word of Jahweh, and speaks of it as if it were a material thing, achieving its effect simply in virtue of its physical weight:

> The Lord has sent a word against Jacob,
>   and it has lit upon Israel.
>
> (Is. IX. 7 [8])

The prophet's way of speaking of the "word" here is very absolute, as if it were something known to everyone. What is even more remarkable is that the people are given no explanation of the subject matter of this word; there is no mention of the prophet who spoke it or of any audience to whom it was spoken. Since this word was directed against the Northern Kingdom, and the event referred to possibly lay now in the past, it is not even certain that it was spoken by Isaiah himself. Yet the prophet, whoever he was, speaks of the word's coming down to earth and its historical effect as if they were objective realities. In some respects the poem presents difficulties for exegesis, but one thing is quite clear: it speaks throughout of repeated sendings forth of this word which, as it makes its way through history, is not quickly spent:

[18] The logion Am. I. 2 must be taken entirely by itself; it has no connexion either with what precedes it or follows it. The words of threat which Seraiah was to read aloud in Babylon also required no one to hear them; they were simply to be proclaimed aloud; the sheet was then to be cast into the Euphrates (Jer. LI. 59ff.).

For all this his anger is not turned away,
and his hand is still stretched out.[19]

While such expressions are rare in the eighth-century prophets and
only serve to show that in certain circumstances these men see the
word of Jahweh operating in a way which is quite different from the
normal one, with Jeremiah they occur frequently, and suggest that
here some change has come over the prophet's basic conception of the
word.[20] Even in the call itself, through which Jeremiah is summoned
to prophesy "against nations and kingdoms," everything is made to
depend upon the power of the prophet's word. How is it possible for
one solitary individual like Jeremiah "to pluck up and to break down,
to build and to plant" in respect of whole nations (Jer. I. 9f.)? Clearly
only by means of the word of Jahweh which Jahweh injects into history;
for this word is very different from that of his degenerate professional
fellow-prophets—it is like a fire, like a hammer which breaks the rocks
in pieces (Jer. V. 14, XXIII. 29). At the very same moment that Ezekiel
was voicing the words he had been inspired to speak against Pelatiah
the latter fell down dead (Ezek. XI. 13). Thus, the reason why these
men were hated and feared was this power inherent in the word. Their
power to bring about disaster, and the possibility that they might do so,
were not contested. If the "wrath of Jahweh" which filled Jeremiah
was to be poured out, this meant catastrophe and death (Jer. VI. 11f.).
For the prophets themselves, however, the word held more than
simply terror. Jeremiah tells us something of its effect on him: he says
in one place that the word became a joy to him, and that he ate it like
a starving man. We cannot assume that he made any exception in
principle of the oracles portending calamity (Jer. XV. 16). When he
speaks of eating the divine words, we should not take this in too
spiritual a way, and regard it as metaphor and hyperbole: it is perfectly possible that a prophet even felt physically dependent on the

[19] Is. IX. 11, 16, 20 [12, 17, 21], X. 4.
[20] The widespread use of the very characteristic phrase, "the word of Jahweh came
to . . ." also occasions thought. It is found—in each case of course only in a very
small number of instances—in practically all the older prophets. In contrast however,
there is a sudden increase in Jeremiah (30 times) and Ezekiel (50 times) (O. Grether,
Name und Wort, pp. 76f.). This must link up with the new emphasis now laid on the
word of Jahweh as event, and indeed with a "theology of the word" which is now
appearing in these prophets.

word and so, in a sense, was kept alive by it. The idea of eating the word of Jahweh reappears in Ezekiel in a very radical form; at his call he was ordered to eat the scroll which was offered to him (Ezek. II. 8 – III. 3). Later on we shall have to consider how the entry of the message into their physical life brought about an important change in the self-understanding of these later prophets. (We may ask whether this entry of the word into a prophet's bodily life is not meant to approximate to what the writer of the Fourth Gospel says about the word becoming flesh.) Earlier, of course, Amos had spoken of a famine of the word of God which was to press so hardly upon men that they would stagger hither and thither in exhaustion seeking the word, and would faint (Am. VIII. 11ff.). This looks very much as if the prophets regarded Israel's whole life as in some special way dependent upon the word of Jahweh, and thought of her as directed towards it right down to the most elemental levels of her life. When Deuteronomy makes Moses exclaim, "this word is your life" (Deut. XXXII. 47), and when it draws from the miracle of the manna the lesson that man does not live by bread alone, but "by everything that proceeds out of the mouth of Jahweh" (Deut. VIII. 3), there can be no doubt that it was making use of ideas generally current among the prophets. Yet, while this idea of man's total dependence upon the word of God originates with the prophets, it apparently only came to the surface, at least in so emphtaic a form, in the seventh century; and the prophets themselves were certainly the first people to realise that their own lives were totally dependent on Jahweh.

In the case of Deutero-Isaiah, the tradition gives no information about the prophet's own relationship to the word. This is, however, offset by the great place which he gives to expatiating on the efficacy of the word in history. At his call a voice from heaven sharply contrasts men's whole being ("all flesh") with the word of Jahweh. The former— the prophet is thinking first and last of man as he behaved in history in the great empires—is utterly transient; the breath of Jahweh will blow upon him in wrath and destroy him completely. As for the latter, however—"the word of our God stands for ever" (Is. XL. 8). The phrase is extremely terse, but it is perfectly clear that by "the word of our God" the prophet means to point to that other power which confronts the first one, the power of man as displayed in the historical empires. He is not, therefore, thinking of the word which will endure because it calls forth an echo in the inner realm of the heart, but of the word which Jahweh speaks into history and which works creatively on that plane: it will "arise" (יקום). Nor will anything endure except that which this word brings about; for the bewildered exiles in Babylon it is the one solid ground under their feet. The book ends as it began on this same note:

"Verily, as the rain and the snow come down from heaven and return not thither without watering the earth, making it bring forth and sprout, giving seed to the sower and bread to the eater, so it is with my word that goes forth from my mouth. It does not return to me empty without accomplishing that which I purposed or fulfilling that for which I sent it" (Is. LV. 10–11).

This is prophecy's most comprehensive statement about the word of Jahweh and its effects. As with the audition at a call, the words here used tend strongly towards a theological radicality; the dimensions are extended to the furthest limits of thought and even right into theological radicality. At the beginning of the prophecy the word was contrasted with "all flesh"; here it comes down from heaven, down from the lips of Jahweh on to earth, in order there to give effect to (עשה) its task and bring it to a successful conclusion (הצליח), and then at the end to return to Jahweh.[21] When the word of Jahweh is likened to rain and snow, what comes into a modern reader's mind are simply the laws of nature; ancient Israel, however, regarded both of these, the sending of the rain and the sending of the word, as contingent events which took their origin from Jahweh alone (Ps. CXLVII. 15ff.). Deutero-Isaiah thus sets the word of Jahweh in the grandest of perspectives. The most important part of its universal activity is admittedly its action in history, yet this is only one part. There is absolutely no saving event not foretold (Is. XLII. 9, XLVI. 10, XLVIII. 5). If, however, Jahweh sends this word which heralds what is to come and allows his chosen people knowledge of it, this is only a concession to Israel's lack of faith:

> Because I knew that you were obstinate,
> and your neck is an iron band
> and your forehead brass,

---

[21] The idea that the word in the end returns to Jahweh as in a circle is odd, and is not found elsewhere. Is this only an *ad hoc* formulation, in order to carry the comparison through? It is to be assumed that the figure of the rain which begets like chthonic force (cp. the הוליד in v. 10) has an old mythological idea as its basis; but it is very unlikely that the prophet was aware of this.

> I declared it to you from of old;
>   before it came to pass, I announced it to you.
>
> (Is. xlviii. 4f.)

If we ask what it is that this word of Jahweh effects in history, we must turn to the content of the message—Deutero-Isaiah thinks above all of the return of the community of Israel, the second Exodus with all its wonders. That the prologue and epilogue of the book, the frame of our prophet's total preaching, deal so radically with the word of God, is a statement of policy of great importance.

The passages quoted here suggest that there was a strong element of theological reflexion in Deutero-Isaiah—something which Jeremiah and Ezekiel had foreshadowed. This "theology of the word"[22] was intended to give a systematic explanation of the phenomenon of the word of Jahweh, and this explanation, in its turn, was to serve as a basis for the huge project of surveying the phenomenon of prophecy itself. In such words as those contained in Is. lv. 10f., prophecy thus also to a large extent presents the results of reflexion on its own nature; for through this view of the word of God, prophecy gave itself the central place in the whole interaction of God and the world.

In this theoretic attempt to come to a proper understanding of the nature and effects of the word of Jahweh, another work should be placed beside that of Deutero-Isaiah; and this, though the two must have been roughly contemporary, is of a very different kind. It is the Deuteronomic history. As we have already seen, it pictured Israel's history as a history of Jahweh's effective word; it postulated a number of predictions as the real causes of events, and at the appropriate places drew special attention to the way in which each particular one was fulfilled ("this came about in order that the word spoken by the prophet . . . might be fulfilled"[23]). The Deuteronomist here applies these ideas to the past in order to show it as a scheme of history shaped

[22] On the "theology of the word" in the prophet Ezekiel, see Zimmerli, *Ezechiel* p. 89.

[23] See vol. I, pp. 343f. The Deuteronomist had an established set of theological terms at hand to show how this word functioned in history: the prophetic word "does not fail"; Josh. xxi. 45, xxiii. 14; I Kings viii. 56; II Kings x. 10; "it will be established" (הקים): I Sam. I. 23, xv. 11, 13; II Sam. vii. 25; I Kings II. 4, vi. 12; "it comes to pass" (בא): Josh. xxiii. 15; "it is fulfilled" (מלא): I Kings II. 27, viii. 15, 24; cp. also Ezek. xii. 25, 28: "Thus has the Lord Jahweh spoken: None of my words will be delayed any longer; the word which I speak is performed, says the Lord, Jahweh."

by Jahweh: but they are undoubtedly prophetic in origin. At the same time, within the larger framework of the Old Testament, it is he who gave the word of God in its form as the dynamic of history its broadest theological basis, for he saw the word of Jahweh, whether in salvation or in judgment, as the real motive-force and creator of Israel's history. The word is extremely active, "it runs swiftly" (Ps. CXLVII. 15); "it [even] hastens" to its fulfilment, and people must be able to wait for it (Hab. II. 3)[24]; for God's thoughts and designs began their historical fulfilment at the point they became words on the lips of the prophet.

In the Wisdom of Solomon the divine word is the subject of some verses of great poetic merit, and in one respect these have close affinities with the prophetic utterances mentioned above. The subject is the night in which Jahweh smote the first-born of Egypt: "While deep silence enveloped all things, and night in its course was now half gone, thy all-powerful word leaped from heaven, from the royal throne, a stern warrior into the midst of the land that was doomed. Carrying as a sharp sword thy unalterable command, it came and filled all things with death. It touched heaven as it strode about on earth" (Wis. Sol. XVIII. 14ff.). This obviously departs from the prophets' line of thought, for they never spoke of the word of Jahweh as an independent entity to this extent, as if it were a being with an existence of its own. For them the word was mobile to the highest degree, and they could never have tied it to places in such a way, or described it like this. Here faith has fallen silent and given place to speculative thought.

The articulate word was not, however, the only means used by the prophets to express the future. They also performed all kinds of symbolic actions, some of which were extremely odd. Ahijah the Shilonite tore his garment into twelve pieces and gave them to Jeroboam (I Kings XI. 29ff.), Isaiah drew up a tablet with a name written on it (Is. VIII. 1–4) and went about "naked," that is, in modern language, in the dress of a deportee (Is. XX. 1ff.), Jeremiah broke a flask (Jer. XIX. 1ff.), wore a yoke of wood (Jer. XXVII. 2ff.), and bought a field (Jer. XXXII. 6ff.), and Ezekiel in particular is credited with a whole series of extremely curious "symbolic actions" (Ezek. IV–V). It took scholars a long time to recognise the special significance of these prophetic signs—indeed, they did not do so until they realised that such signs are not to be regarded simply as symbols intended to bring out the meaning of oral preaching. While in some cases the prophet's purpose was to

[24] The rendering of יִפֵחַ as "pant," "hasten" is not, of course, certain.

reinforce in visual ways what he had said, or was about to say, it is clear that this idea does not give the full picture.[25] For antiquity, the sign, like the solemn word we have already discussed, could not only signify a datum but actually embody it as well; this means that it could act creatively, and in early cultures it probably had an even greater power to do so than the word. For us to-day, this way of looking at a sign is difficult to understand, whereas we can still perfectly easily experience the creative properties of the word; there are situations where it matters very much whether a word is spoken or not—even when it is in everyone's minds. But in primitive cultic practice especially, solemn word and solemn sign lie in the closest possible co-ordination, and this is not just in the sense that the sign is the servant of the word and so merely an additional accompaniment of it; on the contrary, in the form of a sacred rite, for example, the sign can be taken as completely independent from the word.

Like other ancient peoples, Israel was aware of the efficacy of sacred signs, and this not merely in the restricted sphere of the cult but also in the realm of the law (in legal symbolism and symbolic actions in connexion with oaths), in medicine, and even in the language of gesture in the dance.[26] Thus, symbolic actions were by no means simply the prerogative of the prophets. Their contemporaries were not surprised that the prophets performed such actions: what shocked them was the meanings which the prophets expressed in this way. Jahweh himself acts in the symbol, through the instrument of his prophet. The symbol was a creative prefiguration of the future which would be speedily and inevitably realised. When the prophet, by means of a symbolic act, projects a detail of the future into the present, this begins the process of realisation, and on that account the prophetic symbolic act is simply an intensified form of prophetic speech. The only difference is that in the case of the sign, it was less important that its full implications should be understood by those who saw it performed. Do not symbolic actions sometimes seem to conceal more than they reveal? In both of Isaiah's symbolic acts, the command to perform them anticipates the

[25] Research is indebted to H. W. Robinson's article "Prophetic Symbolism" in O.T. Essays, London 1924, pp. 1ff. for the decisive break-through to the new understanding. Cf. at the present time particularly G. Fohrer, Die symbolischen Handlungen der Propheten, Zürich 1953; id. "Die Gattung der Berichte über Symbolhandlungen der Propheten," in Z.A.W., LXIII (1952), pp. 101ff.

[26] Fohrer, op. cit., pp. 10ff.

full disclosure of their meaning by some years (Is. VIII. 1ff., xx. 1ff.)!
Even if we do not adopt the extreme position that the prophet himself
was, to begin with, ignorant of the significance of what he was ordered
to do (though in both cases this is what the text apparently suggests), it
is quite certain that for a long time the people did not understand his
behaviour; and this completely rules out the idea that the function of
symbolic actions was to teach and illustrate. For to do this they would
have had to be visual illustrations chosen by the prophet to produce a
better understanding of a message which his audience had already
received.

This way of regarding symbolic actions, which was only opened up
by the study of comparative religion, is therefore basic for exegesis.
Exegesis will, of course, discover that this idea of the power of the
symbol which acts creatively in history is by no means present in its
pure form in every case. Examination of the way in which the symbolic
act is related to the spoken word reveals a variety of concepts of the
former's function, with the result that exegesis has in each specific case
to ask what the action was intended to signify.

Prophetic symbolic actions were originally directed towards a future
event (II Kings XIII. 14ff.): but the classical prophets also applied the
sign to their own times, and it thus became a little ambivalent. The idea
that the sign had power to create history is clearly still present: but it
now contains a proclamation as well. Because greater emphasis is now
put upon its appeal to the mind, it turns to the people of its own day, in
order to prepare them for the future. Thus, Isaiah's going about naked
becomes a "sign" for the nation once Jahweh discloses its meaning; it
becomes the portent of a deportation which still lies in the future (Is.
xx. 3). In just the same way Ezekiel in making no mourning at the
death of his wife becomes a "sign" for his people, a pointer to a
calamity in which no one will make ritual mourning for his relatives
(Ezek. XXIV. 15ff.). These symbolic actions come much closer to being
actual prefigurations of the events to which they refer; unlike Ahijah's
torn garment, they do not merely foretell the bare fact, but also
actually portray what it will entail (prisoners going naked, no proper
rites at funerals), and to this extent they can be the better understood
by those who witness them.

In the story of Jeremiah's wearing of a yoke the concept underwent
an even more radical change, for Jeremiah used the yoke as a warning
—only the nations who submit to Nebuchadnezzar will escape deporta-

tion (Jer. XXVII. 1ff.). Here the form the future will assume is still completely open, and the symbolic action lays upon the witnesses themselves the decision whether it will be weal or woe. Here Wheeler Robinson's sacramental significance of the symbolic action has completely disappeared.[27] It is, of course, possible that the responsibility for the way in which the symbol loses its earlier meaning lies at the door of the narrator of the incident, for elsewhere in the book of Jeremiah there are symbolic actions quite identical with the older understanding of them (particularly Jer. XIX. 1–2a, 10–11a, 14–15, and Jer. XXXII. 1ff.).

[27] H. W. Robinson, "Prophetic Symbolism," p. 16.

CHAPTER G

ISRAEL'S IDEAS ABOUT TIME AND HISTORY, AND THE PROPHETIC ESCHATOLOGY

I. THE ORIGINS OF HEBREW THOUGHT ABOUT HISTORY

THE question of the specific way in which Hebrew thought understood time and history brings us into an area of great importance for the correct understanding of the prophets. Earlier exposition was quite unaware that there was a problem here, and uncritically assumed that its own Western and Christian concept of time also held good for Israel. To-day, however, we are beginning to realise that her experience of which we call time and ours are different.[1] Yet this in itself does not bring us very much further forward, for we find it extremely difficult to move beyond the terms of our own concept, which we naïvely believe to be the only possible one, and to understand the specific details of another in such a way as to be able to make much of reconstructing it. The attitude of Western man to linear time is, generally speaking, naïve; time is seen as an infinitely long straight line on which the individual can mark such past and future events as he can ascertain. This time-span has a mid-point, which is our own present day. From it the past stretches back and the future forwards. But to-day one of the few things of which we can be quite sure is that this concept of absolute time, independent of events, and, like the blanks on a questionnaire, only needing to be filled up with data which will give it content, was unknown to Israel. It is true that in the Deuteronomic history the notices which synchronise the concurrent reigns of the kings in Judah and Israel presuppose a high degree of intellectual and scholarly activity (as is well

---

[1] C. H. Ratschow, "Anmerkungen zur theologischen Auffassung des Zeitproblems," in *Z. Th. K.* LI (1954), pp. 360ff.; T. Boman, *Hebrew Thought compared with Greek*, trs. J. L. Moreau, London 1960, pp. 123ff. G. Pidoux, "A propos de la notion biblique du temps," henceforth cited as "Temps," in *Revue de Théologie et de Philosophie* (1952), pp. 120ff.; J. Marsh, *The Fulness of Time*, London 1952, pp. 19ff., 35ff.; W. Eichrodt, "Heilserfahrung und Zeitverständnis im Alten Testament," henceforth cited as "Heilserfahrung," in *Th. Z.*, XII (1956), pp. 103ff.

known, they have their parallel in, and are perhaps modelled on, the synchronistic lists of the kings of Babylon and Assyria).[2] Yet, these chroniclers failed to go on to what we should expect to be the next logical step—they did not take these two chronological series together in order to enter them on one single time-line. Each of the two lists of kings keeps its own time. Are we to say that what prevented this simple logical conclusion was certain intellectual limitations of the age? What is much more likely to have made the step absolutely impossible is the ancient world's concept of time. If exegesis regards this way of viewing time as merely a stage of cultural infancy, it bars the way to understanding. It should rather be ready to accept that Israel's perception of time was taken from a different angle than ours.

In addition to being without any idea of absolute and unlinear time, it also seems evident that Israel was not capable of thinking of time in the abstract, time divorced from specific events. She found the idea of a time without a particular event quite inconceivable; all that she knew was time as containing events. Hebrew completely lacks a word for our modern concept of "time." Leaving aside עולם, which means the distant past or future, the most important term which comes under discussion here is עת, but it means "time" in the sense of "a point in time" or "a period of time." There is a time of giving birth (Mic. v. 2 [3]), a time for animals to be gathered together (Gen. XXIX. 7), a time when kings go forth to battle (II Sam. XI. 1). When something out of the ordinary was projected, such as the rebuilding of the temple (Hag. I. 4), there could be debate whether this was the time to undertake it. The tree yields its fruit "in its time" (Ps. I. 3), and God gives his creatures food "in due time" (Ps. CIV. 27); that is to say, every event has its definite place in the time-order; the event is inconceivable without its time, and *vice versa*.[3] This is, of course, self-evident in the case of processes determined by the cycle of the natural year. As antiquity understood it, however, this temporal ordering holds good for all the concerns of mankind—even for the emotions—because every matter under heaven has its own time: a time to be born, to die, to plant, to pluck up, to weep, to laugh, to mourn, to dance, to seek, to lose, to rend, to sew, to keep silence, to speak, to love, to hate (Ecclesiastes III.

[2] E. F. Weidner, "Die Könige von Assyrien (Neue chronologische Dokumente aus Assur)," in *Mitteilungen der Vorderasiatischen Gesellschaft* (1921), pp. 2ff.

[3] Marsh, *op., cit.*, p. 27; Eichrodt, "Heilserfahrung," p. 107; cp. also H. W. Robinson, *Inspiration and Revelation in the Old Testament*, Oxford 1946, pp. 109ff.

1ff.). This profound insight is not, of course, simply that of Ecclesiastes alone, it was one of the basic insights of the people of the age in general, and the utmost degree of wisdom was necessary not to miss the times appointed for things and their discharge, and to recognise their mysterious *kairos*. Finally, on the basis of these leading ideas it is not surprising to find that Israel could also speak of "times." This plural form, which on our lips is properly rhetorical hyperbole, had a realistic significance for her. When a man at prayer says: "my times are in thy hands" (Ps. xxxi. 16 [15]), we must remember that he had no idea at all of time as such; in his eyes human life is made up of a series of many times.[4]

The statement just made, that our concept of time is linear, requires to be supplemented by saying that to a large extent it is actually eschatological. For a thousand years in our Western world it was eschatological in the strict Christian sense of that term; and even when our way of looking at the world and history became a secular one, time itself was still in a certain sense thought of eschatologically— mankind, or a particular nation, was thought of as moving towards some ultimate fulfilment. Even the nihilist is to-day conscious of being in a time-stream; indeed, his precise trouble is that he cannot master its onrush. What puts such a question mark to man in his now secular existence is simply the fact that while other Christian concepts have crumbled away, an eviscerated eschatological concept of time still lives on. Old Testament exegesis must therefore completely exclude this concept.

We may notice in passing that this concept is not found in Greek thought either; our abstract idea of time has no place at all in the ancient world.[5] "According to Herodotus, the law of time which events obey is not chiliastic, does not press on towards a future, cannot be compared to a stream, nor is in any sense whatsoever eschatological, but it is cyclical, periodic, always turning back to its beginning once the end has been reached. His [Herodotus's] philosophy is . . . that human affairs run in a cycle. . . . This mode of viewing events in time . . . asserts that in, with and under the causal nexus visible and comprehensible to man there is one which is invisible, and which shows itself covertly in, and peeps out enigmatically from, gestures, words,

---

[4] Further references for this use of the plural, Ezek. XII. 27; Job XXIV. 1.

[5] "The idea that the course of the world could lead to any goal or end seems originally to have been alien to the Egyptian"; E. Otto, "Altägyptische Zeitvorstellung und Zeitbegriffe," in *Die Welt als Geschichte* (1954), p. 142.

signs and prophecies, until in each specific case the end makes the connexion with the beginning plain. . . . The co-incidence between the
seen and the unseen becomes accomplished fact in the cycle. . . . No
Greek historian would close his work with a glance into the future, as
we are so prone to do. . . . As we understand the terms, the world of
history and historic time are unknown to antiquity."[6]

To return: in more than one respect the comfortable words which
form the close of J's account of the Flood, "while the earth remains,
seedtime and harvest, cold and heat, summer and winter, day and
night, shall not cease" (Gen. VIII. 22), are characteristic of the concept
of time held in Israel in the early period. In the first place they are in
the highest degree non-eschatological, in that what they expect from
the future is precisely the absence of the abnormal: the future (though
the term is not really appropriate) is the extension of the present. The
words "while the earth remains" are a solemn assurance, equivalent
to "for all time," and they certainly do not imply any consciousness
of a limit, meaning that the sentence was to be interpreted in the sense
of "only" while the earth remains. Next, it is typical that the only way
of conveying the idea that the earth will remain in being for ever is to
construct a series of times having various contents. Thirdly, the words
show that this series follows a definite rhythm: it is not arbitrary, but is
subject to a fixed order. This we should call a natural order, since it is
determined by the rhythm of earth and of the heavenly bodies.

Any description of the concept of time in the ancient world in
general and in Israel in particular would, however, be perfectly inadequate unless something was said of the significance of the festivals,
for these were not merely the high-lights of peoples' lives: rather
in fact, the rhythm of festal and non-festal times gave their own
lives their rhythm in time. Indeed, one might even go a stage further
and describe the time of cultic festival as the one and only "time" in
the full sense of the word, for it alone was time furnished with content
in the truest sense of the term; because the observance of these cultic
festivals did not rest upon any human arrangement, and besides, earlier
on there were no ecclesiastical and civil years running parallel.[7] We

---

[6] Karl Reinhardt, Herodots Persergeschichte, in Geistige Überdieferung, hsg. v.
E. Grassi, Berlin 1940, pp. 141ff. Cp. here the important observations on Greek
thought about time as distinct from Biblical and Christian thought made by K.
Lowith, *Meaning in History*, Chicago 1949, p. 6ff.

[7] For this supreme importance of the cultic festivals one may compare what

meant to people who completely lacked any concept of absolute and linear time to which these festivals had then to be related. The festivals, not time, were the absolute data, and were data whose holiness was absolute. There were days of which it could be said that Jahweh "has made" them (Ps. CXVIII. 24). The sabbath was an objectively hallowed day, that is to say, a day set apart for Jahweh, on which the community shared in the divine rest and, in so doing, was conscious that this rest upon which it entered was as it were an ontological reality. The Feast of Tabernacles was a time of joy, whose appointment by Jahweh was absolute. It was holy time absolutely, and even the most wretched must have been filled with delight as they entered upon it. Besides these, there were times of mourning and fasting, which, from the sacral point of view, were negative in character. Failure to observe a time of fasting was not the infringement of a mere human arrangement but of a divinely appointed fixed order. There might occasionally be uncertainty; it might be asked whether the community was misunderstanding a divine order and misconceiving the nature of a time—whether it was, for example, observing a time of mourning where God had already ordained a time of blessing (Zech. VII. 1ff.). Such questions were not just ritual niceties, but affected the very basis of these men's faith, and in dealing with them exegesis has no right to withdraw into its own supposedly superior understanding of time.[8]

The rhythm of Israel's great festivals was originally determined by nature's ordering of the Palestinian year. The festal calendar is, of course, Canaanite in origin, and as such is the expression of a farmer's

W. F. Otto says on the festivals in ancient Greece (*Die Gestalt und das Sein*, Düsseldorf 1955, p. 255): "The festival always means the recurrence of a great hour in the world when what is most venerable, august and splendid is once again present; a return of the golden age, when the forefathers associated so intimately with the gods and spiritual beings. This is the reason for the festal sublimity which, when there are real festivals, is different from any other kind of solemnity and any other kind of joy. Hence the awe-inspiring forms, striving towards magnificence, of genuine worship, whose style cannot possibly belong to the realm of practical purposes. It testifies to a holy plenitude, to an enraptured geniality of the soul which appropriates the extraordinary, the primeval and eternal, the divine. Men have entered into the heights; the return of the great hour has exalted them."

[8] The introduction of the "Spring calendar," *i.e.*, the transference of the beginning of the year to the spring, which took place under Assyrian influence in the later monarchical period, did not indeed affect the cycle of the cultic festivals, but nevertheless it must have been regarded as a sign that the old sacral understanding of time was breaking down.

course, Canaanite in origin, and as such is the expression of a farmer's religion which looks on the processes of sowing and reaping as direct sacral events. Obviously however in Israel, very soon after the settlement, and in spite of the fact that she herself had become a completely farming people, the content of these festivals underwent a change. At Unleavened Bread, the festival which falls at the beginning of the barley harvest, the Exodus from Egypt was commemorated (Ex. xxIII. 15), and at the great harvest and vintage festivals the sojourn in the wilderness and the dwelling in booths (Lev. xxIII. 42f.). Before this the festivals had been purely agrarian, but Israel "historicised" them. We can scarcely overestimate the importance of such changes, brought about as they were by a unique understanding of the world and of human existence.[9] Israel's belief that she was not bound primarily to the periodic cycle of nature but to definite historical events, was the expression of a faith that was probably at the time still completely unaware both of its absolute difference in kind from the Canaanite religion, and of its own vigour. While, therefore, it is perfectly correct to say that Jahwism is founded in history, this does not, of course, involve any thought of the modern concept of history which, as we know, lays great stress on the idea of relativity and of the transitoriness of all events. The historical acts by which Jahweh founded the community of Israel were absolute. They did not share the fate of all other events, which inevitably slip back into the past. They were actual for each subsequent generation; and this not just in the sense of furnishing the imagination with a vivid present picture of past events—no, it was only the community assembled for a festival that by recitation and ritual brought Israel in the full sense of the word into being: in her own person she really and truly entered into the historic situation to which the festival in question was related.[10] When Israel ate the Passover, clad as for a journey, staff in hand, sandals on her feet, and in the haste of departure (Ex. xII. 11), she was manifestly doing more than merely remembering the Exodus: she was entering into the saving event of the Exodus itself and participating in it in a quite "actual" way. The same

[9] Cp. also R. Rendtorff, "Kult, Mythus und Geschichte im alten Israel," in *Sammlung und Sendung, Festschrift für H. Rendtorff*, pp. 121ff. For the process of "historicising" mythical concepts, see A. Weiser, *Glaube und Geschichte im Alten Testament*, Stuttgart 1931, E. Kutsch, in *Die Religion in Geschichte und Gegenwart*, henceforth cited as *R.G.G.*, 3rd edn. Tübingen, vol. II, cols. 911ff.

[10] On the cult as sacral mime, see Mowinckel, *Psalmenstudien*, vol. II, pp. 19ff.

at Shechem, when she celebrated the giving of the commandments and the making of the covenant respectively.[11] As we shall see, this vivid experience of the contemporaneousness of the divine saving acts began to diminish at a later stage of her faith.

This transformation of what were once agrarian festivals, itself the result of the character of Jahwism as a historically determined religion, was, however, only one stage of development, Israel's first step, as we might call it, towards the understanding of her historical existence. For she did not stop short at basing her existence on a single historical event: she went on to specify a whole series of them, and it was this series of events as a whole which called the people of Israel into being. The Exodus from Egypt was prefaced by the patriarchal age, and rounded off by the events connected with the entry into Canaan, and from the aggregate of a whole series of saving acts developed a span of historical time. Israel's faith began to take as its basis not just one single event alone, not even one as momentous as the Exodus commemorated at Passover, nor again a number of disconnected events, but she began to think of a series of consecutive data, or, to put it in another way, she began to realise that her present was based on an earlier series of creative events, a somewhat involved historical development. How was Israel led to this way of conceiving her history? All that can be said is that there must have been a time when each of the individual historical

[11] On the festival of the renewal of the covenant at Shecham, see VOL. I, p. 17f. This cultic experience, which is so hard for us to-day to understand, becomes rather more comprehensible when it is remembered that in olden days the worshipper regarded himself as an individual to a much less extent than we do. He knew himself entirely as a member of a collective body, and in religious matters he could only be moved and filled by the experience of the totality of the worshipping community (see VOL. I, p. 30, p. 37).

Psalm CXIV gives us a good idea of what this actualisation of saving events looked like in the cult. The Exodus event and the choice of Zion are almost brought together in point of time (vs. 1f.). The crossing of the Red Sea (Ex. XIVf.) and that of Jordan (Josh. IIIf.)—separated, according to the Pentateuch's reckoning, by forty years—are mentioned in the same breath (vs. 3), as if it were a matter of one event and not of two. And all this is so contemporaneous for the paslm, which is of course centuries later, that, as this saving event is enacted, it can address it and ask it questions (vs. 5)! On the other hand, this contemporaneousness is not so exclusive as to prevent mention of an event of the wilderness days, the miracle of the water from the rock (Num. XX. 11), which in point of time lay after the crossing of the Red Sea and before that of Jordan. This kind of thing cannot be explained as "poetic freedom," but only on the basis of the thought-world of the cult.

is that there must have been a time when each of the individual historical events was cultically celebrated in isolation and, indeed, at entirely different places. Bethel kept alive a tradition about Jacob, Shechem was the scene of the festival of the renewal of the covenant, it seems likely that at Gilgal there was a commemoration of the conquest which in many respects overlapped the Passover-Exodus festival, and so on.[12] Later, however, these traditions were amalgamated to form a sequence of events from which no single component part could be omitted. At the same time, each of them was to be understood only as a part of the whole which was itself very much more than simply the sum total of all its various parts. The oldest known results of this certainly revolutionary procedure of assembling the various saving acts commemorated in the cult into a historical sequence are those concise summaries of the saving history which were mentioned in VOL. I.[13] Israel had in this way broken through to the concept of a linear historical span, and she achieved this break-through not by means of philosophy or mythology, but by gradually building up the time-span through the summation of the various divine saving acts as they were remembered in various places. Or, more properly, Israel came to realise that Jahweh had a definite plan for her, and that her ancestors had made a long journey with him during which Israel gradually obtained her identity. This realisation—that Israel was not founded upon one single event, but that there was a long road, that is to say, a history, which led up to her formation—is an epoch-making step. What we see here is not what we are accustomed to understand as history: the idea of history which Israel worked out was constructed exclusively on the basis of a sequence of acts which God laid down for her salvation. Thus, Israel's history existed only in so far as God accompanied her, and it is only this time-span which can properly be described as her history. It was God who established the continuity between the various separate events and who ordained their direction as they followed one another in time.

[12] H.-J. Kraus, "Gilgal," in *V.T.*, I (1951), pp. 181ff. There is no evidence making it probable that, as has recently been maintained, in the annual cycle of festivals Israel also celebrated a festival commemorating the creation of the world, that she celebrated not only events in the saving history, but also, year by year in the ritual of Tabernacles, the creation, and that she periodically re-enacted the quelling of chaos and the cosmogeny. The assumption is not supported by Gen. I, which is the beginning of an irreversible time-sequence.

[13] On the historical summaries in Deut. XXVI. 5ff. and Josh. XXIV. 2ff. see VOL. I, pp. 122f.

principle as early as the period of the Judges.[14] She became able to make it more comprehensive and, with it as the theological basis, to see and describe her history from many different angles. But the fundamental thought that history can only exist as the times in which God performed his acts and gave his guidance never altered. Israel was constantly at work in extending the period of time included in the old canonical picture of her history. Reaching from the patriarchal age to the conquest, E still keeps to the original limits. J and P, however, begin with creation and end at the conquest. The Deuteronomic history begins with Moses, but it reaches beyond the others to include the period of the Monarchy, and it ends with the disaster of 587.[15] Chronicles, which stretches from Adam to the post-exilic period, takes in the longest time-span. There was thus a growing desire to survey a linear time-span and to come to a theological understanding of it; the periods considered become wider and wider, though, of course, this does not mean that the process of increasingly consistent expansion of the length of time surveyed finally links up with our present-day concept of history, for not even in her large historical surveys did Israel abandon her own peculiar view of her history as a history with God, a road on which she travelled under God's guidance. It is particularly important to realise that this did not as yet open a door to understanding universal history also as history. Israel only succeeded in doing this in the book of Daniel, in which for the first time Apocalyptic drew up an eschatological picture of world-history taken as a whole.[16] The idea that history has a beginning was established by implication in Gen. 1, for, as we have already shown, the creation story with its subtle ordering of the time divisions sees in creation the beginning of Israel's history with God.

This idea of history which Israel developed theologically in various directions over a period of centuries is one of this people's greatest achievements. (It is well known that the only other people in the

[14] Cp. here what is said in Noth's *Pentateuch*, pp. 46f. about the beginning and end of the "productive stage of the history of the Pentateuch."

[15] As is well known, the point at which the Deuteronomic history begins is a disputed question. Noth proposed to regard it as Deut. 1. 3 (*Überlieferungsgeschichtliche Studien (Schriften der Königsberger Gelehrten-Gesellschaft*, 1943), pp. 12ff.).

[16] But even Apocalyptic pictured the new aeon as a time range of "countless weeks in eternity," Enoch XCI. 17. And, when the prophets made statements like Am. IX. 13; Is. LX. 19f.; Zech. XIV. 7, were they not perhaps intending to point to something beyond time, at all events to a cessation of the present rhythm of time?

ancient world who also wrote history, though of course in an entirely different way, were the Greeks.) We have still, however, to consider the question of the interrelation of this linear and chronological idea of history to which Israel gave birth and the actualising of the saving history at the great festivals which was discussed above. Was not an actualisation of the saving history, as this took place within the framework of the cult, excluded in principle by this chronological concept of history? The idea of contemporaneousness—at least in the strict sense of the term—in virtue of which worshippers at a festival were enabled to enter into the saving occurrence in a real and actual way (that is, into *the* saving occurrence, and not into a long sequence of successive events), was certainly shattered; for the cult in the ancient world was essentially "anti-historical."[17] Were there, then, two ways open for Israel by which history could be actualised, one cultic and the other chronological? As a matter of fact, one can only assume that, for some time at least, both of these persisted side by side.[18] It is extremely unlikely that worshippers at one of the pilgrimage festivals at Bethel or Beersheba had any idea that scholars in Jerusalem were producing more and more comprehensive versions of Israel's history. And in Jerusalem itself people did not stop celebrating Passover in the traditional way after the chronological view of the saving history had been established.

Nevertheless, the case was hardly as simple as the peaceful co-existence of these two ideas, which we can here only sketch. Even once the saving events were dissociated from the sphere of the cult and made available for the construction of a linear period of history, the old form, cultic actualisation, could certainly have persisted for some considerable time alongside the other. Yet, out of this concept of the saving event as a historical series composed of more than one divine act an attitude of mind developed so sweeping in its consequences that it was bound, in the long run, to affect the cultic form of actualisation. It was now no longer really possible to regard history as turning back on itself, to say nothing of the fact that this new view of history was bound to develop beyond its original conception. The exodus from the sacral sphere made it possible for rational understanding to contribute to the construction of a picture of the history; a critical way of thinking sprang up which learned how to select, combine, and even reject, data

[17] The anti-historical element in the earliest cult is mentioned by M. Eliade, *Myth of the Eternal Return*, trs. W. R. Trask, henceforth cited as *Myth*, London 1955, p 76, p.125.
[18] So Pidoux, "Temps," pp. 121f.

from the wealth of the tradition, and which was also able to use its own
insight to draw attention to particular high-points in the long chain of
events, as for example by ordering the course of history under various
covenants.[19] It is, of course, difficult to decide whether from the very
beginning this advance into the dimension of history was assisted by a
certain exhaustion, that is to say, an eclipse of the naïvety of cultic
actualisation, or whether the advance itself was the cause of such
weakening. However this may be, there is evidence pointing to a
crisis in the cultic actualisation of Jahweh's saving acts. In Deuteronomy
the preacher makes it apparent that the generation which he addresses
is well aware of the distance which separates it from the one with
which the Sinai covenant was originally made. In these circumstances,
the covenant, contemporaneous for earlier generations, now requires
to be put on a new basis in order to be valid:

"Jahweh our God made a covenant with us in Horeb; not with our
fathers did Jahweh make this covenant, but with us, the living, with all
of us who are here to-day" (Deut. v. 2–3).

In a later passage, where the method of argument takes a different
line, the preacher's endeavour is the same:

"You stand this day all of you before Jahweh . . . that you may enter
into the covenant with Jahweh, your God. . . . But it is not with you
only that I make this covenant and this oath, but also with those who
stand with us this day before Jahweh, our God, as well as with those
who are not here with us to-day" (Deut. xxix. 9–14 [10–15]).

Here, too, the speaker is trying to establish the present-day validity
of the old covenant at Sinai. The theology which voices such ideas is
obviously determined not to allow the saving events to belong simply
to the past. Here Israel is still within the sphere of the cult. The scene
described in Neh. viii shows us how, after Ezra's reading of the law,
the Levites addressed the solemn assembly and explained the situation
to them, but this is no longer in the old style of cultic celebration—
rational considerations and arguments have now to be adduced in order
to keep the actuality of the saving events. It is also this which gives its
tone to the constant "to-day" which the pareneses in Deuteronomy
drum into their hearers' ears. Furthermore, we should also remember
the remarkable way in which the Deuteronomic history makes the
transition from the age of Joshua, that is to say, from the end of the
canonical saving history, to the period of the Judges. It makes a clean

[19] See VOL. I, pp. 129ff.

break after Joshua (Josh. xxi. 43–5), and then brings on the scene a generation which knew nothing either of Jahweh "or the work which he had done for Israel" (Jg. ii. 10). The clarity with which it was recognised that a thoroughgoing historical understanding of the saving events could create definite problems for faith is simply amazing.

Looked at from the point of view of comparative religion, this idea of history made a radical division between Israel and her environment. While it is possible to recognise in her cultic celebration of the saving acts, which followed the rhythm of the year, certain continuing lines of connexion with ideas which belonged to neighbouring religions of the ancient east, with her idea of saving history she completely parted company with these religions. Not one of them understood the dimension of history in the way that Israel did! The most that can be said of their concept of time is that there is a "primeval time," which is not, however, one era amongst others, but a beginning which remains determinative for all further periods.[20] The various conditions of creation were given their divine orders at that time, and the task assigned to cult and ritual was that of giving continuing effect to these primordial orders; for from the cult issue the creative forces which keep safe and stable a cosmos which is always exposed to danger. The religions of the ancient east did not, however, regard this divine process by which the world was sustained as historical, but as cyclical. The ancient east's view of the world bears to a greater or lesser degree the clear impress of cyclical thinking in terms of myth, that is to say, of a way of thinking which understood the cultic event on the basis of the rhythm of the fixed orders of nature. This comprehensive range of concepts originated in the contemplation of the heavenly bodies and of the rhythm of nature on earth dependent on them. In myth, early man reflected upon natural powers with which he met as he lived his life— and fixed orders too are powers. These he sees as the basis of the world and of the rhythmic event which sustains it, and he looks on them as divine.[21] It was always this basically cyclical order of nature on which the ancient peoples of the east confrered the dignity of divinity and

[20] On the concept of "primeval time," an important concept for comparative religion, see G. v. d. Leeuw, "Die Bedeutung der Mythen," in *Festschrift für Bertholet*, Tübingen 1950, pp. 287ff. Eliade means the same thing by the mythic "archetype" and its cultic repetition and imitation (*Myth*, pp. 34-37, and *passim*).

[21] On myths as fixed orders, see G. v. d. Leeuw, *Phänomenologie der Religionen*, Tübingen 1933, p. 517.

which they regarded as a divine event, both in the myths which deal with theogenies and in those which have as their subject the ἱερὸς γάμος of the gods or the dying of gods. This sacral understanding of the world is essentially non-historical; at least, it leaves absolutely no place for the very thing which Israel regarded as the constitutive element in her faith, the once-for-all quality of divine saving acts within her history. The Babylonian sanctuary at Uruk, the Erech of the Old Testament (Gen. x. 10), was a well-known cultic centre as early as the third millennium; but the finds in the latest strata, from the Seleucid period, show the worship of the same gods, Ea, Shamash, Marduk, and Ishtar, still going on just as in the earliest times.[22]

The overwhelmingly cyclical stamp borne by the sacral concepts of Old Babylonia comes to light in, for example, the annual enactment of the creation myth at the *akitu* festival, or in the annual "fixing of destinies," or in the myth of Ishtar's descent to the underworld, which, no matter how the details are to be taken, reflects the processes of the natural year, or in the cult of Tammuz. The same is true to an even greater degree of the cults of those weather gods who fructified the soil worshipped nearer home to Israel in Palestine and Syria, Hadad, Rimmon, and Baal. This does not, of course, deny to these religions an awareness of the operation of the gods in history and politics as well as in nature, or imply that, where mythic thinking was paramount, the dimension of the historical was totally ignored.[23] Still, because of the way in which the ancient east saw the divine powers which made for order as resident pre-eminently in nature and in the heavenly bodies, the cyclical element must have come quite automatically to prominence in its sacral thought about such orders. The beneficent powers of the deity were also experienced in the realm of social life, as for example in the foundation and maintenance of the state, though the state too was conscious of resting upon natural data and the rhythm of these conceived in terms of myth, as is shown by the cults of certain cities, as for example in the annual celebration of the god Tammuz's sacral marriage. Jahwism too experienced Jahweh as a power who established fixed orders, but with a difference. In the other religions the deities exercised their functions and received their worship *within* these orders—they in fact embodied the orders on which

[22] J. Bottéro, *La Religion Babylonienne*, Paris 1952, p. 138.
[23] In this respect H. Gese, "Geschichtliches Denken im alten Orient und im Alten Testament," in *Z. Th. K.*, 55 (1958), pp. 127ff. has much to the point.

ship *within* these orders—they in fact embodied the orders on which the cosmos and the state rested—whereas for the faith of Israel Jahweh was *outside of* these. He was their creator and guarantor; but he could not be identified with them.

We are thus confronted with an intensely interesting fact of comparative religion. The view of the world current throughout the ancient east, which originated in and stemmed from the age-old cults of Mesopotamia, and to which even the nations within the orbit of Syria freely submitted, is confronted with an entirely different understanding of the divine beneficent action, and that by a tiny people. This is not, of course, to say that Israel forthwith declared war on it, or that by gigantic efforts she extricated herself from its embrace. Rather, what we see is that it was in the earliest period of her life that, with great and unconscious assurance, she rested in her own peculiar religious ideas, and grew stronger and stronger in them. Struggle and temptation came only much later.

2. HISTORY RELATED TO ESCHATOLOGY

When we turn to the prophets, we find many other examples of this same understanding of history. Indeed, the prophets paid serious attention to the theory that Jahweh accompanied Israel along her road through history, and they were particularly concerned with the obligations which this involved, in a way which was markedly different from their contemporaries who were, apparently, no longer very greatly aware of these things. In addition, however, the prophets also show something else that is quite new—a keen and unprecedented awareness of the great historical movements and changes of their own day and generation. Their whole preaching is characterised by an unrivalled ability to adjust itself to new historical phenomena, and by a power of adapting itself to these phenomena which, on occasion, leads them to the point of self-contradiction and makes it very difficult to give any coherent explanation of the prophetic message. The relationship between that message and the events of world-history is so close that it has to be accepted as one of cause and effect: Amos and Isaiah work in the shadow of the threat from Assyria, Jeremiah sees disaster coming from the north, from the neo-Babylonians, Deutero-Isaiah is full of the emergence of the Persian Cyrus, and Haggai and Zechariah take account of convulsions which shook the Persian Empire in 521. This correlation between the prophets and world-history is the real key to

God which they saw around them in exactly the same category as the old basic events of the canonical history—indeed, they gradually came to realise that this new historical action was to surpass and therefore, to a certain extent, to supersede the old. They were in fact called forth by their conviction that Jahweh was bringing about a new era for his people. It would be entirely wrong to suppose that this glance into the future was no more than a kind of prognosis of the likely course of historical events based on evaluation of some of the leading political characters of the day. What makes the difference between the prophetic outlook on the future and any sort of political calculation is their unshakable conviction that in the coming events God was to deal with Israel in the most direct way: in other words, from the theological point of view the meaning of what was about to happen was absolutely clear. Political calculation depends on seeing analogies within history: the prophets looked forward to historical events planned by the sovereign freedom of the will of Jahweh. As will presently be shown, however, they too understood this new action of Jahweh in history in terms of an analogy.

Theology was surprisingly slow to abandon the idea that it was enough to say that the prophets were the embodiment of their nation's conscience, and to recognise what is the prime characteristic of the wide range of their preaching. If the prophets were more than particularly characteristic representatives of Jahwism, the sole reason for this lies in their turning toward the future. The new element which in a certain respect differentiates them from all previous spokesmen of Jahwism is—to use the controversial but unavoidable term—the eschatological element.[24] This is now almost universally accepted, for all that there is no agreement on the minute definition of the term.

Gressmann is responsible both for the rediscovery of this new element and for its establishment as a subject of research. He is also responsible for the mistaken view that eschatology should be understood as a great, consistent body of ideas, made up of complex cosmic and mythological expectations about the future, from which the prophets drew what they wanted. It was a long time before research was delivered from this erroneous view. The first step was to discover the

[24] We deal here with prophecy from the time of Amos and Hosea. Whether the prophecy of Elijah or Elisha can be described as eschatological is open to question. That of a Nathan (II Sam. VII) or a Gad (II Sam. XXIV. 11ff.) was certainly not.

provenance of this complex of ideas. Did it owe its existence to the influx of non-Israelite mythical ideas about cosmic calamities (Gressmann), or was it already present in embryo in Israel's ancient "Sinai experience" (Sellin), or did it originate in an Israelite cultic observance which has only recently become known, the festival of Jahweh's enthronement (Mowinckel)?[25] But, as the term "eschatological" became used more and more widely—and its meaning therefore became more and more vague—it was rightly insisted that the concept must be kept precise and should only be applied to one definite, well-marked phenomenon.

The proper definition of "eschatological" is still anything but settled even to-day. Not a few scholars fight shy of the term: they want an exact use of terms, but this one, they say, obscures rather than clarifies. They are only prepared to let it stand when it is used in connexion with the end of this world's time—that is to say, when it refers to a consummation of the historical process in events which lie beyond the scope of the world's history.[26] This would mean that it can only be used of the very latest of the prophetic writings—indeed, it can only be properly applied to Apocalyptic literature, and even there not with absolute precision, for Apocalpytic envisages the continuation of time and history after the historical consummation. But to define "eschatological" so narrowly would mean that the term has no place at all in the Old Testament and can only properly be applied to Christian doctrines. In this view, every application of the term in the Old Testament is more or less *ab extra* and has nothing there to which it exactly corresponds. We can therefore understand the uneasiness of scholars when the term is used to interpret predictions of the prophets. We must, however, realise the price that has to be paid for such a narrow definition—the most outstanding element in the prophetic message is

[25] Mowinckel, *Psalmenstudien II, Das Thronbesteigungsfest Jahwäs und der Ursprung der Eschatologie*; previously Gressmann, *Ursprung*; E. Sellin, *Der alttestamentliche Prophetismus*, Leipzig 1912, pp. 102ff.

[26] Thus G. Hölscher wished to restrict the term exclusively to the idea of an "end of the world" (*Die Ursprünge der jüdischen Eschatologie*, Giessen 1925). Mowinckel too has recently given it as his conviction that genuine eschatological ideas are only to be found in the last period of prophecy. He holds that Deutero-Isaiah still has no concept of a definitive end (*He that Cometh*, p. 149). G. Fohrer also wants to understand prediction of events that take place "in time" as non-eschatological (*Ezechiel, H.A.T.*, p. xxix, p. 216). But do not these definitions all take as their standard a concept of time which was quite alien to the prophets themselves?

left without proper explanation and without a name, and this practically brings research back to the point from which Gressmann started. But perhaps, there should be a different definition of the term, in the light of prophetic prediction.

The characteristic feature of the prophet's message is its actuality, its expectation of something soon to happen. This should be the touchstone of the use of the term "eschatological". It is also the point on which criticism of the admissibility of the term is based, for the fact that these expectations exist is made the ground for disputing that the prophetic predictions embrace the idea of an absolute end of time and history. To do this, however, is tantamount to applying a concept of time to the prophets' teaching of which they themselves were quite unaware. If, as I have already suggested, this concept of time simply did not exist for the prophets, it is perfectly possible to say that the event which they foretell is a final one even if we, with our different presuppositions, would describe it as still "within history."[27] Of course, the idea of "something final" does not itself describe what is specific in the prophetic teaching; there is also the contribution made by what has been called the "dualistic conception of history," the idea of the two "aeons," including the break which is preceded by Jahweh's great act of demolition, and followed by the new state of things which he brings about.[28] The relevant passages do not, in my view, call for a distinction to be drawn between Jahweh's action within history and his action at the end of it, and there is consequently no need to confine the term "eschatological" to the latter. To my mind, it is far more important to realise that there is this break which goes so deep that the new state beyond it cannot be understood as the continuation of what went before. It is as if Israel and all her religious assets are thrown back to a point of vacuum,[29] a vacuum which the prophets must first create by preaching judgment and sweeping away all false security, and then fill with their message of the new thing. Here, it is important that history has recently been brought in again to provide a definition

[27] On the concept of finality, see W. Vollborn, *Innerzeitliche oder endzeitliche Gerichtserwartung*, Diss. Greifswald 1938, pp. 1ff. J. H. Grønbaek speaks in the same sense of the characteristic "final aspect" of prophetic prediction, *Zur Frage der Eschatologie, Svensk exegetisk Årsbok* XXIV, Lund 1959, pp. 5ff.

[28] Mowinckel, *He that Cometh*, p. 125. J. Lindblom, "Gibt es eine Eschatologie bei den alttestamentlichen Propheten?" in *Studia Theologica*, VI (1952), p. 79.

[29] H. W. Wolff, *Dodekapropheten*, Bib. Komm., p. 78.

of eschatology, and the prophetic vision has been described as "the renewing act of the historical drama."[30]

With this as starting-point, we soon arrive at a proper understanding of the eschatological message of the prophets. Briefly, within the horizons of eschatology as elsewhere, Israel's ideas about saving history must be given back their proper place and their due weight.[31] It is impossible to understand the eschatological message of the prophets in the light of any kind of mythological or specifically cultic complexes of ideas, or in that of disappointed hopes. It can only be understood from the point of view of the distinctive character of Israel's thought about history, a subject in which the prophets engaged with the utmost intensity and to which they in fact gave a new dimension by drawing attention to an entirely new action in history on the part of Jahweh.[32] Like the writers of the canonical history, the prophets regard certain

[30] Th. C. Vriezen, "Prophecy and Eschatology," in Supp. *V.T.*, 1 (1953), pp 218, 229.

[31] For what follows see E. Rohland, *Die Bedeutung der Erwählungstraditionen für die Eschatologie der alttestamentliche Propheten*, Heidelberg Dissertation 1956. It is not surprising that in their pictures of the new the prophets introduce here and there ideas which were not current in earlier periods, but which had in the interval come into Jahwism from other religions. In any case, this process is of no importance for the determination of the phenomenon of the eschatological. Cp. A. Jepsen, Art. in *R.G.G.*, col. 661.

[32] The psychological explanation of the phenomenon of eschatology is very prominent in Mowinckel's first work. "The origin of eschatology must be explained psychologically, otherwise it is not explained at all. . . . Eschatology is to be conceived as a flight into the future due to the disillusioning burden of a new and hard experience of the world round about to which its bearers were not yet accustomed, which took place at a time when the old experiences could no longer be felt with complete genuineness; it is to be conceived as an evasion of the burden along the line of least resistance" (*Psalmenstudien* II, p. 324). M. Buber also speaks of the hope for history which was then "eschatologised" because of growing "disillusionment with history" (*Königtum Gottes*, 2nd edn., Berlin 1936, p. x, quoted by Mowinckel, *He that Cometh*, pp. 152f.). In his second book Mowinckel himself laid much stronger emphasis on the specifically Old Testament way of thinking of history. "We are justified in saying that Israel's unique conception of God as the God of history is the root of eschatology" (*He that Cometh*, p. 153). We do not mean that the idea of experience of disillusionment should on principle be left out in this investigation. Disillusionment would have been one of the contributory factors in the "rise" of eschatology; only, the object by which the disillusionment was called forth ought to have been given more exact theological definition, and also the experience of disillusionment should have been assigned its due place within the total phenomenon. If we hold by what the prophets say, it will not do to put the "experience of disillusionment" at the head as the evocative factor proper.

election traditions as normative, that is to say, they hold a view of history in which Israel was given legitimation as she was called and founded by Jahweh. Indeed, the preaching of some of them can actually be regarded as a great continuing dialogue with the election tradition which they inherited. This tradition is not, of course, the same for each and every prophet. While Hosea stands within the Exodus tradition, Isaiah only knows of the saving institutions connected with the David-Zion tradition. The Exodus tradition is also prominent again in Jeremiah and Ezekiel, and especially so in Deutero-Isaiah. One point, however, is very remarkable. On the one hand, we see with what force and ardour the prophets catch up these election traditions in their preaching; on the other, their relationship to them is a broken one; for they regard the coming judgment as sealing the end of Israel's present existence; the security given her by these election traditions is cancelled out because of her guilt. The only thing she can hold on to is a new historical act on the part of Jahweh, the outlines of which the prophets already see, and to which they point with kindled emotions. The prophetic message differs from all previous Israelite theology, which was based on the past saving history, in that the prophets looked for the decisive factor in Israel's whole existence—her life or her death—in some future event. Even so, the specific form of the new thing which they herald is not chosen at random; the new is to be effected in a way which is more or less analogous to God's former saving work. Thus Hosea foretells a new entry into the land, Isaiah a new David and a new Zion, Jeremiah a new covenant, and Deutero-Isaiah a new Exodus. There are, of course, differences in the prophets' ideas of the completeness of the break between the old and the new situations; there are even considerable theological differences. For Isaiah the old saving acts and institutions are still valid enough to allow Jahweh to link his coming to them. This is true both of the new Zion (Is. I. 26), and of the new David (Is. XI. 1). On the other hand, for Jeremiah and Deutero-Isaiah the break is so complete that Jahweh has to re-enact his former deeds— the covenant is to be made anew (Jer. XXXI. 31ff.), and there is to be a new Exodus (Is. XLIII. 16ff.). This was never Isaiah's way of putting it; he never said that Jahweh would choose Zion, and make the covenant with David, afresh. In contrast, Deutero-Isaiah's vision could lead him to demand that the former saving history should be remembered no more (Is. XLIII. 16ff.). This again could not have been said by Isaiah of Jerusalem. However, such differences are only relative; for even

Isaiah had no doubt that Israel's sole ground of salvation lay in the new actions in history.[33]

On this view of the matter, the message of the prophets has to be termed eschatological wherever it regards the old historical bases of salvation as null and void. But we ought then to go on and limit the term. It should not be applied to cases where Israel gave a general expression of her faith in her future, or, as does happen, in the future of one of her sacred institutions. The prophetic teaching is only eschatological when the prophets expelled Israel from the safety of the old saving actions and suddenly shifted the basis of salvation to a future action of God.

This view of the eschatological message differs from the earlier one in that it does not presuppose either a whole "complex" of eschatological expectations on which the prophetic preaching could draw or an already made eschatological *schema*. The eschatological phenomenon is simplified once more; it is reduced to the extremely revolutionary fact that the prophets saw Jahweh approaching Israel with a new action which made the old saving institutions increasingly invalid since from then on life or death for Israel was determined by this future event. The reason for this change in outlook is to be found primarily in history, which had begun to move again in a quite unprecedented way: but it is also to be found in the realisation that Israel under the Kings had become quite detached from the old relationship to Jahweh. How little the prophets drew on any predetermined "complex of ideas" (whose origin would still have to be discovered) is made plain by the fact that they expected the new saving action to take exactly the forms of the old one, and that therefore, even in expounding the new, they had recourse to Jahweh's saving appointments of the past. We can thus see how close was the attachment of even the prophets to the saving history; it was in fact the norm for their representation of the most distant last things. To be sure, their hearers must have felt that this call to prepare themselves for a coming act of God and to

[33] Here we are concerned initially only with the understanding of the phenomenon in itself. As against this it is of secondary importance whether it was developed in its full range by the prophet in question in his own message, or whether it only appears in its final interrelations after those who handed on the texts worked them over and made additions. Thus, for example, in our view the question, whether Jer. xxxi. 31ff. comes from Jeremiah himself or is later than him, is not so important in respect of the whole process.

seek their salvation in it made very strong demands on their religious faith. They are bound to have thought that they were being led to a realm which lay beyond the ken of their religious knowledge and experience. They had no way of conceiving a dimension outside the saving area of Jahweh's canonical saving acts: in their eyes this could only have appeared to be strange in the highest degree.

3. THE DAY OF JAHWEH

Special consideration needs still to be given to the expectation of the Day of Jahweh, which has often been regarded as the very heart of the prophetic eschatology.[34] Do we not have here, at any rate, attaching to this day a relatively well-defined complex of eschatological expectations? There is in fact something peculiar about the expectation of the Day of Jahweh, for wherever it occurs in prophecy, the statements culminate in an allusion to Jahweh's coming in person. It has often been asked how this concept originated, and rightly so; for, could we find the answer, we would come much nearer to an understanding of the thing itself.

There are not very many passages which refer to the Day of Jahweh in so many words.[35] Of the sixteen, Am. v. 18–20, which has always been regarded as a key passage, offers little towards clarification of the term; also, the long poem in Is. II. 9ff. with its repeated refrain deals much more with the general results and effects which the coming of Jahweh is to have than with the thing itself and its concrete accompaniments, though we do read of people fleeing, and throwing away their now worthless idols in the process. Let us, however, suppose that the correct procedure in the elucidation of an exegetical problem such as this is that we should not confine ourselves to examination of the occurrences and their meaning in their own immediate context. Form criticism and the investigation of the history of tradition have taught us that terms as important as these seldom appear alone, but are as a rule

[34] Gressmann was the first to recognise that the concept of the Day of Jahweh raised problems of a peculiar kind (*Ursprung*, pp. 141ff.). Mowinckel's identification of the Day of Jahweh with the festival of Jahweh's enthronement (*Psalmenstudien*, II) had a great influence, cp. more recently Mowinckel, "Jahves Dag" in *Norsk Teologisk Tidskrift* (1958), pp. 1–56, and L. Černy, *The Day of Jahweh and some Relevant Problems*, Prague 1948.

[35] Is. II. 12, XIII. 6, 9, XXII. 5, XXXIV. 8; Jer. XLVI. 10; Ezek. VII. 10, XIII. 5, XXX. 3; Joel I. 15, II. 1, 11, III. 4 [II. 31], IV. 14 [III. 14]; Am. v. 18–20; Ob. 15; Zeph. I. 7, 8, 14–18; Zech. XIV. 1.

associated with a whole complex of ideas which have definite recurring themes of whose presence careful account must be taken. In this respect, therefore, we must adopt a broader exegetical basis than can be provided by an examination of the term itself, and must include the whole of the textual unit in which the term appears along with its constitutive concepts.

We start with the poem on Babylon in Is. XIII, which is generally taken as an anonymous prophecy of the sixth century. It begins with a call to the fighting men to muster for Jahweh's host; signals are to be raised. Jahweh himself summons his "consecrated ones," his mighty men, and they come in such numbers that there is an uproar of nations. Then Jahweh musters the host in person.

> Wail, for the day of Jahweh is near;
>   as mighty power from the Mighty One it comes.
> Therefore all hands are feeble . . . every man's heart melts. . . .
>   they look aghast at one another.   (Is. XIII. 6–8)

Jahweh comes in person to the battle, the stars are to withhold their light, the earth quakes, the carnage is terrible. The poem ends with an allusion to the complete desolation of the empire. Its concepts are all of the same kind; it tells of a war which begins with the muster of the fighting men and ends with a description of the devastated and de-populated land. The war is made to take on gigantic dimensions; not single warriors but whole nations stream to the muster. At the same time, the events described have their parallels in real warfare.

The oracle against Edom in Is. XXXIV, which again is not the prophet's own, is constructed in just the same way as Is. XIII, and even if it does not contain the actual term "day of Jahweh," but speaks instead of "the day of recompense for Jahweh" (vs. 8), it should be mentioned here. It begins with the announcement of Jahweh's furious wrath against Edom, then goes on to a description of the destruction of Edom by the sword of Jahweh, and ends, like Is. XIII, with a picture of the land completely desolate and inhabited only by wild creatures. Here again the concept of the holy war of Jahweh is prominent. This is expressed in the words that Jahweh has put his foes to the ban (החרים vs. 2). Here also terrible changes appear in the heavens in connexion with the war; "the skies roll up like a scroll, and all their host shrivels" (vs. 4). The comparison made between this war and the slaughter of animals for sacrifice (vs. 6) will be taken up later.

Ezekiel's oracle against Egypt (Ezek. xxx. 1ff.) is also an elaborate poem, though it is a single unit. It begins with a call to lamentation because of the Day of Jahweh: "a day for Jahweh is near." It is a day of clouds; the sword shall come upon Egypt, the Egyptians and their allies shall fall, and afterwards the land and its cities shall lie waste. Though shorter, Ezek. xxx. 1–9 also obviously parallels the course of the prophecies in Is. xiii and xxxiv. This raises the question whether all three are not dependent on an already existing prophetic *schema*.

The same is also true of the great picture given in Ezek. vii. Here again, in view of the exclamations, "the day is near" (vs. 7), "behold, the day" (vs. 10), and "the day has come" (vs. 12), the fact that the full term, "the day of Jahweh," is not used makes no difference. Practically every verse makes plain that the prophecy deals with the Day of Jahweh. Here again it is only the basic concepts in which we are interested: the end is coming, and this upon the whole earth, though of course upon Israel in particular. In contrast with the previous examples, the opening cry is here developed to an unusual length. The description of the war itself does not begin till vs. 14. The enemy is said to have made ready, "but none takes the field" (vs. 14); sword and famine ravish. "All hands are feeble" (vs. 17); the city's riches are to fall into the hands of foreigners, and it itself is to be profaned. These verses describe practically the same final state as was signified in the other poems by the word "depopulation." Jer. xlvi. 3–12, with its description of "that day," "the day of vengeance" on Egypt, also fits exactly into this group.

There are important occurrences in Joel which confirm the picture just arrived at. Little, of course, can be said of Joel i. 10; this has constantly been regarded as a secondary interpolation in its present context.[36] In the case of Joel ii. 1–11, it is to-day generally agreed that a real plague of locusts is envisaged. However, the prophet's conception of this event and, in particular, the means which he uses to describe it, are interesting. Joel is clearly dependent on traditional and, to a greater or lesser degree, conventional, prophetic concepts for the vivid way in which he illustrates the distress; that is to say, on concepts which he only secondarily relates to the distress itself. He equates the locusts with the armies of the Day of Jahweh marching into battle, and is thus able to draw on the whole range of war concepts connected with the Day of Jahweh.

[36] *E.g.*, by T. H. Robinson, *H.A.T.*, *in loc.*

> Blow the trumpet in Zion, sound the alarm on my holy mountain;
>   all the inhabitants of the land shall tremble, for the day of Jahweh
>   is coming.
> Verily, it is near, a day of darkness and gloom,
>   a day of clouds and thick darkness.   (Joel II. 1–2)

An army advances, mightier than has ever been hitherto seen. "Before it people shudder, all faces glow" (vs. 6). Before it the earth quakes; the heavens tremble. Sun and moon are darkened, and the stars lose their brightness (vs. 10). "Great is the day of Jahweh, and terrible; who will endure it!" (vs. 11). At this point the poem passes into a call to repentance and the demand to gather together for a fast; for Joel II. 1–11 is in fact only a part of a great liturgical composition. It is therefore all the more striking to realise how very little influence the actual starting-point, the locust plague itself, was able to exert on the traditional picture of the sequence of events once the catchword, "the day of Jahweh," had been introduced. The traditional sequence of summons to war, dismay, earthquakes, darkness, and the voice of Jahweh, has certainly not very much in common with the advance of a locust plague.

Zephaniah's prophecy concerning the Day of Jahweh is certainly one of the most important sources of material at our disposal for the various concepts connected with this subject (Zeph. I. 7–18). The form of this passage is difficult since it involves a continuous change in style between objective descriptions of events and words spoken by God in the first person. Nevertheless, it would be a mistake to break the passage up into a number of smaller units. It is a single unit in itself. What we have here is a description of the day of Jahweh into which various *logia* have been inserted in certain places. For our purposes, only the first of these two component parts is important (vss. 7, 10–11, 13–18). The description apparently begins with the cry that the day of Jahweh is near. This day is designated as a sacrificial feast which Jahweh prepares for the guests whom he invites. This is a metaphor which we have already met in Is. XXXIV. 6, and it is obviously a concept which belongs to the stock subjects connected with the day.[37] Its clearest expression occurs in Jer. XLVI. 10: at the great festivals the blood of the victims

---

[37] Since in Zeph. I. 7; Is. XXXIV. 6; Jer. XLVI. 10; Ezek. XXXIX. 17 the word זבח is not used with its proper meaning but metaphorically, it will not of course do to adduce these references as a proof of the cultic character of the Day of Jahweh.

flows in streams—Jahweh's war against his foes will be equally bloody. What follows also shows that the event is war: crying and wailing are to be heard in all the quarters of Jerusalem (vss. 10–11). This day is a day of distress, of darkness and gloom, a day of trumpet blast and battle cry against fortified cities. Men will be overcome with fear; the panic which is to break out shows itself in the fact that they "go about like blind men" (vs. 17); they will be unable to save themselves, for the earth is to be consumed with the fire of Jahweh's zealous wrath. This closes the description, the main outlines of which correspond with those given in Is. XIII. 34, Ezek. VII, and Joel II.

The first result of this survey is to show that the prophets expect the day of Jahweh to bring war in its train. Now, the widespread employment of this concept in the prophets suggests that we are dealing with a well-established component part of eschatological tradition. But this runs counter to the fact that the expression "the day of Jahweh" could occasionally be used in connexion with past events (Ezek. XIII. 5, XXXIV. 12; cp. Lam. I. 12, II. 22). In view of this somewhat ambivalent reference, the proper procedure for investigation is first to rule out all possible interpretations based on a rather far-fetched mythology, and then to ask whether Israel herself did not have, in her own old traditions, some knowledge of the concept of Jahweh's coming specifically to wage a war, with its accompaniment of miraculous phenomena.[38] This is, of course, the case. In itself, the almost stereotyped connexion of the day of Jahweh with intervention in war reminds one of the holy wars and all the phenomena which traditionally accompanied them. In this concept of Jahweh's coming to an act of war we have at least one concept clearly stamped with Israel's own tradition, and we should establish its relationship with the prophetic utterances about the day of Jahweh before we try any other methods of interpretation. This becomes even more obvious when we consider that a prophet himself twice connects the eschatological event of war quite directly with one of the holy wars of the past (Is. IX. 4 [5] = Jg. VII; Is. XXVIII. 21 = II Sam. V. 20, 25). People recounted all manner of miracles which accompanied these wars once waged by Jahweh (thunder, I Sam. VII. 10; stones falling from heaven, Josh. X. 11; darkness, Ex. XIV. 20, Josh. XXIV. 7;

[38] Mowinckel's suggested derivation of the Day of Jahweh from the cultic enthronement festival breaks down on the textual evidence, for none of the above references which speak explicitly of the Day of Jahweh makes the link with the concept of Jahweh as king.

clouds dripping water, Jg. v. 4f.). A particularly important part is played by the terror caused by God himself, a panic confusion and demoralisation of the enemy, whose effect was to paralyse their confidence in their fighting powers and so lead them to compass their own destruction.[39]

In view of all this, there can be no doubt that the same principle is at work both in the old stories of the theophanies in bygone wars and in the prophets' descriptions of the future Day of Jahweh. The various constitutive elements and conventional stock subjects of the former reappear one after another in the prophets' predictions. To refer just once more to the sacral panic, we read in Jeremiah:

> What do I see? They are dismayed, they turn back!
> Their warriors are scattered, fleeing hither and thither. . . .
> The swift cannot flee away, nor the warrior deliver himself
> (Jer. XLVI. 5f., following Rudolph's translation)

The concepts connected with the Day of Jahweh are therefore in no way eschatological *per se*, but were familiar to the prophets in all their details from the old Jahwistic tradition. The prophets, however, also believed that Jahweh's final uprising against his foes would take the same form as it had done in the days of old. It is beyond question that the prophetic vision of the concept of Jahweh's intervention in war became greatly intensified; for the war was now to affect all nations, even the fixed orders of creation, and even Israel herself. The event has been expanded into a phenomenon of cosmic significance. Thus, under the influence of this traditional element the prophetic concept of the *eschaton* was also to some extent systematised, that is to say, predictions connected with the expectation of the Day of Jahweh which began from different traditions were to some extent blended. One can well imagine that Amos's contemporaries cherished the expectation of such an uprising to war and victory on the part of Jahweh. Amos, however,

---

[39] Ex. xv. 14f., xxiii. 27f.; Josh. ii. 9, 24, v. 1, vii. 5, xxiv. 16ff. The term "Day of Jahweh" first occurs in Amos; there, however, it is, as has often been insisted, something already well-known. Since the cry, "the Day of Jahweh is near," has particularly deep roots in the whole cycle of tradition (cp. Is. xiii. 6; Ezek. xxx. 3; ob. 15; Joel i. 15, ii. 1, iv. 14 [iii. 14]; Zeph. i. 7, 14), we may ask whether this was not the stereotyped cry by which men were summoned for military service in earlier times, or a cry with which men once went into battle with Jahweh.

S. Herrmann draws my attention to the fact that this "Day concept" lived on in the usage of the ancient Arabians, who called their days of battle "days of the Arabians." W. Caskel, "Ajjam al Arab, Studien zur altarabischen Epik" in *Islamica* (1930), pp. 1ff.

asks them if they never think that this day is to bring a darkness that might also be fraught with danger for them. It is most improbable that Amos's contemporaries already possessed a fully developed "popular eschatology." In this connexion far too much weight has been given to Am. v. 18.

PART TWO

Classical Prophecy

CHAPTER A

AMOS AND HOSEA

I. INTRODUCTION

AFTER these more general theological considerations on prophecy and the way in which it was proclaimed, we must now try to describe the message of the various prophets individually. Here, it is all important not to read this message as if it consisted of timeless ideas, but to understand it as the particular word relevant to a particular hour in history, which therefore cannot be replaced by any other word. The prophetic word—far more than any of the other forms of speech used by Jahwism—has its origin in an impassioned dialogue; yet the dialogue never tries to climb into the realm of general religious truth, but instead uses even the most suspect means to tie the listening partner down to his particular time and place in order to make him understand his own situation before God. In order to reach this partner in the specific situation in which he has to make a decision and which, as stated above, cannot be replaced by any other, the prophets use every possible rhetorical device—they are not afraid to use extremely radical forms of expression or even caricature. With certain exceptions, their concern is not the objective proof of what was generally believed: but rather to be highly critical of Israel's religious traditions. Yet this too could be a misleading statement, for nothing was further from the prophets' minds than a theoretic solicitude about teaching for teaching's sake. Their concern was not the faith, not even the "kerygma": it was to deliver a message from Jahweh to particular men and women who, without themselves being aware of it, stood in a special situation before God. But since the prophet's partner in the dialogue (and it is not simply "the nation") is constantly changing, this allows us to admire the unexampled inner versatility and power of adaptation of the prophetic address, which, though it has in fact a minimum of "basic thoughts" upon which it rests, yet functions as if it had a splendid abundance upon which to draw. By the same token, however, any confidence that we might have of being able to think of the message as an interconnected whole necessarily disappears. It would, nevertheless, be a mistake simply to sit back in face of this; it is, on the contrary, wise to realise from the very start that what we are in the habit of calling a prophet's "kerygma" is a very problematic entity. We do not gain understanding of the prophet's "message" either by reducing the sum total of his sayings to general basic religious concepts, or by co-ordinating the separate *logia* to make a synthetic whole. As was stated above, each *logion* was, for those to whom it was addressed, *the* word of Jahweh. There is therefore, strictly speaking, no such thing as a "message" to which each single word was subordinate and from which each single announcement was derived; all that we have are the various individual words in which, on each specific occasion, *the* word of Jahweh was proclaimed in a different guise.[1]

Nevertheless, however bewildering the ease with which the prophets pass from one form of address to another, there are two constant factors which never fail to find a place with them all. The one is Jahweh's new word for Israel which he allowed the prophet to read off from the horizon of world-history. The other is the election tradition, within which the prophet and his hearers alike stand. The comfortable words of the tradition are, however, both called in question by the prophet's message of judgment and reconverted by him into an anti-typical new form of prediction. Thus, tensions created by three factors bring the prophet's *kerygma* into being. These are the new eschatological word with which Jahweh addresses Israel, the old election tradition, and the personal situation, be it one which incurred penalty or one which needed comfort, of the people addressed by the prophet. It is obvious that these three factors do not all appear in the same way in each prophet; we shall, instead, find a great difference in treatment. With Amos for example, projection of the election tradition into the realm of eschatology is almost completely absent.

2. AMOS[2]

We must not imagine that Amos's home, Tekoa, which lies about two hours' walk south of Bethlehem, was a remote country place, for from

[1] See above pp. 87f. This is different in Apocalyptic; for at every point there the total course of the great apocalyptic drama, of which the specific detail is a part, has more or less to be kept in view.

[2] V. Maag, *Text, Wortschatz und Begriffswelt des Buches Amos*, henceforth cited as *Amos*, Leiden 1951; E. Würthwein, "Amosstudien," henceforth cited as "Amos-studien," in *Z.A.W.*, LXII (1950), pp. 10ff.; A. S. Kapelrud, *Central Ideas in Amos*, Oslo 1956. For earlier literature see L. Köhler, *Th. R.*, IV (1932), pp. 195ff.

the time of Rehoboam onwards it had been a garrisoned fortress.[3] Amos himself was also, so far as we can judge, a man of some reputation and substance. The only reason why a man of solid peasant stock came to join the ranks of the prophets was a very remarkable call from Jahweh. The words which have given rise to so much debate, to the effect that he was no prophet ("I am, or I was, no prophet") and did not belong to any prophetic guild (Am. VII. 14), are not meant as disparagement of the neᵇi'im as a class, but only to explain the strange fact that he suddenly began to speak by inspiration (הנבא, Am. VII. 15), though as a peasant he was not entitled so to do.[4] When, therefore, Jahweh was forced to fall back on a man from the peasantry, he did so as an emergency measure.

The prophetic call itself is a fact which needs no further discussion than was given on pp. 50ff. The peasant Amos's call is almost certainly to be connected with the reception of the five visions (Am. VII. 1–9, VIII. 1–3, IX. 1–4). Surprisingly enough, none of these contains any explicit instruction to proclaim what he had seen. They are reports of communications made by Jahweh to Amos and to him alone; and their sequence shows the various steps he had to take before he finally realised the inevitable end. These visions record a drama between Jahweh and Amos played out in the deepest solitude. Initially, since he did not understand, Amos cast himself on Jahweh's mercy, and twice— on the occasion of the vision of the locusts and on that of the judgment by fire—he even succeeded in averting the disaster. But when it came to the burden of Israel's piled up guilt, he ceased to intercede. In the third vision, that of the plumb-line, Jahweh anticipates the prophet in a word which he speaks concerning it, and from then on Amos begins to yield. The vision of the basket of fruit brings the word: "the end has come upon my people," and to this Amos listens in silence; while the final vision, the most circumstantial, makes known that Jahweh is to

---

[3] II Chron. XI. 6; see Beyer in *Zeitschrift des deutschen Palästina Vereins* (1931), pp. 113ff.

[4] It is debated whether Amos meant to say: I was not a prophet, but now I am one (so H. H. Rowley, "Was Amos a nabi?" in *Festschrift Otto Eissfeldt zum 60. Geburtstage 1 September 1947 dargebracht von Freunden und Verehren*, ed. J. Fuck, Halle 1947, pp. 191ff.) or whether he wished to repudiate all connexion with the prophetic profession (so E. Baumann, "Eine Einzelheit", in *Z.A.W.*, 64 (1952), p. 62). Cp. for the understanding of Am. VII. 14 the careful study made by H. Stoebe, "Der Prophet Amos und sein bürgerlicher Beruf," in *Wort und Dienst, Jahrbuch der theologische Schule Bethel* (1957), pp. 160ff. Stoebe understands Amos's answer as implying the present tense.

let no one, not one single person, escape from the coming calamity, which is perhaps to take the form of an earthquake.

This series of visions is virtually isolated in prophetic literature. Unlike Isaiah or Ezekiel, Amos seems to have no older tradition on which he depends for the contents of his visions. There is also a remarkable absence of any very close connexion between these and his message; for the final catastrophe of Israel's exile which he spoke of again and again and in unmistakable terms in the prophecies is not even hinted at here. Obviously, all that was initially communicated to the prophet was the bare fact of the end and judgment; certainty as to its manner only came under special conditions, and clearly not without reflexion and observation on his own part. Still less do the words which describe Jahweh as roaring from Zion, his voice penetrating far and wide throughout the land and causing disturbances in the world of nature (Am. I. 2), speak to any human ear which had to note a particular communication and pass it on; rather, all that we are told of is the resounding of a so to speak as yet inarticulate voice of divine wrath. The greater part of Amos's message must, then, be ascribed to his own pondering on the situation which he saw before him. He had first to put his own stamp on everything he had learned from Jahweh, for it constantly needed interpretation *ad hominem*. Such knowledge, as we have already observed, must have given the man to whom it was entrusted a unique status far above any human grade of honour, and placed him in a position where all social and sacral distinctions of rank became irrelevant. What is even more important, however, is that intensive intellectual process which must have followed such a revelation. Amos went about amongst a people who had been condemned to death; and as a result his environment at once assumed a different appearance and he became acutely aware of the abuses around him. Thus we see Amos particularly engaged in the task of giving convincing reasons for the coming disaster and, as he goes about his business, we see the man's vitality and intellectual acumen brilliantly at work. No doubt fresh oracles kept coming to him and inspiring him, but the contribution made by his own alert mind must not be underrated.

Since Amos was a Judean, we must assume that he took his stand on the election traditions of the South, those attaching to David and Zion. Unfortunately, there are no real clues to help us to determine his own personal attitude to the Exodus tradition which was the most cherished one in the Kingdom of Israel. Was it so alien to him that he could only regard it as positively heretical and illegitimate?[5] When he spoke to the North Israelites about their traditions, did he do so only as an outsider? In view of the urgency, the ardour even, of the historical retrospect in Am. II. 9–11, this is far from likely. In particular, the insistency with which he pins his hearers down to these traditions, and the conclusions which he draws from their indifference to them, suggest that he, as well as they themselves, took these saving data very seriously. Israel's election as he states is there in actual fact the very reason given for Jahweh's imminent act of judgment (Am. III. 2). We have no understanding of Amos's preaching at all unless we note the way in which he over and over again comes to grips with the election concept, and how it was the nerve of a great part of his message.

Amos was also concerned with the changes and tensions in Israel's political world. David's empire did not endure. The Philistines regained their independence, as did the Edomites and Moabites; and the secession of Aram-Damascus had particularly momentous consequences. Certainly, under Jeroboam II (786–746) the Kingdom of Israel was enjoying another time of peace, and had in fact increased its power to some extent, but the Assyrians had appeared on the fringe of the Palestinian scene long before this, and the year after Jeroboam's death saw the accession of the great Tiglath Pileser, whose campaigns ushered in the beginning of the end for Israel. Even the few references to political matters which Amos does make are enough to leave us amazed at the clearsightedness of his observation of history. How accurate he was when he connected the so-called "Armaean migration" with the entirely different movement of the "sea-peoples" (Am. IX. 7)! Both thrusts occurred at nearly the same time (i.e., c. 1200), and political conditions in Palestine were fundamentally affected by them for long afterwards. The long poem comprising Am. I. 3ff. supplies us with acute comments on what was going on within the Palestinian national group. The prophet has his own opinion of the value of minor successes against Damascus, such as the capture of Lo-Debar and Karnaim (Am. VI. 13). His gaze ranged wider too. He spoke of what befell the north Syrian cities of Calneh and Hamath; and when he cryptically announced exile "beyond Damascus," of course he had the Assyrians in

[5] S. Herrmann, *Die Ursprünge der prophetischen Heilserwartung im Alten Testament*, Diss. Leipzig 1957, pp. 135ff.; Maag too stresses Amos's Judean standpoint, *R.G.G.*, VOL. I, col. 330.

mind (Am. VI. 2, v. 27). In his keen interest in political matters, Amos must have been head and shoulders above his contemporaries.

It would be a complete misunderstanding, however, if the modern reader were to consider the prophet as a detached observer who foresaw the inevitable march of events in the realm of world politics. Certainly, Amos's actual prophecy of the future can be reduced to the simple statement that Israel is to suffer a calamitous military defeat and to be taken into exile.[6] Just as certainly, concrete observation of the way in which Assyria was accustomed to treat her subject peoples contributed to this picture. Yet Assyria was of little importance. It is no accident that the name never appears in the text as we have it to-day.[7] The culminating point of Amos's message is that Israel now has to deal direct with Jahweh; not the Jahweh of the sanctuaries and pilgrimages, but an unknown Jahweh who was coming to perform new deeds upon Israel. It must have been this closeness to Jahweh, the "I, Jahweh" of the coming events, that most surprised and upset Amos's audience. "I smite the winter house" (Am. III. 15), "I take you into exile" (Am. v. 27), "I pass through the midst of you" (Am. v. 17), "I rise against the house of Jeroboam with the sword" (Am. VII. 9), "I destroy it from the surface of the ground" (Am. IX. 8)! Any hope that Jahweh would leave a remnant was regally discounted in a discussion (Am. III. 12; the scraps of the torn animal are the proof that it is dead, cp. Ex. XXII. 12 [13]). Amos hardly ever spoke in such a way as to suggest that Jahweh had not as yet pronounced his final sentence on Israel: but there must have been occasions when, in the company of a few chosen men, even he indulged in a faint-hearted "perhaps" (Am. v. 15, 6).

All that Amos learned in his visions was that Jahweh would no longer forgive his people. But Israel's actual offences were not named by Jahweh—they were left to the prophet to interpret. Almost without exception, the reasons for the coming judgment are to be found in the diatribes—that is, in terms of form-criticism, in the section which the prophet himself prefixes to his threat and which he uses in every case to direct the oracle to those whom it particularly concerns.[8] The reader, therefore, inevitably feels an unevenness in Amos's preaching. While the subject matter of the threats tends to be rather monotonous, the diatribes reveal a really rich variety of observation, of striking snap-

[6] Military disasters: Am. II. 13ff., III. 11, v. 3, VI. 9f., 14, VII. 9, VIII. 3, IX. 10.
[7] In Am. III. 9 "Assyria" is generally read instead of "Ashdod."
[8] See above, pp. 37f., 73.

shots, and of examples of normal or abnormal human behaviour. Each
one of these glimpses of the full life of humanity is intensely alive, and
is yet at the same time ominous and foreboding. Little is gained by
attempting to order and inter-relate them, for each unit really stands
on its own. Nevertheless, it is not an inadmissible simplification to say
that the charges point in two directions, contempt of God's law and
religious complacency.

1. The poem against foreign nations revealed the strength of Amos's
reaction to breaches of the unwritten law of international relations—and
not simply of those breaches which brought suffering to Israel. In this
respect, the stanza against Gaza is of particular interest, since its subject
is injuries done by the Philistines to the Edomites, that is to say, injuries
which did not affect Israel at all (Am. I. 6–8). Amos's Jahweh watches
over the established orders of international law not only in Israel but
also among the other nations, and whenever they are broken he imposes
a historical punishment upon the culprits. Israel's breaches are, of course,
immeasurably more serious, since she was the nation with whom
above all others he had made himself intimate (Am. III. 2). Actually,
Amos shows us a society whose social life is cleft in two—a property-
owning and therefore economically self-sufficient upper class lived at
the expense of the "little people" (דל, Am. v. 11, VIII. 6), and the
wrongs done were particularly apparent in the administration of justice,
since only full citizens could sit and speak in the law courts; at the same
time, however, as owners of property, these men were interested
parties and, often enough, judges in their own cases; slaves, foreigners,
orphans, and widows had no one to uphold their just claims.[9] Bribery
was the order of the day (Am. v. 7ff., 12), and there was also dishonesty
in business (Am. VIII. 5b). At the same time, however, great zeal was
shown in religious matters. People went on pilgrimages (Am. IV. 4f.,
v. 4), and took part in noisy festivals (Am. v. 21ff.). In Amos's eyes,
however, these were provocations of Jahweh. Sacrifices offered by
people who scorned his will as expressed in law could have no value
in Jahweh's sight.[10]

Amos says absolutely nothing about the way in which Jahweh's will
as expressed in law became known to Israel. Yet the way in which he
raises God's claims suggests that his audience would at once acknowledge
their validity. He never appeals to any tradition, written or oral, to

[9] See VOL. I., pp. 64f.
[10] On the prophets' polemic against the cult, see below, pp. 400f.

support their authority. Nevertheless, it is highly unlikely that he based himself on no other authority than "the ethical element."[11] Rather, as recent research has made clear, these fixed orders are to be found point by point in the older tradition of sacral law, especially in the Book of the Covenant.[12] Now, comparison of the charges brought by Amos with the older legal tradition makes it plain that Amos ties his contemporaries down to the simple, obvious, literal sense of these commandments. It cannot properly be said that he made them more radical, and that on his lips their content is intensified, given a keener edge. Yet, in spite of this, the whole thing feels different. There is a new factor, the element of threat, which questions the continued existence of the whole people of Israel. The old commandments were regarded as possible to fulfil, the apodictic formulae stood almost as acts of confession; at all events, in the earlier period reflexion on whether the commandments could or could not be fulfilled had not become widespread. There must always have been individuals who broke the commandments; these the law dealt with. Now, however, at one fell swoop not individuals but the whole of Israel—or at least her leading men—were sharply accused of flagrant breaches of the law. This was something entirely new.[13] We cannot reconstruct the history of popular understanding of the commandments, so we do not know whether Amos's attitude was an entirely new departure or whether there had been considerable preparation for his ideas. Whatever the case may be, we do see how with him the commandments which Israel had once received from Jahweh's hands with love and praise, because the people saw in them evidence of his faithfulness towards her, now turned against her. Even Israel's right to profess her loyalty to these commandments (as in the ritual of the liturgies at the gate) was called in question by the prophet's charges.

2. Since the prophets' polemic, and especially that of Amos himself, is couched in very radical terms, it is difficult to reconstruct the spiritual and religious climate of the time on the basis of this source, and yet we have no other. Amos gives us a picture of a thoughtless upper class complacent in its material prosperity. As we listen to him upbraiding

[11] Wellhausen, *Prolegomena*, p. 474.

[12] Würthwein, "Amosstudien," p. 47; R. Bach, "Gottesrecht and weltliches Recht in der Verkündigung des Propheten Amos," in *Festschrift für G. Dehn*, Neukirchen 1957.

[13] Elijah probably only attacked the royal house and its protegés, the cult officials.

it for its luxury, we have to remember that all asceticism and any kind of suspicion of material good was really very alien to Jahwism as such. Eating and drinking, taking one's enjoyment, in a word, every material blessing that enhanced the quality of life, were accepted in simple thankfulness from Jahweh's hand. It can only have been extreme indulgence which necessitated the raising of such complaints about the enjoyment of material things. Amos reproaches those who are "secure on the mountain of Samaria" with not "being sick" (נחלו) because of the "ruin of Joseph" (שבר, Am. VI. 6). Like so many others of his pregnant enunciations, this matchless statement is not more closely defined. It is probably the havoc in social life which is particularly in the prophet's mind. At all events, it is a quality of heart and mind that he finds lacking in the upper classes; the breach of particular commandments is certainly not in question, for there was no commandment which forbade reclining on ornate beds or anointing oneself with choicest oil, no more than there was any which obliged people to be grieved at the damage done to Joseph. What Amos refers to, therefore, is a general attitude, the way men should live together, and jointly and severally be fellow sufferers in the experiences of God's people. Indeed, did not Amos here unconsciously use himself and his own suffering and injuries as the criterion? His contemporaries were all in the grip of a cruel delusion. They looked for a "Day of Jahweh," when Jahweh would rise up to vanquish their enemies, and did not fear the night which Jahweh's coming was to bring.[14] They knew of Israel's election by Jahweh, and no doubt they took comfort in the fact of it, as guaranteeing them salvation, but they never thought that this very thing would bring them so much the closer into the light of the divine holiness (Am. III. 2). For men who had become so complacent, even the great event of the Exodus had to be reduced to the rank of a part of God's general guidance of history; the saving aspect of that divine redemptive act had to be extinguished for them (Am. IX. 7). But they had no inkling of their true position *vis-à-vis* Jahweh! Time and time again, with one calamity after another, famine, drought, failure of the harvest, failure in war, and epidemics, Jahweh kept knocking at their door, but they paid no heed (Am. IV. 6ff.). Now, however, this time of indirect warning is over. Israel must now hold herself in readiness to meet her God in person—Amos was no doubt thinking of the judg-

[14] The new thing is not that Amos spoke of darkness at the Day of Jahweh, but that the believed that the darkness would also threaten Israel (see above, pp. 124f.).

ment at which the "I, Jahweh" mentioned above would himself appear on the scene.

At the end of the book of Amos comes the prophecy of the future raising up of the "booth" of David that is fallen (Am. IX. IIf.). Grave doubts are raised as to its genuineness, and this was, of course, inevitable as long as Amos's prophecy was regarded as the deposit of some kind of "prophetic religion," the outcome of spiritual struggle and personal conviction. If Amos's prophecy had been of this nature, then we might have expected it to be free of major contradictions. Things wear a different look, however, once we see the prophets as men who addressed themselves to definite sacral traditions as these still survived in the nation, and once we regard their whole preaching as a unique discussion of these ancient inherited traditions, a discussion which submitted them to criticism and made them relevant for the prophets' own day and generation. Now, Amos was a Judean. Would it not surprise us if there had been absolutely no mention of the traditions in which he was most at home? This Messianic oracle is distinctly restrained in the matter of its content.[15] There is no hint of any sensational upheaval in world events as a result of which the heavens and the earth are shaken (cp. Hag. II. 20ff.). The sole thing mentioned is the rebuilding of the fallen house, solely the restoration of an edifice whose foundations were laid long ago. And what will thereafter follow is an integration of the old Davidic empire, which in the interval has suffered severe damage. Jahweh is not to blot out what he once "built"; in particular, he is not to surrender his claim upon the nations "who had been called by his name."

3. HOSEA

It was at one time generally believed that we knew more about Hosea's personal circumstances than about those of the other prophets —except, of course, for Jeremiah. But this idea collapses once we interpret the much-discussed pericope containing the symbolic representation of his marriage (Hos. I–III) as an account of a prophetic symbolic action, that is to say, as a part of his preaching; for this limits any attempt to interpret it biographically.[16] In actual fact, the book of Hosea has extremely little help to give us about the prophet himself. Practically the only thing certain is that he lived and worked during

[15] So, rightly, Maag, *Amos*, pp. 248f.
[16] So for example T. H. Robinson still, *H.A.T.*, I, 14, 2nd edn., 1954, p. 2.

the calamitous last years of the Northern Kingdom up to about the time of the capture of Samaria by the Assyrians (721). We know as little about his home as we do of the place where he made his appearance, or of any conflicts in which he may have been engaged, or of other personal circumstances. It has been assumed, with some probability, that he was closely connected with the Levitical movement in the Northern Kingdom, which, like the prophetic one, had been pushed aside in the general Canaanisation; both reforming groups fostered and preserved the old traditions of Jahwism.[17]

As to the general tenor of Hosea's message, the first impression it makes upon expositors is the extraordinary difference between it and that of, say, Amos or Isaiah; and this difference they try to pin-point. But its really disturbing feature is the unique factor in it. Hosea is the only "writing prophet" of the Northern Kingdom. This means that there is no one with whom we can compare him, and that we cannot separate what is his own in his message from those matters of style, subject-matter, and prophetic tradition which he may have inherited. For his writings allow us to gather that the situation in the Northern Kingdom was, even for a prophet, very different from that in, say, the Jerusalem of Isaiah, and that, to a very great extent, it had its own peculiar problems. Only two basic data specific to the north need be mentioned; the disintegration of patriarchal Jahwism in the Canaanite fertility cult, and the peculiar political and governmental system which existed there, which meant that even a prophet's intervention in public affairs and their problems took on an essentially different aspect from that in the Southern Kingdom. These are also the two factors which give us a clear picture of Hosea.

There is a further difficulty. Hosea's message is different from that of his contemporaries Isaiah, Micah, or Amos in respect of form. Instead of short, clearly contoured units easily detachable from one another, what are most prominent in Hosea are larger entities with a relatively uniform subject-matter. The messenger formula is certainly still found: but with Hosea the process of combining short sayings into larger units seems to have gone on side by side with the permanent establishment (perhaps in writing) of the component parts of the tradition.[18] On the

[17] H. W. Wolff, "Hoseas geistige Heimat," in *Th. L.*, 81 (1956), col. 83ff.

[18] The thrice repeated לכן within the large unit of Hos. II. 4ff. (vss. 8, 11, 16 [2ff. (vss. 6, 9, 14)]) allows us to conclude that originally smaller units have here been deliberately shaped into a large composition. The original units, which must be pre-

other hand, the borrowing from non-religious literary categories which
is so marked a feature of Amos or Isaiah is almost completely absent in
Hosea. The result of these factors is to give Hosea's way of speaking,
taken as a whole, a much greater uniformity. Using his diction to
draw conclusions about his person, we are given the impression that
Hosea was a man of extremely strong feelings. His preaching, more
than that of any other prophet, is governed by personal emotions, by
love, anger, disappointment, and even by the ambivalence between
two opposite sentiments. Since the prophet lends this emotional ardour
to the words of God himself—or, to put it better, since Jahweh catches
the prophet up into his emotions—in Hosea the divine word receives a
glow and a fervour the intensity of which is characteristic of the
message of this prophet alone.

Hosea's whole preaching is rooted in the saving history. It might
almost be said that he only feels safe when he can base his arguments in
history.[19] Jahweh is Israel's God "from the land of Egypt" (Hos. XII. 10
[9], XIII. 4); by the prophet Moses, Jahweh brought Israel up from
Egypt (Hos. XII. 14 [13]). This early history of Israel was the time when
Jahweh was able to give her his entire love (Hos. XI. 4). What an
appalling contrast the present shows! Israel has forsaken Jahweh like a
faithless wife who runs after her lovers. Hosea depicted this completely
subverted relationship of Israel to Jahweh under the image of his own
marriage, and used the symbolic names of the children born of it to
announce the message of Jahweh's wrath and his turning away from
his people.

A note on the marriage of Hosea. The passages in question raise a
considerable number of exegetical problems. The existence of one
account in the third person (Hos. I) and another in the first (Hos. III) is
itself remarkable, and the explanation is certainly not that both of them
are reports of the same incident. Since the second story bears quite
another hall-mark—its subject is the wife's re-education—we must
assume two successive events. In this case, the same woman is the subject of both accounts.[20] It is now generally accepted that the stories
represent an actual happening, and are not merely an allegory as was
formerly believed—on the grounds that God could never have ordered

supposed in Hosea's case also, can consequently be much less clearly separated off.

[19] Hos. I. 4, VI. 7, IX. 9, 10, X. 1, 9, 11f., XI. 1–4, XII. 4f., 10, 13f., XIII. 4–6.

[20] So H. W. Wolff, *Bib. Komm.*, XIV *in loc.* See on p. 6 there the extensive literature
on Hos. I–III.

so objectionable an action! Incidentally, אשת זנונים does not signify a woman of particularly depraved moral character, but a woman who took part in the Canaanite fertility rites. In fact the woman is not exceptional, but serves as a typical representation of Israel.[21] There is less agreement on the question as to how far the texts afford a glimpse of the prophet's own personal relationships and experience. The view has often been put forward that bitter experience in his married life, particularly his unhappy love for his faithless wife, taught the prophet understanding of God's love for his people, and in retrospect made him aware that this marriage was divinely predestined.[22] In my own view, the two chapters provide far too few data to allow of such a psychological and rationalising interpretation. The primary thing was not an intimate personal experience, but Jahweh's command to perform a symbolic action. On this the text gives sufficiently clear information; but it has practically nothing to tell us about what lies beyond this "vocational" task and its execution—something which might possibly give us some biographical information. More particularly, Hosea had absolutely no need to look to his own private life to find a symbol for the relationship between Jahweh and Israel. The idea of marriage between a deity and an earthly partner had long been familiar to him and his contemporaries through the rites of the Canaanite nature religion (the marriage of Baal to the earth is an example).[23] It was, to all appearances, an extremely bold move to transfer this idea which belonged to a religious ideology absolutely incompatible with Jahwism as Hosea understood it, to the covenant relationship with Jahweh. Yet, the very fact that the partner to whom this relationship was now applied was conceived altogether in historical terms eliminated the mythological element from this range of concepts. Interestingly enough, the earthly partner in this covenant of love is pretty well obscured, for Hosea sometimes speaks of the land (Hos. I. 2, II. 5 [3]), and sometimes of Israel (Hos. II. 16 [14], III. 1, 4). In this respect the borrowed material was obviously not completely reduced to order. Hosea himself, of course, places the emphasis on the nation.

To return: of course, this symbolic action, Hosea's marriage, is only one part of what the prophet proclaimed; yet, especially when it is taken along with its closely related context (Hos. II. 4–25 [2–23]), it gives the keynote for practically all the topics characteristic of Hosea

[21] H. W. Wolff, *Bib. Komm.*, pp. 12ff.
[22] A. Weiser, *A.T.D.*, 24.   [23] See VOL. I, p. 22.

—his passionate indignation at Israel's disloyalty, her approaching punishment, and also what lay beyond these, and about which it was difficult to be precise—the hint of a fresh saving activity, and indeed of an entirely fresh start with Israel, to which God's love impels him.

Hosea was the first to describe Israel's submersion in the Canaanite nature religion as "harlotry," "leaving Jahweh in order to play the harlot"; the term expresses both the idea of the indissolubility of Jahweh's covenant and abhorrence of the fertility rites and sacred prostitution of the cult of Baal.[24] Yet, while Jahwism's reaction to this sexual aspect of the nature religion was particularly sensitive, this was not the only reason which brought the prophet on the scene: he was also prompted by Israel's general breach of faith, her violation of the first and also the second commandments (Hos. IV. 12, 17, VIII. 4-6, XIII. 2). The trouble was that Israel's husbandry was prospering: but she believed that it was the Baals whom she had to thank for these blessings. Israel "does not know that it was I who gave [her] the grain, the wine, and the oil, and lavished upon her silver and gold" (Hos. II. 10 [8]). These amazing words represent Jahweh as the bestower of all the precious gifts of the soil. Israel, however, misunderstood both the giver and the gifts; she failed to see that she had been brought into a *status confessionis* before Jahweh because of these gifts; rather, she fell victim to a mythic divinisation of husbandry and of its numinous, chthonic origins. The Rechabites followed a different and much simpler course when they were faced with just such a hopeless perversion of the blessings of the soil. They embarked on a programme of radical separation, and roundly denied that use of the products of the land was compatible with obedience to Jahweh.[25]

Hosea clearly grades the charges which he brings against the parties responsible. Because of his interest in cultic matters, he inevitably laid a particular measure of failure at the door of the priesthood (Hos. IV. 6, 9, V. 1, VI. 9). They—though this is also true of the whole nation—lack the proper דעת אלהים. Unfortunately, this term, so characteristic of Hosea, is not easy to translate.[26] "Knowledge of God" points too much in the direction of what is theoretical in the problem of religious and philosophic epistemology. On the evidence of its occurrences, however,

[24] Hos. I. 2, II. 7 [5], III. 3, IV. 10, 12, 13, 14, 15, 18, V. 3, IX. 1.

[25] See VOL. I, pp. 63f.

[26] For what follows cp. H. W. Wolff, " 'Wissen um Gott' bei Hosea als Urform von Theologie," in *Ev. Th.*, XII (1952–3), pp. 533ff.

the term must also mean something much more specific than simply a general inner disposition towards God; in fact it seems actually to convey the essence of the priestly service, for in Hos. IV. 6 it is parallel to *torah*. It must therefore describe a particular form of knowledge of God which, to her hurt, Israel had lost; the term will therefore have to be related in particular to familiarity with the historical acts of Jahweh. It could also be put in this way—Israel had lost her profession of loyalty to Jahweh.[27]

The apparent split between religion and politics in Hosea is a modern distinction. For Hosea himself, living more fully than any other prophet in the old sacral thinking which saw life as a whole, Israel's political experience was in no way on a different plane. We must again remind ourselves that the charismatic structure of monarchy in the Kingdom of Israel was actually dependent on the active co-operation of the prophets. Thus, in his keen participation in political affairs, particularly in the revolutions at the court of Samaria, Hosea acted the part of a genuine prophet of the Northern Kingdom, and continued the line of action already illustrated by Elisha.[28] Of course, a radical change had come over the situation as compared with the time of Elisha and Jehu in as much as Jahweh wants to have nothing more to do with the ever more frequent palace revolutions and coronations which took place in these last years before the fall of Samaria. "They made kings, but not through me" (Hos. VIII. 4). While the people still believed that in these coronations in Samaria they could see Jahweh in action as the protector of his people, Hosea recognised precisely in these political events that Jahweh's judgment upon Israel was already in full sweep. "I give you a king in my anger and take him away in my wrath" (Hos. XIII. 11). This is, in fact, quite one of the most essential elements in Hosea's view—while his fellows eagerly strive to repair the ravages in the state of affairs, and to guard themselves against threats by taking political measures, Hosea sees that the root of the trouble goes much deeper. It is God himself who has turned against them; the nation is suffering from God, who is seated like an ulcer in its belly.

> But as for me, I am as pus to Ephraim
> and as worm grub to the house of Judah.

---

[27] Cp. here particularly Hos. XIII. 4: "I, Jahweh, am your God from the land of Egypt; you have no knowledge of God except by me."

[28] See above, pp. 28f.

> But when Ephraim saw his sickness,
> and Judah his ulcer,
> then Ephraim went to Assyria and sent to the great king.
> But he is not able to cure you,
> or rid you of your ulcer.   (Hos. v. 12f.)

When he speaks of the judgment itself, which Israel cannot possibly avoid, he gives only brief general hints. The political and historical side of the process is seldom outlined very clearly. Once or twice the prophet speaks of disaster at the hands of enemies (Hos. VIII. 3, X. 14f., XI. 6, XIII. 15), and sometimes of the prospect of deportation. In this connexion, the thought of Assyria is paralleled, surprisingly enough, by that of a "return" to Egypt (Hos. IX. 3, 6, VIII. 13, XI. 5). On the one hand, Hosea follows a very old line of thought in representing this judgment as brought upon Israel by herself, that is to say, by her evil deeds. She is so firmly entangled in the despotic power of the evil which she herself unleashed that she can no longer extricate herself from it (Hos. v. 4f.). "Their deeds encompass them"; they are so completely blockaded by the evil they have brought about that no real freedom of movement is left them (Hos. VII. 2).[29] This concept of the "sphere of action which creates fate" does not, however, in the least imply that it is simply an impersonal law which is working out on Israel. On the contrary, it is Jahweh, who now remembers her deeds (Hos. VII. 2, VIII. 13, IX. 9)—they are "before his face" (Hos. VII. 2). Indeed, it is the fact that the whole force of the prophet's utterance is channelled into showing that Jahweh himself is now rising up against his people that makes his descriptions of the concrete accompaniments of the judgments rather blurred. Jahweh is to chastise his people (Hos. v. 2), he will be a lion to them (Hos. v. 14); he captures them like a hunter (Hos. v. 2, 12, VII. 12). Compared with this "I" who is to engross and determine the whole compass of history from then on—"I, even I, rend" (אֲנִי אָנִי Hos. v. 14b)—the actual way in which the judgment will take historical form almost loses all interest.

In view of prophecies foretelling such a merciless darkness, the accompaniment of Israel's judgment, one hesitates to go on to discuss Hosea's prophecies of salvation; for this gives the impression that the almost intolerable gloom to which he continually alludes is not after all the final word, with the result that the darkness is lightened. Can we be

---

[29] On this set of concepts see VOL. I, pp. 264ff.

sure, however, that the men to whom he announced the judgment and those to whom he spoke of the coming salvation are the same in both cases? It is enough to say that—no matter to whom or for whom—Hosea quite undoubtedly also spoke of a coming salvation. More than this, he was himself aware of the paradox; he saw how the struggle between wrath and love came to be resolved in God's own heart. This led him to an utterance whose daring is unparalleled in the whole of prophecy:

> How could I give you up, Ephraim, abandon you, Israel?
> My heart recoils within me; all my compassion is set on fire;
> I will not execute my fierce anger, I will not again destroy Ephraim,
> For I am God, not man, a Holy One in your midst. . . .
>
> (Hos. XI. 8f.)

Hosea gives us further assistance in understanding his juxtaposition of judgment and salvation: it is his idea of training, which plays a greater role with him than with any other of the prophets.[30] In Hosea, Jahweh's dealings with Israel seem at times to be something like an educative plan aimed primarily at setting the erring ones on the right path by depriving them of certain things and circumscribing their actions. This leads—at least in one or two passages—to the achievement of something like a rational balance between God's action in judgment and his action in salvation.

> Many days shall the Israelites remain
> without king, without officials, without sacrifice,
> without ephod and without teraphim;
> then the Israelites will return
> and seek their God.
>
> (Hos. III. 4f.)

The things of which Jahweh is to deprive his people are so numerous, and so important for Israel's life, that it is impossible to say what kind of existence Hosea envisaged for them in this interim period; they are not only to be without the fixed orders of civil life, but even without those of the cult! To elucidate the matter we may bring in the passage from the great poem on Israel's re-education in which Jahweh's plan for her is disclosed in terms so intimate as to be almost overwhelming. After blocking his people's way to the Baals, he purposes to "allure"

[30] Hos. II. 11ff. [9ff], III. 3-5, XI. 1ff.

them, he intends to "speak tenderly" to them, and to bring them again into the wilderness (Hos. II. 16 [14]). This means nothing less than that God is going to take them back to the place where he originally began with them, back, as it were, to the beginning of the whole road.[31] There, in the wilderness, no gods of fertility can come between Jahweh and his people; there Israel will be thrown back completely upon Jahweh; Jahweh will have her all to himself, in order that from the desert he can once more grant her the land. Hosea thus sees the new saving event as typologically prefigured in the old one, though, of course, everything that marred the first saving event and all its imperfections, which the older saving history did not conceal, are to be cancelled out by the marvels of the final one. The valley of Achor—the place of sacrilege and of the stoning of Achan—is to become "the door of hope" (Hos. II. 17 [15]; cp. Josh. VII), and Jahweh is to be betrothed anew to Israel. A final oracle has a form which suggests that of an incantation, in as much as it depicts the free circulation of the powers of blessing which emanate from God; there is no break in the tightly closed circle (God—heaven—earth—the blessings of the soil—Israel) for the possible entry of Baal and his functions (Hos. II. 23ff. [21ff.]).

The word of promise at the end of the book, which is couched in very antiquated, almost mythological, metaphors, also speaks wholly in terms of the natural world. Jahweh will love Israel, he will be a green cypress, and dew for Israel, and Israel will blossom and strike root, and her fragrance will be like that of Lebanon (Hos. XIV. 5–8 [4–7]). It is a remarkable fact that the same prophet who thinks so emphatically in terms of saving history can at the same time move Jahweh's relationship to Israel over into the horizons of an almost vegetable natural growth and blossoming, where all the drama of the saving history ebbs out as if in a profound quiet.

[31] H. W. Wolff, *Bib. Komm.*, p. 78.

CHAPTER B

ISAIAH AND MICAH

THE preaching of Isaiah represents the theological high water mark of the whole Old Testament. Such at least must be the judgment of all who regard the theological range encompassed by one single man as more impressive than any body of anonymous tradition, however vast. Not one of the other prophets approaches Isaiah in intellectual vigour or, more particularly, in the magnificent sweep of his ideas. Even the ideas which he took over from tradition were usually remodelled in the most daring way. Isaiah's versatility is only fully apparent when we remember that as a man of the ancient world his whole intellectual apparatus was very much more bound by tradition than ours is. So great is the supple power of his message to adapt itself to every change in the political situation that it can show us the specific historical situation simply in the clear-cut contours of the items of the messages themselves, just as in a photographer's negative. Apart from one or two quite meagre biographical references, we only have his style from which to form some idea of him as a man. Yet, what a wealth is here disclosed! Its compass ranges from the incisive diatribe to texts which express depth of feeling with a stately amplitude, from the curt conciseness of an oracle to the sonorous hymn that revels in words.[1] The chief characteristic of everything Isaiah says is, however, moderation; and it is this restraint, preserved even in moments of deep passion, which gives us such a strong impression of nobility in the man. Though we have no exact statement of this, the most obvious assumption is that Isaiah belonged to Jerusalem, and was therefore a townsman. We would expect to find him among the higher ranks of society there. Only such a station as this could account for his freedom of intercourse with the king or with high officials. He was married, and had children to whom he gave symbolic names (Is. VII. 3, VIII. 3). We know nothing more of his personal circumstances; there is no evidence that he held formal office in connexion with the temple—indeed, there are weighty arguments against this theory.

[1] Isaiah's similes with their striking points of comparison form a distinctive side of his rhetoric: Is. I. 8, VII. 4, XVIII. 4, XXIX. 8, 11f., XXX. 13, 17, XXXI. 4.

A note on the history of Isaiah's time. Whereas in the ninth century the Kingdom of Israel was in constant conflict with enemies who sometimes represented a serious danger to her, and had to defend herself against the Syrians, the Philistines, the Moabites, and even the Assyrians (Ahab fought against an Assyrian army at Karkar in 853), the Kingdom of Judah was spared such serious threats. This trend continued in the eighth century and only changed with the end of the reign of Uzziah, which approximately coincided with the accession of the great Tiglath Pileser (745–727)[2] Significantly enough, Isaiah's call came at this turning point (Is. VI. 1). In a very short time the Assyrians were to appear on the immediate horizons of Judah: in 734 Tiglath Pileser advanced along the coastal plain of Palestine as far as the frontiers of Egypt. In the following year Judah was to be compelled by main force to join an anti-Assyrian coalition. In the ensuing Syro-Ephraimitic war Jerusalem, of course, suffered nothing worse than siege; for the Judeans appealed to the Assyrians themselves for help (II Kings XV. 37, XVI. 5ff.). Tiglath Pileser did in fact then turn his attention to the Kingdom of Israel and took away a considerable part of its territory (II Kings XV. 29). Then in 732 came the end of Syria-Damascus as an independent power, and in 721, after the capture of Samaria, Israel was incorporated into the Assyrian provincial system. This made Assyria Judah's nearest neighbour: the imperial boundary ran only a few miles to the north of Jerusalem! From this time onwards there could be no more peace for the still independent nations of Palestine. Three events stand out in the prolonged effort to maintain independence from Assyria by means of coalitions and, particularly, of Egyptian help. The first was the rebellion of Hamath and of King Hanun of Gaza, who was in alliance with Egypt, c. 720. The Assyrian victory at Rapihu ended that hope. The movement towards revolt in the years 713–711, whose moving spirit was Ashdod, involved the Kingdom of Judah much more closely; for in this case, under Hezekiah, she broke off her allegiance to Assyria, whose vassal she had been since 732, and joined a movement in which Edom and Moab also took part. This rebellion, too, Assyria stamped out by sending the *turtānu* against it (Is. XX. 1). Judah was once again successful in escaping with impunity, but unfortunately we do not know how. In contrast to these, however, the third movement of rebellion, which broke out in Askelon at the time of a change on the throne in Nineveh (705) and in connexion with which Judah was again

[2] The year of king Uzziah's death is not certain; it may have been 746.

a partner, was destined to lead to a great calamity for her and for Jerusalem. Admittedly, it was not till 701 that Sennacherib appeared in Palestine, and even then, to begin with, he confined his attention to the coastal plain, and to reducing the Philistines; but after his defeat of the Egyptians also near Altaku, the coalition's power was broken, and there followed the well-known capitulation of Hezekiah, which cost him the greater part of his kingdom.[3]

As we have already said, historical events are very exactly reflected in Isaiah's prophecy. The last on which he commented was the fall of Jerusalem in 701 (Is. XXII. 1ff., 1. 7–9). Of course, Isaiah saw the history of his own time in entirely different colours than does the modern historian. Perhaps his prophetic view of it would come out more clearly if we did what we actually can do and presented his preaching not in its chronological sequence, but according to its roots in tradition. It can be shown, of course, that, wide-ranging and comprehensive as his message is, it rests on a quite small number of religious concepts, all of them furnished him by tradition, and in particular by the Jerusalem tradition.

Like Amos, Isaiah watches inexorably over the divine law of which he is spokesman. He carries forward Amos's indictments of every form of miscarriage of justice and of exploitation of the weak on so broad a front and with such passion that we may fairly assume that the eighth-century prophets must already have fallen heir to a certain tradition, a heritage which furnished them with the subjects on which prophets spoke. Isaiah's concern for the divine law cannot be stressed too strongly.[4] It is society's attitude to this law which determines whether its relationship to God is in good order. For Isaiah, the administration of justice displays most clearly man's attitude to God; and this explains why his predictions are full of references to a Jerusalem with irreproachable judges and an anointed one who is a guarantor of justice (Is. I. 26, XI. 3ff.). In his eyes, the divine law is the greatest saving blessing. In this connexion, the modern reader has to remember that in Isaiah's time legal decisions lay in the hands of the general body of citizens, and were not the concern of professional law-officers.

---

[3] II Kings XVIII. 13–16. On the resultant demarcation of the boundaries, see Alt, K.S., II, p. 242.

[4] This is already apparent in the use of the terms "righteousness" and "justice," which have a central function in Isaiah's preaching: צדקה (צדק) Is. I. 21, 26, 27, V. 7, 16, 23, IX. 6 [7], X. 22, XXVIII. 17; משפט Is. I. 17, 21, 27, IV. 4, V. 7, 16, IX. 6 [7], X. 2, XVI. 5, XXVIII. 6, 17.

What we have so far seen—and we should also remember the cry, "Obedience, not sacrifice" (Is. I. 10–17)—strongly reminds us of Amos, and also of Micah.[5] Nevertheless, Isaiah's concern for law has one or two features that are absent in Amos. The passages cited above which deal with the restored city of God and the rule of his anointed in themselves show clearly that in Isaiah's eyes the real significance of the divine law does not lie in this law in itself: it only becomes significant in wider, i.e., political, contexts. Quite a number of Isaiah's utterances reveal a remarkable concentration of thought about questions concerning the national life, that is to say, a concern for the forms of government appropriate to a society whose founder is Jahweh, and also for the necessary offices.[6] In this connexion, he never once thinks in terms of the amphictyony; first and foremost, he thinks of the chosen people as a *polis*. At the *eschaton* Jerusalem is to be restored as a *polis*, complete with all its officials (Is. I. 26), and in the *polis* the delivered are to find refuge (Is. XIV. 32). As will presently be shown more clearly, all that Isaiah has to say about Israel's deliverance and renewal rests on this *polis* concept. As token of this keen interest in the problems of state affairs, we need only refer to Is. III. 1–5, where Isaiah conjures up something almost like a vision of the complete dissolution of the civil order. With the disappearance of the duly appointed officials, the judges, the officers in the army, and the elders, anarchy breaks in. Youngsters and political failures rise up from the dregs of the populace to become officers of state; "the youth is insolent to the man greyhaired with age and the scoundrel to the honourable," and people seek a man to "rule over this heap of ruins." These wider contexts of the life of the *polis* are

---

[5] Isaiah and Micah are particularly close in their opposition to the *latifundia* economy of the ruling classes in Jerusalem, in whose hands the hereditary land of many impoverished peasants was joined together (Is. v. 8; Mic. II. 1–5). Micah of course differs from Isaiah in that he envisages the complete blotting out of Jerusalem from the pages of history (Mic. I. 5, III. 12), and, as a Judean who lived in the country, looks for the "assembly of Jahweh" to restore the patriarchal arrangements for land tenure. On Mic. II. 1–5, see Alt, *K.S.*, III. pp. 373ff. On Micah's roots in tradition see W. Beyerlin, *Die Kulttraditionen Israels in der Verkündigung des Propheten Micha*, F.R.L.A.N.T., N.F. 54, Göttingen 1959.

[6] A study of the administration and offices of the Jerusalem of the time would derive important material from Isaiah: "judge" Is. I. 26, III. 2; "leader" (קצין) Is. I. 10, III. 6f., XXII. 3; "governors" (נגש) Is. III. 12; "major domo" (על הבית) Is. XXII. 15; "steward" (סכן) Is. XXII. 15; "prince" (שר) Is. I. 23, III. 3, 14; "patron" (אב) Is. IX. 5 [6], XXII. 21.

the place where Isaiah's charges concerning the violation of the divine law are at home.

There is, however, one striking feature peculiarly Isaiah's own, namely the fact that these charges are not only, as in Amos, directed *ad hoc* against the specific transgressors, but are sometimes set in a wider context, that of the saving history. Thus, in Is. I. 2f. Jahweh complains that his people have renounced their obedience to him (פשׁע). This oracle, however, is given the form of a charge made by a father who, in terms of Deut. XXI. 18ff., has recourse to the last desperate expedient of handing over a rebellious son to the jurisdiction of the civil court. Here, a long road in history—Jahweh shows what trouble he has had in bringing up his child—has come to a completely negative end. In Is. I. 21–6 the road runs in an opposite direction, from woe to weal; yet here too the violation of the commandments has its place in a comprehensive divine design for history. This historical perspective, within which the divine disappointment at the demoralisation in law is set, is shown with particular clarity in Is. v. 1–7—again in allegorical form. The poem is short: but consider the detailed description of the man's painstaking work in his vineyard—work which proved completely fruitless.

Yet God erected a terrible barrier against Isaiah and his preaching: he hardened Israel's heart. Isaiah was told as early as the time of his call that it was his task to make the heart of this people "fat," and their ears dull, and to "plaster over" their eyes, that they "might hear with their own ears and yet understand nothing, and see with their own eyes and yet perceive nothing" (Is. VI. 9f.). It may perhaps be that these words were given their present extreme form some time after Isaiah had received his call, when he was able to make some estimate of the results of his work. On the other hand, there are striking similarities between Is. VI and I Kings XXII. 21, and both have been described as typical stories of a prophet's commissioning.[7] If this is so, then it was the prophetic tradition which furnished Isaiah with this very *motif* of hardening of the heart. However this may be, the *motif* holds so prominent a position in Isaiah that we must take the trouble to assign it its proper place within the wider context of Jahwism.

Many commentators have found no great difficulty in this. They appealed to the undisputed fact that when the word of God is continually rejected, the capacity to hear and understand it dies away. "Delib-

[7] Zimmerli, *Ezechiel*, p. 19, Engnell, *Isaiah*, p. 26.

erate neglect of God's truth and habitual deafness to God's warnings inevitably bring indifference to God's working in their train."[8] "Will not" is punished by "cannot." But this interpretation of the hardening of the heart is open to an objection. It depends entirely on the conditional clause, and so becomes a general truth of religion which can be constantly confirmed in the broad realm of religious experience. This means that the process would be a rational one which could be explained in psychological terms; and the most that could be said for the prophet would be that he fulfils "a necessary moral ordinance."[9]

This interpretation of the condemnation to obduracy as only a particular form of the *lex talionis* is not, however, consistent with statements made about it in the Old Testament; for there, hardening of the heart is always represented as an act of God and not as the result of a law of human nature. Each time that God addresses man he finds him in a state of alienation, and this is true even of his contact with his chosen people. But this raises the real question: how is it that Jahweh sometimes elects his chosen and sometimes hardens their hearts? How is it that in Isaiah's message Jahweh suddenly withdraws into an obscurity such as Israel had never before experienced? If Israel's alienation from God was due to a psychological process, then it could surely have been brought to its conclusion without waiting for a message from Isaiah. Any attempt to come to terms with what Isaiah says about hardening of the heart by the way of understanding the words indirectly, that is

[8] Eichrodt, *Theologie III*, p. 112; similarly O. Procksch, *Theologie des Alten Testaments*, Gütersloh 1950, p. 616; H. Schultz, *Old Testament Theology*, trs. J. A. Paterson, Edinburgh 1895, VOL. I, p. 207; J. Seierstad, *Die Offenbarungserlebnisse der Propheten Amos, Jesaja und Jeremia*, Oslo 1946, p. 126.

[9] Schultz, *op. cit.*, VOL. II, p. 207. F. Hesse understands the idea of the hardening of the heart as the result of an intellectual difficulty. On the one hand, it was observed that persistence in sin often makes men blind to the "reality of God." Since, however, it was impossible for Jahwism to derive such baffling phenomena from the sphere of demonic powers, "the only way out was to make a connexion between Jahweh and even such things as could properly have had nothing to do with him his nature being what it was" ("Das Verstockungsproblem im Alten Testament", henceforth cited as "Verstockungsproblem," Bei. *Z.A.W.* 74 (1955), pp. 41–3. That, "his nature being what it was," Jahweh had nothing to do with the idea of the hardening of the heart, is precisely what is open to question. In addition, for the explanation of the idea of hardening the heart as due to difficulty in the solution of a theological problem, there are no exegetical indications whatever which would give us the right to interpret the statements in question in reverse, in the sense that Israel made Jahweh the one who hardened, and not Jahweh Israel the one who was hardened.

to say, by taking them as the secondary result of theological reflexion, and therefore as the way out from a theological dilemma or an account of a general law of the psychology of religion, is, from the point of view of hermeneutics, *a priori* to import a standpoint from outside the text itself. But exegesis can do this only when every attempt at understanding the subject in its direct sense has failed. In the particular case of Is. VI. 9f., however, this has, generally speaking, never been attempted.

There is no tolerably uniform, consistent pre-history of the concept of hardening the heart. Nevertheless, it is certain that from the very first Israel believed the act of deluding or hardening the heart to be prompted by Jahweh, and this is in one way or another the background to Isaiah's saying. The "evil spirit" which brought about an upheaval in the Shechem of Abimelech's day (Jg. IX. 23), the evil spirit which came over Saul (I Sam. XVI. 14, XVIII. 10, XIX. 9), the deception practised on Absalom's council of war whose result was the rejection of the wise advice given by Ahithophel (II Sam. XVII. 14), and last, Rehoboam's decision which, foolish as it was, was nevertheless ordained by Jahweh (I Kings XII. 15), are all precursors of this saying of Isaiah. They offer no escape from the theological dilemma; indeed, in a sense they enhance it, for they show that Jahwism had little difficulty in accepting even such obscure acts from the hand of Jahweh. We must also consider another factor: infatuation, a form of political madness whose inevitable end was self-destruction, meant much more to the whole of the ancient east as to the Greeks than it does to us, and they found it impossible to regard the causes of something so atrocious, such a plunge into madness and ruin at one's own hands, as lying simply on the human and immanent level: in the last analysis they could only be the inscrutable working of the deity. The case of the hardening of Pharaoh's heart is, of course, somewhat different; for the sources regard it as the first event in a comprehensive historical design.[10] Yet this rather isolated cycle of tradition can itself prove all the more important for the understanding of the concept of hardening of the heart in Isaiah. For some kind of logical reason for Jahweh's attitude is given here, and, of course, it was there from the beginning. The hardening took place, Pharaoh is told, "to show you my power, and that my name may be declared throughout all the earth" (Ex. IX. 16, J?).[11]

It is not my purpose to abstract a general concept of hardening the

[10] Ex. IV. 21 (J), IX. 12 (P), X. 1 (J), 20 (E), 27 (E).
[11] Cp. also Ex. VII. 5 (P), XI. 9 (P), XIV. 4 (J), 17 (P).

heart from the various references to it. Our task is to understand Isaiah; and to do so we have to realise two things. On the one hand, as far as this concept was concerned, he inherited an outlook which was unchallenged in Israel, and indeed, in the whole of the ancient world. But on the other hand he voiced something entirely new and unprecedented. This was his radical opinion that Jahweh himself was to bring about Israel's downfall, his conception of the creative word of Jahweh (Is. IX. 7 [8]), and, finally, his concept of Jahweh's "work," the far-reaching nature of God's designs in history. It is this range of theological concepts which forms the framework for what Isaiah has to say about the hardening of Israel's heart. The declaration of a hardening of the heart to be brought about by the prophet himself is not to be understood apart from the concept of the creative word of Jahweh, which was treated in fuller detail above[12]; indeed, it would appear that this ancient concept was given its ultimate and sharpest theological determination in Isaiah's saying. No doubt the idea that the prophetic word was able to effect acts of judgment and calamity by its own power alone had on occasion been very forcibly expressed before Isaiah's time; now, however, with him it is suddenly seen that this word effects judgment not only in the external world of history, but in human beings, in the most hidden recesses of their own hearts, namely, their refusal of the appeal by which Jahweh would save them.

The saying about hardening of the heart in Is. VI sounds as if it shut the door on everyone, and it was intended to be understood in this way. This cheerless background makes it all the more amazing that Isaiah's message was nevertheless accepted by a little group. A few years later the prophet was to sum up the net result of his earliest efforts in the words, Jahweh "has hidden his face from the house of Jacob" (Is. VIII. 17), and he returns to the same point in his last statement of accounts—Judah and Jerusalem were resistant, which means that in this context the obduracy is expressly shown as blameworthy (Is. XXX. 8ff.). Because of this, Is. VI. 8f. ought not to be called a "peripheral saying"[13]; for the enigma of obduracy to Jahweh's offer runs through the whole of Isaiah's activity; it is nothing less than the foil which sets off Jahweh's reiterated invitation.

Stupefy yourselves and be in a stupor! Blind yourselves and be blind! Be drunk, but not with wine, stagger, but not with strong drink;

[12] See above, pp. 89ff.   [13] So Hesse, "Verstockungsproblem," p. 72.

for Jahweh has poured out upon you a spirit of deep sleep
and has closed your eyes and covered your heads. . . .
. . . Therefore I again do a marvellous thing with this people,
wonderful and marvellous, so that the wisdom of the wise men
    perishes,
and the discernment of their discerning men is hid.

(Is. XXIX. 9–14)

"Therefore I act on this people," says Jahweh; thus for Isaiah the
hardening of Israel's heart is a particular mode of Jahweh's historical
dealings with her. One of our chief tasks in what follows will be to
demonstrate that what Isaiah speaks of is always an action, the "work"
of his God. The first thing he has to say in this connexion is his utterance about hardening of the heart; it is not to be the last.

This means, however, that we must learn to read the saying about
hardening of the heart with reference to the saving history. Any psychological or devotional explanation, or any understanding of it merely as
punishment, means understanding it as the end, the final stage of a
process which operates in a greater or lesser degree according to fixed
laws. This is not consistent with the plain evidence found in Isaiah; for,
paradoxical as it may be, its position there is emphatically at the beginning of a movement in the saving history. It was at the beginning, at
his call, that Isaiah was given this word, and in Is. VIII. 17 he says paradoxically that his hope is founded precisely in this God who hardens
the heart; here, too, hardening of the heart is an event, from which the
prophet looks out into the future; and in Is. XXX. 8ff. the position is no
different. As we have already seen, the fact that a prophet's word is not
heard is far from meaning that this is the end of it. The message against
which Jerusalem hardened its heart is to be written down for a generation to come. At that time—such is Isaiah's meaning—all that had fallen
on completely deaf ears in his own day and generation will be fulfilled.
Absolutely everything in Isaiah points out into the future—even the
saying about the hardening of Israel's heart which is the action of
Jahweh himself.[14]

I. ZION

We spoke a moment ago of God's invitation without defining it in any
way: we must now briefly attempt to give a more precise account of it
as we find it in Isaiah.

[14] See above, pp. 42f.

In giving an account of Isaiah's message, we must keep in mind from the outset the question of the sacral tradition on which, as a native of Jerusalem, the prophet could have taken his stand, and we have also to remember the special conditions which obtained in that city: because of its relatively late incorporation into the cultic sphere of Jahwism, it lived a life of its own in respect of tradition.[15] To this question the prophet's message in fact gives a perfectly definite answer. During the course of his long years of activity, Isaiah certainly clothed his preaching in different dresses to suit the hour and the audience whom he was addressing; yet there is one form—indeed it is almost a *schema*—for which he had such a preference that, if we wish to understand him, it is wise to take it as our starting point. It is only Isaiah's amazing ability to vary and diversify the different component parts in his discourse which blinds the reader to its schematic construction. The way in which these units are built up can be seen with almost model clearness in Is. XVII. 12–14. A thunderous throng of nations dashes against Zion; Jahweh rebukes them: thereupon they flee far away. "At evening time, behold, terror! Even before morning, they are no more."[16] Oddly enough, the nations here spoken of are not historically determinable; they appear rather as a formless, surging mass completely without political configuration, an idea which was made necessary by the inclusion of *motifs* from the myth of the struggle with the chaos dragon. Neither is their defeat a military one; it is achieved by a miracle, and takes place unobserved between nightfall and dawn. Only when day breaks can the astonished onlookers see that they have been delivered. It is not easy to date the passage; the old idea that Isaiah is speaking of the siege of Sennacherib has long been abandoned, for, when the prophet speaks of that event, he uses completely different terms. There can be little doubt that he was thinking of an event that could quite easily have taken place: but it also seems certain that the prophet was here making use of a tradition, and that neither the form of the story nor its various components were *ad hoc* creations.

[15] On the question of the inclusion of Jerusalem within the earlier traditions of Jahwism, see Noth, "Jerusalem und die israelitische Tradition," in *Ges. St.*, pp. 272ff. The evidence there should however have been supplemented by reference to the existence of a specific Zion tradition and its inclusion in Jahwism, see E. Rohland, *Die Bedeutung der Erwählungstraditionen Israels für die Eschatologie der alttestamentlichen Propheten*, Heidelberg Dissertation 1956, pp. 119ff.

[16] After G. B. Gray, *Isaiah I–XXIV*, *I.C.C.*, Edinburgh 1912, pp. 303f. (*Trs.*)

The tradition which springs immediately to mind is that contained in the so-called Songs of Zion (Pss. XLVI, XLVIII, and LXXVI), for they belong specifically to Jerusalem—which means they have nothing to do with amphictyonic tradition—we have already noticed them in another context.[17] All three songs tell of Jahweh's mysterious defeat of royal armies which attack Zion—"they saw it and were terrified, they were in panic and took to flight, trembling took hold of them there" (Ps. XLVIII. 6f. [5f.]). Before Zion "he [Jahweh] broke the flashing bow, the shield, the sword, and the weapons of war," "at thy rebuke, O God of Jacob, they lay stunned with their horses and chariots" (Ps. LXXXI. 4, 7 [3, 6]). The event upon which these poems draw has no ascertainable place in the history of the Davidic Jerusalem; neither, on the other hand, is the material mythological in the narrower sense of the term. Does it perhaps originate in the pre-Davidic Jerusalem? These psalms probably date from before the time of Isaiah: but their date is in fact of little importance; for their tradition of an unsuccessful attack on Jerusalem is quite certainly of very much earlier origin. Now, Isaiah's connexion with this tradition of early Jerusalem is abundantly clear, particularly in the way, both moving and mysteriously allusive, in which the prophet depicts the divine intervention. This becomes even more obvious when we bring in further evidence from his writings, although, of course, in each case the prophet makes the old tradition into something entirely new. Thus, in Is. X. 27b–34, a passage which may perhaps date from the same time as Is. XVII. 12ff., that is, c. 715, the picture of the enemies' onslaught is not in the least vague and featureless; instead, the text goes into full geographical detail, naming in order the towns and villages which were affected by the attack, until the point where the foe "shakes his fist at the mount of the daughter of Zion." At this point, however, Jahweh intervenes "with terrifying power." The cause of the enemies' destruction is Jahweh's own personal intervention, and not any battle. Here too deliverance comes only at the eleventh hour; the country districts of Judah are already overrun, and the enemy's power is only to be broken at the gates of Zion itself.

Isaiah shows the same calm assurance in connexion with the revolt of the year 720—he dismissed the ambassadors who certainly intended to incite the people of Jerusalem to join in the revolt with the calm words, "Jahweh has founded Zion; in her the afflicted of his people will find refuge" (Is. XIV. 28–32). Both in point of time and of subject matter

[17] See VOL. I, pp. 46f.

there is a close connexion between this prophecy and the one which announces the destruction of Assyria in Jahweh's own land (Is. XIV. 24–7). Later in his career, when the prophet was waiting for Sennacherib's attack, there are no less than three more or less complete variations of this inherited *schema* and all its component parts. Of course, at the very beginning of the great poem on Ariel (Is. XXIX. 1–8), a highly paradoxical view is expressed: Jahweh himself is to rise up against Zion ("for I will distress Ariel. . . . I encamp against you round about"). This naturally alters the whole tone of the tradition; the event now means utter humiliation for Zion (vs. 4). But it is followed by the turning point of grace; Jahweh will intervene with storm and tempest, and the oppressors will become as chaff and dust that pass away. When the enemy first makes its assault on Zion, therefore, Jahweh takes part in the most personal way against her: but thereafter he turns against the enemy.

And it will be, as when a hungry man dreams he is eating,
and when he awakes, his hunger is not satisfied,
and as when a thirsty man dreams he is drinking,
and he awakes parched and longing for drink—
so will it be with the multitude of the nations that fight against
    Mount Zion.   (Is. XXIX. 8)

In contrast with this, one of Isaiah's most powerful sayings (Is. XXX. 27–33) deals only with the repulse of Assyria, for which Jahweh appears in person, burning with his anger, letting his voice sound forth in majesty, and making the stroke of his arm plain. Finally, in Is. XXXI. 1–8, Jahweh turns against those who rely on alliances and armaments to meet the danger. Zion's protection is Jahweh himself. He will himself come down, "he will protect and deliver, spare and rescue" (vs. 5).

We must deal more fully with Isaiah's message in the earlier part of his career, during the Syro-Ephraimitic war. In the first place, Is. VII. 1–9 is completely different in form. The section is admittedly a narrative about a prophet, but this in turn only serves as the artistic framework into which are inserted a prophetic exhortation and an oracle of promise. What we then have is a rather unusual combination of two literary categories. Here too, in this exhortation to remain calm and fearless, and in this promise that the confederates' attack on Jerusalem will achieve nothing, the basic idea of the *schema* can again be easily recognised. But while in all the passages previously considered the interest was more or less exclusively concentrated on the external events, the attack and its repulse, in this case the inner feelings of the people in whose immediate neighbourhood so terrible and wonderful an event occurs are also important. They are asked whether they can hold out in "faith" even in face of all these troubles; for only if they can will they be established.[18]

This saying on faith seems to some extent to strike a solitary note in Isaiah, and this would suggest that it did not belong to any tradition. But in fact the very opposite is true; for it is precisely at this point that Isaiah is particularly clearly restoring an old tradition to use. We have merely to observe the very extensive use which he makes of ideas which derive from the old cycle of traditions about Jahweh's holy wars. Just as in bygone days Jahweh came from afar to these wars (Jg. v. 4f.), so now he will "come down to fight on Mount Zion"; and just as in bygone days he used to destroy the foe alone and without any help from men, so "the Assyrian shall fall by the sword, no human sword and no earthly sword" (Is. XXXI. 4*b*, 8). Jahweh will draw near, he will let his voice ring out, and do battle "with storm and tempest and hailstones" (Is. XXX. 30); he will visit Zion "with thunder, earthquake and great noise, with storm and tempest" (Is. XXIX. 6). In bygone days, in battle with the Canaanites, he threw stones down from heaven (Josh. x. 11), and in battle with the Philistines thundered with a mighty voice (1 Sam. VII. 10) and made the earth quake (1 Sam. XIV. 15)—according to Isaiah's predictions, it will be exactly the same when Jahweh manifests himself at the final day. The demand for faith too has its home in this old cycle of traditional ideas about Jahweh's saving help. We have already discussed the part played by the demand for faith, even though the word itself is never mentioned, in the account of Gideon's struggle with the Midianites (Jg. VII). The account of the miraculous crossing of the Red Sea, which actually reads almost like a prefiguration of Is. VII. 1ff., not only contains the exhortation "not to fear" and "to be still" since present help is at hand, but also mentions that to some extent as a result of this Israel then "believed" in Jahweh (Ex. XIV. 31). Thus there can be no doubt that in his own day and generation Isaiah gave fresh currency to the concept of the holy wars in which Jahweh both de-

[18] "There is a play upon words here, which may be reproduced in English by the help of a North-England term: If ye have not *faith*, ye cannot have *staith*." G. A. Smith, *The Book of Isaiah, I–XXXIX*, London 1902, p. 106n. There is a similar play in the German, *überstehen* and *überstanden*. (*Trs.*)

livered his people and at the same time demanded faith from them, and that he did so with great vigour. We are not, of course, to think that in the process he went right back to the concepts current in the time of the Judges; the concepts which he took up were rather those which had become established at about the beginning of the period of the Mon-archy. One of their characteristics is that they conceive the holy war as sheer miracle; Jahweh's saving act is entirely self-sufficient and does not allow any human co-operation.[19]

It is precisely at this point, the passionate elimination of all reliance on oneself, that Isaiah's zeal begins. That he saw a great act of deliver-ance lying in the immediate future was only one side of his message. Ahaz and the leaders in Jerusalem had to leave room for this act of God. And this is what Isaiah called faith—leaving room for God's sovereign action, desisting from self-help. Thus in Isaiah the demand for faith is actualised in an emphatically polemical and even negative sense—only do not now usurp God's place by your own political and military plans. For men, the only attitude appropriate to the situation was "to be quiet" (הַשְׁקֵט Is. VII. 4). Isaiah reiterated the same thing many years later, in face of the threat from Assyria, in the paradox that "being still" (נַחַת) would then be "strength" (Is. xxx. 15). When Isaiah speaks in this way of being still, he is quite certainly not thinking only of an inward condition of the soul, but also of an attitude which must be expressed in a perfectly definite mode of political conduct.[20]

[19] Cp. here von Rad, Heilige Krieg, pp. 42ff., 56ff.

[20] The question as to whether this demand to be still should be described as "Utopian" from the standpoint of practical politics (so since, E. Tröltsch, Das Ethos der hebräischen Propheten, Ges. Schriften, VOL. IV, Tübingen 1925, p. 36; especially F. Weinrich, Der religiös-utopische Charakter der "prophetischen Politik" Giessen 1932), or whether, as Prosksch asserts in his commentary (p. 15, 118, etc.), it was even there a shrewd one, introduces viewpoints which were far from the prophet's thoughts; for the question examines the practicability of his advice from outside the situation. It is clear that we, who no longer see the coefficients of the forces which were then in play, can hardly decide it along these lines. For Isaiah, being still was of course also the shrewder political course, but only because Jahweh had commanded it! If Würthwein's idea is correct, that Isaiah saw the breach of faith with Jahweh as lying only in the appeal to the Assyrians for help, and had no thoughts of ruling out all military action, but on the contrary advised that the war should be undertaken in quietness and confidence, this makes no essential difference, since, according to all the relevant passages, Jahweh had promised even so to carry the whole burden of defence. But since even the pre-Isaianic tradition shows the increasing tendency to exclude all human participation in war, and since Isaiah never speaks of such participation, but

The "object" upon which this faith should be based did not, however, as yet exist for his contemporaries; it lay in the future. The astonishing thing was therefore this: Isaiah demanded of his contemporaries that they should now make their existence rest on a future action of God. If they should succeed in taking refuge in Jahweh's future act of deliverance, then they would be saved. Later, when it was all over, when Jerusalem had capitulated and the land lay waste, Isaiah once again balanced accounts with the people of influence in the capital. In the matter of military protection, these men had left nothing undone; every conceivable attention had been paid to the city's fortifications and its water-supply:

> but you did not look to him who did it,
> or have regard for him who planned it long ago.
>
> (Is. xxii. 11*b*)

"Looking to" Jahweh's action in history seems an odd expression; yet it too comes from tradition; for, according to J's account, Moses himself commanded the Israelites to fear not, to stand firm, and to "look to" the help of Jahweh (Ex. xiv. 13), and the story also ends with the note that Israel "saw the mighty hand of Jahweh" (vs. 31). The term, "looking to the action of Jahweh," used just as absolutely as that of "faith," occurs elsewhere in Isaiah, and is almost a synonym for faith; at all events, like the term "being still," it describes a very important aspect of what Isaiah calls "faith."

Isaiah's conception of faith, of being still, and of looking to Jahweh must itself be set within still wider prophetic contexts, namely those connected with Jahweh's "work" and with his "purpose."

Isaiah once attacked the careless revellers in the capital thus:

> But they do not see the work of Jahweh (פֹּעַל),
> nor do they regard the work of his hands (מַעֲשֵׂה).
>
> (Is. v. 12)

This concept of a "work" of Jahweh can scarcely originate in a sacral tradition; it really looks like an independent coinage of Isaiah himself.

rather uses extreme language to show that he looks to Jahweh's intervention to settle the whole issue, Würthwein's idea does not seem to me very probable (E. Würthwein, in *Theologie als Glaubenswagnis, Festschrift für Karl Heim*, Hamburg, pp. 47ff.). On the problem, see also H.-J. Kraus, "Prophetie und Politik" in *Theologische Existenz Heute, N.F. 36* (1952); K. Elliger, "Prophet und Politik," in *Z.A.W.*, 53 (1935), pp. 3ff.

A few verses later, in another oracle of threatening, Isaiah quotes those who were saying:

> Let [Jahweh] speed his work (מעשה), that we may see it;
> let the purpose (עצה) of the Holy One of Israel draw near and be
> fulfilled, that we may know it.   (Is. v. 19)

It is perfectly obvious that these mocking words take up phrases used by the prophet himself in his preaching. Here the term "purpose" of Jahweh is used more or less synonymously side by side with that of his "work." The former term is also very likely the prophet's own creation. It is quite secular in origin, and signifies the decision arrived at in a council. Very probably what is thought of is the royal council in heaven, in which a political project was discussed and then resolved upon (I Kings XXII. 19–22). This idea of a plan to which Jahweh gives effect in history is a new element in the preaching of the eighth-century prophets. In this connexion, the present-day reader is well advised to lay aside all ideas of a general guidance of history by divine providence; for when Isaiah speaks of "purpose," he is thinking of something planned for the deliverance of Zion, that is to say, of a saving work. Isaiah sets this saving act of Jahweh in the widest possible historical context, namely that of universal history. Nothing is improvised here: Isaiah says very definitely that Jahweh "predetermined" (יצר) his work "long ago" (מרחוק Is. XXII. 11; cp. Is. XXXVII. 26). This work of Jahweh thus enfolds the whole realm of world history as it was understood at that time; and the way in which the great world empires who were proudly strutting about on this very stage of history came into collision with God's plan is one of the great themes to which Isaiah returned again and again.

> Jahweh of hosts has sworn:
> As I have planned it, so shall it be,
>   and as I have purposed it, so shall it stand,
> to break Assyria in my land;
>   upon my mountains will I trample him under foot . . .
> this is the purpose, resolved concerning the whole earth,
>   this is the hand, stretched out over all the nations.
> For Jahweh of hosts has resolved it, and who can annul it?
>   His hand is stretched out, and who will turn it back?
>   (Is. XIV. 24–7)

In this passage, which apparently dates from the time when Assyria first became a serious danger, it is perfectly clear that Zion occupies the centre of the stage in Jahweh's plan. For her safety Assyria has to be broken in pieces "upon the mountains of Jahweh." This event, though it is concentrated on one tiny place, also involves the whole world; "all nations" must bow before it; for none can bend back Jahweh's outstretched arm.

The same atmosphere pervades Is. x. 5–19, a great passage which in respect of form alone is one of Isaiah's most powerful poems, and which is also unusual because of its baroque development of the diatribe, into which the prophet has packed so much as to give rise to a disproportion between it and the threat (vs. 16ff.). Assyria had been given a definite, though, in Isaiah's view, a strictly limited, commission by Jahweh: she was sternly to chastise his people. But she is about to exceed this commission. Nothing has happened as yet: but the very fact that she "has it in mind" to exceed, that she "intends" destruction, is sufficient reason for threatening her with punishment. There is hardly any other passage which so clearly shows the nature of the prophetic view of history. Isaiah does not consider the question of how the Assyrians came to have this task allotted to them, but he is in no doubt about the fact itself. Everything stands or falls on the precondition that the prophet claims to know the divine plan which lies behind an actual political event of his time, in this case the Assyrian invasion of Palestine. From this standpoint he sees the event divided up into its divine and its human constituent parts, and is able to separate between that which Jahweh had intended and the guilty human addition, the element imported into it by man's high-handedness. The prophets did not use this way of interpreting history at its very deepest level, as Jahweh planned it, as a rational *modus operandi* which they could apply as they pleased. Yet in moments of great tension they claimed authority for such a view of it which they based on some unexplained inspiration.[21]

[21] The words, Jahweh "will finish all his work on Mount Zion" are also found in this context (vs. 12). Unfortunately they come at a bad place in relation to the whole passage, and therefore possibly derive from a different context; they may however be claimed without hesitation as Isaianic. They show more clearly than other references the way in which what Isaiah liked to call the "work" of Jahweh, which fills the whole world of history, applies to Zion, and will also be brought to its consummation there.

It would appear that Isaiah only once spoke in a very fundamental and theoretically didactic fashion about Jahweh's action in history, namely in Is. xxviii. 23–9—that is, if the understanding of this text as a parable which alludes to a supernatural order,

In the light of the passages so far examined, and particularly of Is. VII. 1ff. and XVII. 12ff., it would seem as though Jahweh would protect Zion from the Assyrians in all circumstances. In actual fact Isaiah said so quite plainly more than once. Nevertheless, he was never completely free from ambiguity in his view of this matter, least of all perhaps in his earliest period, when what he looked for from the coming of the Assyrians was almost entirely a devastating judgment and chastisement for Judah (Is. VII. 18, 20). At no time, however, did the prophet ever completely lose sight of this dark reverse side of the work of Jahweh. This aspect of it again becomes important in his later period—for example, in the Ariel poem which, as we have already noticed, sees Jahweh himself as the one who distresses Zion. There is to be "moaning and lamentation," and Jerusalem is to be like a "ghost" whose thin voice is "to sound from low in the dust." Such is the depth of humiliation which will precede the deliverance (Is. XXIX. 2, 4). Jahweh's work for Zion is here given a remarkable theological ambivalence: it judges and saves at one and the same time. Isaiah expressed the same idea in even stronger terms to the ruling classes in Jerusalem who believed that they could make "lies their refuge" in order to "take shelter in falsehood." He gave them this warning:

> For Jahweh will rise up as on Mount Perazim,
>   he will storm as in the valley of Gibeon,
> to do his deed—strange is his action,
>   and to work his work—alien is his work!
>
> (Is. XXVIII. 21)

Here again we meet the concept of the "work of Jahweh"; and this is the most remarkable of all the references to it. Its terms are once more allusive rather than direct, and leave a great deal open. The only thing certain is that Jahweh will rise up to do terrible battle; the words make one feel how even the prophet himself was seized with terror at the "barbaric alien element" (Duhm) in this self-manifestation of Jahweh. Jahweh will rise up once again. The future act thus stands in a typo-

---

i.e., to Jahweh and his action in history, is correct. Perhaps however it is not altogether easy to believe that the text gives us no indication that it is not to be taken in the literal sense, but as parabolic discourse. In Vergil's *Georgics* there is a poem on the countryman's activities in the successive seasons of the year which includes a reference to the deity who taught the peasants (I. 35ff.). Its only real difference from Is. XXVIII. 23ff. is its compass, and it has never been understood as a parable.

logical relationship to the one which once founded David's empire. Therefore the coming act will, like the former, in the end effect the deliverance of the city of God. What was this to signify for the "scoffers"? For them only the dark side of this appalling sudden appearance of Jahweh comes into the picture.

Who would be affected by the salvation which Jahweh's work was to bring? The usual answer to the question is to point to Isaiah's concept of the holy *remnant*; and in actual fact the prophet did on occasion put it in this way. The main reference to the remnant is the symbolic name Shear-jashub (a returned remnant) which he—no doubt at the command of Jahweh—gave to one of his sons (Is. VII. 3). Yet the concept as understood in this sense of a remnant to be saved at the *eschaton* is remarkably rare in Isaiah (Is. X. 21 is post-Isaianic). As we have already seen, the remnant concept as such belongs to the language of politics, and describes what remained over of a people who had survived a campaign whose aim was their total destruction.[22] This negative use is also found in Isaiah, as for example when he speaks of the remnant of Syria (Is. XVII. 3, 5f.), of Moab (Is. XVI. 13f.), of Kedar (Is. XXI. 17), or of the Philistines (Is. XIV. 30). Indeed, he sometimes employed it in this negative sense of a pitiful remnant with reference even to his own nation (Is. XXX. 17, I. 9). Therefore it cannot be said that Isaiah made the remnant concept a leading one where his concern was his proclamation of salvation. Nor is it probable that in this matter he was basing himself on a fairly firmly defined prophetic tradition which he for his part resumed and developed in accord with his own ideas. If such a "remnant tradition" did in fact ever exist, Isaiah echoes it only infrequently. There can be no doubt that the prophet envisaged a radical process of sifting: and if, for the sake of terminological simplicity, this is called a remnant concept, no exception can be taken to this. A reference to the remnant could then be seen in the Immanuel sign, and, more particularly, in the prophet's disciples (Is. VIII. 16–18), or in the poor who are to find refuge in Zion (Is. XIV. 32), etc. Nevertheless, it has to be remembered that Isaiah himself seldom used such an all-embracing term for the miraculous preservation of a minority. This could be said with much more truth of a number of post-Isaianic passages in which the remnant concept does in fact appear as a clearly defined idea (Is. IV. 3, XI. 11, 16, X. 20, XXVIII. 5).

The reader of Isaiah who appreciates how the prophet's whole

[22] See above, pp. 21f.

preaching is permeated from its very beginning by the theme of Zion
threatened but finally delivered, is bound to sense something of the
yearly increasing tension which must have burdened Isaiah until events
finally reached a climax in the reign of Sennacherib. In 701 the Assyrians,
who were never out of the prophet's mind his whole life long, did not
simply make an appearance in Palestine; on this occasion they even
marched into the hill country of Judah and surrounded Jerusalem.
Hezekiah submitted to them—obviously after a short siege—and had
to agree to pay a heavy tribute of silver and gold, and to cede part of
his territory (II Kings XVIII. 13–16). He did not "show faith," at least not
as Isaiah conceived the term, but by an act of political common-sense
saved the city from the worst possible fate. The sheer joy of relief
expressed by the besieged inhabitants is easy to imagine; but Isaiah
turned away ashamed and angry from the mob and its jubilation. This
was the great moment to which he had looked forward for years—but
Jerusalem was not equal to it.

> Look away from me; I must weep bitter tears.
> Insist not to comfort me for the ravishing of the daughter of my
> people.
>
> (Is. XXII. 4)

This is one of the very few places where, in the midst of the austere
atmosphere of his prophetic message, Isaiah's own human feelings
assert their right and demand a hearing. He must have been shattered
to the depths of his being when events turned out so completely
different from what he had expected. Who could dare even attempt to
comfort a prophet in the hour of his despair!

There is one other passage, Is. I. 4–9, which, even if only indirectly,
reveals in a rather unique way something of Isaiah's frame of mind in
the period after the disaster which befell Jerusalem. It begins with a
diatribe of unusual pungency ("a people laden with guilt," "offspring
of evildoers, sons who deal corruptly"). But these words of burning
anger are not followed, as we should have expected, by the threat. As
he describes the body of the people, so stricken by physical punishment
that it really cannot be smitten any more, the prophet finds that he
himself is caught up in the misery of it all: "They [the wounds] are
none of them pressed out, or bound up, or softened with oil" (vs. 6b),
and this now moves the prophet from anger to pity. His own personal
pain drove from him his original intention to rebuke and threaten. He

ends with a description—notice the metre, the *kinah*—of the country-side devastated by the Assyrians, in which Jerusalem is left "like a lodge in a cucumber field." This passage probably belongs to the last phase of Isaiah's preaching, so far as records have survived.

In the light of what we have so far seen, the total result of Isaiah's work appears overwhelmingly negative. Not one of all his great sayings about Zion came true. The nation showed no faith, and Jahweh did not protect his city. Did the prophet demand too much of the people, or—a hard question—in prophesying the assured safety of Zion, did he encroach upon God's prerogative? It is beyond dispute that Isaiah's disappointment was very deep. On the other hand, there is no indication that the prophet was in any way puzzled by Jahweh. It was his fellow-men who puzzled him. This is one of the important differ-ences between Isaiah and Jeremiah, whose relationship to Jahweh was much more critical. Isaiah apparently acquiesced in the failure of his work. This he could do, because for him the word of Jahweh with which he was charged was beyond all criticism. If his own generation had rejected it, then it must be put in writing for a future one. The very fact that Isaiah did write it down makes clear that in his eyes the prophetic message was far from being a dead letter even if it had failed.[23] And had not Jahweh told him at the time of his call that he would have no success as a prophet? What was said then about the remnant is also found in Is. I. 8f.; and so we have the right to say after all that even at the end of his work Isaiah had this comfort to cling to. Yet, whether he himself regarded his work as a failure, or whether he found comfort, is not so very important—and in any case we do not have the material to give a proper answer to such a question. It is much more important that his message was written down and handed on. More important still, successors took up the themes of Isaiah's message; they added pro-phecies in the Isaianic style to the old Isaianic texts, and thus kept the old message most vitally alive and made it contemporary for later genera-tions. Thus, for example, in Is. IV. 2ff. a word of grace was added to the oracle of judgment on the women of Jerusalem (Is. III. 16ff.). It looks beyond the hour of punishment envisaged by Isaiah and speaks of ignominy washed away and of salvation on Mount Zion. As we now have it, the judgment pronounced on the Egyptians in Is. XVIII. 1–6 ends with a prospect of the blessings of the last time: the Egyptians are then to bring offerings to the God of Israel on Mount Zion. The

[23] See above, pp. 40ff.

"spurious" addition (vs. 7), though phrased in the style of the genuine prophecy of Isaiah, is certainly later. Again, the words, "the proud crown of the drunkards of Ephraim" (Is. xxviii. 1) are repeated a few verses later, but are now given a saving and eschatological reference: Jahweh will himself be a crown and a diadem of beauty for the remnant of his people (vs. 5). The Messianic prophecy in Is. xi. 1-8 was also subsequently enlarged. The Gentiles are to enquire about the shoot from the stem of Jesse: it is to become an ensign for the nations. Critical exegesis has no great opinion of these additions or of many others like them. In so far as this verdict is literary and aesthetic, one can largely agree. The difference in the form and in force of expression is in some cases quite unmistakable: the diction is more diffuse and less colourful, it heaps up the terms used, and the result is often enough the sacrifice of clarity. Nevertheless, we ought to exercise reserve in differentiating between what is original and what was added by successors, since the men of the ancient world were quite unfamiliar with such differentiations used as standards and measures of value. We must particularly remember that such judgments are quite meaningless as far as the theological adequacy of the additions is concerned. For how may we determine the rightness or wrongness of such subsequent actualisations of old Isaianic prophecy? All we can see is that the tradition of this prophet's message was not preserved in archives: it remained a living organism, speaking directly to later generations as it had done to its own, and able even of itself to give birth to new prophecy.[24]

Finally, the subject of the continuing effectiveness of the message and also of the reinterpretation it was later given takes in the complex of narratives concerning the Assyrians' threat to Zion and their withdrawal (Is. xxxvi-xxxviii). Here themes recur which have an important place in our prophet's message—the question of the deliverance of Zion (Is. xxxvi. 14, 18, 20, xxxvii. 12, 20), Jahweh's zeal (xxxvii. 32), the remnant (Is. xxxvii. 32), and above all the question of confidence and of what can be properly relied upon (Is. xxxvi. 5-7, xxxvii. 10). At the same time, however, the differences from Isaiah are unmistakable. For these stories the Assyrian withdrawal is already a thing of the past. Accordingly they lack the specifically historical interest in the political aspect of the event which is closing in on Zion. For the narrator, the Assyrian king is little more than the type of the wantonly insolent foe of Jahweh; he could equally be called Nebuchadnezzar or

[24] On the prophets' message as living bodies of tradition, see above, pp. 46ff.

Antiochus. Corresponding to this waning of interest in the saving history and its uniqueness, and in comparison with the real Isaiah, the demand for confidence is obviously more spiritualised. Faith is now on the way to becoming something almost divorced from history and belonging to the individual's encounter with his God.

2. JAHWEH'S ANOINTED ONE

If Isaiah's preaching had concentrated only on the threat to Zion and her defence it would have shown a single-mindedness unparalleled in the Old Testament, despite the astonishing number of variations the prophet played on this theme. But it contained another idea which, though it occupies less space, is expounded in texts of considerable scope and importance. This is the theme of David and the Messiah.

The idea that Jahweh had established David's throne in Jerusalem and made him far-reaching promises was current even during David's lifetime.[25] It is not certain how large a part this played in the faith of the common people as opposed to the faith practised at court. In Deuteronomy indeed, which is later than Isaiah, we still find the deposit of a theology whose orientation was "amphictyonic," and therefore expressly non-monarchical and non-Messianic. We do not know the attitude taken by the farmers and herdsmen of the Judean south: but in the royal city, the seat of the administration, the probable home of Isaiah, this sacral theology, stemming from the court, was very much alive. Our knowledge of it is derived chiefly from the so-called royal psalms; we do not, however, know it with enough precision to allow us to draw far-reaching conclusions about it by comparing Isaiah's utterances with the royal psalms—as, for example, about the particular nuances which each gave to the component concepts.

In Is. XI. 1–8, the Messianic theme is arranged under three headings. First comes the equipment of the anointed one for his office (vss. 2–3a). His authority is not conferred by one single *charisma*—as had been usual in Israel up to this time—but by a number of them. When Isaiah says that the possession of the spirit is to "rest upon" the anointed one he probably intends to rule out the possibility that the possession should be temporary, as had so far always been the rule. In the second section (vss. 3b–5) we are shown the anointed one exercising his office in virtue of this gift of the spirit. His principal office is that of arbiter, in which he cares particularly for those whose legal standing is weak.

[25] See VOL. I, pp. 39ff., 310.

Like the royal psalms—cp. particularly Ps. LXXII. 12–14—Isaiah regards the anointed one's commission as consisting pre-eminently in the establishment of the divine justice on earth. The prophet's insistence that the anointed one has at his disposal, both for his investigations and for punishing the guilty, such divine properties as omniscience and the power to cause instant death by word alone probably takes him beyond the traditional teachings of the royal theology. The third part (vss. 6–8), which agrees with traditional concepts, tells of the paradisial peace which is to accompany the reign of this anointed one, and to bring order even into the world of nature and to resolve its conflicts.

While Isaiah is here seen to be moving essentially within the traditional courtly concepts and adapting them to his own day, he did at one point abandon and break with these in an almost revolutionary way. He does not, as had hitherto been the case, attach what he has to say to a contemporary and present anointed one seated on the throne of David, but to one who is to come in the future, who is to spring from "the root of Jesse." The reference to the father of David makes it probable that Isaiah is not thinking simply of any future anointed one seated on the throne of David, but of a new David, at whose advent Jahweh will restore the glory of the original Davidic empire.[26] The Messianic prophecy of his contemporary Micah can hardly be taken in any other sense; for when Micah addresses the Ephrathites of Bethlehem, the clan from which David came, and prophesies that a "ruler in Israel" (מושל Mic. v. 1 [2]) shall come forth from it, this can only mean that Jahweh is once more taking up his Messianic work from the beginning, in that he again starts at the very same place as he began in the past, namely in Bethlehem. Both passages are highly poetic in feeling; they are expressed in language remote from that of daily life, which, of course, makes it extremely difficult to analyse their concepts: but the fact that both of them look to the historical town and family from which David came, can only mean that they expect the new anointed one to appear from there. There is, however, one difference: for Micah this new beginning is bound up with the elimination of the old royal

---

[26] This alone makes the fact that Isaiah speaks of the root of Jesse comprehensible. Otherwise it would have been much more natural to speak of the line of David. Admittedly, it cannot be assumed for certain on the basis of Is. XI. 1 that Isaiah expected a new David; but since Jeremiah (XXX. 9) and Ezekiel (XXXIV. 23), explicitly make the assumption, and since Isaiah's contemporary Micah looks to Bethlehem and not to Jerusalem, it is very natural to presuppose that Isaiah also had the idea of David's return.

city, the total obliteration of Jerusalem from the pages of history (Mic. III. 12),[27] whereas, as we have already seen, Isaiah looks for a renewal of Jerusalem. In both cases, the contemporary monarch or monarchs of the Davidic line are dismissed by the prophets. The fact that they so expressly look for salvation in the anointed one of the future is tantamount to saying that the contemporary descendants of David have lost the saving function so emphatically attributed to them in the royal psalms. In this respect, they have relinquished all that caused the singing of their praises in favour of the coming anointed one. It is, of course, remarkable that our only guide in such an important matter is inference. We have no evidence that such a Messianic prophecy was badly received at court, or regarded as highly seditious— which, indeed, it was. All the evidence suggests, however, that these prophets increasingly wrote off the reigning members of the house of David of their own day, and even that they regarded the whole history of the Monarchy from the time of David as a false development. If they did not, what meaning could there be in their expectation that Jahweh would once again make an entirely new beginning? Was it only amongst their intimate friends that the prophets talked about these matters? The literary form in which these prophecies are clothed might suggest that this is so; for they do not look like open proclamations designed for a wider public; there is never any sign of an audience whom the prophet addresses, nor are they formulated as divine oracles, revelations made by Jahweh. Their literary category is really unique. Had they a somewhat esoteric character from the very beginning?

We must not think that the prophets only looked for the coming of an anointed one sometime in a vague future. Isaiah clearly envisaged the enthronement in the immediate future, that is to say, within the context of the Assyrian crisis and its defeat. His other great Messianic passage, Is. VII. 23b – IX. 6 [IX. 1b–7]) starts out from a definite, concrete contemporary situation, Tiglath Pileser's annexation of a considerable part of Israel's territory, and its incorporation into the Assyrian provincial system (II Kings XV. 29). Cut asunder from the people of God, cast out into the darkness where there can be no talk of history, these are "the people that walk in darkness"; and "the light which shines on them" is the fact that they are given knowledge of two epoch-making events. First, Jahweh has broken the yoke and rod of the oppressor, which is the might of Assyria. This came about like one of the miracles

[27] Alt, K.S., VOL. III, pp. 374ff.

of the old holy wars—there is no explanation of the enemy's defeat; all that needs to be done is to clear away and burn the bloodstained implements of war still scattered round about (vss. 2–4 [3–5]). The other piece of knowledge given is that of the accession of the anointed one which, the prophet imagines, is to follow directly upon Jahweh's act of deliverance. The child who is born, the son who is given, is indeed no mere babe; he is the anointed one who, in terms of Ps. II. 7, is at the moment of his "coronation" brought into the relationship of son to Jahweh. In Jerusalem, however, as everywhere in the ancient east, a courtly accession ceremony was described in strictly conventional language; therefore this text is the last place from which we to-day may hope for personal information concerning the anointed one. Isaiah's prophecy too is in the fixed language of a characteristic ritual. Its interest lies in the questions of the office of the anointed one and his authorisation by Jahweh. Now, it is very significant that this coming anointed one is designated as שׂר and his rule as מִשְׂרָה. A שׂר is never an independent ruler, but always an official commissioned by a higher authority; even though he is like a king within his sphere of jurisdiction (Is. x. 8), and has greater power than many who have no one above them, he nevertheless remains himself a commissioned official; in the language of the east, he is not sultan but vizier, and as such is responsible to higher authority.[28] The anointed one is therefore not "king," but is subordinate to a king, namely Jahweh, to whose throne he is summoned as "governor."[29] This deliberate avoidance of the title of king—Micah too eschews the word "king" and speaks of a "ruler" (מוֹשֵׁל)—may again involve an attack on the kings in Jerusalem who were now emancipated from Jahweh and behaving as independent rulers. When the anointed one is invested with powers to govern in God's stead, he has also the customary throne-names conferred upon him. Here the details are not all equally clear. The first is particularly important, for when the anointed one is called "wonderful in giving counsel," the reference is to the advice he receives from the universal king (cp. II. Sam. XVI. 23); he is in constant conversation with Jahweh about the

[28] W. Caspari, *Echtheit, Hauptbegriff und Gedankengang der messianischen Weissagung Jes. 9. 1–6, Beiträge zur Förderung christlicher Theologie*, 1908. Of the picture of the anointed one, Caspari says very aptly that it contains "office rather than person," "function rather than character"; see p. 300.

[29] On the throne of David's successors in Jerusalem as the throne of Jahweh, see VOL. I, p. 320.

government of the world. The supports of his throne are justice and righteousness, and "there is no end of blessing" in his kingdom.

Here we may notice Is. VII. 10–17. While nineteenth-century church tradition could still regard Is. VII. 10–17 as the Messianic prophecy *par excellence*, critical investigation since then has so complicated the understanding of the passage that, apart from the quite preliminary questions of the meaning of the words and of the various statements it makes, we are still very far away from any satisfactory agreement on it.[30] Upon Ahaz's refusal to ask for a sign from Jahweh, Isaiah announces that Jahweh himself is to give a sign: the young woman will conceive, will bear a son, and will call him Immanuel. . . . Clearly, the first consideration here is the idea of the sign; and all interpretation of the passage must keep this firmly in mind. Where is the sign to be seen? In the child, in the strange food he is to eat, or in his name? The first idea that comes to mind is that the sign is the name given to the child, Immanuel. A prophetic symbolic name like Shear-jashub or the names in Hosea I, it indicates weal in the near future. Only we must notice that "therefore" (לכן vs. 14), here as elsewhere in the Old Testament, should be understood in a threatening sense. Moreover, this message is spoken to Ahaz who has already cut himself off from the coming blessing by his refusal of a sign. The coming event therefore brings judgment for him. The alliance of the Syrians and Israelites, the danger which threatened Jerusalem and terrified her inhabitants, was soon to be broken (vs. 16): but Ahaz, his royal house, and his people are to face hard times. Thus, as has often been pointed out, Is. VII. 10ff. seems to have close affinities with Is. VIII. 1–4. Here too there is mention of a child who is still to come into the world, and who is to have a symbolic name, "spoil is speedy, plunder hasteneth," while a time limit is also mentioned (Is. VIII. 4), which corresponds to that of Is. VII. 16. This might suggest that we should think of the "young woman" of Is. VII. 14 as the prophet's wife: Immanuel would then be a son of Isaiah's own,

---

[30] On Is. VII. 10–17, cp. J. J. Stamm's discussion of the most important of the newer ideas, "La Prophétie d'Emmanuel," in *Revue de Théologie et de Philosophie*, 132 (1944), pp. 97ff.; *id.*, "Neuere Arbeiten zum Immanuel-Problem" in *Z.A.W.*, 68 (1956), pp. 46ff.; J. Lindblom, *A Study on the Immanuel Section in Isaiah*, Is. VII. 1 – IX. 6 (*Scripta minora Reg. Societatis humaniorum litterarum Lundensis*, 1957–8: 4, Lund 1958; H. W. Wolff, *Immanuel (Eine Auslegung von Jes. 7. 1–17) (Biblische Studien 23)*, henceforth cited as *Immanuel*, 1959; W. Vischer, *Die Immanuel-Botschaft im Rahmen des königlichen Zionsfest (Theologische Studien*, 45), Zürich 1955.

like "a remnant shall return" and "spoil is speedy, plunder hasteneth." There is more to be said, however, for Wolff's interpretation. He explains the incident, exactly like Is. vii. 1–9, entirely in terms of the concepts of the holy war, themes which were already touched upon in the prophet's utterance about the Syro-Ephraimitic war (Is. vii. 4–9), and which are now simply continued in the announcement of the sign (cp. Jg. vi. 36ff.) and in that of the birth of the deliverer (cp. Jg. xiii. 5).[31] In either case, the statement that the child is to eat curds and honey until he reaches the age of moral discernment, is extremely difficult. Does "curds and honey" signify shortage of food, the sole products of a land ravaged by enemies (cp. Is. vii. 21f.), or does it on the contrary mean the mythical food of the gods, the food of paradise? Above all, however, does vs. 15 form part of the original oracle? It is often regarded as an interpolation, and in actual fact the logical connexion of vs. 16 with vs. 14 is excellent. In this case, it is the interpolator who shifted the centre of gravity in the saying from the child's name to the child himself. In Is. viii. 8b too, though this verse is also to all appearance a later addition, Immanuel is spoken of as a person, the actual ruler of the land. In face of this background, we have therefore to reckon with the possibility that in Is. vii. 10ff. genuine words of the prophet himself, in which he used the symbolic name Immanuel to prophesy weal for believers and woe for unbelievers, have been reinterpreted in a Messianic sense. Some commentators, of course, introduce a much richer set of concepts deriving from the cult and mythology and try to interpret the passage in their light. The pioneer here was Kittel,[32] and Gressmann, Mowinckel and Hammershaimb have gone further.[33]

As a result of this study, it can be said that the whole of Isaiah's preaching is based on two traditions, the Zion tradition and the tradition about David. Both are election traditions: that is to say, they were adopted by court circles in Jerusalem as the basis of their own legitimation before Jahweh. These men founded their whole existence before Jahweh, their faith and their confidence upon the God-given institutions of which these traditions were the guarantee. Isaiah was also at home in

---

[31] Wolff, *Immanuel*, pp. 34f.

[32] *Die hellenistische Mysterienreligionen und das Alten Testament*, Stuttgart 1924.

[33] Thus for example, E. Hammerschaimb, "The Immanuel Sign" in *Studia Theologica cura ordinum theologorum Scandinavicorum edita*, iii, 1949, pp. 124ff.; see however the criticism of it by J. J. Stamm, "Die Immanuel-Weissagung. Ein Gespräch mit E. Hammershaimb," in *V.T.*, iv, 1954, pp. 20ff.

these traditions: but he also brought a completely new concept into them. The songs of Zion were based on the fact of Jahweh's past choice of Zion, and the royal psalms on Jahweh's past choice of David: Isaiah turned completely to the future—Jahweh is about to deliver Zion, he is about to raise up the anointed one, the new David. It is here, in the future event, and not in any historical event of the past, that Jerusalem's salvation lies. Men must have faith in this future deliverance; for there is no other. We who have been brought up with a European outlook find it strange to see how detached and almost unconnected the two traditions are even as late as Isaiah. Yet this very fact has something important to tell us about the kind of men these prophets were. Their message was not, as was long supposed, an independent entity, based so to speak on its own principles, and possibly of an entirely new kind. Instead, they regarded themselves as the spokesmen of old and well-known sacral traditions which they reinterpreted for their own day and age.

CHAPTER C

THE NEW ELEMENT IN EIGHTH-CENTURY PROPHECY[1]

CAREFUL consideration of the distinctive features in the prophecies of Amos, Hosea, Isaiah, and Micah might well lead us
to the conclusion that all comparisons are dangerous, because
once we have discovered the radical differences between them it is
difficult to avoid the temptation of going on and smoothing these out.
What, in actual fact, do Hosea and Isaiah have in common? Hosea
came from the farming world of the Northern Kingdom, he was
opposed to everything that in his day was implied by the word "king";
of all the prophets, he was the most deeply involved in patriarchal
concepts deriving from the cult, and he paid particular attention to
problems in the sacral sphere and to cultic irregularities. Isaiah was a
townsman, brought up in a *polis* tradition, and a sharp-sighted observer
of world politics; he explained all the changes in the political kaleido-
scope as part of Jahweh's rational scheme, he placed his confidence in
the divinely guaranteed protection of the city, and he looked for a king
who would bring peace and righteousness. Much the same can be said
of Amos and Micah. Amos was apparently quite unmoved by Hoesa's
main topic, the threat of Jahwism from the Canaanite worship of Baal;
and he is also different from Isaiah, for he does not inveigh against
mistaken policies, against armaments and alliances. Finally, there is
absolutely no bridge between Micah and the hopes cherished concerning Zion by Isaiah, his fellow-countryman and contemporary; Micah
in fact expected Zion to be blotted out of the pages of history. Even the
kind of prophetic office surprisingly discovered in the state documents
of Mari, which makes it clear that the prophet could threaten even the
king in God's name, does not give us any standpoint from which to
summarise and categorise the prophetic role. If their close connexion
with the king and their interest in political and military affairs is a
particular characteristic of the "prophets" of Mari, then Israel has comparable figures not only in Isaiah, but in a whole series of prophets
beginning with Ahijah of Shiloh, including Micaiah ben Imlah and

[1] Eichrodt, *Theology*, pp. 345–53; Vriezen, *Outline*, pp. 62–6.

Elijah, and going down to Jeremiah.[2] On the other hand, it is impossible to bring Amos into this category. Nevertheless, in spite of all these great differences, there is a great deal of common matter which links the eighth-century prophets to one another; for their religious ideas led them to an absolutely common conviction, one so novel and revolutionary when compared with all their inherited beliefs, that it makes the differences, considerable as these are, seem almost trivial and peripheral. We shall now make another attempt to find out which element in the prophets' teaching struck their contemporaries as being a departure from the religious standards of the time.

To begin with a very simple statement: these men were set apart from their contemporaries and they were very lonely. Their call gave them a unique knowledge of Jahweh and of his designs for Israel. We have already seen how, apparently to a much greater degree than any of their contemporaries, they are deeply rooted in the religious traditions of their nation; indeed, their whole preaching might almost be described as a unique dialogue with the tradition by means of which the latter was made to speak to their own day. Yet the very way in which they understood it and brought it to life again is the measure of their difference from all the contemporary religious heritage of their nation. When Amos said that Jahweh presided over the migration of the Philistines and the Syrians (Am. IX. 7), he was departing pretty radically from the belief of his time. This novel and to some extent revolutionary way of taking the old traditions was not, however, the result of careful study or of slowly maturing conviction; rather, these prophets were all agreed that it was Jahweh who enlightened them and led them on from one insight to another. The reason for their isolation was therefore this—as they listened to and obeyed a word and commission of Jahweh which came to them alone and which could not be transferred to anyone else, these men became individuals, persons.[3] They could say "I" in a way never before heard in Israel. At the same time, it has become apparent that the "I" of which these men were allowed to become conscious was very different from our present-day concept of personality. For first of all, this process of becoming a person was marked by many strange experiences of compulsion, and one at least of its characteristics—we have only to think of the "be still"

---

[2] S. Herrmann, *Die Ursprünge der prophetischen Heilserwartung im Alten Testament*, Leipzig Dissertation 1957, pp. 65ff., 73ff.

[3] See above, pp. 76f. Eichrodt, *Theology*, p. 343.

in Isaiah's demand for faith—was passively to contemplate and make room for the divine action.[4] Yet, at the same time, this opened up freedom upon freedom for the prophet. He could even break out into an "exultation of the spirit" about this, as Micah once did when, as his *charisma* welled up gloriously within him, he became conscious of his difference from other people:

> But as for me, I am filled with power,
>   [with the spirit of Jahweh],
>   with justice and might,
> to declare to Jacob his transgression,
>   and to Israel his sin.
>
>   (Mic. III. 8)

There is a very direct reflexion of the prophets' attainment of personal identity and of their religious uniqueness in their style, the way in which they speak of God and of the things of God. During centuries of reverent speech Israel had created a language of the cult, and had devised a conventional phraseology for speaking about God; yet there were times when he might also be spoken of in the way these prophets loved to do—in monstrous similes, with an apparent complete absence of any feeling for dignity or propriety.[5] These were *ad hoc* inspirations, the provocative inventions of a single person, whose radical quality and extreme boldness was only justified by the uniqueness of a particular situation and the frame of mind of the people who listened to them.

Even if we knew still less than we in fact do of the way in which the concepts of Jahwism were still a living force at the shrines and among the broad mass of the people at the time when these prophets were active, one thing could yet be said for certain—the new feature in their preaching, and the one which shocked their hearers, was the message that Jahweh was summoning Israel before his judgment seat, and that he had in fact already pronounced sentence upon her: "The end has come upon my people Israel" (Am. VIII. 2). The question has recently been asked whether the prophets did not base even these pronouncements of judgment on older tradition. Were there ceremonies

---

[4] Eichrodt, *Theology*, p. 357.

[5] Jahweh, the barber (Is. VII. 20), the ulcer in Israel's body (Hos. V. 12), the unsuccessful lover (Is. V. 1ff.); see also below, p. 375.

in the cult at which Jahweh appeared as his people's accuser?[6] So far nothing definite has materialised; and an answer to this question would not in any way be a complete answer to the other question: why did the prophets proclaim this message? Moreover, the devastating force and finality of the prophetic pronouncement of judgment can never have had a cultic antecedent, for it envisaged the end of all cult itself.

For the proper understanding of what we have called this completely new note in the prophetic preaching, we have not least to remember the changing political situation, Assyria's increasingly obvious and steady advance towards Palestine. When in an almost stereotyped fashion Amos suggests that Jahweh's judgment will take the form of exile, this quite clearly reflects how much the Assyrians occupied his thoughts. The prophets are, however, obviously motivated not merely by one factor but by several. Let us simply say that these men spoke of the divine wrath as a fact, and designated as its proper object their contemporaries' whole way of life, their social and economic attitudes, their political behaviour and, in particular, their cultic practice. At all events, the favourite way of putting it, that this is simply the emergence of new religious ideas, and as such only a new understanding of the relationship between God and man, does not square with the fact that in this matter the prophets most decidedly took as their starting-point the old traditions of Jahwism. It was these that formed the foundation of their attack, and time and again the prophets took them as the basis of arguments with their audiences. Thus, as far as the old Jahwistic tradition was concerned, the prophets and their hearers were on common ground: but they differed in their interpretation of these traditions, which the prophets believed were far from ensuring Israel's salvation. The classic expression of this aspect of prophecy are Amos's words—her very election made the threat to Israel all the greater (Am. III. 1f.)! This is therefore the first occasion in Israel when "law" in the proper sense of the term was preached.[7] This is most apparent in the prophets' castigations of their fellow-countrymen for their anti-social behaviour, their commercial sharp-practice. Here they do not in any sense regard themselves as the revolutionary mouthpiece of one social group. Time and again we can see them

[6] So E. Würthwein, "Der Ursprung der prophetischen Gerichtsrede," in Z. Th. K., 49 (1952), pp. 1ff.; in a different way F. Hesse, "Wurzelt die prophetische Gerichtsrede im israelitischen Kult?" in Z.A.W., 64 (1953), pp. 45ff.

[7] See VOL. I, pp. 195ff.; see below, pp. 395ff.

applying provisions of the old divine law to the situation.[8] Isaiah uses much the same procedure when he measures the behaviour of the people of Jerusalem against the Zion tradition, and looks on armaments or security sought for in alliances as a rejection of the divine help. It is also used by Hosea when he takes the saving gift of the land, which Israel still completely failed to understand, as his starting-point, and uses it to show up the enormity of her faithlessness and ingratitude. Jahweh was known to be the judge of sinners in early Israel also; and early Israel was equally aware that a man's sin is more than the sum total of his several acts (Gen. III). Yet, the prophets' zeal in laying bare man's innate tendency to oppose God, their endeavour to comprehend Israel's conduct in its entirety, and to bring out what, all historical contingency apart, might be taken as typical of that conduct—this was something new, especially since its purpose was to give reasons for Jahweh's judgment. Thus, for example, Hosea included and discussed the whole story of the relationship between God and his people in his poem on Israel's failure to understand that the blessings of the soil of Canaan were gifts from Jahweh. This was a great intellectual achievement. The prophets' chief concern was not, of course, to summarise human conduct under the most general concepts possible by the method of abstraction, though this does sometimes happen[9]; they reached their goal in a different way. For while they seem to be describing only a particular failure of a particular group of men in a particular situation, they have really depicted, by their use of a few characteristic traits, something that was typical of Israel's general attitude to God.[10]

If when the prophets spoke about man, they seldom used general theological concepts, this may also be connected with the fact that they regarded their contemporaries as the product of a definite history. They

---

[8] See above, pp. 135f. H. -J. Kraus, "Die prophetische Botschaft gegen das soziale Unrechts Israels," in *Ev. Th.*, 15 (1955), pp. 295ff.

[9] Here one might think, for example, of Isaiah's characteristic reproach of pride (גבהות אדם Is. II. 11, 17) or of Hosea's equally characteristic term "spirit of harlotry" (רוח זנונים Hos. IV. 12, V. 4), or also of Amos's word about the "pride of Jacob" (גאון Am. VI. 8). The comprehensive term "return" and the statement that Israel does not return, also belong here. H. W. Wolff, "Das Thema 'Umkehr' in der alttestamentlichen Prophetie," in *Z. Th. K.*, XLVIII (1951), pp. 129ff.

[10] The courtly monologues which the prophets put into the mouth of foreign kings also belong to this tendency to make types, Is. X. 8ff., XIV. 13ff., XXXVII. 24, Ezek. XXVIII. 2, XXIX. 3, 9, XXVII. 3.

never took their hearers by themselves, standing in isolation in their opposition to God; those whom the prophets addressed were already "the offspring of evil-doers, corrupt sons" (Is. 1. 4), and this did not excuse them, but made their case utterly hopeless.

The way in which the prophets' charges occasionally plumb the depths of history is particularly characteristic; and this gave them the opportunity of radically reviewing the history of God's people. Of course, these extreme ideas do not claim to be universally valid: but the very arbitrariness of their formulation, their concentration on a single idea, makes them a wonderful testimony to an independent conception and understanding of history. Thus, Amos recounts a long series of divine interventions in Israel's history which caused disaster—drought, famine, blight and mildew, locusts, and disasters in war—all designed to bring the nation to its senses; but they failed to move her to repentance (Am. IV. 6-11). The series reads almost like a parody of the saving history, as if Amos wanted to contrast the generally accepted tradition with a completely different aspect of Jahweh's history with his people, one which, on this interpretation, was also a succession of drastic historical acts. In Isaiah Jahweh complains, in the manner of a father accusing his rebellious sons (Deut. xxi. 18-21), that he had "reared and brought up sons" (Is. 1. 2). These few words open up great vistas in the divine action in history. But the song of the vineyard is much fuller and even bolder in its metaphorical dress. Here Jahweh appears as the steadfast lover who devotes great care to his "vineyard" —"vineyard" is the cypher for "beloved" (Is. v. 1-7). While we should not give an allegorical interpretation to all his labours (digging the vineyard, clearing it of stones, building a watch-tower and a wine vat), the recapitulation of all that the lover did for his vineyard does give the hearer some idea of the patience and sense of purpose with which Jahweh tended Israel throughout her history. The picture of Jahweh as father reappears in Hosea, this time the father who taught Israel to walk like a little child and who loved her (Hos. XI. 1ff.).

Yet these ways of picturing the history, however bold and arbitrary they were, are not in themselves new. What is new is the verdict which the prophets passed on the history up to their own time, namely, that it was one great failure, and that at whatever page it was opened, it bore witness to Israel's refusal. These prophets did not hesitate to include even the figure of the patriarch Jacob within this revolutionary view (Hos. XII. 4f., 13 [3f., 12]); indeed, they took only the first steps along this road; Ezekiel, in particular, following their example, was to take in very much wider vistas still (Ezek. xx).

Jahweh was, however, to have further dealings with Israel; he did not intend to withdraw from her history because of this failure. On the contrary, something tremendous was standing at Israel's door. And this brings us to what is unquestionably the heart of the prophets' message. As was said in VOL. I, one of prophecy's greatest achievements was to recapture for faith the dimension in which Jahweh had revealed himself *par excellence*, that of history and politics.[11] Israel had always, of course, been occupied with the history of her past, but since about the time of David, she had increasingly written off Jahweh as her God as far as the present and the future were concerned; she had taken politics and the shaping of her future into her own hands. The saving history had come to a standstill; now it was rather a thing of the past to be looked back to with respect.[12] We can therefore well imagine the perplexity which these teachings on universal history given by the eighth-century prophets must have caused. They most certainly did not revive the old patriarchal conception of Jahweh's action in history, as this is seen in the accounts of his holy wars in the Book of Judges. The old sacral conception of history, particularly after the development of historiography during the enlightenment in the time of Solomon, had been superseded by a new way of looking at it. One of the most interesting aspects of the prophetic theology is that these men brought the maelstrom of world politics, which involved all nations, great and small, into contact with Jahweh's actions. Even a glance at the verses of Amos mentioned above (Am. IV. 6ff.) shows how completely the prophets were able to look on history in this new fashion—and it is most essentially history brought about by Jahweh; for these disasters (drought, famine, and plague) were acts of Jahweh though in a different sense: they were not miraculous, and they did not break the concatenation of events by means of something completely new—drought and famine can happen everywhere. Such historical acts of Jahweh, one might inevitably conclude, are harder for faith to recognise, because they participate at a deeper level in the ambiguity of all historical phenomena. The prophets, however, would flatly have denied this. Amos's poem is full of growing amazement at Israel's failure to understand this language which her God spoke in her history. Isaiah went even further in asserting that Jahweh's action in history is plain to see:

[11] See VOL. I, pp. 95f.   [12] See VOL. I, pp. 95, 69.

"In that day it will come to pass that Jahweh will whistle for the fly which is beyond the streams of Egypt and for the bee from the land of Assyria, and they will come and settle all together in ravines, in clefts of the rock, on thornbushes and on all the watering places.

"In that day the Lord will shave with a razor hired and chartered from beyond the Euphrates the head and the pubic hair . . ." (Is. VII. 18–20).

These are two saying from Isaiah's early period in which the prophet foretells the coming of the Assyrians to Palestine and the judgment which they will execute; and they can be regarded as characteristic expressions of classical prophecy, because their form and content are quite different from those of all earlier ways of speaking about Jahweh's action in history. The metaphorical dress—Jahweh summoning an empire by whistling for it as if it were an animal, Jahweh as a barber, borrowing a razor, an empire—speaks of God's absolute power in history. This power is so absolute that it seems as if there is room for no other activity in history.[13] When an ordinary individual is confronted with the might of an empire he can see nothing beyond it, and so is faced with the problem of reconciling its war-potential with God's omnipotence. The prophet sees things quite differently. The empires on the Tigris and the Nile are absolutely nothing; they are no more than a borrowed tool in the hand of Jahweh. Though it is true that from the beginning of the monarchical period Israel began to take a more secular and realistic view of history, this does not mean that history had correspondingly moved away from God. On the contrary: in the older historical tradition we look in vain for evidence of such a conception of God as is given here, one in which he fills the whole realm of history and reduces the mightiest factors of the political world to insignificance ("I, even I, rend and go away, I carry off, and none rescues," Hos. v. 14).

We may therefore describe the characteristic feature of the prophetic view of history as follows: not only does it recognise most clearly Jahweh's designs and intentions in history, it also sees the various historical forces involved in quite a different light from other people. The great powers which occupied the centre of the political stage did

[13] There is, however, a slight difference between the two logia. In the first Jahweh calls, and the unclean flies come and spread over the land. In the second Jahweh hires the razor and himself acts by its means. In the second case too all trace of "synergism" is ruled out. In the Ariel poem (Is. xxix) Jahweh is at the same time the one who attacks and humiliates Jerusalem (vss. 2–4), and the one who saves her (vss. 5–8).

not blind the prophets to God; these empires shrivel up almost into nothingness before Jahweh's all-pervasive power. It is the "I" spoken by Jahweh that pervades the historical field to its utmost limits. It is moving to see how Isaiah and his subjective certainty about his own view of history came into collision—a proof of its completely undogmatic flexibility and openness. As Assyria advanced, the interpretation he had put upon her as an instrument of punishment in the hands of Jahweh proved to be inadequate, or at least partial. The way in which she exterminated nations and the danger that she would treat Jerusalem and Judah in the same way gave rise to a question: did she not intend also to overrun Zion? Nevertheless, Isaiah was still able to interpret Jahweh's design; he explained the difficulty by saying that the Assyrians were exceeding the task assigned to them. The scope of their commission was merely to chastise, not to annihilate (Is. x. 5–7). This change in Isaiah's views is a further remarkable confirmation of the prophets' claim to be able to see history in its relation to God clearly and with perfect understanding. In Isaiah's view history can be analysed into the divine design and the co-efficient of arbitrary human power.[14] To come to this explanation—and we should make no mistake about this—Isaiah wrestled with the whole force of his intellect as well as of his faith. Written evidence of this expressly rational grappling with history is furnished by the generally accepted interpretation of the didactic poem in Is. XXVIII. 23–9, in which Isaiah makes the multifarious and carefully considered actions of the farmer's sowing and reaping into a transparent parable of the divine action in history. "Wonderful is his counsel and great his wisdom."[15]

So far, however, we have dealt almost too much with history in a general sense, with the result that misunderstanding could arise: it might be supposed that the prophets shared our concept of objective history. This is contradicted by the very fact that, as the prophets use the term, wherever history is spoken of, it is related in some sense to Israel. Even Isaiah's famous universalism still keeps to the idea that Jahweh directs history with reference to Israel. Yet, closer consideration of the prophecies of salvation shows that Jahweh's coming action in history upon Israel has still another peculiar characteristic. What comes in question here are not designs which Jahweh formed so to speak in perfect freedom, but only the fulfilment of promises he had already made to Israel in the old traditions. Whether we think of Hosea's

[14] See above, p. 163.   [15] See above, p. 163, n. 21

prophecy that Israel will once more be led into the wilderness and once more be brought through the valley of Achor into her own land (Hos. II. 16ff. [14ff.]), or of the prophecy that Jahweh will once more gather nations together against Zion, though he is again to protect it, or of the prophecies about the anointed one who is yet to come in Amos, Isaiah, and Micah, we everywhere see to what an extent even the prophets' predictions of the future are bound to tradition; and this in the sense that on the prophets' lips the coming and, as we may safely call them, eschatological events of salvation are to correspond to the earlier events as antitype and type. Thus, even in what they say about the future, the prophets function largely as interpreters of older traditions of Jahwism.

At the same time they introduce a fundamentally new element, which is that only the acts which lie in the future are to be important for Israel's salvation. The old traditions said that Jahweh led Israel into her land, founded Zion, and established the throne of David, and this was sufficient. No prophet could any longer believe this; for between him and those founding acts hung a fiery curtain of dire judgments upon Israel, judgments which, in the prophets' opinion, had already begun; and this message of judgment had no basis in the old Jahwistic tradition. They believed, therefore, that salvation could only come if Jahweh arose to perform new acts upon Israel, an event which they looked on as certain—and they entreated those who were still able to hear not to put their trust in illusory safeguards (Mic. III. 11), but to "look to" what was to come, and to take refuge in Jahweh's saving act, which was near at hand.[16] The prophets were therefore the first men in Israel to proclaim over and over again and on an ever widening basis that salvation comes in the shadow of judgment. It is only this prediction of a near divine action, with its close relation to old election traditions and its bold new interpretation of them, which can properly be defined as eschatological.[17] Everywhere there were pious hopes and confident statements about the continuance of the divine faithfulness. What the prophets foretold was something completely different theologically. They take as their basis the "No" pro-

[16] See above, pp. 160ff.

[17] See above, pp. 118f. and 239. The term "prophetic," too, urgently requires a suitable restriction. There is no profit in expanding it, as for example Vriezen does, so as to see what is prophetic as something implanted into Jahwism by Moses (*Outline*, pp. 137, 257f.). In my opinion, what is specific to the prophet only appears with the determination of his characteristic attitude towards tradition (see below, p. 299).

nounced by Jahweh on the Israel of their day, her relationship to Jahweh which had for long been hopelessly shattered. They were sure,
however, that beyond the judgment, by means of fresh acts, Jahweh
would establish salvation; and their paramount business was to declare
these acts beforehand, and not simply to speak about hope and confidence.

Summing up, it may be said that in regard to both their "preaching
of law" and their proclamation of salvation, the eighth-century prophets put Israel's life on completely new bases. The former can only be
seen in its true light when it is considered in relation to the latter. We
have already emphasised the fact that the prophets did not derive their
conviction that Jahweh purposed judgment from any special revelation,
independent of his saving acts, but from the old saving traditions themselves; thus, they interpreted the message in a way different not only
from their contemporaries but also from all earlier generations. For
them the traditions became law. Yet, they were not precursors of
legalism; they did not reproach their fellows with not living their lives
in obedience to law; their reproach was rather this, that as Jahweh's
own people they had continually transgressed the commandments and
not put their confidence in the offer of divine protection. How little
the prophets' work was aimed at a life lived under the yoke of the law
is made particularly clear in those places, which are, of course, few in
number, where they go beyond negative accusations to positive demands. "Seek good, and not evil; hate evil, love good!" "Seek Jahweh,
that you may live!" (Am. v. 14f., 6). This is not the language of a man
who wants to regulate life by law. In Amos's view, what Jahweh
desires from Israel is something very clear and simple; if not, how could
he have described it by the perfectly general term "good" (cp. also
Hos. VIII. 3; Is. v. 20; Mic. III. 2)? And listen to Micah. The prophet
answers the excesses in the performance of legal and cultic rites to
which Israel's anxiety was driving her: "he has showed you, O man,
what is good and what Jahweh seeks from you: to do justly, to love
kindness, and to walk humbly before Jahweh" (Mic. VI. 8).[18] This is

[18] The meaning of הצנע is not perfectly certain. The term seems to belong to the
language of Wisdom (Ecclesiasticus XVI. 25, XXXV. 3), and tends in the direction of the
idea of "measured." In his study, "Und demütig sein vor deinem Gott," in Wort und
Dienst, Jahrbuch der theologischen Schule Bethel, 1959, pp. 180ff., H. J. Stoebe also finds
the term principally in the language of Wisdom and translates it as "to be discerning,
circumspect."

the quintessence of the commandments as the prophets understood them. There is no demand here for "ethics" instead of a cult, as if the prophet's desire was to lead men from one set of laws into another. No, something quite simple is contrasted with the arduous performance of works which can end only in destruction—a way along which men can walk before God. Exactly the same is true of the verse in Hosea which "reads like the programme of an opposition party," to the effect that what counts with Jahweh is not the offering of the proper sacrifices, but "loyalty to the covenant and knowledge of God" (Hos. vi. 6). The vow which this same prophet puts into the mouth of those who turn to Jahweh is given in negative terms, doubtless because it follows a literary category used in worship, but in principle it takes the same line. It does not expect the fulfilment of a legal demand:

> Assyria shall not save us, we will not ride upon horses;
> and we will say no more "Our God" to the work of our hands.
>
> (Hos. xiv. 4 [3])[19]

Isaiah says practically nothing about the inner disposition of the purified remnant, with the result that it is not easy to imagine what this is. The remnant is composed of those from whom Jahweh has not hidden his face (Is. viii. 17), those who have had faith. On one occasion he calls those who take refuge in Zion "the poor of his people" (Is. xiv. 32).

The eighth-century prophets were, of course, only the first to tread this new theological path. Their successors were to go further along it, and in particular were to have still more to say about the question of the new obedience. In general they were to take up the topics they inherited and to develop them in their own way; but they were also to enrich the prophetic preaching with new topics which for eighth-century prophecy had not as yet appeared on the horizon.

[19] The negative formulation of the confession corresponds to model confessional formulations; von Rad, *Ges. St.*, p. 292.

CHAPTER D

THE AGE OF JEREMIAH

I. THE TRANSITION TO THE BABYLONIAN ERA
(NAHUM, HABAKKUK AND ZEPHANIAH)

THE Assyrian empire, which had for so long threatened the Kingdom of Judah, finally collapsed ninety years after Jerusalem capitulated to the army of Sennacherib. To those who witnessed it, the collapse was extremely swift; for in *c*. 664, which saw the subjugation of Egypt, Assyria seemed to have reached the zenith of her power. In 612 Nineveh fell to a coalition of the Babylonians, who had sometime earlier thrown off Assyria's yoke, of the Medes, who had recently appeared on the political scene, and of a horse-riding people from Scythia. To be sure, Assyria was not dashed in pieces before the gates of Zion, as Isaiah imagined that she would be; on the other hand, she never came to the point of incorporating Judah into her provincial system. It would be perfectly astonishing if such an epoch-making event as the downfall of Assyria remained unechoed in the pages of the prophets, the keen-sighted observers of all the changes in the political scene.

The man who was first inspired by this event was Nahum, and in some poems of more than ordinary magnificence he celebrated it as a judgment of Jahweh on the "bloody city" (Nah. III. 1). The little book is perfectly attuned to the mood of joy and satisfaction evoked by Jahweh's manifestation of himself in the world as the avenger of wrong. The book contains only a single word directed to Judah herself, and this by the "messenger who brings good tidings" who exhorts her to be aware of the hour of feasting before Jahweh (Nah. II. 1 [I. 15]). Nahum has often been accused of being unlike his near contemporaries among the prophets in saying not a word about the sins of the people of God itself. This would only be remarkable if the prophets as a body were the spokesmen of a single idea—that of ethical monotheism, or of a general moral relationship between God and man. But if we understand that their preaching was completely dependent on the historical events of the hour, this criticism does not apply to Nahum, just as when times of cultic feast are distinguished from those of cultic fast, those to be presumed responsible are the men who thus interpreted such specific time.[1] Nahum is the only prophet who may possibly have had a function within the framework of the cult. His message, too, though it has at least intimate connexions with the literary category of oracles against foreign nations, can be seen as following the traditional threats against the enemies of God's people used in a sacral ceremony.[2] As far as the absence of words of judgment against his own people is concerned, it must also be remembered that Nahum's prophetic message very probably dates from the time of Josiah, and in the period after the "discovery" (II Kings XXIIf.), that is, after the reform, a time which perhaps the prophets as well as the king looked on as having made a return to Jahweh which held promise for the future.

It is easy to see in retrospect that this joyous hour was soon over. In 609 Josiah was defeated and killed by Necho; Judah was thus brought under Egyptian domination for the first time, though we know next to nothing about the political effects of this. Only a few years later, in 605, the Egyptians were defeated by Nebuchadnezzar, and this victory made the neo-Babylonians masters of Palestine too (II Kings XXIV. 7). Jehoiakim, the successor of Josiah, was, however, an unreliable vassal, and as a result his land suffered greatly at the hands of the Babylonian armies (II Kings XXIV. 1f.).

It is very probably within this period, that is, 609–597, that Habakkuk was active. The first part of his prophecy (Hab. I. 2 – II. 4) consists of an almost liturgical dialogue between the prophet and Jahweh. The prophet twice lays a complaint before Jahweh, and Jahweh twice answers him.[3] The first complaint tells of wrongs and violence; the *torah* "grows cold," and the wicked lie in wait for the righteous (Hab. I. 2–4). It is hard to say whether this complaint is a reference to oppression by enemies within or by enemies without. It is given a most surprising answer: Jahweh says: Be astounded! now am I arousing a terrible

[1] See above, p. 103.

[2] Recently the little book of Nahum has been frequently interpreted along these lines, especially by P. Humbert, "Le problème du livre de Nahoum," in *Revue d'histoire et de philosophie religieuses*, XII, 1932, pp. 1ff.

Help towards the understanding of the oracles against foreign nations has come from notice of the connexion between Am. I. 3ff. and the ceremonial of the sacral execration of enemies in Old Egypt. A. Bentzen, "The ritual background of Amos I. 2 – II. 16," in *Oudtestamentliche Studien*, VII (1950), pp. 85ff.

[3] The liturgical character of Hab. I. 2 – II. 4 has often been emphasised; yet, what comes in question here is probably only a "prophetic" liturgy, *i.e.*, not a liturgy deriving directly from the cult, but the prophetic imitation of a cultic form.

people, the Chaldeans (the neo-Babylonians, Hab. I. 5–11). The prospect here opened up by the divine words, that worse is still to come,
that the enigmas of the divine guidance of history are to grow even
darker, takes the prophets completely by surprise.[4] This leads to a
further complaint: how can Jahweh behold so much iniquity and not
intervene? In this case the "wicked" who swallows up the "righteous"
is certainly a foreign power. Men fall into his nets like fish. The way in
which he makes idols of his instruments of war ("therefore he sacrifices
to his net and burns incense to his seine," vs. 16) is absurd. Jahweh again
answers, with a word which is to be written down, because it is not to
be fulfilled at once; indeed, postponement of fulfilment is to be reckoned
with from the very start; whatever happens, "the righteous shall live
by his faith" (Hab. II. 1–4). Recent critics have argued that this cannot
be the full account of a "vision" which was given such an elaborate
introduction and which was obviously very comprehensive, and they
suggest that the theophany described in ch. III, a tremendous picture
of Jahweh arising to do battle with the nations and with the wicked
one (vs. 13), should also be considered.

Apart from one or two unsolved problems, Habakkuk's prophecy
yet shows several characteristic features. The reader who comes to it by
way of Amos, Micah, or Isaiah cannot but be surprised at the change
which has come over the prophet's relationship to Jahweh. The roles
seem to be reversed: the initiative lies with the prophet, for it is he who
is discontented and impatient, while Jahweh is the one who is questioned.
It is, of course, possible that prophets who were commissioned to act
primarily within the cult always made intercession and were recipients
of divine answers: but it is open to question whether Habakkuk's
prophecy can be classified as cultic. One thing is certain: the way in
which he puts his questions and the kind of trials he suffered show
Habakkuk to be a child of his own age. The topics of the relationship
between Jahweh and the Monarchy during its final period and of the
prophetic attitude to theological problems of the time are ones to
which we must return later.[5] Meanwhile we must consider the answer

---

[4] Unfortunately the translation of the last verse of this oracle, on which it is possible
that the understanding of the whole unit largely depends, is not certain. With a slight
emendation F. Horst renders: "they, whose own might was their god, withdraw and
make atonement" (*H.A.T.*, *in loc.*). This would indicate future punishment of this
nation of whom use was made.

[5] See below, pp. 266f. Cp. also VOL. I, pp. 391ff.

Habakkuk received to his complaint. In the first place, it is not in any sense a comforting one (has Jahweh destroyed an old cultic form here?). Jahweh is on the point of shaping history even more ominously. (In Jeremiah we shall meet with a similar instance of cavalier treatment given to a prophet's question.) But those who hold fast to Jahweh will be saved. What Habakkuk says here about the saving power of faith (אמונה) sounds like an echo of the prophecy of Isaiah, particularly since Habakkuk also speaks mysteriously of Jahweh's imminent "work" (פעל Hab. III. 2), and thus suggests that Jahweh will appear to do battle with his foes. But Habakkuk differs from Isaiah in that he mingles the very ancient *motif* that Jahweh will appear from the south with a *motif* taken from Canaanite mythology—Baal–Hadad's battle with the powers of chaos.

Zephaniah also is chiefly concerned with the imminent advent of Jahweh and a universal battle against the nations on this day: but with him very much more emphasis is laid upon the resulting judgment of Jerusalem and threats against the complacent (Zeph. I. 10–13).[6]

There was, however, a contemporary of Habakkuk and Zephaniah whose preaching covered a very much wider field, and whose task it was to explore new realms in the relationship between Jahweh and Israel and to mark out new theological horizons such as Israel had never before suspected.

2. JEREMIAH

Jeremiah received his call to be a prophet in the year 627–626, and, characteristically, there is a close connexion between this and events on the world political scene—trouble was to come from the north and to threaten Palestine among other places (Jer. I. 13ff.). It is uncertain whether this is an early reference to the neo-Babylonians who, in 625 under Nebopolassar, had made themselves independent of Assyria. In actual fact, thanks to Assyria's collapse and the appearance of the Scythians and the Medes, the situation in Mesopotamia had become dangerously fluid. From the very beginning of his life as a prophet this foe from the north was a determinative factor in Jeremiah's predictions, and it continued to be so amid all the many political exigencies of which the Babylonians were the authors in the years that followed, right down to the time when Jeremiah fell silent. This is the first factor upon which the prophecy of Jeremiah depends. The other derives not from

[6] On Zephaniah's prophecy about the Day of Jahweh, see above, pp. 122f.

politics, but from tradition. Jeremiah came from a priestly family which lived in Anathoth. Near relatives of his were landowners there (Jer. xxxii. 6ff.). Though the village lay only a few miles north-east of Jerusalem, it belonged to the tribe of Benjamin. Benjamin was the son of Jacob by Rachel. Yet if she, and not Leah, was the ancestress of Jeremiah (Jer. xxxi. 15), we may at once assume that the traditions cherished both in Benjamin and in Ephraim were those specific to Israel, those of the Exodus and the covenant at Sinai, which we have to differentiate from the traditions of Judah. Once aware of this distinction, the reader who comes to Jeremiah from, say, Isaiah enters a different theological world. The Zion tradition which was determinative for the whole of Isaiah's prophecy has no place whatsoever in Jeremiah; in contrast, what resounds there—even in the prophecies of salvation—are the Exodus, Covenant, and Conquest traditions. No doubt, after his call the scene of Jeremiah's work was Jerusalem; here he had to deal even with kings, and here he also met the sacral tradition of David.[7] He took this seriously, and he used it from time to time in his prophecy. But the limited way in which he employs it, as compared with the predominance of Israelite traditions, makes it plain that here was something quite alien to Jeremiah. There is a further factor. In his early years, Jeremiah was dependent on Hosea. This dependence extends even to his choice of words, and far transcends what was traditional among the prophets, which was at most a dependence in subject matter. This forces us to assume that Jeremiah had close contacts with Hosea's disciples, and possibly even that he had a thorough knowledge of the writing which Hosea left behind. And, as we have already seen, Hosea stood exclusively within the Israelite tradition.

Had these two basic preconditions of Jeremiah's prophecy been all that had to be taken into account, then—making due allowance for various special features either personal or historical—we should have expected from Jeremiah a message fundamentally similar on the whole to that of Isaiah, Micah, or Amos. But this is far from being the case. The actual differences need more than a sentence to describe them; they go to the very heart of this prophet's message and find the most varied forms of expression in specific passages, with the result that we can only proceed step by step to their nearer definition.

One way of determining the special elements in Jeremiah's prophecy

[7] M. Sekine, "Davidsbund und Sinaibund bei Jeremia," in *Vet. Test.*, ix (1959), pp. 47ff.

is, again, by the examination of literary categories. In fact, the radical differences between the form of Jeremiah's preaching and that of earlier prophets is in itself enough to justify the conclusion that the substance of his message must also have been peculiarly his own. The category of diatribe and threat, which was formerly the prominent one, falls into the background—it is quite remarkable how seldom Jeremiah delivers a message he has received from God tersely and objectively, as for example in the "messenger formula" form. Further, the line which previously had been so clearly drawn between the prophet's own words and the actual words of God begins to disappear. Jeremiah makes much freer use of divine words spoken in the first person; he makes Jahweh launch forth into long complaints, and in other places he raises his own voice to utter most comprehensive complaints. Where is this to be found in Isaiah or Amos? We meet in Jeremiah— perhaps for the first time—with what we to-day should describe as lyric poetry. It is because of this as much as anything that his preaching has such a uniquely personal note. To put it briefly: in Jeremiah all the forms of expression to be found in classical prophecy are obviously breaking up. It would, of course, be stupid to view this process solely from its negative and destructive aspect, and then go on to describe Jeremiah as "in decline" as compared with Isaiah. It is far more important to discover the co-efficient in Jeremiah's prophecy which provides the background for these changes in form, what it was that brought them about, that demanded the creation of new forms for its proper self-expression.[8]

1. Jeremiah's preaching in his early years (Jer. I–VI) may be summarised thus: disaster is coming from the north upon an Israel which has forsaken the worship of Jahweh and given herself up to the worship of Baal. We must, however, notice particularly the outward form which Jeremiah gave this message, for such a statement of its content is far from giving an idea of its real characteristic quality.

The very first major unit (Jer. II. 1–13) is quite characteristic. Jahweh remembers the time of Israel's first love: he defends himself, just as a

[8] A relatively large strand of the Jeremiah tradition bears the marks of the influence of Deuteronomy and the Deuteronomists; i.e., it is dependent on the Deuteronomistic terminology and is in prose. For prophetic diction, the latter suggests in principle secondary redaction. The passages in question are (according to Rudolph, H.A.T., p. xvi) the following passages: Jer. VII. 1 – VIII. 3, XI. 1–14, XVI. 1–13, XVII. 19–27, XVIII. 1–12, XXI. 1–10, XXII. 1–5, XXV. 1–14, XXXIV. 8–22, XXXV.

man on trial might do, by appealing to the kindnesses he did her as he led her through the wilderness into the promised land (vss. 5–7). After the settlement, however, Israel forsook Jahweh. But who has ever heard of a people changing its God? The passage culminates in the paradox that Israel's apostasy runs absolutely contrary to common sense. There is no precedent for it in the whole world (vss. 10f.). In the next two units also (Jer. II. 14–19, 20–8) Jeremiah again starts from the fact that Israel has forsaken her God. This apostasy has its roots in the far distant past (מעולם vs. 20a). This same point of view—the divine— is again expressed in the image of the choice vine planted by Jahweh: what Israel ruined was a design with a far-reaching historical effect; but by falling away to Baal she put herself outside the reach of all that Jahweh had been trying to do for her. Yet, how was this possible? Can a maiden forget her ornaments? "Yet my people have forgotten me days without number" (vs. 32). In human marriage a woman who for-sakes her present husband is legally forbidden to go back to her former one; how then could Israel annul her divorce from Jahweh (Jer. III. 1–5)? There is in fact still something belonging to a more primitive time in the way in which the young Jeremiah places Israel's whole failure in the sphere of the cult, at the altar, and how he still thinks in cultic categories. (For example, in Jer. III. 2f. the reasoning is still com-pletely sacral—the land was polluted because of worship which was an abomination to Jahweh, with the result that in return the rain was with-held from it.) Much less space is given to reproof for breaking legal enactments than to complaints against Israel's cultic apostasy (Jer. II. 8b, v. 1f., vi. 6b, vii. 27f., XIII. 27). Jer. IV. 5 – VI. 30 is a collection of prophecies, in the form of discursive poems, speaking of an enemy from the north, a mysterious horse-ridnig people which is to chastise the nation's forgetfulness of God and punish the many offences it has committed in the sight of Jahweh.[9]

In trying to grasp the precise content of Jeremiah's preaching in the

[9] Even to-day these poems are still sometimes connected with the "Scythians," though it has become more and more a question whether they can be connected with what appears to be the rather legendary account given by Herodotus (I. 105) of the Scythians' incursion into Palestine (between 630 and 625). Cp. Eissfeldt, "Das Skythen-problem," in H.A.T., I, 14 (Die zwölf kleinen Propheten, 2nd edn., 1954), pp. 188f., and W. Rudolph, Jeremia (H.A.T., 2nd edn., 1958), pp. 44f. These have made the enemy envisaged by Jeremiah quite uncertain. It may be that he thought of a speedy advance of the Neo-Babylonians even into Palestine.

first phase of his activity we come upon one remarkable fact—political prediction and the threat of judgment which earlier prophets had outlined so clearly is very much less prominent. In Jer. II. 1–13 it is entirely absent; all that the passage contains is Jahweh's complaint, and reflexions on the incomprehensibility of Israel's apostasy. In Jer. II. 14–19 it is certainly said that Judah is bringing chastisement upon herself by her apostasy (vs. 19), and in Jer. II. 36 that Jahweh will also disappoint the confidence that was being placed in Egypt. Not, however, until we come to the war poems in Jer. IV. 5 – VI. 26 do we find genuine prediction in the old prophetic style concerning a nation running headlong towards judgment (Jer. IV. 5f., 13, V. 15–17); yet these show at the same time a particularly clear impression of Jeremiah's own characteristic stamp. Strange to say, the express threats cannot be called the climax of these poems, or their real subject. This is clear from the very fact that they do not come at the end, as the goal to which everything is moving. Rather, they are embedded in cries of alarm, descriptions of the misery which the war brings over the land, laments, exhortations to repent, and reflexions on the enormity of the nation's offences, and they form an inseparable whole with all these. If, then, we ask what these poems say, it is at once apparent that they contain very much more than invective or the announcement of impending judgment. Jeremiah's speech has a strong tendency to become diffuse, and it has epic and even dramatic qualities. No doubt both in their diatribes and their threats Amos or Isaiah, like Jeremiah, not only announced what was to come, but also on occasion gave a very graphic description of it, even if it was generally only a thumbnail sketch. With Jeremiah, however, firstly this descriptive element occupies a much larger place, and secondly—this is still more important—it has a very characteristic theological tendency: the dominant feeling is that of complaint and suffering. In Jer. II. 1–13 there are utterances on the subject of God's feelings of yearning for his lost people, his sense of injustice, and his emotions of dismay at the exchange of gods. Thus, what is said about Israel's apostasy is not said directly, but we derive knowledge of it rather at second hand, from the divine complaint, and this is all that there is to it. The complaint is therefore in no sense the prelude to a word of judgment, but stands in its own right. The case is practically the same with the war poems in chs. IV. 5 – VI. 26, the only difference being that here it is the prophet's own pain that serves as a mirror.

OTT O

> My anguish, my anguish! I must writhe in pain!
> Oh, the walls of my heart! My heart is beating wildly; I cannot
>   keep silent;
> My soul hears the sound of the trumpet, the alarm of war.
>
> (Jer. IV. 19)

This is a cry with which Jeremiah interrupts the description of the coming war, but in fact it is not a real interruption at all, for elsewhere also the distress is portrayed through the medium of the prophet's soul and its suffering.

> I looked on the earth, and lo, chaos . . .
>   I looked on the mountains, and lo, they were quaking . . .
> I looked, and lo, there was no man . . .
>   I looked, and lo, the fruitful land was desert. . . .
>
> (Jer. IV. 23–6)

Here too the future is described wholly from the standpoint of a man who is feeling its pain before it takes place, and it is as much as he can bear. Compared with this, how objective and detached the earlier prophets' announcements seem, even when they were spoken with very deep feeling! In Jeremiah we are conscious of a prophet's feeling of solidarity with his people in their danger, and even with the land itself in hers, such as we shall never meet with again.

Finally, it must be said that in this first phase of his activity, Jeremiah was still far from regarding Jahweh's relationship to Jerusalem and Judah as broken for good and all. He envisaged severe testing. Yet, be the danger ever so great, Jahweh had so far "not torn his soul away from Jerusalem." Because of this, the prophet's task was "to give Jerusalem warning" (Jer. VI. 8). We therefore find the literary category of "exhortation" used more frequently in this earliest section than anywhere else. Jerusalem is to wash her heart from wickedness, and then she will be saved (Jer. IV. 14). What is needed is that the fallow ground be broken up, and no seed sown among thorns—or rather, the circumcision of the heart (Jer. IV. 3f.). Jeremiah attached particular hopes to the "repentance" of the Northern Kingdom (Jer. III. 6ff.), though in this he perhaps shared a hope which everyone cherished during the reign of Josiah.

2. There is good reason for believing that Jeremiah was silent in the years which followed Josiah's reform (621). We may well assume that

his attitude at this time was at least one of goodwill, all the more so since this was the king of whom he was later to speak in more than usually appreciative terms (Jer. XXII. 15f.). The reason for this break in his activity is not, however, sufficiently clear to allow us to take it as the basis for definite conclusions as to his attitude towards the "Deuteronomic" reform.[10] After Josiah's ill-starred death Jehoiakim succeeded to the throne, and he was unhappily in every respect the very reverse of his predecessor. Immediately we find Jeremiah active once more. To a people which pays no heed to the decalogue, even the temple itself has no security to offer—so Jeremiah proclaims in his famous temple address (Jer. VII. 1–15). Jahweh has earlier shown that he can utterly destroy a shrine with a long and honourable history (Shiloh). What worth does a shrine have if men who hold Jahweh's commandments in contempt think that they can find security there! This ruthlessness, which does stop short of criticising the holiest of things, and shatters in pieces all pious attempts to attain security, sets Jeremiah completely in line with the classical prophecy of the eighth century. But while the source which gives Jeremiah's own words does no more than report the address itself, a further account by a second hand adds a number of details, in particular those concerning the perils and hostility incurred by the prophet as the result, and from which he was only delivered by the intervention of certain Judeans from the country districts (Jer. XXVI. 10). This is the one case in the prophets where we have the benefit of both a prophet's own account of an incident and that of a narrator. The conjunction is not, however, coincidental; for this shift of the centre of interest from the message to the messenger is in fact characteristic of the whole tradition connected with Jeremiah. The earlier prophets had also been repeatedly exposed to hostile threats. With Jeremiah these apparently took on a more menacing aspect. This is not itself important. What is important is the change in the idea of what went to make a prophet; and from this arose a growing interest in the prophet's life as well as in his message, and in the complications in which his message involved him. It began to be appreciated that the two were very closely

[10] The situation is rather different in the case of the much discussed question of Jeremiah's attitude to Deuteronomy. It is unlikely that Jeremiah could have come out forthrightly against the digest and "codification" of the will of Jahweh as ancient tradition had handed it on and as this was published in Deuteronomy. H. H. Rowley thinks that he agreed with it at the beginning, but that he later criticised it (*Studies in Old Testament Prophecy*, Edinburgh 1950, pp. 157ff.).

connected. Jer. xix. 1 – xx. 6 is a good example of this new interest.[11]
Jeremiah had broken an earthen flask in the sight of certain men, and
had said that Jahweh would break the nation and the city in exactly the
same way. The narrative goes on to report that as a result of this
incident Jeremiah was beaten by the chief officer Passhur and put in the
stocks for a night; and this is part of the original account, not the
insertion of a redactor.

Though the temple address was in the form of an exhortation
directed to a nation which wanted to find safety in an illusory security,
its ending leaves open only the prospect of complete rejection. The
verses which follow also forbid the prophet to intercede, for Jahweh is
to reject the "generation of his wrath" (Jer. vii. 29); even those who
survive the catastrophic events will long for death (Jer. viii. 3). This has
a much sterner ring than anything in Jeremiah's earlier prophecies. In
the same way also, the liturgy for the great drought ends with an
appalling word of judgment which leaves all pleas for mercy unheeded
(Jer. xv. 1ff.). The oracle on the jars says that it is to be Jahweh himself
who fills the nation, even the priests and prophets and kings, with
drunkenness, so that they end by destroying themselves (Jer. xiii.
12–14). In this connexion, Jeremiah was thinking of events that were
soon to come to pass, plundering by enemies (Jer. xvii. 3), slaughter
of the young men (Jer. xv. 8f.), and exile (Jer. x. 18, xiii. 8–10, xvii. 4).

Yet, even although Jeremiah realised that Jerusalem was apparently
to be finally rejected, this did not prevent him from occasionally
speaking as if there were still hope, as if it were still possible for the
nation to be reached, as though there could still be a decision "before it
grows dark, before your feet stumble on the twilight mountains, while
you hope for light; but he turns it into gloom" (Jer. xiii. 16). Jeremiah's
revelation at the potter's workshop also belongs here. For Jahweh's
words as the prophet watched the potter knead the spoiled vessels together in order to remould new ones from the lump, "can I not do
with you as this potter has done?" are really only a question, and they
leave the door still open for the call to repentance (Jer. xviii. 1ff.).

(In this last passage, the content is somewhat obscure, and this detracts
from its impressiveness. In the opening verses Jeremiah is dealing with
his own people who, by being shown the immense freedom at God's
disposal, are to take warning. Then, however, it suddenly passes over
into general terms. If Jahweh has purposed evil against a particular

---

[1] Vss. 2b–9 and 12–13 can be seen to be later additions.

nation, and it "turns," then he repents of the trouble he intended to cause; and if he has purposed good for another nation, but it is disobedient, then he will alter his design and punish it. This part, too, is meant to indicate Jahweh's freedom as he directs history, but it does this in an oddly theoretical way by giving imaginary examples which are quite contrary to the sense of the passage, for they almost make Jahweh's power dependent on law rather than on freedom. This middle passage (vss. 7–10), after which Judah is once more addressed, should probably be regarded as a theological expansion.)

Jeremiah did not threaten only his own nation with disaster. There is a collection of oracles in which he prophesies the destruction of a number of foreign nations (the Egyptians, Philistines, Moabites, Ammonites, Edomites, Syrians, Arabs, Elamites, and Babylonians).[12] The disasters which these oracles picture are always those of war: but, oddly enough, the power which is the source of such destructive effects remains almost completely obscure.[13] These oracles thus all the more emphatically see Jahweh at work; it is he himself who acts; his is the sword that is to rage against these nations. Since these oracles contain still further elements which derive from the usage of the old holy wars,[14] it becomes all the more probable that this form, the war oracle, belongs to the earliest prophetic tradition. This was the way in which the prophets of Israel who functioned in these wars had once actually spoken when Israel—or rather, Jahweh—went into battle against the foe. The passage of time had brought considerable changes over the category, and it had become detached from its original context, Israel's sacral warfare; its horizons widened to embrace universal history, for it now addresses nations with whom ancient Israel had never had dealings in her wars. Jeremiah's oracles against foreign nations very nearly comprise a judgment on the whole world. The element of reproof of the arrogance and godless self-confidence of the foreign nations (Jer. XLVI. 7f., XLVIII. 1f., 7, 14, 42, XLIX. 4) probably only derives from the ideas of a later period, that of classical prophecy, but others which come down from the earliest tradition have maintained their place with an astonishing tenacity. This early tradition is the only possible explanation

[12] Jer. XXV. 15–38, XLVI–LI. In the latter, the oracles against Babylon (Jer. I.f.) are certainly post-Jeremianic.

[13] According to XLVII. 2, the enemy comes from the north; only in XLIX. 2 is Nebuchadnezzar mentioned by name.

[14] On the summons to do battle or to flee, see above, p. 36, n. 6.

of the prediction that Jahweh is to do battle in person and of the vague
language used in the poems to speak about the human instrument of
judgment—Babylon was undoubtedly in Jeremiah's mind.

Thus, like his predecessors, Jeremiah looked into the future and
noticed the movements on the horizon of universal history. Nor does
he fall short of them in the boldness with which he interpreted events,
or the certainty with which he saw Jahweh taking the most direct
action. However, while with Amos or Isaiah we can grasp all the
essentials of their preaching simply by looking at what they have to
say about the future, with Jeremiah the case is different; for, as well as
predictions, there are a great many passages which deal exclusively with
the present, and which are particularly characteristic of this prophet.

> Grief rises within me,
>   my heart is sick within me.
> Hark, cries for help of the daughter of my people from the length
>   and breadth of the land:
> "Is Jahweh not on Zion,
>   is her king not in her?"
> Why have they provoked me with their images,
>   their foreign vanities?
> The harvest is past,
>   the summer is ended and no help has come for us.
> Because of the wound of the daughter of my people am I wounded.
>   I mourn, and dismay has taken hold of me.
> Is there no balm in Gilead,
>   is there no physician there?
> Why is there no healing for the daughter of my people?
> O that my head were waters,
>   my eyes a fountain of tears,
> that I might weep day and night for the slain of the daughter of my
>   people!
>
> (Jer. VIII. 18–23 [VIII. 18 – IX. 1.])

It is impossible to classify this passage under any specific literary
category. There are certainly echoes of a community lament and of
something like an answer from Jahweh (vs. 19); but these are perceived
only, as it were, from the outside; whereas the very first sentence
places us inside Jeremiah's thought, and this is where all the essential
action takes place. Here, first, is the realisation of a calamity overtaking

the land; the prophet looks for deliverance; then it becomes clear to him that all is lost; and he finally expresses the wish that he could weep out his eyes in tears of grief. This is the "event" of which we are told! How far is this prophetic proclamation? Verses such as these in fact come very close to being what we describe as free lyric poetry. This again shows us that Jeremiah is much more keenly inflamed, and in an entirely novel way, by a poetic impulse which exists quite independently from prophecy. It also raises the question of how we are to evaluate this remarkably large increase of the element of pure poetry. The answer might, of course, be that the essential element of prophecy in Jeremiah was weakened by his yielding to the poetic impulse: it could also be that this apparent weakness gave his words a new strength. Those who took the view that these passages mark the first appearance of a free, personal *ego* and that Jeremiah is the father of free, personal prayer, found this question relatively simple; and there is, of course, an element of truth in their theory. But it is very doubtful whether it does justice to the special character of these passages. Because of the special nature of God's relationship with Israel, and particularly with Jeremiah, it is probable *a priori* that the specific form of these passages and their message can only be understood in the light of their specific preconditions.

3. This also comes out, much more clearly, in those passages which, while still being laments, do not remain pure monologue, but rise to the level of conversation with Jahweh. They are usually called *Jeremiah's Confessions*. In form and content, of course, they vary considerably. Their common factor is that they are not addressed to men, as is the case with divine oracles, but are a result of Jeremiah's own musings with himself and with God. It has long been recognised that the form and style of these most private utterances of the prophet are more or less closely linked with the ancient literary category of the individual lament.[15] It is therefore quite fascinating to watch the way in which, as occasion arose, Jeremiah interpenetrated the conventional usage of the old cultic form with his own concerns as a prophet, and transformed it. The poem which most closely adheres to the traditional usage is Jer. XI. 18–23. It contains a complaint about attacks on the prophet himself,

[15] W. Baumgartner, *Die Klagegedichte Jeremias*, Bei. *Z.A.W.*, 32 (1917). H. J. Stoebe, "Seelsorge und Mitleiden bei Jeremia," henceforth cited as "Seelsorge," in *Wort und Dienst* (*Jahrbuch der theologischen Schule Bethel*) 1955, pp. 116ff. The texts in question are Jer. XI. 18–23, XII. 1–6, XV. 10–12, 15–21, XVII. 12–18, XVIII. 18–23, XX. 7–18.

and a plea that the one to whom he has committed his cause should protect him. It is a prayer which might have been made by anyone suffering persecution. This cannot however be said of the prayer contained in Jer. xv. 10–18. This, too, includes many of the conventional requests: but they are so intimately expressed that they can only have come from Jeremiah's personal experience.

> Words coming from thee were found, so I ate them.
> Thy word became to me a joy and the delight of my heart;
> I was called by thy name, Jahweh, God of hosts!
> I do not sit rejoicing in the company of the merrymakers,
> bowed down by thy hand, I sit alone;
> for thou hast filled me with indignation.   (Jer. xv. 16–17)

God then answered this complaint. This itself corresponded with the normal order of events in the liturgy; for there, through the mouthpiece of the priest, Jahweh answered a prayer of lamentation with an "oracle of weal."[16] Here, however, where it is no longer a cultic ritual form, there is a change—Jahweh answers with a rebuke; indeed, when Jahweh reaffirms the great promises he made to Jeremiah at the time of his call—on condition that the prophet returns to him—he tells Jeremiah that he has betrayed his prophetic calling. But if he does return, Jeremiah may once more "stand before God" and "serve [him] as his mouthpiece" (vs. 19).

Jer. xii. 1–5, too, contains a question and answer conversation between God and the prophet. Jeremiah wants to plead his case before Jahweh; yet, in the very first words, he gives up his whole case— "Jahweh is always in the right." The prophet's subject is the prosperity of the godless, whose chain of success seemed secure in every link. Here Jeremiah is undoubtedly contributing to a question which occupied his whole generation. How is the individual's share in Jahweh's gifts apportioned?[17] The question has become personally important for Jeremiah, for he has burnt his boats far more than others, and his dependence on Jahweh has made his life one of danger and solitude. Here too God's answer is a stern one:

> If you run with men on foot, and they weary you,
>   how can you compete with horses?
> And if you only feel safe in a land at peace,
>   how will you fare in the jungle of Jordan?   (Jer. xii. 5)

---

[16] See VOL. I., pp. 401ff.   [17] See VOL. I., pp. 400ff.

Jahweh demolishes the prophet's question with a counter question. The answer shows amazement that Jeremiah is threatening to founder on such difficulties, for they are as nothing compared with what he ought to be able to bear. It is pointed out that he is still only at the threshold of his trials, and that, as Jahweh's prophet, he ought not already to be complaining about such problems.

Jeremiah probably discussed the trials of his office with Jahweh in this way throughout his life. He was given special commissions; for example, he was appointed a gleaner (Jer. VI. 9), that is to say, he was to look for the unnoticed fruits of goodness. His answer was that it was useless to make such a search. On another occasion God gave him the task of going about amongst his people as an assayer, to test, as is done in a refinery, whether the dross could be separated from the pure metal; but again his answer was that it was impossible (Jer. VI. 27-30). One thing stands out—both the passages in which Jeremiah holds converse with God and those in which he alone is the speaker always shade off into darkness, the impossibility of the prophet's task. There is not one single instance of hope, no occasion when he gives thanks to Jahweh for granting him redemptive insight or for allowing him some success. What a difference from the defiant boasting of Micah![18] Reading the passages in the order in which they occur—and they are best taken as arranged according to the course of the prophet's life— one is haunted by the impression that the darkness keeps growing, and eats ever more deeply into the prophet's soul. It is no accident that the last two passages of this kind also describe the extremity of Jeremiah's despair. Israel's language when she addressed God in prayer, and particularly in the prayer of lamentation, was never exactly timid: she was not afraid to use positively audacious expressions. But here Jeremiah went far beyond anything in the traditional form of lamentation which, though freely expressed, did keep more or less to conventional cultic language.

> Thou hast deceived me, Jahweh; and I let myself be deceived.
> Thou wast too strong for me, and prevailed over me.
> Now I have become a laughingstock all the day;
> everyone mocks me. . . .
> Yet, if I thought, I will know no more of him
> and speak no more in his name,

[18] See above, p. 178.

> then it was in my heart like a burning fire,
> shut up in my bones.
> I tried to hold it in, but I could not.   (Jer. xx. 7, 9)

The word which we have rendered as "deceived" in fact designates the act of enticing and seducing a young girl—"you took advantage of my simplicity" (Rudolph). The prophet cannot really blame himself: his power and Jahweh's were too unequal. He admits that he attempted to escape from this intolerable service: but the word with which he was inspired was like fire in his breast. Therefore he had to continue to be a prophet. But what is to become of him as a result! His days are to end in shame (vs. 18). And so finally—and this is the supreme consequence—Jeremiah curses the complete abandonment of his life (vs. 14f.). These last passages are soliloquies—the God whom the prophet addresses no longer answers him.

The confessions are central for the interpretation of Jeremiah. They must be understood as the written testimony to an intercourse between Jahweh and his prophet that is both striking and unique. The external circumstance of the order in which they appear in itself outlines a road which leads step by step into ever greater despair.[19] Each one of these passages tells of a separate experience. The areas in which these experiences were made are also different. Yet, the passages all point alike to a darkness which the prophet was powerless to overcome, and this makes them a unity. It is a darkness so terrible—it could also be said that it is something so absolutely new in the dealings between Israel and her God—that it constitutes a menace to very much more than the life of a single man: God's whole way with Israel hereby threatens to end in some kind of metaphysical abyss. For the sufferings here set forth were not just the concern of the man Jeremiah, who here speaks, as it were, unofficially, as a private individual, about experiences common to all men. In every instance these confessions grow out of his specific situation as a prophet; what lies behind them is a call to serve in a quite particular way, a relationship of particular intimacy with Jahweh, and therefore they have in the highest degree a typical significance for Israel. This does not, of course, mean that commentary on Jeremiah

---

[19] This would of course still remain substantially true even if the order of the texts as given does not correspond to the succession of the incidents in the prophet's life; for what is important is not the phases of his passion in which Jeremiah had these experiences, but the fact that he did have them.

should pay no attention to the human side of the matter. The intimacy of spiritual intercourse with God here revealed, the maturity of self-expression, and the freedom in admitting one's own failure and making no concealment of God's censure is a manifestation of the human spirit at its noblest. But here we are particularly concerned with the circumstances in which this phenomenon occurred and the place in Israelite prophecy occupied by these confessions and what they add up to. When they are set in this wider context, their most striking feature is seen to be a questioning reflexion. We should not think of the earlier prophets as unconscious organs of the divine will in revelation, but what happened with Jeremiah was an increasing inability to see where he was going. It was not merely that he pondered on the lack of success which attended his work. The failure was not only an outward one, stemming from other people, it was also personal, in that the prophet was no longer at one with his office and his tasks—at all events, he now called the first in question. With Jeremiah, the man and the prophetic task part company; indeed, serious tensions threaten the whole of his calling as a prophet. As a result of this parting between the man and the prophet, the prophetic calling as it had been known up to Jeremiah's own time entered upon a critical phase of its existence. As the child of his age, it was no longer possible for Jeremiah to resign himself to the will of Jahweh; he had to question, and to understand. In his sensitiveness and vulnerability, his feeling for the problems of religion, he was certainly at one with many of his contemporaries. He was undoubtedly very much more spiritually complex than Amos or Micah. Thus, there was also a large element of the refractory in him, a rebellion against decrees of the divine will which earlier ages, more secure in their faith, would probably have accepted with greater submissiveness. On the one hand, he was bound to Jahweh and remained subject to him more than any other prophet; on the other, however, he had to let his thoughts have free range. And the seriousness with which he took this intellectual state, which of course lay outside his prophetic calling proper, is shown precisely by the wide range of his reflexion on theological problems.

There is no doubt that from this point of view Jeremiah is to be regarded as a late-comer in the prophetic series. At the same time, he is completely conscious of his spiritual ancestry—he speaks more than once of the prophets who preceded him.[20] During his lifetime, there

[20] *E.g.*, Jer. VII. 25, XXVI. 5, XXVIII. 8. Stoebe refers the sentence "thy words were

was certainly something very like a tradition even among the free prophets. This included not only the subjects and topics traditional in prophetic preaching, but also the experiences and disappointments of many generations. There was certainly also an awareness of an unchanging pattern of failure, to be found only amongst these free prophets and transmitted by them alone. If it is only with Jeremiah, and not earlier, that the earthly vessel broke, the reason is primarily that the prophetic office assumed by Jeremiah was far greater in its range and depth than that of any of his predecessors. In proportion, he also required the continuous support of God. At the same time, however much we attempt to place Jeremiah in the correct historical framework of his age, and this is essential, a great deal remains that we cannot explain. It is still Jeremiah's secret how, in the face of growing scepticism about his own office, he was yet able to give an almost superhuman obedience to God, and, bearing the immense strains of his calling, was yet able to follow a road which led ultimately to abandonment. Never for a moment did it occur to him that this mediatorial suffering might have a meaning in the sight of God. Again, if God brought the life of the most faithful of his ambassadors into so terrible and utterly uncomprehended a night and there to all appearances allowed him to come to utter grief, this remains God's secret.

4. Surprisingly enough, besides the confessions the book of Jeremiah contains another source which traces the prophet's steps. This is the narrative of Baruch (Jer. XXXVII–XLV). However, just as the confessions are confined to the development of the prophet's inner life, so the Baruch narrative is only concerned with describing the outward circumstances of this *via dolorosa*.[21] Although it does sometimes contain oracles spoken by the prophet, the accounts here given are not to be understood, as in many other cases (*e.g.*, chs. XXVI–XXIX), as no more than the narrative framework for the oracles; no, the subject described here is the dramatic events in which the prophet was involved and which brought him into greater and greater dangers. Baruch begins with Jeremiah's imprisonment and dispassionately traces the subsequent events, recording the prophet's various conversations and ending with

---

found, and I ate them" (Jer. XV. 16) not to the prophet's own reception of the word, but to Jeremiah's familiarity with the oracles of earlier prophets ("Seelsorge," pp. 122f.).

[21] H. Kremers, "Leidensgemeinschaft mit Gott im Alten Testament," in *Ev. Th.*, 13 (1953), pp. 122ff.; L. Rost, "Zur Problematik der Baruch-Biographie" in *Meiserfestschrift*, München 1951, pp. 241ff.

his exile in Egypt. Jeremiah's death apparently formed no part of this account. The narrator's strict concentration on events in space and time is made clear in the résumés with which he likes to round off his description of the various stages in the story.[22] The man who so exactly describes the stations of Jeremiah's cross was obviously most closely associated with the events; there can therefore be no doubt that his description is trustworthy. Yet, what can be said of his intention? To what end did he make a written record of the events? What was it he wanted to document with such a circumstantial account? The author in fact gives the true cause of all Jeremiah's suffering.

As everyone knows, it was Jeremiah's firm conviction that, at this time by the instrumentality of Nebuchadnezzar, God was about to effect great changes in the international situation, and that he would bring Judah also under the dominion of the Babylonian empire (cp. Jer. XXVII. 5f.). Consequently, during the months when the danger from Babylon was at its greatest, all that Jeremiah could prophesy was that the capture of the city was certain (Jer. XXXVII. 8, 17, XXXVIII. 3, cp. XXXIV. 2), and his advice was to capitulate as quickly as possible (Jer. XXXVIII. 17). This conviction, which Jeremiah also expressed in public, was therefore the reason for the prophet's sufferings, for the nationalists in Jerusalem found a man with such convictions quite intolerable.

Jeremiah's sufferings are described with a grim realism, and the picture is unrelieved by any divine word of comfort or any miracle. The narrator has nothing to say about any guiding hand of God; no ravens feed the prophet in his hunger, no angel stops the lion's mouth. In his abandonment to his enemies Jeremiah is completely powerless—neither by his words nor his sufferings does he make any impression on them. What is particularly sad is the absence of any good or promising issue. This was an unusual thing for an ancient writer to do, for antiquity felt a deep need to see harmony restored before the end. Jeremiah's path disappears in misery, and this without any dramatic accompaniments. It would be completely wrong to assume that the story was intended to glorify Jeremiah and his endurance. To the man who described these events neither the suffering itself nor the manner in which it was borne had any positive value, and least of all a heroic value: he sees no halo of

[22] "So Jeremiah came into the vaults of the cistern, and remained there many days" (Jer. XXXVII. 16). "So Jeremiah then remained in the court of the guard" (Jer. XXXVII. 21, XXXVIII. 13, 28). "So Jeremiah came to Gedaliah at Mizpah and remained there with him" (Jer. XXXIX. 14). Kremers, "Leidensgemeinschaft," p. 131.

any kind round the prophet's head. On the contrary, Jeremiah sometimes appears in situations which even a reader in the ancient world
might have regarded as somewhat dubious (Jer. xxxviii. 14–27).[23]

As with all the rest of Israel's pure narrative, the actual theological
substratum in the account of Jeremiah's sufferings is fairly slight. Its
author is not one who is aware of connexions between things and the
necessity which brings them about. On the other hand, he does give
some leads. It is only to be expected that in a writing which is so un-
communicative in the matter of theology, a particular hermeneutical
significance should attach to its conclusion, and this has been rightly
emphasised in recent literature. The conclusion here has something
special about it, since Baruch tells of an oracle which Jeremiah spoke to
him himself regarding his complaints[24]:

"You said, 'Woe is me! Jahweh adds sorrow to my pain; I am weary
with groaning, and can find no rest.'... Thus hath Jahweh said:
'Behold, what I have built I am breaking down, and what I have
planted, I am plucking up'... and do you seek great things for your-
self? Seek them not! For, behold, I am bringing great evil upon all flesh,
says Jahweh, but to you I give your life as a prize of war wherever you
may go" (Jer. xlv. 3–5).

Here we meet again with the idea of the reorganisation of world-
history and of the destruction it is to bring with it. An undertone of
sadness accompanies Jahweh's words: they hint almost at feelings of
pain at this work of pulling down what his own hands built up. At this
time of judgment, when God has to tear down his own work in history,
no human being can look for any good for himself; it is no wonder if
the prophet and those about him are drawn in a quite exceptional way
into this demolition. Thus, the reason why Baruch so conscientiously
traces all the details of this *via dolorosa* is that the catastrophic events into
which the prophet was drawn do not after all come by chance; instead,
they bring the divine demolition to pass; here a human being has in a
unique fashion borne a part in the divine suffering.[25]

[23] For an example of an entirely opposite idea, cp. the way in which the martyrs
were made heroes in ii. Mac. 7.

[24] Kremers, "Leidensgemeinschaft," pp. 132ff.; A. Weiser, "Das Gotteswort für
Baruch, Jer. 45 und die sogennante Baruchbiographie," in *Festschrift für K. Heim*,
Hamburg 1954, pp. 35ff.

[25] Even if the addition of Jer. xlv is not to be attributed to a particular purpose
which Baruch wished to serve—it could indeed also be regarded as a rather chance

5. The oracle just mentioned ended with the mysterious words that Baruch was to preserve "his life as a prize of war," that is to say, he was to survive the destruction following this judgment. The saying naturally leads us to ask about the special features of Jeremiah's *prophecies of salvation*. Prophecy of this kind is not, of course, to be looked for in the early part of his activity, for, as we have already seen, at that time he hoped that Israel could still decide for or against Jahweh. In his final period, however, during the reign of Zedekiah, the case was completely different. The Babylonians had already administered one shock—in 598 the young king Jehoiachin was deported, along with his officials and members of the upper class. Even those who had never before considered the question were now asking what action Jahweh would take next. We have already seen that Jeremiah expected the Babylonians to win a complete victory. But his was an isolated position, opposed to an overwhelming war party and, still more serious, a group of prophets who stirred up religious ferment and prophesied that Jahweh would speedily intervene for the honour of his people and of his pillaged temple. Jeremiah's clashes with his own colleagues were probably among his hardest battles (Jer. XXIII. 9ff, XXVIII).[26] He seems at times almost to have been overwhelmed by the problems thus raised. We can see him searching deliberately for practical criteria to identify the false prophet. At one moment he compares the content of their message with the prophetic tradition, at another he is suspicious of the forms in which they received their revelations, because they appealed to dreams, and not to a word from Jahweh, and were therefore in danger of self-deception. Further, their offensive conduct spoke against them. The very fact that Jeremiah could not point to any criterion that might in principle answer the question—who was the false prophet and who the true—showed him the full difficulty of the problem; for there could be no such criterion in respect of form or content. Just because Jahweh was not "a God at hand," but a God "far off" (Jer. XXIII. 23), there could be no standard method of any sort by which he granted revelation. On the other hand, it is surprising to see a prophet

appendix, since the event it records is twenty years earlier than what is recorded in the chapter immediately preceding—even so, the word is still of great importance for the Baruch narrative, because it so clearly defines his place within the divine destruction of history: he cannot stand outside it.

[26] On this see G. Quell, *Wahre und falsche Propheten: Versuch einer Interpretation*, Gütersloh 1952.

so much at sea with a problem. At times in his famous encounter with
Hananiah Jeremiah's arguments are almost groping (Jer. xxvIII. 5–9).
The splendid certainty and straightforwardness which characterises the
way in which classical prophecy saw things was no longer vouchsafed
to Jeremiah in the same measure. Two centuries before, the problem
of prophets who contradicted one another was given a completely
different solution by Micaiah ben Imlah. Micaiah did not look for
criteria to deal with his opponents. He saw the whole matter as lying in
the transcendental sphere, in the council of Jahweh, who himself
inspired the false prophets in order to entice Ahab (1 Kings xxII. 21ff.).
With such a point of view he could accept his opponents' *bona fides* and
their subjective certainty of having been commissioned much more
calmly than did Jeremiah.[27]

These last ten years of Judah's independence thus constituted a high
water mark of prophetic activity in which Jeremiah's message of doom
made his position very difficult. But perhaps even greater difficulty
was caused by his message of salvation, for, of course, it was entirely
different from that of his colleagues. The letter which he sent to those
exiled to Babylon in 598 was written in a spirit of calm certainty. It was
aimed at their faithless feelings of depression and their equally faithless
fervent hopes, and clearly reveals the tension between the two.

"Build houses and live in them, plant gardens and eat their produce.
Take wives and have sons and daughters. Take wives for your sons,
and give your daughters in marriage, that they may bear sons and
daughters, that you may multiply there and not decrease. Seek the
welfare of the city where I have sent you into exile, and pray to Jahweh

[27] Deuteronomy too tries—not very successfully—to draw up objective criteria by
means of which the false prophet might be recognised (Deut. xvIII. 21). The contradiction between prophet and prophet, each speaking in the name of Jahweh (cp. Jer.
xxvII. 4, xxvIII. 2) must have been particularly confusing in the final period of the
Monarchy. As far as we can see from the relevant texts, their colleagues' proclamation
of salvation was particularly suspect in the eyes of the "true" prophets (1 Kings xxII.
11ff.; Mic. III. 5ff.; Jer. vI. 14, xIV. 13, xxIII. 9ff., xxvIII. 5–9; Ezek. xIII. 16). It is
probable that the false prophets and their predictions of salvation coincided with the
interests of the national cult (H. -J. Kraus, *Prophetie und Politik* (*Theologische Existenz
Heute*, N.F., 36), München 1952, pp. 41ff., 53ff.). But even this is no assured criterion.
Did not what they predicted coincide with the faith of Isaiah? The falsity cannot be
seen either in the office itself, or in their words themselves, or in the fallibility of the
man who spoke them. It could only be seen by the person who had true insight into
Jahweh's intentions for the time, and who, on the basis of this, was obliged to deny
that the other had illumination. (Quell, *op. cit.*, p. 66.)

on its behalf, for its welfare is also your welfare" (Jer. XXIX. 5–7).

The words are an unexampelled exhortation to sober thinking and an attack on fervent high hopes fostered by religion. The exiles were obviously quite unable to appreciate the real seriousness of the situation, and therefore Jeremiah counselled them to do what lay to hand and prepare to settle down. This meant, of course, a change in the deportees' attitude to Babylon. She is no longer the enemy. She carries the people of God upon her bosom, and therefore it was fitting for prayer to be made for her. Times had changed. Prayer for Babylon is now a prayer for the people of God. For the latter has still a future in his sight.

"For I know the thoughts I have for you, says Jahweh, thoughts for welfare and not for evil, to give you a future and a hope" (Jer. XXIX. 11).

In this passage it is possible that Jeremiah's whole message on Jahweh's will for the salvation of Israel is contained in the two words "future and hope," for vs. 14b, which speaks of a return from among all the nations, is perhaps an interpolation. He was more explicit about the nation's future on the occasion when he was ordered to purchase a field, for in the context of this piece of family business he received a word from Jahweh. Jeremiah had the deed of purchase duly witnessed and placed in safe keeping at a time when besiegers were already throwing up earthworks against the city and famine was raging within it, as a symbol that "houses and fields and vineyards shall again be bought in this land" (Jer. XXXII. 15). In this glance towards the future Jeremiah had in mind equally the exiles of 598 and those who still remained in Jerusalem. In the vision of the two baskets of figs, however, those in exile are now ranked much higher than those still in the land of Judah. They alone are the subject of the promise:

"Thus hath Jahweh, the God of Israel, spoken: Like these good figs, so do I regard as good the exiles from Judah, whom I have sent away from this place to the land of the Chaldeans, and set my eyes upon them for good. I will bring them back to this land, I will build them up and not tear them down, I will plant them and not uproot them, and I will give them a heart to know that I am Jahweh, and they shall be my people and I will be their God, for they shall return to me with their whole heart" (Jer. XXIV. 5–7).

The eschatological salvation which Jahweh purposed for his people is therefore this. Both the exiles of 587 and those of 721 are to return home. Jerusalem is to be rebuilt (Jer. XXXIII. 4ff.), people will once more buy fields and vineyards, and there will also be Rechabites who take upon themselves particularly rigorous vows of abstinence and serve Jahweh in a very strange way (Jer. xxxv. 18f.). This picture of the future is almost disappointingly sober. Jeremiah has nothing to say of any changes in the natural world of the land where God's chosen people are to dwell; and nothing of any paradise-like fertility. All he says is that, in the land which at the moment is lying waste, conditions will return to normal and life will go on again. Pilgrimages to Jerusalem will be arranged once more (Jer. xxxi. 6), and laughter and rejoicing be heard in the villages (Jer. xxx. 18f., xxxiii. 10f.). Of Jahweh it is said that he will look upon them "for good" (Jer. xxiv. 5). This apparently rounds off the picture of Israel's new life before Jahweh and, reading it, one might feel that the time of salvation of which Jeremiah speaks is in all essentials a restoration of previous conditions. The truth is quite the opposite. With Jeremiah, the gulf between old and new is far deeper than with any of his predecessors among the prophets, for in our account of these prophecies of salvation we have still to consider the statement that Jahweh is to give his people a heart to know him (Jer. xxiv. 7). If we neglect this we never grasp the characteristic feature of the salvation envisaged by Jeremiah, for here is his prophecy of the new covenant compressed into one sentence.

Jeremiah addressed his words about the new covenant to the exiles of the former Northern Kingdom (Jer. xxx. 1–3), but the saving event which he had in mind was certainly to be shared by the whole of Israel, in particular by the exiles of 721 and 598.[28] What is important, and towers right above any previous prophetic prediction, lies in the *prophecy of a new covenant* which Jahweh intends to make with Israel. This is clearly something quite different from Jahweh's saying that days were coming when he would again remember his covenant which he made with Israel. No, the old covenant is broken, and in Jeremiah's view Israel is altogether without one. What is all important is that there is no attempt here—as there was, for example, in Deuteronomy—to re-establish Israel on the old bases. The new covenant is entirely new, and in one essential feature it is to surpass the old. To us to-day, however, the greatness of the difference between the two ordinances is not at once obvious, and so we must take the much-interpreted passage Jer.

[28] The date of the "little book of comfort for Ephraim" (Jer. xxxf.) is a matter of controversy. The fact that Jer. xxxi. 31ff. bears a direct resemblance to both Jer. xxiv. 7 and Jer. xxxii. 37ff. makes it probable that this prophecy belongs to the later period of the prophet's activity.

XXXI. 31ff., examine it with particular care, and safeguard it against some common false expositions.

The content of the Sinai covenant was the revelation of the *torah*, that is to say, the revelation of Israel's election and appropriation by Jahweh and his will as expressed in law. This *torah* is also to stand in the centre of the new covenant which Jahweh is going to make with Israel "in these days." Thus, as far as the content of Jahweh's self revelation is concerned, the new covenant will make no change. Jeremiah neither says that the revelation given at Sinai is to be nullified in whole or part (and how could a revelation given by Jahweh ever be nullified or taken back!), nor does he in any sense suggest any alteration or expansion of its content in the new covenant. The reason why a new covenant is to ensue on the old is not that the regulations revealed in the latter have proved inadequate, but that the covenant has been broken, because Israel has refused to obey it. And here is the point where the new factor comes into operation—there is to be a change in the way in which the divine will is to be conveyed to men. At Sinai, Jahweh had spoken from the mountain top, and the Elohist—thus early—reports that Israel could not endure this address, and begged Moses to receive the revelation of the divine will in her stead (Ex. xx. 18ff.). If we understand Jeremiah correctly, the new thing is to be that the whole process of God's speaking and man's listening is to be dropped. This road of listening to the divine will had not led Israel to obedience. Jahweh is, as it were, to by-pass the process of speaking and listening, and to put his will straight into Israel's heart. We should completely ignore the distinction between outward obedience and obedience of the heart, for it scarcely touches the antithesis in Jeremiah's mind. As we have already seen, every page of Deuteronomy, too, insists on an obedience which springs from the heart and conscience. It is at this very point, however, that Jeremiah goes far beyond Deuteronomy, for in the new covenant the doubtful element of human obedience as it had been known up to date drops out completely. If God's will ceases to confront and judge men from outside themselves, if God puts his will directly into their hearts, then, properly speaking, the rendering of obedience is completely done away with, for the problem of obedience only arises when man's will is confronted by an alien will. Now however, the possibility of such a confrontation has ceased to exist, for men are to have the will of God in their heart, and are only to will God's will. What is here outlined is the picture of a new man, a man who is able to obey perfectly because of a miraculous change of his nature. It is very significant that Jeremiah, writing comparatively late in Israel's history, should lay so much emphasis on the anthropological side of Jahweh's work of salvation.

Behold, days are coming, says Jahweh, when I make a new covenant with the house of Israel < >, not like the covenant which I made with their fathers when I took them by the hand to bring them out of the land of Egypt, which they broke, so that I had to show myself as lord, says Jahweh. But this is to be the covenant that I will make with the house of Israel after these days, says Jahweh: I will put my instruction within them and write it upon their hearts, and so I will be their God, and they shall be my people. Then no man needs any longer to teach his neighbour, and no man his brother, saying, "Know Jahweh," but they shall all know me, from the least to the greatest, says Jahweh, for I will forgive their iniquity, and I will remember their sin no more.

(Jer. XXXI. 31-4)

Behold, I will gather them from all the countries to which I drove them in my anger and my wrath and in great indignation, and will bring them back to this place and make them dwell in safety. They shall be my people, and I will be their God, and I will give them a heart and a way, that they may fear me for ever, for their own good and the good of their children after them. And I make an everlasting covenant with them, that I will not turn away from doing good to them. And I will put the fear of me in their hearts, that they may not turn away from me. And I will have joy in doing them good, and I will plant them in this land in faithfulness, with all my heart and with all my soul.

(Jer. XXXII. 37-41)

These two passages almost read like two targums on a text. At any rate, they are so alike in content that we ought not to miss the opportunity of amplifying the exposition of Jer. XXXI. 31ff. by comparing them. Both texts have the same event in view, but there are considerable differences in the way in which they describe it. We cannot say very much about their literary relationship. We can be certain that Jer. XXXII. 37ff. is not simply a copy or twin of Jer. XXXI. 31ff. The phraseology of the second passage is too distinctive, and the distinctions occur at the central points of the argument. If Jer. XXXII. 37ff. is to be regarded as later than Jeremiah himself, then it might be taken as something like an interpretive paraphrase of Jer. XXXI. 31ff. But the dependence is not close enough for this. Furthermore, even Jer. XXXI. 31ff. can hardly be the form of the oracle as it was originally spoken by Jeremiah, for he, like the other prophets, usually gave his oracles a verse form. Jer. XXXI. 31ff. is, however, prose, though there are one or two places where the outlines of an original verse form can still be recognised.

The best explanation is therefore that Jeremiah spoke of the new covenant on two different occasions, both times in a different way, and that each of the passages as we now have them has been subsequently worked over.[29]

God's promise to put his will in men's hearts is only slightly altered in Jer. xxxii. 37ff.—he is to put the "fear" of him "in their hearts." Here we have only to recall that in the Old Testament the expression "the fear of God" is the equivalent of obedience to the divine will.[30] As a result of this creative grafting of the will of God on the hearts of men all theological teaching offices become unnecessary and there is no further need for admonition. This agrees with ch. xxxii. 39, where it is said that in their fear of Jahweh men are to have one heart and one way. The will of God is one, and each man is to know it in his heart. In the same way too, it was prophesied in ch. xxiv. 7 that, when the Israelite tribes of the North return home, Jahweh will give them a heart to know him. This is Jeremiah's way of speaking of a future outpouring of God's spirit, for what he thinks of is nothing other than a spiritual knowledge and observance of the will of God. Ezekiel after him is to speak in the same sense of the spirit's being planted in what had hitherto been the stony heart. The fact that Jeremiah never actually employs the word "spirit" means nothing when we remember the very concrete terms in which he describes the way in which this transfer takes place. There is nothing in the second passage corresponding to the forgiveness of sins in the first.

The road whose end Jeremiah glimpsed when he spoke of the new covenant is a long one. In terms of prophetic speech it might be called Israel's full and final return to her God.[31] Had the prophets been preachers of revival, we should expect to find their statements on conversion in the form of exhortation. But this is not the case, for these are found rather amongst their preaching of judgment. What the prophets have to say on this subject is that contemporary Israel is not returning to Jahweh,[32] and by the word "return" they mean not so much our

---

[29] S. Herrmann goes much further. In his exhaustive analysis of the whole of Jer. xxxi. 31ff., he reckons it as part of the Deuteronomic redaction, and also separates it in content from Jeremiah (*Der Gestaltwandel der prophetischen Heilserwartung im Alten Testament*, Habilitationsschrift, Leipzig 1959).   [30] Köhler, *op. cit.*, pp. 55f.

[31] For what follows, cp. H. W. Wolff's work, "Das Thema 'Umkehr' in der alttestamentlichen Prophetie," in *Z. Th. K.*, xlviii, 1951, pp. 129ff.

[32] Am. iv. 6, 8, 9, 10, 11; Is. ix. 12 [13], xxx. 15.

individualistic and spiritual idea of "conversion" as the nation's turning back to the serenity of its original relationship with Jahweh. Jeremiah also takes up the complaint that Israel refused to return (Jer. VIII. 5); indeed, on occasion he went so far as to say that a return to Jahweh was actually inadmissible, for it would contravene the law (Jer. III. 1). Yet, in spite of this, it is precisely with this prophet—and in speeches of exhortation at that—that the call to return is suddenly found on a broad basis.[33] In Isaiah (Is. VII. 3) and Hosea (Hos. III. 5, XIV. 2ff. [1ff.]) Israel's return was a subject of promise; but just for that very reason Hosea could also exhort Israel to return, call upon her to close with God's offer (Hos. XIV. 2 [1]). Here again, therefore, Jeremiah is Hosea's disciple. The call bulks larger with him, however, in as much as he recognised—and here he goes far beyond Hosea—that such a return was Jahweh's work upon Israel (Jer. XXIV. 7). So far, then, there is no essential difference in basic theology between Isaiah and Hosea on the one hand and Jeremiah on the other, for in all alike what is said about returning is found within the proclamation of salvation. Where, however, the later prophet does differ from his predecessors is in the much greater emphasis he places on the human side in the divine saving work. Jeremiah is also the prophet in whose preaching one constantly comes across reflexions on whether man's disposition can or cannot be changed. God appointed him an assayer (Jer. VI. 27), and he knew that the human heart was deceitful (עקב) and incurable (אנוש) (Jer. XVII. 9). As he thus ruminated on the nature of man, he arrived at a very profound understanding of elements in it. His thoughts constantly revolve round the tremendous bondage in which man is the prisoner of his own opposition to God. It is simply not in his power to determine his way; to no one is it granted to direct his own steps (Jer. X. 23). Any attempt to make oneself clean in God's sight would be even less successful—man would still remain stained in his guilt (Jer. II. 22).

> Can an Ethiopian change his skin
> or a panther his spots?
> Then also even you can do good
> who are accustomed to do evil.
>
> (Jer. XIII. 23)

It is only in the light of this devastatingly negative judgment on the possibility of Israel's setting her relationship to God aright again by her

[33] Jer. III. 12, 14, 22, XVIII. 11, XXXV. 15.

own efforts that one can understand not only what Jeremiah says about the new covenant, but also his imploring entreaty to return. Jeremiah gained ever increasing insight into man's actual condition, and for this reason he did not unthinkingly demand that man should follow a road on which he would again inevitably come to grief. His appeals to return increasingly emanate "from God's decision to save."[34] They urge the nation to settle for what God has promised to do for it. No matter how many reservations we may have about interpreting a prophet's message in terms of his own psychology, we may nevertheless assume in the case of Jeremiah that he constantly reflected on the problem of man; that is to say, he reflected on the question of what must come about in man as man if God is to receive him into a new communion with himself. If God is again gracious to him, how can he in any way stand before him as man without once again coming to grief because of his heart's opposition to God? The answer which Jeremiah received to this question was the promise that God would himself change the human heart and so bring about perfect obedience. No prophet before Jeremiah was so much at pains to provide a basis for the human side of God's saving event. None the less, Jeremiah was not the only one to wrestle with this particular set of theological problems, and because of this we shall have later to consider his prophecy of the new covenant not merely as something isolated, but as set within still wider contexts.[35]

6. So far as we have found Jeremiah's prophecy to have roots in tradition the case is clear—Jeremiah stands and acts upon the Exodus-Sinai tradition, and this gives his preaching a very broad foundation. He shows his indebtedness to tradition both when he looks back (Jer. II) and when he looks forward (Jer. XXXI. 31ff.). At the same time, however, it is perfectly obvious that Jeremiah also took up the Messianic tradition associated with David. Linked with a diatribe against the nation's useless shepherds comes the following prophecy—the connexion between the two literary categories is not altogether clear:

[34] Wolff, op. cit., p. 142.

[35] See below, pp. 269ff. This peculiar prophetic interest in what may be called the eschatological man who is justified in God's sight also lies behind the prediction in Zeph. III. 11–13: God himself will remove the proud boasters; "you shall no longer be haughty in my holy mountain, for I will leave in the midst of you a people humble and lowly, that seeks refuge in the name of Jahweh, the remnant of Israel."

> Behold, days are coming, saith Jahweh, when I will raise up
>   for David a righteous branch.
> He shall reign as king and deal wisely,
>   he shall execute justice and righteousness in the land.
> In his days Judah will be saved
>   and Israel will dwell securely.
> And this will be the name by which he is called:
> Jahweh is our righteousness.   (Jer. xxiii. 5–6)

The fact that the oracle employs the terminology which had long
been conventionally applied to the monarchy is, of course, no reason
for suggesting that it does not come from Jeremiah himself. The
designation of the king as shepherd, the special significance attaching
to his throne names, and the righteousness and wisdom of his rule, all
form part of the language of the court. Nor should Jeremiah's authorship be questioned on the grounds that the prophecy may be felt to
show a certain colourlessness, a lack of that personal emotion which
almost everywhere else characterises his diction. The impress of his own
personality on a piece of old traditional matter, so as to make a new
thing of it, varied from case to case, nor was there always the same
need for the prophet to alter: there were cases when it was enough for
him to actualise the tradition in the form in which he received it. It is, of
course, remarkable that in ch. xxiii. 5f. he speaks of an anointed one of
the line of David, but in ch. xxx. 9 of the return of David himself. In
the complex of prophecies concerning the lost Northern Kingdom
(Jer. xxx–xxxi) there is, however, an oracle on the subject of the
coming of the anointed one in which we meet with something special
that Jeremiah had to say.

> His ruler shall come forth from his midst;
> I will make him draw near to me, that he may walk before me;
> for otherwise who would risk his life to draw near to me? says
>   the Lord.
>
>   (Jer. xxx. 21)

Of the many powers and functions of the anointed one only one is
here singled out; however, it is apparently the most important, as it is
also the hardest—Jahweh is to "make him draw near" to himself. Since
the term "to draw near" is a technical term of the priesthood, its use
here might indicate a sacral and specifically priestly function of the

anointed one.[36] Yet, on the basis of traditional Messianic concepts, it is much more probable that the expression here indicates a specific privilege at court. The anointed one is Jahweh's representative on earth; as such he shares the throne with him (Ps. cx. 1), and has most personal converse with him. Among the things which testify to and emphasise the intimacy of the anointed one's association with Jahweh, and his part in the divine government of the world, is included the right of free access to Jahweh. What Jeremiah means is that the anointed one deals directly with Jahweh: he has access to the most secret counsels of the ruler of the world.[37] However, the special feature of this prophecy lies pre-eminently in its reflexions on the uniqueness of this access. It can only truly be attributed to this one person, the anointed one. No one else would be ready "to give his heart in pledge." This expression comes from the legal sphere, and denotes the deposit of a pledge or the giving of security. Thus, the rhetorical question that so strangely interrupts the prophecy is meant to suggest that this access on the part of the anointed one to Jahweh is only possible on the condition that he yields up his life. No indication is given as to where Jeremiah thought the particular danger lay. The commentaries think of early Jahwism's belief that he who sees God must die.[38] It seems to me to be extremely characteristic that even in a Messianic prediction Jeremiah is particularly interested in the preconditions of the saving event as these affect the person involved. In his view—and here again we recognise Jeremiah— the most important thing is that the anointed one risks his life, and in this way holds open access to God in the most personal terms possible. "Who is it who gives his heart in pledge to come near to me?" This is one of the hardest questions that was ever put in ancient Israel. What knowledge of God and of man was required for it even to be asked!

[36] So, for example, Mowinckel, *He that cometh*, pp. 179f., 238.

[37] קרב occurs with this specifically courtly sense in II Sam. xv. 5. It is significant that the verb is also used when the "son of man" is presented to the council of the king in heaven (Dan. vii. 13*b*). In this connexion, when the prophecy speaks not of the king, but of the "ruler" (משל), this is perfectly correct, for Jahweh is the king. Cp. here also Zech. iii. 7*b*.

[38] Jg. vi. 23f., xiii. 22; Is. vi. 5. The prophecy ends in vs. 22 with the old covenant formula, an indication of how strands of tradition with completely different origins are now beginning to be woven together.

CHAPTER E

EZEKIEL[1]

THE fact that Jeremiah and Ezekiel were more or less contemporaries has always led to their teachings being compared.
Even a child can see that, although both came from priestly
families, they are extremely different not only in temperament, but
especially in their way of thinking, speaking, and writing. But to be
able to pin-point the difference, to define Ezekiel's specific standpoint
as a prophet and his use of traditional material as opposed to those of
Jeremiah, would be to solve not only the unusual measure of perplexi-
ties in Ezekiel's message but also those in Jeremiah's.[2] As far as the
outward course of Ezekiel's life is concerned, intensive research has
made clear that the reasons which led some critics to deny that the
scene of his work was the exile are inadequate.[3] To divest his message of
its exilic dress and assume that he worked exclusively in Jerusalem
before 587 entails a radical criticism which makes deep inroads into the
very nature of the prophecy itself. We may therefore start by supposing
that Ezekiel arrived in Babylon with the first deportation in 598, that
he was there called to be a prophet in 593, and that he exercised his
office from then on until about 571. The great interest with which he
followed the course of events in Jerusalem—so great that at times he
even seems to be living rather with the people in the homeland than
with those around him in Babylon—is something he has in common
with exiles of all times. The well-known very careful arrangement of
his book (chs. I–XXIV oracles of doom against Jerusalem and Judah,

[1] G. Fohrer, *Die Hauptprobleme des Buches Ezechiel*, Bei. *Z.A.W.* 72, 1952; *id.* "Das
Symptomatische der Ezechielforschung," in *Th. L.* 83, 1958, pp. 241ff.; C. Kuhl,
"Neuere Hesekielliteratur," in *Th. R.*, N.F. 20, 1952, pp. 1ff.; *id.* "Zum Stand der
Hesekielforschung," in *Th. R.*, N.F. 24, 1957/58, pp. 1ff.; H. H. Rowley, "The Book
of Ezekiel in Modern Study," in *Builetin of the John Rylands Library*, 36, 1953, pp.
146–90; W. Zimmerli, "Das Gotteswort des Ezechiel," in *Z. Th. K.*, XLVII, 1951, pp.
49ff.

[2] J. W. Miller, *Das Verhältnis Jeremias und Hesekiels, sprachlich und theologisch
untersucht mit besonderer Berucksichtigung der Prosareden Jeremias*, Assen and Neukirchen
1955.

[3] So V. Herntrich, *Ezechielprobleme*, Bei. *Z.A.W.*, 61, Giessen 1932.

chs. xxv–xxxii oracles against foreign nations, chs. xxxiii–xlviii oracles of salvation for Judah) is beyond all doubt due to fairly complicated redaction, but present-day criticism once more thinks of a considerable basis of genuine prophecy. This conviction rests not least on the autobiographical form in which his work has come down to us and the careful dating of many of the oracles, for these, with recognisable exceptions, must derive from the prophet himself.

Like all his predecessors, Ezekiel followed events on the political scene with a keen interest. Assyria had left the stage (Ezek. xxxii. 22f.). The two empires in whose sphere of influence Palestine now lay were Babylon and Egypt. In grave danger from the former, Judah sought help from the latter, and was bitterly disappointed (Ezek. xvii. 1ff., xxx. 20f.). After this the prophet follows the advance of Nebuchadnezzar (Ezek. xxi. 23ff. [18ff.]). The Babylonian emperor is first of all to deal with Tyre, and Ezekiel is very well informed about conditions there (Ezek. xxvi–xxvii). After this the Babylonians advance against Judah and Jerusalem, whose fall a messenger announces to the exiles (Ezek. xxxiii. 21). Similarly, the prophet is aware of the hostile attitude of the lesser neighbouring peoples, the Ammonites (Ezek. xxv. 2ff.) and the Edomites (Ezek. xxv. 12ff.). As has already been said, there is nothing surprising in the fact that Ezekiel was *au fait* with all that went on in the homeland, even in detail, for this is how exiles have behaved down through the ages.

In matters of general knowledge and culture alone Ezekiel's intellectual horizons were unusually wide. More detailed consideration of his knowledge of the traditions connected with the saving history and with sacral law will be given later: this fell within the more restricted sphere of his professional knowledge as a priest. Yet, his casual remark about the exceptional ethnic position of early Jerusalem is amazing: "as to your origin, your father was an Amorite and your mother a Hittite" (Ezek. xvi. 3), because the two terms exactly fit the actual historical conditions which obtained in Jerusalem before the time of David—a Canaanite population and a "Hittite" governing class.[4]

As well as possessing such historical knowledge, Ezekiel was familiar with a variety of traditional material of a mythological or legendary kind (the primeval man, Ezek. xxviii. 11ff.; the foundling, Ezek. xvi.

[4] Ezekiel also knows of the consequences of the disasters of the year 701, the transfer of Judean territory to the Philistines. On Ezek. xvi. 26f. see O. Eissfeldt. *Palästinajahrbuch* 27 (1931), pp. 58ff.

1ff.; the marvellous tree, Ezek. XXXI. 1f.), which can hardly have been common or general at the time. At least, the use which he makes of this material, and the way in which he grafts and fuses it into the quite dissimilar elements in his preaching, point to an unusual intellectual ability to integrate material. When we further notice that Ezekiel is as well-informed about the technical details of shipbuilding as about the places from which the necessary materials had to be imported (Ezek. XXVII. 1ff.), we arrive at a picture of a man of not only all-round general culture, but of intellectual powers of the first rank. For Ezekiel, more even than Jeremiah, needed to express his prophetic message in writing—in an ordered form. He makes scarcely any use of the shorter units of expression, the diatribe and the threat, which classical prophecy had employed. When he speaks, the results are as a rule literary compositions, even large-scale dissertations, for example, the literary category of the dirge, which he develops to almost baroque proportions.[5] In these compositions which, as we have said, are often considerably extended in length, Ezekiel more than any other prophet likes to subsume his subjects by a figure or type. The prophets had from the very first stimulated their hearers' attention by use of the parable (משל) or the riddle (חידה) with the veiled element which they contain.[6] With Ezekiel, however, the disguised form of expression no longer derives from the prophet's public dispute with his audience; it is much more a question of an artistic literary form. To this category belong the *mašal* of the vine, which approximates more closely to the parable proper (Ezek. XV. 1ff.), the allegory, called a "riddle," of the two eagles and the topmost twig of the cedar tree (Ezek. XVII. 1ff.), that of the girl whom Jahweh first found and later espoused (Ezek. XVI), the two laments over Zedekiah (Ezek. XIX. 1–9 and Ezek. XIX. 10–14, the lioness and the vine), and again the allegories in Ezek. XXI. 2ff. [XX. 46], and XXIV. 3ff. A different but just as characteristic indirect method appears where Ezekiel uses typical cases to shed light on problems and point the way to their solution. The three successive generations in Ezek. XVIII. 5ff. are a schematic abstraction, and the three intercessors Noah, Daniel, and Job (Ezek. XIV. 12–23) are equally types serving as

---

[5] Ezek. XIX. 1ff., 10ff., XXVII. 1ff., XXVIII. 11ff., XXXI. 1ff., XXXII. 1ff. See above, p. 38.

[6] K. von Rabenau, "Die Form des Rätsels im Buche Hesekiel," in *Wissenschaftliche Zeitschrift der Martin-Luther-Universität Halle-Wittenberg*, Ges.-Sprachw. Jahrg. VII (1958), pp. 1055ff.

examples. Imagery of this kind and the tendency towards abstractions and types enable Ezekiel to some extent to stand back from his subject —his expositions largely breathe an atmosphere of cool didactic detachment: and, where the prophet allows himself to be coarse and even shocking in his descriptions, this can have a positively icy effect. Here the difference from Jeremiah, whose preaching is so shot through with the emotions of his own troubled heart, is particularly great. In fact, Ezekiel must have been a man of completely opposite temperament. None the less, this very coldness and hardness upon which the commentators all remark, produces an impression of grandeur and aloofness. It would of course be completely wrong to see in Ezekiel the detached judge of his age and its abuses, for within this man glowed a strange fiery zeal, and this not merely for Jahweh, but also for Israel. What is really remarkable and intriguing, however, is that Ezekiel finds a place for rational reflexion beside the visionary and inspired elements in his work. No other prophet feels so great a need to think out problems so thoroughly and to explain them with such complete consistency. In other words, Ezekiel is not only a prophet, but a theologian as well. And this double office was essential for him, because he confronted a presumptuous and indeed rebellious generation for which a prophet's preaching was not enough: he had to debate and argue with it.

1. The account of Ezekiel's call at the river Chebar (Ezek. I. 4 – III. 15) is itself a complex of traditions of baroque proportions. It is built up of several kinds of traditional material, but none the less it passes as a unity in its present form. Ezekiel sees the "glory of Jahweh" (כבוד יהוה) coming down from heaven, and then receives his commission in the form of a kind of state paper written in heaven. The message which he is to preach as an "ambassador" is handed to him in a roll. Each part of this unit has a long history of tradition behind it[7]; and this applies not least to the disclosure that in the exercise of his prophetic office he must preach to deaf ears and dwell among scorpions (Ezek. II. 6). The burden of no prospect of success laid on the prophet in the first hour of his ministry must continue to increase; this, too, is traditional.[8] But Jahweh arms him for this road on which he will find opposition too

---

[7] See above, pp. 63ff.

[8] Heedlessness of the prophet's message must have taken curious forms; there even seem to have been people who gave him the kind of hearing that a singer with a beautiful voice receives (Ezek. XXXIII. 32).

great for any human power to support—he makes the prophet's face harder than flint. Yet the message of doom which Ezekiel is given to eat—it is written in a book which exists already in heaven—tastes as sweet as honey to him. This means that from now on he is entirely on God's side; the prophet and his message are the same. Unlike Jeremiah, therefore, he does not rebel against it.

The roll which the prophet had to eat had "lamentations and mourning and woe" (Ezek. II. 10) written on both sides of it; thus, his commission, like that of all his predecessors, was "to declare to Jacob his transgression and to Israel his sin" (Mic. III. 8). Our task must now be to understand what is peculiar to Ezekiel's conception of Jacob's transgression and to his method of argument.

Even a cursory reading of the text makes one thing plain. Where Ezekiel speaks of sin, he thinks in particular of offences against sacral orders. Complaints about transgression of the social and moral commandments are very much less prominent. For Ezekiel, the cause of Israel's approaching fall lay quite indubitably in a failure in the sphere of the holy. She had defiled the sanctuary (Ezek. v. 11), turned aside to other cults (Ezek. VIII. 7ff.), and taken idols into her heart (Ezek. XIV. 3ff.)—in other words, she had "rendered herself unclean" in the sight of Jahweh, and this is the reason for her punishment.[9] The richest quarries for information are of course the great historical retrospects in chs. XVI, XX and XXIII. There is no mistaking that these are written from a priestly point of view. No doubt, Ezekiel is above all else a prophet, but the world of ideas in which he lives, the standards which he applies, and the categories according to which he sees Israel's existence ordered before Jahweh, are expressly those of a priest. Another outcome of a priestly, sacral way of thought is the importance which Ezekiel attaches to the land of Israel and its cultic status (Ezek. XXXVI. 17). Indeed, to the prophet the people of Israel and its land are so closely united that he often speaks to "the land of Israel" or the "mountains of Israel" as if they were Israel herself.[10] The standard by which Ezekiel measures Israel's conduct are the "ordinances" (חקות), the "judgments" (משפטים), which Jahweh gave to his people (Ezek. v. 6, etc.).[11] When

[9] טמא Ezek. XX. 30f., 43; XXIII. 7, 13, 30; חלל Ezek. XXII. 26, XXIII. 39, XXXVI. 22f. Cp. also VOL. I, pp. 272ff.

[10] Ezek. VII. 2, XXI. 7f. [2f.], XXXVI. 6, VI. 2f., XXXV. 12, XXXVI. 1, 4, 8.

[11] Texts like Ezek. XVIII. 5ff. or XXXIII. 25 allow us to see the "ordinances" which the prophet has in mind.

Amos accused Israel he, too, was concerned with transgressions of the commandments. The difference in Ezekiel, however, comes out characteristically in the remarkable changes in the forms he uses. Exact analysis of Ezek. XIV. 1–11 has made it clear that while the unit begins as a prophetic diatribe, this form is presently abandoned, and the discourse proceeds in the impersonal form used for regulations in sacral law ("Any man of the house of Israel who cherishes his idols . . ." vs. 4).[12] The same thing is found with the threat. After the usual לכן, God speaks in the first person in vs. 6, but again the words pass over into the form characteristic of the language of sacral law ("Any one of the house of Israel, or of the aliens that sojourn in Israel, who separates himself from me . . ." vs. 7). This is not simply the prophet arrogating an alien form, applying it *ad hoc*, and then dropping it. Such a remarkable use of forms is much more than just a casual game with an unaccustomed form; it points to a profound difference in Ezekiel himself. He makes use of the old sacral ordinance not only in the diatribe; what is of greater import is that, when he announces the punishment, again, without further ceremony, he uses the wording of the old ordinance and the punishment it prescribed. He does not give a judgment based on his own prophetic outlook: here it is enough for him to cite the age-old penalty prescribed in the ban (יכרת)—this is an old sacral formula—in the words of the old ordinance. This gives an important clue towards answering the question of what traditions form the basis of Ezekiel's preaching, and so helps us to a better understanding of him. Ezekiel's roots are in the sacral tradition of the priesthood. It is from this that he took these basic categories by which all sacral thought understands the world, the categories of the holy and the secular. At the same time the sacral tradition also supplied him with a number of standards still then in existence by which those who were in contact with the holy had to live. Ezekiel had, of course, no priestly function. His message went far beyond priestly theology, and, indeed, can easily be shown to have shattered its bases at certain points. Ezekiel's relationship to this sacral tradition is curiously ambivalent: he was dependent on it, and yet free from it. The effect of this attitude on his prophecy was that sacral understanding of the world shaped even the prophecies of the new Israel.

2. It is to this priestly tradition that Ezekiel also owes his picture of

[12] W. Zimmerli, "Die Eigenart der prophetischen Rede des Ezechiel," in *Z.A.W.*, LXVI, 1954, pp. 1ff.

the history of Israel's origins. Like others, Ezekiel summoned up history to demonstrate her lost condition and sinful depravity. He drew up three such indictments, basing them on a broad historical foundation (Ezek. XVI, XX and XXIII). The recapitulation, in ch. XX, of the history from the time when the nation was first elected down to her taking possession of the land is of particular interest, because here the prophet follows on the one hand an ancient and well-known *schema* of the saving history long ago established in tradition—though it was apparently not that of any of the source documents which form our Hexateuch—while on the other he gives the traditional material a completely new twist by means of a highly individualistic interpretation and arrangement of it. The election, that is to say, the beginning of this history of Israel's dealings with Jahweh, took place in Egypt with the revelation of the name Jahweh and the giving of the first commandment. Yet here, right at the very start, we at once meet with novel features in this historical survey. Even in Egypt the people refused to obey this revelation: they did not forsake the cults practised there, and even in Egypt Jahweh all but rejected them (vss. 5-10)! Then a second phase follows—Jahweh leads Israel into the wilderness and reveals the commandments to her. However, this attempt to bind the nation to himself also failed (vss. 11-14). The result is the third phase—Jahweh urged his commandments on the second generation as well, again, of course, without meeting with any obedience (vss. 15-17). In the fourth and last phase Jahweh gives his people commandments "that were not good," in particular the commandment to offer up their first born sons, because of which Israel was inevitably defiled in God's sight (vss. 18-26). Here the description ends—more or less at the point designated by the traditional summaries as the conquest.[13] We cannot say for certain that details of this account of the sacred history were not found in tradition: yet this travesty of it, a succession of divine failures and acts of chastisement, must be exclusively the work of Ezekiel. The prophet has made the venerable tradition into a monstrous thing, and he shows a quite paradoxical mixture of close attachment to it on the one hand and audacious freedom in its interpretation on the other. He divides the history into four phases, each of which has four acts (1. Jahweh reveals himself; 2. Israel disobeys; 3. Jahweh acts in wrath; 4. Jahweh spares Israel). It is easy to see that the prophet was working with material which did not really lend itself to his interpretation. This

[13] See VOL. I, pp. 121ff.

is, of course, particularly true of the passage dealing with the commandments which were "not good," where prophetic interpretation reaches its boldest limits.[14] It is also quite clear that the traditional material has had an alien *schema* forced on to it where it is said that on each occasion Jahweh was obliged to refrain from pouring out his wrath "in order not to profane his name in the sight of the nations" (xx. 9, 14, 22). The first three phases of the history close by saying that Jahweh restrained his anger out of "pity" for his people, and resolved to go on leading Israel (vss. 9, 14, 17). This enabled the prophet to make the link with the earlier summaries which, of course, only recounted the actual facts of the way by which Israel was led. In the final phase this refrain is lacking. This phase therefore, which really lasts down to the prophet's own time, is still open.

It cannot, of course, be denied that Ezekiel's intellectual mastery of this history led to a slight distortion of its real nature. The prophet schematised it and divided it into phases: but these, with the exception of the last, have an absolutely cyclical course, for each returns to the point where the one before it ended. The old summaries, compact as they are in detailing the history, had an element of progression in each phase: here, however, divine action is characterised by repetition. This, of course, makes the question of how Jahweh will act in this final and still open phase all the more exciting.

Such, then, is Ezekiel's understanding of the canonical saving history —on Jahweh's part a series of unsuccessful actions, and on Israel's a constant failure to comply with the divine will. The one thing which allowed the whole story to go on was a lasting divine "inconsistency," namely, God's regard for the honour of his name among the nations. Ezekiel's real intention in making these historical excursions is this— what can be expected of a people with such a prehistory, a people that all this long time had been wearing the patience of its God to shreds? Moreover, the history of Jahweh's dealings with Israel has actual pro-

[14] Theological interpretations of this commandment are also to be found in the priestly tradition (Num. III. 12ff, VIII. 16). In Ezekiel this meaning put upon a commandment which, while it was certainly recognised as having been given by Jahweh, had however for long ceased to be taken literally, is an extremely bold one. Since however Ezekiel too understood the commandments given at Sinai as commandments by whose observance men live, this interpretation of an isolated commandment does not allow us to draw radical conclusions as to the theological significance of the commandments in Israel. Ezekiel himself describes the thing as exceptional.

phetic force, for, just as it was a history of divine judgment, so Jahweh will again bring his people into the "wilderness of the peoples," in order there again to enter into judgment with them (vs. 35f.). However, this judgment again will not exterminate Israel: it is to be a purifying judgment.

Ezekiel also reviewed the history of the monarchical period. But here he had far less documentary material on which to draw than for his recapitulation of the "canonical" saving history. Excerpts from annals did not supply his needs: what he needed was a conspectus which again considered the age not from the political angle, but as the story of God's action; and this did not yet exist, for the Deuteronomic histories only came into being after the time of Ezekiel. He was therefore thrown back on his own resources, and had to depend on such recollections, either of his own or of his contemporaries, as were still available. The consequence was one with which we are already familiar —factually, the account of this period proves to be much less vivid, with actual historical events much less clearly set down and described, than was the case with the earlier saving history.[15] In both chapters the prophet chose the form "allegory," though, of course, he continually abandons metaphorical language to speak directly of historical events. In ch. XVI he represents the history of Jerusalem as the story of a girl exposed at birth but ordered by Jahweh, as he passed by her, to live: she grew up to marry him, but thereafter broke her covenant with him by her continual unfaithfulness. Such a picture of the history is again as black as it can possibly be. Even when we bear in mind that in Ezekiel's time people were particularly conscious of their unworthiness in the sight of Jahweh ("you are the fewest of all peoples," Deut. VII. 7), the cutting pungency of his description of the paradox of the divine act of election far transcends anything that had ever been said hitherto. Judah-Jerusalem was like an abhorred foundling, on whom not the slightest care had been bestowed: but Jahweh, who saw her "weltering in her blood," commanded her to live; he bathed her, washed off her blood, clothed, and adorned her; but when she grew up, she lapsed into harlotry. Now Jahweh is about to summon her lovers; they are to execute a ghastly judgment upon her who was once the bride of Jahweh. The verdict passed in the other allegory, that of the two sisters Oholah and Oholibah, who are the two kingdoms with their capitals Samaria and Jerusalem (ch. XXIII), is even more sweeping. Although

[15] See VOL. I, p. 123.

they played the harlot even in Egypt, Jahweh took them to wife, and they bore him children; but they never gave up their harlotry. Oholibah-Jerusalem was the more corrupt. Now Jahweh has had enough of her also, and the end is the same as in ch. xvi—the lovers are to come and execute judgment.[16]

These three reviews occupy a special place in Israel's conception of her own history, and this for one reason in itself—leaving aside the Chronicler's history, they add a final and completely new version to Israel's long series of pictures of her history. Israel's view was never a heroic one. It was never herself she glorified, but the deeds of Jahweh. Yet Ezekiel brought everything connected with the human factor under Jahweh's judgment in an entirely unprecedented way. With him the human partners—and they are men who had been called into fellowship with Jahweh—are shrouded in utter darkness. Hardly anything more could be said than is done here about Israel's unfaithfulness, her indifference to the love of God, and her inability to render the slightest obedience. For a proper understanding of this, however, we have to notice the theological standpoint of the message. Two things need to be kept in mind. Ezekiel speaks as he does in order to give the reason for a divine judgment which is to come about in the very near future. He also speaks in the light of a saving event, whose outline he can already discern, an event which Israel is to take to herself and which is entirely unmerited on her part. In a sense even these three sombre chapters are the prelude to the glory of Jahweh's saving act, a glory which is all the greater simply because it cannot be based on any merit of Israel herself.

Ezekiel thus brings a new direction to the old prophetic task of exposing sin. He is, perhaps, more concerned than his predecessors were to demonstrate its total dominion over men. These excursuses on the history are intended to make clear that it is not a matter of separate transgressions, nor simply of the failure of one generation, but of a deep-seated inability to obey, indeed of a resistance to God which made itself manifest on the very day that Israel came into being. What makes Ezekiel's pictures of Israel's history so unvarying is that in his eyes the end is no better than the beginning. There is no difference, no moment of suspense—the same state of affairs exists in every age of her history.

[16] Here and in ch. xvi Ezekiel uses the term "whoring" in a double sense. He understands it as cultic apostasy to the nature deities, but he sometimes uses it with reference to politics, seeking security with the great powers.

Now, however, Jahweh is making an end to this: he revokes his historical design. Proof of his intentions can be seen in an event which at one and the same time is both catastrophic and magnificent for the saving history—the prophet sees the "glory of God," that manifestation of Jahweh which mysteriously dwelt with Israel, solemnly leaving the temple and soaring up in the direction of the east (Ezek. x. 18f., xi. 22ff.).

3. All that has been said so far might give the impression that despite its difficulties Ezekiel's task was basically simple because it was to inform people of their lost condition. Surprisingly enough, we here come upon one of the prophet's most complex functions, for it was Ezekiel's particular task to show great quickness of mind by getting right inside his hearers' exceptional religious situation. His call to be a prophet had, as it were, a supplementary clause, in terms of which his office was extended in a special direction—he was appointed a "watcher" for the house of Israel.[17] His office was thus modified to the extent that he had not only to deliver a divine "word"; when he received a message of doom, he had also, like a sentinel on a city wall, to warn (הזהיר) the inhabitants when danger threatened. However, the comparison is defective at the most important point. A watcher's duty is a simple one—he gives warning of the enemy; but Ezekiel's position is more complicated. Indeed, it is almost contradictory, since it is Jahweh who both threatens Israel and at the same time wishes to warn her so that she may be saved. Here, therefore, the delivery of the message entails a second task for the prophet, that of giving Israel a chance to "turn." The prophet's failure to warn the "wicked" (רשע) will be followed by the latter's death: but Jahweh will hold the prophet responsible. The kind of activity in particular involved in this office of "warning" is not immediately apparent from ch. xxxiii. 1–9 (iii. 16b–21). Elsewhere, however, there are two detailed examples of this special function which clearly show how the prophet thought of this office.

In ch. xviii Ezekiel is dealing with people who were suffering because the divine dispensation took no account of the individual, and who opposed the old collective idea according to which the generations form a great organic body, which is also a single entity in the sight of God. They deny God's right to punish them for the sins of their

[17] The connexion of the prophet's office as watchman (Ezek. xxxiii. 1–9) with his call (Ezek. iii. 16–21) is due to redaction. The intention was to make the entrusting of the former to him a part of his call.

fathers. The prophet helps them to think these problems through, and
tries to comfort their troubled hearts by saying that every life is in a
direct relationship of its own with God. A father's wickedness cannot
prevent his son from approaching Jahweh, nor can a wicked son reap
the benefit of his father's righteousness. Indeed, even in the life of one
individual there is no casting of accounts—Jahweh does not average
out a man's life; for the wicked, the way of turning to him is always
open, and when he does turn, all his previous wickedness will no longer
incriminate him.[18]

The second passage (Ezek. xiv. 12ff.) also takes as its starting-point
religious questions which became acute—perhaps to those in exile too
—because of the inevitable calamity threatening Jerusalem. In this case,
of course, the question apparently worked the other way round—in
the general collapse, will it be possible for someone whom Jahweh
spares to save his children too? Ezekiel's answer is that in a city under
so great a threat even men of exemplary righteousness, like Noah,
Daniel, and Job, could save only their own lives.

In both cases Ezekiel accomplishes his task by handling the problem
abstractly and quite impersonally—he lifts it on to a purely theoretic
and didactic plane, and works it out by means of exaggerated typical
examples. This is in keeping with his priestly way of thinking: but we
must not therefore lose sight of the fact that these expositions are based
on a very independent consideration of the problems, and that the
solution offered by Ezekiel, whose eyes are fixed on an imminent act
of God, is one which could only be given by a prophet. Here Ezekiel
entered upon a completely new sphere of prophetic activity. The subject to which the prophets of the classical period directed their messages
was Israel, i.e., a rather general audience. They then left it to each
individual to take out of them what applied to himself. Even Jeremiah,
who was himself so highly individualistic, did the same. Only with
Ezekiel does this change. He was the first prophet consciously to enter
this new sphere of activity, which may be described as a "cure of
souls," provided we remember that it corresponds to the New Testament paraclesis.[19] In actual fact, the term exhortation, warning and
comfortable address, fairly accurately describes this side of Ezekiel's
office, for his discussions are not intended to satisfy a speculative need,
but speak instead to a man's will, and sometimes at the end pass over

[18] Ezek. xviii has been considered in VOL. I, pp. 393ff.
[19] On παράκλησις see Th. W.B.N.T., VOL, v, pp. 790ff.

into personal appeal (Ezek. XVIII. 30f., XXXIII. 11). The precondition of such a pastoral activity had been given quite automatically by the emergence of the individual from the group, and this process had assumed particularly aggressive forms in the later monarchical period. (This subject has already been considered in VOL. I.)[20] At that time each generation was consciously distinct from that of its fathers, and the problem of the individual's relationship to Jahweh was being discussed as never before; and it was against this background that the prophets were for the first time given the task of caring for individuals as well as for the nation, of thrashing out their problems with them, and of impressing on each of them his own personal situation in the eyes of God. In doing this, it was Ezekiel's special endeavour to hunt men out in their secret fastnesses of religious security and their assumed "righteousness." The individualism of his own day suited his purpose perfectly, because it helped him to bring a man face to face with the living God. The royal word of Jahweh, however, determined the whole basis of his pastoral activity and its direction: "As I live, I have no pleasure in the death of the wicked, but that the wicked turn back from his way, and that he stay alive" (Ezek. XXXIII. 11).

This pastoral office meant much more for Ezekiel than simply an extension of his prophetic calling, or a special nuance given to it. It was his duty to live for other people, to seek them out, and place himself and his prophetic word at their disposal, and this task affected his own life in deadly earnest, for Jahweh had made him responsible for the souls of these individuals: if he allowed the wicked to die unwarned, Jahweh threatened to require their lives of the prophet's own hands. Jahweh had thus imposed on the prophet a special mediatorial office which already entailed suffering. And this is not the only instance of the kind; there are other passages as well which show how for Ezekiel the prophetic office was a matter of life and death, and how the offence of the message he was charged to deliver reacted first upon his own person, and had sometimes to be most strangely and painfully expressed in symbolic actions.

"And you, son of man, groan" With trembling loins and bitterness shall you groan before their eyes! (Ezek. XXI. 11 [6]).

Things of this kind were not cheap playacting. Here the coming disaster, the destruction of Jerusalem, is casting its shadow before it and harnessing the prophet, body and soul alike, with a hard yoke of

[20] See VOL. I, pp. 391ff.

suffering. Yet Jahweh had so decreed, for Ezekiel was to be made "a sign for Israel" (Ezek. xII. 6b). He was not to present a symbolic action which did not involve him personally; his own condition was to prefigure the suffering of the coming judgment.[21] The other symbolic action which compelled him to lie for a considerable time first on one side and then on the other, in order to bear the guilt of the house of Israel (Ezek. IV. 4–8), must have affected the prophet's inmost being even more profoundly. Here there is as yet no idea of a vicarious bearing of guilt, for what happens to Ezekiel is above all a prediction, a drastic prefiguration of what is about to come. It is very significant, however, that the method of prediction is not confined to oral communication, but that Jahweh draws the prophet's whole being into the disaster as its sign, and in the "days of his siege" makes him the first to suffer what is to come.[22] We shall have to discuss later how near Ezekiel's mediatorial office comes to that of the servant in Is. LIII, and how it yet falls short of it.[23] Ezekiel himself once gave a very clear statement of what he reckoned to be the heart of the prophetic service. It was made when he was dealing with false prophets. He reproaches them that, at the time when the threat from Jahweh was grave, they "did not go up into the breaches" or "build a wall round the house of Israel" (Ezek. xIII. 5). The picture indicates war, siege, and extreme peril for the people of God. In Ezekiel's view, the prophet's task is to set himself in the front line before Jahweh, in order to protect the people with his life. In this conception of the prophetic office Ezekiel again has affinities with the mediatorial office of the servant of Deutero-Isaiah.

4. Classical prophecy's abrupt juxtaposition of predictions of doom and predictions of salvation which, as we all know, raised so many misgivings in the minds of more than one generation of scholars, does not occur to the same degree in Ezekiel, because even before the destruction of Jerusalem he spoke of the possibilities of deliverance. It was his theological "individualism" which above all else gave his preaching a more flexible form; for he was free to allow men a considerable latitude in their decision for or against Jahweh. With Ezekiel then, the transition from doom to salvation is apparently much more intelligible from a logical point of view—those who receive salvation

[21] So also Ezek. xII. 17ff.
[22] W. Zimmerli, *Ezechiel* (*Bib. Komm.*), p. 117.
[23] See below, pp. 274ff.

are those who have remained true to Jahweh, who "sighed and groaned over all the abominations" that were committed in Jerusalem (Ezek. IX. 4), or at least those who at the eleventh hour took warning from the prophet and repented. The fact that Ezekiel sometimes expressly envisages the judgment as a purging (Ezek. XX. 37f., XXII. 17ff., XXIV. 11) seems only to reinforce this. Yet the point is not as easy as this for the logic of religion. On the contrary, it may be said that no other prophet tore open so deep a gulf between doom and salvation, or formulated it in so radical a fashion. The guardian "glory of God" departed from the temple before men's eyes (Ezek. XI. 22f.); Israel is dead in the true sense of the term (Ezek. XXXVII. 1ff.). These are the theologically relevant events which the prophet believes to lie between doom and salvation. Such a prospect makes the chances of Israel's return to Palestine— which does not surprise the historian—seem possible only as the result of a miracle.

Whenever Ezekiel speaks of the lot of the new Israel, he always assumes an historical, and also a political, existence for God's people within their own ancestral land.[24] Their members are to be enrolled in the register of Israel's citizens and to return to the land of Israel (Ezek. XIII. 9). Jahweh will then multiply the nation and bless the land with fruitfulness (Ezek. XXXVI. 9, 29f., 37). In this connexion, Ezekiel compares the once desolate land with the Garden of Eden (Ezek. XXXVI. 35), but clearly the prophet was not envisaging any mythological "paradise-like" conditions, or some kind of Elysian fields. Farmers will till the land for the future (Ezek. XXXVI. 34), and the cities will even be refortified (Ezek. XXXVI. 35).

Though these external conditions are important and even essential for the new Israel, it is the saving event which Jahweh is to bring about in the heart of man which is of the greatest moment.

"I will take you from the nations and gather you from all the countries and bring you into your own land. I will sprinkle you with clean water, and you shall be clean from all your uncleannesses, and from all your idols will I cleanse you. A new heart I will give you, and a new spirit I will put within you. I will take out of your flesh the heart of stone and give you a heart of flesh. My spirit will I put within you, and cause you to walk in my statutes and be careful to observe my ordinances. Then you shall dwell in the land which I gave to your fathers and be my people, and I will be your God" (Ezek. XXXVI. 24-8).

[24] The "sketch of the future" is not considered here. See below, p. 296, n. 23.

The best starting-point for interpreting this passage is the last of the verses quoted, for in "you my people, I your God," it contains the old formula of the covenant, and this puts it beyond all doubt that Ezekiel is speaking of a saving appointment of Jahweh analogous to the making of the old covenant. The fact that the word "covenant" is not here mentioned means nothing—there are other passages where he did designate the saving event as covenant (Ezek. XXXIV. 25, XXXVII. 26)—for the content of the passage shows it to be closely parallel, feature by feature, to Jeremiah's pericope on the new covenant (Jer. XXXI. 31ff.). Here too the purpose of God's saving activity is the re-creation of a people able to obey the commandments perfectly. Here too this is connected with a forgiving expurgation of previous sin (Jer. XXXI. 34b = Ezek. XXXVI. 25); above all however, with both prophets the saving work consists in God's making men capable of perfect obedience by as it were grafting it into their hearts. Ezekiel, of course, goes into very much greater detail over the human aspect than did Jeremiah—God takes away their hardened heart and gives in its stead a "new heart," a "heart of flesh." Moreover, God will bestow his spirit on Israel, and thus equipped she will be able to walk in the path of the divine ordinances. There are striking parallels with Jer. XXXI. 31ff.; one feels that Ezekiel must somehow have had Jeremiah's prophecies in front of him (in particular, Jer. XXXII. 37ff.). Jeremiah's wording, "I will put my law in their hearts," seems almost too undefined compared with the theological precision with which Ezekiel describes the process of renewal. There is another feature, concerned not with the process itself but with its result, where Ezekiel goes far beyond Jeremiah—when in her completely transformed state Israel looks back on her evil past and remembers it, she will loathe herself (vs. 31).

5. This remains, however, an incomplete account of Ezekiel's picture of the new Israel, for God's people are once more to be led by a monarch. Even the grievous harm done to the royal office by those who had last worn the crown did not vitiate the prophet's hope that Jahweh would redeem the promise attached to the throne of David, "until he comes whose right it is" (Ezek. XXI. 32 [27]). Thus mysteriously—with silence rather than speech—did Ezekiel once speak of the anointed one to come. At another time he expressed himself with somewhat greater clarity, in the parable of the twig which Jahweh was to plant on the lofty mountain of Israel; this twig (cp. Is. XI. 1) is to become a great life-giving tree, and Jahweh is to make the dry tree

sprout again (Ezek. XVII. 22-4). Twice, however, Ezekiel took up the topic of the Messiah directly. In Ezek. XXXIV. 23-4 a shepherd is mentioned whom God is to set over his people, his "servant David," and in Ezek. XXXVII. 25ff. the prophet again speaks in exactly the same way of the shepherd, the servant David, who is to rule over "Judah and Joseph," now finally reunited as one nation. There is, of course, no mistaking the fact that in Ezekiel also the topic of the Messiah and the traditional concepts specific to it are not altogether properly drawn. He is strangely unable to expound the Davidic tradition. One looks in vain in Ezekiel for an exposition of the subjects connected with it: instead, in both passages he glides into the wording of the Exodus-covenant tradition. In Ezek. XXXIV. 23f. the formula belonging to the Sinai covenant—I their God, they my people—follows upon the heels of what is said about the Messianic advent of the king, and in Ezek. XXXVII. 23 it immediately precedes it. How then is the covenant concept which appears in both places to be understood from the point of view of the history of tradition? Is it a renewal of the covenant with David, or of the Sinai covenant? Undoubtedly the latter. We have just seen how little Ezekiel expounds the once-widespread Messianic-Davidic tradition. Thus Ezekiel fuses the Sinai tradition and the David tradition which Jeremiah still kept essentially separate. But the Sinai tradition dominates his thought—under the new David, Israel will obey the commandments (Ezek. XXXVII. 24).

Ezekiel sometimes looked at this whole saving work from a theological viewpoint which is highly characteristic of his whole message. By gathering Israel and bringing her back to her own land, "Jahweh manifests his holiness in the sight of the nations."[25] This "manifestation" is therefore much more than simply something inward or spiritual; it is an event which comes about in the full glare of the political scene, and which can be noticed by foreign nations as well as by Israel. Jahweh owes it to his honour that the covenant profaned by all the heathen should be re-established. There is an unmistakable element of reason in this method of argument. In order to make the whole saving work theologically comprehensible, Ezekiel takes the radical course of relating it to Jahweh's honour, which must be restored in the sight of the nations.

"Therefore say to the house of Israel: Thus says the Lord Jahweh: It is not for your sake, O house of Israel, that I act, but for the sake of

[25] Ezek. XX. 41, XXVIII. 25, XXXVI. 23.

my holy name, which you have profaned among the nations to which you came. I will vindicate the holiness of my great name, which has been profaned among the nations, and which you have profaned among them; and the nations will know that I am Jahweh—oracle of Jahweh —when through you I vindicate my holiness before their eyes" (Ezek. XXXVI. 22–3).

These words remind us that in Ezekiel Jahweh concludes many of his predictions of coming events with the words: "that they may know that I am Jahweh."[26] The final goal of the divine activity is therefore that Jahweh should be recognised and worshipped by those who so far have not known him or who still do not know him properly.

[26] On the theological significance of this formula which occurs 86 times in Ezekiel see W. Zimmerli, *Erkenntniss Gottes nach dem Buche Ezechiel*, Zürich 1954, in particular pp. 65ff.

CHAPTER F

DEUTERO-ISAIAH

SCHOLARS have had to invent a name for the prophet whose mouth Jahweh filled with words of an unparalleled splendour which charm the reader and carry him forward. The anonymity of the message meant that its derivation from a special kind of prophet was only recognised by Biblical criticism. The messenger himself—a man who would be of the greatest interest to scholars—is completely hidden behind his message, so completely that we do not know his name, the place where he worked (though this is generally believed to have been Babylon), or anything else about his life. His literary style too is quite different from that of, say, the first Isaiah. The latter's style led us to believe that he was no ordinary man: but the high emotional tone of Deutero-Isaiah's words, and the richness of his language, which leaves the reader spell-bound, are closely linked with the diction of the hymn and other cultic forms and therefore are less personal.[1] On the other hand—and this is also characteristic of a prophet of Jahweh—it is easy to recognise the new epoch upon which the history of Israel was about to enter, and which this prophetic voice sets itself to interpret. Cyrus was on the throne of Persia and rising to power, and his successive victories were convulsing the world. His career naturally aroused great interest among the deportees in Babylon, as everywhere else. He did, in fact, later demolish the neo-Babylonian empire.[2] The preaching of Deutero-Isaiah is most intimately connected with these

---

[1] L. Köhler's *Deuterojesaja (Jesaja 40–55) stilkritisch untersucht*, Bei. *Z.A.W.*, 37, Giessen 1923, is basic for the understanding of the form of Deutero-Isaiah's diction, J. Begrich's *Studien zu Deuterojesaja*, henceforth cited as *Studien*, *B.W.A.N.T.*, 4. Folge, 25, Stuttgart 1938, is still the standard work for the delimitation of the units and for the determination of them in terms of form-criticism.

[2] The subjugation of Lydia (Croesus) *c.* 547/6, which has always been regarded as taking place about the time when Deutero-Isaiah appeared, was an event of particularly far-reaching significance. It may be taken as certain that Deutero-Isaiah's preaching preceded the collapse of the Babylonian Empire. (It is true that W. B. Stevenson regarded a few of the oracles of Deutero-Isaiah as an echo of the fall of Babylon: *Successive Phases in the Career of the Babylonian Isaiah*, Bei. *Z.A.W.*, 66, Berlin 1936, pp. 89ff.) Anything but a general date is, however, hypothetical.

events which, after a period of fairly peaceful transition, changed the face of contemporary history.

Before considering this message, however, it is perhaps once more worth while to make ourselves familiar with the theological traditions in which Deutero-Isaiah stood and lived. It is now, of course, apparent that when the prophets spoke of coming events, they did not do so directly, out of the blue, as it were; instead, they showed themselves bound to certain definite inherited traditions, and therefore even in their words about the future they use a dialectic method which keeps remarkably close to the pattern used by earlier exponents of Jahwism. It is this use of tradition which gives the prophets their legitimation. At the same time, they go beyond tradition—they fill it even to bursting-point with new content or at least broaden its basis for their own purposes. The three election traditions (of the Exodus, of David, and of Zion) which are constitutive for the whole of prophecy are all, we find, taken up by Deutero-Isaiah and used by him in striking poems. On the whole, however, in his view of the future, the most prominent tradition is undoubtedly that of the Exodus.[3] The position of the Exodus in Jahweh's saving activity for Israel is such a central one that this prophet can only imagine the new saving acts in the form of another Exodus. We shall have more to say about this later. Since Deutero-Isaiah was familiar with the Exodus tradition, it is not surprising that he sometimes also speaks of the election of Abraham (Is. XLI. 8, LI. 1ff.), and touches on the dim figure of Jacob (Is. XLIII. 22), for the patriarchs were, of course, the starting-point of that saving history which led on to the Exodus.

Besides what he owes this, the oldest and most important of all Israel's "election traditions," Deutero-Isaiah is also indebted to the Zion tradition; for the Exodus, of course, leads to a city destined to be rebuilt, guaranteed by Jahweh (Is. XLI. 19, XLIX, LIV. 11ff.), and the future home of God's scattered people and even of the Gentiles (Is. XLIX. 22ff., XLV. 14). Deutero-Isaiah's thoughts dwell continually on Zion. He likes to use the term, which is, after all, simply a place name, to address God's people as a body.[4] In his predictions about a pilgrimage to be made by the nations to the holy city, it is easily seen that Deutero-Isaiah took up traditional matter of a peculiar kind (Is. XLV.

---

[3] Is. XLIII. 16f., 18–21, XLVIII. 20f., LI. 10, LII. 12. Abraham is mentioned in Is. XLI. 8, LI. 2, and Jacob in Is. XLIII. 28.

[4] Is. XLI. 27, XLVI. 13, XLIX. 14, LI. 3, 11, 16, LII. 1, 7, 8.

14f., XLIX. 14–21, 22–3, LII. 1–2). In point of the history of tradition, these prophecies belong to a complex which overlaps the Zion tradition proper, for they occasionally appear in later prophecy. Their characteristic is the idea of the eschatological coming of the nations to Jerusalem, and they form a remarkably self-contained body of prophetic concepts. They will therefore be discussed later.[5]

On the other hand, Deutero-Isaiah's relationship to the David tradition is a very strange one. He mentions it once and, using a traditional description, grandly calls it the חסדי דוד, "the sure and gracious promises made to David" (Is. LV. 3, cp. II Chron. VI. 42). He does not, however, interpret Jahweh's promises concerning the throne of David and the anointed one of Israel in the traditional way, for he understands them to have been made not to David but to the whole nation. It is, therefore, for all Israel that the promises made to David are to be realised: Israel is to become the sovereign ruler (נגיד) of the peoples (Is. LV. 4). In thus "democratising" the tradition Deutero-Isaiah actually robbed it of its specific content. Indeed, the Messianic hope had no place in his prophetic ideas. This bold reshaping of the old David tradition is an example, though admittedly an extreme one, of the freedom with which the prophets re-interpreted old traditions.[6]

Very surprisingly however, there is still another tradition in Deutero-Isaiah, one upon which no previous prophet had called. It deals with the creation of the world by Jahweh. Because Jahweh had the power to subdue chaos, appeal could also be made to him to help his people in times of tribulation in the historical realm (Is. LI. 9f.); and because Jahweh created the ends of the earth, the message which he is now sending to Israel is also trustworthy (Is. XL. 27ff.). A special feature in Deutero-Isaiah's thought about creation is, of course, that he does not regard creation as a work by itself, something additional to Jahweh's historical acts. Indeed he seems to make no clear distinction here—for him creation is the first of Jahweh's miraculous historical acts and a remarkable witness to his will to save. This has already been discussed in VOL. I.[7] The certain evidence for this "soteriological" conception of creation is the fact that Deutero-Isaiah can at one time speak of Jahweh, the creator of the world, and at another of Jahweh, the creator of

[5] See below, pp. 294ff.

[6] The same reinterpretation in the collective sense is seen in Ps. CV. 15 ("Touch not my anointed ones!").

[7] See VOL. I, pp. 137f.

Israel.[8] Jahweh is Israel's "creator" in the sense that he called this people in its whole physical existence into being, yet he is creator in particular because he "chose" Israel and "redeemed" her. When the prophet speaks of Israel's "creation," however, he is thinking of the historical acts which the old Exodus tradition had ascribed to the God of Israel, and especially of the miraculous crossing of the Red Sea. In Deutero-Isaiah "to create" and "to redeem" (גאל) can be used as entirely synonymous.[9] When, taking the literary form of the hymn, he pictures Jahweh as the creator and redeemer of Israel, he does not allude to two separate activities, but to a single one, the saving redemption from Egypt (Is. XLIV. 24, LIV. 5). The fact that this saving act is never mentioned for its own sake, but only because it is the type and pattern of one to come, will be dealt with later.

We thus see in Deutero-Isaiah a remarkable combination of two traditions which originally had nothing to do with one another.[10] The reason for this sudden incorporation of the creation tradition into the prophet's preaching is to be found in the new situation in which Israel was placed. Abruptly confronted with the Babylonians and with the power of so great an empire, appeal to Jahweh and his power needed to range more widely than it did in the days when Israel was still more or less living a life of her own. If this explanation is correct, then it again presupposes that the prophet used considerable freedom in his handling of the creation traditions. His relationship to the old saving traditions seems to have been even freer still. Deutero-Isaiah could choose among them, he could combine them, and sometimes he could even interpret them in a new way. This positively eclective attitude is also something new, as form-criticism bears out. It has long been recognised that Deutero-Isaiah makes particular use of the literary category of the priestly oracle of response for his proclamation of salvation. This was the cultic form in which God's help was promised to a suppliant. Such characteristic expressions as "fear not" and "I redeem, I strengthen you, I help you, I am with you" or "you are mine" (Is. XLI. 10, 13f., XLIII. 1, 5, XLIV. 2, etc.) belong to this category,[11] but the discourses which speak of Jahweh as the creator of the world and of

---

[8] Is. XLIII. 1, 7, 15, XLIV. 2, 21.

[9] In Is. XLIV. 1f. Israel's creation is co-ordinated with her election.

[10] See R. Rendtorff, "Die theologische Stellung des Schöpfungsglaubens bei Deuterojesaja," in Z. Th. K., 51 (1954), p. 11.

[11] J. Begrich, "Das priesterliche Heilsorakel," in Z.A.W., lii (1934), pp. 81ff.

Israel, with which these are combined, certainly do not. Deutero-Isaiah has thus moulded the contents of the old traditions into a form of his own choice which was originally alien to them. Here again it is instructive to glance back to First Isaiah: when he, too, proclaimed salvation for Zion, he kept the form of the old Zion tradition.

Was Deutero-Isaiah really a prophet in the specialised sense of the word? Is it not more likely that this great unknown, whom it is so difficult to imagine speaking in public, was not a prophet but a religious writer of the greatest skill?[12] The question is easily answered, for the pivot on which his whole preaching turns is an awareness of the reality of Jahweh's creative word. At the time of his call a voice from heaven pointed him to the word of Jahweh, which "stands" tor ever. He finds it important to be able to think of himself as in the succession of earlier prophets (Is. XLIV. 26, XLV. 19). What they prophesied long ago is now beginning to be fulfilled (Is. XLIII. 9ff., XLIV. 7, XLV. 21), and in the case of the words which are put into his own mouth, realisation will follow in their wake (Is. LV. 10ff.). Indeed, Deutero-Isaiah sees the whole business of world-history from the viewpoint of its correspondence with a previously spoken prophetic word. In this he reminds us strongly of a near contemporary, the author of the Deuteronomic history,[13] the only difference being that with Deutero-Isaiah this theological aspect of history has much more practical application—he uses it for apologetic purposes, to counter the anxiety that in the long run the Babylonian gods may prove to be more powerful than Jahweh. In fact, Deutero-Isaiah puts in bold relief the question of who is the controller of world-history, and the answer he gives almost takes one's breath away—the Lord of history is he who can allow the future to be told in advance.[14] This is something the gods of the heathen cannot do, and therefore they are "nothing." In Jahweh's contest with the idols, the power to foretell proves his specific difference from them. Of course, in the arena of history, which is the scene of the mighty contest,

---

[12] The dangerous political situation of the time is not really a satisfactory explanation of the anonymity of the Deutero-Isaiah tradition. On the contrary, ought he not to have been remembered, and his name all the more dutifully connected with his message, some twenty or thirty years after he appeared, and after the great change in the situation which he foretold? Did Deutero-Isaiah appear in public? Or did he work only indirectly, as a writer? Not a few critics have taken the latter view (Begrich, *Studien*, p. 93, O. Eissfeldt, *The Old Testament, An Introduction*, trs. P. A. Ackroyd, Oxford 1965, pp. 339f.

[13] See VOL. I, pp. 343ff.   [14] Is. XLI. 25ff., XLVIII. 14.

Jahweh is thrown back on his people, for Israel is his witness. Poor as this witness is (Is. XLII. 19), it can perform this service at least:

> All the peoples are gathered together and the nations assembled;
> Who among them declared this, and tells us the former things?
> Let them bring their witnesses, that they may be justified,
>   let them tell it, that we may say, It is true.
> You are my witnesses, says Jahweh, and my servant,
>   whom I have chosen.

(Is. XLIII. 9-10)

The power of Jahweh's word in history is shown particularly in its shaping of the future of God's people (Is. LV. 10ff.).

Deutero-Isaiah has the almost gnostic vision of the word of Jahweh as the only source of creation. History and all its peoples are the realm of the transient (Is. XL. 6–8). Yet it is a sphere where prophecy is genuinely fulfilled, the battlefield where the witness borne by the servants of the true God is ranged against the presumptuous powers of the heathen gods and their prophecies (Is. XLIV. 25). Everything depends simply upon the word of God. Surely such a vision carries with it the title prophet. The fact that theological reflexion and rational argument, almost prolix on occasion, occupy a large space with Deutero-Isaiah corresponds with the spiritual climate of his age, and links him with Jeremiah and Ezekiel.

I. THE NEW SAVING EVENT

On the first occasion when Deutero-Isaiah heard Jahweh speak to him, he was given the content of his message[15] in a nutshell—Jahweh's advent is imminent; but he is not only to reveal himself to Israel: this time his advent is to be a final theophany for the whole world; he is to reveal his glory (כבוד) in the eyes of all the nations. In Israel only one man knows this, but in heaven the angelic beings are already astir— they are already summoned to the task of preparing the miraculous highway for this advent of Jahweh the king (Is. XL. 3–5). The new turn given to world-history by Cyrus has set events in motion that are swiftly leading to the end. "My deliverance is near, my help draws nigh" (Is. LI. 5, XLVI. 13). Jahweh has already bared his arm before the eyes of the nations (Is. LII. 10); a wonderful event is about to take place.

[15] On this cp. Begrich, *Studien*, pp. 92ff., 112ff; J. Linbdlom, *Die literarische Gattung der prophetischen Literatur*, Uppsala 1924, pp. 52ff.

OTT R

Deutero-Isaiah has a variety of ways of alluding to the new political direction given to history by Cyrus, and, contrary to the custom of the older prophets, he twice mentions him by name.[16] It is Jahweh himself who makes Cyrus the centre of attention not only for Israel but also for the whole world. Jahweh has "stirred him up" (Is. XLI. 2, 25), he addresses him in the courtly language of the ancient east as the one whose hand he has grasped, whom he accompanies as friend, whom he has called by name, and whom he loves.[17] Jahweh has now given Cyrus a free hand in world-history; he is to cut asunder bars of iron, and unsuspected treasures are to fall to him (Is. XLV. 2f.). The words are reminiscent of Jeremiah's thoughts about the dominion over the world which, at that time, Jahweh had given to Nebuchadnezzar (Jer. XXVII. 5ff.). His day is past, and it is now Cyrus who, as master of the world, accomplishes the will of Jahweh. Yet again Israel is and remains the object of these world-wide historical designs of Jahweh: it is for her sake that Cyrus has been "stirred up," and it is for her sake that he must be furnished with a world empire.[18] For it is he, Cyrus, who is to vanquish Babylon and to allow the captives to return home "without price or reward" (Is. XLVIII. 14, XLV. 13).

This could be described as the sole topic of the prophecy of Deutero-Isaiah, or at all events as a relatively self-contained set of ideas concerned with the impending historical events. What we have seen is, however, only the preparations, knowledge of which is given to the prophet, by whose means Jahweh mobilises history for the real subject. The saving event proper is the departure of the exiles from Babylon and their return home, and the advent of Jahweh himself, who is to

[16] It is certainly remarkable that Jahweh calls Cyrus "his anointed" (Is. XLV. 1), but this is no more than a rousing rhetorical exaggeration inspired by the actual situation. How could Deutero-Isaiah have meant more than this, since Cyrus was not of the line of David, and since the prophet had already imparted to his nation his prophecy concerning David (Is. LV. 1ff.)? Cyrus was Jahweh's instrument in basically the same way as the Assyrians were this for Isaiah of Jerusalem. So, his emotions kindling as he spoke, Deutero-Isaiah applied to Cyrus that title which his own preaching had left without any rightful bearer. If Cyrus had a *charisma*, its activity is exclusively restricted to the political field.

[17] Is. XLV. 1–3, XLVIII. 14. Notice has always been taken of the parallelism with the courtly form of language used on the so-called Cyrus cylinder about the relationship of the god Marduk to Cyrus. H. Gressmann, *Altorientalische Bilder zum Alten Testament*, 2nd edn., Berlin and Leipzig 1927, pp. 368ff.; J. B. Pritchard, *Ancient Near Eastern Texts relating to the Old Testament*, 2nd edn., Princeton 1955, pp. 315f.

[18] Is. XLV. 4; Begrich, *Studien*, p. 69.

accompany his people. It is only now that the prophet's message reaches its climax and his language soars to the highest flights of passion. The stir of emotion, the quiver of excitement felt in these passages is almost unmatched in the whole of prophecy. At one moment he calls upon the exiles to touch no unclean thing, to make ritual preparation for the departure, because Jahweh in person accompanies them on the march (Is. LII. 11–12, XLVIII. 20), at another he speaks of the miraculous conditions which are to attend this march through the desert.

> They shall not hunger or thirst,
> neither scorching wind nor sun shall harm them,
> for he who has pity on them will lead them,
> and by springs of water will he guide them.
>
> (Is. XLIX. 10)

Those who go forth will not thirst nor feel hunger (Is. XLVIII. 21). The road will not be hard for them, for all obstacles are to be removed, so that they will travel on a level highway (Is. XLIX. 11). Myrtle trees are to grow instead of thorns (Is. LV. 13), and Jahweh is to turn darkness into light (Is. XLII. 16); indeed the whole of nature it to take part in the beatitude of this saving event—the mountains are to break forth into singing and the trees to clap their hands (Is. XLIX. 13, LV. 12), when the redeemed of Jahweh return "with everlasting joy upon their heads" (Is. LI. 11). On another occasion Deutero-Isaiah shows us these same events from the standpoint of the holy city, telling how the "messenger of good tidings" (מבשר) speeds before the marching column, and how the watchmen see him and break out into songs of joy.

> How beautiful upon the mountains are the feet of him who brings
>   good tidings,
> who publishes salvation, who brings tidings of good, who publishes
>   deliverance,
> who says to Zion, "Your God has become king."
> Hark, your watchmen lift up their voice, together they sing for joy;
> for eye to eye they see their delight at the return of Jahweh to Zion.
> Break forth and rejoice together, you waste places of Jerusalem,
> for Jahweh has comforted his people, he has redeemed Jerusalem.
>
> (Is. LII. 7–9)

Thus, as the prophet understands him, this man is a εὐαγγελιζόμενος (Is. LII. 7, LXX): one who makes speed before the advent of the Lord and proclaims the dawn of God's kingly rule! In another place Deutero-Isaiah entrusts this office of herald of victory to Zion herself. As yet the wonder is all unknown to men; only on Zion is there knowledge of it; therefore she has the duty of proclaiming the tidings of Jahweh's advent far and wide throughout the land (Is. XL. 9–11).

However, the proper significance of the event only becomes clear when it is seen within that context of the saving history in which Deutero-Isaiah himself set it. There can be no doubt that the prophet regards the exodus of the redeemed from Babylon as the counterpart in the saving history to Israel's departure from Egypt in the far off past. He in fact stresses the parallel course of the two events—Jahweh is once more to go forth as a warrior (Is. XLII. 13), as he then did against the Egyptians, and at the new exodus, as at the first, he is miraculously to make water flow from the rock for his people to drink (Is. XLVIII. 21). At the same time, the new exodus will far surpass the old in wonders, for this time they are not to depart in "haste" (חפזון)—an idea which formed an important element in the old tradition (Ex. XII. 11; Deut. XVI. 3)—but Jahweh is to lead them in person (Is. LII. 12). One must be clear about what is implied here. In referring as he does to the new exodus, Deutero-Isaiah puts a question mark against "Israel's original confession"[19]; indeed, he uses every possible means to persuade his contemporaries to look away from that event which so far had been the basis of their faith, and to put their faith in the new and greater one. Does this mean then that Deutero-Isaiah thinks that God's saving activity for his people falls into two phases? As a matter of fact, the prophet stated this in plain terms by drawing such a sharp distinction between "the new," that which is "to come to pass hereafter," and the "former things."[20] By the former things he can hardly mean anything other than that saving history which began with the call of Abraham and the exodus from Egypt and ended with the destruction of Jerusalem.[21] Deutero-Isaiah attaches great importance to the fact that the

[19] See VOL. I, pp. 175f.

[20] "The former things" (קדמוניות) Is. XLIII. 18, "the former things" (ראשנות) Is. XLI. 22, XLII. 9, XLIII. 9, 18, XLVI. 9, XLVIII. 3, "the new thing(s)" (חדשות) Is. XLII. 9, XLIII. 19, XLVIII. 6, "what is to come hereafter" (אתיות) Is. XLI. 23. In the discussion of the problem raised by the juxtaposition "the former things" and "the new things," C. R. North, "The 'Former Things' and the 'New Things' in Deutero-Isaiah," in *Studies in Old Testament Prophecy*, ed. H. H. Rowley, Edinburgh 1950, pp. 111ff., deserves special mention.

[21] Rohland, *Erwählungstraditionen*, pp. 99ff. A similar interpretation of the "former

events in this history were all foretold, and came to pass accordingly; for they plainly show the importance Jahweh attaches to his word, and this allows men to put their trust in the new event prophesied. It is worth note in passing that in the idea that all saving history is history foretold by Jahweh Deutero-Isaiah agreed with his contemporaries—cp. the Deuteronomist. By the "new" event he means the saving act about to come after a long pause in the saving history, and which he as a prophet can foresee from the course of secular history. A remarkable aspect of Deutero-Isaiah's message is that on the one hand he so depicts the departure of the exiles from Babylon as to recall the first exodus from Egypt and the miracles which accompanied it; yet he is also aware that Jahweh's new revelation is something which cannot possibly be represented—no one is to imagine that he knew of it and anticipated it on the basis of the earlier event (Is. XLVIII. 7f.). And because the task Jahweh is now undertaking is so marvellous and will so completely eclipse his previous ones, Deutero-Isaiah believed that his contemporaries should concentrate all their thought upon it and turn away from the events which had previously given their faith its content. On one occasion he stated this very bluntly, in words which the pious in particular must have felt to contain an element of blasphemy:

> Thus says Jahweh, who made a way in the sea, a path in the mighty waters,
> who brought forth chariot and horse, army and warrior together
> —they lie there, they rise not up, they are extinguished, quenched like a wick!—
> "Remember not the former things, nor consider what is past!
> Behold, I am doing a new thing, now it sprouts forth, do you not perceive it?
> Yea, I make a way in the wilderness. . . ."
>
> (Is. XLIII. 16–19a)

The verses first make clear that by the former things Deutero-Isaiah means the act of deliverance at the Red Sea on which the saving history was based, and the exodus from Egypt. We may conclude from the

things" and in particular of "remember not" in Is. XLIII. 18 had already been given by A. Bentzen: "But Deutero-Isaiah exhorts his people no longer to look back to the Holy Past of their nation, the 'old' history of salvation embodied in the story of the Exodus from Egypt." "On the Idea of 'the Old 'and 'the New' in Deutero-Isaiah," in *Studia Theologica*, I, 1947, p. 185.

style of vss. 16f. that the account of the saving act with which Deutero-Isaiah was familiar was one given in hymns used in worship. From now on, however, Israel is to turn her back on this venerable tradition of Jahwism. This can mean one thing only—Jahweh's first dealings with Israel have come to a full circle. As the prophets viewed history, the exile was an end; as a threat which had received fulfilment, it was the end of a road leading from prophecy to fulfilment. Now, however, in Deutero-Isaiah's eyes, the "new" event is on the point of beginning, for its first dawning rays are already visible. "The first has passed away" and only remains valid as a type of the new. Never before had a prophet so sharply marked off the inauguration of the *eschaton*, nor so strictly dissociated it from all Jahweh's previous actions in history. In actual fact, there was also a great danger inherent in this sharp discrimination. Must it not have meant for the prophet's hearers that Jahweh's action was completely torn in two, with the result that justifiable doubts must have arisen about the credibility of the new prophecy? If there was no sort of continuity between the old and the new, was it really the self-same Jahweh who was at work in both parts? This caused Deutero-Isaiah no trouble, however, for the new as well as the old had been foretold long ago. This gave his message its legitimation: it was legitimised by the continuity of prediction.[22]

This proof from prediction, which Deutero-Isaiah is conspicuously eager to use, has a wider significance than for Israel only. As we have already seen, its strength depends on the theological judgment passed on the power—or rather, the lack of power—of the heathen gods. Indeed, there is something absolutely new in the way in which Deutero-Isaiah always pictures Jahweh's total saving action as at the same time relating to the heathen, "the nations," as well as to Israel, that is, as relating to the influences which these acts upon Israel are to have on the political world round about her. Deutero-Isaiah is firmly convinced that their effects will be on a world scale. Once Jahweh has performed his work upon Israel, there will be a universal "twilight of the gods" among the nations, for the heathen will realise the impotence of their idols. The heathen will be put to shame (Is. XLI. 11, XLII. 17, XL. 24),

[22] Is. XLIV. 7f., XLV. 21. It is not easy to say what Deutero-Isaiah is thinking of as he speaks of this already fulfilled prophecy. Is he thinking of earlier oracles against Babylon such as Is. XIII or XIV? Or did he, perhaps like his predecessor Hosea, understand the old saving history as prophecy? He obviously believes that he stands himself in a prophetic tradition.

they will come to Jahweh (Is. XLV. 24); indeed, because they are convinced of the greatness and glory of the God of Israel, they will even bring home the Lord's scattered people (Is. XLIX. 22f.). "Kings shall see it and arise, princes, and prostrate themselves" (Is. XLIX.7). Then, again by Deutero-Isaiah's lips, Jahweh can make a direct appeal to the nations to avail themselves of this hour of the dawn of salvation: "Be saved, all the ends of the earth" (Is. XLV. 22); "let the coastlands put their hope in Jahweh and wait for his arm" (Is. LI. 5). This ought not to be called a "missionary idea," however, for when Deutero-Isaiah describes Israel as a "witness" for the nations (Is. XLIII. 10, XLIV. 8, LV. 4), he is not thinking of her sending out messengers to them. In the prophet's mind Israel is thought of rather as a sign of which the Gentiles are to become aware, and to which, in the course of the eschatological events, they will resort of their own accord. They will come to Israel and confess that "God is with you only, and nowhere else, no god besides him"; "only in Jahweh are salvation and strength"; "truly, thou art a God who hidest thyself" (Is. XLV. 14f., 24).

Did people believe the prophet when he said this? The question introduces us to another peculiar side of his activity, his discourse with those of little faith and those who had grown weary, for whom reality wore a very different appearance, because they felt themselves forsaken by God and were unable to believe that Jahweh cared about their "way."

> Why do you say, O Jacob, and speak, O Israel,
> "My way is hid from Jahweh, and my right is disregarded by my God"?
>
> (Is. XL. 27)

> Fear not, for I am with you, look not in dismay, for I am thy God.
>
> (Is. XLI. 10)

> But thou, Zion, sayest, "Jahweh has forsaken me, my Lord has forgotten me."
> Can a woman forget her sucking child, that she should not have compassion on the son of her womb?
> Even if these forget, yet will I not forget you; see, I have graven you on my hands. . . .
>
> (Is. XLIX. 14–16a)

For a brief moment I forsook you,
  but with great compassion I will gather you.
For mountains may depart and hills be removed,
  but my grace shall not depart from you,
    and my covenant of peace shall not be removed.

(Is. LIV. 7, 10)

Never before had Jahweh spoken in such a way by the lips of a prophet. Never before had he come so close to his people when he addressed them, laying aside anything which might alarm them in case he should terrify one of those who had lost heart. In these dialogues the prophet brings every possible means of persuasion into play. He appeals now to reason, now to emotion. He gives arguments and proofs. As Deutero-Isaiah entices and woos the heart of Israel, hardened by excessive suffering, he uses terms which expose the heart of his God almost shamefully. He almost makes light of the divine wrath which lies upon Israel and of the judgment that has been executed. Israel has already made too great expiation (Is. XL. 2); or, the wrath lasted only a brief moment, and it is now past (Is. LIV. 7). To be sure, Jahweh kept silent when the enemy exulted over his people. Yet, how he had to restrain himself and hide his pain (Is. XLII. 14)! No one is to think that Jahweh has rejected his people in wrath for all time. "Where is the bill of divorce?" There is none (Is. L. 1)! And if the question be put, why does Jahweh still hold on to this people, the answer is, "because you are precious in my eyes, and honoured, and I love you" (Is. XLIII. 4). And if the further question be put, why the accusations which were so prominent in the pre-exilic prophets fall into the background with Deutero-Isaiah, and why it is only with him that the message of Jahweh's invincible love bursts out with such mighty power, the answer is that Jahweh has forgiven his people. The prophet looks upon this forgiveness as an unlooked for event which it is his task to voice in this special hour of history.

2. THE NEW SERVANT

The Servant Songs are discussed separately, perhaps because we cannot fully understand them.[23] We see that, both in diction and in their theo-

[23] For the extensive literature the reader is referred to the list compiled by W. Zimmerli and J. Jeremias, *The Servant of God*, trs. H. Knight and others, henceforth cited as *Servant*, London 1957, pp. 105ff.

logical subject-matter, they have much in common with the rest of
Deutero-Isaiah—for there is no reason to think that their author is not
Deutero-Isaiah himself. On the other hand, we still cannot dovetail
these songs smoothly and successfully into the prophet's ideas as outlined above. For all their close connexion with his preaching, they still
stand in a certain isolation within it, and have their own peculiar
enigmas enshrouding them. Not a few of the questions which are of importance for their understanding can no longer be answered—or at
least, the expositor ought to allow that, in places, more than one
answer is possible.

> Behold, my servant, whom I uphold, my chosen, in whom I delight.
> I have put my spirit upon him, he will bring forth truth to the nations.
> He does not cry, or lift up his voice, or make it heard in the street.
> The bruised reed he will not break and the dimly burning wick he
>   will not quench.
> Faithfully does he bring forth justice, he is not extinguished nor
>   broken,
> till he has established truth in the earth; and the coastlands wait for
>   his teaching.   (Is. XLII. 1–4)

In this first song, the speaker throughout is God. Jahweh introduces
his Servant, and he does so in a form apparently borrowed from the
court. This is the way in which, on some solemn occasion, an emperor
might have presented one of his vassal kings or a provincial governor
to his nobles and legally defined the new official's duties and powers.[24]
After the presentation, a statement is made about the equipment received by the official to help him in the discharge of his grave responsi-
bilities—that is to say, his *charisma*. Then comes a brief description of
the responsibility itself—he is to bring forth "truth" to the nations who,
indeed, already await his teaching. Finally, we are also told something
about the way in which he is to work. There is nothing violent about
it: it is something that spares, something that saves. The meaning of the
word מִשְׁפָּט, which occurs three times, is important for the understanding of the passage. It could be taken as meaning a "pronouncement
of judgment," that is to say, the clement judgment which the Servant
has to speak to the nations.[25] A more probable view, however, is that

[24] We should think of an act such as David's presentation of Solomon as his
successor in I Chron. XXVIII. 1ff.
[25] So Begrich, *Studien*, pp. 161ff.; Zimmerli, *Servant*, pp. 27f.

מִשְׁפָּט has a very general sense, and means the God-given fixed orders for cult and life. It could in fact be equated with true religion.[26]

> Listen to me, you coastlands, give heed, you peoples from afar.
> Jahweh called me from the womb, from the body of my mother he named my name.
> He made my mouth a sharp sword, in the shadow of his hand he hid me;
> he made me a polished arrow, in his quiver he hid me away;
> and he said to me, "You are my servant <   > in whom I will be glorified."
> But I thought, I have laboured in vain, spent my strength for nothing and vanity.
> Yet my right is with Jahweh, and my recompense with my God.
> But now Jahweh speaks, who formed me from the womb to be his servant,
> to bring Jacob back to him, and that Israel might not be cut off.
> So I am honoured in the eyes of Jahweh, and my God is my strength.
> He said: "It is too light a thing that you are my servant to raise up the tribes of Jacob
> and to restore the preserved of Israel—
> I make you a light to the nations, that my salvation may reach to the end of the earth."   (Is. XLIX. 1–6)

Here the speaker is the Servant himself. The partner whom he calls upon to listen to him is the whole body of the nations of the world. He speaks—exactly in the manner of a prophetic account in the first person—first of all of his call. Like Jeremiah, the Servant was called by God before he was born, and before he had been used (while he was still hidden in God's quiver), God had confided to him his plan: he himself was to be glorified in the Servant.[27] When the Servant complained that his efforts were nevertheless vain—the complaint and God's answer which follows are strongly reminiscent of the form in which Jeremiah's Confessions are couched—God renewed his commission, this time in specific terms. On the one hand, the Servant had a mission to Israel. This was to restore those who had been preserved and to raise

[26] As for example the use of God's מִשְׁפָּט in II Kings XVII. 27 and Is. LVIII. 2; cp. Jer. v. 4, VIII. 7. Our word "truth" would be closer than "justice."

[27] We regard "Israel" in vs. 3 as a later interpolation, with the majority of expositors. See the Note in Mowinckel, *He that Cometh*, pp. 462f.

up again the tribes of Jacob. Behind this mission, however, as yet entirely unaccomplished, already lies a second, namely, to be a light to the Gentiles and to mediate Jahweh's salvation to the ends of the earth. No inner causal connexion is apparent between the two, they are indeed far removed from one another. The phrase "raising up the tribes of Jacob" seems to indicate a re-establishment of the old clan alliance, and not the organisation of the new Israel as a nation.

> The Lord Jahweh has given me a disciple's tongue,
> that I may know how to feed the weary;
> the Lord has opened my ear to know the word.
> Morning by morning he waked my ear, to listen like a disciple,
> and I was not rebellious and I turned not backward.
> I gave my back to those who smote me, and my cheeks to those who
>   pulled out my beard.
> I hid not my face from shame and spitting.
> But the Lord Jahweh helps me, therefore I shall not be confounded,
> therefore I set my face like a flint, and know that I shall not be con-
>   founded.
> He who vindicates me is near; who will accuse me?
> Let him come near to me!
> Who has a claim against me? Let him take his stand before me!
> Behold, the Lord Jahweh helps me; who is it who condemns me?
> Behold, all of them wear out like a garment; the moth eats them up.
> (Who among you fears Jahweh, let him hearken to the voice of his
>   servant.
> Who walks in darkness and has no light, let him trust in the name of
>   Jahweh and rely upon his God.
> But all of you who kindle a fire, who sets brands alight,
> walk by the light of your fire, by the brands which you have kindled).
>   (Is. L. 4–11a)

The form and content of this song too is reminiscent of Jeremiah's Confessions, and it is best defined as a "prophetic psalm of trust."[28] The relationship of the Servant to Jahweh is that of a prophet—he has an obedient tongue, which finds its special employment in comforting the weary, and an ear which is unceasingly open to receive revelation. Since revelations come to him continuously and without interruption, his experience differs from that of his predecessors—the Servant's con-

[28] Elliger, *Deuterojesaja*, p. 34.

verse with God is constant. His ministry has certainly brought him sore suffering, but he has never lost the conviction that he is secure in Jahweh. This gives him strength to endure and to look ahead to his vindication. The fact that the language used here is the language of the law courts does not necessarily indicate that the Servant held a specific legal position; such language forms part of the imagery which is proper to these expressions of confidence (cp. Job xiii. 18f.). It is not certain that vss. 10f. are part of the song, for here suddenly someone else— probably the prophet, but it may even be Jahweh—speaks about the Servant. But in view of what they say about the Servant's suffering and his faith I prefer to include these verses. They contain an exhortation— or rather, a threat—against those who ignore the Servant or who are even, perhaps, the authors of his sufferings.

> Behold, my servant shall prosper,
>   he is lifted up and will be highly exalted;
> even as many were shocked at him,
>   his appearance was so marred, beyond human semblance,
>   and his form not like that of men,
> so he will make expiation for many nations,
>   kings shall shut their mouths before him.
> For that which has never been told them they shall see,
>   that which they have never heard they shall understand.
>
> Who believes what we have heard?
>   And to whom is the arm of Jahweh revealed?
> He grew up before us like a young plant,
>   and like a root out of dry ground.
> He had no form, no majesty,
>   we saw him, but there was no beauty that we should love him.
> He was despised, forsaken by men,
>   a man of sorrows, acquainted with grief.
> As one from whom men hide their faces
>   —he was despised—we esteemed him not.
> Yet it was our sicknesses he bore,
>   and our pains he carried,
> and we reckoned him as stricken,
>   smitten by God and afflicted.
> But he was wounded for our transgressions,
>   bruised for our iniquities.

Chastisement that makes us whole lies on him,
   and with his stripes we were healed.
All we like sheep have gone astray,
   we looked every one to his own way,
But Jahweh laid on him the iniquity of us all.
Racked, he suffered meekly
   and opened not his mouth;
Like a lamb that is led to the slaughter,
   and like a sheep that before its shearers is dumb. . . .
He was taken from prison and judgment,
   and his state,[29] who still thinks of it?
For he was cut off out of the land of the living,
   for our transgressions he was put to death.
And they made his grave with the wicked,
   and his place with evildoers,
although he had done no violence
   and there was no deceit in his mouth.
Yet it was the purpose of Jahweh to smite him [with sickness].
When he makes his life an offering for sin,
   he shall see his offspring, he shall prolong his days.
And the purpose of Jahweh shall prosper in his hand.
After the travail of his life he shall cause him to see light,
   and satisfy him with his knowledge.

My servant . . . makes the many righteous
   and takes their guilt upon him.
Therefore I will give him the many for his portion,
   and he can apportion the strong as spoil,
because he poured out his soul unto death,
   and was numbered with the transgressors,
while he bore the sin of the many,
   and made intercession for the transgressors.

                    (Is. LII. 13 – LIII. 12)

Since the passage is arranged as a sequence—a speech by Jahweh (Is.
LII. 13–15), a chorus (Is. LIII. 2–10), and another speech by Jahweh (Is.
LIII. 11–12)—it may be called a prophetic liturgy, though it must be

---

[29] For the translation of דור as "state," see G. R. Driver, "Linguistic and Textual
Problems: Isaiah XL–LXVI," in *J.T.S.* XXXVI (1935), p. 403.

remembered that not only several of its component forms—as, for example, the presentation of the Servant to all the kings of the earth—but also the specific contents of the "dirge" in particular, go far beyond anything which could have been found in the context of worship. The speech of Jahweh with which the song begins draws attention to the Servant's future, his exaltation. It displays him before all the nations of the world, and it envisages the precise moment at which they will become aware of the true position of the man who has been despised and mutilated beyond human semblance. Greatly astonished, they become acquainted with something "that had never been told them." The unusual aspect of this great poem is that it begins with what is really the end of the whole story, the Servant's glorification and the recognition of his significance for the world. This indicates, however, one of the most important factors in the whole song—the events centring on the Servant can in principle only be understood in the light of their end. It is only thus that all the preceding action can be seen in its true colours.

Accordingly, when the chorus which now follows describes the events of which the Servant is the centre, it does so in retrospect; it therefore expresses insights which could only be seen from an eschatological standpoint. There is some dispute about the identity of those who sing the song. If we begin with its context, then it seems that the singers are the contemporary Gentile world: but some commentators believe that because of its resemblance to a lament for the dead the song could only have been sung by Israel.[30] Following the form of a dirge, the chorus launches into a description of the dead man: but what is emphasised here is not the Servant's renown, as in the customary eulogies, but his wretchedness and the contempt in which he is held. The singers accuse themselves of blindness: they had been unable to understand the event which had taken place before their eyes—the Servant suffered for others; the man to whom they had refused fellowship was the man who was truly one with them. The choir never tires

[30] The decision is also to some extent dependent on the way in which we understand vs. 1b onwards. The question "to whom is the arm of God revealed?" is probably to be related to the Servant (it therefore has the sense of "to what sort of a person"). A different interpretation relates the revelation to a group of people who are for their part opposed to another group to whom Jahweh did not reveal himself. But the idea of a group which pays no heed to the Servant is nowhere suggested in the text, whereas everything turns on the "qualis" of the Servant.

of finding new ways with which to reiterate the one fact that the
Servant took it upon himself to act vicariously, that submissively and
unresistingly, and therefore deliberately, he took this mediating office
upon himself even unto death, and that in so doing he complied with
Jahweh's purpose.[31] Nor does the song spare words in describing the
depth of his suffering, though there is no definite information about its
nature, because, as is the custom in laments, various afflictions are
heaped upon the Servant—his outward appearance, his origin, the
disdain in which he was held, sickness (the idea that he was a leper is
old[32]), stripes: he was put in prison, disfigured, pierced (vs. 5a), and
bruised, and was given a degrading burial. The song thus endeavours
to depict the Servant's sufferings as supreme. At the same time there is
an awareness that Jahweh's purpose in appointing the Servant does not
fail and that he will have life and "offspring" (vs. 10b)—obviously
beyond the grave.[33]

Jahweh's speech at the end of the song introduces a further important
concept in describing the Servant's saving work—he "makes the many
righteous," i.e., he brings them back into the proper relationship to
God, and does so by "removing their guilt." As with his sufferings, so
too the Servant's saving function is described in several different ways
—he "cleanses" (חזה), he bears sicknesses (נשא), carries sorrows
(סבל), chastisement is laid upon him (מוסר עליו), his stripes heal
(רפא), he makes his life a substitute (שים אשם), he makes righteous
(הצדיק), he pours out his life (הערה), he acts vicariously (הפגיע).
Interpretation of these "songs" must from the very first be subject
to the limits imposed by the very flowery language in which they are

---

[31] The statement that the Servant gave his life as "an offering for sin" (אשם vs. 10)
is another of the variations played on the theme of vicarious suffering. If this alludes
specifically to the sacrifices offered in the cult, a special importance would accrue to
the expression from the theological point of view; for the suggestion that the Servant's
sacrifice surpassed the sacrificial system would certainly be unparallelled in the Old
Testament, and it perhaps also contradicts Deutero-Isaiah himself (Is. XLIII. 22f.). It is
perhaps best to understand אשם in the more general legal sense of "substitute,"
"compensation" (I Sam. VI. 3).

[32] For the idea—a very old one—that the Servant was a leper, see Zimmerli,
Servant, pp. 62ff. The translation in the Vulgate is "quasi leprosus."

[33] In the song, the "many" with whom the Servant is contrasted, and for whose
sake he suffered, are mentioned on four occasions (Is. LII. 15, LIII. 11, 12a, 12b). The
term is to be understood in the inclusive sense of "all" (and therefore not as exclusive:
many, but not all). J. Jeremias, Art. "πολλοί," in Th. W.B.N.T., VI, pp. 536ff.

written. The reader is often completely unaware that the author is using metaphor, and even where he uses direct speech he does not become any more precise, for he so piles up his words that, while what he says gains in force and emotion, the terms he uses are not exact, with the result that a certain vagueness still remains.[34] The same is true of the forms he employs. Though the writer certainly uses definite literary categories, he much expands them by the content he gives them. But his method is completely eclectic, so that even the forms have a limited usefulness as exegetical guides. They are all to a greater or lesser extent "disintegrated," i.e., they are divorced from their proper *Sitz im Leben* and broken apart by the special content they are now made to carry. Once this has been noticed, however, it provides a clue for the understanding of the songs as a group. Such extreme language can never have been applied to a living person—or even to one recently dead. If the Servant had been a contemporary prophet, Deutero-Isaiah himself for example, there would have been no need to hark back to forms from the court tradition; and the same holds true of the lavish use made of prophetic forms if he had been a former king. This transcendence of all familiar human categories is characteristic of discourse which foretells the future.

The only way to understand the songs completely is by understanding the nature of the office allotted to the Servant—the title "Servant of Jahweh" is itself too ambiguous to be much help.[35] The first thing that we can take for granted is that he does hold a definite office, though it may be thought of in an entirely novel way, and, secondly, he is not an imaginary figure standing outside all the familiar and traditional *munera*. This being so, only two possibilities are open

[34] Deutero-Isaiah's metaphorical way of speaking has been fully treated by Lindblom, *Servant Songs*, pp. 75ff.

[35] The patriarchs, Moses, David, the prophets, and Job have all been designated as the Servant of Jahweh. The idea that Cyrus disappointed Deutero-Isaiah's hopes, and that the latter thereafter transferred the title of Servant to someone quite different, the Servant of God, falls to the ground because of the lack of particularity in the title alone. Did not Jahweh have many servants? Above all however, this psychological interpretation goes beyond what exegesis can permit. In the case of a prophet of whose personality we know absolutely nothing, we are not in the position to raise such delicate psychological considerations. There may be something in this interpretation; the case may, however, be quite different. J. Hempel, "Vom irrenden Glauben," in *Z.S.T.*, 7 (1930), pp. 631ff. Begrich too presupposes that Deutero-Isaiah suffered disappointment, though it is in a different respect, *Studien*, pp. 112ff.

—the Servant's function is either that of a king or that of a prophet. In my judgment, only the second of these can be correct.[36] There are, certainly, one or two expressions (though they are not so numerous as many people think) which are typical kingly predicates, but they can be easily enough explained as incidental expansions of the traditional picture of a prophet.[37] The basic function of a king, that of ruling, is absent. The songs have as their theme proclamation and suffering—the basic prophetic functions at that time. How can the office allotted to the Servant in the "oracle of presentation" (Is. XLII. 1ff.) be understood as anything other than prophetic? In the second song, the Servant's first reference is to his mouth, which Jahweh made into a sword (Is. XLIX. 2), and in the third—again it is the first thing said—he conceives himself as an obedient speaker and recipient of revelation (Is. L. 4). We have abundant evidence that by the seventh century the idea of the prophetic role had changed, and the prophet was portrayed as a suffering mediator. Where is there such evidence for a suffering king?[38]

This conception of the Servant's office does not, of course, answer the second question: is the Servant pictured as an individual, or is he a symbol for the whole of Israel in its mission to the world? The second interpretation is a very old one; indeed, as the interpolation in Is. XLIX. 3 and the Septuagint's rendering of Is. XLII. 1 show, it is the oldest that we know.[39] It is also supported by the fact that Deutero-Isaiah elsewhere applies the term "Servant of Jahweh" to the nation of Israel,[40] and that much of what he says about Israel is used in the songs to refer to the Servant.[41] Yet this "collective interpretation" raises insuperable difficulties. The old objection, that according to Is. XLIX. 6 the Servant has a mission to Israel, is still valid. In addition, there is something forced in

[36] This interpretation is very impressively represented by Mowinckel, *He that Cometh*, pp. 187ff., 213ff., 218f. So also Zimmerli, *Servant*, pp. 25f.

[37] Here belong in particular the presentation by Jahweh (Is. XLII. 1ff.), the release of the prisoners (Is. XLII. 7) and the exaltation of the Servant before the kings who shut their mouths (Is. LII. 13f.). For a representation of this particular piece of court ceremonial see *Archiv für Orientforschung*, 1937/39, p. 21, figs. 23 and 24.

[38] See below, pp. 274ff.

[39] In early times, however, this collective interpretation was far from being the only one in the field. In Palestinian Judaism there are instances of the individual and Messianic interpretation, Zimmerli, *Servant*, pp. 54ff.

[40] Is. XLI. 8, XLII, 19, XLIV. 1, 2, 21, XLV. 4, XLVIII. 20.

[41] See H. H. Rowley, *The Servant of the Lord and Other Essays on the Old Testament*, London 1952, pp. 7f., 49f.

assigning to a group such an individualistic literary category as that of prophetic confession (Is. XLIX. 1ff., L. 4ff.). Above all, however, it is impossible to identify the lack of faith and unwillingness of Deutero-Isaiah's Israel with the willingness, complete self-surrender, and strength of faith of the Servant of the songs. Deutero-Isaiah did not think Israel's suffering to be innocent (Is. XL. 2, XLIII. 24, L. 1) as in the last song the Servant's is said to be.

Nevertheless, recent research has established that not even a thorough-going individualistic concept of the Servant resolves these difficulties, because the boundaries between the two ideas are fluid at certain points. It can certainly be said that the figure of the Servant embodies all that is good in Israel's existence before Jahweh. There are therefore theological cross-connexions between the Servant on the one hand and Israel on the other; Jahweh says of both that he chose them (Is. XLII. 1, XLI. 8), that he upholds them (תמך Is. XLII. 1, XLI. 10), that he called them from the womb (Is. XLIX. 1, XLVIII. 12).

These common features should, of course, be seriously considered by commentators: but they must not be allowed to obscure or veil the fact that the Servant depicted in these songs is a person entrusted with a prophetic mission to the whole world. But to what point in time does he belong? We may rule out those interpretations—some of which are grossly fanciful—that see in the Servant a figure of the past. The idea, long popular, that the Servant is none other than Deutero-Isaiah himself, is also unsatisfactory, because it leaves too many questions open, especially in connexion with the last song. This biographical method of interpretation which connects the songs with some individual breaks down on one particular feature which criticism has for too long ignored, because it set the songs in much too narrow a frame—the expressions used go far beyond biography, indeed they go far beyond the description of anyone who might have existed in the past or the present. The picture of the Servant of Jahweh, of his mission to Israel and to the world, and of his expiatory suffering, is prophecy of the future, and, like all the rest of Deutero-Isaiah's prophecy, belongs to the realm of pure miracle which Jahweh reserved for himself.

It is, of course, probable that Deutero-Isaiah included a number of his own experiences during his prophetic ministry in his picture of the Servant. That is not to say that he and the Servant were one and the same person. Jeremiah's suffering and converse with God also played a part in the picture of the Servant, yet Jeremiah is not the Servant. There is, however, one strand of tradition which we must recognise as particularly important for the origin of these songs; this is that of Moses, especially as he is represented in Deuteronomy. Moses is there designated the Servant of God,[42] indeed, he stands there as the prophetic prototype; and he also had the mission of allotting to the tribes of Jacob the various districts which they were eventually to inhabit (Num. XXXII. 33; Josh. XIII. 8, 15ff., XIV. 1f. [XIII. 32f.]). He too acts as mediator between Jahweh and Israel, he suffers, and raises his voice in complaint to Jahweh, and at the last dies vicariously for the sins of his people.[43] "Chastisement was laid upon him"—are not these traits which all recur in the Servant? And now consider further that the Servant is given the task of raising up the tribes of Jacob and restoring those who have been preserved. Here is struck up the message of the new Exodus, which is of course one of Deutero-Isaiah's main topics. Does not this message actually demand the foretelling—as antitype—of a prophetic mediator who is to be greater than Moses in the same degree as the new Exodus is to outdo the old? He ought not, of course, to be spoken of as a "second Moses" or a *Moses redivivus*, but as a prophet "like Moses." In my opinion, it is very probable that, as with Deuteronomy, Deutero-Isaiah stood within a tradition which looked for a prophet like Moses.[44] Deutero-Isaiah did not draw upon Deuteronomy. It is much more likely that both used an existing Mosaic tradition, about his office as mediator, and about the prophet who was to come. Deutero-Isaiah, of

[42] In the Old Testament Moses is 40 times called a servant of God. Eleven of these references are post-Deuteronomic (they are practically all to be found in the Chronicler's history and are therefore dependent on the Deuteronomic phraseology), and only five are pre-Deuteronomic (Ex. IV. 10, XIV. 31; Num. XII. 7, 8, XI. 11). Thus, by far the greatest number of references occur in Deuteronomy and the Deuteronomic history. This cannot be a matter of indifference for the interpretation of the almost contemporary texts concerning the Deutero-Isaianic Servant of God.

[43] Deut. III. 23ff., IV. 21, IX. 9, 18ff., 25ff. See VOL. I, pp. 294f. The correspondences between this picture of Moses and the Servant Songs were noticed a long time ago; they are particularly emphasised by J. Fischer, *Isaias 40-55 und die Perikopen vom Gottesknecht* (= *Alttestamentliche Abhandlungen* VI, 4-5), Münster 1916, pp. 191, 193; and more recently particularly by A. Bentzen, *King and Messiah*, trs. author, London 1954, pp. 66, 108. See also H.-J. Kraus, *Gottesdienst in Israel*, Munich 1954, p. 116.

[44] I am increasingly uncertain whether it is correct to understand the well-known verse, Deut. XVIII. 18, in the distributive sense ("a prophet on and on for ever"). Perhaps it rather contains the promise of a new Moses. However, even if the traditional way of taking the verse is the correct rendering of its meaning, a connexion can obviously still be made between the Servant Songs and this expectation.

course, developed it far more fully than did Deuteronomy. The tremendous new factor which he introduced—and it goes far beyond all previous prophecy—was the universal sweep of his prediction; and Deutero-Isaiah adapted the tradition about the prophet who was to come, a tradition which he certainly inherited, to suit this new dimension. Unlike Deuteronomy, what he stresses is the significance of the prophetic mediator for the world.[45] If the interpretation of the Servant of Jahweh as "a prophet like Moses" is correct, this would also close the uneasy gap which makes itself felt between the Servant songs and the rest of the message of Deutero-Isaiah.

[45] For final observations on the prophecy of the Servant, see below, pp. 273ff.

CHAPTER G

THE NEW ELEMENTS IN PROPHECY IN THE BABYLONIAN AND EARLY PERSIAN PERIOD

I

THEIR very succession in time prompts the question of what the three great prophets of the neo-Babylonian and early Persian periods have in common. Ezekiel was a younger contemporary of Jeremiah—the two must have known one another; and at the time when Ezekiel's prophecy ceased (after 571), Deutero-Isaiah may already have been alive. What specially links them, however, is that they lived during the period when the never ending crisis which began with the birth of the Mesopotamian empires' interest in Palestine had now entered upon its tensest and most acute phase. No one living in Jerusalem about the year 600 could fail to see that world-shaping events were already in preparation. But what was Jahweh's purpose behind them? Was it, indeed, entirely certain that Jahweh was still in control of events?—the element of sense in his control of history, and even his power, had, after all, been questioned. Zephaniah speaks of people who were saying that Jahweh "does neither good nor evil" (Zeph. I. 12); these were no atheists, but they no longer reckoned with divine action in the present day; and when the storm broke, and the Southern Kingdom suffered the same fate as had the Northern, and saw its upper classes deported to Babylon, the question of Jahweh's relationship to his people became completely uncertain. Indeed, to many of them it seemed already to have received a negative answer (cp. Jer. XLIV. 15ff.). Deutero-Isaiah, too, belongs to this period of acute crisis in that at a time when other answers seemed much more plausible, he came forward with the message of Jahweh's passionate concern for Jerusalem, and with the prophecy that Jahweh was even now about to raise up a world power in order that he might avow his loyalty to his people and glorify himself in history.

On the other hand, in considering the question of the common element in these three prophets, we must remember that they belong to a time when men had become even more detached than before from the ties of religion—a process which left its mark even on the prophets of the day. This does not mean that their prophetic passion was feebler as a result of the contemporary undermining of religious belief, but it does mean that there was some change in their relationship to the traditions of the faith. In VOL. I we have already mentioned the great extent to which, in the last days of the Monarchy, the individual emancipated himself from the group and asked questions about his rights as a person.[1] Thus, the prophets, too, of the monarchical era are much more of individuals, they are religious and literary personalities to a far greater extent than are Amos and even Isaiah. In short, the specifically human element and all the problems which this entails now claim a much greater place. Accordingly, these three prophets' relationship to the sacral traditions is looser and more eclective. How arbitrary Ezekiel or Deutero-Isaiah could be in handling a time-hallowed tradition (cp. Ezek. xx; Is. LV. 1ff.)! Jeremiah is generally taken to be the prophet who went furthest along the road of isolation and individuality, and in comparison with him Ezekiel may seem much more bound to tradition. And yet, in his very lavish use of elements taken from tradition, Ezekiel illustrates more than the change in the times in general. Indeed, it is probable that he was ahead of his time in the "modernity" of his interpretation and his use of a subtly rational and completely novel point of view to master his material. It is Ezekiel who makes it absolutely clear that his mental world is miles away from the world of traditions which he forces into some sort of relevance for his own day. Therefore, in order to give a proper answer to the question of what these prophets had in common, we have to start from the fact that they had all travelled far along the road towards becoming individuals.

To take an external point first, a new element in these prophets is that, as far as forms are concerned, their preaching stands on a very much broader basis than did that of the earlier prophets. The picture of the prophetic tradition has now far more colours to it. As well as the traditional literary categories (the messenger formula or oracles against foreign nations), we find in the prophets of this age large-scaled allegorical compositions (Ezek. XVI, XXIII), a theological excursus (Ezek, XVIII), a pastoral letter (Jer. XXIX), dialogues of the prophet with God.

---

[1] See VOL. I, pp. 391ff. As well as the sceptical utterance of the people of Jerusalem: "the way of Jahweh is not just" (Ezek. XVIII. 25, 29; cp. VOL. I, p. 391), another saying is quoted in Ezek. XII. 22: "every [prophetic] vision comes to naught."

long soliloquies of lament, etc. Two things are here characteristic. With Jeremiah and Ezekiel at least, the prophetic "I" suddenly becomes very much more prominent—indeed, the Book of Ezekiel is practically a long prophetic autobiography. These men are actually much more distinct personalities, they are more detached, and in their spiritual and theological aliveness much more self-dependent than were their predecessors.[2] In the same measure, they are also much more free not only in their choice of expression and in the forms in which they clothe their message, but also in their whole dealings with Jahweh. Nothing is more characteristic of the last than the fact that they could sometimes even turn on Jahweh with complaints and reproaches (Habakkuk, Jeremiah). The second feature is unquestionably closely connected with their versatility as individuals—their relationship to the "thou," the people to whom they spoke, has also changed, for it has become much more intense. Their message enters much more into the hearers' religious situation, indeed, it absolutely pursues them, and this means that the prophets' debate is at a much deeper level. Their audience was largely critical, if not positively sceptical, and if they wanted to be heard at all, they had to adapt themselves to this. Accordingly, their endeavours are directed even more than their predecessors' were towards being really understood by their hearers. They try to clear up misconceptions, they are urgent in their efforts to persuade, and they take care that their arguments are cogent. These efforts reach their climax in, for example, Deutero-Isaiah's discussions or his proofs from prophecy, with their broad theological basis (Is. XLI. 26f., XLIII. 9f., XLVIII. 14). This implies that theological reflexion played a very large part in giving its characteristic features to the preaching of these prophets. It is certainly no accident that the prophets of this era are the first with whom we see an effort to give an axiomatic definition and explanation of the phenomenon of the word of Jahweh. One notices how engrossed they are not only with each separate "word" which they have to deliver, but also with the phenomenon of the word of Jahweh in general. In the context of a purely abstract consideration of

[2] The direct result of this individualisation of prophecy was the increase in the number of collisions with those who saw the same situation with different eyes, and whom we call "false prophets." The collisions must have grown more and more in proportion as this individualising process progressed. It was only in this period that the latent problem of the authority of the prophetic word appeared in all its final acuteness.

the value which belongs to different modes of revelation, Jeremiah calls "the" word of Jahweh a hammer that breaks the rocks in pieces, and he contrasts it with the less authoritative form of revelation by means of dreams (Jer. XXIII. 28f.). Again, Deutero-Isaiah's statements on the word of Jahweh are demonstrably those of a theoretical theologian. There is something almost schematic about the way he divides the empirical world into two realms. On the one side is the world of flesh and the transience of everything in it; on the other, the word of Jahweh, the only thing creative and productive of blessing (Is. XL. 6–8, LV. 10f.). This unsurpassable value which is accorded to the word of Jahweh naturally increased these prophets' self-confidence. As the bearers and spokesmen of this word they occupied an absolutely key position between Jahweh and his government of the world.

2. One of the central subjects upon which they reflected was God's "justice," that is to say, the question of how Jahweh's faithfulness to the covenant was made effective. It was a question which had not only become a source of serious perplexity to the people of the day: it was also one which even the prophets were no longer able to answer in the same way as Israel had hitherto done. With Habakkuk it was the arbitrary action and arrogance of stronger political powers that raised doubts as to whether Jahweh was still gracious to his people. Jeremiah and Ezekiel faced the same problem from a different angle—how did Jahweh's will to save work out in practice for the individual? Did not his actions prove that he paid no heed to the individual, and that he was indifferent both to his guilt and his devotion and obedience? Did Jahweh's actions afford a reasonable basis for faith? It is not surprising that the prophets' answers to this perplexing contemporary problem do not follow any set pattern—why, different prophets even framed the question in different ways! Ezekiel countered the complaint that Jahweh lumped the generations together in wholesale acts of judgment by roundly asserting the contrary—each individual stands in direct relationship to God, and Jahweh has the keenest interest in the individual and the decisions which he takes, because he wants to preserve his life (Ezek. XVIII). In advancing this view, Ezekiel abandoned the old collective way of thinking. How modern and revolutionary the prophet appears here, this very prophet whose thinking is at the same time so conditioned by sacral orders! Jeremiah too has heard it said that the children had to bear their fathers' guilt, and he too used what was a radically individualistic view to counter the saying (Jer. XXXI. 29f.).

The answer that Habakkuk and Jeremiah received to the question "why" was different from that received by Ezekiel. Whereas Ezekiel had no hesitation in speaking of a clearly perceptible logic in the divine action in the case of an individual's responsible decision, with Jeremiah and Habakkuk the answer to the question why there should be such great and mysterious suffering is so remarkably veiled and obscure that it makes one feel as if Jahweh were retreating before the question, and withdrawing into ever deeper seclusion. At all events, both cases are alike in that they give no answer to the question "why," but only disclose horizons of still greater sufferings and trials. Jeremiah has to learn that he is still at the very start of his road, and that Jahweh can make no use of him if he is already failing in "a land that is safe" (Jer. XII. 5). While this oracle confines itself to directing the prophet's troubled eyes to greater problems and suffering, the one received by Habakkuk contained more comfort: it speaks of the promise that accrues to perseverance in faith (אמונה) on the part of the righteous (Hab. II. 4).

There was another respect in which the relationship between men of this time and Jahweh had been called in question. Not only had Jahweh's צדקה become a problem for them, but there must also have been many who came increasingly to doubt whether it was possible for Israel, that is, for the human partner, to maintain the covenant relationship offered her by Jahweh. For these people, therefore, what we call "assurance of salvation" had been shaken by doubts as to the possibility of men's צדקה. This brings us to the deeply perplexing questions which Jeremiah answered with the message of the new covenant and Ezekiel with that of the new heart.

In this connexion, we must first of all say something more about the great theological contexts to which these belong. For in this matter Jeremiah and Ezekiel were, of course, far from being lone voices crying in the wilderness. On the contrary, it can be easily shown that, in certain circles at least, religious thinking was very much alive during these years, and that it apparently concentrated on the question of the covenant, on how far men might rely upon it and how much it could bear. Here we must first mention Deuteronomy and the people who gave it its final form; for Deuteronomy is, of course, the outline of a comprehensive covenant theology, directed solely towards making the people of the time believe that the covenant had a meaning for their own day and generation. It covers a huge time-span, from Moses and the events at Sinai down to its own day, and it cries out to this late generation: now is the accepted time, now is the day of salvation! Here we must particularly consider the two passages Deut. v. 2f. and xxix. 4ff. [3ff.], which have already been discussed in VOL. I, for they reveal more clearly than anything else the effort to make the "contemporaneousness" of the Sinai covenant plausible for the present. The way in which Deuteronomy presses this offer of salvation also shows a concern lest Israel should reject what was almost an ultimatum (Deut. xxx. 15ff.); nevertheless, Deuteronomy still has a lively confidence that, if Israel harkens to the voice of Moses and obeys the commandments, she will have "life."

3. Some decades after the great occasion of the publication of Deuteronomy, in the reign of Josiah, saw the birth of the Deuteronomic history. This splendidly conceived theology of history does not, it is true, deal particularly with the problem of the covenant, but it works out, with a fascinating theological precision, that it was on Jahweh and his commandments alone that Israel, along with her kings, came to grief. Nowhere is this crushing verdict so forcefully expressed as in the words put into the mouth of Joshua at the assembly at Shechem, with which he cuts clean through Israel's declaration that she is prepared to serve Jahweh:

"You cannot serve Jahweh, for he is a holy and a jealous God" (Josh. xxiv. 19).

Like the sentence passed by the Deuteronomic history, these words —which are quite without parallel in the Hexateuch—must in some way link up with the verdicts passed by the prophets, particularly those of Jeremiah and Ezekiel; they are in line with what Jeremiah says about the Ethiopian who cannot change his skin (Jer. xiii. 23), and with Ezekiel's understanding of man. No one in Israel had yet realised with such clarity as Ezekiel the incapacity of human beings to live with and belong to God. His representation of the saving history as a series of entirely fruitless attempts on God's part (Ezek. xx) is almost blasphemous, and it too is connected with Josh. xxiv. 19.

It is clear, therefore, that a radically new factor had at this time entered into men's understanding of the will of Jahweh, a factor which specially affected the prophets. The change in their outlook as compared with that of the earlier prophets is shown by the fact that Jeremiah and Ezekiel made the concept of the will of God addressed to Is. el into something concrete by speaking summarily of Jahweh's

Torah or of *the* statutes.[3] They no longer judge single transgressions in the light of single commandments, but measure Israel against the whole body of Jahweh's will, and to this degree they recognise Israel's complete incapacity to obey. For these prophets the hardest problem lies in the realm of anthropology—how can this "rebellious house," these men "of a hard forehead and a stubborn heart" (Ezek. II. 3f.), who are as little able to change themselves as an Ethiopian can change the colour of his skin (Jer. XIII. 23)—how can these be Jahweh's people? Here, then, Jahweh's commandments have turned into a law that judges and destroys. The change can be clearly seen in a prophetic utterance which may well come from this time. It is couched in the form of a liturgy of the gate, that is to say, the ritual of question and answer which took place on entering the precincts of a shrine.[4] Now, however, the usual question runs in a completely different way—it has almost become a rhetorical question answered by "the sinners" themselves:

> Who can dwell with the devouring fire?
> Who can dwell with everlasting burning?   (Is. XXXIII. 14)

What was once a ritual used in worship has become an insoluble problem.[5]

If we are to understand the prophets' answer to this, the hardest question they faced, we must once again reflect on the idea of Jahweh's covenant with Israel, so clearly and impressively presented in Deuteronomy, for the Israel which Moses addresses is actually the Israel of the last days of the monarchy. Deuteronomy sets the scene in the past, but it is really Josiah's Israel which had just made the covenant with Jahweh and which was still looking forward to the fulfilment of his great promises; this Israel had certainly not as yet found rest, which means that the redemption of the great promise of blessing was still to come.[6] A comparison between this basic concept in the theology of Deuteronomy and Jeremiah's prophecy of the new covenant immedi-

---

[3] Characteristic examples of these summary quotations of *the* Law are Jer. VI. 19, VIII. 8, IX. 12 (13), XVI. 11, XXXI. 33, XXXII. 23; Ezek. V. 6, XI. 12, 20, XVIII. 5ff., XX. 5ff, XXXVI. 27. With some of these references, of course, account has to be taken of the Deuteronomic stamp given to the prophet's words.   [4] See VOL. I, pp. 377f.

[5] Another example of this prophetic radicalisation was pointed out by Zimmerli, "Die Eigenart der prophetischen Rede des Ezechiel," in *Z.A.W.*, LXVI (1954), pp. 24f.

[6] See VOL. I, p. 321.

ately reveals their similarity. Deuteronomy also looks forward to the future, to a time when Israel, obeying the commandments, is to live in the promised land. Neither Deuteronomy nor Jeremiah expect there to be any miraculous change in the outward conditions of Israel's future life. According to Deuteronomy, Israel is to be a true nation and to enjoy Jahweh's blessings in the realms of history and nature alike (מנוחה, ברכה). According to Jeremiah, Jerusalem is to be rebuilt, there is again to be buying and selling, people will again go on pilgrimages, and the laughter of those who rejoice will again be heard in the villages (Jer. xxiv. 5ff., xxxiii. 4ff., xxx. 18f.); this corresponds line for line with the picture in Deuteronomy even down to the latter's injunction to rejoice (Deut. xii. 7, 12, 18, xiv. 26, xvi. 11, etc.). There is only one point of difference: Jeremiah speaks of a new covenant, while Deuteronomy preserves the old one and goes to the limits of theological possibility as it extends its force to apply to contemporary conditions—the final period of the Monarchy. The difference highlights the crucial feature in the prophetic teaching; for Jeremiah places his entire confidence in the expectation of a new saving act with which Jahweh is to eclipse the Sinai covenant: but Deuteronomy hopes that Jahweh is now to give effect to the promises of the old covenant. Here is a remarkable and deep distinction which must be linked, as we have already seen, with the fact that for Deuteronomy the question of Israel's obedience had not yet become a problem,[7] whereas Jeremiah and Ezekiel take Israel's total inability to obey as the very starting-point of their prophecy.

We have already seen, of course, that the new thing looked for by Jeremiah did not mean that the Sinai covenant and its contents became obsolete. The prophet did not expect Jahweh to put his relationship to Israel on an absolutely new basis. The new thing is part of something else, for Jeremiah believed that Jahweh's old offer to Israel, that she should be his people and obey his commandments, was still valid. Here his view of the fulfilment of the Sinai covenant is exactly the same as Deuteronomy's. The new thing lies in the human sphere, in a change in the hearts of men.

Ezekiel's ideas are so much his own that it is unlikely that his pericope about Israel's spiritual renewal was taken directly from Jer. xxxi. 31ff. It is therefore all the more significant that the climax of his forecasts in Ezek. xxxvi. 25ff. should correspond almost exactly to Jeremiah. The

[7] See VOL. I, p. 230.

only difference is that Ezekiel's description of the process of man's re-
creation is very much more precise and detailed. He goes further than
Jeremiah in that for him Jahweh's work of re-creation is divided into a
whole series of separate divine acts, and the first of these is the promise
that Israel will be cleansed from her sins—something which Jeremiah
only includes as an appendix. Jahweh is next to give Israel a heart of
flesh instead of a stony heart; and finally he is to give her the most
important gift of all, the gift of his spirit so that she can keep his divine
commandments.[8]

We may notice in passing that Deutero-Isaiah too speaks of a new
covenant which Jahweh is to make with Israel. Is. LV. 3 clearly shows
that this future event is not seen as the actualisation of an already
existing covenant. Here it is the covenant with David which in its new
form is to embrace the whole people and bring glory to it (Is. LV. 3ff.).
Though Deutero-Isaiah differs from Jeremiah and Ezekiel, we can
see how much the problem of the covenant was exercising men's
thoughts during this whole period, and how the prophets also felt
themselves challenged to define their attitude to it.

We have still to consider the revolutionary significance of the amazing new factor which the message of Jeremiah, Ezekiel, and Deutero-
Isaiah must have contained for its hearers. The adjective "new" in
Jer. XXXI. 31 implies the complete negation of the saving events on
which Israel had hitherto depended. Such a judgment was infinitely
harsher than any previous one for it was an out and out challenge to the
validity of the basis of salvation on which Israel relied. It is as though
these prophets had changed the outlook of faith by 180 degrees. The
saving power of the old ordinances is abolished, and Israel can only
find salvation in new, future saving appointments on Jahweh's part.

Now, the message of the end of the old and the need to turn to a
future act of Jahweh was not itself new—it is also to be found in the
eighth-century prophets.[9] With the prophets of our period, however,
the gulf between the old and the new has become much wider, the
new beginning, which is the future saving event, is much more sharply,
and indeed aggressively, marked off from the end of the old—consider
words such as "not like the covenant which I made with their fathers"
(Jer. XXXI. 32), or "remember not the former things!" (Is. XLIII. 18),
or the mention of a time when the confession "as Jahweh lives who

[8] For the exposition of Ezek. XXXVI. 25ff., see above, pp. 234ff.
[9] See above, pp. 184ff.

brought up Israel out of the land of Egypt" will be done away with (Jer. XXIII. 7). Jeremiah's comments on the ark are also properly to be brought in here (Jer. III. 16f.). Obviously the creation of a new ark was being considered. Jeremiah abruptly rejects the proposal, however, for he envisages a time when "people shall no more say, 'The ark of the covenant of Jahweh' "; it will no longer be remembered, far less remade, for Jerusalem, and not the ark, will be called "Jahweh's throne." When we remember that for centuries the ark had been the sacral focal-point of Israel's worship we can see again the gulf between past and future in the saving history. In this matter, as well as in the words "they shall not remember," the oracle links up with Is. XLIII. 18. How could the prophets' hearers countenance such words, which blasphemously challenged everything that they held most sacred? Yet the men who spoke in this fashion were zealous devotees of Jahweh and spoke of him more seriously and with greater fervour than did any of their contemporaries.

The perplexing element in the message of these prophets was therefore what they said about a deep gulf in Jahweh's saving action towards his people, a gulf in whose depths God's people lay dead (Ezek. XXXVII). Theologically speaking, they consigned their audience, and all their contemporaries, to a kingdom of death where they could no longer be reached by the salvation coming from the old saving events. In this state, nothing remained for them but to cast their whole being on the future saving act which was already imminent. The task confronting such a man as Deutero-Isaiah was to use every means in his power— tender invitations, comfort, or theological argument—to overcome their scepticism and lack of faith. At the same time, it would be wrong to speak of a complete breach in the saving history, of its falling apart into two unrelated segments. For these prophets believed that when the new event was accomplished it would exactly follow the pattern of the old, as a new Exodus, a new covenant, a new David, etc. The old is therefore renewed, it is present in the new, in the mysterious dialectic of valid and obsolete. The prophets obviously set great store by this typological correspondence, for they work it out in their prophecies, and in so doing they are very careful to show how the new overtakes and surpasses the old. The new covenant will be better than the first, the new Exodus more glorious, and the suffering of the eschatological servant greater and, just because of this, also more effectual, than that of Moses.

4. In order to understand the last of these concepts, the prophetic Servant of Jahweh, we must add something to our previous summary.[10] Though the picture of the suffering Servant of God portrays a man of almost superhuman qualities, there are still one or two things to say about its origin, for it is not so completely isolated in the prophets' message as might at first sight appear. Let us take as our starting point that the Servant's office is manifestly prophetic. He proclaims the divine will and he is entrusted with a ministry of mediation which can only be called prophetic. Although our knowledge of Deutero-Isaiah is very slight, we can still be sure that he must have been specially competent to paint such a picture of the Servant's office. He had in fact to describe his own office raised to the nth degree; it was his own experiences and suffering from which he formed the description of one greater than himself.[11] The time was now long past when to be a prophet was something which carried with it its own evidence and required no justification, when a man prophesied because Jahweh had spoken.[12] In the period to which Jeremiah, Ezekiel, and Deutero-Isaiah belonged, the prophetic office itself had become the subject of theological reflexion. If we are correct in regarding the preaching of the eighth-century prophets as in some sense a continuous dialogue with tradition,[13] the same thing is certainly true of the prophets of the Babylonian and early Persian period. There is, however, one difference. In the interval the tradition had been enriched by a new factor, a store of experiences, and also of problems, which from generation to generation had attached themselves to the office and its representatives like a growing burden. The tradition in question must have been unique, and it was actually formed in unfavourable circumstances, for, as we are firmly convinced, the prophets under discussion should be regarded as an independent body of men and not as duly authorised officials. The best proof that there was such a tradition of the prophetic office at the end of the monarchical period, and that it in turn would have moulded the prophets of this age, is the presence of a relatively fixed—indeed, by now

[10] For the exposition of the Servant Songs, see above, pp. 250ff.

[11] Jer. XXIII. 5f. could be given as an example of the opposite case, a prophet's failure to expound traditional material due to his not having certain presuppositions concerning the tradition. In one of his prophecies Jeremiah did not succeed in duly bringing the Messianic tradition to life. See above, pp. 192, 217ff.

[12] On Am. III. 7, see above, p. 58.

[13] See above, p. 177.

almost conventional—picture of the prophet which is to be found in various contemporary versions.

One of the most important factors affecting the prophets of this time is the way in which their office increasingly invaded their personal and spiritual lives. Here again one must guard against exaggerating the difference from earlier prophecy into a difference in principle. Elijah and Amos, too, must have been keenly affected in their own persons by the opposition and vexation they encountered. Nevertheless, anyone who reads Jeremiah feels that at one vital spot something has broken. The very forms which he uses proclaim this—he expands his message into lyrics into which a new element enters: in these poems the prophet opens up a dimension of pain. It is a twofold suffering, the suffering of those upon whom judgment has come, but at the same time also God's grief over his people. And then—and this is the really important thing —Jeremiah himself enters into this twofold suffering; it weighs upon him, and he speaks of it as his own personal affliction. There is a difference here compared, for example, with Amos, for in his case we may unreservedly assume that his innermost spiritual and personal being remained less impaired. Jeremiah shifted the ground, and came over in sympathy to the side of the men under judgment. Indeed, Jeremiah's Confessions particularly showed us how, as a result, his prophetic office went to pieces, how the fragments of this utterly fruitless office fell away from him, and how then, simply as a human being vulnerable at every point, he was step by step led nearer to the terrifying night of abandonment by God.[14] Baruch then gave an objective account of this suffering and failure, and the main purpose of his writing was probably to counter any doubts as to Jeremiah's work as a prophet. The catena of mounting suffering and increasing failure is not evidence against Jeremiah's prophetic role. On the contrary, just because Jeremiah was a genuine prophet of Jahweh, his path inevitably ended in the way it did. His failure and collapse prove beyond doubt that he was a genuine prophet. Was Baruch in this passion story only describing, almost as a modern writer might, what he actually observed in Jeremiah, or did he have some preconceived idea about the suffering prophet which Jeremiah seemed to him to fulfil? Whatever the answer may be, he too expresses a very changed idea of the prophetic office.

Yet we meet the same idea in Ezekiel also. His very appointment as the responsible watchman resulted in his having to discharge his office

[14] For more detail, see above, pp. 201ff.

at the risk of his own life (Ezek. XXXIII. 1f.); on one occasion Jahweh even gave him the strange command to lie for a long time on the one side to bear the guilt of the house of Israel, and then on the other to bear that of the house of Judah (Ezek. IV. 4–8). The prophets had from the first performed symbolic actions: but here is something much more than the realistic demonstration of a tremendous guilt: it is the imposition of this guilt on one man whose task it is to bear it. Here again, then, the office with which the prophet is charged deeply affects the sphere of his personal life, and causes him to suffer; and here the suffering is expressly vicarious.[15] The difference is significant. In the case of the earlier symbolic acts, the sign was something exterior to the soul and spirit of the prophet concerned (wearing horns, breaking jars, etc., see above pp. 95ff.). Now, however, the prophet himself becomes a sign (Ezek. XII. 6), and this consists in the fact that he has been drawn by God himself into enduring the judgment sooner than all others and by way of example (cp. also Ezek. XXI. 11 [6], and see above pp. 232f.). We also meet this greatly changed conception of what is incumbent on a prophet in the judgment which Ezekiel passes on the false prophets. He reproaches them for not building a wall round Israel and not going up into the breaches when Jahweh threatened the nation (Ezek. XIII. 5), that is to say, they ought to have protected Israel, taken up their posts in her defence. Without question Ezekiel is thinking of omission to plead for the nation in prayer, though perhaps he may also have had some other form of intercessory work in mind.[16] We are taken a stage further by a verse in Ps. CVI—vs. 23—which sings Moses's praises for entering into the breach (עלה בפרץ) when Jahweh was resolved to destroy the people for the sin of idolatry, and was only deflected from his purpose by Moses's intercession (Ex. XXXII. 9ff.). Intercession was, to be sure, one of the particular functions of a prophet from the

[15] "When the prophet bears something, he at the same time obviously bears it along with others. His own life is caught up in the עון [guilt-punishment] of his people. Bound up in the bundle with them, as his symbolic action shows him to be, he lays the burden of Israel's guilt upon his own shoulders. One can hardly fail to notice here the presence, in embryo, of thoughts which are later fully developed in Is. LIII, which, too, probably has a prophetic figure in mind. . . . The Ezekiel tradition too seems to have contributed to the development of the picture of the Servant of Jahweh who takes the guilt of the many upon himself." W. Zimmerli, Ezechiel, Bib. Komm., p. 117.

[16] F. Hesse, Die Fürbitte im Alten Testament, Dissertation Erlangen 1949, pp. 56f.

[17] See above, pp. 51f.

OTT T

earliest times.[17] Yet, what a change must have come over this ministry now that it was exercised by a prophet who was ready to throw his own life into the breach between God and Israel! Nevertheless, this was the way in which later prophecy, the subject of the present section, understood the prophetic office. In the case of Jeremiah, his suffering had still no particular relationship to his office as intercessor. Jeremiah cannot, in fact, explain his suffering, and it obviously never occurred to him that there could be something vicarious about it, or that Jahweh had imposed it upon him actually for Israel's salvation.

There is, however, a picture of a suffering intercessor which must be almost contemporary with Jeremiah, a picture whose dimensions surpass the merely human. This is Deuteronomy's picture of Moses. Moses makes himself the intercessor for Israel. He speaks of his fear (יגרתי Deut. IX. 19) of the wrath of Jahweh which drove him to make intercession for the people and for Aaron, and recounts the words of the prayer which he then spoke. Yet, he made entreaty for himself as well, for Jahweh had cast his wrath against Israel upon him ("he was angry with me for your sake"), and had laid on him a terrible punishment for Israel's sake—he was not himself to set foot on the promised land, but was to die before it was reached. His plea that Jahweh should avert this fate was peremptorily silenced—he had to acquiesce in this hard decree (Deut. III. 23–8, IV. 21–7). The detailed way in which the whole story is told, with the prayers and answers set forth at length, shows how keen an interest there was at this time in this aspect of the prophetic office. Here, indeed, the act of intercession is more than just mentioned—Deuteronomy wants to move its readers with the picture of a man who, while greatly afraid, took God's wrath on himself, and who was to die vicariously outside the promised land. And if we consider with this the expectation Moses gave voice to that Israel should expect just such a prophet as himself in the future (Deut. XVIII. 18), then we are at once brought face to face with Deutero-Isaiah's prophecy of the suffering Servant, for God himself is to bear witness before the whole world "that he bore the sins of the many, and espoused the cause of the transgressors [making intercession for them]" (Is. LIII. 12). This is not meant to imply that Deutero-Isaiah took Deuteronomy's picture of a prophet as his immediate starting-point and went on to build upon it. It does mean, however, that his ideas about the nature of the prophetic office were familiar at the time and held by definite

[17] See above, pp. 51f.

prophetic message as it has often been supposed to be. On the contrary, what it says was prepared long beforehand. The formula of its theological prehistory may be said to rest on two antecedents. The first is the intercessory office, which from the very first the prophets knew was entrusted to them. The other is that inroad which the prophet's role made upon his soul and spirit which we have already mentioned. It is only by seeing Is. LIII in its proper context that we can see how unique it was. There are five specific points which separate the prophecy of Is. LIII from the current ideas of the time. 1. What is said about the depth and comprehensiveness of this prophetic suffering far surpasses all that had ever been said before. 2. Where however the Servant songs go especially far beyond all that had been said before them is their description of the Servant's readiness to suffer and of his paradoxical confidence of his safety in God. 3. Is. LIII foretells the Servant's advance into a realm beyond suffering where he is glorified before the whole world. 4. In Is. LIII the people for whom the Servant suffered overcome their initial blindness and acknowledge him. Their actual words are given. 5. The songs speak of the Servant as having a significance which reaches far beyond Israel. He confronts all the nations of the world. Kings are to shut their mouths before this Servant of God.

THE PROPHETS OF THE LATER PERSIAN PERIOD AND THE PROPHECIES OF THE NEW JERUSALEM

I. TRITO-ISAIAH, HAGGAI, ZECHARIAH, MALACHI, AND JONAH

DEUTERO-ISAIAH had spoken of the imminent restoration of the exiles, led by Jahweh in person, but we do not possess any document which gives us information about the actual return itself. It took place, but we do not know how, or even when. There are reasons which make it probable that the first move to the homeland only took place in the reign of Cambyses and not as a result of the edict of Cyrus. It is remarkable, however, that the event made no particular impact either on its own or on future generations. The return was obviously not accompanied by miraculous events— indeed, those who took part in it did not in any way regard it as a saving event. If they had done so, they would never have allowed it to fall into oblivion as if it were of no particular significance. It was obviously not celebrated as the fulfilment of a great prophetic prediction. Deutero-Isaiah's prophecies had therefore still to be fulfilled. None the less, Israel's situation had altered. The great hardship of the deportation had given way to the lesser ones of the resettlement and reconstruction. Yet for this era too Jahweh had raised up prophets who carried on the message of his advent. The theological judgments passed on these prophets of the later Persian period are usually guarded, if not actually negative. There can, of course, be no question of comparing messages of such matchless depth and range as those of Jeremiah, Ezekiel, and Deutero-Isaiah, each one of whom represents a whole world of prophecy and theology, with those of Trito-Isaiah, Joel, Haggai, Zechariah, and Malachi. None the less, we ought to be more chary of such summary judgments as "men of the Silver Age." To say nothing of the fact that these involve the setting up of an idea of spiritual originality which was unknown to Israel in general and to the prophets in particular, the only proper question is whether these prophets, in giving the message they did, were true ministers to their own day, or whether, in the light of all the understanding of Israelite prophecy we think we have reached, they failed in their task. No one can detract from the greatness of a Jeremiah or an Ezekiel, but this does not at all mean setting up the concept of "greatness" as a theological norm and measuring the later prophets by it.[1] Because of the inevitability of the approaching disaster, the final years before the fall of Jerusalem were not without greatness, and in the same way, because its hardships were so clear, the situation of the exiles in Babylon had greatness. The period after the return was neither clear nor great. Yet it and all its problems were what concerned these prophets, and their only success could lie in the way in which they dealt with them.

The situation of the community in Jerusalem towards the end of the sixth century—obviously by no means a clear one—is reflected in the messages which are subsumed under the name of Trito-Isaiah (Is. LVI–LXVI).[2] This prophet's call certainly speaks quite clearly of an office of comfort entrusted to him which has a very strong pastoral stamp upon it, namely "to bind up the brokenhearted, to proclaim liberty to the captives" (Is. LXI. 1). Yet, as prophet he had also to deal with grave abuses, with almost catastrophic social and legal conditions (Is. LVII. 1ff.), and with the failure of the ruling class to do its duty (Is. LVI. 9ff.).

---

[1] No one can prove "that Malachi, for example, was a poorer prophet than the others, although he obviously appears to have less inspiration than they did, and although the themes upon which he touches are pale in comparison with those of the great prophets. These men who received a call, whether they were major or minor prophets, were every one of them the right men for their day and generation, and they wore themselves out in their service." G. Quell, op. cit., p. 12.

[2] There is no agreed answer to the question of the authorship of the last eleven chapters of Isaiah. Elliger's thesis, that they come from a prophet who lived towards the end of the sixth century, and that the chapters are therefore a unity, has repeatedly been opposed (K. Elliger, Die Einheit des Tritojesaja, Stuttgart 1928; "Der Prophet Tritojesaja," in Z.A.W., XLIX, 1931, pp. 112ff.). In actual fact, the passages where Deutero-Isaiah's influence is unmistakable are very few (Is. LX, LXI, LXII), while others lack it completely. It is therefore possible that the chapters do not represent an absolutely uniform tradition—may it have been that of a school? Even so, the most probable assumption is that the texts are to be taken as deriving from the time just before or after that of Haggai and Zechariah. (Only in the case of Is. LVII. 7–13 could an essentially earlier origin come in question—does it date from even before 587?, cp. Eissfeldt, Einleitung, p. 417; similarly A. Bentzen, Introduction to the Old Testament, VOL. II, Copenhagen 1949, pp. 109ff.). The designation "Trito-Isaiah," which we retain for the sake of simplicity, thus leaves the question of the authorship open.

Here the keenness of his insistence on justice and righteousness hardly falls short of the charges made by the pre-exilic prophets. This is particularly true of the prophetic criticism which he levelled at the vain cultic observances, which, he says, are far less pleasing to Jahweh than compassion for others would be (Is. LVIII. 1ff.). Unlike the pre-exilic prophets, however, the people with whom Trito-Isaiah was concerned were not outwardly arrogant: rather, they were men of little faith. He therefore discusses with them whether Jahweh's arm is too short (Is. LIX. 1); he uses theological arguments to make the delay in the coming of salvation intelligible as due to the community's mounting guilt: "Therefore [Jahweh's] justice is far from us" (Is. LIX. 9). Indeed, Jahweh actually protests by his lips that he was ready to be sought out and found by those who did not seek him; he spread out his hands all the day to his people. Yet, a terrible retribution will overtake those who still repulse these hands (Is. LXV. 1ff.). Thus, like the old prophets, Trito-Isaiah tears open a gulf where one was not hitherto seen, and separates Israel from Israel. Unfortunately, we know too little about the cultic conditions of the time to be able to be more precise about those who "provoke" Jahweh (Is. LXV. 3)—the offences in question must have been grave cultic abominations. These sinners are contrasted with the servants of Jahweh whom the prophet addresses in rapturous terms and to whom he promises Jahweh's salvation. In his proclamations of salvation he not only takes up central themes of Deutero-Isaiah's message, but he also shows himself to be so strongly influenced even by the latter's diction and emotions that we are right in guessing that Trito-Isaiah's relationship to Deutero-Isaiah is something like the close one of pupil or disciple.[3] Thus, such phrases as "build up," "make the way plain" are re-echoed in Trito-Isaiah (Is. LVII. 14, LXII. 10), and so is the saying about Mother Zion's astonishment at the abundance of her children (Is. LXVI. 7f. = XLIX. 21). The tradition is followed particularly strongly in the rapturous words which describe the city of God which Jahweh has again taken in his care, and the arrival of the first pilgrims (Is. LXII). Nevertheless, it is easy to see how the phraseology taken over from Deutero-Isaiah has here been adapted to meet a situation which had changed considerably both externally and internally.[4] With Deutero-Isaiah Zion is the climax of the prediction, the

[3] Thus in particular K. Elliger, *Deuterojesaja in seinem Verhältnis zu Tritojesaja* (*B.W.A.N.T.*, IV, 11), Stuttgart 1933.

[4] For a compendium of the prophetic traditional material which Trito-Isaiah took

goal of the eschatological restoration; here, however, Zion is the starting-point of the prophet's thoughts, and she is Zion unredeemed, still waiting, forced to importune Jahweh, constrained to give him no peace, begging him to give effect to that glorification of the city of God which still tarries. This is not the language of Deutero-Isaiah. The background to Trito-Isaiah's message was a dangerous situation— characterised by the feeling that a divine promise was long overdue. Yet Trito-Isaiah calmly takes up the oracle of Jahweh's imminent advent to his city. Indeed, the climax of his message comes with his attempt to warn his contemporaries and make them see that Jahweh's transfiguration of his city by his coming, despite its delay, is a genuine and world-shaking event.[5]

The prophetic message of Haggai and Zechariah also culminates in the approaching advent of Jahweh and the imminent establishment of his kingdom, but, to the great embarrassment of not a few of the commentators, this message is linked most closely to the rebuilding of the Temple in Jerusalem which had been destroyed by the Babylonians; the link is, indeed, so close that for these two prophets the rebuilding of the Temple is actually the necessary precondition of Jahweh's advent and of his kingdom. It is perfectly true that no such idea can be found in Isaiah or Jeremiah. The reason can hardly be that these prophets were so much more "spiritual" than Haggai and Zechariah, for the pre-exilic prophets too had very down to earth ideas about the eschatological salvation and its fulfilment. The difference is explained simply by the completely different spiritual condition of the people to whom the later prophets were sent. In the earlier period, Israel was faced with the alternatives of political alliance or trust in Jahweh; failing these, the question of proper justice in the gate was made *status confessionis*; these were the factors which determined whether or not Israel still belonged to Jahweh. Now, the people of Jerusalem were living in a state of "resigned security," and because of their concern with economic matters, which prevented them from looking any higher, the question of the rebuilding of the Temple had become *status confessionis*. The Temple was, after all, the place where Jahweh spoke to Israel, where he forgave her her sins, and where he was present for her. The attitude taken towards it therefore determined the attitude for or

over and actualised and a discussion of the alterations which he made to it, see W. Zimmerli, "Zur Sprach Tritojesajas" in *Schweizer theologische Umschau*, 1950, pp. 62ff.

[5] Is. LVI. 1, LVIII. 8, 10f., LXII. 1-3, 11, etc.

against Jahweh. People had no great interest in the place however; because of economic hardship they kept putting off rebuilding it—it was "not yet the time" for it, they said (Hag. I. 2). Haggai completely reverses this scale of priorities: Israel is no longer Israel if she does not seek first the kingdom of God; if she does this, then the other thing, the blessing of Jahweh, will be given her as well (Hag. I. 2–11, II. 14–19). What he said and demanded was not in principle different from Isaiah's call for faith during the Syro-Ephraimitic war. Haggai's only reason for saying what he did was his belief that the eschatological Israel was to have a sacral centre, and that this alone would guarantee her existence. It is very doubtful whether Isaiah would have opposed him. Is it not better to see the genuineness of Haggai's prophecy in the fact that against all the evidence he interpreted the period as one of salvation and that even in the poor conditions of his time he saw Jahweh beginning something new, and begged his followers to prepare for the event which Jahweh was to accomplish for them and to place themselves at his disposal? Had he thought otherwise, he would have admitted that the prevailing despondency was justified, and that it was right to assume that Jahweh could naturally have nothing to do with such wretched conditions. When in the end a start was made to the rebuilding of the Temple, and when the foundations already gave some idea of its area, Haggai addressed the older people and expressed the sentiments which their own hearts probably did not dare even to admit: "Is it not in your sight as nothing?" (Hag. II. 3). There is a prophetic grandeur in this little scene and its blunt words about the insignificance of God's new start. Haggai did not narrow Israel's world by binding her once more to the Temple; rather he enlarged it by wresting from his contemporaries some acknowledgment of Jahweh's eschatological work.[6]

One thorny problem was still unanswered, however. Who were to be the future participants in Temple worship and who were therefore to have a part in rebuilding the Temple? Was it not arguable that, like all pagan temples, it should throw open its doors to everyone who felt himself drawn to worship within them? It was, after all, the Persian government which arranged for the rebuilding and supplied the necessary materials.[7] But Samaria was at that time still the seat of the provincial government in whose jurisdiction Jerusalem lay. It is there-

---

[6] M. Schmidt, *Prophet und Tempel, Eine Studie zum Problem der Gottesnähe im Alten Testament*, Zollikon-Zürich 1948, p. 197.   [7] See VOL. I, pp. 93ff.

fore not surprising that, once the building was in process, official circles there became interested, and wished to have a share in it, even if only to have a finger in the pie. It is also perfectly possible that on plain economic grounds this desire found support even in the Jerusalem community itself.[8] Using the form of a prophetic parable, Haggai gave a blunt No in answer to this question.[9] For the present the Temple is built solely for and by Israel; not everyone who offers gifts within the framework of its cult will be "well-pleasing" to Jahweh. To us to-day it sounds a harsh decision; many would rather that the prophet had given the opposite verdict. But it ought not to be difficult to see that Haggai was only being true to the first and second commandments, and that he insisted upon a separation such as Elijah or Deuteronomy had also battled for in their time. Jahwism was not a religion of which one could become an adherent at will, while possibly still maintaining other cultic connexions; it went back to a divine act of election and remained tied to a definite national entity. Thus Haggai's importance lies in the fact that he, like a second Elijah, saw in the difficult question of religious exclusion, a question which had disturbed Israel in days gone by also, a clear cut "Either—Or" at exactly the point where his contemporaries were no longer aware of it. We must stress again that had he made a different decision, he would have denied Isaiah's whole struggle against the policy of alliances, a struggle which Isaiah hoped would detach the relationship between Jahweh and Zion from all political stratagems and standards of judgment.[10] Neither Isaiah nor Haggai saw their decision as a spiritual one; for them it was a question of keeping an appointed historical place free for Jahweh's action.

It was Haggai himself who envisaged the time when all the nations were to worship Jahweh and bring him their treasures, and, surprisingly enough, he believed that this time was already imminent (Hag. II. 6–9). It was for this time, when Jahwism would throw off its national limitations and become a universal religion—the time of the Messiah—that the temple had to be built. It is to be preceded by a fearful shaking of the heavens and the earth; the nations are to wage internecine war, and

---

[8] K. Elliger, *Das Buch der zwölf kleinen Propheten II* (A.T.D.), p. 94.

[9] The question of who are meant by "this people" in Hag. II. 14 is answered by most commentators in the sense that these people who had been refused a share in the building of the temple are to be identified with the non-Israelite ruling class in Samaria. Cp. also Ezra v. 1–6, 15, and the more recent commentaries.

[10] H. W. Wolff, *Haggai* (Biblische Studien), Neukirchen 1951, p. 41.

Jahweh is to destroy the weapons of war—it is a "day of Jahweh."[11] Thereafter, however, the anointed one is to enter upon his office as the signet-ring of Jahweh, *i.e.*, as the one who gives effect to Jahweh's decrees. When Haggai made this prophecy, he was not thinking vaguely of some unspecified anointed one. He clearly and unequivocally designated as the coming anointed one David's descendant Zerubbabel, the grandson of the unfortunate Jehoiachin.

It is common to point out that Haggai here differs radically from the pre-exilic prophets by naming a living member of the house of David as the coming anointed one; and this raises the question whether he so showed himself to have been a dreamer. Since we know nothing of the contemporary circumstances, it is quite possible to reconstruct a plausible picture of a great freedom movement breaking out in Judah, connected with the convulsions shaking the Persian empire, and finding a spokesman in Haggai, though Zerubbabel's participation would remain uncertain.[12] But, quite apart from the fact that the little Book of Haggai does not give the slightest impression that the prophet was carried away by a popular movement, our sources are simply not adequate for any such reconstructions. All we can do is acknowledge that Haggai regarded Zerubbabel as the coming anointed one, but that in fact Zerubbabel never came to the throne. If this leads to a derogatory judgment of Haggai's prophecy, how then is, say, Deutero-Isaiah to be exempt from the same verdict, when we remember his prophecy of the returning exiles' miraculous journey through the desert? We must also remember the situation revealed in the royal psalms. Did not the writers of these psalms in each case regard the subject of their praises as Jahweh's anointed one? And were those to whom they were first addressed still on the throne of David when, in the post-exilic age, these poems were read and handed on with a mounting Messianic interest?[13] The differences between these men and Haggai was that Haggai was thinking of a throne which no longer existed. But in any case, is it so very important that Haggai included a contemporary historical figure in his predictions? Isaiah must have believed that the anointed one whose coming he foretold was also in some respects an historical figure. And even such an anointed one as Haggai's is only a vice-gerent for him in whom all Old Testament predictions are Yea and Amen.

[11] See above, pp. 119ff.
[12] Hölscher conjectures the latter, *Profeten*, p. 342.
[13] Cp. *e.g.*, I Chron. XVI. 7ff.; II Chron. VI. 41f.

How are we to decide whether a prediction is visionary or sober? Is it not possible that a prediction which was defined as "visionary" at the time of its delivery afterwards became absorbed in the great complex of prophetic tradition, because like other such predictions it was applied, after the failure of its first objective, to a future act of God?

The message of the prophet Zechariah is very similar to that of Haggai. His preaching too is closely co-related to the Temple, now in process of re-erection, and to the Davidic Zerubbabel, for whom, as he looks for the imminent eschatological saving event, Zechariah also holds out the prospect of a Messianic office. Zechariah appeared on the scene in 520, only a few months after Haggai, and, according to the dates given in his Book, he prophesied for two years longer than Haggai. Thus, when he first began to preach, the rebuilding of the Temple was already under way. It has been pointed out, quite correctly, that Zechariah does not, as one might easily have expected, reiterate Haggai's summons to persevere in this work without slackening. Zechariah never admonishes or drives when he speaks; rather, his words about the completion of the Temple are most usually in the indicative mood. For example, those adverse factors which look like towering mountains will be levelled out and "the hands of Zerubbabel will complete this house" (Zech. IV. 6–10). Of course, Haggai and Zechariah do not contradict each other, for in spite of his admonitions Haggai too regarded Jahweh himself as the real initiator of the work which was to be undertaken—it is the spirit of Jahweh that authorises the community to rebuild and gives it the strength to do so (Hag. I. 14, II. 5), while in an oracle with a keen polemical edge Zechariah opposed any idea of bringing in human or political means to defend the new Jerusalem:

Not by might and not by power, but by my spirit, says Jahweh of hosts.
(Zech. IV. 6)

This was Israel's old watchword when she waged holy wars: it was also to apply when the final saving event came to pass.[14]

As with Haggai, the subject of Zechariah's message is the proclamation of the imminent advent of Jahweh (Zech. II. 14 [10], VIII. 3). It is characteristic of both that they try to bring their hearers to a right understanding of the signs of their time. This time had been one of calamity, and, since the Temple was a complete ruin, it may also actu-

[14] Von Rad, *Heilige Krieg*, p. 66.

ally have been reckoned, from the viewpoint of the cult, as a time of fast. The blessing of Jahweh had been withheld, and men's labours met with no success (Hag. I. 5f.). From now on, however—and the way in which they exactly fix the "now" is characteristic of the realism of the two prophets' thoughts about saving history (Hag. II. 15, 18; Zech. VIII. 11)—from now on it is a time of salvation. These two prophets therefore regard themselves as placed exactly at the point of the sudden great critical change. Trito-Isaiah was still almost completely in the dark—think of the moving prayer of lament in Is. LXIII. 7 – LXIV. 11, and also of Is. LIX. 9–15. The hour in the saving history at which Haggai and Zechariah speak is under different auspices—the night is far spent, the day is at hand. The building of the Temple brought the dawn of the time of salvation. The time of adversity is at an end, and blessing—understood in a completely material way as agricultural prosperity—will begin immediately (Hag. II. 15–19), and has indeed begun already (Zech. VIII. 10–12). It is important that the great turning-point for these prophets which brings the final saving act had its way prepared by an historical event to which particularly limited sacral significance was attached. Neither the edict of Cyrus nor the return of the exiles were happenings which were given any special dignity as saving events.

We have just seen that Zechariah envisaged the early advent of Jahweh to his dishonoured city. The cycle of his night visions reveals many details connected with the eschatological new order which precedes this advent.

As the first vision (Zech. I. 7–15) makes clear, the outward condition of the world gives as yet no indication of the advent of Jahweh and his kingdom. The heavenly messengers who have patrolled the earth and observed it carefully can only bring back to heaven's gate the depressing report that they found the earth at peace and the nations living in security. It would, however, be a mistake to conclude that nothing is now to be looked for from Jahweh. He is in fact exceedingly jealous for his city, and his imminent salvation is already prepared, even down to the last detail. This is still unknown on earth; but it will soon be experienced. For—this is the second vision (Zech. II. 1–4 [I. 18–21])—the powers which are to smite those empires opposed to Jahweh are already drawn up. The third vision (Zech. II. 5–9 [1–5]) is full of dramatic excitement. The prophet sees "a man with a measuring line in his hand," who is about to measure the new Jerusalem, clearly in order to prepare in advance for the building of her walls. However, an angel excitedly recalls him, for the new city of God is actually to be without defences; her sole protection is to be the wall of fire provided by the glory of God. This vision undoubtedly reflects certain plans of the returned exiles to rebuild the demolished walls. Zechariah opposed them. History, of course, came to ignore this prophetic protest, as it did others, for the wall was in fact later rebuilt, at the particular instigation of Nehemiah (Ezra IV. 6ff.; Neh. III). The fourth vision (Zech. III. 1–7) sketches a court action in heaven over which the angel of Jahweh presided, and in which the accuser (שׂטן) appeared against the high priest Joshua. The crime of which the latter is accused is not specified, but the fact that he appeared clothed in mourning suggests that the charge was a just one. However, it is better to see Joshua here as the representative of the community which is guilty in the eyes of Jahweh than to think of personal transgression on his own part. Here again there is an episode—the angel of Jahweh dismisses the charge with a sharp rebuke to the accuser. Joshua is invested anew; jurisdiction over the Temple and the offering of sacrifice in the forecourts are put under his charge; indeed, he is even given free access to the company of the heavenly beings. (How real the divine world is, and how near to human beings: if Jahweh so authorises it, it is but a step!) In contrast to this vision, in the fourth (Zech. IV. 1–6a, 10b–11, 13–14) Joshua is shown a picture in which there is no movement at all. A lampstand with forty-nine lights is flanked by two olive trees. These are "the two anointed"—Joshua and Zerubbabel—"who stand before the Lord of the whole earth." Zechariah thus sees—and this is unique in prophecy —the new Israel constituted as a dyarchy; the representative of the priestly office stands with equal rank next to the representative of the royal office. Later, in the fifth vision (Zech. V. 1–4), thieves and those who swear falsely have been driven out of the community and evil itself (this is the sixth vision, Zech. V. 5–11) has been removed; the seventh vision (Zech. VI. 1–8) reverts to the picture given in the first. In the meantime morning has come; the heavenly chariots are ready to go out into the world. Nothing is divulged of the duties assigned to them except that those going towards the north—and this certainly means Babylon—have to "lay down" Jahweh's spirit in the north country, obviously to encourage the Diaspora there to return home and enter into the Messianic kingdom.

After these pictures had appeared to his spirit during the course of a single night, Zechariah awakened. What had they done for him? He learned that at a time of calm in the world's history, when the nations believed themselves secure in their own powers alone, the kingdom of God was already prepared in heaven. He became aware that Jahweh was jealous for Jerusalem and that he had already made all the preparations for his own advent—he had appointed his representatives and provided for and overcome all complications and opposition. The clear-cut way in which the heavenly world is differentiated from the earthly is important. The eschatological saving orders and offices are already present in the world above. Indeed, even the events which must necessarily precede the advent of the kingdom of God—as, for example, the removal of evil—are already accomplished in the sight of the world above, so that they have anticipated the course of events on earth. This is not how either Isaiah or Jeremiah regarded the eschatological event. Isaiah was, of course, aware of a world above which was the abode of Jahweh and his heavenly court; but the emphasis now placed upon the archetypal existence of the final things in heaven is something new. Ezekiel shows the change beginning; he received his message in the form of a heavenly book (Ezek. II. 8ff.). Deutero-Isaiah hears how the processional road for Jahweh's return to Jerusalem is already prepared in the world above (Is. XL. 3ff.), and this brings him quite close to Zechariah. In this late period Israel apparently gave a greater place to certain ideas common to the whole of the east; for in the Babylonians' sacral-mythical picture of the world, it was an established fact that everything on earth, particularly if it had sacral value, had its corresponding archetype in the world above.[15] In the same way also, according to the Priestly Document, the tabernacle was modelled on a heavenly pattern (תבנית Ex. xxv. 9, 40). In Apocalyptic these age-old concepts were once again expressed in a completely new way.

The little Book of the anonymous prophet which bears the name of Malachi only contains six oracles. The man who addresses us is exclusively concerned with abuses practised by the community. He attacks priests who are careless in ritual matters, divorce, and, above all, blasé scepticism in religious matters. This suggests that he was writing after the religious revival under Haggai and Zechariah and the completion of the rebuilding of the Temple. It is remarkable that this prophet's message contains practically no clues which might determine the tradition to which he belongs. He gives less of a broad exposition of

[15] See below, p. 365.

eschatological ideas than any other prophet, perhaps because he uses the form of the polemic. He mentions God's eschatological action in only two of his oracles (Mal. II. 17 – III. 5, III. 13–21 [III. 13 – IV. 3]). Jahweh is to come unexpectedly, and his day is to bring judgment upon the godless; but for those who fear God, "the sun of salvation" will shine forth. The idea that Jahweh will send a messenger before his own final advent (Mal. III. 1) is only found in Malachi. There is debate about whether the prophet thought of a heavenly or an earthly messenger— did he perhaps think of himself as this messenger? In an appendix to the little Book the return of Elijah, who had been taken up to heaven at his death, is expected immediately before the terrible day of Jahweh: he is to turn the hearts of the fathers and the hearts of the children towards one another (Mal. III. 23f. [IV. 5f.]).

The little Book of Jonah, perhaps more than any other in the Old Testament, calls for special appreciation of the literary form in which its message is clothed.[16] At all events, the straightforward message contained in this Book has been distorted ever since people began to be puzzled by Jonah's sojourn in the belly of a fish. The minor detail whether this could be accepted as an event that actually happened became the all-important matter of contention, and it was left to modern criticism, which has been able to restore to so much of the Old Testament its pre-scriptural form, to explain the story properly. Quite obviously, it is a story with a strong didactic content, and should not be read as an historical account. It deals with a man of God who— from the narrator's standpoint—lived in times so remote as to be almost legendary, the time of Jeroboam II (II Kings XIV. 25), and who had received an order to go to Nineveh, the capital city of Assyria, and "to preach against it."

He did not go there: but immediately fled from Jahweh's presence. On the voyage to the farthest west a terrible storm overtook the little ship. The crew did all they could to cope with the danger: but Jonah lay in the inner part of the ship and slept. Yet, he could not contract out of the situation, as he no doubt wished to do, and when the truth about this passenger came to light, the sailors cast him into the sea—at his own suggestion, because he preferred to die rather than go on with

---

[16] The text seems to be seriously disturbed at one point only; vs. 5 in ch. IV is wrongly placed; it should be put after III. 4. The psalm of thanksgiving in II. 3–10 [2–9] is a later addition. For the exposition of this story told about a prophet, see E. Haller, *Die Erzählung vom Propheten Jona* (*Theologische Existenz Heute*, 65, 1958).

Jahweh's purpose. However, a great fish swallowed Jonah and cast him up on the country from which he had sailed. When Jahweh reiterated his command to go to Nineveh, Jonah could no longer avoid it.

He delivered his message, that the overthrow of the city was close at hand, in Nineveh itself, and then sat down outside the city to observe what was to take place. Things did not turn out as he expected, for the city was moved to repent at the foreign prophet's message; the king arose from his throne, and removed his robes: a royal proclamation was made calling for a general act of national penitence, in which even the domestic animals shared. Jonah recognised that God's thoughts towards Nineveh had changed, and that he was ready to forgive her.

"But it displeased Jonah exceedingly, and he was angry, and he prayed to Jahweh and said, 'I pray thee, Jahweh, this is what I thought to myself while I was yet in my country. That is why I made haste to flee to Tarshish, for I knew that thou art a gracious and merciful God, slow to anger and abounding in kindness . . ." (Jon. IV. 1–2).

Here then for the first time the real reason for his disobedience becomes clear—he had foreseen that God would ensure the triumph of grace, and so he casts in Jahweh's teeth the gracious words with which Israel had from of old made her confession in worship. God did not fulfil the prophet's wish to let him die in his anger. On the contrary, he caused a broad-leafed bush to grow at the place where the disgruntled man of God was lodging, and in its shade Jonah's ill-humour quickly changed into gladness. Thereupon the Lord of all creation appointed a worm, which attacked the plant, so that it withered. When the terrible sirocco began to blow and the sun to burn, the prophet's strength and patience again gave out; he became angry and wanted to die. The Book ends with the answer which God gave to his refractory ambassador. It takes the reader's mind away from all that is ridiculous and impossible in the story, away too from all the blindness of men's vision, and brings him directly to the heart of God:

"You pity the plant, for which you did not labour, nor did you make it grow, which came into being in a night, and perished in a night. And should I not pity Nineveh, that great city, in which there are more than a hundred and twenty thousand persons who do not know their right hand from their left, and also much cattle?" (Jon. IV. 10–11).

The material of the Book is laid out with great artistry, for it falls into two exactly corresponding halves, Jonah in the ship and Jonah at Nineveh. In both cases the heathen appear in a much better light than the prophet. It was they who took the initiative during the storm and who saw that Jonah was the cause of the trouble; and how happily things turned out through them in Nineveh! They are simple and transparent in God's presence, but Jonah is an unknown quantity, and psychologically complex. He is at his worst when he speaks of his faith in confessional and cultic terms—witness on the one hand when he talks religion in the ship's cabin ("I am a Hebrew, and fear Jahweh, the God of heaven . . ." Jon. 1. 9), and on the other his words with God about forgiveness. At the end of the first section comes the sacrifice which the sailors offer to Jahweh. That they become believers in the God of Israel means that one of God's aims has already reached its goal. Yet this was, of course, merely a prelude to what was afterwards to be repeated on a grand scale in the savings of Nineveh.

The story of Jonah thus falls within the literary category, which we have already met, of a story told about a prophet, with the difference that this has now actually become didactic narrative to a greater degree than the earlier stories were. Indeed, it seems to have been the last and strangest flowering of this old and almost extinct literary form. Consider how the story is told—with a grace and ease unmatched in the prophetic literature. And yet, it deals with grave matters, with a city whose days are numbered in the sight of God, with evil men, and above all with a prophet whose attitude to his office was outrageous. Of course, even in the earlier narratives about prophets, the "hero" of the story was never the prophet himself, but rather Jahweh, who was glorified through the prophet. In this respect there is really no great change; the only difference is that God is here glorified not through his ambassador, but in spite of his ambassador's complete refusal. The ridiculous, stubborn Jonah, grudging God's mercy to the heathen, but filled with joy at the shade of the castor-oil plant, and then wanting to die when he sees it withering away, is unable to impede God's saving thoughts— they achieve their goal in spite of everything. Indeed, this constitutes the particular enigma of the Book—for all his disobedience Jonah is nevertheless a figure whom God used as a king might a subject: it was because of him that the sailors' attention was drawn to Jahweh and the men of Nineveh repented. Thus, there is no indignation or complaint over the man of God's refusal. Considering God's victorious work, even a refusal like this could be related in these non-tragic, and even gay, terms.

It is best not to let conjecture about the contemporary causes of the

Book cloud our interpretation of it. We have no knowledge of any "universalistic" opposition to the "particularist" measures taken by Ezra and Nehemiah, and the Book itself contains no evidence to support such a theory. Moreover, polemical and tendentious writings usually wear a different appearance. Further it is wrong to suggest that the Book's universalism wished to see covenant and election finally severed from their restriction to Israel; it addresses those who know covenant and community; and it is these men whom it warns against the temptation of using their peculiar position in God's sight to raise claims which compromise Jahweh's freedom in his plans for other nations. It is not at once obvious why the story portrays a prophet as the embodiment of such a grudging faith, for the great prophets did try to open their fellow-countrymen's eyes to the fact that Jahweh's plans embraced the whole world of nations. For all his orthodoxy the really bad thing about Jonah is his aloofness. This was displayed on board ship, and also before Nineveh: when life and death were at stake, he remained withdrawn, in a very sinister position. It would certainly be wrong to interpret the story as a final judgment on prophecy in Israel. This would be to misjudge prophecy entirely. Yet the prophetic proclivity for self-questioning—one of the best aspects of its spirit—once again sprang to life in this little Book. It is worth noticing that one of the last utterances of Israelite prophecy is so devastatingly self-critical; for in the way in which in this Book it strips itself of all honours, and turns men's gaze away from itself in order to give the honour to him to whom alone this is due, it reveals something of the "he must increase, but I must decrease" spoken by the last in the line of these ambassadors (Jn. III. 30).

2. THE PROPHECIES OF THE NEW JERUSALEM[17]

The subject of Haggai's and Zechariah's prophecies of salvation was the eschatological restoration of the Temple and of the city of God. The outward form given by Zechariah to what we may properly call eschatological Israel was that of a *polis*, and this undoubtedly reflects the historical situation of the time: for at that time Jerusalem was the scene of everything that was vital and concrete in Israel, whether hopeful or despairing. If the prophets wanted to speak at all relevantly to the

---

[17] A. Causse, "Le Mythe de la nouvelle Jérusalem du Deutéro-Esaie à la IIIᵉ Sibylle," in *Revue d'Histoire et de Philosophie religieuse*, XVIII (1938), pp. 377ff. K. L. Schmidt, 'Jerusalem als Urbild und Abbild," in *Eranos-Jahrbuch*, XVIII (1950), pp. 207ff.

men of their time—*ad hominem*—it had to be within the frame of reference of this restricted area; and they had to declare that, in spite of everything, this was not too narrow a basis for Jahweh to begin his saving work. No wonder that it was the Zion tradition which came back to life at this precise time. The concepts which these late prophets use to express the glory of the new Jerusalem are, of course, of various kinds and have, traditio-historically, no single root.

1. The announcement of the failure of a hostile attack on Zion apparently forms part of the oldest traditions of pre-exilic Jerusalem; indeed, there are indications that this tradition derives from the pre-Davidic Jerusalem.[18] We have already seen how it was suddenly developed by Isaiah, and how he used it like the theme of a fugue, playing ever new variations on it as he applied it to his own day.[19] No other prophet employed this range of concepts at such length. In comparison, the brevity of Micah's presentation (Mic. IV. 11–13) makes him seem to belong really to the past, an impression which is strengthened by the fact that here Zion is herself summoned to fight against the enemy, a feature which is absent in the later variations of the theme. The picture which portrays the eschatological assault by the nations on the largest scale is the prophecy of the coming of Gog and Magog and of their destruction "on the mountains of Israel" (Ezek. XXXVIII f.). The description in these chapters is of baroque proportions. Though like Isaiah they enter into great detail in other respects, they say practically nothing about the battle itself, particularly about the disposal of the dead and the collection of the weapons that is to keep Israel busy for all of seven years. Interestingly enough, this prophecy expressly appeals to earlier predictions (Ezek. XXXVIII. 17); it regards itself as based on an earlier prophetic tradition. In Joel IV. 9–17 [III. 9–17] too, we meet with the idea earlier expressed in Isaiah that the nations advancing against Zion do not in the least come by their own initiative and choice, but because they are summoned by Jahweh (cp. Ezek. XXXVIII. 4, XXXIX. 2). Here again what comes in question is a day of Jahweh with earthquake and darkness (vs. 14).[20] Jahweh is to judge the

---

[18] On Pss. XLVI, XLVIII, LXXVI and the Zion tradition, see VOL. I, pp. 46ff.

[19] See above, pp. 155ff.

[20] From the point of view of the history of tradition we have thus the fusion of two cycles of tradition which originally had nothing to do with one another, that of the attack of the foreign nations on the city of God, and that of the Day of Jahweh. Incidentally, the same thing is also to be found in Ob. 15ff.

nations in the valley of Jehoshaphat; Zion will be preserved. The final development of these variations on the theme of the foreign nations' assault on Zion comes in Zech. XII and XIV, where the basic component parts of this cycle of concepts—Jahweh's assembling of the nations, the battle, and the preservation of Zion—are set out in full side by side. A unique feature here is the idea that the enemy will actually force their way into the holy city itself and work dire havoc within her; the text also gives many grisly details about the chastisement of the enemy (Zech. XIV. 12). Another unique feature of this text is the interweaving of *motifs* which derive from entirely different eschatological concepts— from henceforward, the survivors of the foreign nations will make pilgrimage to Zion and worship Jahweh. External conditions are to be miraculously changed—the whole land is to become a plain, only Jerusalem will remain aloft on the mountain, and living waters are to flow out from it. There is to be no alternation of light and darkness in the city: there is to be perpetual daylight. This elaboration of the usual cycle of concepts by means of a number of different ideas of what was expected to happen shows that the passage is of late composition. But since there are certain gaps in the picture, we have also to reckon with the possibility that later interpolations may have been added to it.

2. The other cycle of concepts which is attached to the eschatological city of God, and is also frequently taken up and transformed in a variety of ways by the prophets, is that of the pilgrimage of the nations to the city on Mount Zion. This concept differs from the one just considered in that it describes a peaceful event: its subject is the salvation of the nations, and not their judgment. In the oldest version in which we have it, Is. II. 2–4, the first stage in the eschatological event is a miraculous change in physical geography. At the end-time, the mountain of the house of Jahweh is to rise aloft and be exalted high above all the hills round about it, so that it will be visible to all nations. These will immediately set out and stream to it from every side, because they can no longer endure the desperate condition in which they live. They therefore come as pilgrims to Jahweh, "for out of Zion goes forth instruction." Just as the bands of Israel's pilgrims year by year made the journey to Zion where, at the climax of the festival, Jahweh's will as expressed in law was proclaimed to them, so the prophecy expects that "at the end of the days" the nations will present themselves on Zion for a final settlement of all disputes, and to receive those fixed rules for living by which Jahweh grants salvation, and that thereafter—once

they have returned home again—they will reforge their weapons of war into the implements of peace. If this passage had been the only reference to the concept, we should have been blind to the fact that Isaiah only selected some features from what is obviously a rich and living cycle of concepts.

In Deutero-Isaiah too, only parts of the total range of concepts are in each case actualised. None the less, it is characteristic of the importance and independence which attached to these ideas that, when the prophet makes use of such prophecies, he does not confine himself to incidental allusions, but always fills up a whole unit with them. It is interesting to see the way in which he transposed the traditional material into the situation of his own day. In Is. XLIX. 14–21 he turned it into an oracle of comfort for despairing Jerusalem. Those who stream to her from round about are her own children! In the following unit (Is. XLIX. 22–3), the prophet takes up the traditional *motif*—he foretells the coming of the nations. This time, however, it is Jahweh himself who gives them the signal to come. Yet, here again Deutero-Isaiah wove something of his own into the material: the nations are to come and bring the sons and daughters of Zion in their arms. "Kings shall be your foster fathers." In Is. XLV. 14–15 it is again the foreign nations who come, bringing their precious treasures. The special feature of this passage, however, which makes it unique among all the adaptations of the material, is the confession which Deutero-Isaiah puts into the mouth of the nations who are brought to worship the God of Israel:

"God is with you only, and there is no other, no god besides him" (Is. XLV. 14).

The fullest development of this traditional material is to be found in Trito-Isaiah (Is. LX), and this makes the chapter very important for the correct evaluation of others which are related to it. Like the beginning of Is. II. it speaks of a transfiguration of the city of God, the "coming of a light," as a result of which Jerusalem emerges from her previous insignificance and thus sets in train the pilgrimage of the nations.[21] Here the poet did not miss the chance of giving a magnificent description of this coming of the nations. On the sea the sailing ships can be seen hastening like flights of doves from the west, and from the east the caravans and camels of Midian and other Arabian tribes. They bring sheep for sacrifice, gold and incense for the Temple—they even bring

[21] This command "to become a light" has a precursor in Is. LII. 1: "Awake, awake, put on your strength, O Zion; put on your beautiful garments, O Jerusalem."

the exiles from among God's people. Thereafter lawlessness and social oppression will cease. Peace will be the overseers and righteousness the governors in the city of God; the days of her mourning will be at an end.

The briefest mention of the pilgrimage of the nations is in Haggai (Hag. II. 6ff.). Jahweh is to shake the nations, then they will arise and bring all their precious things to Zion, for "the silver is mine, and the gold is mine," says Jahweh. Haggai really took only one feature from the whole range of concepts, that of the solemn conveyance of the treasures of all the nations to Jahweh. Jahweh alone has a rightful claim to all the valuables which now lie scattered among the nations; only at the *eschaton*, once the Temple has been prepared, will the treasures which are his by right, and which have meanwhile been apportioned amongst the nations, revert to Jahweh's possession. On the other hand, First Isaiah also took only one detail from the complex. His interest is concentrated not upon the cultic aspect of the event, the entry of the nations into the worship of Jahweh and the presentation of their offerings, but upon the reception of Jahweh's ordinances, on whose basis alone there can be lasting peace among the nations in the latter days.

This belief in a future pilgrimage of the nations to Zion is thus seen to be a very fluid tradition, which the prophets could actualise in quite different ways. The author of Zech. IX–XIV apparently connected it with the wars of the nations.[22] He too knows of the land being changed into a plain and the holy city being exalted above it, of the pilgrimage of the nations "who survive" to worship Jahweh, and also of the perfect holiness of the city of God (Zech. XIV. 10, 11, 16, 20).[23]

The theme of the eschatological pilgrimage of the nations to Zion is also found several times in the Apocryphal literature, as for example Tob. XIII. 9ff., XIV. 5ff.; Enoch XC. 28–33; and Syb. Or. III. 703–31.

[22] Similarly Zeph. III. 8ff.

[23] The vision of the new temple and the new city of God in Ezek. XL–XLVIII also fits in here. Traditio-historically, it can be set alongside Zech. XIV. 10, where the city set aloft (cp. Ezek. LX. 2) and its gates are again mentioned. The traditional element, the waters that issue from the temple, is also found in Zech. XIV. 8 and Ezek. XLVII. The difference of course lies in the fact that Ezek. XLff. took the description of the structural features and the institutions of the new temple as almost its sole theme, and in consequence goes into much fuller detail concerning what it depicts. For an exact analysis of this far from uniform body of tradition, which can hardly be ascribed to the prophet Ezekiel, see H. Gese, *Der Verfassungsentwurf des Ezechiel* (*Beiträge zur historischen Theologie*, 25), Tübingen 1957.

Finally, in Apocalyptic there arose the idea that the new Jerusalem in all its perfection would come down from heaven to earth (Rev. XXI. 2; IV Ezra VII. 26, XIII. 36).

POSTSCRIPT

Apart from some lesser units, prophecy in Israel ended with Malachi and Trito-Zechariah. There is, especially in Malachi, an impression that prophecy was flagging: but the subsequent silence inspires several questions. Was it the sign that eschatological expectations had actually become extinct—that is to say, did it indicate that the line of those who carried on the prophetic tradition had come to an end? The psychological concept of exhaustion does not altogether cover all the data concerned. A more valid reason might be that in the period after Alexander the Great Palestine was left untouched by any events of world-wide scale, and it was always in the shadow of such events that the prophets operated. We must also particularly remember the internal religious structure of the post-exilic community.[24] Haggai and Zechariah saw the rebuilding of the Temple wholly within the perspective of a great eschatological event. But, as a result of the Priestly Document, which may have been brought to Jerusalem by the returned exiles, and its non-eschatological cultic theology, this vision must have become lost. As time went on, the consolidation of the post-exilic community, which apparently corresponded to the restoration which many of the returned exiles hoped for, had become more and more bound up with an increasingly consistent elimination of eschatological ideas. This does not mean that these ideas were no longer represented: but the ruling priestly aristocracy in Jerusalem tended to push eschatological expectation more and more on one side, and finally forced it into separation. It is indeed hard to believe that the writer of, say, Zech. XIV held the same faith, and worshipped in the same way, as did the author of Chronicles, who was in all likelihood his contemporary. It is possible that this was the time when the prophets' eschatological expectation broke for ever with the theocracy. Thereafter the latter developed into the service of a law which, now divorced from the saving history, itself became an absolute entity.[25]

At this point, however, we must again notice a brief theological consideration. At the very beginning of this book we considered the

[24] For what follows, cp. O. Plöger, *Theokratie und Eschatologie*, Neukirchen 1959, pp. 41–68, 135ff.   [25] See VOL. I, pp. 90ff.

question of the proper designation of the new element which prophecy constituted in Israel.[26] In earlier exegesis of the prophets two basic ideas in particular were constantly brought forward. The first was that in the prophetic preaching ethical monotheism came for the first time to the fore. Amos was regarded as almost "the incorporation of the moral law," and Isaiah as the preacher of "the universal moral order."[27] The other was the appearance of the spiritual man who stood in a direct religious relationship to God.[28] This whole way of looking at prophecy, which tried to make an over-hasty break-through to basic religious and philosophic truths, has now been abandoned, for what is peculiar to prophecy comes neither from the peculiarity of its spiritual experiences and encounters nor from its religious ideas taken by themselves. In all probability, the questions considered by earlier criticism will one day require to be taken up again, though under different theological presuppositions. Our particular concern has been to put the prophets back into the saving history and to pay heed to the aspects of prophecy which result from this. We began with a fact already established by exegetical investigation—each of the prophets occupied a place of his own in the history of the relationship between God and Israel. This place was a determining factor in their message, and is the only standpoint from which to understand their whole discourse. They are conscious of being placed inside a historical continuum with wide perspectives over both past and future. Within it, however, each prophet stands as it were at the cross roads where God's dealings with Israel, which have been almost stationary, suddenly and dramatically begin to move again. The place at which they raise their voices is a place of supreme crisis, indeed almost a place of death, in so far as the men of this period of crisis were no longer reached by the saving force of the old appointments, and were promised life only as they turned to what was to come.

[26] See above, p. 5.

[27] "In Amos we have, so to speak, the incorporation of the moral law. God is a God of justice; religion the moral relation of man to God...." C. H. Cornill, *The Prophets of Israel*, trs. S. F. Corkran, Chicago 1909, p. 42. "The Israelite prophets anticipated the Greek philosophers in discovering the law of moral casuality which reigns uniformly in the world," Hölscher, *Profeten*, p. 188.

[28] "In prophetic religion, which increasingly parted company with the sacrificial system and with cultic mantic ideas, the layman entered into direct connexion with the Deity without priestly mediation. The time when such individual religious needs, were beginning to be felt was the beginning of personal religion," Hölscher, *Profeten*, p. 87.

All the prophets shared a common conviction that they stood exactly at that turning point in history which was crucial for the existence of God's people. This is the standpoint from which one has to understand their passionate demolition of the old, in particular of all false means of security before God, as well as what they say of the approach of entirely new and terrifying divine acts of salvation. Yet, they also shared a common certainty that the new thing which they expected was already prefigured in the old, and that the old would be present in the new in perfect form. Thus, the old actually seems to have had a prophetic significance for them, at least to the extent that they were certain that Jahweh was not going to nullify what he had himself begun and established, but would link on to it, in order to bring it the more splendidly to completion. Or, to put it in another way, they shared in a common, spell-bound watching for the new thing, and along with it in a denial of the saving power of Jahweh's old appointments, though the latter was not of course expressed in its full consistency until Jeremiah, Ezekiel, and Deutero-Isaiah. For them Israel's life and death depended solely on the meeting with the Lord who was to come. Western man with his philosophic equipment has here to remember that this recourse to, and actualisation of, old traditions was much more than merely an effective rhetorical device. Projecting the old traditions into the future was the only possible way open to the prophets of making material statements about a future which involved God.

In my opinion, the most effective way of making this aspect of Old Testament prophecy once more central—and I judge it to be prophecy's most important specific content—is still the way of taking the prophets and their message individually. (This does not naturally imply that this is the only possible way of presentation.) Of course, any "systematic" treatment of the prophets has to face the gravest difficulties inherent in the expressly charismatic character of practically all their utterances. Such a treatment must also in no case obscure their position in the saving history. For during its course of more than three centuries, prophetic teaching developed in very varied ways. The message of every prophet was exactly directed to meet a specific time, and it contained an offer which was never repeated in precisely the same form as it had with the original speaker. In the matter of God's requirements and offers, the time of Nebuchadnezzar was completely different from that of Sennacherib. Therefore, in the time of Jeremiah—indeed, in fact, any time after the disaster of 701—no one could any longer adduce the safeguarding of Zion in the sense that Isaiah had foretold it. The Jerusalem of the day did not recognise the hour; the waves of history rolled over Zion.[29] Deutero-Isaiah's prophecy that Jahweh would lead his people home was valid in that precise form only for the exiles of Babylon. Even Trito-Isaiah could only take it up in a considerably altered form, because the historical situation had altered. Thus, the message of every prophet was closely bound up with the point in history at which it was delivered, and after this point no message could be repeated exactly in its original sense. This is where creative interpretation begins. How such interpretation was put on a completely new basis by the saving event which the New Testament describes must be discussed more fully in Part III.

[29] See above, pp. 165ff. Cp. VOL. I, pp. 65f.

CHAPTER I

DANIEL AND APOCALYPTIC

I. APOCALYPTIC

EVEN after prophecy had ceased Israel continued to look into the future and to speak of the eschatological events still to be realised. She had learned much from the prophets, and a number of their predictions were absorbed into the language in which she expressed her hope. This is shown, for example, in the last words of the aged Tobit (Tob. XIII and XIV). At the same time, she spoke of her history and God's historical consummation in an even entirely new form which may be called apocalyptic.[1]

For the sake of clarity, it is wise to confine the term "apocalyptic" to what lies within the compass of the evidence. So taken, it is a literary phenomenon of late Judaism, that is to say, the group of pseudepigraphical apocalypses from Daniel to IV Ezra. Everything beyond this, particularly the background to these written works, cannot be evidenced in the same way as the purely literary phenomenon can. It therefore cannot be the starting-point for research, but must be its goal. Nevertheless, this definition of apocalyptic (as a literary phenomenon of a peculiar kind) is inadequate; for such a new and striking literary phenomenon should be seen within the context of a general intellectual movement. It must have had a *Sitz im Leben* in the Israel of the day, and also its own definite representatives. Thus the many definitions of apocalyptic attempted at different times have not confined themselves simply to the understanding of a peculiar literary phenomenon, but they also try to describe a theological phenomenon with its own view of the world. The discoveries at Qumran mean the opening of an entirely new phase of the problem.

The characteristic of apocalyptic theology is its eschatological

---

[1] For the relevant literature, see H. Ringgren, "Apokalyptik," in *R.G.G.*, VOL. I, col. 466; A. Oepke, "Die Apokalyptik," in *Th. W.B.N.T.*, VOL. III, pp. 580ff.; R. Meyer, "Die apokalyptische Literatur", in *Th. W.B.N.T.*, VOL. VI, pp. 827f. More recently O. Plöger, *Theokratie und Eschatologie*, Neukirchen 1959; D. Rössler, *Gesetz und Geschichte, Eine Untersuchung zur Theologie der jüdischen Gemeinde im neutestamentlichen Zeiten*, Neukirchen 1960.

dualism, the clear-cut differentiation of two aeons, the present one and the one to come.[2] A further characteristic is its sheer transcendentalism —the saving blessings of the coming aeon are already pre-existent in the world above and come down from there to the earth (Dan. VII. 13; Enoch XXXIX. 3ff., XLVIII. 3, 6, XLIX. 2; IV Ezra XIII. 36, etc.). The idea that the final events were determined far back in the past and foretold in detail to certain chosen men many centuries before they were to occur is also characteristic. This is linked in turn with the pseudonymity of apocalyptic writings. Such writings purport to be revealed knowledge imparted to chosen sages long before the decisive moment at which the two aeons coincide. These men wrote down the exact historical and cosmic course of events to be expected. But they did not publicise their knowledge, either to warn or to comfort their contemporaries. On the contrary, they kept everything which had been revealed to them absolutely secret, for it was something which even they themselves did not fully understand (Dan. VIII. 27), since it would only come into effect at a very much later date (Enoch I. 2; Dan. VIII. 26, XII. 9). This introduces us to another characteristic of apocalyptic writing, its esotericism and gnosticism. The last things can be known; indeed, they can be exactly calculated; but this is only possible for the initiated, who understand the art of decoding these predictions, for they are mostly in cypher. Then, corresponding to the esotericism and gnosticism is the notion of "mystery," "secret," found at every point in this literature. He who understands the secrets understands what holds the world together in its inmost being.[3] This list of characteristic features could, of course, be extended: but even a full list of them would not be entirely satisfactory, for we would thus achieve only a transcription of the phenomenon, not a description of it.

[2] Cp. here the frequently quoted verse of II Esdras: "God has made not one world but two" (II Esd. VII. 50). A detailed characterisation of Apocalyptic thinking is given in P. Volz, *Die Eschatologie der jüdischen Gemeinde im neutestamentlichen Zeitalter*, henceforth cited as *Eschatologie*, Tübingen 1934, and in J. Muilenberg, *The Interpreter's Bible*, VOL. I, New York and Nashville, 1952 onwards, col. 340. W. Baumgartner also gives an excellent definition of the characteristics of Apocalyptic: "pseudonymity, eschatological impatience and exact reckoning up of the time of the end, comprehensive and fantastic visions, a horizon which takes in universal history and is even cosmic, numerical symbolism and cryptic language, the doctrine of angels and the hope for the life beyond." "Ein Vierteljahrhundert Danielforschung," in *Th. R.*, N.F. II (1939), pp. 136ff.

[3] G. Bornkamm, Art. μυστήριον in *Th. W.B.N.T.*, VOL. IV, p. 821.

Where are we to look for the representatives of such apocalyptic ideas?

In view of its keen interest in the last things and of the significance it attaches to visions and dreams, it might seem appropriate to understand apocalyptic literature as a child of prophecy.[4] To my mind, however, this is completely out of the question. In this connexion, too much importance should not be given to the fact that apocalyptic literature never understands itself as prophecy, and that it sometimes speaks of prophecy as ended ("the prophets have fallen asleep," Syr. Baruch LXXXV. 3). The decisive factor, as I see it, is the incompatibility between apocalyptic literature's view of history and that of the prophets. The prophetic message is specifically rooted in the saving history, that is to say, it is rooted in definite election traditions. But there is no way which leads from this to the apocalyptic view of history, no more than there is any which leads to the idea that the last things were determined in a far-off past. In the panorama of history given in Daniel's two great night-visions, the picture of the empires and the vision of the four beasts, there is absolutely no mention of Israel's history; here God deals only with the empires, and even the son of man does not come from Israel, but "with the clouds of heaven." All that is said of Israel is that she will suffer great tribulation from one of the horns. The entire saving event is eschatological and future. Admittedly, Israel's history is re-counted at length in other visions.[5] Yet, is this still the same way in which Israel, and particularly Israel's prophets, had from the very beginning interested themselves in the saving history? For Israel, history was the place in which she experienced her election by Jahweh and from which alone she could understand her own identity. No generation was exempted from that task; each one in succession was obliged to achieve this self-understanding in faith. Thus, even the Chronicler planned his work in the light of the saving appointments in the time of David.[6] Now, contrast this with the accounts of the history of God's people as we met them throughout apocalyptic literature—they are really devoid of theology! This view of history lacks all con-fessional character; it no longer knows anything of those acts of God on

---

[4] So O. Procksch, *Theologie des Alten Testaments*, Gütersloh 1950, p. 401; H. H. Rowley, *The Relevance of Apocalyptic*, 2nd edn., henceforth cited as *Apocalyptic*, London and Redhill 1947, p. 13.

[5] So, for example, in the vision of the oxen in Ethiopic Enoch, LXXXV-XC, in the apocalypse of the ten weeks in Enoch XCIII, in the Assumption of Moses II-X, or in the vision of the clouds, Syriac Baruch, LIII-LXXI.   [6] See VOL. I, p. 350.

which salvation was based and in the light of which previous accounts of the nation's history had been constructed. Good and evil certainly occur in it, but they are spoken of in a way that gives the impression that they are quite timeless. Apocalyptic literature could only alter the form of the traditional material available to it. Thus, by means of allegory it could put the tradition into code—almost playfully—and break it up into time divisions. Basically, apocalyptic literature was only concerned with the last generation of Israel, those who, it was convinced, were just about to enter upon the last events; consequently, it is relatively unimportant that the history of God's people is sometimes recounted in greater detail, and sometimes in less.

This gives the question of the way in which apocalyptic literature understands history, so entirely different from that previously understood by Israel, all the greater urgency. Indeed, we may even ask whether apocalyptic literature had any existential relationship with history at all, since it had abandoned the approach by way of the saving history. This question must be directed to the very conception from which apocalyptic literature gains its splendour, that of the unity of world history. This unity is already expressed in Daniel's picture of the empires (Dan. II. 31ff.); and again in the vision of the four beasts, the empires appear as a connected entity (Dan. VII. 2ff.).[7] The empires have an origin, an existence, and a goal; their course is predestined, and fulfilled. In the sphere of world history, a "measure," that is, something which has already been defined, the measure of transgression (Dan. VIII. 23), has to reach fulfilment. So far, this view is extremely determinist. Isaiah's picture of Assyria was very different, very much more pliable. With him nothing was predestined, and certainly not from the beginning of history—Israel could "turn," or Jahweh could "repent" of the evil. In addition, Isaiah was of course only concerned with one phase of world history, and not with the whole of it from Adam down to its eschatological consummation!

We must also notice the methods used by apocalyptic literature. The prophets certainly used allegorical code to present historical events of a certain kind (Is. VIII. 5–8; Ezek. XVII. 1ff., XXXI. 1ff.): but what they dealt with was isolated events in history, whereas apocalyptic literature tries to take the whole historical process together and objectify it conceptually. To this end it reduced the endlessly varied shapes and forms of history to a number of relatively simple allegorical

7 Volz, *Eschatologie*, p. 6.

and symbolical representations (an image, Dan. II; four beasts, Dan. VII; cloud, Syr. Baruch LIIIff., etc.). The fact that the whole historical process could be represented, with some success, by the allegory of an upright human figure must be due to the ability of the writers of apocalyptic literature to reduce history to the primary forces at work within it, and to schematise and unify it to the highest possible degree. Some representations are much more expressive than others. The picture of a human form composed of various metals seems quite unsuited to represent a sequence of historical events, however schematised it may be; for the image in itself is static, and movement only comes into the picture with the stone which drops from the realms above. In contrast, the picture of the four beasts which come up out of the sea, or that of the cloud which rains clear and dark water, leave at least some place for movement in history. In Dan. II and VII, however, the meaning of the pictorially represented movement is perfectly plain—it indicates a growth of evil. Apocalyptic literature's view of history is therefore pessimistic in the extreme—world history is moving towards an "abyss" and a "great destruction" (Enoch LXXXIII. 7). According to apocalyptic literature, this growing evil is clearly due to the nature of man and of the empires founded by him; to this extent all that evolves and manifests itself in world history is something inherent in it from the beginning. Here apocalyptic literature differs from prophecy, for prophecy attributed all catastrophic events to the direct intervention of Jahweh in history.

One further characteristic of apocalyptic literature's own peculiar way of looking at history seems to me to be important. When they made their predictions, the prophets had always openly taken their standpoint in their own day and age; it was from that point that they saw the vistas of history roll back into the past or forward into the future. In contrast, the apocalyptic writers veiled their own standpoint in time,[8] though scholars are generally able to deduce it from the way in which they describe the period immediately preceding the *eschaton*, (and it is thus possible to date the various apocalyptic writings with some precision). But what these writers are concerned with is to offer a survey of history in which everything turns upon the fact that the epochs of world history are predetermined. Again we may be tempted to ask whether such a conception is not indicative of a great loss of historical sensitivity, whether history has not been excluded from the

[8] Rowley, *Apocalyptic*, p. 36.

philosophy which lies behind this gnostic idea of epochs that can be known and calculated, a philosophy which has dispensed with the phenomenon of the contingent. Our concern here, however, is simply to mark the great gulf which separates apocalyptic literature from prophecy.

Once it is realised, however, that knowledge is thus the nerve-centre of apocalyptic literature, knowledge based on a universal Jahwism, surprisingly divorced from the saving history, it should not be difficult to determine the real matrix from which apocalyptic literature originates. This is Wisdom, in which, as we already noted in VOL. I, exactly the same characteristics appear.[9] We understood Wisdom as the effort made by the people of Israel to grasp the laws which governed the world in which she lived, and to systematise them. In course of time this developed into a really encyclopedic science which applied itself not only to matters of natural philosophy but also to questions of history. And here, in Ecclesiasticus XLIV–L, is to be found the first example of the history of Israel presented without reference to the saving history and merely as a catalogue of the events concerned. And are not the matters with which apocalyptic literature is occupied expressly those of wisdom and its science? In the Apocalypse of Enoch there is an enormous accumulat. _n of knowledge about the development of civilisation (Enoch VIII), the heavenly bodies (Enoch LXXII–LXXIX), the calendar, meteorology, and geography. Further, the literary category of "figurative discourses" (מֹשׁלִים) is in principle to be described as a form of teaching traditional to Wisdom. Daniel is educated as a wise man (Dan. I. 3ff.), and in consequence he is enrolled among the wise men (Dan. II. 48); charismatic wisdom gives him his ability to interpret dreams (Dan. II. 30, V. 11), and his Book, which contains an "almost overwhelming admixture of erudition,"[10] actually ends with an apotheosis of the Wisdom teachers (Dan. XII. 3). Enoch designates himself as a unique representative of true wisdom (Enoch XXXVII. 2–4), and Ezra, who had apocalyptic knowledge granted him, is called "scribe of the knowledge of the Most High" (IV Ezra XIV. 50). This is a good description, for these apocalyptists were scholars and researchers. Certainly, they were aware that all human striving after knowledge, especially where it is directed upon the things of God, the future, and what lies beyond the end, requires revelation, and that it can only exist as charismatic knowledge. This, however, is far from

_____

[9] See VOL. I, pp. 446, 450.   [10] Eissfeldt, _Einleitung_, p. 653.

making them prophets. The notion of wisdom as a divine *charisma* has its own tradition in ancient Israel.[11] Foretelling the future was in no way the sole prerogative of the prophets. Least of all do we find them occupied with the interpretation of dreams, something which is prominent in apocalyptic literature. From the earliest times this fell in the province of Wisdom (Gen. XLI. 8, 39). Thus, if we pay attention only to apocalyptic predictions about the *eschaton* we narrow the whole field of reference for these writings. This is not possible even with Daniel; and how, for example, could the astronomical details in Enoch LXXIIff. be included in such a compass? In these chapters the form of prediction is abandoned; instead, they give the results of a comprehensive study of astronomy with scholarly exactitude.[12]

Can we not interpret this interest in time and in the secrets of the future shown by the apocalyptic writers in the light of Wisdom teaching that everything has its times, and that it is the part of Wisdom to know about these times (Ecc. III. 1ff.)?[13] An exact examination of the various materials used by apocalyptic writers—among which one would certainly have to reckon onomastica[14]—would clarify still further the imposing range of the scholarly knowledge on which it is based. It is possible that the cultivation of these branches of knowledge is of more ancient origin than we imagine. Probably all that is new is that at a specific point in history this branch of scholarship came out of the seclusion of the study with a preaching mission, and that it set itself to console men. For the apocalyptic writers make one thing plain. Wherever we are to look for them—and one must think of the Wisdom teachers much more than of "the quiet in the land"[15]—what they

[11] See VOL. I, p. 442.

[12] We may note that such learned traditions have to be presupposed as early as Daniel. The battle between the ram (the Persians) and the he-goat (the Greeks) in Dan. VIII. 2ff. can only be understood on the basis of astral-geographic ideas, according to which the various lands are assigned to certain constellations, Cumont, "La plus ancienne géographie astrologique," *Clio*, Leipzig 1909, p. 273.

[13] See above, pp. 100f. and VOL. I, p. 456. "The great principle in the divine economy is this: everything has its time and its measure, great and small, the universe and its parts considered spatially and temporally; everything has its day, its appointed hour, its duration; so also the acts of the eschatological drama and the end. This is pre-eminently a part of Apocalyptic's stock-in-trade." Volz, *Eschatologie*, p. 138.

[14] Cp. Enoch LX. 17ff.; on Enoch VI. 7 ("angel of thunder, of smoke, of cloud, of lightning, of rain"), see G. Kuhn, "Beiträge zur Erklärung des Buches Henoch," in *Z.A.W.*, 39 (1921), pp. 240ff. On the onomastica, see VOL. I, p. 425.

[15] So A. Oepke, Art. ἀποκαλύπτω, in *Th. W.B.N.T.*, VOL. III, p. 580.

ventilated in their pages were very hard theological problems. They undertook, from their own individual standpoint, and underwriting this with all the insights they derived from scholarship or *charisma*, to deal publicly with the great problems of their time.[16] There can be no doubt—though this applies least of all to the Daniel apocalypse—that in the process their scientific presuppositions themselves exposed them to the danger of teaching a great cosmological gnosis. This perhaps marks the point at which apocalyptic literature stands at the farthest remove from prophecy. In this respect the concept "secret," which is absolutely fundamental for apocalyptic literature, but which has no basis in the preaching of the prophets, is particularly illuminating, since the prophetic message, which was proclaimed absolutely openly, has nothing to do with esoteric knowledge.[17] There can, of course, be no question but that prophetic traditions contributed to the great heritage which the apocalyptic writers held in trust; but they had probably only encountered these as literature—the prophetic books were studied and interpreted like the others of the ancient tradition. The Habakkuk commentary in the Dead Sea Scrolls shows that the actualisation of a text from Jeremiah in Dan. IX was only one example among many practised at the time. Generally speaking, the apocalyptists' intellectual achievement may be fairly completely summed up in the term "interpretation." The time-divisions of world history, typical of apocalyptic writers, are simply the interpretation and actualisation of earlier cosmological schemata found in myth. This work of interpretation grew so large that on occasion—it was only a question of time—it became self-contradictory, one interpretation being ranged against another.[18]

2. DANIEL

Coming now to Daniel: in view of what has just been said, no one will expect a prediction based, like that of the prophets, on definite election traditions. In fact, the traditions connected with the patriarchs,

---

[16] "In the apocalyptic writers prophecy consists in the scholarly disclosure of the organic plan of the divine government of the world," F. Baumgärtel, *Verheissung: zur Frage des evangelischen Verständnisses des Alten Testaments*, Gütersloh 1952, p. 31.

[17] For the term "secret" only a Persian loan-word, רז, was available; Dan. II. 18f., 27, 29, 30, 47, IV. 6, 9 [9, 12].

[18] The interpretation of the eagle as Rome, and the reference in II Esdras XII. 11 which corrects Daniel's interpretation (VII. 7), are well-known.

Exodus, or Zion all seem to lie quite outside Daniel's mental world.[19] The songs of praise which occur here and there in the text (Dan. II. 20-3, III. 33 [IV. 3], IV. 31-4 [34-7], VI. 27-8 [26-7]) are remarkably different from the earlier ones which, as we all know, had as their chief subject Jahweh's wonderful works in creation and in the saving history.[20] Here, the speaker's religious horizon has almost no connexion with the actual events of history; he extols the greatness of God's power, which can make and unmake kings, deliver men and set them free. God's enlightening wisdom is also praised, and so is the indestructibility of his kingdom. This does not mean, of course, that in Daniel's time Israel had completely severed her links with the saving history tradition. Even for Daniel the ground of Israel's well-being is loyalty to the traditional commandments, and her greatest danger anything which prevents this loyalty. These commandments themselves are now set forth, however, in a surprisingly absolute way, and their old connexion with the saving history is broken. They have a completely self-contained and once for all time meaning. God's will is therefore no longer to be re-interpreted to meet new situations, as had been the usual practice in the past.[21]

The legends of Daniel (chs. I-VI), the oldest traditional material in the book, very clearly illustrate the way in which Israel remained bound by the commandments, as they also do all the possibilities of conflict which this entailed. They depict the members of God's people as quite separated and isolated from the community in which they lived: yet they are quite sure that it was possible for the Israelites and their heathen neighbours to co-exist in a pagan empire. The heroes of these stories successfully adopt the difficult career of a state official—Daniel shares in the educational facilities of the land (Dan. I), just as he does in the honours which were Nebuchadnezzar's to confer (Dan. II. 48f., VI. 29 [28]). The Nebuchadnezzar or the Darius of these stories can never have been intended to represent the terrible Antiochus IV who set up the "abomination that makes desolate." The trusting loyalty to Nebuchadnezzar shown by Daniel and his friends reflects a much more peaceful time than that of the Maccabean revolt. These legends, with

---

[19] Only in the prayer in Dan. IX. 4ff. is there reference to the law of Moses and to the Exodus. This passage has, however, to be regarded as a secondary interpolation and, also, it is not a prophecy.

[20] See VOL. I, pp. 357, 360.

[21] See here VOL. I, 198ff.

their overtly didactic purpose, were originally addressed to the Jews of the Persian diaspora. The message they brought to their own age was an exhortation to obey the commandments of their own God precisely within the narrow limits of co-existence with the worshippers of other gods. It was also a warning: they were to be on their guard, and ready, if need be, to face very bitter hostility. For hatred of the chosen people and of their way of worship could spring up spontaneously from the very heart of these empires—their cultic philosophies. Three of these six stories (Dan. I, III, VI) give examples of this hostility which would completely have destroyed the chosen people had not God himself carried them through every danger. Here is the other aspect of the legends' lesson—the exiled Jews must know that they are not alone; despite all appearances, they have not been abandoned to the control of a despotic world-empire. Divine help rewards their persistence in obedience (Dan. III, VI). Here there is a widening of the theological horizon, for behind the problem of the threat to the chosen people and their deliverance can be seen the hand of the God who directs world history: who is not mocked (Dan. V), and who has power to depose and reinstate even emperors (Dan. IV). This message was a vital one for a people so closely involved in the life of a pagan empire. The confidence reflected by these legends is based on the conviction that God will keep faith. They bring not only a warning but also a message of comfort.

It seems paradoxical that these same stories which so confidently emphasise the possibility of co-existence with pagans should on the other hand speak openly of the final consequence of obedience, namely martyrdom. The right to apply this term to pre-Christian martyrs has been questioned: it is alleged that we may only speak of martyrdom where the suffering is expressly related to the idea of witness-bearing (and not to loyalty to the Law), and, in particular, only where the martyr is conscious that "a part of God's final discourse with mankind is being fulfilled in him," that is to say, where the martyr is aware of being involved in the eschatological Christ event.[22] This is certainly a correct definition of Christian martyrdom, and is one which we ought to keep in mind, for it points to features in martyrdoms which only became definitive with the coming of Christ and with His passion. On the other hand, the passion of Jeremiah and of the Servant, and even the conflicts described in Dan. III and VI, come very close to Christian

[22] H. von Kampenhausen, *Die Idee des Martyriums*, Göttingen, p. 3 and in particular pp. 106ff.

martyrdom; for even in Israel it became more and more apparent that loyalty to Jahweh logically would lead to suffering.[23] The people who were affected by this paradox did not regard suffering as a sign that their fellowship with God was ended, nor did they refuse to accept its consequences. Here it is important that the three young men do not rely on the miracle, but concede that God is free to allow even his own followers to perish (Dan. III. 18). Further, it cannot be said that the idea of bearing witness is only of secondary importance in Dan. III; for by their obedience to the commandments the youths do bear witness to the God of Israel, and they also say that this is what they are doing. The connexion between witness-bearing and suffering is of course still closer and more logical in the case of Jeremiah; it is he, and not the three youths of Daniel, who is the martyr *par excellence* of the Old Testament.

In the legends the theme proper, the consummation of history, is no more than struck up. The problem of the world-empires, their immense power, their disappearance, and the emergence of new empires to take their place, is already present; the dimensions of history are still however this world. It is only in the visions of the night in Dan. II and VII that the writer carries us to that farthest margin where history touches the realm of the transcendent; indeed, his gaze passes over into the transcendent world itself.[24] In the vision of the four kings, very ancient ideas about a series of world ages (such as occur in Hesiod and others) have been fused with similar ideas about a series of four empires in the political world (which are later found in Latin writers). It can easily be seen that the reference to Antiochus Epiphanes was only brought about by means of an extension of the schema in which the kingdoms are represented by four metals; for, in what may be presumed to be its earliest form, the picture of the four kingdoms probably referred to the empire of Alexander. The process of adjustment to apply it to Antiochus IV and the great tribulations which he caused is itself not a unity, because the text lent itself to increasingly wider interpretations—this is particularly true of the dream's interpretation (Dan. II. 36–45). The main point is, of course, perfectly clear: with the terrible fourth kingdom into which the empire divides, world history will come to an end. The stone which is to be

[23] Jepsen, *Nabi*, p. 183.
[24] On what follows cp. M. Noth, "Das Geschichtsverständnis der alttestament-lichen Apokalyptik," in *Ges. St.*, pp. 248ff.

cut "by no human hand," and which is to destroy the kingdom and itself to become a great mountain, is an image of the kingdom of God that fills the whole earth. The same is true of the vision of the four beasts; here too, what is obviously older material has been made—though not without some difficulty—to refer to the persecution of Israel for her faith by Antiochus IV.[25] Of course, in this vision the scene is changed. We are shown a throne room in heaven, and the description of everything that takes place here goes far beyond what is said in the vision of the kings. In the first part of the vision of the four beasts it is clear that some power is controlling the kingdoms. This is signified by the indeterminate passives, "its wings were plucked off," "it was made to stand" (vs. 4), "it was given" (vs. 6). But in the vision of the throne the site of this controlling power is made visible.[26] It is the throne room of Jahweh, in which a court of judgment is held, and in which the final transference of dominion over the world is solemnly made to the "man." Apocalyptic ideas are far removed from the tradition of the Davidic Messiah—the anointed one of the prophets comes from the line of David and from Bethlehem (Mic. v. 1 [2]), and not down from heaven: but at the same time there can be no doubt that the son of man described in Dan. VII. 13 is initially presented as a Messianic figure in the wider sense of the term.

We still do not know the origin of this concept: but we can say this much. The vision speaks of an individual who comes from the heavenly world, and whom God authorises to take "dominion and glory and kingdom" over all the nations of the world.[27] Oddly enough, this figure of the "man" which, as we have just said, was quite certainly

[25] Like the four rivers in Gen. II. 10ff. or the four horns in Zech. II. 1 [1. 18], the four beasts represent the world in general. In Dan. VII. 3 an idea that the four beasts came up contemporaneously out of the sea is still clearly visible. This would then completely correspond to Zechariah's picture of the four horns.

[26] On these characteristic passives see M. Noth, "Zur Komposition des Buches Daniel," in *Theologische Studien und Kritiken*, 98/99 (1926), pp. 144ff.

[27] Of the countless attempts to determine the origin of the Son of Man concept, that of Procksch seems to me to merit special consideration. According to it, the concept of the man who comes with the clouds of heaven is connected with that of the coming of the "glory of Jahweh," especially as this worked out in Ezek. I. 26. Ezekiel too sees "something like a man" come down from heaven. Besides, the coming of the divine *kabod* with the cloud is already characteristic of the account given in the Priestly Document. O. Procksch, in *Christentum und Wissenschaft*, Dresden 1927, pp. 427ff.; id., *Theologie des Alten Testaments*, pp. 416f.

understood initially as an individual, is given a collective interpretation
in the passage which explains it (Dan. VII. 17–27): the "man" is the incorporation of "the saints of the Most High." The view—hitherto
almost unchallenged—that the saints of the Most High mean the people
Israel, has recently been shaken; in face of both the linguistic usage of
the Old Testament and of extra-canonical texts, we should more probably understand them as heavenly beings: that is to say, the reference is
to the idea that at the end of the ages dominion over the world is to be
put into the hands of the angels.[28] However this may be, the subject
matter of this dream vision has a greater width than any of the visions
of the prophets, for it embraces all that takes place from creation down
to the coming of the kingdom of God. The kingdoms come up out of
the realm of chaos; their nature and behaviour is pictured in bizarre
fashion. Apart from the excesses of the fourth beast, they are passive
rather than active, and over them all, even over the havoc wreaked by
the "horn," Jahweh bears sovereign and unending sway. All that is
needed to strip the horn of its power and to destroy it is a sentence
passed by the court. On the other hand, the "man" does not come
from the realm of the unformed, but from the divine world on high.
All this is described as from a spectator's point of view; the vision is not
conceived as projected from its recipient's own historical standpoint,
he does not stand within the events he beholds, but outside, and as he
looks, all world history passes before his spirit like a film.

Where, in vs. 25b, it comes to its climax and refers to Antiochus
Epiphanes, the vision of the four beasts itself cryptically named a period
up to which the persecution would continue. It is, however, only in the
latest material in the Book of Daniel, Dan. VIII–XII, that this desire to
give precise times for the duration of the persecution and the beginning
of the turning of the tide towards salvation becomes prominent. It is
not at all surprising that the various calculations set forth in these
chapters do not completely agree, for at that time the Wisdom teachers
had different ways of going about their involved calculations. One
particular desire was to determine the time of the end on the basis of the
exposition of older prophetic texts. The exegesis of the seventy years
prophesied by Jeremiah (Jer. XXV. 12, XXIX. 10) is certainly only one of
many examples, and it shows the way in which the prophetic books
were read at the time. This method of interpreting old and valued texts

[28] M. Noth, "Die Heiligen des Höchsten," in *Ges. St.*, pp. 274ff. Only one reference, Dan. VII. 21—and Noth concedes this—cannot be fitted into this interpretation.

gave the apocalyptic writers a completely new understanding of them. For it gave such texts a possible second meaning in a perfectly clear form. The seventy years were interpreted as "seventy weeks of years" (Dan. IX. 24), that is, as a time span of 490 years.

This is probably the first instance of that form of scriptural exegesis which was to become so important for both Judaism and early Christianity. It is entirely probable that the three and a half times which play such a part in the calculation of the end (Dan. VII. 25, XII. 7) also derive from some old tradition, though, of course, the source upon which Daniel here drew has not yet been discovered. In other places too, the statements made about the future are simply exegesis of older words of scripture. Thus, in Dan. IX. 26, in the prophecy of the end of Antiochus Epiphanes, the term שטף occurs. This is certainly not a random choice, but goes back to Is. X. 22; for the very next verse to that (Is. X. 23) is used in the same passage in Daniel, the only difference being that the "decreed end" (כלה ונחרצה) is now made to refer to the Seleucid king (Dan. IX. 27), and the "rumours" (שמועות) which terrify him and impel him to his final effort are taken from Is. XXXVII. 7.[29] In Dan. XI criticism has always noted the transition from vs. 39 to vs. 40 as the break where *vaticinium post eventum* passes over into genuine foretelling. To think of it in this way is, however, to obscure what the writer wanted to suggest, for for him the whole thing is foretelling. Both history which was (for him) already in the past and the future looked forward to in the old prophetic writings were alike revealed as a complete course of historical events foretold by God. Without any doubt, a delicate exegetical touch was necessary in order to interpret the old prophetic books in such a way; for the expositors presupposed that these books only contained as it were an initial revelation, which still required the proper key-revelation which apocalyptic exegesis gave.[30]

Where the course of history is predestined to such a degree, man's power of choice can only have a subordinate significance; men are only in a limited sense agents in what takes place, and therefore apocalyptic literature's pictures lack the genuine tension of history. The oppressor must "fill his measure full" (Dan. VIII. 23), and the oppressed are

[29] Might not the presentation in Dan. XI actually be described as a *pesher* of Isaiah? So I. L. Seeligmann, "Midraschexegese."

[30] K. Elliger, *Studien zum Habakkuk-Kommentar vom Toten Meer*, Tübingen 1953, pp. 156f.

ordered to wait for "the end of the indignation" (Dan. XI. 36). Here, it is true, the writer distinguishes between the unfaithful who "violate the covenant" and those who "know their God" (Dan. XI. 32). Among those who stand firm, the wise men (משכילים) have a leading part to play—they "help many to understand" (Dan. XI. 33), "they lead them to righteousness" (Dan. XII. 3); indeed, their very death has a purifying and cleansing effect, reminding one of the atoning function of the Servant (Is. LIII. 11). Without any doubt, the writer of Daniel sides with those who endure persecution rather than those who take up arms against it, and in so doing he is only being true to his own basic conviction that what must be will be. He is far removed from the Maccabees and their policy of active resistance; their large following is actually suspect in his eyes. There is something almost sublime about the way in which, as he tells the story, he sets down a whole series of their amazing victories simply as something relatively unimportant, "a little help" which the oppressed receive at this time (Dan. XI. 34). His gaze is imperturbably fixed on the goal which God has appointed for history, and this forbade him to glorify this mighty upsurge of human fortitude.

PART THREE

The Old Testament and the New

THE ACTUALISATION OF THE OLD TESTAMENT IN THE NEW

I

ALL these writings of ancient Israel, both those which were concerned with her past relationship to God and those which dealt with her future one, were seen by Jesus Christ, and certainly by the Apostles and the early Church, as a collection of predictions which pointed to him, the saviour of Israel and of the world. How could they do this—for the Old Testament never mentions Jesus Christ, nor does it visualise such a man as appears in the Gospels and Epistles? The Old Testament can only be read as a book of ever increasing anticipation. The oldest layer in this huge amalgam of expectations was the promise of a land made to the pre-Mosaic patriarchs. Of this, however, there was, oddly enough, never any satisfactory historical fulfilment and consummation. The conquest under Joshua which was in fact its historical fulfilment was described and documented in great detail: but the Conquest was clearly never regarded as the full and final realisation of this divine promise. Even as late as Deuteronomy—about 600 years after Joshua—Israel believed that this promise concerning the land was still in abeyance and she expected it to be realised in terms of God's word only in the future. In the interval Jahweh had brought new saving institutions into being: Zion had been "founded," and David "chosen."

These new foundations were at first celebrated in Israel's praise in the form of statements made about the past, but they suddenly led to predictions about a new saving action for Israel. We have seen this in the case of the prophets' Messianic predictions and their predictions concerning the new city of God. The history of Jahwism is thus characterised by repeated breaks. God appoints new institutions and fresh starts which inaugurate new eras of tradition. Yet scarcely had Israel come to terms with these before she was again startled by being pointed to new acts of God, and by being forced to leave behind ideas in which she had just made herself at home. This shows us once again how completely different Israel's religious ideas were from those of other countries of the ancient East. In Egypt or Babylon the only possible salvation after any political or religious disturbance—of which there were many—was that the nation should return to these primeval sacral orders which found expression in myth and the cycle of the festivals: but Israel emphasised the unique character of any events that had occurred. Consequently a survey of the great movements of her history gives us the impression of a lack of repose—the nation is always on pilgrimage—and the constant emergence of new religious ideas seems to leave her a stranger in time. The impression that she was travelling along a road which could not be retraced is undoubtedly strengthened by the self-portrait drawn in her surviving literature. Her cultic life probably contained rather more constant and recurrent elements—that is, more of the "cyclic"—than is evident here[1]: but Jahwism achieved its fullest self-expression precisely in this concentration upon the uniqueness of each of God's new saving acts.

Jahweh's covenant with the patriarchs, the revelation of his name, the events at Passover, the miraculous crossing of the Red Sea, the making of the covenant at Sinai, the establishment of Zion, the covenant with David, Jahweh's entry into the temple with his Ark, are all points of departure into a new form of Israel's existence, and all from the very start contained far-reaching divine promises. As we have seen, however, in the predictions of the prophets some of them were, as archetypes of mighty predictions, projected into the future. Israel's expectations thus continually grew wider. It is amazing to see how she never allowed a promise to come to nothing, how she thus swelled Jahweh's promises to an infinity, and how, placing absolutely no limit on God's power yet to fulfil, she transmitted promises still unfulfilled to generations to come. In this way she increased God's debt to her.

Even those writings which actually have no kind of eschatological expectations whatsoever, as for example the Deuteronomic history or the Book of Job, nevertheless still have something that points mysteriously to the future. Were the acts of guidance and chastisement, the saving orders which were so strong a feature of the monarchical period, finally justified by an unhappy king's being allowed at the last to put off his prison clothes and to sit as a vassal at the table of the king of Babylon (II Kings xxv. 27ff.)? Was the great issue to be decided be-

[1] Behind texts like Ex. xii (the institution of Passover), II Sam. vi, Ps. xxiv. 7–10 or Ps. cxxxii (the bringing of the Ark into the Temple) lie cultic observances which were repeated in the cycle of the festivals.

tween Job and God resolved by the rebel's being silenced before God and by an old man's having children and herds given him again? We shall have more to say later about this peculiar discrepancy between such endings and the themes which had been raised before them. We must stress again that the Old Testament can only be read as a book in which expectation keeps mounting up to vast proportions. For this reason alone it has to be given a place of its own within the framework of comparative religion. Yet of itself this does not answer the question whether it is also to be read as the book which foretells Jesus Christ. Historical and critical Old Testament scholarship which sees it as a body of independent religious documents to be interpreted in its own light and that of its religious environment, gives the question no certain answer. On the contrary, on its basis it is perfectly possible to argue that the Old Testament with all its expectation "points straight into the void."[2] From this standpoint, one can hardly say more than that in the case of the literary legacy of Israel we are dealing with a particular enigma among the many in the history of religion. The question before us, however, is this: does not the way in which comparative religion takes the Old Testament in abstraction, as an object which can be adequately interpreted without reference to the New Testament, turn out to be fictitious from a Christian point of view?

Because of the confusion of views on the relationship of the Old Testament to the New and the way in which theological definitions of this contradict one another, it may be worth while to anticipate and say that in the chapters which follow we are in fact going to discuss the question from one point of view only, the one which we have already taken as our guide in expounding the traditions within the Old Testament itself, that of the traditio-historical. Everything that follows is really intended simply to carry this familiar procedure a stage further by trying to understand that the way in which the Old Testament is absorbed in the New is the logical end of a process initiated by the Old Testament itself, and that its "laws" are to some extent repeated in this final reinterpretation. There is therefore no need to emphasise that there will be nothing about any mysterious hermeneutic device— something which is not in the least necessary for understanding the relationship between the early Church and the Old Testament. Initially therefore our method does not begin from the New Testament and its manifold references to the Old Testament. This is a method which

[2] Barth, *Dogmatics*, VOL. I, Pt. 2, p. 89.

has often been adopted, and it is a right and proper one. It has also, of course, led all too often to contrasting the one with the other with a sharpness which does not do justice to the great hermeneutic flexibility of the relationship between the two Testaments. The method will be an attempt to show one characteristic way in which the Old Testament leads forward to the New. We shall first now deal with the question of "form" displayed in the process, and our interest will be concentrated on the way in which such processes were developed within the Old Testament itself.

2. We have already noticed that, as regards the cult, Jahwism was preceded by a phase which we call the religion of the Gods of the ancestors, and that the traditions which went with these forms of worship—or at all events the basic ones—were adopted by the Jahwism which followed. This incorporation did not, however, lead to merging or coalescing; on the contrary, it was for long remembered that the revelation of the name "Jahweh" involved a fresh start (Ex. III. 1ff., VI. 3). Admittedly, this pre-Mosaic worship has characteristics which seem in a very remarkable way to anticipate the Jahwism which succeeded it (the deity is not attached to a place, as was so common in the ancient East; his personal relationship to a particular group of men and women and his concern for what happens to them in their history is therefore all the stronger[3]). On the other hand, there are important differences too. Jahweh was the God of the twelve clans and had revealed himself in a number of different ways, while the God of the ancestors was only the God of a small band of nomads. Now however, the nomadic traditions had been absorbed into Jahwism; in the promise of a land made to the ancestors, Jahwism recognised the voice of its own God. Jahweh now made his entry into the age-old traditions: it was he who had had dealings with Abraham, Isaac, and Jacob. This at once brought the old patriarchal stories into an entirely new light, for what a difference it must have made when Jahweh took the place of the "strong one of Jacob"! From the hermeneutic point of view, this meant a complete reinterpretation of the old tradition. There is one point at which this is particularly clear—Jahwism transferred the old promise of a land to the horizon of a different and much more distant point of fulfilment, namely the conquest under Joshua. The patriarchs' stay in the land of Canaan was now looked on as a temporary thing, as the time when "in the land of their sojourning" they still awaited the

[3] See VOL. I, pp. 7f.

real fulfilment.[4] While we cannot name many details, we can say that the incorporation of this earlier form of worship into Jahwism certainly meant that some elements were lost at the same time. Jahwism would not have preserved its character if it had not quietly discarded what was incompatible with itself. Thus, even at this early date, we have to reckon with a kind of selective process in virtue of which some things were to be handed on while others were to be deliberately forgotten, a process which was to be repeated later.

A very much clearer instance of a comparable procedure is to be found in the prophets' relationships to the time-hallowed election traditions of Jahwism. In this case there is clear written evidence, which can be followed even in detail. At this point it is unnecessary to repeat that there was a radical break in the relationship between the prophets and the saving election traditions of the patriarchs, Sinai and the Exodus, and Zion and David. They believed that same Israel, who still thought of herself as under God's protection and blessing, to be rather subject to his final judgment. They did not act as reformers, however, and summon her to render more strict obedience to Jahweh's saving will as it had been revealed in these traditions. The important thing about them was that they actually denied their fellows the right of appeal to the salvation offered there, and saw only a very narrow way forward to a salvation which Jahweh was only to create in the future. On the other hand, they had no intention of "abrogating" the old revelations; we saw good reason for believing that they took these much more seriously than did their fellows. At the same time, however —and this is what we are here concerned with—they speak of them as if from a theological standpoint which lies beyond the traditions themselves; for what engrossed the prophets' attention was God's new saving action, whose dawn they had discerned. The reason why they made any use at all of these old traditions in their preaching is that they ascribed to them something like a predictive character. They looked for a new David, a new Exodus, a new covenant, a new city of God: the old had thus become a type of the new and important as pointing forward to it. Undoubtedly, however, the prophets allowed themselves very great freedom in their typological utilisation of the old traditional elements. Here again some things were accepted and others passed over. Since their prediction of the "new things" is mainly in the form of positive statements, what they pass over as made obsolete by

[4] See VOL. I, pp. 168f.

the new saving event is, in the nature of the case, much less apparent. Obviously there was less reason to speak about what was to be "done away" with than of that which was to be fulfilled as the antitype of the original type. Sometimes, however, in order to make matters clear, the prophets did condescend to contrast the new with the old, and in these cases the words "no more" are to be looked on as polemical. This is most clearly expressed in Jeremiah's pericope on the new covenant (Jer. XXXI. 31ff.), which therefore serves as a standard type of prophetic prediction, that is to say, of the mysterious combination of close attachment to the old saving tradition and its radical supersession. The direct inference of Jeremiah's words is that the new covenant will make no difference as far as God's revealed will for Israel is concerned. Thus at first sight it might seem that the new was not itself a complete thing, that it was simply a modification of the old procedure by which God's will was conveyed to Israel—a modification by which God is not only to proclaim his will but is also actually to plant it in the hearts of men. Yet this seeming incompleteness in fact puts the whole process on a new basis. Even if Jer. XXXI. 31ff. goes far beyond many other prophetic predictions in its definite separation of the new from the old, it still does not actually contrast the two. Jeremiah's concern is not to provide even only a partial description of what is to be done away with and what is to remain valid, but to give a brief indication—by using what are really catchwords—of his message to his contemporaries about their problems.[5] But this leads to a related fact of very great importance. The whole way by which old traditions are actualised in the prophets' predictions, these men's close attachment to the old, their habit of carrying over the old into the new, and their contrasting but connected habit of ignoring some aspects of the old which they believed to be superseded, can only be understood as fundamentally charismatic procedure, or, to put it more exactly, as an eclective process based on *charisma*. It is, of course, quite obvious that in making their

[5] See above, pp. 212ff. and 269ff. Commentators frequently understand Jer. XXXI. 31ff. too "dogmatically," as if what comes in question is the unfolding of a great and, so to speak, broadly-based body of theological ideas. The reason for this may be the didactic "Deuteronomistic" diction. However, what the whole thing leads up to in the contrast between the covenants is simply the way by which the divine will is conveyed. Even Jer. XXXI. 31ff. is completely akin to those prophetic *ad hoc* actualisations already noticed made to suit a particular occasion. The difference between the covenants could equally well have been illustrated from some other point that is characteristic of the new one.

predictions the prophets were guided by the old traditions: but it would be quite wrong to suggest that they used any fixed method of actualising them. Their relationship with them, their dependence on them and freedom from them, was determined by their own particular circumstances, which explains why the relationship altered with different individuals. Sometimes the link with the old is more prominent, at others the prophet's independence from it and his freedom to reinterpret it. If we were to take a particular prediction and try to define precisely its relationship with the old—that is to say, if we were to try to make a hermeneutic distinction between dependence on the old and transcendence of it—we should see that any such prediction was the product of a highly complicated process. Indeed, we might well ask whether it would not be better for exegesis to leave hermeneutics to itself, since the old and the new are in fact altogether inseparably interwoven. At all events, as far as we can see, this was a distinction of which the prophet took no account: on his lips old and new together became something completely actual and an entity in itself. When Deutero-Isaiah transfers to Israel the predicates of the promise made to David, exegesis can still descry in various details—e.g., that Jahweh purposes to make Israel a נָגִיד—elements of the old which the prophet used in actualising the divine promise; but exegesis has at the same time to say that the old has been completely absorbed into the new and fused with it.[6] Another example of extreme freedom in actualising the old was found in the recapitulation of the saving history in Ezek. xx.[7] Such are the completely original interpretations of the venerable traditions of the Exodus and the events in the wilderness period that were possible in the sixth century!

We may note in passing that the pericope which describes Jacob's wrestling at Jabbok can be taken as a good example of the hermeneutic alterations which sometimes resulted from this handing on of old traditions (Gen. xxxii. 23ff. [22ff.]). It is to Gunkel in particular that we owe the recognition of the great age of the saga material here, which goes far back into the early history of Canaan, or at all events, far back into pre-Israelite and pre-Jahwistic times. Later, however, it was absorbed by Jahwism. Where is one to begin interpretation? It is perfectly proper to attempt a scientific reconstruction of the saga in what may be regarded as its earliest form. Still, now that the story has been incorporated into Jahwism and there is no doubt that Jahweh is the God who encountered Jacob, there is not much point in speaking of the lurking "river demon."

[6] On Is. LV. 3f. see above, pp. 46 and 240.   [7] On Ezek. xx, see above, pp. 225ff.

In what way did Jahweh encounter Jacob? Did he ambush him, and did he take fright, as demons do, when dawn broke? The moment that Jahweh came into the story—Jahweh the creator of the world, the Jahweh of the Abraham stories, who was later to become Moses's Jahweh—the story received a completely new meaning, and interpretation has, as it were, to start all over again. It must, of course, be said that we seem to-day to know much more about the content of the pre-Jahwistic saga than about the one which results from the appropriation of the material by Jahweh.[8] Careful interpretation, however, concerned to understand the story from within the context of Jahwism, will not, of course, fail to notice that some elements that were important in the old saga now fall quite automatically into the background, while others, as, for example, the wrestling with God, or Jacob's words, "I will not let you go," appear in a new light. We are given some idea of the way in which the prophets viewed this story from the casual remarks upon it in Hosea (Hos. XII. 4f. [3f.]). They are all too brief, but they do show us that the prophet read something into the story—Jacob's deceit and importunity—which was not present in the Jahwist's understanding of it as given in Gen. XXXII. 23ff. The Christian however—and here, of course, we anticipate—will see the story in the light of Jesus Christ, and interpretation will again have to make a fresh start.

Exact definition and classification of the character of such forms of Israel's theological utterances still eludes us. From our point of view, of course, their particular interest lies in the "diction" they use; for they make no attempt to express the specific new insight in a new way. The new makes use of the traditional form, yet it is still able—often simply by means of some apparently insignificant alteration, or in particular by the help of the context, that is to say, helped by a totally different way of understanding the whole thing—to work in what is really an out of date "form" with an amazing freedom. When seen in the light of the process just described, how many of the radical conclusions which have been drawn from the fact that Israel "took over" traditions from alien cults are reduced to their proper proportions. To establish that something was "taken over" means in itself very little: yet it is extremely hard to say whether Jahwism could properly express itself in a form that derived from Canaan, or whether this of necessity misrepresented it.

[8] G. von Rad, *Genesis*, pp. 35f., 40ff.

The purpose of these considerations is not to reconstruct successive stages of the saving history. Indeed, one would have to ask whether this acceptance of the old into the new and the form adopted to actualise it does not actually modify the idea of saving history. All we have tried to do was to shed some light on the hermeneutical side, first on the problems raised by the absorption of the Old Testament into the New and its actualisation there, and second, on the sometimes tacit and sometimes openly expressed thesis that the Old Testament is "incomplete"; for when the Old Testament and the New are contrasted with each other in the way in which they are to-day, it certainly looks as though the divisions we draw are much too rigid. And we must certainly assume in this connexion that the freedom which the Apostles and the writers of the Gospels allowed themselves in taking over, revising, or rejecting Old Testament material was no less than that which Ezekiel already claimed for himself. It is still more true of them that in the witness they bear they now stand at a point outside the Old Testament tradition, and yet, in spite of this, we see that their relationship to it—taking it up or revising or rejecting it—involves them in breaking it down in quite the same way as we have already found within the Old Testament material itself. We said earlier that the prophets do not improvise, that they show themselves to be bound to definite traditions, that they move about within the realm of older witnesses to Jahwism in an extraordinarily dialectic fashion, that they take their own legitimation from these and at the same time, because of new content which they give them, go beyond them and even break them up, that, while they certainly select from among the traditions, at the same time they keep them as the broad basis of their arguments— does not this also describe the relationship of the Apostles and the writers of the Gospels to the Old Testament?[9] Thus, a new name was once again proclaimed over the ancient tradition of Israel: like one who enters into an ancient heritage, Christ the Kyrios claimed the ancient writings for himself. A characteristic feature of this appropriation is the transfer to the new Kyrios of those sayings in the LXX where Jahweh is called Kyrios, with the result that the old statements were at once given new theological frames of reference.[10] Yet, who would care to define hermeneutically how far the old sense was still preserved and how far something new had been added in such texts? This is that

9 See above, p. 239.
10 Mk. I. 3; Acts II. 21; Rom. X. 13; Heb. I. 10; Pet. II. 3, III. 15, etc.

process of "adaption" which was mentioned above, and towards which exegesis should show itself much more open and flexible than it generally is.[11] Because the Old Testament is not dominated by any uniform "conception of God" but, as we have tried to show, reflects a series of new revelations and divinely given saving appointments and the constant fresh actualisation of these, this process of adapting older traditions to suit the new situation was the most legitimate way by which Israel was able to preserve the continuity of her history with God and prevent it from disintegrating into a series of unrelated acts.

It may be objected that the taking over of Old Testament material into the New Testament is not a comparable process, since here it is a matter of a tradition which is already fixed in writing, indeed of "holy scripture," whereas in the other case it was a matter of an oral tradition, which is *per se* much more flexible and therefore much less able to resist reshaping. This is, of course, true. In this sense the Old Testament tradition was no longer flexible in the hands of the Apostles; it had become holy scripture, and in many respects this implied a change in the way it was handled, since interpretation had now to hold to "texts." The difference is not a radical one, however, but affects the "formal" aspect more than anything else, since, where a document is concerned, the process of hermeneutics and interpretation must of course bring definite requirements along with it ("proof from scripture," etc.). Indeed, if we take this difference quite openly into account, then the amazing freedom with which the old tradition was handled only comes out more strongly; for the fact that the old was now in the form of holy scripture made the exercise of such freedom all the harder.

3. Even a cursory glance at the New Testament reveals that right down to its latest writings it is absolutely permeated with a sense of wonder at the advent of a tremendous new event, an overwhelming awareness of standing at a new beginning from which entirely new horizons of God's saving activity have become visible: the kingdom of God is here.[12] The new event—the preaching of Jesus, his death, and resurrection—led to an understanding of the Old Testament fundamentally different from that of the scribes and also of the Qumran sect. It was no longer read as solely dominated by the law, but by saving history. In other words, the Old Testament was now read as a divine

[11] See above, pp. 48f.
D. M. G. Kümmel, *Promise and Fulfilment: The Eschatological Message of Jesus*, trs.
[12] W. Barton, London 1957, pp. 109ff., 111, 153.

revelation which was the precursor of Christ's advent, and was full of pointers towards the coming of the Lord; and this led to a completely new interpretation of the Old Testament.[13] Every page of the New Testament rings with the exultant awareness of standing in a new era of God's activity—it is sometimes called the era of "fulfilment" (Gal. IV. 4; Lk. IV. 21; Mt. XI. 4–6). Everything in the Old Testament is now referred to Christ. A particularly radical departure from Judaism is the early Church's belief that Moses was not just the mediator of the law— even he prophesied the coming of the Lord (Lk. XXIV. 27; Jn. I. 45, V. 46; Acts XXVI. 22).[14]

As is very understandable, the new saving event, the coming of Christ, which put not only Israel's relationship to God, but also that of the Gentile world, on an entirely new basis, was initially worked out in the New Testament by contrasting it in various ways with the Old. The least in the kingdom of God is greater than the greatest among those who awaited it (Mt. XI. 11). The prophets had longed to see what had now come to pass, and had not seen it (Mt. XIII. 17). This is to say that the New Testament took as its starting point the contrast between this new event and the whole of Israel's previous experience; and this must always be the starting-point for Christian interpretation of the Old Testament. But study of the New Testament clearly shows that this negative contrast is not a complete statement of its relationship with the Old. The writers of the Gospels saw even the details of Jesus's life on earth, his passion, his death and resurrection as the fulfilment of Old Testament predictions. One particular way by which the Old Testament was understood as a prediction which pointed forward to Christ is the well-known typological interpretation which the New Testament applied in various ways, and whose purpose was to establish a correspondence between an event in the Old Testament and another in the New; and here as a rule the element of enhancement is important. "Something greater than Solomon is here" (Mt. XII. 42). Here again there is an element of supersession, since the prediction differs somewhat from the fulfilment and the type is less important than the antitype to which it points. In actual fact however, both proof from scripture and typological interpretation are equally concerned to bring out

---

[13] Not that reflexion on the Law ceased; but the new saving aspect became normative in this very matter of the understanding of the Law.

[14] This difference in the understanding of Moses was pointed out by M. Wittenberg, *Heilige Überlieferung*, Neuendetteslau 1958, pp. 5ff.

a continuity between Israel's previous experience of Jahweh and what had come to pass "at the end, in these days," with the coming of Jesus Christ; both are, indeed, based on the assumption that all Israel's experience of Jahweh had been planned with reference to Jesus Christ, and that it was only for those who believed in him that the long-transmitted writings became fully and finally actual: "they were written down for us" (I Cor. x. 11); the Old Testament prophets "serve you" (I Pet. I. 12); it was written for our instruction (Rom. xv. 4; I Cor. IX. 10).

The New Testament writers show the utmost freedom in their appropriation of Old Testament material. They are able to actualise it in many different ways which range from showing the continuity and unity of the message to sharply contrasting the Old and New Testament themes. A particular example of the latter is Paul's opposition of law and gospel, or the disquisition in the Epistle to the Hebrews on the "imperfection" of Israel's cultic institutions. On the other hand, Hebrews is one of the strongest testimonies to the fact that the old saving history was full of pointers to and predictions of the Christ-event of the New Testament. And Paul too thinks in terms of saving history and typology; he sees in Abraham's faith a prefiguration of Christian faith, and on one occasion he equates the rock from which the Israelites drank in the wilderness with Christ himself (I Cor. x. 4). Nevertheless, such expressions are always rather casual; they are inspirations of the moment, and in many cases are not introduced because they are necessary parts of some great topic, but are dropped into the argument by the writer's use of specific expressions, which themselves open up references to the Old Testament. Often they are *ad hoc* associations which occur to him and he uses them. "Proof from scripture" is much too weighty a term for many of these spur-of-the-moment allusions to the Old Testament.[15] On the other hand, it is just these *ad hoc* allusions which make things difficult for exegesis, because they often seem to be quite arbitrary, and to take no account of the real sense of the particular Old Testament passage cited. We must be quite open about it and admit that much of the interpretation of scripture practised by the New Testament writings is conditioned by its own generation, and that we can no longer concur in it. This does not mean that early

---

[15] On the New Testament proof from Scripture, see E. Fuchs, *Hermeneutik*, Bad Cannstatt 1954, pp. 201ff.; but see also the criticism of the concept in H. Diem, *Dogmatics*, trs. H. Knight, Edinburgh and London 1959, pp. 154ff.

Christianity could only resort to venturesome exegetical methods in order to absorb material which was in principle quite alien to it. There was a very much greater continuity between the old and the new than is expressed in the quotations and allusions. "Proof from scripture" is not the only bridge between the Testaments; for this whole practice of quotation rested on the awareness of a large element common to both.[16] This common element may to some extent be revealed in the more comprehensive disquisitions of Paul or the Epistle to the Hebrews; yet even Paul never put his views in a fundamentally theological way, that is, without regard for the actual requirements of those whom he specifically addressed. We should, therefore, in theory make a distinction between on the one hand the cases of absorption into the New Testament of Old Testament tradition which were conditioned by the needs of one particular audience, and on the other those cases where references to the Old Testament are one-sided and exaggerated, so that everything is concentrated on the distinctive aspect of the reference in this particular context. In the first case, everything is subordinate to the specific theological subject under discussion: in the second a charismatic process is undoubtedly at work.[17] The great variety of ways in which the Old Testament is cited and made actual, and, as has already been pointed out, the small part played in the New Testament by the question of hermeneutic method, are certainly all bound up with this char-

[16] "The postulate of the New Testament proof from Scripture is this: Jesus' human Being was, both as a whole and in detail, 'formed' in the light of what it was God's will to do with Israel and what he is now realising. . . . Therefore God's action in and through Jesus, too, is only to be 'understood' on the basis of the Word in the Old Testament. This postulate of the proof from Scripture has not merely an existential character for the Israelites of the time. The proof from Scripture claims to make a 'categorical objective' utterance about Jesus. God's action in the Old Testament is not just something added to the Jesus-event by way of confirmation and corroboration, that is to say, with a cognitive significance, but it has a causative, axiomatic importance for Jesus, and therefore forms a constitutive part of this event itself." C. H. Ratschow, *Der angefochtene Glaube*, Gütersloh 1957, p. 70.

[17] "A closer look at the way in which [the church of the New Testament took over the Old Testament as holy Scripture] reveals that it did not act like the Jews of Palestine, who materialised its sacred letter, nor like the Jews of Alexandria, who spiritualised this. It took the way of inspired realism and drew the consequences which follow upon the soteriological continuity between the fulfilment which was now taking place and the prophecies made in the Scriptures; and it did this in every case with untrammelled freedom, as need arose," O. Schmidt, "Das Alte Testament im Neuen Testament," in *Wort und Geist, Festgabe für Karl Heim*, 1934, p. 67.

acteristic type of actualisation.[18] In the last analysis, it was the risen Lord himself who "opened up" the scriptures to his own (Lk. XXIV. 32, 45).

This *ad hoc* actualisation necessarily presupposes, however, the existence of a general understanding of the relationship between the old and the new upon which it could draw if necessary. This appears only indirectly in the New Testament writings themselves; but its existence must be presumed, for it can always be seen marginally. Paul obviously had rather definite ideas about what was meant by Christ's rising from the dead "according to the scriptures," but he did not elaborate them (1 Cor. XV. 4). The same is true of the conviction which is frequently expressed in the Gospels that Christ "must" suffer.[19] What kind of an understanding of the Old Testament lies behind this idea? Or consider the transference to the Kyrios of the New Testament of the (Jahweh)-Kyrios sayings of the LXX. This only appears occasionally in the New Testament and is nowhere theologically substantiated, but it does presuppose some fairly general agreement. If we could discover this understanding of the Old Testament which lay before the Apostles and the writers of the Gospels, the various authors would no doubt show even considerable differences in their idea of it, but the picture would certainly not be as lacking in uniformity as it necessarily appears when only the sometimes extremely subtle methods of proof demanded by practical exegesis are considered. Their exegesis often runs counter to our own understanding of scripture: it nevertheless indicates that for Christians the Old Testament only has meaning in so far as it refers to Christ and was able to speak in the light of Christ.

As we have already seen, Israel's history with God thrusts forward violently into the future, and in the New Testament this phenomenon of ever more powerfully concentrated expectation appears in a new light; for there, following upon the numerous earlier new saving beginnings, it reaches its last hermeneutic modification and its full and final interpretation. But if we look at Christian interpretation of Old Testament traditions from this angle, and realise that here for the last time a law which determined the whole saving history of the Old Testament comes once again into operation, then we see that the way in which the Old Testament was cited and interpreted and made to

---

[18] G. Ebeling, *Evangelische Evangelienauslegung: eine Untersuchung zu Luthers Hermeneutik*, Munich 1942, pp. 102ff.

[19] Mk. VIII. 31; Lk. XVII. 25, XXII. 37, XXIV. 7, 26; Acts XVII. 3. On this δεῖ see W. Grundmann, Art. δεῖ, *Th. W.B.N.T.*, VOL. II, pp. 21ff.

supply proofs was entirely proper. Such a transformation of the traditional material in the light of a new saving event was as proper for early Christians as were many other such transformations which had already taken place in the Old Testament itself. There can be no impartial proof of the legitimacy of the new interpretation given to the Old Testament in the New; but the fact that it was so successful and convincing—that indeed the Old Testament as interpreted by Christianity was able to win such a new power to illuminate and could be applied in so many new ways—was for the early Church reason enough for seeing in the Old Testament a book which belonged to itself. We have already noticed that the great new beginnings in the saving history cannot be understood without reference to other events. The history of tradition showed us how old material could suddenly be put on a new basis and into new theological horizons, and the question therefore is whether the reinterpretation of Old Testament traditions in the light of Christ's appearance on earth is not also hermeneutically perfectly permissible. It is not a valid objection to say that in such a case the original meaning of the old material is abandoned, that therefore one cannot rightly speak of citing the old, and that it is rather a case of the new having a colloquy with itself. This is wrong, since form and content cannot be completely separated. There can be no such thing as an Old Testament form emptied of its content and filled with New Testament material. The question should be put the other way round: how was it possible for the Old Testament traditions, and all the narratives, prayers and predictions, to be taken over by the New Testament? This could not have happened if the Old Testament writings had not themselves contained pointers to Christ and been hermeneutically adapted to such a merger. Here, it is still an open question whether the Christian exegete ought to concentrate exclusively on the Old Testament's understanding of itself. The Apostles clearly take the view that the texts of the Old Testament only attain their fullest actuality in the light of their fulfilment. In the Qumran sect also it was believed that the Old Testament prophet could only have had a partial understanding of his predictions, because the "perfection of the end-time" had not been revealed to him (Comm. on Hab. VII. 1f.), and in this respect the sect is not essentially different from the New Testament point of view.

A glance at the Magnificat and the Benedictus (Lk. 1. 46–55, 68–79) helps to clarify the hermeneutic process by which statements made in the Old Testament were taken up in Christianity. It is at once obvious that these hymns are entirely written in the phraseology of those of the Old Testament. They speak of God the saviour (מוֹשִׁיעַ), who does great things (גְּדֹלוֹת), and of his mercy (חֶסֶד) and his opposition to the mighty (vs. 52). He has visited (פָּקַד) and redeemed (גָּאַל vs. 68) his people, and remembered his covenant (vs. 72). Even the theme of deliverance from "enemies" reappears (vss. 71, 74). Yet consider that this language, which is certainly not neutral, but carries extremely heavy theological overtones, is made to celebrate the coming of Jesus Christ. In this new guise what are meant by "redemption," "feeding the hungry" (vs. 53), "horn of salvation" (vs. 69), and "deliverance from enemies"? What is the difference between these two songs and the hymns in the Psalter? Now the same expressions as are found here and there in the hymns of the Old Testament are applied to a completely new saving event. In the process they do not lose the meaning they originally had; it still remains true that God redeems, that he shows mercy, satisfies his own, etc. Still, even so, there has been some change, in that the same expressions have been put into an entirely new theological perspective. A considerable change has taken place, for example, in the concept of men's deliverance from "enemies"; now it can only be understood in its transferred sense.

A second example may illustrate the process. It has long been recognised that Jesus's appeal, "Come to me, all who labour, etc." (Mt. XI. 28-30) is couched in a form and in terms which originally belonged to Wisdom's invitation. She too called men to her, bade them take her yoke upon them, and promised them rest (Ecclesiasticus LI. 23-7, VI. 24-30). How is the Matthean passage to be interpreted? Unquestionably, the use of this unusual diction signifies more than merely a casual and uncommitted rhetorical borrowing. The fact that this appeal is clothed to such an extent in an Old Testament form is of the utmost theological importance. Jesus enters authoritatively into the realm to which these Old Testament expressions belong and claims for himself the form and content of this final Old Testament offer of salvation.[20] Here too then there are considerable hermeneutic complications. It would be too naïve to say that the form belongs to the Old Testament, but the content to the New. Going far beyond the merely formal aspect, a considerable number of the actual expressions used in this saying of Jesus's were already in existence—the invitation, the idea of the yoke, and of the peace which men can find. Yet, the

---

[20] On the offer see VOL. I, p. 443.

very fact that it is Jesus who says this, and says it with reference to himself, puts the whole thing on a different plane. The fact that Jesus describes his yoke as "easy," and, in particular, that he calls attention to his relationship with the Father, and speaks of himself as merciful, puts the old invitation into an entirely new perspective. Jesus speaks as the one who "fulfils" the Old Testament.

Both these examples, which could easily be multiplied, do not actually cite Old Testament material but take it up in a still more immediate way. Any citation of the Old Testament does, of course, give a sense of continuity with the New: but it also conveys the separation in time between the two. In this form of taking up the Old Testament, it retains a life of its own within the New. But in Mt. xi, for example, this separation is done away with through an act of identification. In both cases, this absorption of Old Testament sayings into the sayings of Christianity is a process with very far-reaching hermeneutic consequences. With the Magnificat and the Benedictus it was a matter of phrases found in the hymns of the Old Testament, and to this very day we use them in our liturgies to express our faith in Christ and to praise him. Yet there is no difference in principle when it is a question of taking up Old Testament narratives or predictions. We are therefore faced with the fact that the new faith actually needed the Old Testament for its own self-expression. It is, of course, easy to ask whether this auxiliary function of the Old Testament was not perhaps merely time-conditioned, and whether, once Christianity severed its ties with Israel, it might have been dropped. The answer to this, the hardest problem raised by the survival of the Old Testament, can be given from two angles of approach. We can and must discover whether the citation and incorporation of the Old Testament within the New was nothing more than evidence of a transitional and polemical period. This is a question for New Testament theology to answer. But an answer can and must also be given by the Old Testament, because we must be quite clear that the foundations of Christianity rest on the Old and New Testaments together. I shall try in the following chapters to expand this statement.[21]

---

[21] N. W. Porteous is correct in demanding that a theology of the Old Testament ought not to confine itself to a phenomenology of the faith of Israel. "The Old Testament and some theological Thought-forms," in *Scottish Journal of Theology* (1954), p. 159. Among present-day writers, F. Baumgärtel in particular has repeatedly emphasised the need for a basic theological attitude.

CHAPTER B

THE OLD TESTAMENT'S UNDERSTANDING
OF THE WORLD AND MAN, AND
CHRISTIANITY

A LL that was said in the last chapter shows the impossibility of defining Christian interpretation of the Old Testament by comparing the constitutive characteristics of the religion of ancient Israel and those of the religion of the early Church, both taken in isolation, and basing one's conclusions on the similarities and differences between them. For the first Christians the Old Testament was not the official writings of a religion: it was holy scripture; and therefore the only possibility is to ask whether the Old Testament texts begin to speak with a new voice in the light of Christ's revelation. More exactly, the question is no longer to define the message of the old texts before the era of the New Testament, but to discover whether they still preserved their kerygmatic reality after Christ's coming, and if so, to what extent. Indeed, the matter goes deeper; it has to be shown that it is only with the coming of Christ that the true actuality of these writings was revealed and that they had from the very first foretold this very event. Only if this is established are we justified in speaking of a word of God which comes to us from the Old Testament.

Down to the present day the Churches in their Confessions have put the Old Testament on the same level as the New as a book which contains a God-given revelation; no difference is made between either the inspirational source of the Testaments or their character of being the absolute doctrinal standard.[1] Admittedly, in the course of its history the Church has had several different ways of giving practical effect to this understanding of the Old Testament as a word of God. There is no lack of methods of scriptural exposition which we to-day can only term unacceptable. Indeed, a review of the whole history of the Church's interpretation of the Old Testament might suggest that, as far as theological concepts go, she has seldom arrived at a satisfactory clarification of the relationship of the two Testaments to each other.

[1] So for example the Formula Concordiae (Sol. Decl.), which ranges the prophetic writings alongside those of the apostles "ut limpidissimos purissimosque Israelis fontes.'

Whatever the truth of this, it seems that the Old Testament did not for long continue to be so freely interpreted as it was at the time of the origin of the New Testament, when the writers of the Gospels and the Apostles could take what they wanted from the old writings, and when they found in every part of them testimonies which could be applied to their own theological, Christological, and ecclesiological arguments. As far as the unsatisfactory, and largely forced, element in later exposition of the Old Testament is concerned, it must, of course, be remembered that theoretic and theological reflexion on the Old Testament only represents one side of its impact on the Church, and this the one which is in no sense the most convincing. The picture would be different if we took into account the sermons or the poetry of any period, or, in particular, the way in which the Old Testament was reflected in the fine arts.

Although the New Testament shows a freedom and breadth and vitality in interpreting the Old Testament such as the Church has hardly ever achieved since, all the possible ways of relating the Old Testament to Jesus and his Church are far from being exhausted in it. The list of theological themes taken from the Old Testament which Paul enumerates in Rom. IX. 4–5 is unlikely to be a complete one: but the subjects he mentions—"sonship," "glory of God," "making of covenants," "giving of the law," "worship," "promises," "patriarchs," "Messiah"—show which Old Testament subjects could be developed theologically by the Apostle when he had particular cause to express himself doctrinally upon them from the standpoint of Christian faith. Thus, the New Testament does not display the whole possible range of the word of God in the Old Testament as it spoke to the early Church; and, as we said, the references to the Old in the New often appear quite casual. The Old Testament has spoken differently to different ages, and each must therefore be responsible for its own interpretation of it. Each has, of course, in the process to pay careful attention to the interpretations of earlier ages and constantly to test its own understanding on the touchstone of theirs. But no age must allow past interpretations to hinder it from venturing its own judgment. As everyone knows, present-day Old Testament scholarship sees a deep gulf separating its own theological ideas about the Old Testament from those of earlier times. The wealth of new knowledge which it has acquired from historical, archaeological, and literary research, as well as from comparative religion, and the questions which these raise, have, from roughly the middle of last century, led almost to a breaking off of theological debate proper. This is the particular difficulty under which interpretation labours to-day. It is probably inevitable that debate is therefore rather tentative at times, and that it must even decide to leave problems open in places where the subjects are not yet sufficiently clarified theologically—even in places where earlier ages were perfectly sure of themselves.[2] On the other hand, about a quarter of a century ago we made a new beginning; and this very difference from earlier theological ideas may even be particularly auspicious.[3]

The starting-point of our attempt to define the importance of the Old Testament for Christianity is a proposition which is still hotly disputed: that it is in history that God reveals the secret of his person,[4] a proposition valid for Old and New Testament ideas alike. (Here of course we are able only to cite certain examples, and not to consider the whole range of the Old Testament.) It seems at first a very general proposition, and it needs more precise definition for its great distinctiveness to become apparent. It will, of course, be necessary to widen the contemporary meaning of the concept of "history"—which does not, in any case, coincide with its Old Testament meaning. It is therefore better for us to enquire about the *distinctive features in the Old Testament's understanding of the world*: we thus recognise from the first that Israel's understanding of the world is determined entirely by her distinctive faith.[5]

1. We have already said that the Greek conception of the world as a cosmos, that is to say, as an ordered organism in repose, was foreign to ancient Israel.[6] For her, the world does not have unity in itself, and certainly not in any "principle"; it has unity solely in its relationship

---

[2] Here too Bonhoeffer's words are apposite—we are again "thrown back to the initial stages of understanding" (*Widerstand und Ergebung*, Munich 1951), p. 206.

[3] Only, there ought not to be so much argument about the danger inherent in certain trends of theological thought. All dealing with the Old Testament is dangerous, with this difference only, that the danger inherent in the opinions approved by a majority only become apparent to their children and grandchildren.

[4] The formulation is taken from Zimmerli, *Erkenntnis Gottes*, p. 71.

[5] "World (κόσμος) is here (in the New Testament), in distinction to the Greek concept of *cosmos*, an historical concept, *i.e.*, it is orientated on the life of man in history. World means initially the sum of the given conditions and possibilities of human life; and to this extent the world is called God's creation," R. Bultmann, "Das Befremdliche des christlichen Glaubens," in *Z. Th. K.*, 55 (1958), pp. 197f.

[6] See VOL. I, pp. 152, 426f.

to God, in its origin in his creative will, in his continual sustaining of it, and in the goal he appointed it. It has its unity in its property as creature and as being the realm of his sovereignty, for it belongs to him (Ps. xxiv. 1f.). When the Old Testament speaks of creation, it sees the world in contrast to God: as a realm with its own splendour, of which the Psalms and the Wisdom literature can never say enough, but which is nevertheless created, *i.e.*, it was called into being by the creative word with complete effortlessness. Israel particularly opposed her view that the world was created to the view of the nature religions which saw the world more as an emanation of the deity.[7] This view of the world was given a particularly polemical form in the second commandment.[8] She challenged the idea that the world was a place where there were a number of ways by means of which God directly revealed himself. She knew that she was poles apart from the basic presupposition of all forms of idolatry, namely, the belief that the divine nature is represented by a variety of earthly embodiments and cultic symbols.

The statements made about God as creator, particularly those in Genesis, seem to stand rather apart; nevertheless, they are closely allied to Israel's characteristic understanding of the world as it is expressed in the historical books and the prophets. This springs naturally from the fact that Israel did not make so sharp a distinction between "nature" and "history" as we are apt to do. Admittedly, we cannot say that when Israel's beliefs about creation were put at the head of all the testimonies of the Old Testament, this needs no comment; but we can say that the chapters which speak of Jahweh as the creator do not in the last analysis express a different concept of the world from that given in the prophets' polemic against idolatry or in the historical books of the Old Testament. Israel's understanding of the world had very varied tasks confronting it, and, consequently, it had also to express itself in different ways. The rather theoretic and programmatic reduction of the world from divine status which Israel carried out in the creation story (Gen. I. 1 – II. 4a) did not end when the section in question was finally written down. The so-called "concept of creation" was not a philosophical insight which was accepted because it was self-evident to any thinking person; it was far more a doctrine of faith which had constantly to be justified in the face of new temptations. Here, however,

---

[7] This conception is to be sharply distinguished from the specifically Israelite conception that a testimony to God, its Creator, issues from the world as creature. Ps. xix. 2 [1], cxlv. 10 [11].   [8] See vol. i, p. 216.

OTT Z

the soil had been long prepared in Israel by the cult, particularly by the proclamation of the commandments. For, paradoxical as it perhaps sounds, the first and second commandments of the Decalogue are also the key to Israel's understanding of the world. She declared war on the gods and the idols and waged it with vehement intolerance, and she thereby kept alive her knowledge of the living God. This knowledge was also the source of life for her understanding of the world, for she was debarred from understanding the world in terms of myth. In her eyes the world was not constructed as a realm of fixed sacral orders which rested on the shoulders of a multiplicity of quasi-divine powers. Ancient man's mysterious capacity to objectify his experiences of the elemental powers of the natural world in which he lived—to him even fixed orders are powers!—and to regard these as divine, met with no encouragement in Israel. She rejected the sensual interpretation of the world which the nature myths provided, and on that account she also fought against, for example, the divinisation of sex and its sacral objectification in bull images; the same holds true of the divinisation of the heavenly bodies, etc. Myth, just because it is myth, is a way of thinking by means of symbols and images: but Israel fought with all the resolve she could command against the most important thing in all the mythic symbols which her religious environment offered her, namely, their capacity to serve as means of revelation. This awareness of the barrier which men erect between themselves and God by means of images is, however, Israel's greatest achievement. This, and this alone, her insight into idolatry and myth, furnished the key to her loneliness in the company of the religions of the world. She was not, of course, in the exalted position of knowing better than they did. Over a long period of time she had enough to do to extricate herself from the temptation to idolatry and image-worship. We find even the prophets still engaged on the task of smashing to bits their nation's graven image of a national god who offered protection and bestowed the blessings of nature, because they knew that Israel was finished if she put her trust in "worthless gods."[9] Once the struggle was over, however, she occasionally even burst into laughter at this eager fashioning of idols and at the nations dancing before the work of their own hands (Is. XLIV. 9ff.; Jer. X. 1ff.).

[9] The deities of other nations are frequently described as "worthless gods" (אלילים) in the Old Testament: Lev. XIX. 4, XXVI. 1; Is. II. 8, 18, 20, X. 10f., XIX. 1, 3; Ps. XCVI. 5, XCVII. 7, etc.

Any description of Israel's understanding of the world is made more difficult by our different interpretation of the concepts involved. Wherever we speak of "nature" or "history"—and how can we avoid doing so?—we have already thrown Israel's ideas out of gear by using concepts which differ from hers.[10] Her understanding of the world did not follow such absolute concepts as those we are accustomed to use. Thus, we have to ask ourselves how did Israel experience the world in which she found herself if she had no way of defining it by using the terms "nature" and "history"? Israel did not have that familiarity with the world which comes from a knowledge of its laws: and she apparently was also unaware of the emotion known to the student of myth as "terror in the face of nature".[11] Israel could only master the world by reference to its creator and controller. But we should not assume that Israel always maintained her understanding of the world in its entirety. The Old Testament pictures of her history suggest that the mass of her population were never conscious of the dependent status of creation, and that it was only a few historians and prophets who fought against the seductions of idolatry or the cults of foreign gods. And even such men exposed only one aspect of the world. This means that Israel had continually to re-define the nature of the world for herself and that hardly a generation fully understood the world's created status. In this matter Israel was in a constant state of flux, and one can distinguish a whole series of advances, thrusts forward to a specifically new understanding of the world.

Here what first calls for mention are the efforts made by the different theologies of Israel's history to understand the world as the sphere of Jahweh's historical action. We have already spoken of the way in which the Priestly Document brought the creation of the world into close connexion with the beginning of the saving history. With the creation of the world (the six-day *schema*) the dimension of history opens up. Only by referring history to the creation of the world

[10] "The concept of endless self-existent nature . . . is the myth of modern science. Science began by destroying the myth of the Middle Ages; now its own consistency forces it to see that it had set up another myth in its place." C. F. von Weizsäcker, *Die Geschichte der Natur*, Göttingen 1948, p. 53. This modern way of looking at nature is therefore the very reverse of what Israel had in mind when she spoke of the world as a created thing upon which God acted throughout. The same is true of the modern way of looking at "history."

[11] E. Grassi, *Kunst und Mythos*, Hamburg 1957, pp. 39ff.

could the saving action within Israel be brought into its appropriate theological frame of reference, because creation is part of Israel's etiology.[12] We also noticed how the saving action which began in Israel was divested of all mythological character by means of the insertion of the Table of Nations. The Biblical primeval history, which has as its climax the world of the nations, gives Israel the same creaturely status as the nations, and excludes any mythological primacy assigned to her in primeval times. Her future experience of God will be in the realm of secular history and, indeed, according to Gen. x, in the realm of universal secular history.[13] The Priestly Document's primeval history does no more than lay down a few strictly theological propositions. We may assume that as it does so it gives a theological evaluation to insights and experiences which Israel had acquired over a long period in the history of her faith and of her understanding. In any case, there was, centuries before the Priestly Document reached its final form, a tempestuous breakthrough into the secular world in the historical works ascribed to the humanists of the age of Solomon.[14] The way in which these disclose the out-and-out secularity of an age and, in particular, reveal men in their full secular human nature, represents a *ne plus ultra* of insight beyond which even the Christian faith does not go.

There is another aspect of the advance towards the understanding of the world which is inspired by this view of history—that of the Wisdom which derives from experience. Its concern was not only the careful ascertaining of fixed orders operative in the realm of human life, but also the acquisition of knowledge of the world outside man. It endeavoured particularly to master the secrets which lie on the frontiers of human life (numerical proverbs).[15] We meet with instances of this matter of fact observation in more than one place in the Old Testament. It is perfectly true that, in the teaching given by Wisdom of this kind, the world is seen as secular, and not at all in terms of myth, and that there is even an attempt to master its secrets by means of reason and science. Yet, this rational aspect of the world never became entirely autonomous in Israel; one way or another it remained within the ambit of the faith, and there was always a consciousness of the limits imposed on it by God and by his control of the world. In Job xxviii, which was

[12] See VOL. I, p. 138.   [13] See VOL. I, pp. 161f.

[14] For more detail about the picture of history and of man in these works, see VOL. I, pp. 48ff., 308ff.   [15] See VOL. I, p. 425.

the last attempt to shed light on the nature of the world by this method, there is a resigned ackowledgment that all man's mastery of the world has not brought him one step nearer to understanding the secret which God implanted in it.[16]

Again, an entirely different advance into the realm of the secular, which brought equally far-reaching results, had its origin in the prophets, for these men tore open the horizons of world history to reveal perspectives of a vastness such as Israel had hitherto never imagined. At the same time, as they taught men to see the world of the nations in the fullness of its non-sacral secularity, the prophets did not in the least withdraw this aspect of the world from the sovereign sphere of God. On the contrary, they are the very people who proclaim that God makes greater and greater claims on the nations. We can therefore say that in proportion as they subordinated the nations to God and regarded them as belonging to him alone, so for them the nations became part of the world. For these were now no longer under the jurisdiction of their own gods, as Israel had earlier believed them to be (cp. *e.g.*, I Sam. XXVI. 19; II Kings III. 27).[17] The fact that Deutero-Isaiah's concept of

[16] See VOL. I, p. 446.

[17] It should not be imagined that it was an easy thing for the prophets to come to this view. Here and there it can be shown that concepts from the cult helped them in this expansion of the theological horizon. For example, they transferred to the dimension of history self-revelations of Jahweh which for Israel had hitherto only been connected with certain cultic activities. Thus, as far as we can see, ancient Israel encountered what the Old Testament terms the "zeal of Jahweh" exclusively within the realm of the cult, and this in the form of Jahweh's abhorrence of the worship of foreign nations by Israel (see VOL. I, pp. 203ff.). In contrast, it must have been a revolutionary thing when Isaiah saw Jahweh's "zeal" operative behind the effect which the latter gave to his historical designs (Is. IX. 6*b* [7*b*]), or when Zephaniah expects the eschatological punishment of the disobedient nation, and indeed even that of foreign nations, to come about by the instrumentality of Jahweh's zeal (Zeph. I. 18, III. 8). In the terms of Ezekiel's prophecy, Jahweh is to "vindicate his holiness" by vanquishing Gog, and to be jealous for his holy name in the eyes of the nations (Ezek. XXXVIII. 16, 23). The little book of Haggai also shows one such process which is typical of the prophetic way of thinking. The prophet derives the norms for solving an actual political problem from the attitude of the priests to and the ritual assessment of a cultic condition of things (Hag. II. 12ff.). The same thing is found in Jer. III. 1, where Jeremiah deduces the irreparable quality of Israel's apostasy from a regulation in the old sacral law of marriage. It was particularly in their intellectual thrust out into universal history that the prophets used ideas and norms that hitherto had been at home only in the cultic sphere. Since they greatly expanded the old content of these, they could make use of them—to some extent as a first conceptual tool—to express

universalism goes hand in hand with the proclamation that the gods of the nations are dethroned and that their cults are futile is in keeping with a profound logic of Old Testament faith. That faith must have been very clearly thought through, and the nations undergone a radical process of demythologising, before God was able to say "Nebuchadnezzar, my servant" and "Cyrus, my anointed" (Jer. xxvii. 6; Is. xlv. 1)![18]

Another example of such secularisation—again it is a fairly forceful procedure—may be examined briefly, because it takes us another step forward. It is to be found in the cultic regulations of Deuteronomy, as a result of which the people who lived outside Jerusalem were at one fell swoop deprived of their little sanctuaries. Attention has often been drawn to the hardships involved in this measure. It killed off much of the old cultic usage. Through it the life of the peasant population, which up to then had been sheltered by many sacral institutions, was suddenly thrust out into the dimension of the secular. It cannot be said that Deuteronomy was unaware of the problems which this readjustment raised, for a great part of what it tries to do is precisely to give men a helping hand in their now secularised lives by regulating and guiding them. The one reason why the drastic nature of the secularisation of Israel's whole life is not more sharply apparent is Deuteronomy's many references to the sanctuary and to what is to be done there. In this whole matter, however, there is no difference in principle between Deuteronomy and the advances into the secular which took place elsewhere in Israel, for she never came to think of the word as being completely without a divine element. It is true that we find extreme advances in this doctrine which expose the secularity of Israel's sphere of existence with great consistency: but we should misunderstand these if we failed to notice that even their most radical exponents presuppose, tacitly at least, that there is a place which houses

that universal action of Jahweh in history which had recently come within their range of vision.

[18] Intellectually, this view had incalculable results, for it at the same time determined the whole of the European way of thinking about history. It would however be wrong to assume that in Israel this is to be understood only as the harvest accruing from a continual polemic against the mythological concept of history. Israel no doubt became involved in serious conflicts of this kind from time to time; but over a quite large sector of her literary legacy no polemical tendency of any kind can be seen. These texts are therefore all the more emphatic witnesses to Israel's innate inability to think effectively in terms of myth.

what is more than secular: that is to say, that even with these men we must take into account an awareness of the cult as an important factor in their theology. Indeed, the only explanation of their calm and courageous advance into the secular world, so baffling to the student of general religious phenomena, is that they had the support of the cult behind them. Israel's sphere of existence never became entirely worldly because she knew that in every age Jahweh had established a sphere where the holy was operative, where he himself was present in the most personal way possible, and to which the secular was external.[19]

It is particularly interesting to see how Israel conceived of those places where the holy was operative in her midst. She did not think of them as the mythic centre of her world, as an *omphalos*, to which the world thinks of itself as eternally related as the cosmic mid-point spoken of in myth. Granted, Ezekiel once speaks of Jerusalem in this way, as if she were the navel of the world (Ezek. v. 5); this idea of the *omphalos* (Heb. טבור) quite certainly goes back in the end to Canaanite ideas, and Israel may have taken it up more than once (cp. Jg. ix. 37).[20] This makes no difference, however, to the fact that her ideas about the place of worship did not derive from a belief in an absolute and inherent holiness belonging to such a place. This could never have been combined with her ideas about Jahweh. Certainly, even in Israel there had to be a *temenos*, a small area separated off from the world, in which quite different arrangements applied from those outside, as, for example, the right of sanctuary. If one observes what is characteristic of P's tabernacle—and the source P gives us our best insight into Israel's theology of worship—one thing is noticeable: how little outward para-

[19] K. Elliger, "Sinn und Ursprung der priesterlichen Geschichtserzählung," in *Z. Th. K.*, 49 (1952), p. 127. It is conceivable that P's cultic theology and its efforts to restore the old were actually an endeavour to check the advance of the world into the cult. P is only concerned with the place of worship, the cult, and the cultic personel, and with Israel assembled in the "camp" round this spot. P's efforts are aimed at creating the preconditions for the indwelling of holiness in Israel (see K. Koch, "Die Eigenart der priesterschriftlichen Sinaigesetzgebung," in *Z. Th. K.*, 55 (1958), p. 41). The prophet Hosea makes it particularly clear that this courage to go out into the secular world had basically a theological reason. It was Jahweh who gave Israel "grain, wine and oil, and who lavished upon her silver and gold" (Hos. II. 10 [8]). On the contrast with the attitude of the Rechabites, who rigorously opposed settlement on the land, see VOL. I, pp. 63f.

[20] On the *omphalos* see W. Caspari, "tabur," in *Zeitschrift der Deutschen Morgenländischen Gesellschaft* (1933), pp. 49ff.

phernalia was needed for the erection of a sanctuary. It was, indeed, erected only to be taken down again. There was no idea of an absolute holiness belonging to the place; everything depended on the resting or moving of the pillar of cloud (Num. IX. 15ff.).[21] It was a sanctuary which, as it were, kept on the move until God had appointed a fresh place for his cultic dealings with his people. Deuteronomy's way of dealing with the problem of Jahweh's relationship to the place of worship was quite different. It contemplates an Israel now settled in Palestine, and as a result a fixed place of worship; but it designates it as the place "where Jahweh will put his name." It is no natural or mythological holiness, but an historical act of election, that makes this place a place of worship; in this connexion the formula, "putting the name of God," is particularly interesting. Undoubtedly the idea of the cultic significance of the divine name is in itself extremely old. In Deuteronomy, however, its use is particularly deliberate and serves a theological end, for it guards against a direct identification of the place of worship with Jahweh himself, who sits enthroned in heaven, and at the same time guarantees the salvation which comes from his gracious presence, for in his name Jahweh is in a mysterious way present in person.

Many more reflexions on Jahweh and his relationship to the place of worship are to be found in the Old Testament. It is, in fact, absolutely amazing to see how the most varied ideas about Jahweh's "dwelling places" maintained themselves within Israel without being harmonised.[22] Was his dwelling place Sinai, from which he sometimes appeared (Jg. v. 4; Hab. III. 3), or was it the Ark, with which he went into battle, or was it Zion (Am. I. 2; Is. VIII. 18), or was it heaven? It is unsatisfactory to explain this variety of ideas simply as the result of the devious history of the cult. The odd flexibility of these ideas and the open way in which they are mentioned must themselves have been in line with the insight which Israel had into Jahweh's nearness and presence, and with her lack of need to reduce them to a fixed dogmatic standard and harmonise them. When, however, Israel ceased to do justice to the special nature of Jahweh's dwelling in her midst, when she misused the place of worship, then Jahweh destroyed it and made it over to the chaotic powers of secular history (Jer. VII. 12; Mic. III. 11ff.).

In conclusion, one other peculiarity of the Old Testament under-

[21] Num. IX. 15ff., X. 1ff.; cp. VOL. I, pp. 278, 234ff.
[22] Although in many respects it is out of date, cp. here G. Westphal, *Jahwes Wohnstätten nach den Anschauungen der alten Hebräer*, Bei. Z.A.W., 15 (1908).

standing of the world has still to be noticed. The increasing total threat offered by the nations to God's chosen area and, as a result, to his whole saving work, makes the prediction of the total destruction of the nations come to play a greater and greater part in prophecy. The familiar world surrounding Israel is therefore in the last resort a world which was passing away in Jahweh's sight. Here is a further characteristic of Old Testament understanding of the world. This idea did not, of course, dominate Israel at every period. It emerged only in prophecy, and was really only consistently developed in later prophecy.[23] All the same, even the Priestly Document teaches men to understand the world as one whose existence is continued by God only because of the special provisions of the covenant with Noah made after his sentence was passed on it in the judgment of the Flood (Gen. IX. 8–17).[24] Since Israel's faith is based on history rather than cosmology it follows that the dominant feature in prophecy is the prediction of the destruction of the historical world—that is, the world of the nations. This prediction is occasionally modified, for example in Trito-Isaiah's saying about the new heaven and the new earth (Is. LXV. 17), or in several of apocalyptic literature's perspectives of the absolute end of the whole present existence of heaven and earth (Is. XXIV. 17–23). Incidentally, the distinction between the world of history and the world of nature is never made in the Old Testament; even when prophecy spoke about the sudden disaster which would overtake the nations it envisaged the destruction of the whole world.

2. The preceding section listed Israel's main advances towards an entirely unique understanding of the world. More detailed examination would certainly reveal other movements as well.[25] We may therefore say that since Israel's doctrine contained a number of such aspects which are not necessarily compatible she never completely realised the full secularity of creation. The case is apparently similar with her picture of man.[26] As was said above, in the last analysis Israel's idea about the

[23] Jer. XXV. 15ff., XLVI–LI; Joel IV. 1ff. [III. 1ff.]; Hag. II. 21f. Zech. II. 1–4 [I. 18–21].

[24] See VOL. I, pp. 156ff.

[25] Because of the breakdown of the concept of a sphere of action which creates fate, Israel entered upon a great crisis in her understanding of the world (see here VOL. I, pp. 264ff., 384ff.). The best expression of the crisis are Job's soliloquies.

[26] As well as the relevant sections in Old Testament Theologies, cp. W. Eichrodt, *Man in the Old Testament*, trs. K. and R. Gregor Smith, London 1951; K. Galling, *Das Bild vom Menschen in biblischer Sicht* (*Mainzer Universitäts-Reden*, Heft 3, 1947);

world can only be understood in the light of the distinctive nature of her faith: this is certainly even more true of her ideas about man. In particular, it must be remembered that Israel very seldom spoke of "man." She always sees men *vis-à-vis* God, either turning to him or turning away from him; she never sees them in detachment from history, but always as set in the context of a history with God; *i.e.*, for the most part, the man of whom the Old Testament speaks is not "man" at all; rather, he belongs to Israel (or to her enemies), and his experience is in no sense merely that of humanity in general. This, of course, does not mean that Israel never properly saw into the phenomenon of man. The very opposite is true, for in the primeval history (Gen. I–XI) which precedes the saving history, she expressed a real wealth of insights into the nature of man. Jahwism had, therefore, opened up a wide range of insights into man; we cannot repeat them in detail here. As is well known, it is in general a "contradictory" picture of man, for although he originated in the heavenly world, in some incomprehensible way he broke the tie of obedience to God which would have given him security.[27] Disturbances of the gravest sort, affecting both body and spirit, entered his life, disturbances which in the end led to the destruction of that unity of mankind proposed in creation.[28] And it is this man whom God found waiting him in Israel as his partner; she bears the same created traits, and the marks of the same disturbances. Each of the Old Testament histories shows in its specific way this man freely exercising all his potentialities. The picture of his relationship with God is fairly uniformly presented. Man is everywhere ready to oppose God and to fall away from him; he is in constant need of forgiveness, and of God's support. Only very seldom, and then to some extent rather against his own nature, is he able to realise the special possibilities of the saving relationship offered him—faith, obedience, and surrender. Where the narratives turn, however, to the relationship between man and man—and we have already seen that in this connexion a new horizon opened up at a particular time—the picture of man is painted with all the colours of the rainbow.[29] The heights and the depths, trivialities and events of great psychological complexity, are depicted

W. Zimmerli, *Das Menschenbild des Alten Testaments* (*Theologische Existenz Heute*, N.F. 14, 1949).

[27] In contrast to Gen. III, Ecclesiasticus XXIV develops a completely different idea of man's original sin—Wisdom came down from heaven, but man gave her no dwelling-place.   [28] See VOL. I, pp. 157ff.   [29] See VOL. I, p. 54.

with a matchless realism. This secularity of man and the ruthless secularity of the powers to which he believes himself to be abandoned does not, of course, indicate an outlook which, as some critics have maintained, has completely parted company with the religious viewpoint proper.[30] It is, rather, a theological datum of the utmost importance.

Israel did not reach this view of man by accident—as it were, a harvest reaped more or less outside the fields of her own faith. Had she done so, the same view would be expressed elsewhere in the cultural and religious environment from which she is known to have appropriated so much. This is exactly what we do not find. Investigation of the cultures and religions of Israel's neighbours shows that she is absolutely unique in taking man out of the sphere of myth. She dropped the mythological realm of spirits and magical powers. As a result, man became poorer, abandoned far more to the adverse elements in life than the man who thought of the world in terms of myth, and who could counter all that was hostile by means of magic and exorcism. Sex in particular was taken out of the world of myth; the door was closed on the possibility of entrance into the mystery of the ἱερὸς γάμος, and so of having at the centre of Israel's life and its continuance participation in something which, according to myth, the gods also shared. Even Israel's kings were not a mythic primeval datum of the created order as was the case with some of her neighbouring nations. They were men who, more than other mortals, were at the mercy of the secular powers of history. They were fallible, and open to particularly severe criticism.

3. We should also mention Jahwism's attitude to death, for here again it was particularly zealous in stripping death of the dignity allowed it in myth. Jahwism regarded the actual event of dying as something caused directly by God himself (Deut. XXXII. 39; 1 Sam. II. 6; Ps. LXXXVIII. 7 [6]). This meant, however, that the dead were excluded from fellowship with Jahweh and were in the highest degree unclean. We find in Ps. LXXXVIII a definition of the state of being dead which, theologically speaking, leaves practically nothing more to be said: the dead were cut off from praising Jahweh and from hearing him proclaimed, and above all, they were cut off from him himself. On the other hand, since Israel was strictly forbidden to ascribe any numinous power to the dead lying outside the possibilities of Jahwism, i.e., by way of an additional private cult, an extremely odd theological vacuum

[30] For example, E. Meyer judged the Succession Document as a completely secular presentation (*Geschichte des Altertums*, VOL. II, pt. 2, Stuttgart 1931, p. 286).

resulted. Jahwism's tendency to destroy myth in all its forms was not abandoned in its understanding of death. What is astonishing is the way in which this mysterious world is entirely divested of its sacral character. But in this case the process was not the same as in the cases previously discussed, those of the world, man, and history. In each of these, by destroying the world of myth Jahweh appropriated them more fully. The realm of the dead remained an indefinable third party between Jahweh and his creation. Apart from isolated questionings (*e.g.*, Job XIV. 13–22), it was not a subject of real interest to faith. Poetic fancy alone took it up now and then (Is. XIV. 9ff.; Ezek. XXXII. 20ff.).[31] Should we not see this theological vacuum, which Israel zealously kept free from any sacral concepts (see VOL. I, pp. 276f.), as one of the greatest theological enigmas in the Old Testament? The prediction that God will provide a resurrection from the dead of his own people is found in it only peripherally (Is. XXVI. 19; Dan. XII. 2).

4. In what way, however, is this wide range of extremely striking Old Testament ideas about the world, man, and death related to the message about Jesus Christ contained in the New? The latter says that in Christ the word became "flesh" (Jn. I. 14), and that he was born of a woman (Gal. IV. 4); it places the coming of Christ in historical con- nexion with Israel (Mt. I. 1ff.), and, indeed, with world-history (Lk. II. I, III. I); it unfolds the saving event as a series of historical occur- rences, and speaks of time fulfilled, of word fulfilled, and of the "mighty works of God" (Acts II. 11), which begin with Jesus's birth, include the ministry in Galilee, lead to the crucifixion and, finally, to the resur- rection and ascension. Once more, therefore, the great concern is not to unfold a new teaching, but primarily to describe a series of historical events which put the relationship between Israel and God, and, indeed, between God and the whole world, on a completely new basis. Thus one intrinsic likeness between the message of the New and Old Testa- ments is that both speak of man and his potentialities, of the "flesh," and of the world and the realm of secular history, as the sphere in which God reveals himself. These ideas as they are expressed in the New Testament are no different in principle from ideas which were current in ancient Israel.[32] We must face the fact that the Old Testament

---

[31] "Ideas connected with the shades had no importance for Israel's faith," Zimmerli, *Erkenntnis Gottes*, p. 17.

[32] "It is clear that the early Christian doctrine of man is diametrically opposed to that which prevailed in the Greek tradition. Man is not regarded as an instance of

has at any rate a preparatory importance, and that therefore we must, as best we can, define more precisely this idea of "preparation" which we constantly meet, for it is indispensable to any discussion of the relationship between the Old and the New Testaments.

There can, of course, be no question of regarding the characteristically non-mythic Old Testament understanding of the world as being a neutral phenomenon from the philosophic and religious point of view. It was not something which, like Palestine's soil, or its landscape and climate, was a given datum for the New Testament saving event and could at most be described as a general dispensation of providence with which Christ's coming in the New Testament could naturally be linked, and which gives this event its intellectual basis. Such an explanation is contrary both to the Old and to the New Testaments. The assertion that Israel's understanding of the world and of man is a fortuitous and non-essential factor of her life derived from culture and philosophy is quite contrary to Old Testament teaching. For the Old Testament view was rather one which always only developed in the shelter of a particular saving action, and which needed the constant support of Israel's faith to re-establish and maintain it in the face of the temptations offered by an environment where the determining factor was myth. The crucial point, however, is this: if the New Testament saving event is as absolutely unique as Christianity believes it to be, and differs entirely from all the ideas about God, the world, and man developed by other religions, and is, indeed, offensive to them, what talk can there be of "linking"? Yet, to say that the Old Testament has a preparatory function means considerably more than that the New Testament may be linked to it.

universal human Being, which in its turn is seen to be an instance of cosmic Being in general. There is no attempt to escape from the questionableness of man's own individuality by concentrating on the universal law or the cosmic harmony. Like Gnosticism, primitive Christianity was totally uninterested in education or training. It had no use for the Greek dualistic anthropology, with its tension between spirit and sensuality, or the view of life which that implied, viz. the realization of the ideal of the 'gentleman' as a 'work of art'. Man's essential Being is not Logos, reason or spirit. If we ask primitive Christianity where the essential Being of man resides, there can only be one answer: in the *will*. To be a man or to live a human life, means to strive for something, to aspire after something, to will." R. Bultmann, *Primitive Christianity in its Contemporary Setting*, henceforth cited as *Primitive Christianity*, tr. R. H. Fuller, London and New York, 1956, p. 180. On the non-Greek understanding of the world in the New Testament, see above, p. 338, n. 5.

What was the nature of this entity which prepared the way for Christ's coming to earth? Even if the Old Testament's function was just to provide the appropriate concepts which alone could lead to a proper understanding of Christ's coming in the flesh, and it achieved this without involving disastrous explanations in mythic terms, this would be of far-reaching theological importance; and it would really be impossible to say that there is any point in the Old Testament where this preparation for the New Testament saving event is not present. We cannot restrict it simply to the concepts connected with the doctrine of creation, for here everything is interlocked. The phenomenon which needs theological explanation is in fact this: the Old Testament does not supply Christianity just with single ideas but with whole catenas of statements (chiefly of a cultic and prophetic kind), whole "texts," in which Christianity could, and still does, find its own expression. Moreover, these Old Testament texts and statements are not completely isolated in their bearing on the New; they also refer back to their own Old Testament context, and the New Testament may therefore claim this vast range of reference also. For the New Tesatment does not "quote" so atomistically that any citation of an Old Testament statement refers only to itself and to nothing beyond it. Yet, how was it possible for the New Testament to make this claim upon the Old? The question is the more important to the extent that we see something radically new in the new event—a point of view which is entirely reinforced by the witnesses to the new faith. But this seems to be contradicted by the very free way in which the New Testament witnesses make their link with Old Testament material.

We cannot determine the relationship between the two Testaments, which is connected with the question of "linking" the material used in each, just by considering the actual quotations, or other somewhat occasional allusions and references, which appear in the New Testament. Should we try to answer the question of what connects the two by a study of their *language*—here understanding the word in its wider sense, *i.e.*, as man's ability to name and describe the data of his existence? As is well known, in naming and describing an act of genuine discovery, indeed even of re-creation, takes place. All enunciation of the experienced data of existence in itself presupposes a positive knowledge of them. Language understood in this way is always an intellectual whole because everything it says is based on a concrete knowledge of the datum involved. Here no phenomenon is isolated; one thing depends on the other. Language has a tremendous creative power; for at the same time as it places itself at man's disposal it also prescribes a particular knowledge of the datum and a particular way of expressing it. It is only rarely that a man can break down its domination and make the language in which he has been brought up subservient to his own new insight. There is, of course, no single way of speaking of things. Different ways of speaking of the data of existence correspond to different apperceptions of them. There was no real possibility of mutual understanding between the priests of Egypt, with their mythological speculative language, and Herodotus; his question about the history of Egypt meant something which simply did not exist for the language of the Egyptians and their knowledge of things.[33]

Israel's world was exposed in all its parts to God. Her language is appropriate to such a world. It can therefore be said that when God began to reveal himself to her in history, he also gave her her language. For the peculiar thing is that in conversation with her God Israel learned to know and name her world, *i.e.*, to know and name her world as history. This is the origin of that extremely specific linguistic and conceptual tool, a specific form of naming which exactly corresponded to the peculiar nature of Israel's encounter with her God (think, for example, of the "prayer language" of the Psalms). Now, it is simple fact that the primitive Christian community was able to continue to use the language of the Old Testament, to link on to it, and to avail itself of this linguistic tool. This is a theological phenomenon of great significance. The New Testament contains no evidence of tension or doubt in connexion with Old Testament sayings. Yet, considering the character of the new event, these might have been present to an even greater and more disturbing degree than in the discussion between Herodotus and the Egyptians. Instead, what surprises the reader is the unbroken continuity, the lack of break at the transition; for, in the beginning at least, it was possible to express the new event effortlessly in the language of the old. It is, of course, extremely important that the language of the New Testament is Greek and not Hebrew. Never-

---

[33] Herodotus had asked the Egyptian priests about the *history* of their land, whereupon they stated to him a time-span of more than 11,000 years. "Four times in this period (so they told me) the sun rose contrary to his wont; twice he rose where he now sets, and twice he set where he now rises; yet Egypt at these times underwent no change, neither in the produce of the river and the land, nor in the matter of sickness and death." Herodotus II, 142, trs. A. D. Godley (Loeb).

theless, almost because of this difference, we are soon made aware that in a deeper sense the language of the Old Testament and the New are the same.

(Of course, the facts which lie behind this very compressed statement are very complex; for important terms and concepts appear in the New Testament which correspond with nothing in the Old and which derive from a realm of language and thought which is quite alien to it. Nevertheless, in so far as it is not a question of bringing such terms back to their place of origin, they must be understood in the context of a much greater number of genuine Old Testament terms. Because of this co-ordination, neither the old terms nor the new remained unchanged; it brought about manifold inner changes and enlargements of them. To put it in another way, the language did not remain at the phase represented by the Old Testament and late Judaism; it grew, and this being so, its passage into the Greek-speaking world opened up new possibilities of speech, and also possibilities of asking new questions— to say nothing of the new dangers which it also met with in the process. Any language which remains spoken, and does not persist merely as a "dead" language, is constantly changing. And in the New Testament we are dealing with a language which actually was incredibly alive. This, however, does not contradict our thesis of its "unity." Christ's own preaching comes closest to Old Testament language. Yet it includes a range of terms deriving from gnosticism. They do not seem out of character but fall naturally within its scope.[34] For these Hellenistic and gnostic terms had gradually grown away from the realm of mythical speculation in which they originated, and had been co-ordinated to a realm of concepts about God, the world, and man which bore a specifically Israelite stamp. It was only in this conceptual world that the ἐφάπαξ which occurs from Rom. VI. 10 to Heb. VII. 27, IX. 12 could have been spoken and also really kept its ground. It was not, however, until the post-New Testament period that the Greek form of the Christian message came to its full flowering; with this, of course, begins an increasing divorce from the specifically Old Testament language and concepts. We are all the more justified in speaking of the uniformity of the language of the Old and New Testaments in our particular sense.)

---

[34] Cp. e.g., terms like κόσμος, στοιχεῖα, ἀφθαρσία, εἰκών, ψυχικός, πνευματικός. But for her own part Israel from a very early period in her long history incorporated foreign words and concepts into the vocabulary of her faith and so enriched it. Cp. Ratschow, *Angefochtene Glaube*, p. 71.

This is a very bold assertion; for each word has a specifically hermeneutic function in that it gives a place in the general world-picture to
the thing it represents. A word—at all events in an ancient language,
and we are not here concerned with modern ones—does not stand by
itself as a descriptive label, which can if necessary be replaced by
another. Rather, it lives in its linguistic and conceptual province as if
this was a living organism, and it has its indispensable place therein. It
is woven into the linguistic organism to which it belongs by a thousand
threads. One word always suggests others which lie closely round
about it. It can never be taken entirely by itself, but once it is captured,
it brings practically the whole linguistic province to which it belongs
in its train. When the New Testament speaks of "election," "fulfilment,"
of "acts of God," his "wrath," his "righteousness," of "faith," yes,
even when it speaks of ἀλήθεια or of the λόγος, it links on to Old
Testament terms and concepts in the process; at least, that non-
mythological understanding of the world of which we have already
spoken is not separable from these terms. This in itself, however, credits
the Old Testament with a preparatory function of great scope; for, as
was said above, these terms and concepts belonged to a faith which was
constantly re-shaping them and which was warranted only by God's
revelation of himself in Israel. Here is the real link between the Old and
New Testaments; it is in this that the "preparation" took place. What
there occurred is not something alien to the New Testament revelation
of Jesus Christ, and it did not occur against the background of a neutral
view of the world. This preparation started at the very first revelation
of the secret of Jahweh's person, and we must go back to this point to
clarify the relationship between the two Testaments. Thus Jesus could
appeal to the God of the Old Testament without having to give any
special explanations or preparations.[35] Mankind and the world only
had an identity in their relationship with God. Surely this means
that all the Old Testament witnesses, who taught men to understand
the world and themselves not in terms of myth but as creatures in the
sight of God, are in the last analysis to be seen and understood as pointing directly to Christ's coming. As we saw, they for their own part
express insights which could only have been produced in the context
of a particular saving activity. This precedes the New Testament
one in time, yet it only reaches its true goal with the coming of Christ.
What is described in the New Testament as "his own" (Jn. I. II), to

[35] Ratschow, *Angefochtene Glaube*, p. 71.

which he came, is already heralded in clearly recognisable terms in the Old Testament.

The fact that we are to-day still without clear concepts with which to express this preparatory function of the Old Testament saving history cannot deter us from giving attention to the thing itself. The great task which confronts us at present is the redefinition of the noetic and heuristic importance of the Old Testament witnesses for the understanding of the saving event of the New. Perhaps there are still unexhausted heuristic possibilities of understanding Christ even in the theological subtlety of the Old Testament sayings on the exceptional features of God's "indwelling" in Israel on which we have already touched. There is no doubt that God's self-revelation in Jesus Christ is different from that of the Old Testament in that all material and sacral mediation is there dropped for good and all. God has become man's partner in person—as man—more immediately and personally than he ever was in a cultic revelation. Therefore, strictly speaking, the astonishment expressed in an old story, that God spoke to a man "face to face, as a man speaks to his friend" (Ex. xxxiii. 11), finds its proper point of reference only in the New Testament. For only in the saving event of the New Testament did this art of speaking dispense with all cultic media and become completely personal. On the other hand, it is also true that what is said of God's self-revelation in Israel and of his cultic indwelling within her can also largely be applied to Christ—indeed, that the full assurances contained in these statements often seem actually to transcend the Old Testament cultic reality. We should therefore reconsider whether Christological matters are not foreshadowed even in Old Testament utterances about, for example, the appearance of "the glory of God" covered by a cloud to protect men from it,[36] or the presence of the divine name, which almost took on an objective existence of its own vis-à-vis Jahweh,[37] or the theological characteristics of the tent concept (cp. here the use of σκηνοῦν in John i. 14)—whether everywhere here Christological matters are not already foreshadowed. However, the question to which this brings us, that of the importance of Israel's specifically historical experiences, requires separate discussion.

[36] See VOL. I, pp. 239f.   [37] See VOL. I, pp. 185f.

CHAPTER C

THE OLD TESTAMENT SAVING EVENT IN THE LIGHT OF THE NEW TESTAMENT FULFILMENT

IF, as we do, we put Israel's ideas about the world and man and her ideas which relate specifically to the saving history in separate chapters, this is only a matter of convenience, and can hardly appeal to any lines of separation which she herself drew. The most that can be allowed is that her cosmological ideas have a relative autonomy of subject. Israel was in fact sometimes able to speak of the world as creation without making any particular mention of Jahweh's saving activity (cp. *e.g.*, Ps. CIV). But apart from the fact that such cases are exceptional, the relative independence of certain groups of concepts does not mean that they derived from any other root than belief in Jahweh, the God of Israel. The impressive phenomenon of Israel's language is something exclusively her own and does not allow any interpretation of the concepts it voiced except as being derived from the centre of her existence, the fountain-head of all knowledge and specification. Consideration of the language has already shown us that we can make little headway by separating various aspects of the language or by assuming the "adoption" of foreign ideas. This language, which gave names to God, the world, man, and death, was minted by a faith on which it directly depended. The faith, in turn, was constantly driven forward by specific revelations in history; and it was also constantly subjected to new transformations because of this. We have now to consider particularly the specifically "saving" words spoken by Israel's faith, especially in relation to the corresponding sayings in the New Testament.

1. The Old Testament is a history book; it tells of God's history with Israel, with the nations, and with the world, from the creation of the world down to the last things, that is to say, down to the time when dominion over the world is given to the Son of Man (Dan. VII. 13f.). This history can be described as saving history because, as it is presented, creation itself is understood as a saving act of God and because, according to what the prophets foretold, God's will to save is, in spite of many

acts of judgment, to achieve its goal. This saving history has its beginning in Israel; it is characterised by the revelation that God is at
work in acts of election and in the making of covenants which long
precede any action of man's will. This self-revelation of God thus "comes
about in history," and it does so in the form of words and acts of God
which are accordingly pin-pointed in the history in each case as events
of a special kind. It is in this way alone—and therefore an extremely
non-speculative way—that knowledge of God was attained in Israel.
There is, however, a surprising discord in the answers which the Old
Testament gives to the question of the particular way in which this
knowledge of God was attained in Israel. At a first glance, two sets of
statements seem to be opposed to each other without any interconnexion—God revealed himself by means of his words, and God
revealed himself by means of his acts. Much has been written about
the variety of forms which revelation by word could assume in
Israel; they range from the oracle mediated in the cult to the *alloquium
vocis articulatae* experienced by the prophets. It seems more difficult to answer the question of the way in which the knowledge of
God given in his acts was attained. However, the Old Testament
believes that God always and for ever "glorified himself" in his
acts, that is to say, that the *doxa* of his activity was made visible beyond all possibility of doubt, and that therefore the event could be
recognised as a "sign," and indeed as an actual miracle. Here—of
course always only at particular times—an event became addressed
to Israel quite directly, so that in it she could learn God's historical
will.

Even so, it is worth while to enlarge upon this double nature of the
ideas about Jahweh's intercourse with Israel, for it is a characteristic
factor in the Old Testament revelation of God. History becomes word,
and word becomes history. Exposition has, however, to guard against
premature resolution of the tension which this causes. There are texts
which describe Jahweh's relationship to Israel as if its sole basis were his
acts—take, for example, the *credo* in Deut. XXVI. 5ff., which covers the
time from the patriarchs to the conquest, and in the process confines
itself exclusively to recapitulating Jahweh's historical acts.[1] In contrast
to this, a mark of relatively later accounts is, in general, that there the
event which Jahweh brings about is already in some measure interpreted

[1] These confessional "first elements" are collected and examined by Noth, *Pentateuch*, pp. 48ff.

since the narrator refers it back quite directly to a word spoken by Jahweh. Thus for example, according to J's ideas, a word of Jahweh preceded the whole of the patriarchal history, set it under way, and gave it its goal (Gen. xII. 1–3). Later Israel knows Jahweh as the one who is ready to speak, and even to have questions put to him (Is. xLV. 11); he does nothing without taking his prophets into his confidence beforehand (Am. III. 7). And if, as is said in a very bold utterance of Deutero-Isaiah, he at one time held his peace, he had had to do himself the greatest violence (Is. xLII. 14). Israel is conscious of being the only nation that is not dependent on omens and soothsaying (Deut. xvIII. 9ff.); in Israel there is no enchantment and divination: "at the proper time she will be told what God does" (Num. xxIII. 23). These statements, and others like them, presuppose not only a robust religious self-consciousness, but also a fairly firmly fixed idea of a relationship to Jahweh which stands or falls as he speaks to her, and speaks to her in such a way that she not only gets to know him, but is ever led to fresh knowledge of herself and of her situation before God. In the Old Testament tradition, however, as of course also in the synoptic tradition about Jesus in the New Testament, we constantly come across accounts which may be described as "pre-theological," using the term "theological" quite simply as meaning the endeavour to place the phenomena under discussion in wider contexts. In the nature of the case, it is not possible to delimit these texts with precision; also, it must be remembered that redaction has placed all of them in wider contexts, which react back upon them and illumine them. Even so, it is not wasted labour to pay particular attention to this strand in the tradition which stands so close to the events themselves or which so preserves the original form in which they were related that its clear endeavour is to be open to recapture the event in every detail. These accounts are dominated by a concentration on the specific event and all its details which leaves no room for interpretation or theological reflexion. There are examples of such narratives in the patriarchal stories (the stories about Jacob and Laban are particularly good examples), in the Book of Judges, or in the stories about Saul and David. Of course, every time a story is told, a particular understanding of its subject is presupposed, and to this extent even the Song of Deborah (Jg. v) gives an interpretation of the great event it celebrates, even though the author was probably very close to it in time. However, it makes a difference whether the narrator is engrossed in an almost laboured "pacing in the midst of the event,"[2] or whether he leads us on to understand it by means of general theological ideas and to set it in larger contexts. In the latter case, his aim is to make something that has happened comprehensible within a wider theological horizon; in the former it is to show it in its uniqueness. And it is this second series of accounts which more than any others make the Old Testament as a whole so much an historical book, for they bring us face to face in the most direct possible way with actual, mysterious history which reflexion has not yet brought under any kind of control.

These thoughts on the way in which Israel dealt with the events of her history lead further. Compared with these pre-theological accounts, there are a greater number of stories which interpret the events and try to open them up to the understanding of faith. Yet, even the "pre-hheological" accounts underwent new interpretations. A very ancient pre-literary fixed form of a given incident in the patriarchal stories was taken up, after a period of oral transmission, by the genius of the Jahwist. It reappears with a different ring in the Elohist. And finally perhaps it was adapted to suit the rigorism of the Priestly Document. An incident in the period of the Judges appears in an entirely different light within the framework of the Deuteronomic survey of the history, while the history of the monarchy as given by the latter, itself the deposit of years of work on a theology of history, reappears in Chronicles with some parts unchanged, but with others told from a point of view which is all the Chronicler's own. We therefore see the historical material of the Old Testament passing on from one hand to another and from one generation to another. More could doubtless be seen from a later point in time than was possible earlier—wider contexts and more of the general principles of God's way with Israel became discernible. At the same time, we must reckon with the other possibility, that of a decline in understanding. Which of the interpretations was ultimately valid—that given by the last redactor of the Hexateuch, that of the Deuteronomist, or that of the Chronicler? And after these, the New Testament once more took up the interpretation of Israel's history with God on the basis of an entirely new saving event. The question of the meaning of this course of history was posed once more in the light of Jesus Christ. It led to a great survey of that history, and the question of its meaning was posed in a very radical way. It was also assumed that the real tenor of this course of history had never been properly under-

[2] See Buber, *Prophetic Faith*, p. 8.

stood until this time, for it was full of pointers to the saving event of the New Testament and from the very beginning was written "for us" (Rom. xv. 4).

This phenomenon—that even within the Old Testament one and the same event could be given so many interpretations—forces us to define more precisely a characteristic of the Old Testament's way of thinking about history; for not every presentation of history could stand up to such repeated reinterpretation without suffering harm in the process. (Thucydides's views are certainly to be preferred to those of later historians.) All presentation of history in the Old Testament is in one form or another inherently open to a future. "Radical openness for the future" has been rightly called the characteristic of the understanding of existence in the Old and New Testaments alike[3]; in this connexion "future" is always a future to be released by God. This is, of course, seen in its purest form in the preaching of the prophets. Do the presentations of history differ in principle however? As we have already seen, even the creation story in Genesis looked to a historical future, namely, the saving events in Israel. The stories of the patriarchs, for all the realism of the representation of the ancestors' experiences, are told with a future in view, that of the birth of the nation and of the conquest. The same is true of all the stories of Moses and of the wanderings in the wilderness. A temporary resting-point was apparently reached with the conquest, but in the stories in Judges we see God setting the history under way afresh. This forward-looking is certainly not always the same. Sometimes it is more obvious, sometimes less: but it is present everywhere, for even the stories which were concerned only with their own day were adapted to a larger literary context, in whose light they are now to be interpreted, and this points them forward to the future.

This, however, establishes an important point. This continuous reinterpretation to which, as we have seen, the old stories about Jahweh were submitted, did not do violence to them. Rather, they were predisposed to it from the very start. Their intrinsic openness to a future actually needed such fresh interpretations on the part of later ages; and for the latter it was essential to their life to take up tradition in this way and give it a new meaning. Their own relationship to the God of Israel was clarified in a direct ratio to their understanding of their own position in their fathers' history with God, and, more particularly, with

[3] Bultmann, *Primitive Christianity*, pp. 180ff.

their ability to become an actual part of this history. Thus, the words "written for us" were already true of the many changing stages in the pre-Christian interpretation and appropriation of the old material, which, of course, in view of the interpretation of the Old Testament in the New, has the character of a great first act.

2. At one time there was a movement in Protestant theology which believed that it was in the position to give a very plausible theological explanation of this way in which the Old Testament saving history continues in the New Testament. In the sequence of the two Testaments these men saw described a divine plan of salvation, an "economy," whose connectedness could be demonstrated down to the last detail. They were not, of course, as conscious as they should have been of the great degree in which the philosophic climate of their own day contributed to this unified view.[4] To-day, under the impact of a history of the cult which is worked out in very much greater detail, and of investigation of the history of tradition, Biblical theology is much more impressed by the opposite point of view, namely the extreme discontinuity between the revelations which it was Israel's lot to experience. We see how sacral institutions were set up by divine initiative and then destroyed by divine word, in order to give place to new institutions, and we see calls to office which are followed at once by the rejection of the man called. We also see hallowed traditions growing up in association with great saving events and then being called in question, and actually held in derision, by the prophets, and we find it impossible to see in all of this an "organic evolution of salvation," with all its parts co-ordinated and, indeed, with the end already "given along with" the beginning. Initially what we see is only that this people had not been destined to find rest in a single revelation of its God.

Thus, on the basis of the Old Testament itself, it is truly difficult to answer the question of the unity of that Testament, for it has no focal-point such as is found in the New. The day is past when we could designate Moses's spiritual and prophetic religion as the hidden axis of the Old Testament; this was a criterion imported *ab extra*, and besides, it proved quite incapable of bringing the content of the Old Testament under one head. If it were to be said, however, that Jahweh is the focal-point of the Old Testament, this again would not be

---

[4] What we have primarily in mind is the theological exposition of the Old Testament such as that of J. A. Bengel, J. T. Beck, and J. Chr. K. von Hofmann. Cp. G. Weth, *Die Heilsgechichte*, Munich 1931.

sufficient; for, as we have seen, Israel was hardly ever really at rest in her relationship with God. She was always being driven forward by his constant new promises to constant new moments of fulfilment. Indeed, the moments of fulfilment within her internal history—and there was no lack of them—themselves unexpectedly turned into new promises, as can be seen, for example, in the case of the establishment of the monarchy and the Messianic prophecy connected with it. It is, then, impossible to speak of a focal-point within the Old Testament which might have served as a constant standard for Israel. But the situation in the Old Testament does correspond to the view variously expressed in the New that the true goal of God's relationship with Israel is the coming of Jesus Christ. In the rest of this section we shall now try to arrive at a clearer definition of the relationship of the Old Testament saving events to those of the New.

Our first point is that an unmistakable "structural analogy" can be seen between the saving events in both Testaments.[5] Initially it consists in the peculiar interconnexion of revelation by word and revelation by event which is so characteristic of both Testaments; it therefore consists in that divergence from all forms of mythological speculation which was mentioned earlier. The way in which the prophets give the exact time at which they received certain revelations, dating them by events in the historical and political world, and thereby emphasising their character as real historical events, has no parallel in any other religion. Words such as "in the year that King Uzziah or King Ahaz died . . ." (Is. VI. 1, XIV. 28), or "in the year that the Tartan marched against Ashdod . . ." (Is. XX. 1), set the tone for the Christian "suffered under Pontius Pilate." But the supreme analogy between the Old and New Testaments is the way in which men are confronted more and more painfully with a God who continually retreats from them, and vis-à-vis whom they have only the gamble of faith to rest on. Something more will have to be said of this later. This means, however, that the correspondences go far beyond the purely formal establishment of a general structural analogy between the saving events in the two Testaments. Within the orbit of the word of God addressed to Israel there are constant occurrences—promises, calls, acts of rejection, of judgment and guidance, of comfort and trial—which are absolutely without analogy in the religions and cultures of Israel's environment, but which correspond to the saving events of the New Testament. The

[5] Ratschow, *Angefochtene Glaube*, pp. 72, 78f.

writers of the Gospels and the Apostles were aware of the specific forward-looking character of these analogies in the Old Testament, and liked to refer back to them in order to shed some light on the special nature of the saving event of Christ's coming or of being a Christian. Such freedom of reference to the Old Testament is very surprising when we consider how strongly the New Testament emphasises the uniqueness of the saving event of Christ's coming. The only possible explanation is that the writers of the Gospels and the Apostles were firmly convinced that the God of Israel was none other than the one who, when the time was fully come, sent forth his son (Gal. iv. 4). The typological understanding of the Old Testament was an important way of putting its correspondence with the New in a theological frame of reference and of using it in preaching and parenesis.[6]

Typological thinking is in itself very far from being an esoteric form of proof which belongs only to theology. It rises out of man's universal effort to understand the phenomena about him on the basis of concrete analogies, an effort to which both philosophers and poets of every age have devoted themselves. As everyone knows, Schiller's poem "The Bell" is typological in structure—there is the world of manual work, the world of secular affairs subject to strict law. This world is also, however, full of symbols—or at any rate, it is related to something higher, an ultimate fixed order in the spiritual world, glimpses of which can be seen even in the insignificant world of the manual worker. The background of this analogical thinking is the philosophy of German idealism, but in the sacral thinking of the ancient East the world is ordered in quite a different way, namely by means of a correspondence between the heavenly and the earthly worlds which is understood in terms of myth. "The view is taken that, in terms of the law of correspondence between the macrocosm and the microcosm, the prototypes of all lands, rivers and cities exist in heaven in certain constellations, while the lands, etc., on earth are only copies of these."[7] This idea is, of course, particularly important for the assess-

---

[6] L. Goppert, *Typos* (*Die typologische Deutung des Alten Testaments im Neuen*) Gütersloh 1939; R. Bultmann, "Ursprung und Sinn der Typologie als hermeneutischer Methode," in *Th. L.* (1950), cols. 205ff.; *id.*, "The Problem of Hermeneutics" in *Essays Philosophical and Theological*, trs. J. C. S. Greig, London 1955, pp. 234ff.; Fuchs, *Hermeneutik*, pp. 192ff.

[7] Meissner, *Babylonien*, VOL. I, p. 110; cp. here also Eliade, *Mythos*, the section entitled Himmlische Archetypen von Ländern, Tempeln und Städten, pp. 16ff.

ment of sacral institutions—temples are merely the copies of their originals in heaven. Jahwism was not unfamiliar with such ideas which may have come to it through the Canaanites. But Jahwism apparently never achieved a vital relationship with them. There is no evidence that it adapted them or worked them out according to their presuppositions; and the few references in Israel's literature to this mythological and speculative way of analogical thinking are somewhat isolated. But there is an important reference to the heavenly pattern (תבנית) of the tabernacle revealed to Moses, to which the earthly sanctuary was to correspond (Ex. xxv. 9, 40). Generally speaking, however, a different form of theological speaking in terms of analogy was developed in Israel by the prophets, that of a typology based not on myth and speculation, but on history and eschatology. We have already spoken more than once of the way in which the correspondence between original and copy was projected into the temporal realm, *i.e.*, these were understood in the sense of historical succession (the original and the eschatological Exodus, the original and the eschatological David, Zion, and Covenant).[8] This typological thinking, which was not altogether a stranger to late Judaism either, was once again given a new development in the New Testament. Not only in Paul and Hebrews, but in the Synoptic Gospels as well, the New Testament saving events are frequently regarded as the antitypes of events and institutions in the Old. Thus, for example, in the presentation of the saving work of Jesus there are not infrequent references to an Old Testament prototype.[9] This is in no sense always done by means of formal citation of Old Testament texts. Very often it is merely a matter of fairly trivial references to attendant circumstances, by means of which the connexion between the New Testament saving events and prototypes in the Old become clear for those who understand ("And he gave him to his mother," Lk. VII. 15*b*=1 Kings XVII. 23). The ways in which New

---

[8] See above, pp. 116ff., 272. It is unlikely that we should assume that this typological thinking is to be connected with the ancient oriental doctrine of recurrent periods. There is nothing cyclical in the linear way which leads from type to antitype, even less when the antitype surpasses the type, and therefore in a certain sense does away with it; it is not a repetition, but only stands in a relationship of correspondence to the original. This typological thinking is diametrically opposed to cyclical thinking. With the prophets the weight lies unequivocally on the final and definitive last act among all Jahweh's actions.

[9] Mk. I. 12f. (Gen. IIf.; Ex. XXXIV. 28); Mk. XV. 16–20 (Is. L. 6); Matt. XXVII. 34ff. (Ps. XXII); Jn. I. 51 (Gen. XXVIII. 12); Jn. VI. 9ff. (II Kings IV. 42), etc.

Testament narratives parallel Old Testament texts vary greatly in detail; as is well known, the passion story is absolutely full of such references to things foretold in the Old Testament. Compared with this typological understanding of the Old Testament, allegorical interpretation falls almost completely into the background.[10]

Allegorical exegesis of the Old Testament, which first occurred in the early post-Apostolic age and later became the most dominant method used in the West because of the work of Augustine, ended with the Reformation and the subsequent return to an attempt to understand the historical sense of scripture.[11] It was at that time too that the typological method of scriptural exposition began to be distinguished from the allegorical, and during the seventeenth century it took on a new lease of life, more from the support of Calvin's followers than Luther's (Cocceius). Its subsequent decay is an interesting phenomenon in the history of thought. The damage was not so much due to the way in which it was allowed to run wild, i.e., by the fanciful production of extremely far-fetched "types." This could have been corrected if the theological bases had still been sound. In the secular world, however, classical and historical scholarship had by now begun to undermine the old idea of saving history. Typology began unconsciously to alter completely. It more and more lost its old connexion with historical facts and concerned itself—as for example in Michaelis—with "the general truths of religion," which were regarded as "symbolically set forth for all time" in the Old Testament.[12] Typology thus turned into a general study of symbols and pictures, and so it is understandable that Herder could enthusiastically appeal to "the Bible's finest branch of study," namely its symbolism.[13] At this juncture then, there was not the least concern for the special phenomena in the saving history, but only for the light which the symbolic language of the Bible threw on

[10] According to L. Goppelt (R.G.G., 3rd edn., see under "Allegorie") it occurs in pure form only in 1 Cor. IX. 9. Gal. III. 16 and 1 Cor. V. 6–8, X. 4 are allegorical expositions within the framework of typological interpretations.

[11] H. Bornkamm, Luther und das Alte Testament, Tübingen 1948, pp. 74ff.; H. J. Sick, Melanchthon als Ausleger des Alten Testaments, henceforth cited as Melanchthon, Tübingen 1959, pp. 19ff.

[12] J. D. Michaelis, Entwurf der typischen Gottesgelahrtheit, Göttingen 1763.

[13] J. G. Herder, Briefe das Studium der Theologie betreffend (39. Brief): "It will be a proper, wise and good employment to restore its honour to the whole symbolism of Scripture, and to show it forth in its natural, lasting and pleasant language that speaks to the heart."

man in general. Even those who still upheld the traditional concept of saving history set great store on the fact that, even in the case of each specific growth, the organic succession was determined by the law of the type.[14] This borrowing from general philosophy was fatal to the final phase of the typological exposition of the Old Testament; for, once the "organic view of history" was shown to be a philosophic fiction, the basis of the typology was completely destroyed (all the more because a century before Delitzsch Semler had given it as his opinion that theology would suffer no loss if it turned its back on typological exposition). This opened the door to the spiritual interpretation of the Old Testament which in the nineteenth century was almost exclusively to hold the field.

Typological exposition of the kind practised in Protestantism from the time of the Reformation down to that of Delitzsch can never be revived. Too much of what it took for granted, not least its underlying philosophy of history, has proved untenable, and the gulf between it and ourselves has become so wide that no great profit could be expected from any discussion of it. But present-day scholarship has recently once more become aware of typological thinking in both the Old and the New Testaments which is quite independent of this old and almost forgotten exegetical tradition. Typological thinking has come under discussion again as one of the essential presuppositions of the origin of prophetic prediction. In addition, it is a characteristic of the road by which early Christianity came to terms with its Old Testament heritage. Since this is so, it suggests that we should ask whether our own theological evaluation of the Old Testament and our own definition of the relationship of the two Testaments can ignore these facts which, as much as any other exegetical facts, have somehow to be taken into account in the search for an overall understanding. And there is something more. Something has happened in our whole understanding of the Old Testament traditions which has inevitably

---

[14] Thus, F. Delitzsch could still say: "Just as natural life presents a series of stages, in which the lower stage of existence points preformatively to that which is next in order above it, and indirectly to that which is highest, so that, *e.g.*, in the globular form of a drop there is announced the striving after organism, as it were, in the simplest fugitive outline, so the progress of history, and more especially the history of redemption, is also typical; and the life of David, not only as a whole, but also most surprisingly even in individual traits, is a *vaticinium reale* of the life of Him, whom prophecy regards as David raised up again." *Biblical Commentary on the Psalms*, trs. D. Eaton, London 1887, VOL. I, p. 92.

had far-reaching effects on the theological interpretation of the Old Testament as a whole. It has been shown that practically the entire literature of the Old Testament is attached, in the form of larger or smaller accumulations of tradition, to a few saving institutions ordained by God; and this means that Israel was incessantly at work upon making her God's saving acts and institutions actual. There never was such a thing as a "religion of the people of Israel," *i.e.*, an integrated abstract complex of all her ideas about the relationship between God and man, beginning with creation, taking in sin and redemption, and ending with eschatology. It is therefore the Old Testament itself which has more and more cut away the ground from under the feet of the scholarship which enquired particularly into the thought-world of its religion, the types of piety represented in it, or the supra-historical truths enshrined in it. When the Old Testament is allowed to speak for itself, in the end it always confronts us with an event, an act of God either past or future. Of course, in the process it often speaks also of piety and godlessness, and of sin and forgiveness, but hardly ever does it do this in a general, absolute sense: in each case it is piety or failure made manifest against the background of special events, acts of God's guidance, or institutions appointed by him. The general experience of the men of the Old Testament, and what they say, and their specifically religious experience cannot be explained on the basis of a general "religion" which they represent: they take their stand in the shelter of a particular word of God, whether it is a promise or a threat, and their experiences are therefore absolutely determined by the specific moment in history when they were confronted by God, or, perhaps, entrusted with office.

This changed understanding of the Old Testament automatically brings about the need for a revision of the definition of its relationship to the New. The Old Testament expatiates much less on abstract religious associations than on saving appointments, it speaks of acts of God in history and of men, often entrusted with responsible offices, who are each entangled in different dealings with God. Can it, therefore, have anything to do with the coming of Jesus Christ, and how should this be defined in theological terms?[15] On what plane, and in

[15] On what follows, cp. W. Zimmerli, "Verheissung und Erfüllung," in *Ev. Th.*, 12 (1952), pp. 34ff.; H. W. Wolff, "Zur Hermeneutik des Alten Testaments," in *Ev. Th.*, 16 (1956), pp. 337ff.; W. Eichrodt, "Ist die typologische Exegese sachgemässe Exegese?" in *Th. L.*, 81 (1956), cols. 641ff.; W. Pannenberg, "Heilsgeschehen und Geschichte," in *Kerygma und Dogma*, v (1959), pp. 218ff.

what sense, are the two Testaments comparable? Is there some typical central feature which binds them together? The term "typical" introduces something very simple into the discussion: namely, the question of the larger context to which the specific Old Testament phenomenon belongs—a context which contains some sort of analogy and in whose light the essential nature of the phenomenon can be better understood.[16] It is only within the larger context that the phenomenon can be properly seen and understood (for a single thing can never be appreciated unless it is set within a larger context). The larger context into which we have to set the Old Testament phenomena if they are to be meaningfully appreciated is not, however, a general system of religious and ideal values, but the compass of a specific history, which was set in motion by God's words and deeds and which, as the New Testament sees it, finds its goal in the coming of Christ. Only in this event is there any point in looking for what is analogous and comparable. And it is only in this way of looking at the Old and the New Testaments that the correspondences and analogies between the two appear in their proper light.

Considered from this point of view the events in the story of Joseph, his brother's conspiracy against him—God's special tool in his plan of salvation—and the mysterious way in which God gave effect to his plan, are the first faint sketches of something far greater which reached its climax in the story of Christ. Reflexion on the key verse of the whole story ("you meant evil against me; but God meant it for good," Gen. L. 20) inevitably however leads a step further; does not this verse which interprets the story also contain at the same time something which reaches out beyond the events? The primary reference is to the Joseph story, but one cannot help feeling that, in its full significance, the verse is not at all co-extensive with that story, and that it is only in the saving event of the New Testament that it receives a full and appropriate application. That in God's providence men's evil is turned to good is certainly no general truth. The words are thus first fulfilled in Christ's

---

[16] Consideration of similar attempts in the realm of general historical scholarship might prove useful for Biblical scholarship, and would perhaps in some degree loosen up not a few all too dogmatic fronts. In general historical scholarship the concept of the type has been given a new importance; for, paradoxically, as exact an understanding of the type as can be reached helps in turn towards a better appreciation of the individual. Here cp. Th. Schieder, *Der Typus in der Geschichtswissenschaft*, Studium Generale, 1952, p. 228.

passion in a way which goes far beyond the thought-world of the Joseph story, but which had already been hinted at there.

If, further, we consider the pericope which is of such importance for the prophecy of Isaiah, Is. VIII. 16–18, we shall not lay the chief stress on the prophet's mood, his disappointment, or the boldness of his hope.[17] What is to be emphasised is the fact that precisely at the moment when he had completely failed to bring his message home to his nation, he calls himself, together with his disciples, "signs" (מופת), indeed, that, even after this failure, he still, by the very fact that he exists, retains his character as a sign, in the midst of a *massa perditionis*—is not this a pregnant hint of the one who in a still more valid sense is the sign of the God who hides himself so deeply? What he says about "signs" will also retain its application for his disciples who, in a world that is rushing headlong to judgment, continue to hope in God.

Finally, if we consider the description of Moses's office in the Pentateuch, where the theological nuances are very carefully brought out, showing it on the one hand as that of the only man in Israel who has been completely set apart for converse with God, and on the other as that of the great intercessor, who in vicarious suffering dies all alone outside the promised land, here again we see what is in some sense a preparation for the saving event of Christ's coming, and it is easy to understand how, because of such earlier pictures, the men of old regarded the Old Testament as having prophetic power.[18]

What are we to say about such a method of understanding Old Testament texts? We must accept that meaning of the text which is revealed by using all available exegetical tools and critical criteria. The story of Joseph is the story as revealed by modern investigation. Even its specifically theological message can only be clearly ascertained once criticism has illuminated the whole context of the story from every angle. It is precisely the same with Is. VIII. 16–18; for it is, of course, to modern literary and form-critical analysis that we owe our understanding of the key position which this text holds. The same applies, finally, to the picture of Moses in Deuteronomy and in the Priestly Document. We must therefore insist that, as clearly as it can be, any specific text is read in the way in which it is understood in the Old

[17] In Kautzsch, *Die Heilige Schrift des Alten Testaments*, 4th edn., ed. A. Bertholet, Tübingen 1922, the pericope is entitled: "Die Stimmung des Propheten: im Schmerz doch Hoffnung"!

[18] On the complex picture of the tradition about Moses, see VOL. I, pp. 291ff.

Testament. However, we do introduce a new element of interpretation which does not derive from the Old Testament in that we presuppose the existence of a particular kind of connexion between the saving events of the Old Testament and the transcendent saving events of the New. Thus, we do not confine ourselves only to the Old Testament's own understanding of the texts, because we see them as part of a logical progression whose end lies in the future. When they are considered simply as they were understood by ancient Israel their forward-looking character is not apparent: but to the man who is aware of the New Testament saving event, the Old Testament texts speak in a new way of the events which overtook Israel during her journey through history. For these events can now be recognised as prefigurations of Christ's coming, and at the same time they keep their preliminary incomplete character.

The name given to such exegesis is relatively unimportant. If it is called typological, the term is a suitable one in that it links up with an earlier form of exegesis which, for all its limitations, was well aware that the bond of unity between the Old Testament and the New is formed by concrete divine acts which appointed salvation and judgment, and does not consist in their common or kindred religious ideas. And yet, the essence of our view differs from earlier typology as understood, for example, in the seventeenth century at one very crucial point; for the latter used the data with reference to a salvatio-historical progress which it objectified naïvely; we, however, can no longer say that the David or Joshua of history, or the Tabernacle, or the Passover lamb, are types of Christ. There can now be no question of declaring certain persons or objects or institutions as, in their objective and as it were static essence, types. Everything depends on the *events* between Israel and her God, on the gradient of the progress in all the manifestations, proclamations, ceremonies, deliverances, conflicts, and punishments which occur, and on what place all these events have in the great area of tension constituted by promise and fulfilment which is so characteristic of Israel's whole existence before God. The historical utterances of the Old Testament cannot be abstracted from their historical context and taken each as at rest in itself. One of the chief concerns of our whole presentation has been to show how, from Abraham to Malachi, Israel was kept constantly in motion because of what God said and did, and that she was always in one way or another in an area of tension constituted by promise and fulfilment. Whether

OTT 2 B

we take a text from the patriarchal narratives, or one from the Book of Joshua, or from the histories, we shall always notice that the event described stands in the shelter of a word of God that is pregnant with the future and points beyond itself to something yet to come. Thus, exegesis of Old Testament words and texts must, under all circumstances, try to understand them in the light of this movement towards a fulfilment, to which, as we have seen, they are already themselves inherently open. The last thing it should do is abstract them into general truths of religion; for God's revelation in Israel was determined by a fellowship which he initiated with an act of election and by the particular road on which he set Israel, which continually led to new goals. The typical element is therefore to be looked for in the progress which is presented.

In the example already taken, the story of Joseph, hindsight noticed in the words of Gen. L. 20 something like a fulfilment; at the same time, however, we saw that these words also reach forward beyond their own place in the saving history, for they include much more than what is disclosed in their application to the conflict of the brethren with Joseph (in passing, this view also coincides with the intention of the story-teller—who was also a teacher—who put into effect only one of many possible applications of the words). Yet, the true significance and the ultimate theological reach of the words of Gen. L. 20 only become clear to us on the basis of the New Testament; it alone enables us to see that the words still failed to find their ultimate and appropriate fulfilment in the Old Testament. The same could be shown in the case of the other two examples.

Another particularly characteristic range of Old Testament saving utterances is that which tells of the calls of charismatic persons and of people summoned to great offices. In VOL. I we conjectured that, in the case of certain descriptions of the call and the failure of charismatic leaders (Gideon, Samson, and Saul), we are dealing with literary compositions which already show a typological trend, in that the narrators are only concerned with the phenomenon of the rise and speedy failure of the man thus called.[19] Here too in each case there is a fulfilment, the proof of the *charisma* and victory. Suddenly, however, these men are removed, Jahweh can no longer consider them, and the story ends with the reader feeling that, since Jahweh has so far been unable to find a really suitable instrument, the commission remains

[19] See VOL. I, p. 329.

unfulfilled. Can we not say of each of these stories that Jahweh's designs far transcend their historical contexts? What happened to the ascriptions of a universal rule made by Jahweh to the kings of Judah (Pss. II, LXXII, CX)? It is impossible that the post-exilic readers and trans-mitters of these Messianic texts saw them only as venerable monuments of a glorious but vanished past.[20] Saul, called to save Israel (I Sam. IX. 16), perished in despair—indeed, his failure was such an embarrassment to later ages that they actually blotted it out of the pages of history.[21] Yet David too fell into sin, and the account of his last years speaks of renunciation and weariness. These men all passed away; but the tasks, the titles, and the divine promises connected with them, were handed on. The Shebna-Eliakim pericope is a fine example of such transmission (Is. XXII. 15–25).[22] The almost Messianic full powers of the unworthy Shebna pass over, solemnly renewed, to Eliakim. Yet he too will fail. Thus, the office of "the key of David" remained unprovided for until finally it could be laid down at the feet of Christ (Rev. III. 7).

It is in this sense—i.e., in the light of a final fulfilment and of the ceaseless movement towards such a fulfilment—that we can speak of a prophetic power resident in the Old Testament prototypes. So too with the conquest, to which any theology of the Old Testament has con-stantly to return: it included the promise of a basis of life given and blessed by God and has therefore typical significance for God's action in salvation. But what happened about the fulfilment of this prophecy of "rest" for Israel? Certainly, when it first became historical reality, this was obediently and thankfully noticed (Josh. XXI. 43–5); but the same historian was obliged to mention a jarring note as well, the fact that Israel was forced to share this land with the Canaanites (Jg. II. 3, 21, 23). Thereafter this rest which God promised is quite frequently mentioned; but always only with reference to temporary conditions and never as a final fulfilment. Thus, this promise too remained open, and the letter to the Hebrews could take it up again and suggest an entirely new meaning for it (Heb. III. 7ff.).[23] It is the old promise, but now, in the light of the saving event of Christ's coming, it reveals completely new facets. In the same way this same letter could say of those who were made promises in the Old Testament that they had died in faith and had not received that which was promised—that which is the ultimate

---

[20] Cp. here the actualisation of Messianic passages in the Psalms in II Chron. VI. 42.

[21] On this see VOL. I, p. 327.

[22] See above, pp. 47f.   [23] Von Rad, *Ges. St.*, pp. 101ff.

goal of all Old Testament promises; they "only saw it and greeted it from afar" (Heb. XI. 13).

3. No special hermeneutic method is necessary to see the whole diversified movement of the Old Testament saving events, made up of God's promises and their temporary fulfilments, as pointing to their future fulfilment in Jesus Christ. This can be said quite categorically. The coming of Jesus Christ as a historical reality leaves the exegete no choice at all; he must interpret the Old Testament as pointing to Christ, whom he must understand in its light. This continual flow of reciprocal understanding is plainly laid down, both by the historical importance of the New Testament saving event and by the ceaseless movement of promise and fulfilment in the Old Testament. *The only question is, how far can Christ be a help to the exegete in understanding the Old Testament, and how far can the Old Testament be a help to him in understanding Christ?* In this connexion some further observations must be made about the Old Testament's statements on the hiddenness of God and on faith.

(a) The mark of the New Testament saving event is a deep *hiddenness on God's part*. In Christ, God divested himself of his power and glory, indeed, he did his work among men *sub specie contraria*, veiled, and in weakness and shame. Ancient Israel also had to bear the mystery of God's withdrawal, and often spoke of the experiences and trials which this entailed. The whole history of the covenant is simply the history of God's continuous retreat. His message that Israel was the one in whom he was to be glorified, and that his salvation and judgment were henceforth to be determined by the attitude adopted towards his historical saving work in Israel ("I will bless those who bless you, and him who curses you I will curse," Gen. XII. 3), is the message of a God who was hiding himself from the world. The enigmatic quality of this peculiar divine plan in history appears in another quite different form in, for example, the extravagant attributes predicated to the Messiah. The man whom the royal psalms envisage as designated by God to be king of the whole world (Pss. II, LXXII), the anointed who redeems all victims of oppression and violence, and in whose sight the blood of the very poorest is precious (Ps. LXXII. 14), is a man who carries little conviction in the world of power politics. We do not know how contemporary Israel got round this contradiction; possibly she was not greatly troubled by it. But this does stress the fact that a petty Judean king was given in God's name a claim to world-wide dominion and a saving office which he could not possibly fulfil. After his death this mandate had to be handed on to his successors, along with the question, "Are you he who is to come, or shall we look for another?"

There must have been times in Israel when certain groups of people became keenly aware of the mysteries and paradoxes of God's action in history and gave their awareness particular expression. Actually, the story of Abraham as given in JE has as its subject the delay of fulfilment: it shows how, although the promise was solemnly announced, its realisation was constantly imperilled, and how it constantly eluded its recipient's grasp. The offering of Isaac was a far greater trial than any that had previously been recorded, for it advanced into the realm of extreme experience where God declares against his own work and which seems to have only one possible climax—complete abandonment by God. The fulfilment of all God's promises was vested in Isaac, and Abraham had been ordered to give him up. But who were the people in Israel who had such experiences with God? How did these experiences come to them, and under what circumstances? Or should such experiences be regarded as premonitions of extremities inherent in any such relationship with God?

Jahweh's hiddenness is given new and still more mysterious traits in the preaching of the prophets. One has really only to look at the range of extremely bold similes which they apply to him in order to gain a view of this aspect of their message; Jahweh, the unsuccessful lover (Is. v. 1–7), Jahweh, the barber (Is. VII. 20), Jahweh, the rock of stumbling for Israel (Is. VIII. 14), Jahweh, rottenness for Israel (Hos. v. 12), Jahweh, the adoptive father of an adulterous foundling (Ezek. XVI. 4ff.), Jahweh, who searches the houses of Jerusalem with a lamp (Zeph. I. 12).[24] Israel's cult strictly forbade her to worship God in the form of images: but the interpreters of his action in history represent him in terms which seem to mock the divine dignity and holiness. The fact that it was possible to speak of him in a manner which outraged pious feeling, and that this was, indeed, essential if the people were to see him as he really was, indicates how deeply he had withdrawn. As early as Isaiah, the prophetic message is characterised by complete lack of success. Indeed, the purpose of his calling had been to produce obduracy. Yet he took up the task. He must have been appalled as he voiced the word of the God who was to bring about a "strange, alien work" in Israel

[24] J. Hempel, "Jahwegleichnisse der israelitischen Propheten," in Z.A.W., XLII (1924), pp. 74ff. The word עש in Hos. v. 12 does not mean "moth" but "putrefaction": see Köhler, Lexicon, p. 743.

(Is. xxviii. 21). Yet even after the first phase of his mission, Isaiah spoke another extremely paradoxical word. The gloom was visibly closing in on Israel, but he said that he looked hopefully "to the God who has hidden his face from the house of Jacob" (Is. viii. 17). And the same message occurs at the end of his ministry:

Therefore I again do marvellous things with this people,
marvellous and wonderful; so that the wisdom of their wise men
    perishes,
and the discernment of their discerning men is hid.

(Is. xxix. 14)

The focal point of revelation at which the Old Testament prophets had to take their stand went however further than Isaiah, even though his insight had reached a pretty final conclusion. Isaiah still envisaged God's coming as an event which lay outside his own experience and that of the people as a whole: but with Jeremiah a crisis overtook the prophetic office. Jeremiah is no longer merely an ambassador: the office laid upon him invaded his own personal humanity. He himself became the scene of God's tremendous encounter with his people. His own soul, and even his own body, had to bear the weight of this clash. Thus, at a fairly late stage in the development of prophecy, a possible new relationship between God and his prophets was developed. It is the way into a dimension of quite exceptional suffering; for, as we have seen, Jeremiah bears God's suffering and at the same time that of his people. It is also the way, however, into a quite new form of responsibility, for the prophet, who is a watchman, answers for the rest of the people with his own life (Ezek. xxxiii. 1ff.); everything depends upon his going up into the breaches (Ezek. xiii. 4f.). All this is set out with the utmost restraint, the restraint of an earnest finality. The men who resign themselves to the endurance of such vicarious suffering have no halo given them. Only in Is. liii is there a glimpse of something lying beyond this suffering, a place from which it is possible to look back and see the recognition given by the nations to God's Servant. Here—and not in Jeremiah—are the first outlines of the New Testament *theologia crucis*.[25] Where else do we find anything which corresponds to the fate over-taking these men? The problems outlined in their conflicts are Christo-

[25] "Hae sunt propheticae tentationes in quibus degustant Prophetae passiones Christi, quas etiam significant hi terrores." Melanchthon on Jer. xx. 14ff., *Corp. Ref.* xiii. 810 (quoted by Sick, *Melanchthon*, p. 112).

logical. Here is the foundation for that insight into the δεῖ which occurs so often in New Testament tradition, particularly in Jesus's sayings about his passion and his acceptance of the necessity of suffering.[26] There is an analogy—seen particularly clearly by Luke—between the road followed by Jesus and that followed by the prophets. In the case of Jesus too, this road led to suffering and death.

There is, however, another body of Old Testament sayings which was cited by the New Testament in order to explain the necessity of Christ's sufferings. These are the psalms of lamentation. They tell of a particular experience which God forced Israel to endure, namely the trial of the suppliant who was isolated from his fellows and who felt that he was increasingly being abandoned by God.[27] It was a bitter experience to find that the very people who had cast themselves entirely on God's mercy, who saw in Jahweh their only refuge from distress, sickness, and the assaults of their enemies, were those whom God had forsaken in the eyes of the whole world. Israel's hardest burden was probably that God had hidden himself so completely from the despairing man who had trusted in his mercy. Yet in the Gospels these utterances of suffering, especially those in Psalm xxii, accompany Christ's path right up to his death on the cross. In all four Gospels the descriptions of the passion are meant to show that these words of prayer about the abandonment of the righteous only reached fulfilment in the sufferings of Christ. So completely had he stripped himself of his glory that he could enter straight away into these sufferers' words, so that they expressed his own suffering.

All true knowledge of God begins with the knowledge of his hiddenness.[28] Israel's experience had already taught her this in very many different ways. The time at which she became fully conscious of this truth theologically is, of course, another matter. We owe the clearest statement in the Old Testament to Deutero-Isaiah:

> Truly, thou art a God who hidest thyself, thou God of Israel, the Saviour. (Is. XLV. 15)

Yet the words of First Isaiah about the nature of God's strange work

---

[26] On this δεῖ see W. Grundmann, *Th. W.B.N.T.*, VOL. II, pp. 21ff.; L. Goppelt, "Allegorie," in *R.G.G.*, pp. 90f., 126. Paul too however seems to take hold of a similar idea when he says that Jesus Christ died "in accordance with the scriptures" (I Cor. xv. 3f.). [27] See VOL. I, p. 398.

[28] Barth, *Dogmatics*, VOL. II, Pt. 1, p. 183.

which confounds all the wisdom of the wise also presupposes a theological awareness; and even the Jahwist must have had some idea of the hiddenness of God's ways, or he could not have organised the material in the patriarchal stories as he did. And even in her earliest days Israel knew that to see God face to face meant death.[29]

(b) So far as Israel's theories on God's withdrawal are concerned, we have to reckon with a relatively late cognitive clarification of the data, though it was founded on long experience; even so, the knowledge that *faith* was Israel's only possible answer to the offer which this God made her seems to have been common to all times. In speaking of Israel's "faith," we have, of course, to begin with the terminological difficulty constituted by the fact that the Old Testament knows no such word as signifies man's turning to God with the whole of his being, and to which every writer could have recourse. Certainly, the verb הֶאֱמִין is of great importance because of the special emphasis and content which it received in a few prominent passages: but this same thing was expressed in a different way at different times and by different people, and quite often it was not spoken of in conceptual terms at all—people simply told a story. Studies of Israel's faith which have recently appeared rightly make the term הֶאֱמִין central; the word was in fact more frequently used than any other to convey succinct statements about faith.[30] Nevertheless the presence or absence of any particular term in the Old Testament is an external criterion, and we must also raise here the question of method. Can investigations which tabulate more or less completely the occurrences of these terms really explain the facts of the case? Can they, for example, bring out how far the "faith" which was demanded by Isaiah became in Jeremiah's time rebellion against God? It can certainly be said that the object of Israel's faith was Jahweh and his action; but Jahweh and his purposes changed —and for the prophetic preaching they changed with every change in the political scene. Thus, the proper approach to the particularly complex question of faith, as this arose in Israel, is, in principle, to consider Israel's peculiar existence in the context of saving history.

The Old Testament has an extensive literary category of stories

---

[29] Gen. XVI. 12[13], XXXII. 30[29]; Ex. XXIV. 11; Jg. VI. 22, XIII. 22.

[30] For descriptions of the Old Testament concept of faith, see R. Bultmann and A. Weiser, *Faith*, trs. D. M. Barton, London 1961, pp. 1ff.; G. Ebeling, *Word and Faith*, trs. J. W. Leitch, London 1963, particularly pp. 206ff.; E. Pfeiffer, "Glaube im Alten Testament" in *Z.A.W.*, 71 (1959), pp. 151ff.

which have wars as their subject; they tell how from time to time Jahweh rose up to protect his people, and their theology is still completely determined by the old ideas connected with the holy wars. These stories are not, however, contemporary with the events of which they tell, for in that the victory is represented as an absolute miracle wrought by Jahweh, to which the fighting men themselves make no contribution at all, they present the action in an idealised form. In consequence, Israel's participation is important more as a confession of faith than as an act of war. Wherever these stories reflect on the disposition and attitude of Israel as the human partner in these events— and this differs from story to story—they are dealing with faith. The story of Gideon (Jg. VII) points to this particularly forcefully although no special word indicates it.[31] But the *motif* of faith is also to be heard in the story of Rahab, the Canaanite woman, who makes confession of Jahweh as the chosen people approaches (Josh. II. 9ff.). The story of the miraculous crossing of the Red Sea, whose theological build-up sets it completely within this category of stories, speaks—though it is rather an exception—*expressis verbis* of Israel's faith in Jahweh. Indeed, the *doxa* of this event was so great that even Moses, who functioned as the means by which it was brought about, was caught up into the *doxa* and therefore became an object of faith as well: Israel "believed in Jahweh and in his servant Moses" (Ex. XIV. 31).[32] The term also appears in the story of the spies (Num. XIV. 11). It does not occur in the story of David and Goliath; nevertheless, David's words that he came not with weapons but in the name of his God, are to be taken as a high water mark in the series of Old Testament utterances on the subject of faith (I Sam. XVII. 45). David's speech here is the first of the series of war-speeches which contain a brief exhortation to the warriors about the battle they are on the point of fighting and about their faith. They appeal to them for faith as an act of obedience which Israel owes to her God because of his promise to protect her.[33] In principle, this faith looks both backwards and forwards. They appeal to an historical event, to a call received, or to guidance experienced, but on the basis of these look towards the future and have faith in the God who promises an act of deliverance or salvation that will only come to pass in that time.

[31] On Jg. VII see VOL. I, pp. 328f.

[32] The incorporation of Moses into the *credenda* in Ex. XIX. 9 is even more forcible —"that they may also believe you for ever."

[33] Deut. XX. 2f., IX. 1–6, XXXI. 3–6, 7–8; Josh. I. 1–9; see VOL. I, p. 17.

The Abraham stories show this clearly, for they go far beyond, for example, the programmatic words of Gen. xv. 6, and their theme of the delay of fulfilment greatly modifies the faith *motif*. Abraham assented to a promise God made him, he believed the historical plan which Jahweh outlined to be something real, and consequently he was set on the road to a fulfilment. The same is in principle also true of Isaiah, the only difference being that the "work of Jahweh" to which faith looks here, Jahweh's final revelation, is sharply distinguished from all the previous saving history and looks out over a much deeper gulf. In Isaiah faith means "looking to" Jahweh, that is to say, not relying on the political relationships of the day. The great powers outside Israel can offer no salvation; indeed, things will become worse ("for from the serpent's root comes forth an asp, and its fruit is a flying fiery serpent," Is. xiv. 29). No "reliance" can be placed on these powers.[34] Deliverance is for that man alone who knows how to leap ahead of the present and take refuge in the coming saving event which Jahweh "is to finish on Zion" (Is. x. 12). This offer of salvation on Zion is no longer mentioned in Jeremiah; in his time Nebuchadnezzar was given full power and lordship over the whole world (Jer. xxvii. 6). The eschatological perspective was completely changed; the demand that the people should resort to faith falls into the background of Jeremiah's preaching. With this prophet the question of faith turned inward, and became, in the Confessions, the question of his own existence. This raises a hard problem: faith can no longer keep in step with a God who hides himself ever more deeply.

Again, and in a quite different way, the Deuteronomic histories pass a negative judgment: the kings of Judah were not "perfect" with Jahweh, their hearts were not "wholly true"; only one of them—King David—"walked [before Jahweh] with integrity of heart and uprightness' (1 Kings ix. 4).

It has been truly said that faith in the sense just mentioned is always directed to a person. It is faith in Jahweh, not in facts.[35] Further, this faith always implies a total concern, a man's existence; by its very nature it always means "an abandonment of oneself."[36] There is no

---

[34] In Isaiah the term "placing one's reliance upon" (הִשָּׁעֵן) has become parallel to "having faith" (Is. x. 20, xxx. 12, xxxi. 1). The term is given fresh currency in the Chronicler's history (II Chron. xiii. 18, xiv. 10, xvi. 7f.).

[35] Bultmann and Weiser, *op. cit.*, p. 11; Ebeling, *op. cit.*, pp. 209f.

[36] This formulation is taken from Ebeling: "Faith in the Old Testament sense dose

difference in the New Testament. There too faith is directed to God and his acts; it has an act of God, the coming of Christ in the flesh, as its precondition—and at the same time, on the basis of this, it holds itself in readiness for an eschatological fulfilment. To this extent the existence of the old Israel in which everything centred on faith, is repeated in the Christian Church. On the other hand, however, it is radically changed because of the fact that God's action took place in the person of Jesus Christ, and because faith, by now becoming faith in Jesus Christ, was given a completely new form of personal confrontation and also a completely new eschatological perspective. At this point the Old Testament and the New part company.[37] Old Testament faith was faith in Jahweh; even in its eschatological orientation it remained faith in Jahweh. For example, in Messianic prophecy it never in any way became faith in the Messiah.

There is, however, something more: to say that Israel's faith was always faith in Jahweh is not enough. Who was this Jahweh? How, and where, was he present for men? Let us remember what was said above about the disconcerting lack of continuity in Jahweh's relationship to his chosen people. The Old Testament tells of sacral institutions set up and then destroyed, of calls solemnly given and rejections which immediately followed them; possibilities of cultic communion with God were opened up and then shattered. There is the Jahweh who commands sacrifice and then abruptly rejects it, and the Jahweh who, as time goes on, hides himself ever more deeply from his people, who kills Israel in order to bring her to life again. Only here, in the encounter with this God, does the Old Testament find its specific difficulty with the question of faith. How often was it not God himself who drove Israel out of her religious heritage; how often was she called upon, explicitly or implicitly, to "remember not the former things" (Is. XLIII. 18)! This always happened when she was complacent about her faith, when she debased it, or when she misused her knowledge of Jahweh to assert herself before God. Israel was not to depend on some

not mean thinking something about God, but expecting something from God. It does not believe in the presence of God, but in the coming of God." Ebeling, *op. cit.*, p. 214.

[37] Cp. here Bultmann and Weiser, *op. cit.*, pp. 82ff. Of course, in this contrast between faith in the Old Testament and faith in New, full justice is not done to the new ground broken by the preaching of the prophets, its break with the past and the radical reference of faith to eschatology.

mythological fixed order which was reputed to be primeval, and her communion with God was not to be carried out by a long-practised oracular technique. She had to live solely by the word which her hidden God constantly spoke anew to her. And this again brings the Old Testament into close proximity with the New.

"But it has an unheard-of breadth of form. The radical nature of its (the prophets') criticisms and judgments and warnings beggars all comparisons. It cannot be explained until we see that we always have here something more than the opposition to concrete aberrations and sins of Israel, which, of course, have to be taken seriously as such. What we have here is at every point the inevitable struggle of revelation against the religion of revelation, a struggle in which the prophets did not even spare prophecy itself. Is it not as if the whole religion of Israel is ground as between two millstones, between the Word of God, which so definitely institutes and orders and forms it, and the Word of God by which, one must almost say, every concrete obedience to this command is no less definitely unmasked as unbelief?"[38]

4. To return, in conclusion, to our main question, the Christian understanding of the Old Testament. The chief consideration is not to be seen in the fact that a great number of Old Testament theological terms recur in the New, even if often with a very different stamp. The chief consideration in the correspondence between the two Testaments does not lie primarily in the field of religious terminology, but in that of saving history, for in Jesus Christ we meet once again—and in a more intensified form—with that same interconnexion between divine word and historical acts with which we are already so familiar in the Old Testament.[39] This is not the place to consider all the connecting lines which the New Testament draws with the Old, beginning with the title Christ, which, of course, initially designates Christ as the Messiah of Israel. As we have already seen, however, the Old Testament too has its contribution to make to the question just posed; for the passages which interpret the various events which took place within the Old Testament sometimes look away from their own standpoint in time and forward to Jesus Christ, to be subsumed in him as their final fulfilment.

So far, and regarded simply in the sense of an historical sequence,

[38] Barth, *Dogmatics*, VOL. I, Pt. 2, p. 329.
[39] See above, pp. 358.

the New Testament saving event appears as the prolongation and conclusion of Israel's history with God which the Old Testament records. This is in fact the way in which the simple historical summaries in the New Testament also represent it, for they produce the line of Old Testament history to connect with the New Testament saving event.[40] Yet, precisely as a consequence of such an actualisation of Old Testament material—it was always undoubtedly only selective—as is carried out in many places in the New Testament and, after the New Testament in Christian exposition, the New Testament saving event has at the same time to be understood in the sense of a repetition, though it is, of course, a repetition on the basis of an entirely new saving event.[41] The Old Testament shows us a nation called by God into a special relationship with himself, a relationship which demanded complete trust in him and which received its impetus from repeated new promises directed towards fulfilments becoming always more universal in scope. We have already seen that Israel recorded in the Old Testament the fulfilments of these promises which occurred within her own saving history (cp. Josh. xxi. 43ff., xxiii. 14). The odd thing was, however, that, even so, the promises were not regarded as having been given final effect; after the time of Joshua the promise of the land retained its character as a promise for all time—indeed, the very fulfilment of this promise in Joshua made it the source of fresh promises. The same thing could be said of, for example, the Monarchy. Israel's proleptic experiences in her history find their completion in the relationship between the saving events of the Old and New Testaments. Christ is fulfiller and so becomes at the same time a promise for those who are his. The New Testament sees the Old Testament promises as fulfilled in Christ; but the "to-day" of the fulfilment (Lk. iv. 21) at the same time opens faith's eyes to a new consummation of salvation. A "new outcome of faith" (1 Pet. i. 9) can now be seen. Thus far, therefore, Israel's experience is repeated in the Christian community—the latter too receives its impetus from an event directed towards a future fulfilment; it too finds itself launched on a journey and moving towards such a goal

[40] Rev. vii; Heb. xi. Cp. also however Lk. xi. 49, and on it E. Stauffer, *New Testament Theology*, trs. John Marsh, London 1955, pp. 239ff., 363f.

[41] On what follows, cp. O. Schmitz's useful study, "Das Alte Testament im Neuen Testament," henceforth cited as "Das Alte Testament," in *Wort und Geist, Festgabe für K. Heim*, Berlin 1934, pp. 49ff.; but also W. Zimmerli, "Verheissung und Erfüllung" in *Ev. Th.* 12 (1952), pp. 34ff., 54; Ratschow, *Angefochtene Glaube*, p. 78.

(Heb. IV. Iff.).[42] That the things which happened to Israel on her way were always "types," and that this Old Testament saving event was full of pointers forward to the New, was, of course, only revealed through the coming of Christ. It was also revealed, however, that what the New Testament designates as fulfilment cannot be understood as a straightforward and literal realisation of the promise, but as a fulfilment which, even from the beginning, far surpasses it. Even where the Old Testament event is a close prefiguration of the saving event of Christ's coming—as, for example, with Jeremiah—it is no more than a shadow of the reality.[43] The saving blessings of the New Testament are, indeed, very different from those which Jahweh used to give Israel her impetus. Thus even prophetic predictions cannot be called prediction in a direct sense, but only the prediction of "prefiguration," in so far as what the prophets say about the future of God's chosen people does not in principle depart from the specific Old Testament concept of the saving blessings.

The early Church's reinterpretation of Old Testament material to make the latter apply to itself is therefore, even from the standpoint of the pre-Christian history of the tradition, a perfectly legitimate procedure. Later Judaism itself carried this legacy of ancient Israel to the threshold of the New Testament period, and, as the Qumran texts have recently shown, made the utmost effort to interpret it correctly and make it applicable to its own day. All that the early Church did was to carry the process further. A great number of the texts which were transmitted within the Old Testament itself show a remarkable diversity of hermeneutical strands. We have seen some examples in the story of Jacob's wrestling at Penuel (Gen. XXXII) or in the prophecy of Nahtan (II Sam. VII). Yet the same exegetical process holds true in principle for all Old Testament texts—even those where it cannot be so closely observed. For the field within which all these texts are interpreted extends from the time when the events they contain were first recorded to their final interpretation in the light of the saving event of Christ's coming. The theological term "prediction" is, after all, simply the discovery that the message of the ancient words holds good right down to the time of Christ and, indeed, that their true message only,

---

[42] On this "way" theology, its possibility and its limits, cp. F. Nötscher, *Gotteswege und Menschenwege in der Bibel und in Qumran*, Bonn 1958.

[43] Strongly emphasised by Barth, Dogmatics, VOL. I, Pt. 2, pp. 88f., VOL. IV, Pt. I, pp. 171ff., etc.

becomes apparent when they are applied to him. The only difference between ancient exegesis and that of the present day is that the former took as its starting point this final meaning which the ancient words gained in Christ, whereas we, who have a keener eye for history, realise that two possible ways of understanding them are open, the Christian interpretation of the Old Testament and the pre-Christian one.

It is quite clear, however, that there are two sides to the way in which the Church has always handled the Old Testament scriptures which it has taken over. On the one hand, when the Old Testament is examined in the light of Christ's coming, it reveals the differences as well as the similarities between it and the New Testament, and thus reveals its own provisional nature. Christian theology must continue to follow Paul's lead and try to reach a fresh understanding of itself at these very points of difference. On the other hand, however, Christianity has always gone almost to excess in its eagerness to link Old Testament material with the life of Christ and to adapt it to the needs of the new faith. This example has been followed right down to the present day in the use of the Old Testament in Christian worship. For here language taken from the worship of ancient Israel is ingenuously used in invocation of God and of Jesus Christ, and in commemoration of the New Testament saving event. This whole transference of Old Testament material into the orbit of the Christian faith is on much too large a scale, and carries too much conviction with it, for the metamorphosis which the process of adaption brings about ever to be accused of being counterfeit hermeneutics. In view of the way in which the Old Testament and New Testament saving events interpret one another, the process is perfectly consistent. It is simple fact that Christian faith can express itself, and indeed elucidate itself, in material drawn from the Old Testament as well as from the New. The patriarchal history, the stories of the wanderings in the wilderness, those of the Judges and Kings, and the ancient prayers and prophecies do in fact all have a point, an aspect, from which they can be made to speak quite directly of Christ. No preacher would hesitate to give Old Testament material a contemporary reference by concentration on this one aspect and so giving it some relevance for a Christian congregation.[44] It is as if Christ himself were entering in the Old Testament events, expanding

[44] Important indications of the variety of possibilities open for preaching on Old Testament texts in C. Westermann, *Verkündigung des Kommenden*, Munich 1958.

their meaning, and extending their reference. We have already indicated that such an interpretation of the Old Testament can only be a charismatic one, and also that it can only proceed by selection.

However, such indications of the light which Christ reflects back on the Old Testament still form only one side of the matter. The New Testament saving event was no doubt the "clue" by means of which the early Church tried to come to terms with the Old Testament, and in the light of which the Old Testament was brought for it into an entirely new perspective.[45] But it is equally true that the Old Testament saving events provided a clue to the Church's understanding of the saving event of Christ's coming. This is clearly demonstrated in, for example, the presentation of the passion with its references to the Old Testament. Each Testament legitimates the other.[46] The first proposition—that the Old Testament is to be understood in the light of Christ —is less challenged by present-day theology than is the second, that we also need the Old Testament to understand Christ. Is it really true, however, that we know exactly who Jesus Christ was and is, and that all that needs to be done is to solve the secondary problem of the correct definition on this basis of the relationship between the Old Testament and the Christ we already know?

If in their discussions with one another the expositors of both Testaments could succeed in making this second proposition clearer, the still debated question of the "retention" of the Old Testament would be answered. As far as this is concerned, it is enough to say that Christianity has never cut itself off from the Old Testament. Attempts to do so have not succeeded in dimming the illumination which Old Testament concepts bring to our understanding of Christ. Moreover, these concepts are unconsciously preserved in theological thought, and may still be heard in our hymns, our church services, and not least in the New Testament itself. In this respect the Old Testament heritage in present-day theology is probably much greater than people are aware. On the other hand, the last generation of theological development has shown that if Christianity is to be saved from falling into the traps of mythology or speculation it needs the Old Testament view of history.[47]

[45] Schmitz, Das Alte Testament, p. 67.
[46] E. Dinkler, "Bibelautorität und Bibelkritik," in Z. Th. K., 47 (1950), p. 73.
[47] Bultmann, Theology, VOL. I, pp. 117f.; W. Zimmerli, Das Alte Testament als Anrede, Munich 1956, pp. 84f.; H. W. Wolff, "Zur Hermeneutik des Alten Testaments," in Ev. Th., 16 (1956), p. 366; Ratschow, Angefochtene Glaube, p. 90.

There is even reason for hoping that the Old Testament itself will force theologians to reconsider the concept of history. Christianity also needs the universalism of the Old Testament doctrine of creation, to prevent Christians from being "a group of esoterics to whom the world is foreign."[48] However, such considerations, and others like them, are not really creative; rather, they help theology to achieve a measure of self-control. The arguments of, for example, the younger Churches who stand outside the Western tradition will differ from ours—for instance, the question of freedom from belief in demons. The Israel to whom Paul appeals in Rom. IX–XI would have something to say about this. But the strongest resistance to any idea of abandoning the Old Testament comes from the New Testament itself. For its testimony to Christ can only be divorced from its Old Testament background at the cost of very radical reinterpretation.

[48] O. Weber, *Grundlagen der Dogmatik*, Tübingen 1955, VOL. I, p. 323.

CHAPTER D

THE LAW

OLD TESTAMENT scholars have hitherto argued that the reinterpretation of the Old Testament in the New Testament and the concept of it as a book which predicts Jesus Christ are subjects which lie more or less outside the scope of Old Testament theology. Can this view be maintained any longer? For New Testament theology on its side is coming to see less and less reason to address itself specially to the question of the relationship between the two Testaments, and we have thus come close to having two independent theologies, one of the Old Testament and one of the New, which firmly ignore each other. It goes without saying that this situation, which has sprung from division of labour and the development of separate departments of scholarship, is unsatisfactory. It means the virtual elimination of such an important phenomenon as the relationship between the two Testaments. A whole category of important theological questions to-day lies in a kind of no-man's-land between Old Testament and New Testament theology. Consequently, discussion of this particular problem is relegated to practical theology where the emphasis falls rather on edification—though even here some serious and worthwhile work has been achieved. On the whole, it will be true to say that practical theology has kept faith with questions which Biblical scholarship has for too long neglected. But for two reasons Biblical scholars must address themselves to these questions. First because, as I hope I have been able to show, the proper interpretation of the Old Testament shows that it foretells a future event and that it poses beyond possibility of neglect the question of God's redemption of the accumulation of his promises, *i.e.*, their fulfilment. The second reason lies in the many echoes of the Old Testament contained in the New which themselves call for a theological explanation and attitude towards them. Here we are only at the very beginning of a road which was lost at the point in time where historical and critical ways of thinking impinged upon theological scholarship. None the less, to-day the conception of Old Testament theology is beginning to be less rigidly defined—at least at the periphery—to the extent that it is becoming apparent that there can properly be no such thing as a theology of the Old Testament which confines itself to the Old Testament only; unless, of course, it disregards the most essential characteristic of the Old Testament, the way in which it points forward to the Christ-event of the New.

We now move on from the topic of Jahweh's saving action to that of the significance of the Law: but this again means that in the sense already mentioned we are going beyond the problems specifically related to the Old Testament. For it is obvious that the question, thus formulated, relates specifically to the New Testament and Christianity. But to make a distinction between "Law" and "Gospel" is not to apply an unfamiliar idea to the Old Testament. For the Old Testament too knows God's revelation partly as prevenient grace, and partly as a demand upon men. Of course, here things are not so simple for us as they were for earlier generations who, while perhaps not actually giving Luther's ideas an extreme interpretation by regarding the whole Old Testament as the deposit of a "legal religion", at the very least took it for granted that the decalogue was "Law."[1] They had a ready-made concept of law which they had only to apply to the texts, and they came to them already strongly influenced by a traditional theological understanding of the Old Testament which has since been greatly modified. We to-day are far from possessing such a generally accepted view of what "law" in the Old Testament means. Here too we are in the same position as with so many concepts of fundamental importance—we must re-learn from the Old Testament what Israel meant by "law," and how this demanding and accusing will of God towards Israel was related to his actions towards her in grace. For this question, which once stood at the centre of all theological discussion of the Old Testament, almost ceased to be raised as a basic theological topic in the compendious works of the nineteenth and twentieth cen-

[1] In certain summary formulations (as for example in the preface to the Old Testament of 1523 and in that to the New Testament of 1545) Luther came in fact very near to identifying the Old Testament with God's Law and the New Testament with the Gospel. The preface to the New Testament begins with the words: "Just as the Old Testament is a book in which are written God's Law and commandment, besides the history of those who have and have not kept these: so the New Testament is a book in which are written the Gospel and God's promise, besides the history of those who believe and do not believe in these." On this cp., however, H. Bornkamm, *Luther und das Alte Testament*, Tübingen 1948, pp. 103ff. and G. Heintze, *Luthers Predigt von Gesetz und Evangelium*, Munich 1958.

turies.[2] Scholarship was preoccupied with special historical problems, with the origin and drafting of the legal norms, and with their custodians and their transmission. Think only of how much research was necessary before gradual elucidation of the history of law in ancient Israel led to the demolition of Wellhausen's revolutionary hypothesis that the law came not before but after the prophets, and to the recognition that the hypothesis is only valid for the literary collection into major theological works (Deuteronomy and the Priestly Document) of traditions which in themselves are very much older than their collection. It is beyond question that God's will as expressed in law was announced to Israel as early as the earliest stage of Jahwism. But the question of how it is to be understood theologically, of how Israel herself understood this demanding will of God in the various phases of the history of her faith, is still far from being satisfactorily cleared up. Yet, for the value which Christianity has to put on the Old Testament, much depends upon the answer. Such summary distinctions as the traditional division of Old Testament law into ceremonial law, law proper, and moral law, do not to-day answer the purpose.

1. Since there are so many different facts to be reckoned with, the best course is to begin by asking what Israel, and this means early Israel, experienced in her worship. It is surely right to believe that it was in the cult that the basic characteristics of the relationship between Israel and Jahweh were given standardised and compact form. As a matter of fact, recent form-critical and traditio-historical investigation has brought to light a considerable body of cultic material which allows certain conclusions to be drawn about procedure in worship. It is now absolutely certain that, in the earliest worship of Jahweh, the demands of God's will in "commandment" form bulked large. It is common knowledge that these commandments generally appear in the form of "series"— and the reason for this is the fact that they were used liturgically, i.e., they were recited. These series are by no means always drafted in identical form.[3] The diversity in the ways available can be shown by a brief conspectus:

[2] In his *Old Testament Theology*, trs. G. E. Day, New York 1883, G. F. Oehler was one of the last who still occasionally spoke of a "tuition of the Law" in the Old Testament (pp. 335, 455). But this idea plays no conspicuous part in his presentation of the Old Testament material.

[3] See VOL. I, pp. 190ff.

Ex. xx. 2ff.; Deut. v. 6ff.	"thou shalt not ..."
Lev. xix. 13ff.	"thou shalt not ..."
Ex. xxi. 12, 15–17 (a fragment)	"he who does ... shall surely be put to death."
Deut. xxvii. 15ff.	"cursed be he who ..."
Deut. xxvi. 13ff.	"I have not ..."
Job xxxi. 5ff.	"If I [have done], then ..." (the form is that of calling down a curse upon oneself).
Ezek. xviii. 5ff.	"and he does not ..." (similarly Ps. xv. 24).

In all these cases what we have are "series"; of course, their position in the act of worship varied. Sometimes it is a ceremony at the gate (Ps. xv. 2f., xxiv. 4)—in this case a worshipper's own personal confession of faith. In the Dodecalogue, however (Deut. xxvii. 15ff.), the subject is the whole community solemnly separating itself from the unworthy, should such be found in its midst. Special prominence is given to the recitation of the Decalogue, which very probably took place at the climax of the regularly recurring festival of the renewal of the covenant.[4] The common factor in all these cases is, therefore, law. Nevertheless, it is still an open question whether the community's situation at each specific recitation can be called a "legal" one from the theological point of view, which would mean that Israel's relationship to Jahweh could only be maintained by the rendering of a particular obedience. As we have already shown in VOL. I, the evidence of the texts is definitely against such an assumption.[5] Israel was elected by Jahweh before she was given the commandments. As a result of this election she became Jahweh's chosen people, and this, in fact, happened before she had had any opportunity of proving her obedience, as Deut. xxvii. 9f., which seems to have derived from some ancient ritual, clearly shows. Moreover, these commandments do not outline anything like an ethos; rather, they only mention, in their negative formulation, possible courses of action which lie at the edges of the sphere of human life, namely practices absolutely displeasing to Jahweh —he who belongs to Jahweh does not commit adultery, remove boundary stones, and murder. Still, this is very important—the saving event whereby Israel became Jahweh's is indissolubly bound up with

[4] See VOL. I, p. 18. [5] See VOL. I, pp. 192ff.

the obligation to obey certain norms which clearly mark out the chosen people's sphere, particularly at its circumference. The same thing, however, occurs in the early Christian community. From the very beginning it too was conscious of being bound to certain legal norms, and it put them into practice unreservedly. It would be quite untenable to say that Paul was legalising Christianity because he sometimes insisted very strongly that certain people should be excluded and that certain boundaries should be drawn (I Cor. v. 5, XVI. 22; cp. Acts VIII. 20). The early Church too saw that it was essential to separate itself from unworthy members—the very fact that it existed meant the division of the community into those who belonged to the Church and those who did not and that the line between the two had constantly to be redrawn.[6] "Let everyone who names the name of the Lord depart from iniquity" (II Tim. II. 19). In this respect, the early Church too was conscious of a "law" imposed upon it to which it submitted. One may therefore ask in all seriousness whether the ritual proclamation of curses in the Shechemite Dodecalogue (Deut. XXVII. 15ff.) is to be regarded, from the theological point of view, as any different from the declaration of the "anathema" which had an important place in the earliest liturgy of the Lord's Supper.[7] In both cases the community solemnly and ritually separates itself from those with whom the Lord chose that it should have no fellowship.

In the Old Testament area there is, however, a further step still to be taken. The whole "ceremonial law," that is to say, the regulations concerning festivals, circumcision, and sacrifice, and the decisions on clean and unclean, may also be designated as "law" from the theological point of view, but only in the sense of standards which follow upon God's establishment of a wide-reaching saving institution, and therefore as regulations which give to an already existing community both its form and the sacramental orders upon which it rests. Admittedly, the Old Testament only gives very bare indications of the theological significance of the sacrifices and other rites, and does it least of all for Israel's earliest days. In our judgment, however, this silence lends very

---

[6] On "outside" cp. Rev. XXII. 15 ("outside are the dogs and sorcerers and fornicators and murderers and idolaters, and everyone who loves and practises falsehood"). See especially E. Käsemann, "Sätze Heiligen Rechts im Neuen Testament," in *New Testament Studies*, 1 (1955), pp. 248ff.

[7] G. Bornkamm, "Das Anathema in der urchristliche Abendmahlstheologie," in *Das Ende des Gesetzes: Paulusstudien,* Munich 1952, pp. 123ff.

strong support to the view that the rites and sacrifices were never understood as services rendered which, as it were, established a claim on the divine favour. In none of the prayers which accompany the offering of sacrifice is any place taken by reflexion on the service rendered and its importance.

The most important arguments against the idea that earlier Israel understood her relationship to God in terms of law are, however, provided by Deuteronomy, for Deuteronomy is essentially a unique and passionate renewal of the old offer of salvation to Israel. Here too there is proclamation of law; but there is no idea that Israel must be frightened by the threats which this law made, or have cause to doubt whether the saving promise which precedes the proclamation of the commandments would be strong enough to make her able to obey them. Deuteronomy of course contains the first appearance in the Old Testament of a new form of proclamation with a broad theological basis, the "paraclesis," whose special theological place alongside the indicative "Gospel" and the imperative "Law" has only recently been more closely investigated.[8] *Paraclesis* is not to be confused with law; it does not call the message of salvation in question; rather, it is a special form of comforting or hortatory address to such as have already received the word of salvation.

"I have commanded you [צוה]; be strong and of good courage; be not frightened, neither be dismayed, for Jahweh your God is with you wherever you go."

(Josh. 1. 9)

The *paraclesis* in Deuteronomy—it is more often called *parenesis*—admittedly has great theological flexibility, for it is aware of a danger which comes from within Israel herself and which might overcome her state of grace. But these long *paracleses* do not mention something which we might expect them to—the question of Israel's ability to fulfil the law. In the view of the Deuteronomic preacher, it is perfectly possible to fulfil the commandments, indeed, they are easy to fulfil. The threat to Israel's state of grace does not come from the law. It is not the question of Israel's ability to fulfil this that worries these *pareneses*, but rather of her possible refusal so to do.

[8] E. Schlink, "Gesetz und Paraklese," in *Antwort* (*Karl Barth zum 70. Geburtstag*), Zollikon-Zürich 1956, pp. 326f. W. Joest, *Gesetz und Freiheit*, Göttingen 1951, pp. 137ff.

A further review of the question, keeping Deuteronomy in mind, brings at least one important fact to light—Jahwism never contained a clearly defined entity which Israel could have identified as "Law." This does not mean she was not constantly faced with stern demands from Jahweh—particularly in the cult but also outside it. The content of the divine will was not given her, however, in the shape of an exactly fixed and easily recognisable law. On the contrary, we have already seen how, in the history of her cult, and under the pressure of the constantly changing dangers to which it was exposed, she regarded herself as repeatedly required to come to a fresh interpretation of the first or the second commandment. In the last analysis this interpretation of the will of Jahweh, at one time tolerating certain customs and at another sternly rejecting them, was always a charismatic process.[9] For the many detailed decisions which had to be taken in the tangled growth of traditional cultic usage and new religious advances, the summary statements of the old sacral law furnished no more than general guidance. In her attempts to learn what constituted obedience to Jahweh and what disobedience, Israel was referred to the conscience of her priesthood. This means, however, that, in principle, this law depended on interpretation. From an early period onwards the understanding of it was never static, as can easily be seen from the way in which certain commandments were given a different form.[10] This leads, however, to an important conclusion: for Israel this law was far from being a known quantity which only needed to be called to mind —it was something learned by experience. When Israel heard the commandments read aloud—in early times at the pilgrimage festivals— she came face to face with her God. Even Deuteronomy itself is a unique actualisation of God's will designed to counter specific dangers which appeared at a definite hour in the already lengthy history of Jahwism. The fact that in its entirety this will of Jahweh was also now put into writing was undoubtedly something new in Israel; for even

[9] See VOL. I, pp. 209f.

[10] On the reinterpretation of older commandments, see VOL. I, pp. 198f. The commandment concerning the offering of the first-born has a particularly chequered history of interpretation. To its citation in Ex. XIII. 2 is added a detailed legal interpretation (Ex. XIII. 11–15), in which the commandment is rooted in history and made specific in its application to the first born of animals and of man. The interpretations given in P, Num. III. 12f., 40f., VIII. 16 (see VOL. I, p. 250), and that of the prophet Ezekiel (Ezek. XX. 25) take us into a much later time.

although the original purpose was probably no more than that of giving a compendium of the will of Jahweh for a time of special crisis, its fixation in written form almost inevitably had the result that God's revealed will to Israel now began to appear in a new form. One expression of this will, which was to begin with no more than one actualisation among many, from then on became increasingly normative, and the time factor was forgotten. Thus the process of forming a canon began. It has often been emphasised that Deuteronomy and its publication in the time of Josiah mark a turning-point; a distinction has to be made, however, between the effect it had upon later ages and its own ideas about the revelation of Jahweh's will to Israel. As far as the latter is concerned, it stood quite outside legalism; indeed, it turned out to be a particularly penetrating sermon on Jahweh's prevenient will to save.

2. Israel's relationship to Jahweh was suddenly and dramatically changed through the preaching of the great prophets. As was shown above, these men are to be regarded neither as preachers of new religious ideas nor as reformers of the old. The key to their whole message lies in the fact that, as far as saving history is concerned, they see an entirely new day dawning for Israel; they see a new action of God approaching her, which will bring with it heavy punishments but also mysterious acts of preservation. In view of this—so the prophets are convinced—it will no longer be enough to appeal to the old saving appointments, for this new saving divine activity, and it alone, is to decide the question of the existence or non-existence of Israel. Thus, the first task upon which we see the prophets engaged is that of using every rhetorical device and argument at their disposal to show their contemporaries how completely illusory their trust in God's salvation was. They did this by preaching the message of God's wrath and by placing their audience under his law. This preaching of law as an end in itself and the tremendous intensification of the preaching of a divine demand which meant men's death, was something completely new.[11]

---

[11] In a certain sense the pre-exilic prophets' message of judgment can be seen as already in preparation in certain accounts of Israel's murmuring in the wilderness, for the possibility of Israel's total destruction appears even in these (Num. xi. 1f., xiv. 11ff.). In this respect interest attaches to Ex. xxxii. 10, where, after the sin of the "golden calf," Jahweh seems to set to work against Moses, to destroy the obstinate people: "but of you I will make a great nation." Here for a moment the outline of an entirely new plan of salvation—Moses as the ancestor of a new chosen people—flashes

To state that the preaching of the pre-exilic prophets is pre-eminently "preaching of law" is, of course, only to put the matter in very general terms. The fact that the prophets use a completely different theological language—in Isaiah the term "law" occurs only marginally[12]—itself forces us once again to look briefly at the question of the norm itself, and to ask in what theological *milieu* and in what contexts within the prophetic preaching this "law" makes its appearance. For there are considerable differences in the accusations made by the prophets of the eighth century and those of the seventh and sixth centuries, and such differences are particularly clearly shown in the arguments used to expose the nation's sin. The position of the eighth-century prophets would be quite consistent if we had only to consider their complaints about the attitude towards those to whom the law gave little protection and their censures on oppression of the poor, perversion of justice, and so on, for here they took as their starting point the divine law as it had been revealed to Israel. Despite the fact that they only occasionally cite chapter and verse for any ancient legal statutes (Hos. IV. 2 and Jer. VII. 9 cite a ten-member or twelve-member commandment series), there can be no doubt that the prophets based their accusations on specific legal statutes, which we can for the most part identify.[13] All this is no doubt true: but it fails to grasp the gravamen of their charges. The point is not simply that in this case there is a breach of one commandment of the old law given by God, and in that the breach of another: the point is Israel's total failure *vis-à-vis* Jahweh. This tendency to look at Israel's relationship to Jahweh in its totality is epitomised in the reviews of Israel's history, of varying lengths, which the prophets so frequently give.[14] In order to bring into focus what was in their eyes the most important thing, they found it necessary to set forth the saving history *in toto*. As we said, the essential thing was Israel's complete failure. But here we come to an important question—exactly where did Israel fail? In regard to the law of Jahweh? If we try to answer the question by

forth side by side with the sentence of destruction. If the passage had not been so isolated (cp., however, Num. XIV. 12), we should have had to imagine some kind of connexion with the prophetic message.   [12] Is. V. 24, XXX. 9.

[13] On the basis of Am. II. 6ff., III. 9, IV. I, VIII. 4, 6, V. 7, 11, VI. 12 (see above, p. 136, n. 12) R. Bach attempted to show that Amos refers only to the demands made by ancient sacral law, that is the apodictic law. On Micah, see W. Beyerlin, *Die Kulttraditionen Israels in der Verkündigung des Propheten Micha* (F.R.L.A.N.T., N.F. 54), Göttingen 1959, pp. 42ff. On Ezekiel see Zimmerli, "Eigenart," pp. 1ff.

[14] Am. II. 9–12, IV. 6ff.; Is. I. 2f., V. 1ff.; Mic. VI. 1ff.; Hos. XI. 1ff.; Jer. II. 1ff.

considering Jahweh's lament over the rebellious sons he reared (Is. I. 2f.), or the beloved's lament over the "vineyard" for which he had done so much (Is. V. Iff.), or that of the father who taught his child Israel to walk (Hos. XI. Iff.), the answer is always the same—what Israel failed to respond to was Jahweh's action in salvation. Israel's sin consisted in the fact that she had paid no heed to the way in which her God had led her, and had despised his gifts. Even allusions to contempt for Jahweh's will as expressed in law are intended to point in the same direction. In any case, it cannot be said that the prophets of this era confront their nation with Jahweh's law (supposing that anything of the kind actually existed at their time); it was not on the law, but on Jahweh's will to save, that Israel foundered. Once this is recognised and established in principle, then there is no obstacle to acknowledging the differences which do certainly exist. The clearest illustration of our proposition that Israel's sin was revealed as sin against her God's action in the saving history would be Hosea, whereas in Amos and Isaiah charges of breaking specific commandments also play a part. Significantly enough however, even Amos contrasts these transgressions (Am. II. 6–8) with the benefits which Jahweh conferred in the saving history (Am. II. 9–12), while for Isaiah lack of faith is above all the great obstacle. The unforgivable sin of the men of Jerusalem was that they did not accept the invitation to take refuge in Jahweh, they failed to "look to" him (Is. XXII. 12f.). It therefore remains true that while the prophets of the eighth century "preach law," or at all events reveal sin, this sin is shown to be immediate sin against God's saving action, and not against a law of judgment which stands over against this saving action. Amos perhaps found the most telling way of putting this—the very saving act by which Israel was elected becomes her judgment (Am. III. 2). However, to say that these prophets preach law necessitates narrowing this term in another direction as well; for, as is well known, the positive summons to be obedient plays a very small part in their preaching. They place no insistence on the need for human obedience as a prerequisite of God's salvation. Thus their message might almost be described as self-contradictory because of the sharpness of their condemnation on the one hand and on the other the absence of any great commands. The two elements are easily explained, however, by the fact that the prophets were looking to the future, to the "destruction decreed" (Is. XXVIII. 22) and to the new salvation which Jahweh promised to bring about.

We can observe very much the same thing in the case of the prophets of the seventh and sixth centuries, Jeremiah and Ezekiel, although with them there is a certain change precisely in the question under consideration. Clearly, the old prophetic calling of exposing sin had now entered on a new phase. In the view of Jeremiah and Ezekiel, Israel has broken the covenant. Of course, Amos and Hosea could also have said this; but what does Jeremiah mean by giving the *torah* a central place in what he says on the subject (Jer. xxxi. 33)? The reason why we now find considerations of the Law which were absent in Amos, Isaiah, and Micah is, first of all, that as a result of current tendencies to revive the past, this whole age had suddenly become interested in the ancient traditions, and was endeavouring to accommodate itself to them. The prophet's contemporaries gave him his catchword; they led him to express himself in opposite terms (Jer. viii. 8). At the same time, however, there is no doubt that the prophets' own insights and experiences also brought them increasingly up against the problem of the *torah* and of Israel's fulfilment of it. While the earlier prophets had spoken of Israel's utter and complete failure *vis-à-vis* Jahweh, Jeremiah and Ezekiel reach the insight that she is inherently utterly unable to obey him. Ezekiel's grim retrospect in ch. xx is initially a further example of the prophets' way of confronting Israel with her saving history in order to show the enormity of her sin. To this extent Ezek. xx is an amplification of what had been in Amos's mind when he said that it was precisely Israel's election that led to the exposure and punishment of her sins (Am. iii. 2). At the same time, however, a new note is struck; for, as it is given in Ezek. xx, what involves Israel in sin is not Jahweh's saving activity in the narrower sense of the term, that is to say, his acts of guidance and the miracles he has wrought; instead, it is demands of a legal character which Israel had been put under obligation to obey. In the era which he surveys, Ezekiel observes. Israel's constant failure to obey the promulgated law (see above, pp. 225ff.). The change in the view taken of the norm here as compared with earlier prophecy is unmistakable; for what Ezekiel speaks of is *lex* in the real sense of the term, and the question of the fulfilling of this law has now arisen. The prophet's answer to it issues in the curt statement that Israel did not comply with these demands. In Ezekiel's view however, the chosen people are so hardened in their opposition to the will of God thus revealed that the question, to which ch. xx gives no explicit answer, whether this disobedience originates in lack of will or lack of power, has very little point. Certainly, these prophets hardly say that the commandments which Jahweh gave absolutely transcend Israel's capacity to fulfil them. Yet, what Jeremiah says about the Ethiopian who cannot change his spots and the leopard which cannot change its skin does seem to point in this direction (Jer. XIII. 23). Such a radical utterance as that of Joshua at the assembly at Shechem, that Israel cannot serve Jahweh (Josh. XXIV. 19), is unparalleled in all the rest of the Old Testament.

The best proof of the radical insights attained by the prophets in this matter are the prophecies on the subject of the new obedience which Jahweh himself is to bring within his people's powers. The theological situation in which this was announced is not without significance. Israel is completely lost. This however—at all events with Jeremiah— really only becomes clear at the point where Jahweh rises up to effect his chosen people's deliverance, that is to say, at the point when the realisation is almost too late. Nevertheless, passages like Jer. XXXI. 31ff. and Ezek. XXXVI. 26ff. show the strength of the legal element in these prophets' understanding of Israel, and also how far they regarded her as threatened because of the problem rising out of the need to fulfil the law. We have already dealt at some length with the prophecy that God would cut this Gordian knot by means of a miracle to be wrought not in the world of external nature but in the hearts of men.[15] Nevertheless, Jeremiah's words about the New Covenant do not exhaust the topic of the new saving event; for in the whole passage only one *differentia specifica*, the new heart, is mentioned. The prophet thus takes one point alone to illustrate the change from the old to the new. (Could he perhaps have cited other differences as well to elucidate the nature of the New Covenant?) This makes no difference to the fact that the prophets Jeremiah and Ezekiel, and their successors, the Deuteronomic historians, expressed the most searching insights on the subject of Jahweh's revealed law, namely that Israel's failure to obey it is punished with death. The prophets also said, however, that there was to be a new saving event through which Jahweh would bring Israel to life again (Ezek. XXXVII. 1ff.).

If we review the prophets' understanding of the Law, we would do well to take it from a point of view which has proved helpful for so many phenomena of the Old Testament tradition, namely that of the reinterpretation of earlier traditions. Certainly, not all of the prophets

[15] See above, pp. 212ff., 235ff., 267ff.

interpreted commandments in a new sense. Amos, for example, prescribed many of them to his contemporaries in their old surface sense.
In his case, the astonishing fact is simply that he himself took these
ordinances so seriously in an age which had long abandoned all obligation to them. In other cases, however, the prophets' demands and
charges are based on a bold reinterpretation of the old ordinances which
can only be understood as charismatic. They adapted them to meet
conditions and problems that lay far beyond the range of their earlier
reference. This is already true of the way in which Hosea and Jeremiah
actualised the first and second commandments; for such a pronounced
syncretism as appeared at the end of the monarchical period did
not lie within the purview of the old sacral directives. Again,
where attacks on economic and social abuses were concerned, the
old regulations could often only be applied by analogy, because the
structure of social relationships had become markedly different from
what it was at the time before Israel became a state, when she was only
an amphictyonic alliance of clans. We have already noticed the way in
which Isaiah actualised the old regulations for the holy war in order to
counteract the policy of a self-conscious state which looked for security
in arms and alliances.[16] We may sum it up thus: confronted with the
eschatological situation, the prophets were set the task of taking the old
regulations and making them the basis of an entirely new interpretation
of Jahweh's current demands upon Israel. Isaiah was probably the first
to do this, when he so emphatically extracted the demand for faith
from the whole complex of the holy war traditions and made it the
pivot on which the whole existence of Judah and Jerusalem turned. In
another respect, the prophets' intellectual flexibility was strongly
challenged by the sudden expansion of the political horizon to include
the whole contemporary world.

We thus see that in passing judgment on the great social, economic,
and political problems of their own day the prophets made use of old
norms derived from the cult. At the same time, however, we see that
they extended the field to which these norms applied, and that with an
amazing daring they pronounced them valid for areas that had long ago
claimed independence from the cultic sphere. This may shed further
light on the much-discussed subject of the prophets' polemic against the
cult; for these attacks presuppose divisions not yet present in the olden
days of "pansacrality." It was something completely new that there

[16] See above, pp. 159f., 178ff.

were such deep differences between cultic and "moral" regulations that the two could be played off against each other. At the same time, however, Israel's development meant that the ordinances given in the cult were now in some respects inadequate, and equally, Jahwism had lost ground in other fields. In its own sacral province, cultic life preserved the even tenor of its way, and its regulations may even have remained largely unchallenged; in any case, there was no need for the prophets to be concerned with them, for they were the province of the priesthood. Clearly, however, the prophets were not satisfied with this, either because the other side of Jahweh's will, which formerly was a single will, was thus ignored, or because people were now quite unconscious of the fact that his will was valid even in areas where no link with him had as yet been forged.

It was therefore a new form of law which Israel encountered in the preaching of the prophets. The fact that the prophets subjected not only Israel but also the other nations to the will of God, and regarded the latter's arrogance as the stumbling-block in their relationship with him, was also new (Is. x. 12). But the main new factor was the radical character of their preaching of law, the vehemence with which they tore the veil from every sphere of Israel's life, even her most secret ones, and dragged these into the light of the divine demands.[17] There is truth in the statement that the prophets' application of old norms sometimes involved them in contradictions. Why appeal to the ancient formula of the ban, in terms of which the malefactor was to be "cut off" from Israel, when in fact the Israel from which he was to be expelled no longer existed, because all her members were under the same condemnation?[18] Thus, when the prophets conscript the old norms of sacral law to aid them in their persistent attempts to prove that the whole nation was lost, this was a bold piece of hermeneutic; for it was certainly not the prophets' business that offences against Jahweh should be duly punished each in its own place. Yet this would have been the simple logical conclusion of the actualisation of the old legal statutes. It could therefore be objected that merely to enumerate the various commandments broken did not prove that the whole nation was lost, because in each specific case the commandment called only for the punishment of the transgressor himself, or, at most, his kindred,

[17] We found an instance of the prophetic radicalisation of the commandments given in a liturgy of the gate in Is. xxxiii. 14f. (see above, p. 269).
[18] On Ezek. xiv. 7f. see Zimmerli, "Eigenart," pp. 24f.

and that the prophets were thus quite wrong in their deductions. Nevertheless it is "proved," for the prophets see their nation as standing on the threshold of an entirely new action on God's part. They put the old commandments into this new perspective, and the commandments thereby receive a new light. An extreme instance of such interpretation of an old statute is to be found in Ezek. xx. 25. The idea that when God commanded the offering of the first-born, he gave a statute that was "not good," by which they could not have life, is a slap in the face to all previous ideas about the nature of the divine commandments, and can only be accounted for by the new view of the world which Ezekiel developed.[19] The full powers with which the prophets pick and choose among these old ordinances, and the way in which they apply and interpret them, are entirely charismatic.

3. Never again was there in Israel a more incisive or menacing "preaching of law" than the prophets'. But it is difficult to measure its effect with any exactness. It most certainly had an influence on Deuteronomy and the Deuteronomists. The monotonous consistency with which the Deuteronomic histories seek to ascertain how far the kings obeyed God, that is to say, how far they were "perfect" with Jahweh, of course relates primarily to their attitude in cultic matters[20]; but the thoroughgoing way in which this standard is applied and, in particular, the straight line drawn here between these kings' decision to disobey and the divine judgment of 586, can only be understood as an echo of the thoroughgoing nature of the preaching of the prophets. If the question of the effect which these had is posed more precisely, then one has particularly to enquire as to the effect of their specifically eschatological message, and here there is little that we can lay hold of. The way in which the Priestly Document greatly increases the number of the sacrifices, and the details into which it enters about them, as well as the emphasis it lays on their atoning function, can also have a different explanation, as the product of the general religious insecurity of an age which was beginning to doubt the bases of the covenant and its validity. We shall therefore here only go on to look at a single idea which was

---

[19] "Undoubtedly this is the language of an age that is deeply affected by the mysterious and that has had the confident possibility of a righteousness of its own shattered, that dares to submit without evasion to the enigma of a divine punishment which is contained in the commandments themselves. In an oddly restricted formulation, the Pauline understanding of the nature of the Law can here be glimpsed from afar." Zimmerli, *Ezekiel*, p. 449.   [20] See VOL. I, pp. 337f.

given a remarkable development because of the prophets' thorough-going preaching of law. This is the idea of a human *mediator* who vicariously steps in between Jahweh and the people whom Jahweh threatens.

This idea did not of course originate as such with the prophets. In a story which has a very old-world ring about it we are told how, when Jonathan came under the ban, he was ransomed by the people. Many commentators take the view that here was a case of a man—not an animal— taking the curse on himself, and this does fit in with the old-fashioned rigorism apparent in the whole story (1 Sam. XIV. 45). Ulti-mately too, the whole ministry of the priesthood was a ministry of vicarious mediation, especially when it is remembered that they ate the flesh of the sin-offering.[21] Again, the idea that the Levites were made over to Jahweh in place of the first-born, thus saving the latter from being sacrificed, must be kept in mind in this connexion (Num. III. 12f., 40f., VIII. 16).

The prophet's office, too, had an intercessory function linked with it from the very beginning. This prophetic ministry of mediation be-comes theologically important at the point at which the prophet's office begins to make inroads into his personal life and imperils the mediator's own human existence. There were certainly not a few in-stances of this even in early times; yet, as is plain to see, it was only in the seventh and sixth centuries that there came a special and intensified development of this picture of the suffering prophet. Jeremiah's case was, of course, exceptional. He plumbed the profoundest depths of suffering in his service as a prophet, and it is apparent to any reader of his book that the clash between Jahweh and his disobedient people took place within the prophet himself. But it is noticeable that neither Jeremiah nor Baruch apparently had any idea that this suffering was specifically mediatorial. Ezekiel's case is essentially different, for he was appointed watchman of the people, and was made answerable with his life for those who were put in his care. Here, therefore, the law which passed sentence of death on Israel quite obviously affected its messenger also. The same thing is apparent in the task of "going up into the breaches," in which Ezekiel obviously sums up the essence of the prophetic calling (Ezek. XXII. 28f., XIII. 4), for this ministry exposes the prophet to greater danger than anyone else. Nevertheless, here again it is uncertain whether this vicarious ministry can, like a real sacrifice,

[21] See VOL. I, p. 248.

avert the punishment of others.[22] Its efficacy probably consists only in the fact that, by the warning it gives, it opens a door for repentance. If people disregard the warning, Ezekiel has no power to deliver them (Ezek. III. 19, XXXIII. 5). On the other hand, it is abundantly clear that it is to the prophet that the rest owe this opportunity to repent, the prophet who has to enter into an area of special danger on their behalf. The most far-reaching expression of this part of Ezekiel's office is the symbolic action in which he had to lie for a certain time on one side "in order to bear the guilt of the house of Israel" (Ezek. IV. 4ff.), for the term נַשָׂא עָוֹן, which derives from the language of the cult, implies a real vicarious removal of guilt, as is shown by its use in connexion with the scapegoat (Lev. XVI. 22).[23] From these hints at a somewhat restricted mediatorial function it is only a step to Israel's two descriptions of a complete vicarious mediation, Deuteronomy's picture of Moses, and the prophecy of the suffering and death of the Servant. The two are almost contemporary in origin, and both outline the picture of a mediator which was never realised in the span of the Old Testament saving history. In both cases vicarious assumption of the guilt of "the many" brings the mediator to an extraordinary death—Moses dies outside the promised land, and the Servant dies the death of one who has been found guilty and rejected.

It cannot therefore be said that the idea of a vicarious mediator is consistently carried through in the Old Testament. It can be contrasted with other sayings which express the idea that it was Jahweh himself who was "wearied" by his people (Is. VII. 13) and who must "carry" the burden of his people's leadership (Is. XLIII. 23f.). Oddly enough it is Deutero-Isaiah, the author of the Servant Songs, who also speaks in bold anthropomorphic terms of the vexation with which Israel burdened her God. What he says of the toil and trouble which the sin of his people gave Jahweh suggests the idea of a different Servant of God, the idea that God himself was to become the Servant for this people.

4. The net result of the prophetic message, in so far as it is possible to formulate such a thing, was a terrifying interpretation of the will of Jahweh for Israel and an equally terrifying prediction of new action in history on his part. But the prophets did not make this the basis for a command to Israel to grapple with her fate through doing her utmost to save herself by once more obeying Jahweh. To imagine that they made the renewal of the broken covenant relationship dependent upon

---

[22] On this see also Ps. CVI. 23.   [23] Zimmerli, *Ezekiel*, pp. 111, 117.

a more meticulous fulfilment of the commandments would be to misunderstand them completely. It is not easy to give an answer to the question of when it was precisely that Israel began to seek her salvation along
the road of the meticulous fulfilment of divine commandments. The
first steps are perhaps to be seen in the Chronicler's history—and, by an
odd paradox, these come in many of the "prophetic" addresses (e.g., II
Chron. xv. 2ff., cp. xiii. 4ff.). However, such passages must be carefully
interpreted in the light of the theology of Chronicles as a whole, and,
considering the earnestness of the demand for faith made there, this
theology can scarcely be called "legalistic." We must also remember
that we know in considerable detail the trials to which post-exilic Israel
was exposed, and the cause of these was not the Law and the question
of its fulfilment.[24] It is well known that Job, for example, was very little
troubled by this question (Job xxxi); and in Ecclesiastes it is never even
looked at. The laments of the *anawim*[25] do touch on the problem of
abandonment by God, but the suppliants are never pictured as being
contrite because of having sinned, but rather as waiting for the divine
promises and as possessing the confidence of men who positively boast
of their righteousness and "integrity" (תמה). We have already said that
these utterances are not to be taken as indications of a legal religion,
but rather of its opposite. Even the psalms of the Law (Ps. xix. 7-14,
cxix) betray no trace of this uneasiness or of the effort to mark off the
measure of obedience demanded which is so characteristic of a legal
religion.[26]

There is no basis in the Old Testament for the well-known idea
which early Lutheranism exalted to almost canonical status, that Israel
was compelled by God's law to an ever greater zeal for the Law, and
that it was the Law and the emotions it evoked which prepared the way
for true salvation in Christ.[27] Had the Old Testament writers believed

[24] Otherwise F. Baumgärtel, who calls this later period taken as a whole the "legal
age" (*Verheissung: Zur Frage des Evangelischen Verständnisses des Alten Testaments*,
Gütersloh 1952, p. 45. Can however the words, "the inability to find a way out, into
which the pious Israelite was brought under the Law, is limitless" be supported by Old
Testament texts? Is "the cult rooted in the Law"? (*op. cit.*, p. 44).

[25] See VOL. I, pp. 399f.   [26] See VOL. I, pp. 200f.

[27] The conception of the Old Testament as Law was recently revived in a radical
form by E. Hirsch. He sees the significance of the Old Testament as consisting in the
fact that it is the most important counterpart of the New historically; it is a similitude
of what was shattered by the New Testament, an eternal picture of the legal religion
repudiated in the Gospel! (*Das Alte Testament und die Predigt des Evangeliums*, Tübingen

that the Law's function was to expose sin they would necessarily have presented sin as easy to understand in theological terms, or at least would have shown an awareness of it as something that was to be made manifest through divine instruction. But the prophetic preaching of law regards Israel's sin as quite incomprehensible, something for which there is no analogy either among the Gentiles or in the animal world (Jer. II. 11, VIII. 7). Certainly, the Old Testament tells of many judgments which overtook the disobedient nation. But who was their author? Was it the Law? It was God himself acting on Israel, and not a legal system of salvation which worked out according to a prearranged plan. In particular, it was God himself who always remained Lord even over Israel's sin, and whose judgments even the pre-exilic prophets —and their successors even more clearly than they—represented as being at the same time evidence of his faithfulness to his chosen people.[28] None of these judgments brings irrevocable rejection. Jahweh never failed to accompany his faithless people, and he always took them back; even Job in his rebellion had to let God find him, in a place far beyond the reach of saving history or the cult. "Where is your mother's bill of divorce?" asks Deutero-Isaiah of his despondent fellow-countrymen (Is. L. 1). There is no such renunciation of Israel on God's part. What the prophet means is that there must be evidence of such a rejection. The Bible's testimony is that God did not dissolve this covenant until the time when Jesus Christ took the people's place as the seal of God's faithfulness to Israel. It was first to Israel that God held out his hands in Christ (Rom. X. 21); Israel, however, did not see what made for her peace. At no time in her history did Israel make the gulf between

1936, pp. 63, 76, 83 etc.). Bultmann arrives at the same result in a different way: Old Testament Jewish history can only be understood as prophecy "in its inner contradiction, its miscarriage" ("Prophecy and Fulfilment" in *Essays Philosophical and Theological*, trs. J. C. G. Greig, London 1955, pp. 182ff.). Bultmann is perfectly right in what he says about the "inner contradictions" in connexion with giving real effect to the Old Testament concepts of the covenant, the kingdom of God and the people of God: the programmatic words uttered by God at the establishment of all the institutions and calls can only be partially recognised in the corresponding fulfilments and realisations; from the beginning these seem to point to an eschatological fulfilment. Did not Jahweh accompany his people all along this road, and was he not already present at the place to which (after much trouble and many a failure) they were to come, in order to speak to them anew there and bear them further? Thus, Israel's "miscarriage" is at best only one side of the matter.

[28] Barth, *Dogmatics*, VOL. I, Pt. 2, p. 91.

herself and the saving action deeper than when she said "No" to Jesus Christ. Even this did not destroy God's faithfulness to her: but it was only those who never pursued righteousness through faith who attained it (Rom. ix. 30), and became heirs of the promises of the old covenant.

5. We revert to the chief question in this section and glance once more at the value set by the early Church on the Old Testament Law. In view of all that we have already seen, we should expect to find, here too, the same thing operative in principle, namely, a reinterpretation in the light of a new saving event. As in the case of the prophetic actualisation of God-given legal statutes so, even more so, with the adaptation of old traditions to suit an entirely new situation in the saving history was it necessary to give a thorough reinterpretation of the old material.[29] Some things were taken up, others were tacitly or in a sharply antithetic way left behind as "obsolete." Does not the Sermon on the Mount's "but I say unto you" have as its parallel in the saving history Deutero-Isaiah's "remember not the former things" (Is. xliii. 18)?[30] In the subject of law, a very free rein was given to the charismatic and eclective factor which is so characteristic of the history of tradition, and this was particularly true of the reinterpretations made at the time of the great fresh beginnings in the saving history. In its expressly charismatic interpretation of the Law, the New Testament goes further back than Judaism and links up with the practice of the prophets. It is therefore not surprising that the Old Testament Law as such often cannot keep up with its new Christian interpretation, and that it does not seem of itself to yield the interpretation given it by Christian understanding.[31] As we saw above, however, the prophets had already "over-interpreted" the old Law in just the same way. And what was their "fresh view" compared with the horizon opened up by Christ's preaching and by his passion, death, and resurrection! Christ proclaimed that transgression of the law brings death; the prophetic message had been the same. But in the case of Christ, the one whom the Law kills is the one who had

[29] The radicalising of the Law is also to be seen in the Qumran sect. H. Braun, *Spätjüdische-häretischer und frühchristlicher Radicalismus*, Bei. zur historischen Theologie, 24, Tübingen 1957.   [30] See above, pp. 247f., 271.

[31] This is above all true for Paul. On his teaching about the Law, see especially Bultmann, *Theology*, VOL. I, pp. 259ff. The most extreme case where Paul's interpretation transcends the Old Testament is probably Gal. iii. 17: the Law was not intended to effect salvation (on this cp. Bultmann, *op. cit.*, p. 263). Also, the clear-cut separation of Law and promise as two redemptive revelations is not found in the Old Testament (Rom. iii. 21, vii. 3; Phil. iii. 9).

been humiliated "for our sins" (I Cor. xv. 3), he whom the New Testament calls "Son of God," "Lord," "Israel's Messiah." This event, the perfect obedience and death of Jesus Christ, could only lead to a new and even more thoroughgoing understanding of the Law (and of death as well); for now something absolutely astonishing had been made plain—the fact that the Old Testament Law was directed towards Jesus Christ (Rom. VIII. 3f., x. 4; Gal. III. 24). This Law was only properly revealed in him, who had fulfilled it. In the context of this universal view, the New Testament method of proof does not hesitate, either, to apply central ideas of the Old Testament cult to Christ; for like everything else the ceremonial law was only a "shadow of what is to come" (Col. II. 17).[32] Thus, Israel's covenant with God only found its true partner in Christ, for he remained in steadfast union with covenanted Israel right to the point of death.[33] He carried the burden of being forsaken by God as had Job and the *anawim*. In him the spiritual self-offering of which the spiritual insight of the Levites had already spoken became reality. He also took upon himself the office in which the charismatic leaders of the Old Testament had failed, and lifted it far beyond the limits the Old Testament had given it. God was thus shown to be in the right after all—here was one whom even his adversaries saw to be blameless (Job I. 8, II. 3). The prophets also had been in the right. In fact, God's whole relationship with Israel had not "fallen into the void," nor had it ended in posing an absolutely intolerable question to God. In Jesus Christ there at last entered into the history of the chosen people one who was "perfect" with God; and in this One, God drew near to his people in the most personal way possible, more personally and directly than could be through any of the institutions or offices in the old Israel. Yet Jesus Christ was also the one in whom, again in accordance with the ancient prophecies, the limitations of God's covenant were removed, and who made the blessings of salvation extend beyond the things of this earth.[34]

It is perhaps inevitable that every kind of Christian interpretation of the Old Testament depends particularly upon that given it by Paul. After all, in the last analysis, Paul was the man who in one respect most consistently demonstrated the continuity between the Old Testament and the saving event of the New. In his exercise of "the dispensation of

[32] Rom. III. 25; Eph. v. 1; I Pet. II. 5; Heb. IV. 14ff., IX. 14.
[33] O. Weber, *Grundriss der Dogmatik*, Neukirchen 1955, VOL. I, pp. 328ff.
[34] Gen. XII. 3; Is. II. 1–4, XLV. 23, LX. 1ff.

the Spirit" (II Cor. III. 8), he was also the boldest in extending the lines of the Old Testament and entirely reinterpreting it in the light of the new event. Paul was, however, only one of many charismatic interpreters of the Old Testament; even he cannot offer—nor does he claim to—an absolute norm for the Christian understanding of the Old Testament. Such a bold interpretation could scarcely be taken as normative. Other views of the Old Testament, those of Matthew, Luke, and the Epistle to the Hebrews, also show the mark of the spirit. There is in fact no normative interpretation of the Old Testament.[35] Every age has the task of hearing what the old book has to say to it, in the light of its own insight and its own needs. Any age which loses this charismatic approach will find no help from either Paul or Matthew or the Epistle to the Hebrews.

[35] To explain the Old Testament as the testimony of a legal religion is to apply to the Old Testament an objective norm which has to serve as a hermeneutical master-key, and this means parting with the intellectual freedom of Paul's interpretation.

CHAPTER E

POSTSCRIPT[1]

SINCE Old Testament theology came into being, it has never
had such a lasting stamp put upon it that generations of scholars
have done further work on the product and improved it.
Indeed, as one looks back over the course of the last hundred and fifty
years (that is, from the time of Vatke) its striking feature is the lack of
continuity. Relatively soon after its "discovery" it was metamorphosed
into a purely historical discipline, a "history of the religion of the Old
Testament." This phase continued, and for several generations work
was dictated by certain dominant questions. This was the time when
the titles "Theology of the Old Testament" and "History of the
Religion of the Old Testament" had the same meaning and were inter-
changeable. Then, within the context of powerful general theological
trends emanating from different quarters during the nineteen-twenties,
the term "Theology of the Old Testament" became fairly generally
established.[2] This was then far from being simply an externality, the
matter of a title. At the start, the decision to use the designation "Old
Testament theology" was the break that emancipated the Old Testament from historicism, and it expressed the conviction of an awareness
that our links with the Old Testament are theological and not simply
religio-historical. At the same time, the decision coincided with the
recognition that the only possible way of developing a theology of the
Old Testament was a "systematic" one, that is to say, a development of
the concepts and terminology contained in it, and that therefore an
historical presentation of the religious phenomena is inadequate. This
was the time when the question of whether exposition should be
historical or systematic became the shibboleth of Old Testament
scholarship. Many scholars persisted in developing the material historically. The future, however, apparently lay with the theological con-

[1] Additional to the German edition. The original essay, "Offene Fragen im Umkreis
einer Theologie des Alten Testaments" is to be found in *Th. Lz.*, 88 (1963), pp. 402ff.
[2] O. Eissfeldt, "Israelitisch-jüdische Religionsgeschichte und alttestamentliche
Theologie," in *Z.A.W.*, 44 (1926), pp. 1ff. W. Eichrodt, "Hat die alttestamentliche
Theologie noch eine Bedeutung innerhalb der alttestamentlichen Wissenschaft?" in
Z.A.W., 47 (1929), pp. 83ff.

ception. In many respects new territory was then opened up by the important works of Köhler and Eichrodt. The question to-day is, of course, whether there was then firmly established a system which allows the contents of the Old Testament to be developed in a really pertinent and organic way. And, in spite of the great stimulus which all Old Testament scholars have received from Köhler and Eichrodt, we have to give the answer "No."

I

There have been further advances. Following the initiative of Gunkel, Alt, and many others, the historical literature of the Old Testament has been subjected to increasingly intensive analysis; units both large (J, P, Deut.) and small have been classified as to their form. In the process, scholars came to recognise three things which, though not absolutely new, promised to open up new horizons when seen in a new context. The first was the recognition that there is a strong confessional element in the books mentioned: different though these are, they all aim at telling of a particular activity of Jahweh as it was revealed in Israel, and they do this in confessional terms. We may give this aspect of research the short name of "the kerygmatic aspect." It also became increasingly clear that Jahweh's historical actions seen in this context did not fall into a historical void. Each was linked to definite foundations, bases of salvation, which Jahweh had instituted in Israel, and each historical action moved and was to be understood in their shadow. The foundations themselves already contained definite promises. The specific historical actions described in the Old Testament indicate a part of the road along which Jahweh manoeuvres history towards a fulfilment of this promise. This aspect we call traditio-historical.

Now, although the number of these initial appointments was quite small (the covenant with the patriarchs, the Sinai covenant, the covenant with David, and the foundation of Zion), the impression they gave was one of marked heterogeneity, both because the specific contents of these original appointments were widely divergent, and because, as a result, each promise gave its own characteristic theological stamp to the progression of historical events which led to its fulfilment. Moreover, the fulfilments towards which Jahweh's historical action moved were themselves widely divergent in their precise content. Yet we also find the same heterogeneity when we analyse the preaching of the prophets, for this too is in each case determined by one or other of the

initial appointments: the only difference is that it looks for an eschatological renewal of these in terms of type and antitype. Thus Isaiah, who
has deep roots in the David tradition, speaks of the coming of a new
David. Hosea's roots were in the Exodus tradition, and he therefore
looked not to a Messianic eschatology but to a new entry into the
promised land, and so on with the other prophets.

In this state of affairs, what can we mean by "Theology of the Old
Testament"? It is evident that, initially, the new insights in fact destroy
what had previously been achieved. The unity of the Old Testament is
even more open to question than before, for traditio-historical analysis
has disclosed a number of theologies which differ widely both in their
conception of the fundamental events of the saving history and in the
way they understand the theology of history, the divine action.[3] We
can no longer share the assurance which led Köhler to continue to treat
in succession "those ideas and thoughts and concepts of the Old
Testament which are . . . important" under a very general theological
schema (theology, anthropology, soteriology), as if these ideas etc. were
all children of the same parents. Köhler did not even begin by proving
this great unity—for him it was a matter of course! In contrast, Eichrodt's starting-point in the covenant is certainly much closer to the
facts. In my own view, however, his *schema* cannot be stretched to
cover the whole range of the Old Testament. (What is there in common
between the royal theology and this covenant theology? The king was
not an organ of the covenant. An inadequate synthesis was achieved
only after much arduous work had been done on the traditions concerned.) Further, is it possible to set forth the relationships between "God
and the world" or "God and man" by means of taking references from
such divergent complexes of traditions, *i.e.*, from completely divergent
"theologies," and arranging them in a fresh complex under the several
theological topics? The answer to this question need not perhaps have

[3] The same problem confronts us even in the New Testament field though, quite
unlike the Old, its material is ordered round a mid-point. . . . "The theology of the
New Testament appears initially as a truly remarkable formation. It consists of a
series of theologies with very different ranges of vision, directions of gaze, ways of
seeing things, with very variously developed and often objectively divergent sets of
concepts, with themes of this kind and that or even only the first notes of themes, and
with much variation in basic structure. Taken altogether, it is a theology, or better, a
collection of different theologies with a very fragmentary character. . . ." H. Schlier,
"Über Sinn und Aufgabe einer Theologie des Neuen Testaments," in *Biblische
Zeitschrift* (1957), p. 8.

been unreservedly negative had not the traditio-historical aspect revealed a further aspect, the so-called aspect of actuality.

In each specific case, Israel spoke in quite a different way about the "mighty acts" of her God. In so saying, we do not mean the truisim that in the course of her history her faith itself underwent considerable changes. (The systematic presentation mentioned above saw this and properly tried to get over it.) No, Israel constantly fell back on the old traditions connected with the great saving appointments, and in each specific case she actualised them in a very arbitrary, and often novel, way. There are three entirely different conceptions of the "call of Abraham" set beside one another (Gen. xv. 1-6, 7-17). The tradition of the covenant with David first appears in what is probably a very ancient text (II Sam. XXIII); afterwards it makes its contribution to the Succession Document; thereafter it is taken up into the Deuteronomic history (in the concept of the "lamp of David"[4]), and finally it is used by the Chronicler. It is therefore a case of the same appointments being actualised in a different way at different times and probably also at different places. Set in different perspectives, the appointments disclosed different contents and—what is equally important—they each opened up aspects of the future which were equally specific. The range of variation in the Exodus theme is quite astonishing. Jeremiah regarded the wilderness period as the time of Israel's first love (Jer. II. 1-3), but Ezekiel regarded it as a time of repeated failure to measure up to Jahweh's demands because of Israel's disobedience (Ezek. xx). Both prophets are actualising one and the same tradition. Thus, even if we confine ourselves to setting forth the content of no more than one of the election traditions, we cannot discharge our task by the method of taking a cross-section and fitting its essential contents into a hard-and-fast set of concepts, for the interpretation of these concepts had varied very considerably at different periods. And we have more than one of such election traditions!

We should here note that the reinterpretation of an older text by a later is often a violent one. The Deuteronomic *schema* in the Book of Judges forces the much earlier and originally separate stories to take on an aspect they did not originally have. In its present literary context the so-called Song of Moses is meant to be understood as, and was transmitted as, a witness against Israel, though its content has thereby had a great deal taken from it (Deut. XXXI. 16ff.). The Succession Document

[4] I Kings XI. 36, XV. 4; II Kings VIII. 19.

is now meant to be understood in the light of the Nathan prophecy (II Sam. VII). Thus, we have not only more than one "election tradition"; these same traditions are also always appearing in new forms—almost with every new generation. This is of the utmost theological importance, for earlier Israel in particular had no knowledge of Jahweh "in himself." When Israel spoke of Jahweh, she had to identify him as the one who had brought Israel out of Egypt, as the God of Abraham, Isaac, and Jacob, as the one who chose Zion, etc. It was therefore only when an old tradition was actualised that Jahweh was made a present reality to his chosen people.

If we seek to extract from the bewildering number of these actualisations some characteristic, common, and continuing feature, it is this— in one way or another (the specific tradition determines the way) Israel was always placed in the vacuum between an election made manifest in her history, and which had a definite promise attached to it, and a fulfilment of this promise which was looked for in the future. Each successive generation had the task of understanding itself as Israel in Jahweh's eyes. Israel therefore had many possible ways of understanding her position before Jahweh as an elect nation; for she had different election traditions which she actualised. The common element in all of these was that Israel was poised between promise and fulfilment and that she saw herself as walking along a road which led from a particular promise to a particular fulfilment. Here is a fact which we shall have to reconsider at the end of this section.

This continual actualisation of the data of the saving history, with its consequence that every generation saw itself anew on the march towards a fulfilment, occupies such a prominent position in the Old Testament that a "Theology of the Old Testament" must accommodate itself to it. As has already been said, this will initially work out as a destruction of many accepted ideas. In this view the idea of the unity of the Old Testament will be called in question, because the Old Testament contains not merely one, but quite a number of theologies which are widely divergent both in structure and method of argument. If I judge rightly, since the nineteen-twenties and -thirties, the process of understanding the Old Testament historically, the realisation that its contents are conditioned by their place in time, has become a more radical one, particularly because it has been recognised that each specific testimony only has force for the specific time at which it was actualised, and this has once again—notice, once again—violently exploded the idea of the unity of the Old Testament which is so characteristic of *Theologies* written up to now, and has set us in a new situation in the field of Old Testament theology. This, it seems to me, is what characterises our present situation in scholarship, and it is a problem to which we must address ourselves. To-day it is not so easy to find the way back to an all-embracing basic concept, a "basic structure" or "basic tendency." At all events, it has to be sought anew, and in different circumstances. Yet, this is precisely what is promising in our present situation. We see sacral institutions most solemnly established by Jahweh at different sanctuaries, and presently rejected. We see traditions growing up in the shadow of divine appointments, the understanding of which changes in an amazing way; then prophecy either abrogates them or takes them up as prophecies of an event still in the future.[5] So we have seriously to ask ourselves whether and in what sense we may still claim to use the title "Old Testament theology" in the singular. Where is its focal point? Of course, it can be said that Jahweh is the focal point of the Old Testament.[6] This is, however, simply the beginning of the whole question: what kind of a Jahweh is he? Does he not, in the course of his self-revelation, conceal himself more and more deeply from his people? Have we not relied for far too long on our illusory idea of the unity of the Old Testament, an idea which must now be refounded? We shall not be able to do so by constructing a frame into which Israel's whole religion must be fitted, for such a frame would be too rigid to disclose much of the way in which Jahweh actually revealed himself to his chosen people and was present with them. Paradoxically, we must keep an open mind towards all the disparate and divergent elements in the field of Israel's political and cultic history which have been discovered by recent research, and at the same time we must pay very close attention to what Israel has to say about Jahweh and her encounters with him. In other words then, we have to ask anew what is the typical element in Israel's faith. Israel certainly tried continually to understand herself and her history as a unit: but such a unity existed only during the particular period in her faith with which she was at the moment concerned. It was not something demonstrable in her political and cultic history, nor was it to be found there: it was a *credendum*. Israel's knowledge of her own future also formed

[5] Cp. the "no more" or "not as" of Jer. III. 16f., XXIII. 7; Is. XLIII. 18, LII. 12.

[6] H. Graf Reventlow, "Grundfragen der alttestamentlichen Theologie im Lichte der neueren deutschen Forschung," in *Theologische Zeitschrift*, 17 (1961), p. 96.

part of this unity for her.[7] It was only in her position in the minimum between a promise and its fulfilment that Israel understood herself as a unit.

We have also to-day to some extent destroyed Israel's understanding of revelation. As things now are, it is quite impossible to express her understanding of revelation in a sentence or even with the help of a viable concept. Otherwise how could there be such a debate as the one continuing at the present moment about so fundamental a question as whether Jahweh revealed himself chiefly in his acts or his words, or whether it was both together, and, if so, how is this collocation of word and history to be more precisely defined? The old summaries of the saving history only set down the *bruta facta* side by side like blocks of unhewn stone, and say nothing of the revelation by word. The Deuteronomist, on the other hand, can only understand Israel's history as a realisation of previous verbal revelations. This question is going to exercise us for some time yet, for in many respects our scholarship is not properly equipped to deal with it. Is there not a gap in our work on the texts here? We know a considerable amount about the literary forms of Old Testament texts. We have learned how to visualise the text in an earlier, that is to say, a pre-literary, shape. We have a whole arsenal supplying the history of terms and concepts which is of the utmost service for the elucidation of details. But when someone then goes on to ask what, with all its details, the text is saying, whether, or how, it is to be interpreted in the light of its context, he generally finds himself alone. It would be a great mistake to regard this establishment of the meaning of a text, which is the final stage and crown of exposition, as something simple, a thing which dawns as it were automatically on the expositor's mind. Here again the latter needs all the acumen he possesses, for he will very soon be brought to see that there is more than simply one possible way of interpreting the text taken as a whole, and that it is often difficult to decide for one way as against another. Yet here is one of the most important decisions which Old Testament theologians would have to make. If a team of expositors were to-day to work upon Gen. xxii, for example, the resulting conceptions of it would be pretty divergent. But such discussion does not take place. Nevertheless we very much need it, because it could force us to abandon a phenomenological exposition of Old Testament theology in favour of a more critical one.

[7] H. W. Wolff, "Das Geschichtsverständnis der alttestamentlichen Prophetie," in *Ev. Th.*, 10 (1960), pp. 219, 231.

In view of a critique of Old Testament material which starts from a variety of standards of evaluation, some of them uncontrolled, and which is, some of it, quite inappropriate, I felt it incumbent on me to distil out the essence of each writer and work in the Old Testament as objectively as possible. We may assume that by following this method we receive from the Old Testament itself standards which will lead us to much clearer presentations, and this to more precise positive and negative evaluations. Here, too, however, we are in a stage of transition.

II

The historical interpretation of the Old Testament has reached a kind of crisis. It furnished us with an entirely new picture of Israel, her life, and her religious ideas: but the question then arose whether a consistently applied historico-critical method could really do justice to the Old Testament scriptures' claim to truth. Is not the great gain here at the same time counterbalanced by a great loss, namely that we tend to beg the questions of their claim to truth? The present situation is made particularly tense by the fact that the historico-critical method did not set the Old Testament in a horizon to which it was not susceptible. On the contrary, the Old Testament's own historical understanding is as intense as our own: but it confronts our modern way of thinking about history with a different one. It passes a different judgment on the same data, because it sees them in a different frame of reference. We must consider whether we have not too naïvely combined the Old Testament's way of thinking about history with our own, either by making it endorse ours, or, what is even more serious, by interpreting it in the light of our present-day theories. Our situation may be eased by looking at the differences between the Old Testament interpretation of history and ours. There is no need to-day to waste words over the amazing versatility and boldness of ancient Israel's way of regarding history. She not only actualised her own history in repeated new historical writings, some of them on a colossal scale: she also carefully noted the historical movements and shifts in the world about her, and had her own thoughts about them. In this respect the Old Testament furnishes modern critical research with a great store of material with which it can at once link up, and which it can go on to elucidate. Initially, therefore, the contact between modern research and Israel's interest in history had a positive result. For both sides it led to an extremely fruitful give-

and-take, and the result was, as has been said, a completely new picture of Israel's history. What then led to the collision?

Let us start from the simple and accepted fact that historical phenomena have a quite chaotic appearance: they never take on an automatic order or present any kind of meaningful pattern. Yet this, and only this, is history. A true picture of history is arrived at only by a long and concentrated intellectual effort, and we know to-day that there are several starting points for this process. Israel herself did not come to an understanding of the great patterns of association in her history by one single road. Even the picture of her history contained in the old historical summaries (Deut. xxvi. 5ff.; Josh. xxiv. 2ff., etc.) must have had a fairly complex pre-history, for it must have been the result of a co-ordination of separate and extremely diverse cultic traditions.[8] It was these ancient materials which gave Israel the enduring common element in all her diverse attempts to understand the theology of history. She could only understand her history as a road along which she travelled under Jahweh's protection. For Israel, history consisted only of Jahweh's self-revelation by word and action. And on this point conflict with the modern view of history was sooner or later inevitable, for the latter finds it perfectly possible to construct a picture of history without God. It finds it very hard to assume that there is divine action in history. God has no natural place in its *schema*. The realisation that the men who give us the history of ancient Israel were not only men of faith, but that however diverse their theological standpoints, their conceptions of history centred completely on God, brings out the tremendous difference between their view of history and the modern scientific one. A question which will occupy theologians for a long time to come is whether it is still possible to say that each view is of equal value in considering the phenomenon of Israel's history in its various conceptions, or whether nowadays we must choose between them.

There is, however, a further collision between modern criticism and certain claims made by ancient Israel's presentation of her history: but, if my judgment is correct, it is of less importance, though it occasions much more lively debate. It concerns certain presentations of Israel's early history (the patriarchal age and that of Moses) which have a mythical character, and whose validity has been questioned by recent research. But since these presentations unequivocally insist that the

[8] See above, pp. 106f.

events and experiences they recount are historical, the question of their historical reliability cannot be avoided here either.[9]

The literary historian is perfectly familiar with the fact that in their early days nations do not give "authentic" accounts of historical experiences and events whether in annals, accounts of war, or any other form of historical writing. What they do is to give a certain refraction of historical reality expressed in figurative form. The story-form is available for this. We cannot know all the reasons that impelled an ancient people to express their historical experiences in story form. In any case, early Israel knew many possible forms of expression, or "literary categories." How far did a deep-seated aesthetic pleasure, sheer joy in the experience and its expression, come in here? (This would not, of course, mean that they did not take the matter seriously. *Res severa verum gaudium.*) The mysterious process of sublimating the experience into the objective realm of words, the story, *i.e.*, the fashioned narratives and songs, is never exactly the same from one text to another. What is more important is that we can never avoid assuming that there was such a leap from the *datum* to its interpretation, in other words, that there was a sublimation of the event into the plane of the potency of words. It would be naïve to imagine that there is no need to make this assumption in the case of authentic and documented presentations of history. The "most objective" annal, containing no trace of story, does not make the matter any easier. Rather, the way in which it refrains from setting the event in a context where it can be more clearly understood makes the annal the more difficult from the point of view of hermeneutics. A modern historian cannot short-circuit the difficulty by interpreting the annal in his own intellectual terms. However, confining ourselves to the early period of Israel's history, we have to ask what there is to say about the details of this process of sublimation. In what follows we mention, in rather propositional form, three characteristic procedures.

1. The advance which authentic, that is to say, documented, presentation of history makes upon the older presentation, more or less "saga" in form, probably lies in its power to bring out the single event

---

[9] "One can perfectly well entertain historical doubts on the subject of the Trojan War or of Odysseus' wanderings, and still, when reading Homer, feel precisely the effects he sought to produce; but without believing in Abraham's sacrifice, it is impossible to put the narrative of it to the use for which it was written." E. Auerbach, *Mimesis*, trs. W. R. Trask, Princeton 1953, p. 14.

in its isolated particularity, that is to say, in its historical contingency. Events presented in such a way as Abimelech's kingship in Shechem (Jg. IX) or Jehu's revolution (II Kings IXf.) occurred only once, and it is this uniqueness which interests their narrator. The saga type of presentation is different. Saga too, of course, has the power to actualise the event in a highly vivid way and often, even to the extent of matters of psychology, in a very "real" way. Yet, all the charm that it radiates in this respect cannot blind us to the fact that its focus of interest lies in a different field. Here the narrator has a different end in view. Whatever tradition we select—the story of Cain, the betrayal of Sarah, the manna, Balaam, or the Blessing of Moses (Ex. XVII)—it is perfectly clear that, while they refer us to the realm of history, yet, in spite of all the concreteness of their presentation, there is always at the same time a certain typical significance. Correspondingly, the men and women involved in the event are also to a large extent types, in that the ways in which they act are not to be regarded as having occurred only once: what makes them important is precisely their more general validity. They therefore possess a coefficient of present-day relevance which the documentary presentation of history lacks. There is no doubt that certain traditions set out to relate an event which occurred only once, yet give it the form of one which occurred over and over again. Yet even in narratives where this is not so apparent, these which actualise the event as a model type, the actuality is more direct for succeeding generations. Much could be said in detail on this subject.

2. Saga is usually said to have an "historical kernel." This formula safeguarded saga's claim to historical truth from the all too rigorous scrutiny of critico-historical scholarship by conceding that even the saga has a modicum of history in it. And this was perfectly proper, and will hardly be seriously contested—one has only to think of the so-called "ethnological" sagas (Gen. XIII, XVI, XIX, XXVII). Yet, this way of putting it, "historical kernel," is not a happy one, for it inevitably raises the question of how one is to regard what is not "kernel." Is it simply fiction? Certainly, no one would deny the obvious part which story-telling's embellishment and reshaping played in these accounts. This is not the important thing, however, which would simply allow it to be said that the historical kernel is overlaid with fiction. What is important is rather what we have already seen: that saga does not envisage the event it describes in isolation. It sets it in the horizon of its own day and generation—this is most obvious in the case of aetiological

sagas. The narrator—historical considerations notwithstanding—reports the events as he himself conceives them as having happened. In the case of the sagas of the Old Testament, which concentrate so much upon the action of God, this means that the event is naïvely placed within the horizon of the narrator's own faith, and he is of a later generation. This implies, however, that the narrator attests not only the once-for-all act done by God at a particular point in history, but also an act which has meaning for himself since in a sense it is contemporary. Thus, it is not the case that only the saga's "kernel" is historical; the experience, which reaches down to the narrator's own day, is also historical. The only difference is that it now refers to a different dimension of history. With such traditions, once we have distinguished between a primary and a secondary experience in this sense, we immediately notice the part taken by one or other experience in each specific case. In the story of the defeat of the Canaanites in Josh. x or in that of Deborah and Barak (Jg. IV), the primary experience takes marked precedence, whereas in the case of the account of the breach between Samuel and Saul (I Sam. xv), the secondary experience, the conflict between the monarchy and the prophets, has very strongly overlaid the primary one which goes back to the time of Saul. Such narratives as once had an aetiological basis which has in the meantime disappeared are dominated by the secondary experience. (Take, for example, Gen. XXII. The earliest strand in this traditional material, which once told of the redemption of a child-sacrifice, is now completely silenced. The subject of the story is now a trial which originated in the singularity of Jahweh's promise; but this is not mere invention: what is here expressed is Israel's definite historical experience of Jahweh and his action.) We must, therefore, take such anachronisms into account. Indeed, it might be said that when saga makes the transition to a narrative form more like that of the short story (the history of Joseph), the secondary experience always becomes the more prominent. Saga is quite unable to safeguard its original content from later alterations. On the contrary, it is a ready vessel for new contents, it adapts itself to new possibilities of interpretation, and in the process it often leaves its original subject far behind. The story of the spies is based on an old Calebite saga of the capture of Hebron. Its present form does, indeed, preserve this element: but it has absorbed a great number of other historical experiences, and the result is a great enrichment of its theological content. Of course—and this disturbs the present-day reader—a certain measure of anachronism remains, for since, as a general rule, saga clings to the historical event in which it originated, and also inserts later experiences in the wrong chronological order, the result is that the historical data often cut across one another. In particular, the event reported and the faith it expresses are no longer from the same period. There is a hiatus between the datum and the way in which it is thought of, as, for example, in the patriarchal stories, where this appears in classic form. For the God of whom they speak is no longer the "god of the ancestors," and their religious ideas are no longer those of a "clan religion," but they speak of Jahweh, the God of Israel, who is the God of the whole world. This cannot, and should not, however, hinder us from making use of these traditions also as unique sources for the history which Israel experienced with her God.

3. We have to assume, therefore, that the old traditions which relate to the time before Israel became a state and even to earlier ages are entirely developed within an historical horizon in which Jahweh, the God of Israel, reigns supreme. It is faith in this God that shapes them, and they are to be interpreted with reference to him. They speak of experiences which Israel underwent in her history with Jahweh, experiences which in each case reach down to the narrator's own time. This still however falls short of being an adequate description of what lies before us. Are these traditions in saga or short-story form solely shaped by past experiences? In answering this question, we should start from a characteristic trait of "Biblical" narration whose significance has only recently been appreciated—its openness to the future. Striking demonstration has been given of the fact that in this these sagas differ radically from, for example, the way in which Homer tells his story, and perhaps also from Greek historical thinking in general.[10] The words, "openness to the future," do not, of course, mean the truism that history continues on its course and that the events narrated will be overtaken by fresh events. It means something very different: it means the conviction that there is an event still to come, from which, and from which alone, the event narrated is to receive its final illumination. The future to which the event is open is not an indefinite one—this is the point—so as sooner or later to deprive what it relates of actuality. It gives it actuality, for the future to which the event narrated is open is a definite happening that will come from God, and it is no less real for the narrator's faith than is what he describes. It has been said that all

[10] As for example in K. Lowith, *Meaning in History*, Chicago 1949. pp. 6ff.

that the narrators described is determined by this end and is narrated with reference to the future. One must only add the further point that this future is in no sense a vague one, hidden, let us say, in the counsel of God, but a definite, and therefore a known, future. And this we term a "fulfilment," the content of which is exactly determined by an antecedent promise. H. W. Wolff has actually described this understanding of history in the light of its future as the essential feature of all prophetic understanding of history.[11] Does it only begin with the prophets? Are not the patriarchal history, the stories of the wandering in the wilderness, and all the rest down to those of David's rise to power related in a very definite and exact sense to something else, a divine future which lies beyond the event narrated? The stories themselves may each contain this forward-looking note (as in the dialogue form), or it may be imposed on them by their place in a whole body of other writings.[12] And what comes in question here is, I repeat, no sort of vague future hidden in the counsel of God: it is a clear one, a future known in the light of a clear promise which has been already made, as, for example, the promise that Jahweh is to make the patriarchs become a great nation, or that the patriarchs' descendants are to take possession of the land of Canaan, or that David is to be exalted as *nagid* of Israel. We shall therefore find it impossible to avoid the paradoxical fact that the saga-like traditions dating from Israel's early days are not shaped solely by experiences which Israel underwent with Jahweh in the past; they are also shaped by a knowledge of the future, *i.e.*, a knowledge of definite fulfilments which stand in the vanishing line of the event reported, and which alone give it its proper place in the history of Jahweh's dealings with Israel. This knowledge of the future occasionally asserted itself so strongly when the material was being shaped that the event is described as having a glory which far transcends the actual historical experience, as for example in the description of the entry of the *whole* of Israel into Canaan (Josh. II–IX).

This then is the way—given rather in the nature of an artist's first sketch, that is to say, omitting all the details, which admittedly are of particular importance here—in which we might outline the processes which, we must suppose, accompanied the birth of narratives in saga

[11] Wolff, "Geschichtsverständnis," pp. 218ff.

[12] The fact that often what comes in question are *vaticinia post eventum* makes little difference. It is then a fulfilment which has been experienced and not merely one seen by the eye of faith, which reacted on the shaping of the events.

or short-story form. There is little reason to fear—and it is the first objection that occurs—that in these descriptions of her early period Israel may have lost contact with actual history. They are rather utterances—one is often tempted to say outbursts—of a people obsessed by its actual history and intensely concerned with the wide range and diversity of the experiences undergone in it. On the other hand (although the only reason for saying this is to counter an all too naïve historical positivism), in none of these traditions, not even in the best attested of them, do we have actual history at first hand, but only its reflexion, a picture of it. The way in which the primary and secondary experiences are interwoven means that to raise the question of their authenticity is to be introduced to a most confusing set of data. I think, however, that we ought to take Israel's utterances about her history in the way that the traditions themselves offer them to us. This means that we should exercise more reserve and not, on the basis of the ideal of accuracy current in modern critical historical scholarship, too quickly dispute their claim to make historical utterances. No doubt, recent historical scholarship, using methods which were unknown in ancient Israel, has worked out a picture of Israel's history which is in one respect more exact than the picture which Israel herself had. This muss not however bar our listening to what, with the means and possibilitiet available to an ancient people, Israel herself said about her historical experiences. The various patriarchal narratives as now compiled into quasi-biographical compositions and already in short-story rather than saga form can no longer be regarded as trustworthy reports which come from these men's actual lives. In the three great *corpora* of tradition we discern at best some bedrock which dates back to those far-off times, but even it yields nothing that can be used in a more restricted biographical sense. This at once raises the question whether, in evaluating the historical traditions in this way, we do not fail to measure up to their specific claim to truth. It is doubtful whether Israel, when she read or listened to these old traditions, was dominated, as we are, by the standpoint of authenticity. Or, to put it better, it is open to question whether she did not understand their authenticity in a different way from the way we do, for they were certainly authentic for her also. One thing can be said with assurance—Israel was not interested in the subjects of these old traditions in the sense that they dealt with self-contained events which suddenly emerge from a very far-off past. Rather, while perfectly well aware of her historical remove from them, she saw them as her own, she found something of importance for herself expressed in them, and therefore they were at the same time contemporary for her. And this brings us back again to what we designated above, for convenience, as secondary experiences. Do not many of these old stories—I think, for example, of that of the peril into which Sarah and Rebekah were put, the story of Hagar, the offering up of Isaac, Penuel, Cain, and Abel—do not these expand, at the dictate of the secondary experiences, almost into parables, that is to say, into very compact and yet rather parabolic actualisations of something that Israel experienced in earlier days and which she still experiences down to the narrator's own time?

III

As we now have them, these separate traditions are no longer independent as once they were, but have been amalgamated into larger literary compositions. This introduces us to a phenomenon which is of great importance from the point of view of theology, for when Israel took this step, she tried to go beyond the presentation of isolated anecdote and in each case to throw light on Jahweh's activities throughout a longer time-span. This still cannot really be designated as "historical writing" in the narrower sense of the term. Relatively soon, however, Israel did find her way to this form of historical presentation too. At the same time it is interesting to notice that, even before this, and with much more primitive means—namely by gathering together entirely different kinds of saga material—she took the very bold step of representing Jahweh's particular intervention in history not merely in anecdotal form, but also as a time-span which embraced several generations. Ignoring the initial stages, such sketches lie before us in final form in the work of the Jahwist and the Elohist, and in the history of David's rise to power. We said earlier that the wide range of historical phenomena does not fall into order automatically as one reviews it, and this is even more true of such disparate and disconnected traditional material as was brought together in, for example, J. The question how, *i.e.*, in what sense, it was possible to build this material, in itself so unyielding, into a unified historical structure is therefore all the more urgent. The answer is this. First of all, this whole material was put within the horizons of a history in which Jahweh exercised sovereign sway and in which he was continuously active. Enough has been said of this above. (Nevertheless, it should be noticed that this is not a self-evident statement. For with his concept of a continuous divine activity, the Jahwist imperceptibly forced on the old material an interpretation which is itself no longer in complete accord with the idea originally contained in it.) Over and above this, however—and this is largely a matter of the forms used—we can speak with greater precision about the way in which these writings conceive Jahweh's action in history. They do this by speaking of distinct acts of election and great promises—promises which God later fulfils, though often only after a period of waiting which is fraught with many trials. As everyone knows, the whole material of the patriarchal stories was worked over in order consistently to weave into it the traditional element of the "promise to the patriarchs" (the making of the nation, the possession of the land). This promise, almost monotonously re-iterated, was the one thing which made the disparate individual units into a connected whole, as it is also the one thing which gives the reader the impression of a course of events leading towards a goal. The goal towards which God's action is directed lies beyond—far beyond—the stories themselves. To this extent they are completely "open" to the future. The same thing could equally well be said of the complex of narratives which make up Josh. II–x, or of the history of David's rise to power. In them something important comes to light; right at the very beginning, in Israel's first efforts to rise above anecdote and to present longer time-spans in narrative form, a way of looking at history was established which may be called salvatio-historical: that is to say, a way of looking at history which in a specific sense understands each period it surveys as a realm of tension between a promise revealed and its realisation, between a prophecy and its fulfilment. This is the bed-rock fact in Israel's way of looking at history. And all that might occur in this field of history was given its particular mark from the fact that it had its place in a progression which began with a precise God-given promise and led on to a precise divine fulfilment. We have already said that this way of looking at history was established in Israel by the time her faith began to comprehend larger historical contexts; and, if my judgment is correct, she held on to this right to the end. The great historical works from the Succession Document and the Deuteronomic histories down to Chronicles certainly exhibit an astounding variety both in possible methods of presentation and in basic aims: but the fundamental conception of history as a continuum of events determined by Jahweh's promise, which flows forward to the fulfilment intended by him, is constant. We spoke earlier of the particular intellectual presuppositions which formed the basis of modern historicism, and of the limits inherent in this way of understanding history. Now, of course, the counter-question must be asked—what are the limitations inherent in ancient Israel's way of thinking about history? Israel, too, was the prisoner of her own intellectual *schema*, and it would therefore be a difficult matter to establish where and how her peculiar way of understanding history was a limitation, and where, bound up as she was in her own "ideology," she distorted actual history. Critical historical investigation does us important service in answering this question; indeed, it alone enables us to take up the task at all. Nevertheless the crucial thing is that we do not form our judgment on the naïve certainty claimed by historical positivism.

In spite of the tremendous diversity in the content of the Old Testament, many people to-day expect a "Theology of the Old Testament" to show us how to understand the Old Testament as a unity. But is this a legitimate demand? The specialist in Romance or German literature would surely be extremely hesitant about attempting to understand as a unity the product of more than a thousand years in the history of a people's thought and literature. And to do this with Israel of all nations! For, was not the characteristic feature of Israel's experience with God that she was positively at pains to oppose the deep-rooted urge towards that unification of concepts which is inherent in myth or ideology? I very much doubt whether the main task of an Old Testament theology is the understanding of Israel's literary legacy as a unity. There is certainly a unity in the Bible—but this is a different matter, even though this is still far from being recognised.[13] The most urgent task to-day, as it seems to me, is that of avoiding all conceptions of unity which are not fully authenticated by the material itself. This appears to me to be the surest way towards a better understanding of what was characteristic of ancient Israel's experience with God.

A theology of the Old Testament will therefore have to do further work upon the question of what is the typical element in Jahwism. If it follows this road, the result may be a restoration of the concept of the unity of the Old Testament, which has become so problematic in our day. It would, however, be more important if asking this question brought us any nearer recognition of the unity of the Bible.[14] It is the

[13] Cp. here H. H. Rowley, *The Unity of the Bible*, London 1953.
[14] "Without raising this question of what is typical in the Old and New Testament

texts themselves which pose this question about what is the typical element; it does not originate from an endeavour to modernise a dust-covered theologumenon. Unquestionably, the re-actualisation of historical saving appointments or events in the eschatological message of the prophets is typical of Jahwism, and is a special form of typological thinking. It was exegesis itself which called our attention to this phenomenon, and its range and fundamental importance is amazing. The student of the New Testament also works with Old Testament material which has been absorbed into the New by typological means. It is therefore the two Testaments themselves which are our instructors, bidding us give more serious consideration to this element which is obviously typical of the Biblical understanding of history. Perhaps, however, it is actually better to probe still further into the Old Testament itself and to find out what is typical there. For what we discover will then quite automatically lead us beyond the Old Testament. For in my opinion one thing is clear: if Old Testament theology allows itself to be guided by the ceaseless process of the handing on of tradition that is so typical of ancient Israel, if it takes seriously this openness to the future which again and again directs the reader's eyes to divine fulfilments, then it can no longer designate, for example, the literary achievement of the Jahwist or the religion of the prophets as the essence and climax of the Old Testament, since it is then using standards imported more or less *ab extra*. If it followed this method, then the material itself would bear it from one actualisation to another, and in the end would pose the question of the final fulfilment.[15]

One final word: only when Old Testament theology takes this final step to the threshold of the New Testament, only when it makes the link with the witness of the Gospels and the Apostles perfectly openly,

texts it will be difficult for us to find the narrow way between (past) historical dismemberment and levelling of actual history through the particularising view of it and existentialistic resolution of history into significant history. By raising the question of what is typical we get over the comparison of phenomena represented from a one-sided point of view, capitulation to the 'omnipotence of analogy' (Tröltsch)." H. W. Wolff, in *Ev. Th.*, 10 (1960), p. 226.

[15] It is perfectly clear to me that, when such a method of writing an Old Testament Theology is followed, the intertestamental field too must be incorporated in an entirely different way; in particular, that deep-going transformation of the religious heritage in apocalyptic must be taken into account. But in the matter of theological and at the same time traditio-historical analysis, too little of the great apocalypses survive for it to be possible to reach back to the actual process.

and when it is able to make men believe that the two Testaments belong together, will it have the right to term itself a theological undertaking, and therefore "Biblical theology."[16] If instead it analyses the Old Testament in isolation, then, no matter how devotedly the work is done, the more appropriate term is "history of the religion of the Old Testament."

[16] It is a hopeful sign that to-day the question of a "Biblical Theology" is again being put from very different standpoints. G. Ebeling, *op. cit.*, pp. 96f. H. Schlier, pp. 19f.

LIST OF ABBREVIATIONS AND
OF WORKS FREQUENTLY CITED

ALT, A. *K.S.* = *Kleine Schriften zur Geschichte Israels.* Munich 1953–9.

A.N.V.A.O. = *Avhandlinger utgitt av det norske Videnskaps-Akademi.* Oslo.

A.T.A.N.T. = *Abhandlungen zur Theologie des Alten und Neuen Testaments.*

BEGRICH, J. "Studien" = "Studien zu Deutero-jesaja," in *B.W.A.N.T.*, 4 (1938).

BEI. *Z.A.W.* = *Beihefte zur Zeitschrift für die alttestamentliche Wissenschaft.*

Bib. Komm. = *Biblischer Kommentar. Altes Testament,* ed. M. Noth. Neukirchen.

BIRKELAND, H. *Traditionswesen* = *Zum hebräischen Traditionswesen (Die Komposition der prophetischen Bücher des Alten Testaments),* *A.N.V.A.O.*, II (1938).

BULTMANN, R. *Primitive Christianity* = *Primitive Christianity in its Contemporary Setting,* tr. R. H. Fuller. London and New York 1956.

B.W.A.N.T. = *Beiträge zur Wissenschaft von Alten und Neuen Testament.*

ELIADE, M. *Myth* = *Der Mythos der ewigen Wiederkehr.* Düsseldorf 1953. *Myth* = *The Myth of the Eternal Return,* London 1955.

ELLIGER, K. "Deuterojesaja" = "Deuterojesaja in seinem Verhältnis zu Tritojesaja," in *B.W.A.N.T.*, IV (1953).

Ev. Th. = *Evangelische Theologie.* Munich.

GEORGIADES, TH. *Musik und Rhythmus* = *Musik und Rhythmus bei den Griechen.* Hamburg 1958.

GRESSMANN, H. *Mose* = *Mose und seine Zeit.* Göttingen 1913.

GRETHER, O. "Name und Wort" = "Name und Wort Gottes im AT," in *Z.A.W.*, LXIV (1934).

HESSE, F. "Verstockungsproblem" = "Das Verstockungsproblem im Alten Testament," in *Z.A.W.*, LXV (1935).

HÖLSCHER, G. *Profeten* = *Die Profeten.* Leipzig 1914.

J.B.L. = *Journal of Biblical Literature.*

JEPSEN, A. *Nabi.* Munich 1934.

KÖHLER, L. *Kleine Lichter.* Zürich 1945.

KÖHLER, L. *Kleine Lichter*. Zürich 1945.

KREMERS, H. "Leidensgemeinschaft" = "Leidensgemeinschaft mit Gott im Alten Testament," in *Ev. Th.* 13 (1953).

MARSH, J. *The Fulness of Time*. London 1952.

MEISSNER, B. *Babylonien* = *Babylonien und Assyrien*. Heidelberg 1925.

MOREAU, J. L. "Temps" = "Apropos de la notion biblique du temps," in *Revue de théologie et de philosophie*. 1952.

MOWINCKEL, S. *Erkenntnis Gottes* = *Die Erkenntnis Gottes bei den alttestamentlichen Propheten*. Oslo 1942.

—— "Prophecy and Tradition" = "Prophecy and Tradition. The Prophetic Books in the Light of the Study of the Growth and History of Tradition," in *A.N.V.A.O.*, II (1946).

NOTH, M. *Pentateuch* = *Überlieferungsgeschichte des Pentateuch*. Stuttgart 1948.

—— *Ges. St.* = *Gesammelte Studien zum Alten Testament*. Munich 1957, 1960.

QUELL, G. *Wahre und Falsche Propheten: Versuch einer Interpretation*. Gütersloh 1952.

RAD, G. VON. *Heilige Krieg* = *Der heilige Krieg im alten Israel*. Zürich 1958.

R.G.G. = *Die Religion im Geschichte und Gegenwart*, 3rd edn., Tübingen 1957ff.

ROBINSON, T. H. *Prophecy* = *Prophecy and the Prophets in Ancient Israel*. London 1923.

ROHLAND, E. *Erwählungstraditionen* = *Die Bedeutung der Erwählungstraditionen für die Eschatologie der alttestamentlichen Propheten*. Heidelberg 1956.

ROWLEY, H. H. *Apocalyptic* = *The Relevance of Apocalyptic*. London and Redhill 1947.

SCHMITZ, O. "Das Alte Testament" = "Das Alte Testament im Neuen Testament," in *Wort und Geist, Festgabe für K. Heim*. 1934.

SEELIGMANN, I. L. "Midraschexegese" = "Voraussetzungen der Midraschexegese," in *V.T.* 1 (1933).

STOEBE, H. J. "Seelsorge" = "Seelsorge und Mitleiden bei Jeremia," in *Wort und Dienst*. 1955.

Th. Lz. = *Theologische Literaturzeitung*. Herrnhut.

Th. R. = *Theologische Rundschau*. Tübingen.

Th. W.B.N.T. = *Theologisches Wörterbuch zum Neuen Testament*, edd. G. Kittel and G. Friedrich. Stuttgart 1930ff.

U.U.A. = *Uppsala Universitets Årsskrift.* Uppsala.

VRIEZEN, TH. C. *Theology* = *An Outline of Old Testament Theology,* trs. S. Neuijen. Oxford 1958.

V.T. = *Vetus Testamentum.* Leiden.

WELLHAUSEN, J. *Prolegomena* = *Prolegomena to the History of Israel,* trs. J. S. Black and A. Menzies. Edinburgh 1885.

WIDENGREN, G. *Aspects* = *Literary and Psychological Aspects of the Hebrew Prophets, U.U.Å.,* 1948.

WOLFF, H. W. *Das Zitat* = *Das Zitat im Prophetenspruch.* Munich 1937.

—— *Immanuel* = *Immanuel (Eine Auslegung von Jes. 7, 1–17)* 1959.

Z.A.W. = *Zeitschrift für die alttestamentliche Wissenschaft.* Giessen, later Berlin.

ZIMMERLI, W. AND J. JEREMIAS. *Servant* = *The Servant of God,* trs. H. Knight *et al.* London 1957.

Z. Th. K. = *Zeitschrift für Theologie und Kirche.* Tübingen.

INDEX OF SCRIPTURE PASSAGES

OLD TESTAMENT

DEAD SEA SCROLLS

Commentary on Habakkuk

NEW TESTAMENT

INDEX OF HEBREW WORDS IN VOLS. I and II

NAME AND SUBJECT INDEX

The index for VOL. I has been worked in here in a considerably expanded form

election (*continued*)
  of Zion: I. 46, 69, 123, 125, 341, 353,
    367, 397
Eliakim: II. 47f., 373
Elijah: II. 6, 14ff., 25, 34, 53, 56, 71, 89,
    136, 177, 274, 289
Eliphaz: II. 68
Elisha: II. 6, 25ff., 34, 56f., 71
Elohim-beings: I. 19f., 23, 138, 145, 146,
    156f., 158, 178, 211, 360, 370, 409,
    416
Elohist (E.): I. 6, 123, 131, 138, 177, 181,
    186, 189, 235f., 292ff., 379. II. 107
emanation: I. 142, II. 339
emotions, God's: II. 63
empire: II. 183, 188, 311, 313
end: II. 313
enlightenment (Solomon): I. 48–56, 140f.,
    157, 316, 425, 429
Enoch: II. 306
  Apocalypse of: II. 306
enthronement, Jahweh's: I. 362ff.
  the king's: I. 40f., 319f., 323f. II. 172
ephod: I. 24
Ephraim: II. 192
Ephrathites: II. 170
epiclesis, cultic: I. 19, 121, 186
error, sins committed in: I. 267f.
eschatology, eschatological: I. 111, 368,
    407. II. 99, 101, 114ff., 118, 185f.,
    288f., 381
  expectation: II. 297
  message: II. 118, 402
  restoration: II. 281
  eschatologising: II. 112ff.
  non-eschatological: II. 102
eschaton: II. 248, 302f.
esotericism: II. 302
Essenes: II. 27
ethics: II. 70
ethos: II. 391
etymology: II. 83f.
examination of terminology: I. 119f.,
    354, 378
exclusive worship, Jahweh's claim to:
    I. 43, 184, 207, 277

exegesis: II. 370f.
exhortation: II. 37, 158, 196, 215f.
exile: I. 67, 80–84, 125ff., 231, 335, 342,
    344, 345. II. 132, 134, 179, 198, 248
exiles: II. 210ff., 244f., 278
Exodus: I. 12f., 115, 122, 137, 175–87,
    192, 281, 291–3, 295, 306, 338
  tradition: II. 117, 132, 192, 217, 236
expectation: II. 319, 321
  prophetic e. of something soon to
    happen: II. 115
experience, wisdom deriving from:
    I. 418–41, 442, 451. II. 74, 342f.
expiation: I. 247, 248, 250, 254–8, 262–
    72, 317. II. 64
evil: II. 74, 305
Ezekiel: I. 28, 141, 156, 194f., 199, 207,
    240, 258, 268, 283, 378f., 391–4.
    II. 59, 63, 65, 91, 94f., 97, 117, 182,
    220ff., 243, 263ff., 266f., 270, 274f.,
    343, 398f., 403f.
Ezra: I. 79, 88f. II. 306
  codex of: I. 79, 88

face: I. 285, 288
failure: II. 65, 167, 206, 226
faith: I. 4, 17, 70, 106–12, 119, 120f., 171,
    176, 177, 302, 365, 378f., 402, 408f.,
    410, 427, 434, 450, 454. II. 159f.,
    191, 249, 355, 378ff.
  demand for: II. 160
  men of little f.: II. 280
faithfulness, God's: I. 225, 373. II. 407
fall, of Jerusalem: II. 279
  of man: I. 147, 154–58, 159f., 163, 268
falling away: v. apostasy
fallow year: I. 16, 300
fasts: II. 103, 286
fate, belief in: I. 172, 390, 459
  act which creates, sphere of: I. 264–6,
    269, 271, 384–6, 391, 392, 412, 427f.,
    436, 458. II. 74, 144, 347
fellowship: II. 256
fertility, fruitfulness: I. 41, 144, 162, 229,
    304